# SYSTEMS
# OF CITIES

# Contributors

William Alonso
Brian J. L. Berry
Hans Blumenfeld
Christopher Board
John R. Borchert
Kenneth E. Boulding
Larry S. Bourne
Martyn Cordey-Hayes
Ron W. Crowley
Ronald J. Davies
Kingsley Davis
Rodney A. Erickson
T. J. Denis Fair

Boris S. Khorev
Paul L. Knox
Elliott Medrich
Koichi Mera
Richard L. Morrill
Peter A. Morrison
Alan B. Mountjoy
John Friedmann
Jean Gottmann
Torsten Hägerstrand
Niles M. Hansen
Douglas Jeffrey
David G. Khodzhaev

Poul Ove Pedersen
Richard Peet
Allan Pred
Richard E. Preston
Harry W. Richardson
Brian T. Robson
Frank Schaffer
Paul J. Schwind
James W. Simmons
Yi-Fu Tuan
Barbara Ward
D. J. Webb

# SYSTEMS OF CITIES

## readings on structure, growth, and policy

edited by
L. S. Bourne and J. W. Simmons
University of Toronto

New York · Oxford University Press · 1978

Copyright © 1978 by Oxford University Press, Inc.
Printed in the United States of America.

**Library of Congress Cataloging in Publication Data**
Main entry under title:

Systems of cities.

Includes bibliographies.
1. Cities and towns—Addresses, essays, lectures.
2. Cities and towns—Growth—Addresses, essays, lectures.
3. Urbanization—Addresses, essays, lectures.
I. Bourne, Larry Stuart, 1939–  II. Simmons, James William,
1936–
HT151.S93     301.36     77-9452
ISBN 0-19-502264-5

# Preface

We know that cities harbor an increasingly dominant share of national wealth in developed and developing countries. What is more recent, however, is our awareness of the intimate but complex relationship between urbanization and national development. The process of urbanization, once viewed simply as an inevitable consequence of development, is now seen as an integral component and a generator of economic growth and social change. To understand and influence either requires us to come to grips with urbanization at this level.

It is also widely known that cities in developed countries interact among themselves in many complex ways. In effect they act as a system. Every introductory urban course includes at least some reference to the idea of systems of cities. Yet it was not until recently that the intensity and diversity of the interactions among cities and the implications of these interactions were fully appreciated. Only very recently has a body of literature emerged to document these interactions.

## OBJECTIVES

The subject matter of urban systems is extremely complex, perhaps too much for any single author to digest. This is the purpose of anthologies. The rationale of this volume is to draw together a representative selection of the best research writings of authors from numerous disciplines on systems of cities, urban growth, and national urban policy. Our focus then is on *interrelated sets or systems of cities*, for which we use the term "urban systems," and on how these cities and the regions they serve behave as social systems.

Specifically we have selected papers to illustrate the following aspects of urban systems: 1) definitional questions on the nature of urban systems and their spatial delineation; 2) the historical evolution and spread of urbanization; 3) the description of size, structure, and differentiation within national urban systems; 4) the variety of linkages among cities that give substance to the concept of a system; 5) recent growth patterns and processes of change; 6) problems emanating from rapid urban growth (or decline), and examples of the debate on national planning and settlement priorities; and 7) suggestions given or positions taken on what alternative policies and strategies are appropriate to these problems.

Our objective, however, is not simply to illustrate these concerns with substantive papers. We also seek to say something original about the nature and role of an interconnected urban system in the social fabric and in the development of regions and nations. The urban system is more than a set of interdependent cities: it creates, transmits, alters, and reflects changes in society as a whole. To this end we have prepared extensive introductory remarks to the book and to each of the sections.

In these introductory remarks and in the papers themselves, the term "national" is used widely but that is not the only level of interest. The papers selected deal with systems of cities at all geographic levels or scales: regional, supra-regional, and national as well as international. Generally, the larger and more diverse the country, in area, economy, and population, the more appropriate it is to examine regional urban subsystems as well as national systems. Similarily, the more open the economy, social structure, and culture of a given country to outside influence, the more international events must be considered in the analysis of that country's urban system. The reference to national urban systems tends to be a matter of convenience as well as a reflection that national governments have prime influence, if not responsibility, over the urbanization process generally. Much of the policy literature and policy-oriented research has been directed at this level.

The focus on urban systems at an aggregate, or macro, scale is not intended in any way to minimize the importance of research or policy on the micro scales of individual neighborhoods or of single cities and metropolitan regions. It goes without saying that it is at these local levels that urban problems are most apparent to all of us. Moreover it is here that solutions to urban problems are likely to show the greatest and the most immediate payoff. However, it is precisely this close proximity to local urban problems as we perceive them that has in the past deflated interest in and concern for urbanization at broader scales. Local problems in housing, social welfare, transportation, and jobs take place within a broader context of social and economic change in the country as a whole, and must be understood within that context.

Although we are now generally aware that most such problems originate, at least in part, outside the individual city or region we live in, we have not effectively linked policy initiatives at these different levels. Solutions to local urban problems must involve action on supra-regional and national levels as well as local levels if they are to have any chance of success. If, for instance, an urban area that is growing rapidly through in-migration wishes to slow its growth rate it cannot do so in isolation, at least not without creating difficulties elsewhere. *Cities are not islands.* Appropriate action in the areas of the origin of this migration is necessary if the rate of movement is to be reduced. To date, many of the policies of senior governments directed toward urban problems have been negated or contradicted by local government policies, and vice versa.

## BACKGROUND

Our initial interest in preparing this volume arose during the preparation of two more specific studies on national urban systems. One study (Bourne, 1975) involved a cross-national comparison of national urban policies in Australia, Canada, Britain, and Sweden, while the second (Simmons, forthcoming) represented an intensive case study of the historical evolution and current structure of the Canadian urban system. In both cases we found a substantial gap in the standard literature dealing with the analysis of urbanization at this aggregate level. Studies of urban systems were included, but aside from a few specialized areas—particularly central place theory, city classifications, and regional economic growth and planning—there was little material displaying the incredibly rich diversity of urban system characteristics and the complexity of how such systems operated. At the same time, in our search for bibliographic materials we were struck by an accelerating but widely scattered flow of articles and reports related to the urban systems theme. The need for a new reference source became more and more apparent.

## THE POLICY CONTEXT

In part our interest in the subject of urban systems also reflects the relatively recent and rapid rise of national growth and urban development as major issues of political and social concern. The "crisis of the cities" brought increased pressures for the direct involvement of all levels of government in planning urban growth, particularly at those senior levels with sufficient resources and power to influence urban growth—usually the central government. The influential but controversial report of the Club of Rome, entitled *Limits to Growth*, stressed the world's shrinking natural resource inventory and shifted the debate on growth to the center of the international political stage. At the United Nations Conference on the Environment, held in Stockholm in 1972, the principal issue that emerged was the deteriorating condition of the global urban environment. This issue in turn became the focus of subsequent U.N. conferences, notably on population (Bucharest, 1974) and human settlements (Vancouver, 1976).

Most national governments have now committed themselves to some degree of guidance or regulation of urbanization at this macro scale. The specific political reasons for their involvement may be different as are the methods employed, but the stated objectives are often similar: to reduce the excessive concentration of population in the large metropolitan regions and to stabilize growth or at least to arrest the decline of depressed areas, while maintaining a reasonable quality of life for those people and areas left behind in the urbanization process. We now recognize that issues of poverty, regional deprivation, and population redistribution are intimately related to urbanization and are embedded in the conceptualizations of large-scale urban systems which we discuss in this volume.

There are both benefits and costs in the rapid evolution of such systems. The benefits seem to center around two themes: efficiency, in terms of higher rates of productivity and economic growth, and accessibility, in terms of improved access for a larger proportion of the population to the wide range of opportunities large cities provide. The costs derive from at least three major sources: the costs of spatial redistribution itself, in terms of new capital requirements in growing regions and abandoned infrastructures in declining regions; the social costs created by the agglomeration of population, activities, and services in large cities, such as congestion, pollution, and alienation; and the costs of dealing with the inequalities and poverty of peripheral regions. These issues are the subject of debate in our last two sections.

## CRITERIA OF SELECTION

The selection of papers included was based on several criteria. Obviously we first sought a sample of the best and the most comprehensive papers on urban systems. Some of these, however, were widely available elsewhere or were inappropriate because of length, difficulty, style, or source. From the initial set we selected core papers. To this core we added those that demonstrated additional empirical and theoretical perspectives on urban systems, as well as different methodologies, or those that studied different countries or conflicting social and political philosophies. In many cases selection involved a trade-off between those papers that are now or will be classics, but which tended to be concentrated in a few subject areas or were highly mathematical, and our desire to produce as complete and balanced a volume on urban systems as possible. For some subjects, such as monetary flows or income movements through an urban system, as will be apparent in the sections to follow, we could find no suitable papers to reprint. In other cases, because of space limitations we were forced to edit papers, some rather severely, to reduce their length for inclusion.

Empirical examples are also drawn as widely as possible—from Australia, Great Britain, Canada, Sweden, South America, continental Europe, Japan, South Africa, Southeast Asia, the U.S.S.R., and of course, the U.S. There is, however a clear bias toward studies set in the developed world and in market-based economies.

With respect to the level of difficulty of the papers, again we have attempted to provide a wide range of perspectives, varying both the level and the techniques of analysis. Given the very recent development of the field and the relative absence of data and empirical studies, much of the substantive research literature is theoretical and often highly mathematical. The beginning student, however, will only have difficulty with a few of the papers, and this should at least encourage him or her to explore the subject further. One might add that selecting from the mountain of political and popular literature has also been difficult. Much of this writing is vague and superficial or overly specific to the country in question.

In any case, we have played down the mathematical material whenever possible to ensure that the concepts and issues involved are brought to the widest possible audience. But some of this material cannot reasonably be avoided. *Urban systems are complex,* and so too are the methods of analysis. If we are able to demonstrate the enormous breadth and importance of problems relating to urban systems without underplaying either the complexity of the issues involved or the uncertainty of our knowledge, then our major goal will have been achieved.

## EDITORIAL INTRODUCTIONS

The editorial introductions in each section, as noted, are meant to be more than per-functory remarks and listings of the papers to follow. Instead, they are intended to be substantive contributions in their own right. An attempt is made in each section to set an appropriate context for the papers, to link the papers with those that have gone before or that follow, and to fill in some of the gaps in the discussions, which are inevitable in any selection of readings. More important we try to use these readings as a basis on which to provide a more comprehensive overview of urban systems than has been made heretofore. We highlight areas of controversy and raise questions for discussion that are not posed in those papers. The reader will judge whether the attempts have been successful.

## THE AUDIENCE

The intended audience is, obviously, anyone interested in urbanization at the macro scale of urban systems and in the relationship between urbanization and the spatial structure of economic and social development. They may be students, teachers, prac-tioners, or policy advisors. More to the point, we visualize several audiences, ranging from those seeking an introduction to the field to those requiring less frequent refer-ence use and more specialized information and analysis. One book can serve both purposes. In the classroom we anticipate that the volume will be useful as supplemen-tary readings to a more general text—in urban and regional planning, geography, political science, economics or in interdisciplinary courses such as policy analysis and urban studies—as well as a reference source for a variety of other courses.

## REFERENCES

Bourne, L. S. 1975. *Regulating Urban Systems. A Comparative Review of National Urbaniza-tion Strategies: Australia, Canada, Great Brit-ain, Sweden.* London: Oxford University Press.

Simmons, J. W. Forthcoming. *The Canadian Urban System.*

# Acknowledgments

We owe a considerable debt to many friends and colleagues who have undertaken the research on which this volume is dependent. In particular we acknowledge the willingness of many authors and editors to allow us considerable latitude to abstract and otherwise manhandle their papers to fit into the extremely tight space restrictions we faced. We apologize for any injustices done to their original contributions. We should also thank the pre-publication reviewers for their valuable comments on improving the editors' introductions. Last but not least we acknowledge the continuing interest and support of our editor, Jim Anderson, at Oxford University Press (New York) and the secretarial skills of Bev Thompson at the Centre for Urban and Community Studies, University of Toronto, who translated our continual revisions into a clearly typed, if not readable, draft.

L. S. BOURNE
J. W. SIMMONS

*Toronto*
*October, 1976*

# Contents

INTRODUCTION: THE NATURE OF
URBAN SYSTEMS   1

# 3 CITY SIZE, LOCATION, AND DIFFERENTIATION  159

# 4 BEHAVIOR: INTERCITY LINKAGES, DIFFUSION, AND CONFLICT    259

# 5 URBAN SYSTEM GROWTH AND CHANGE  341

# 6   THE CONTROVERSY: ISSUES IN THE NATIONAL SETTLEMENT DEBATE      413

# 7   POLICY: ALTERNATIVE SETTLEMENT STRATEGIES AND PLANNING EXPERIENCE      489

*INTRODUCTION:*
*THE NATURE OF URBAN SYSTEMS*

During the last few years the meaning of the term "urban system" has evolved rapidly toward the meaning we use here, that is, an urban system is a set of interdependent cities comprising a region or nation. Figure 1 illustrates this concept for the system of cities in Canada. In this volume we focus on the structural and spatial organization of such systems, on the interrelationships between cities, and on their varied growth paths over time. By examining the cities within one country, and how they interact with one another as a system to create patterns of growth and development, we are emphasizing not only the processes of growth and change but their spatial imprint.

Even within this context, studies of urban systems may vary widely. Some are restricted to rather narrow discussions of the population size, relative location, or the economic role of cities. Others represent static cross-sectional analyses of growth and change or cross-national comparisons of the structural characteristics of urban systems. Still others examine the complexities of financial or power interrelations among urban regions, while others hotly debate the arguments for and against national growth and settlement strategies.

In our terms, studies of urban systems at this scale do not include analyses of relationships within a single city.[1] We have excluded here, for example, studies of structural growth linkages among economic sectors or firms or among various locations within a metropolitan area. Of course, the pattern of growth within any given urban area is related to its role within the larger system, but this is the subject of another book. In the readings presented here the focus is on comparisons of different cities and sets of cities, and how they operate together to make up regional and national as well as international urban systems.

## THE RESEARCH CONTEXT

The concept of the urban system has a number of attractions, but perhaps its major one is that it links together (or forces us to) all studies that examine the relation-

---

1. There are now a number of volumes of readings on the internal organization of cities that parallel this volume in purpose and design. See Bourne (1971), Blowers et al. (1974), and Gale and Moore (1975).

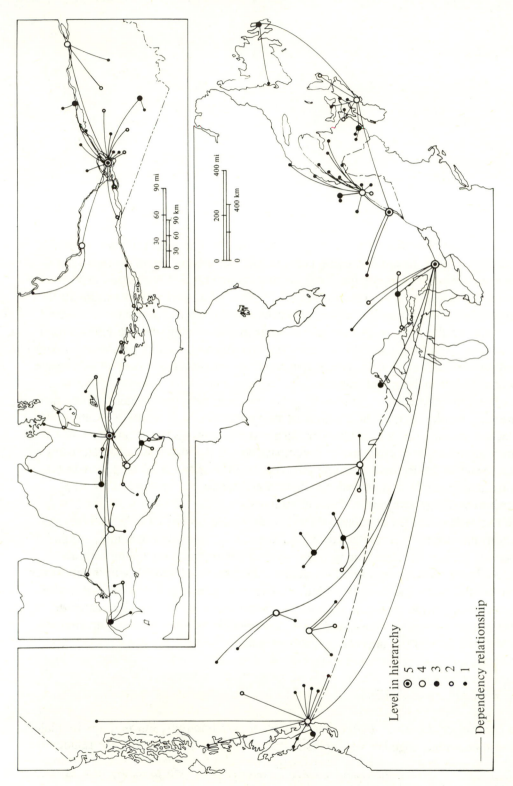

Level in hierarchy

- 5 ⊙
- 4 ○
- 3 ●
- 2 ○
- 1 ·

——— Dependency relationship

Figure 1. The Urban System Concept: The Example of Canada.

ship between the nation and its spatial components. A national geography, for instance, is primarily concerned with the systematic description, comparison, and correlation of spatial distributions over a wide range of phenomena, such as terrain, climate, economy, income, and culture. Increasingly in industrialized societies, the integration of these phenomena occurs *within and through a series of metropolitan nodes* (see Berry, 1973b; Pred, 1974; Stöhr, 1974). For example, Chicago's growth is a response to its particular mix of industry, hinterland accessibility, cumulative capital investment, and human resources. Denver's growth reflects a different combination of the same ingredients.

Any advanced nation, then, is an aggregation of urban-centered regions, that is, a spatial aggregation of differing combinations of resources. These resources are in turn shaped by the interaction among the cities themselves. Again, Chicago and Denver each have their own unique patterns of accessibility, in terms of the time and cost and mode of transportation, to regional, national, and international markets. In the development process, the advantages of initial historical site and location, such as a strategic port, and local specialization are amplified and modified by each city. The potential range of growth, prosperity, and economic structure available to Denver, for example, is in turn limited by the characteristics of the national economy—the price of beef perhaps—as well as by the existence of competing urban locations, such as Los Angeles, Salt Lake City, Omaha, or even Pueblo.

The historical evolution of a nation or of a national urban system can be treated in the same way. The linkages among cities and regions at any point in time and their relative size and locational advantages shape the patterns of settlement, growth, and political organization which follow. The rapid growth of Chicago in the late 19th century reflected the westward expansion of American settlement. One does not first look within Chicago to explain its growth but without, that is, at the growth of the region it serves and to the system-wide linkages of Chicago relative to those of its competitors.

For assistance in understanding these patterns we can draw on the research of many disciplines. Regional economics, for instance, is concerned with explaining patterns of economic growth and income differences among regions within a nation. Again, the dominant approach in this literature is based on the systematic comparison of resource and accessibility advantages and on a set of hypothesized relationships among regions. The latter generally involve a process of exchange, via comparative advantage—or exploitation of peripheral regions by metropolitan-based monopolies. When combined, exchange and exploitation largely determine how the fruits of economic growth (or decline) are distributed spatially among regions, as well as socially. *What you get from the system does depend on where you live*.

In introducing this collection of readings, we argue that the concepts of the city and the region are increasingly interchangeable. The functional or nodal region, centered on a city, is the basic concept. For example, the state of Georgia is increasingly equated with Atlanta; Ontario with Toronto; and Colorado with Denver. For every region we can define an urban node which comprises much of that region's social activities. We can also assume that the economy of the region, as well as its contacts with the outside world, takes place largely at that location. Similarly, on an international scale we speak of agreements or conflicts as taking place between cities, not countries: Washington and Moscow and London and Lisbon act as symbols of their nations.

The use of urban-centered regions also helps to integrate the literature of urban and regional economics with that of comparative urban studies, but both still lack a concern for the networks of interrelations between cities, which are implicit in the notion of an urban system. Partial models of how urban places relate to each other can be drawn from a variety of sources—from the literature of interregional trade and comparative advantage (Richardson, 1969 and 1973), and from the new urban economics (Richardson, 1977); from the ideas of spatial monopoly developed initially by Christaller (1933) and Lösch (1937); from studies of growth and income differentials (Alonso, 1968) and the concepts of regional science (Cripps, 1975); and from the relationships between financial power and resource exploitation (Friedmann, Section IV). However, none are comprehensive. The nature of these networks of interdependencies represents one of the most interesting and controversial aspects of this rapidly growing field of study.[2]

## ORGANIZATION OF THE VOLUME

The arrangement of papers in this volume follows a traditional approach (Figure 2). The definitional concerns expressed in the preceding discussion, which essentially relate to the increasingly close fit between concepts of the city, the metropolitan area, the region and the nation as spatial systems, are taken up in the papers in the first section. Here we examine the urban system as a unit of analysis. How are urban systems and the urban units they represent defined? How are these systems organized, and how might this organization be studied and assessed? What role do cities and urban systems play in the larger context of national development?

These papers provide background for those in Section II, which concerns historical urban growth and the evolution of urban systems. Here the global transition from rural to urban life and examples of the spatial evolution and spread (or diffusion) or particular urban systems are discussed. Section III is largely descriptive. In this section, continuing the definitional theme of Section I is a concern primarily with city size, or if you prefer, with the relative distribution of population and

2. One striking aspect of this field is the very rapid evolution of ideas and of methods, as displayed in the literature. The interested student of urban systems should note a substantial evolution in emphasis and ideas between Friedmann's (1966) classic study of regional development in Venezuela and in the revised reader on regional policy by Friedmann and Alonso (1975). One might also compare the text edited by Berry and Horton (1970) with Berry's later (1973a) overview of contemporary trends in world urbanization.

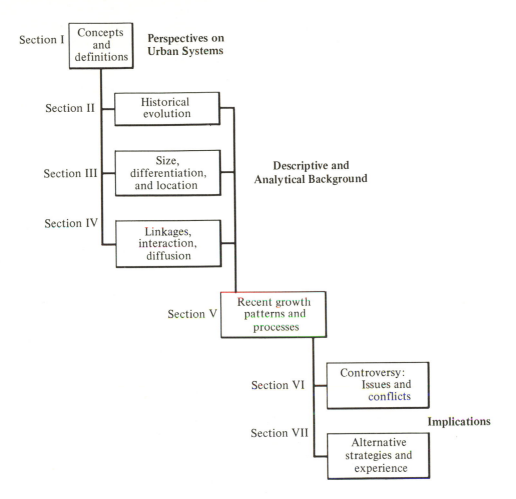

Figure 2. Organization of Papers.

economic activity across a series of urban-centered regions. The discussion is enlarged, however, to include papers which deal with a wide range of other variables
that can be used to describe the cities in an urban system: environmental quality,
political power, and the images that cities present to both visitors and residents.

The concept of an urban system also determines the composition of the other
predominantly analytical sections (Sections IV and V). Section IV is devoted to
examples of analyses of the form, content, and function of intercity linkages.
These linkages are selected to represent the whole spectrum of relationships among
urban regions—relationships which in effect define the *organization* of the urban
system. Section V examines the growth and behavior of the urban system, emphasizing
recent and short-term trends.

The final two sections trace the implications of the growth of the urban system
for generating various kinds of public-policy problems and conflicts (Section VI)

and as a basis for selecting orderly approaches to ameliorate those problems (Section VII). These interwoven problem areas have provided the main thrust for the recent outburst of interest in national and regional urban systems and in national settlement policies.

Unfortunately research has not kept pace with policy needs. The wealth of theoretical models of urban growth now available have not proven to be very satisfactory for empirical analysis, largely because of their inability to specify the external relationships of cities noted above. Data sources are also deficient. In few countries is there any systematic attempt at monitoring the growth of urban systems to the extent that adequate models can be specified and problems can be identified as they are emerging rather than after they are firmly in place.

Yet, these manifest problems, involving differences in income, jobs, and rates of growth among cities and regions as well as the need to match the local resource base to the level of human activity in each region have necessitated increasing public intervention in the urban system. In the last three decades we have observed a massive increase in public programs affecting this system. We do not have as yet, however, very much evidence of the impact of these programs on the system as a whole.

Like many ideas the urban system is not really new; its prominence today is largely a reflection of a growing concern and a sensitivity on the part of academics and public officials about problems at this broad scale of spatial aggregation (Chisholm and Manners, 1971). This concern is partly due to an awareness of the increasing role of urban-centered activities—tertiary (services) and quaternary (services to services)—relative to primary activities in the growth of local economies and to the increasing size and power of corporate and governmental enterprises. In part it is also a result of the realization that many problems facing local communities are directly related to the economic strength of the municipality, to the characteristics of the migrants it receives (or loses), and to the political strength of that community within the broader state or national government framework. The point to start from in understanding these problems is the larger urban system of which that community is an integral unit.

## HISTORY OF THE URBAN-SYSTEM CONCEPT

Many early writers, such as N.S.B. Gras (1922), Christaller (1933), Lösch (1937), Harris and Ullman (1945), and Vining[3] discussed the nature and origin of

---

3. One of the most prolific writers on what we would now call urban systems was Rudyard Vining. During the 1940s and 1950s he wrote over a dozen papers on such topics as regional systems and urban growth. Many of these papers, in concept and orientation, anticipated later studies, but somehow they never had the full impact they might have had. Possibly if he had worked in a more sympathetic discipline than economics, or if his work had been published as a single integrated volume, the result would have been different. See Vining (1945; 1946; 1949; 1953; 1955).

systematic variations in the characteristics of urban places. However, the full range of implications deriving from the urban-system concept was not outlined until much later, notably in the work of Otis D. Duncan and his colleagues in the publication *Metropolis and Region* (1960). This book, representing an extensive statistical compilation, was developed at the request of Resources for the Future. It provided not only a valuable source of urban data for the U.S. but a new view of that nation's economic and social landscape.

In conjunction with the equally important report *Regions, Resources and Economic Growth* (Perloff *et al.*, 1960), the authors of *Metropolis and Region* argued that both the national economy and the national geography of the U.S. could be succinctly described in terms of the urban system. Duncan and his colleagues said that regional metropoles effectively organize the production of regional specialities and then exchange them for the products of other regions. And they demonstrated that Detroit, Seattle, Dallas, and Atlanta, for instance, each serve to integrate a regional economy, while New York, Washington, and Los Angeles provide special services for all areas of the country as well as for their own region. The cities of the northeastern manufacturing belt made up a second, less structured group in their analysis, providing products to each other as well as to the nation as a whole, but linked together in a complex fashion according to the flows among industries. Throughout their book emphasis was placed on the variety of specialized roles of cities within the national system and on the interdependencies among regions and metropolitan areas.

With *Metropolis and Region* as backdrop and additional theoretical and empirical material provided by the compilations of Isard in *Location and Space Economy* (1956) and *Methods of Regional Analysis* (1960), the stage was set in the 1960s for the introduction of two more important components to this conceptual (and analytical) framework. First, Moser and Scott's study, *British Towns* (1961), demonstrated the power of the computer in describing and classifying cities within national urban systems on the basis of a lengthy list of census attributes. The output of these analyses, usually involving factor analytic techniques, identified which characteristics were held in common and which were unique to particular cities and then grouped cities accordingly. Innumerable replications of this analysis have spawned a whole sub-species of urban research now called "factorial ecology." In 1964 Brian Berry proposed a formal link between urban population distributions and the hierarchy of service centers (the central place hierarchy) and linked these to the language of general systems theory; the terminology of urban systems became official.

One other important trend in subsequent years was the gradual extension of the concept of the city and enlargement of the definition of the census metropolitan area to include an even broader area surrounding and functionally linked with the metropolitan core but not part of the built-up area. Concepts such as "megalopolis" (Gottmann, 1961), the "urban field" (Friedmann and Miller,

1965), and the "functional economic area" (Fox and Kumar, 1965) are well-known examples. More recently Berry's now widely quoted work on "daily urban systems" (one map is reprinted here as Figure 3), which defines the United States as a set of structured urban-centered regions on the basis of the ebb and flow of daily commuting and activity patterns, is a formal application of this concept of extended urban areas (see Berry and Horton, 1970; Berry, 1973b).

The final element in the growing interest in urban systems is the increasing world-wide concern with the formulation of national policies for urbanization. Most governments now accept the proposition that to achieve established goals of balanced economic development, regional equality, and orderly population redistribution requires a national strategy or strategies for dealing with urban growth and decline. Most countries consequently have created, or are in the process of creating, institutional structures and extensive programs in an attempt to influence the distribution of growth spatially and to redistribute income, at least in some minor way. Writers such as Myrdal (1957), Thompson (1965), and Rodwin (1970) have brought the universal aspects of these problems and their possible solution to the public's attention. A flood of literature has emerged that analyzes various components of national urban systems, assesses the implications of the continued growth of those systems along new or existing directions, and debates the policy alternatives (see, for example, Cameron and Wingo, 1973; Berry, 1973a; Hansen, 1975; Swain and Logan, 1975). Part of this increased awareness of urban problems at this macro level has been a greater sensitivity on the part of politicians to the role of geographic space in shaping national development (Chisholm and Manners, 1971).

Perhaps no one has provided a more important lead in understanding how urban and region systems operate, and particularly in identifying the policy options in dealing with such systems, than John Friedmann and William Alonso. In a long series of individual papers and notably in their two collections of readings, *Regional Development and Planning: A Reader* (1964) and *Regional Policy: Readings on Theory and Applications* (1975), they have contributed as much as anyone to the rapid evolution of the field which this volume attempts to represent.

Undoubtedly a clear benchmark in the international policy debate was the U.N. Conference on the Human Environment held in Stockholm in 1972. Although few explicit policies or international agreements came out of this conference, what did emerge was a greater awareness of the important role of urban environments in determining the quality of life as well as an appreciation of the strength of the interdependencies between urbanization and national economic development and between both of these and social equality. Most governments now find that they can no longer simply ignore such issues. On paper at least, governments had committed themselves to a more sensitive approach to urban matters. This concern also led in part to the planning of subsequent U.N. conferences on population and food and most recently that on human settlements (the Habitat Conference) held in Vancouver in 1976 (see United Nations, 1976a). It also stimulated, directly and indirectly, a series of national and cross-national studies of urban growth on which this volume draws (O.E.C.D., 1973; E.F.T.A., 1973; Ward, 1976; United Nations, 1976b).


## WHAT KIND OF A SYSTEM?

Having argued above that the urban areas, or urban-centered regions, of a nation constitute a meaningful system begs a number of questions: What kind of system is an urban system? Of what relevance are systems concepts? Are the terms mere window-dressing? Although we do not wish to become involved here in semantic issues nor to address the literature on formal systems analysis as such, these questions cannot be entirely avoided. Most authors acknowledge that the presence of strong interactions among a set of elements (cities) in a bounded area (nation) and the existence of feedback effects which regulate growth and change implies the existence of some kind of system. However, as Richardson notes in his paper in Section III few agree on what are the important interactions and feedbacks among urban regions and thus on what kind of system is involved.

One concept the editors have found useful in previous research (Simmons, 1974; Bourne, 1974), is that provided in the literature on "complex social systems" (Emery and Trist, 1972). The key implication here, aside from the obvious one of complexity, is the recognition that urban systems are in fact social systems. They are not simply mechanical or natural systems. Nor are they strictly economic or political systems. They are, instead, all of these. As social systems, a system of cities may then be characterized as inherently complex, highly unstable, often diffuse, and continually evolving in response to influences from outside. These outside influences are themselves highly unpredictable, creating what Emery and Trist term as the "turbulent" environment of social systems.

Perhaps most important, social systems are what in terms of regional development Dunn (1971) has called "cumulative learning systems." This implies that such systems have internal self-regulating mechanisms that dictate their form and evolution, and that they learn from past experience and thereby adapt to expected future situations. They show an impressive internal capability for adjusting to very different external needs and internal stress conditions.

The importance of these considerations here is that, as complex social systems, cities and systems of cities cannot be conveniently reduced for purposes of analysis to discrete operating parts, as criticisms of Forrester's (1969) "urban dynamics" model have shown. Unlike mechanical systems, cities and systems of cities cannot be taken apart and put back together like a toy train. Nor is it possible, as in most natural systems, to deduce the response conditioned by any given change.

The parts, whether they be entire cities, economic sectors, or infrastructure services may serve very different functions within an urban system at different points in time. Different parts of the system have different time spans (or half-lives) and

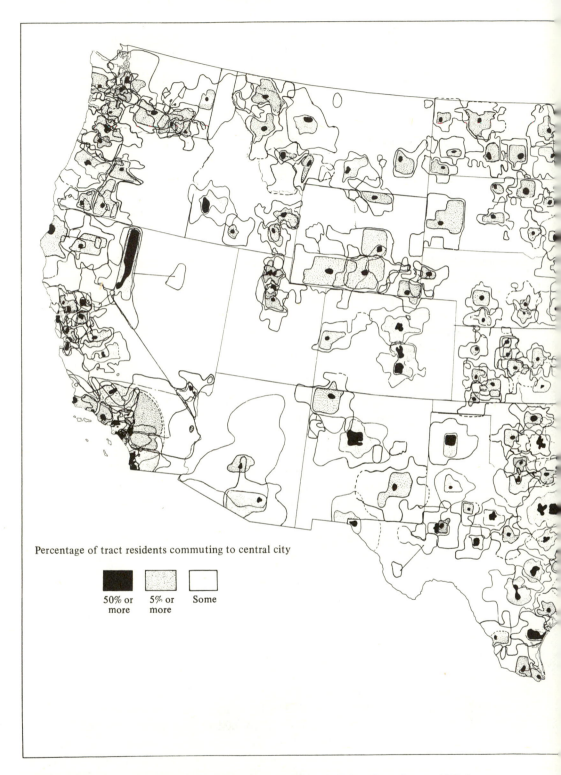

Percentage of tract residents commuting to central city

50% or more    5% or more    Some

Figure 3. Commuting Fields of the Nation's Major Central Cities (from Berry, 1973c).

0    100    200    300    400    500 mi

many parts have more than one role to play at any given time. In some instances the appearance or form of the parts may no longer resemble the original function for which they were defined. In other instances the function disappears but the form persists, or the reverse may occur. Cities founded as trading centers may be transformed into military bases (or vice versa), and then into financial or corporate headquarters. Cities based on a mining boom, or on a railway or a port may at a later date totally disappear.

## CONCLUDING REMARKS

Thus, in these very general terms, we acknowledge that a considerable degree of uncertainty exists in the study and design of large-scale social systems in general and urban systems in particular. None of the papers in the following sections attempt to solve all of these questions. We would not expect them to do so. This uncertainty, however, means that urban-systems strategies cannot at this time, if ever, be rigid master plans which are all-embracing. Planning too must be a learning process.

## REFERENCES

Alonso, W. 1968. "Urban and Regional Imbalances in Economic Development." *Economic Development and Cultural Change,* vol. 17, pp. 1–14.

———. 1971. "Problems, Purposes and Implicit Policies for a National Strategy of Urbanization." Working Paper No. 158, Institute of Urban and Regional Development. Berkeley: University of California.

Berry, B. J. L. 1964. "Cities as Systems within Systems of Cities." *Papers and Proceedings of the Regional Science Association,* vol. 13, pp. 147–164.

———. 1973a. *Human Consequences of Urbanization.* London: Methuen.

———. 1973b. *Growth Centers in the American Urban System.* Vol. 1. Cambridge, Mass.: Ballinger.

———. 1973c. "Contemporary Urbanization Processes," in *Geographical Perspectives on Urban Problems.* Washington: National Academy of Sciences, pp. 94–107.

———, and Horton, F., eds. 1970. *Geographical Perspectives on Urban Systems: Text and Integrated Readings.* Englewood Cliffs, N.J.: Prentice-Hall.

Blowers, A. *et al.,* eds. 1974. *The Future of Cities.* London: Hutchinson.

Bourne, L. S. ed., 1971. *Internal Structure of the City: Readings on Space and Environment.* New York and Toronto: Oxford University Press.

———. 1974. "Forecasting Urban Systems: Research Design, Alternative Methodologies and Urbanization Trends." *Regional Studies,* vol. 8, pp. 197–210.

Cameron, G. C. and Wingo, L. Jr., eds. 1973. *Cities, Regions and Public Policy.* Edinburgh: Oliver and Boyd.

Chisholm, M. and Manners, G., eds. 1971. *Spatial Policy Problems of the British Economy.* Cambridge: The University Press.

Christaller, Walter. 1933; reprinted 1967 *Central Places in Southern Germany.* Translated by C. W. Baskin. Englewood Cliffs, N.J.: Prentice-Hall.

Cripps, E. L. 1975. *Regional Science: New Concepts and Old Problems.* New York: Academic Press.

Duncan, O. D., Scott, W. R., Lieberson, S., Duncan, B., and Winsborough, H. H. 1960. *Metropolis and Region.* Baltimore: Johns Hopkins University Press.

Dunn, E. 1971. *Economic and Social Development: A Process of Social Learning.* Baltimore: Johns Hopkins University Press.

Emery, F. E. and Trist, E. L. 1972. *Towards a Social Ecology: Contextual Appreciations of the Future in the Present.* New York: Plenum Press.

European Free Trade Association (E.F.T.A.). 1973. *National Settlement Strategies: A Framework for Regional Development*. Geneva: E.F.T.A.

Forrester, J. N. 1969. *Urban Dynamics*. Cambridge, Mass.: M.I.T. Press.

———. 1975 *Collected Papers of Jay Forrester*. Cambridge, Mass.: Wright-Allen Press. Fox,

Fox, K.A. and Kumar, T.K. 1965. "The Functional Economic Area: Delimitation and Implications for Economic Analysis and Policy." *Papers and Proceedings of the Regional Science Association*, vol. 15, pp. 57–85.

Friedmann, J. 1966. *Regional Development Policy*. Cambridge, Mass.: M.I.T. Press.

———, and Alonso, W., eds. 1964. *Regional Development and Planning. A Reader*. Cambridge, Mass.: M.I.T. Press.

———, and Alonso, W., eds. 1964. *Regional Policy: Readings in Theory and Applications*. Cambridge, Mass.: M.I.T. Press.

———, and Miller, J. 1965. "The Urban Field." *Journal of the American Institute of Planners*, vol. 31 (November), pp. 312–20.

Gale, S. and Moore, E., eds. 1975. *The Manipulated City: Perspectives on Spatial Structure and Social Issues in Urban America*. Chicago: Maaroufa Press.

Gottmann, Jean. 1961. *Megalopolis*. New York: The Twentieth Century Fund.

Gras, N.S.B. 1922. *An Introduction to Economic History*. New York: Harper.

Hansen, N. M. 1975. *The Challenge of Urban Growth: The Basic Economics of City Size and Structure*. Lexington, Mass.: D. C. Heath.

Harris, C. A. and Ullman, E. L. 1945. "The Nature of Cities." *Annals of the American Academy of Political and Social Science*, vol. 242, pp. 7–17.

Isard, Walter. 1956. *Location and the Space Economy*. Cambridge, Mass.: M.I.T. Press.

———. 1960. *Methods of Regional Analysis: An Introduction to Regional Science*. Cambridge, Mass.: M.I.T. Press.

Lösch, A. 1937. *The Economics of Location*. Translated by W. Woglom and W.A. Stolper. New Haven: Yale University Press.

Moser, C. A. and Scott, W. 1961. *British Towns*. London: Oliver and Boyd.

Mydral, G. 1957. *Economic Theory and Underdeveloped Regions*. London: Duckworth.

Organization for Economic Co-operation and Development (O.E.C.D.). 1973. *National Urban Growth Policies and Strategies: Evaluation of Implementation, Experience and Innovation*. Paris: O.E.C.D.

Perloff, H. S., Dunn, E. S., Jr., Lampard, E. E., and Muth, R. F. 1960. *Regions, Resources, and Economic Growth*. Baltimore: Johns Hopkins University Press.

Pred, A. 1974. *Major Job Providing Organizations and Systems of Cities*. Resourse Paper 27. Washington: A.A.G. Commission on College Geography.

Richardson, H. W. 1969. *Regional Economics*. New York: Praeger.

———. 1973. *Regional Growth Theory*. London: Macmillan & Co.

———. 1977. *The New Urban Economics*. London: Pion.

Simmons, J. W. 1974. "Canada as an Urban System: A Conceptual Framework." Research Paper No. 62, Centre for Urban and Community Studies. Toronto: University of Toronto.

Stöhr, W. 1974. *Interurban Systems and Regional Economic Development*. Resource Paper 26. Washington: A.A.G. Commission on College Geography.

Swain, H. and Logan, M. 1975. "Urban Systems: A Policy Perspective." *Environment and Planning A*. Vol. 7, pp. 743–755.

Thompson, W. R. 1965. "Urban Economic Growth and Development in a National System of Cities," in P. M. Hauser and L. Schnore, eds. *The Study of Urbanization*. New York: Wiley, pp. 431–490.

United Nations. 1976a. *Report of Habitat: United Nations Conference on Human Settlements*. New York: United Nations.

———. 1976b. *Global Review of Human Settlements*. Item 10 of the Provisional Agenda, Habitat: U.N. Conference on Human Settlements, Vancouver, 31 May to 11 June, 1976.

Vining, R. 1945. "Regional Variations in Cyclical Fluctuations Viewed as a Frequency Distribution." *Econometrica*, vol. 13, pp. 183–213.

———. 1946. "The Region as a Concept in Business Cycle Analysis." *Econometrica*, vol. 14, pp. 201–218.

———. 1949. "The Region as an Economic Entity and Certain Variations to be Observed in the Study of Systems of Regions." *Papers and Proceedings of the American Economic Association*, vol. 39, May, pp. 89–104.

———. 1953. "Delimitation of Economic Areas: Statistical Conceptions in the Study of the Spatial Structure of an Economic System." *Journal of the American Statistical Association*, vol. 48, pp. 44–64.

———. 1955. "Description of Certain Aspects of An Economic System." *Economic Development and Cultural Change*, vol. 3, pp. 147–198.

Ward, B. 1976. *The Home of Man*. Toronto: McClelland and Stewart.

**1**

# URBAN SYSTEMS:
# DEFINITIONS, CONCEPTS,
# AND APPROACHES

# Introduction

## THE URBAN SYSTEM AS A UNIT OF ANALYSIS

Our all-embracing view of the urban system as a framework for the discussion of virtually all aspects of the spatial evolution and structure of a nation at the outset requires close attention to problems of concept and definition. Not all the authors of the papers selected for inclusion in this volume have the same view of the urban system, or even of a city itself. In fact many of the apparent contradictions or paradoxes in the literature derive from such definitional differences.

The analysis of an urban system based on cities legally defined as municipal units differs substantially from an analysis based on cities defined as metropolitan areas, or the "daily urban systems" discussed below. Even the visual images presented by maps are strikingly different when varying definitions are used. Contrast a traditional map of urban districts in England and Wales with the maps constructed by Hall *et al.* (1973), showing standard metropolitan labor market areas (see Figure 3 in the paper by Simmons and Bourne). Not only are the definitions of the elements or cities in the urban system important, but so too is the specification of the boundaries of that system. For example, a model of urban growth calibrated for cities in New England or South Australia will give different results from a model calibrated on a national scale (Putnam, 1975).

Three aspects of urban definitions must be discussed here: 1) the external bounding or "closure" of the urban system; 2) the urban-rural interface; and 3) the identification of those relationships among cities most relevant to our focus on "systems" as such. The papers selected for this section provide elaboration of these issues. The editors begin with an overview paper on traditional concepts of the city and its spatial measurement, as exemplified by United States, Canadian, and British census data. These data sources, because they are far more comprehensive than any other data on cities, act as a powerful constraint on the exploration of new empirical relationships in urbanization as well as on the information and insights such research uncovers.

The widening conceptual framework of what we define as urban is perhaps best represented by the concept of the "urban field" as described in Friedmann's paper in this section. This paper is an updated version of the initial landmark paper on the urban field (Friedmann and Miller, 1965), which permanently altered our idea of what the city is. The urban field is a spatially extensive and multi-nodal region, which includes the bulk of the life-space or activity area of urban residents. It extends well beyond the built-up area into recreational zones and areas of exurban residences within 100 miles or more of the urban core. The urban field becomes the basic building block in our concept of the urban system, and the relationships among these fields are in fact the main concern of this volume. The last decade has seen a flurry of studies extending the concept or providing empirical verification of its validity, notably the work of Brian Berry (1970, 1973).

The paper by Gottmann expands on the complexity of urban regions, while introducing some concepts from ekistics (the science of human settlements developed initially by C. Doxiadis), as one approach to understanding urban settlement patterns. Urbanized zones are beginning to emerge and may eventually fill in to produce extensive urban regions or megalopolises, as in northwestern Europe (Robert, 1976). These megalopolises may embrace dozens of metropolitan centers. Some writers (Doxiadis and Papaioannou, 1974) have even reached the point of extrapolating from this trend a prediction of a global ecumenopolis, or world city, formed by the linking of several megalopolises into a world-wide urban network. Fortunately this event is unlikely.

The final definitional theme, the necessity for conceptual models that encompass the interdependencies among cities, is portrayed in a paper by Simmons written specifically for this volume. Implicitly, in any discussion of systems of cities or systems within cities (Steiss, 1975), we draw on many models of how those systems are "organized." However, models of growth and change in the urban systems require that external linkages and the forces they represent be introduced explicitly. In this direction Simmons develops a typology of different *organization models,* each of which reflects a particular phase in the evolution of urban systems, but which may be operating at the same time in varying degrees to shape the spatial structure of those systems.

In the final paper John Friedmann develops the overall theme of the urban system as the necessary link between the evolution of a local urban economy and that of a national and international system, and also as an instrument for achieving national development goals. The paper also serves to link our definitional concerns in this section to the empirical focus of subsequent sections. The selection reprinted here is part of a chapter from his excellent book entitled *Urbanization, Planning and National Development* (1973a). The interested reader is referred to this or more recent volumes (Friedmann and Wulff, 1976) for further elaboration.

## The "Closure" of an Urban System

One neglected aspect of research on city systems is the effect of influences deriving from outside the nation (the "turbulent" environment we cited in the Introduction), on the organization of those systems. It becomes quickly evident in most historical studies of urban systems that many events and forces of change emanating from beyond the borders exert important influences on the location of cities, their size, economies, and rates of growth. Included among these external forces are such varied historical relationships as the origin, location, and direction of evolution of the margin of settlement such as that of the eastern seaboard of the United States, which left an established hierarchy of major cities in the east, and the rapid growth of urban centers on the west coast, the latter partly due to two major wars in the Pacific. More broadly, no nation is unaffected by its trading patterns of international migration or national defense, each of which alters rates, directions, and locations of growth within the country. One can seldom treat a national urban system as an independent entity. The city is also, as Boulding notes in his paper in the next section, an element in the international political system.

Similarly unpredictable (from a study of the nation in isolation) are forces of nature, technology, and social change. Recent students of North American urban systems (Borchert, in the section to follow; Berry and Neils, 1969), often seem bemused by the uncertainty and unpredictability of urban growth. In the short run, the accidents of weather, dramatically altering agricultural production, or the discovery (or demise) of mineral deposits, or the shifts in world commodity prices, or a host of other factors alter the growth and prosperity of many of our cities. In the longer run, changes in the technology of air transportation (such as in Seattle), in defense research (Houston), in where a country's government is situated (Brasilia), or in industrial structure (Manchester) will also alter growth rates and permanently modify the urban system. Other changes are more subtle. Increases in income and changes in preferences for different living environments have created some of the most rapid shifts within the urban system, such as migrations to Miami and Los Angeles, or to Brisbane or Santiago.

Few of these kinds of change are predictable from a knowledge of the pre-existing urban system or a description of its current internal processes of change.* Although looking backward the evolution of an urban system has some apparent logic, there are always many alternative paths of growth the system could have followed. A "Detroit" could have occurred in South Bend or in Toledo. A properly timed hurricane could have prevented the rise of Miami, and may have done so in Darwin, Australia. The nation itself, as a spatial and political entity, is the accidental product of wars, treaties, land purchases, and trade agreements, often undertaken to fulfill some now forgotten imperial needs.

The external or international forces that impinge on a national urban system are so numerous, so varied, and so unique to each nation that systematic analyses of their effects are rare. One continuing research tradition, however, is that of the

---

*There are some exceptions to this generalization. We need more studies of change of the thoroughness of Hägerstrand's study of population change and distribution in Sweden (see Hägerstrand *et al.*, 1974).

imprint on national development of *imperialism*. Imperialism may take several forms. One explicit form is that of colonial rule, which may lead to the kind of dual economy characteristic of much of Asia and described so vividly by Myrdal (1957). Or it may simply be the result of spatially biased development processes deriving from the effects of external technology and market pressures and leading to a core-periphery model of national development (e.g., Friedmann, pp. 00–00). Whatever the origin of imperialism, or its political ideology, however, the implication is essentially the same: that of an external agency, economic system, or country imposing an urban system upon a previously unstructured territory and often polarizing that territory. What we now require from our research is a clearer sense of how such external influences continue at later stages in the development process, hand in hand with processes of concentration, specialization, and interaction operating within each country. Perhaps some of the systematic international comparisons of urban systems now underway may be useful (see Hall, Hansen, and Swain, 1975).

## The Urban-Rural Interface

At the other end of the range of definitional problems is the apparent need among researchers to segregate urban and rural activities. In the past at least, this definitional concern has been of great importance. Perhaps too much so. The assumption was always that regional studies, of whatever discipline, discussed the bulk of the place-to-place variations in the economic and social life of the nation. The field of urban studies was subsequently added in order to focus on those "residual" activities that were carried on in cities. These were activities characteristically dominated by secondary and tertiary economic sectors and whose location was largely determined by agglomeration effects and by intense intersectoral linkages rather than by the location of resources.

When cities were seen to play an important role within a nation and to show differences among themselves in terms of landscape, life-style, and economic specialization, it became necessary to clearly delimit them from their surroundings. The rural-urban boundary question thus became one of considerable research and policy interest. Some researchers continue to place great emphasis on such measures of urbanization—which are actually measures of population concentration—and then correlate them with other processes, such as industrialization, increasing income, and personal mobility. The results are then used to evaluate, either longitudinally or in cross-section, the role of urban systems in social change. (Every urban text contains a graph of urbanization over time and a map of the boundaries of present-day urban areas.)

But as the urban component of the national population total approaches seventy, eighty, or even ninety percent, as it does today in most western nations as well as in parts of the Socialist bloc, the focus of concern must change. The urban-rural boundary becomes so blurred that the dichotomy, at least in terms of life-styles and attitudes, becomes arbitrary and essentially meaningless. No one has been able to demarcate the boundary of a city in a consistent fashion.

Instead we have devised a wide variety of definitions of urban areas which serve various purposes and different kinds of analysis, and we use them simultaneously. Chicago can mean the Loop, or the political city of the late Mayor Daley, or it can include everything between Detroit and the Rockies. London may imply the "City" of bankers, or the GLC (Greater London Council) administrative area, or the entire southeast of England. With increasing frequency, studies of the urban system in highly developed economies use extensive spatial units that ignore rural-urban distinctions. The geographic territory of one city extends to the territory of the next.

The variety of possible definitions is exemplified by Figures 1 and 2, which describe the range of spatial delimitations of Toronto. For some purposes Toronto is about one square mile of high-rise offices, banks, and law courts—an area with few permanent residents but 150,000 workers. At the other extreme Toronto can be treated as coexistent with the province of Ontario (1977 population 8.4 million) or even, for certain functions, all of Canada (population 23 million). In between we see the whole spectrum of units, each used for some purpose: as statistical

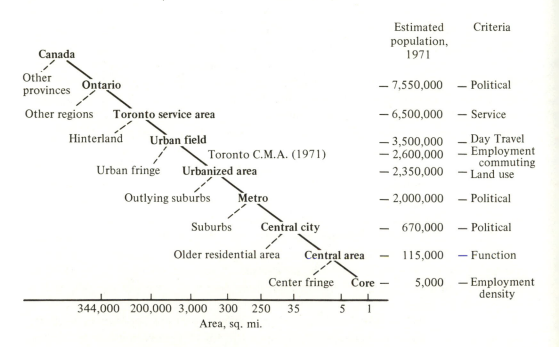

Figure 1. Definitions of Toronto (from Simmons and Bourne, 1973).

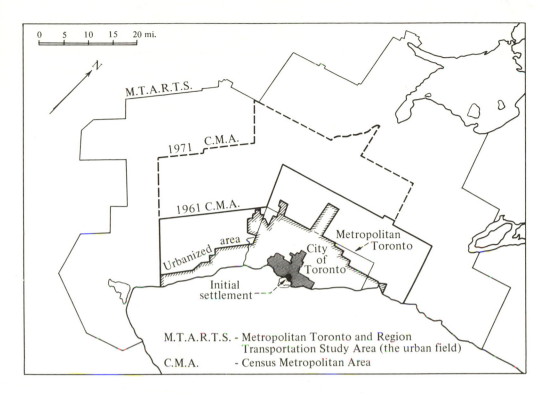

Figure 2. Delimiting Toronto (from Simmons and Bourne, 1973).

reporting units (C.M.A.) for analysis and planning, or as political and administrative units (Metro). The urban landscape itself has extended far into the countryside, in the form of country residences, recreational resorts, public institutions, and speculative land ownership (the urban field). The degree of integration among these components of the urban area is intense, including the movement of millions of people and the exchange of millions of pieces of information daily. Toronto, for example, draws its workers from an area of over 3000 square miles. In two hours one can be anywhere within this area. The same situation applies everywhere in the developed world.

The complexity of the concept of "urban" is displayed in the following papers. Friedmann uses the urban-field concept to describe the spatial interpenetration of urban/rural activities. Gottmann, drawing on the classic works of Doxiadis (1968), suggests in the second paper that many urban areas are becoming coterminous, without any real rural interstices. For urban systems like these—and Berry (1973) puts most of the continental U.S. in this category—the only meaningful boundary between rural and urban may simply be the dividing line between adjacent urban-centered regions. The nation-space becomes almost entirely subdivided into *functional* urban-centered regions. "Rural" is used explicitly to delineate a portion of the urbanized region less tightly linked than others to the urban core. (Those rural areas which are least tightly linked are commonly the zones of economic stagnation.)

This perspective does not in any way deny the importance of rural and agricultural areas. Instead the intention here is to deflate the traditional emphasis attached to the identification of discrete rural/urban boundaries and to suggest the need for a reinterpretation of the role of agricultural activities. These activities then become a major sector of, and a full participating member in, a heavily urbanized national economy, rather than a peripheral activity which is often treated in isolation by policymakers.

The critical definitional criterion then becomes the threshold size of an urban region necessary for consideration in an urban-system perspective. At what scale can a satellite center be considered independent? The size of the urban core, the intensity of the labor-shed, and distance from adjacent centers become most important. Small centers, such as Rapid City, South Dakota (population 43,800) may center an extensive urban region; larger centers, such as Jersey City (population 609,300) often do not. Thus, the city's labor-shed, as defined by commuting patterns, may be the single most meaningful criterion (Berry, 1970). Within the labor-shed, people can change their job or residence independently, thereby adjusting to the need for social mobility or life-cycle changes. A reasonably full range of jobs, occupations, social classes, and housing exists. At spatial scales below the labor-shed, disproportionate concentrations of certain activities (e.g., primary jobs) can occur; while at larger scales, to adjust one's employment may require residential migration as well. As a result the flexibility of response to economic change is limited at either extreme.

### Relationships among Cities

Geographic boundaries are of course a familiar problem in urban studies, but the literature of urban systems raises a new problem: what pattern of relationships is assumed to exist among cities in that system? That is, to use the terminology of the Simmons' paper in this section, "How is the urban system organized?" The problem has three facets. Initially, it comes from the use of extended boundaries for urban areas as suggested above. The number of urban regions designated in an urban system not only defines the threshold size of the smallest urban region but also determines which places are most likely to be closely integrated with the largest center. Any systematic aggregation, or disaggregation, of groups of cities implies some degree of dominance and dependence among those cities. For some purposes, South Bend is independent; for others, it is part of Chicago. But why Chicago, rather than Detroit or St. Louis?

These dependencies can be made more explicit in the notion of a *hierarchical system organization,* in which every city has relations with both higher- and lower-order centers. From the analysis of such relations one can designate different and distinct levels or orders of centers following the terminology of Christaller (1933) and Lösch (1937). Such orders are often a convenient taxonomy for analysis, permitting us to separate out centers of varying size and functional role (Brown and Holmes, 1971).

A strictly hierarchical structure of interdependence is not always realistic, how-ever (see Pred, 1976 and Section IV). It implies regularities in city size, distance, and functional specialization, which frequently do not occur. Highly industrialized urban regions, for instance, may interact in quite different ways with each other than with less industrialized regions. In some situations, then, the specifications of the urban system for study purposes requires an explicit decision at the outset on what interdependencies within the system are important. Do we link cities together because of their complementary economic specializations, or do we assume that linkages are readily apparent in the transportation networks? Do growth impulses move from the largest centers to the smallest, or vice versa? Or do they move among the large centers first, as Pred suggests in Section IV? Intercity interaction is highly structured, and this itself has important implications for most debates on growth and change in an urban system.

## Concepts of the City

Elaborating the notion of an urban system also extends the concept of the "city." We have already noted the development of new definitions of the city, particularly those with differing spatial scales. The broader-scale definitions, because they in-ternalize much of the hinterland economy by bringing it into the urban area, create very different impressions of that region's total economic base and of the factors affecting urban growth. Yet by including more of the surrounding farmland, a more appropriate basis for studying the urban economy is identified. That is, the observed growth in the urban core appears simply to reflect a redistribution within the region, analogous to suburbanization, rather than an inter-regional shift of ac-tivities or population. The specification of the urban system is therefore a critical component of any analysis of population change and redistribution.

The urban system also treats the city essentially as one point, or node, within a large and complex network of external relationships. The size of a city, its power, degree of specialization, and rate of growth are largely determined by its situation within the national urban system. External relationships can sometimes be studied on a disaggregate basis, such as visiting one's aunt in Kansas City or the network of General Motors factories around the globe. More often though it requires us to combine the activities of the urban region into a single integrated complex, which acts for the benefit (or disbenefit) of all its residents. The combined activities of the city then become something more than the sum of its components. Atlanta attracts, Atlanta seeks, Atlanta rejects. This personification is awkward, for it assumes a uniformity of purpose that is not likely to exist. It attributes goals to a city or community that perhaps only a few businesspeople or politicians share. Nonetheless it is a necessary perspective in order to consider more fully the complex operations of urban systems.

# REFERENCES

Berry, B.J.L. 1970. "Commuting Patterns, Labor Market Participation and Regional Potential." *Growth and Change*, vol. 1, pp. 3–11.

———. 1973. *Growth Centers in the American Urban System*. Cambridge, Mass.: Ballinger.

———, and Neils, Elaine. 1969. "Location, Size and Shape of Cities as Influenced by Environment: The Urban Environment Writ Large," in H. Perloff, ed., *The Quality of the Urban Environment*. Baltimore: Johns Hopkins Press.

Brown, L. and Holmes, J. 1971. "The Delimitation of Functional Regions, Nodal Regions and Hierarchies by Functional Distance Approaches." *Journal of Regional Science*, vol. 11, pp. 57–72.

Christaller, Walter. 1933. *Central Places in Southern Germany*. Translated by C. W. Baskin. Englewood Cliffs, N.J.: Prentice-Hall, 1966.

Doxiadis, C. A. 1968. *Ekistics: An Introduction to the Science of Human Settlements*. London: Hutchinson.

———, and Papaioannou, J. 1974. *Ecumenopolis, The Inevitable City of the Future*. Athens: Athens Publishing House.

Friedmann, J. 1973a. *Urbanization, Planning and National Development*. Beverly Hills, Ca.: Sage Publications.

———. 1973b. "The Future of the Urban Habitat," in D. McAllister, ed., *Environment: The New Focus for Land Use Planning*. NSF Press, pp. 96–134.

———. 1973c. "The Future of the Urban Habitat," in S. P. Snow, ed., *The Place of Planning*. The 1971–72 Lectures in Urban and Regional Planning. Auburn, Ala.: Auburn University, The Graduate School, November 1973, pp. 103–141.

——— and Wulff, R. 1976. *The Urban Transition*. London: E. Arnold.

———, and Miller, J. 1965. "The Urban Field." *Journal of the American Institute of Planners*, vol. 31, pp. 312–320.

Hägerstrand, T. *et al.* 1974. *The Biography of a People. Past and Future Population Changes in Sweden*. Stockholm: Royal Ministry for Foreign Affairs.

Hall, P. *et al.* 1973. *The Containment of Urban England*. Vol. 1. *Urban and Metropolitan Growth Processes*. London: Allen and Unwin.

———, Hansen, N. M., and Swain, H. 1975. "Urban Systems: A Comparative Analysis of Structure, Change and Public Policy," *Research Memorandum RM-75-35*. Laxenburg, Austria: International Institute for Applied Systems Analysis.

Hansen, N. M. 1975. "A Critique of Economic Regionalizations of the United States," RR-75-32. Laxenburg, Austria: International Institute for Applied Systems Analysis.

Lösch, A. 1937. *The Economics of Location*. Translated by W. H. Woglom and W. A. Stolper. New Haven: Yale University Press, 1954.

Myrdal, G. 1957. *Economic Theory and Underdeveloped Regions*. London: Duckworth.

Pred, A. 1976. "The Interurban Transmission of Growth in Advanced Economies: Empirical Findings versus Regional Planning Assumptions," RR-76-4. Laxenburg, Austria: International Institute for Applied Systems Analysis.

Putman, S. H. 1975. *An Empirical Model of Regional Growth with an Application to the Northeast Megalopolis*. Philadelphia: Regional Science Research Institute.

Robert, J. 1976. "Prospective Study on Physical Planning and the Environment in the Megalopolis in Formation in North West Europe," *Urban Ecology,* vol. 1, pp. 331–411.

Simmons, J. W. and Bourne, L. S. 1973. "The Area of Interest: Urban Definitions in Canada," in L. S. Bourne *et al.*, eds., *The Form of Cities in Central Canada: Selected Papers*. Toronto: University of Toronto Press, pp. 5–16.

Steiss, A. W. 1975. *Models for the Analysis and Planning of Urban Systems*. Lexington, Mass.: Lexington Books.

# Defining Urban Places: Differing Concepts of the Urban System

JAMES W. SIMMONS and LARRY S. BOURNE

## INTRODUCTION

All descriptions, analyses, and comparisons of cities depend on the validity of the urban definitions employed. Inconsistencies in concept and measurement of the appropriate area for study often render comparisons virtually meaningless. They may even distort our images of cross-sectional relationships at one point in time. For instance, naive researchers have frequently attempted to compare urban population densities for different cities, using simply the population of a municipality divided by its geographic area. Such a measure is so sensitive to the slightest boundary change—the inclusion of another suburb, or water area, or a large park—as to be almost worthless. Most measures of urban growth are almost equally vulnerable to definitional changes. Although there is no single solution to this problem, what we need is both consistent definitions of urban places and an awareness of the effects of modifying those definitions.

One response to the definitional problem is to develop a whole spectrum of urban definitions that are suitable for different purposes. When relationships are compared across these differing sets of units we can then evaluate their sensitivity to changes in boundary lines. Ideally this spectrum of definitions should be continuous and additive. That is, it should be possible to reconstruct an original set of small spatial units, such as census tracts, census divisions or municipalities, from the larger aggregated set, and vice versa. In this way analytical flexibility is maintained without a significant loss of generality.

## INTERNATIONAL CONTEXT

Until recently there has been relatively little interest in attempting to standardize urban definitions across national boundaries. In a series of reports, Kingsley Davis (1972) has provided an overview of world urbanization trends based on the prevailing urban definitions employed in each country (see Section II). His detailed calculations indicate just how complex and seemingly intractable the problems are. On the other hand innumerable specific studies have been undertaken of a few cities or countries or both, but these make little pretense to being comprehensive.

More recently, a number of international agencies and study groups (see Hall, Hansen, and Swain, 1975) have initiated comparative studies of urban development, an initial stage of which is the assessment of definitional criteria. Although formal recommendations as to definitions and measurement problems have not as yet emerged from these studies, a much greater awareness now exists of the importance of the problems.

Most countries now use some definition of the concept of the "extended city" as a basis for measuring the extent of urbanization. In the United States it is the standard metropolitan statistical area (SMSA); in Canada the census metropolitan area (CMA); in Britain the unofficial standard metropolitan labor market area (SMLA); in Australia the census expanded urban district; in France the *agglomération;* in West Germany the *Stadt* region; and in Sweden the labor-market area. They all share at least three common elements: 1) a minimum population threshold for inclusion as an urban area; 2) a geographic scale large enough to encompass the built-up urban area and small enough to maintain a minimum level of population density; and 3) an area from which workers are drawn to the urban central core, effectively the urban labor market.

In each country these criteria are interpreted and applied somewhat differently, and the individual building blocks used in constructing the geographic areas also vary. In the U.S. the basic blocks are usually counties; in Britain, local authorities; in Canada and in Sweden, local municipalities and census divisions. In some instances, notably Sweden

and the U.S., these areas may be exhaustive, that is, they divide all of the national territory into a set of urban-centered regions.

To illustrate certain aspects of these problems Table 1 summarizes data for the United States and Canadian censuses of 1970 and 1971 respectively. Obviously several methods of slicing up the national territory into urban units are possible, but it should again be stressed that any relationships specified for one set of units do not necessarily carry over to others. In aggregate, however, there is not much disagreement about the total size of the "urban" population in either country.

The Canadian-American example illustrates other definitional difficulties as well. It is noteworthy that even the very modest discrepancies in spatial units of measurement (and in the way census variables are defined) have made comparisons of these urban

Table 1. A Comparison of Urban Definitions

| | United States, 1970 | | | Canada, 1971 | | |
|---|---|---|---|---|---|---|
| | Number | Total Population | Average Size | Number | Total Population | Average Size |
| Municipalities 10,000 and over | 2301[1] | 112,451,000 | 48,900 | 207[2] | 10,910,000 | 52,700 |
| Urbanized Areas 50,000 and over | 248[3] | 118,447,000 | 477,600 | 33[4] | 10,754,000 | 325,900 |
| Metropolitan Areas | 243[5] | 139,419,000 | 573,700 | 22[6] | 11,875,000 | 540,000 |
| Urban Population | — | 149,325,000[7] | — | — | 14,727,000[8] | — |
| Total Population | — | 203,212,000 | — | — | 21,568,000 | — |

[1]Incorporated urban places. United States Bureau of the Census, *Census of Population, 1970.* Vol. I, "Characteristics of the Population", U.S. Summary, Section I, Table 6.
[2]Incorporated cities, towns and villages. Canada, *1971 Census of Canada,* Bulletin 1.1–8, Table 7.
[3]Central city of 50,000 or more plus the surrounding closely settled incorporated and unincorporated areas. United States, *op cit.,* Table 20.
[4]Includes the urbanized cores of census metropolitan areas and census agglomerations. Canada, *op. cit.,* Bulletin 1.1–8, Tables 8 and 9.
[5]Standard Statistical Metropolitan Area includes central cities of 50,000 or more plus adjacent counties within the labor-shed. United States, *op. cit.,* Table 5.
[6]Census Metropolitan Area include urbanized cores of 100,000 plus adjacent labor-sheds. Canada, *op. cit.,* Bulletin 1.1–8, Table 8.
[7]Urban includes residents of incorporated and unincorporated places of 2500 or more plus the urban fringe of urbanized areas. United States, *op. cit.,* Table 3.
[8]Urban includes population living in incorporated cities, towns and villages with a population of 1000 or over; unincorporated includes places of 1000 or over having a population density of at least 1000 per square mile The built-up fringes of the above have a minimum population of 1000 and a density of at least 1000 per square mile. Canada, *op. cit.,* Bulletin 1.1–9, Table 10.

systems—so similar and so closely linked in many ways—almost impossible.[1]

The varieties of urban definitions in both countries are worth exploring in detail because of the light they shed on our concepts of urbanization and urbanity. The sections of this paper to follow describe the basic urban units for the United States, and then contrast these first with the Canadian format, and then with the British.

## APPROACHES TO DEFINING THE URBAN AREAS OF THE UNITED STATES

The United States Bureau of the Census pioneered the concept of the extended urban area by delimiting the "Metropolitan District" in the census of 1910. Since that time the concept has been extended and complemented by the variety of alternative approaches listed below, which provide the urban analyst with a full spectrum of data units. Probably the best reviews of this evolution of definitions are provided in Berry *et al.* (1968), and Berry and Horton (1970).

### The Municipality

The basic building block of every empirical concept of an urban areas is the political municipality, that is, the city, town, or township. The simplest approach to defining the elements in the urban system is to choose the central city, say Boston, New York, or Detroit to represent the urban area. This approach can be justified in that census data compiled for individual households are com-

monly aggregated to these units and because additional materials derived by local and state authorities are often only available for such municipalities.

The difficulties with the municipality as a unit of analysis are threefold. Central cities, as commonly delineated, are usually poor fits to most working definitions of the city as a social, economic, or spatial unit. Most often they are spatially underbounded, excluding suburban and exurban areas which are closely integrated with the central city. Conversely, for some western U.S. cities such as Santa Fe or Phoenix, they include vast areas not yet, nor ever likely, to be built up. An equally serious problem with municipalities as units of analysis is the propensity of state and local governments to alter political boundaries frequently by annexation or, on occasion, by their marriage or full integration into some form of metropolitan area or regional government. The municipal reorganizations of Dade County (Miami), Nashville, Seattle, and the Twin Cities (Minneapolis-St. Paul) area are now well documented examples. Each of the above of course varies in purpose and legal form as well as in geographic scope, but all complicate analyses based strictly on municipal boundaries. Most major Canadian cities, Metro Toronto for instance, now have a two-tier governmental structure of some kind. Under these conditions it is difficult to specify which municipality should be the data-reporting unit and difficult also to maintain consistent data files over time.

Finally, because municipalities are so frequently only partial representations of a labor-shed, they can generate quite misleading impressions when statistics are calculated. The industrial suburb, or a wealthy residential suburb, can exist very comfortably without the full complement of land uses, labor force, and social diversity that we expect to see in a city. These muncipalities will appear as extreme points in any analysis, perhaps having one doctor for every sixty people, or $100,000,000 in industrial assessment per worker. It is only when political variables, such as the structure of government or fiscal

1. In some respects Canada can be treated as a subsystem of the North American urban system, centered on New York. Like other regional subsystems in the U.S., such as the west or southeast, it is closely linked to the core urbanized region on the northeast seaboard, but the interdependency is not symmetrical. An enormous volume of trade takes place between the two national systems, amounting to over ten percent of total Canadian economic production, but only one percent of the United States total. Changes in the volume, quality, and locale of trade therefore have disproportionately heavy effects on the Canadian urban system. Interdependencies of this sort are one of the inherent sources of stress within an urban system.

relationships are involved that legal municipalities become a viable unit for urban systems analysis in their own right.

## The Urbanized Area

The most obvious response to the difficulties posed by the use of the central-city or municipality-area definition for research purposes is to define a geographically broader and more functionally based concept of the city. The "urbanized area," first applied in the 1950 U.S. census, is the simplest approximation of this concept and the most widely used because of its visual and intuitive appeal. Its definition is jointly based on a minimum population size threshold and on the level of urban land-use intensity. More specifically (see the 1970 *U.S. Census User's Guide*), it includes:

(1) A central city (or twin cities) of 50,000 or more population, plus

(2) Those surrounding, closely settled, incorporated and unincorporated areas that meet certain minimum requirements of population size and density (greater than 1000 persons per square mile).

A host of other rules cover the application of the above to various special cases, including land-use criteria, whether areas are adjacent or not, etc. Undeveloped portions of the central city can even be excluded under these rules.

The urbanized area embraces the bulk of urban activity (see Table 1) and is useful for cross-sectional comparisons of variables in any given census year. However, because it is delimited by the most rapidly changing boundary in an urban area—the built-up fringe—it tends to be very volatile. The real urbanized area shifts much more quickly than do census redefinitions (usually every ten years), and the complexity of the boundary itself makes it largely incompatible with other data sources. By 1976, for instance, the urbanized area as defined in 1970 already excludes the areas of most rapid social change in a metropolitan region.

## The Standard Metropolitan Statistical Area

The alternative unit of urban aggregation is the "Metropolitan Area," a concept introduced over sixty years ago, which has weathered a number of changes in definition and a considerable evolution in the techniques of urban analysis. The 1970 definition is, as in the past, based on two basic requirements: urban population size and a measure of spatial integration. The Standard Metropolitan Statistical Area or SMSA (see *Census Data User's Guide*) includes:

(1) Either one central city with a total population of 50,000 or more, or two contiguous cities constituting a single community with a combined population of 50,000 and a minimum population of 15,000 for the smaller of the two.

(2) The remainder of the county to which the central city belongs (the central county), and

(3) Adjacent counties, if
   (a) seventy-five percent or more of the labor force is non-agricultural, and
   (b) at least fifteen percent of the workers living in the outlying county work in the central county, or twenty-five percent of workers in that county live in the central county, and
   (c) either fifty percent of the population resident in that county lives in contiguous minor civil divisions with a population density of 150 persons per square mile or more; or the nonagricultural employment (or workers) equals at least ten percent of the nonagricultural employment in the central county (or workers), or it totals 10,000.

These definitions have evolved slowly over time, but their total effect is to include most of the labor-shed of the central county as well as that of the central city within the SMSA. Overall, this set of definitions has strengths and weaknesses, both stemming from the same source: the simplicity of the county as a spatial building block. On the one hand the

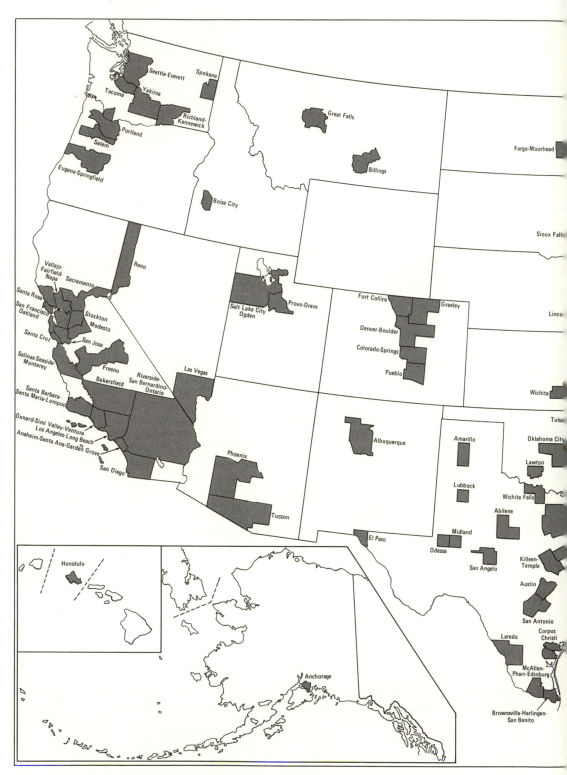

Figure 1. Standard Metropolitan Statistical Areas, 1976. U.S. Bureau of the Census.

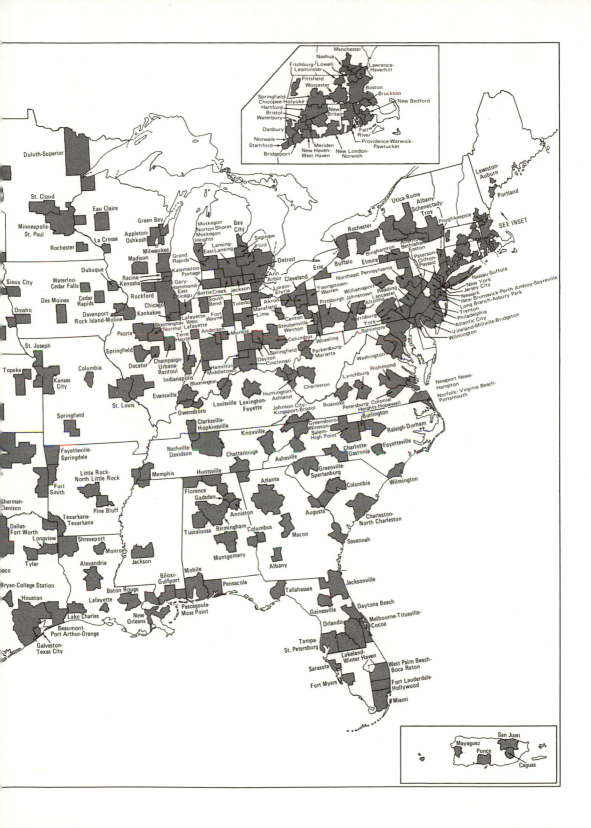

county is a crude and often unwieldy unit. In some states in the western U.S. (e.g., San Bernardino) the county covers an enormous area, stretching for hundreds of miles. A small urban center in one corner of the county linked to an adjacent city results in the whole area being included in the SMSA. In other states, particularly in the northeast, the county is inappropriate for designating the boundaries between adjacent urban centers, the cores of which may be only twenty-five to thirty miles apart. In partial response to the latter problem the Bureau of the Census has also designated two Standard Consolidated Areas. These are:

(1) New York-Northeastern New Jersey (including the New York SMSA, the Newark SMSA, the Jersey City SMSA, and the Paterson-Clifton-Passaic SMSA, as well as adjoining counties), and

(2) Chicago-Northwestern Indiana (including the Chicago SMSA and the Gary-Hammond-East Chicago SMSA).

On the other hand, the very crudeness of the SMSA's spatial delimitation makes them relatively stable over time. They can be readily linked to other data sources and thus are useful for a wide variety of purposes.[2] The boundaries of small metropolitan areas, consisting of two or three entire counties, are unlikely to shift with each census and are thus readily adjustable for time series analysis. These units are also able to absorb and display the effects of decentralization over an extended geographic area. As a result they have developed into useful recording units for marketing research, labor-force studies, and economic-base analyses precisely because they approximate the service area and overall labor supply or catchment area of the central city.

## The Urban-Centered Region

The data gathered on commuting patterns in the 1960 U.S. census permitted, for the first

time, a detailed exploration of the urban-field concept as outlined by Friedmann and Miller (1965). The first comprehensive, nationwide examination of these daily trip patterns by Brian Berry and his associates (Berry *et al.*, 1968; Berry, 1973) suggested that the nation could be treated, for most purposes, as fully urbanized. When smaller urban centers of 25,000 population were added to the adjacent metropolitan areas with which they were closely linked, almost every populated area was included within one commuting field or another. To these fields the name "daily urban systems" suggested by C. Doxiadis has been widely applied (Berry, 1973; see his map in Section III). Later work by Huff (1973) and Berry and Lamb (1974) on retail service fields and newspaper circulation confirmed the basic patterns of these functional regions. Schwind (1971) and Lankford (1972), for example, have also used urban-centered regions, based on Berry's investigations, as units of analysis in studies of migration and income levels in the U.S. with considerable success (see Section V).

## CANADIAN DEFINITIONS

As in the United States, the basic building block in Canadian urban definitions is the political municipality (the city, town, village, or township), which has the legal responsibility to provide municipal services. Differences from the U.S. terminology arise first because of the absence of counties as functional entities in Newfoundland and the western provinces and the peculiar elongated shapes of counties in Québec fronting on the St. Lawrence River. As a result counties cannot be used to build metropolitan regions as conveniently as in the U.S., and Statistics Canada has had to define its own census divisions for the presentation of areally extensive data. The census divisions, however, were defined at an early stage in the settlement process, and are

---

2. The United States Bureau of the Census has also begun to experiment with functional regions when it has the opportunity of defining minor civil divisions, such as in Oklahoma. See the discussion by K. Thompson (1975).

now particularly unwieldy for defining functional urban regions.[3]

Canada, as noted, has also been the scene of extensive municipal reorganization which has altered the traditional meaning of many urban terms. The City of Toronto is now simply one borough among six comprising the regional municipality of Metro Toronto, which is the more meaningful urban unit for most analytical purposes. Ottawa, Hamilton, Niagara, and Kitchener are examples of even more dramatic municipal reorganizations that integrate urban cores and extensive rural hinterlands. Western cities such as Saskatoon, Edmonton, and Calgary have opted for extensive annexation instead.

The response of Statistics Canada to these realities has been to focus on the continuously built-up or urbanized area, which is clearly identifiable from land-use maps, air photos, street plans, etc. A city, town, or village of at least 1000 population, together with an adjacent built-up area of at least 1000 population, which also has a population density of 1000 persons per square mile, then becomes the basis of a *census agglomeration* (C.A.) This unit is enlarged to include the rural portions of those municipalities considered to be part of the original built-up area. About 100 census agglomerations have been so defined, varying in size from 2000 to 110,000 persons, and distributed across the country as follows: the Maritimes, 20, Québec, 35, Ontario, 25, and the western provinces, 20. Although useful, they tend to be inconsistent as data sources since their definition varies over time, and they must be combined with those municipalities that have no externally built-up areas in order to obtain a complete list of urban centers. Census agglomerations do, however, take into account that small centers as well as large ones may have extensive suburban development outside their boundaries.

Once the urbanized core attains a population of 100,000, the entire urban center is then defined as a census metropolitan area (C.M.A.). Its boundaries are extended to in-

clude all other municipalities partly with urbanized area if:

(1) the percentage of the labor force in primary activities is less than the national average, and

(2) the rate of recent population increase (i.e., that between 1956–1966) is larger than the average for all C.M.A.'s.

If only one of these criteria is met, municipalities are included if they are served by a highway of two or more lanes in width. These cumbersome rules are essentially designed to enclose the major labor-shed of the urbanized core but generally fall short of that goal. They will likely be replaced by criteria based on journey-to-work movements (available for the first time in the 1971 census) in future censuses (Ricour-Singh, 1972).

The Canadian metropolitan area as a result tends to be both smaller in area and more precisely bounded than its American counterpart. If appropriately defined for a particular problem, the C.M.A. is a consistent and useful unit; but the intricacy of the definitional criteria makes it inflexible for the study of different kinds of problems, or to carry out an analysis of urban growth over time (Simmons, forthcoming).

Little work has been done in Canada to develop urban-centered regions similar to those in the U.S., although other types of regionalizations have been attempted (Cameron, Emerson, and Lithwick, 1974). This is understandable, perhaps, given the small number of metropolitan areas (22) and the enormous area of the country which is unsettled. In one attempt to overcome the cartographic distortions caused by largely empty wilderness areas, the degree of urbanization in the country has been displayed by an isodemographic map (Figure 2), which assigns an area on the map to each unit in proportion to its population. The significance of the urban system in the geography of Canada is thereby underlined.

## BRITISH URBAN DEFINITIONS

Unlike the United States, Britain has not had an official set of census definitions ap-

3. In the 1971 census, however, the census divisions of British Columbia were completely redrawn (based on urban nodes), to create an excellent set of urban-centered regions.

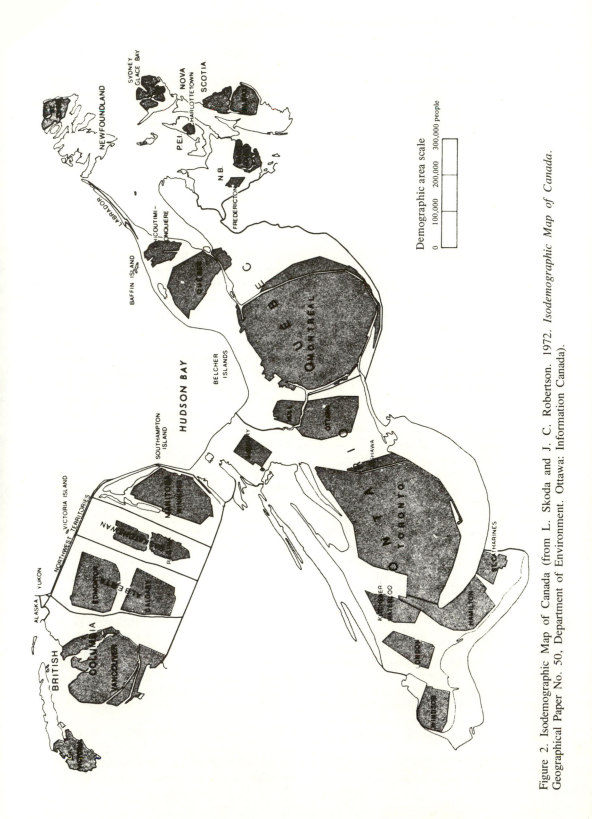

Figure 2. Isodemographic Map of Canada (from L. Skoda and J. C. Robertson. 1972. *Isodemographic Map of Canada*. Geographical Paper No. 50, Department of Environment. Ottawa: Information Canada).

proximating the concept of the "extended" urban area. In most instances the boundaries of a bewildering array of small urban municipalities, districts, and boroughs or local authorities (both urban and rural) have sufficed as statistical reporting units (Clawson and Hall, 1973). Aggregations of such areas into spatial units more closely approximating the extent of economic integration of the British landscape have been primarily those of large-scale planning regions (i.e., "the southeast"). It is argued that these regions, given their size and the density of population in the country as a whole, particularly in England, are the most appropriate units for planning and research. This view has recently been challenged.

The first comprehensive attempt at developing a new set of definitions for urban areas in Britain was undertaken by the Political and Economic Planning (PEP) group. Their results were reported in a two-volume report *The Containment of Urban England* (Hall *et al.*, 1973). After reviewing the definitions used in other countries, particularly the SMSA and Functional Economic Area (FEA) designations in the U.S., the PEP group decided to incorporate both concepts into their definitions. Using the journey-to-work and employment data from the 1961 census of England and Wales they established two principal types of urban units:

(1) the Standard Metropolitan Labour Area (SMLA), and

(2) the Metropolitan Economic Labour Area (MELA).

The latter includes the area of the former plus an outer ring of areas more loosely related to the urban core. These definitions have recently been updated using 1966 and 1971 census data and have been extended to include Scotland (see Drewett, Goddard, and Spence, 1974; Goddard and Spence, 1976). Applying the same criteria in 1971 as in 1961 produces 126 labor market areas compared with 111 in 1961.

## The Standard Metropolitan Labour Area

The SMLA is, as the name suggests, essentially the labor-shed of a major urban center.

It consists of two parts:

(1) a labor center or core and

(2) a metropolitan ring of areas surrounding and strongly related to that core.

The statistical building blocks that are put together to establish these areas are local authority areas (L.A.'s). Over time, new labor market areas may emerge from either of two situations: through the growth of sufficient jobs within the outer rings of the large metropolitan cores to produce a new labor center, or through the growth of new or free-standing towns (towns well removed from existing urban areas), able to meet the population-threshold requirements for inclusion as an urban core.

Three basic criteria (and a long list of special cases) define a core area:

(1) the density of jobs in a local authority area must exceed five per acre (or 2.12 per hectare);

(2) the total number of jobs in those areas constituting the core must exceed 20,000, and

(3) local authorities designated as part of the same core must be geographically contiguous.

Not all local authorities need meet all three criteria for inclusion, however. Any area satisfying only criteria (1) but which is contiguous to another that satisfies all three is then combined with the latter as a "joint labour center." Any authority satisfying only criteria (2) but not contiguous to an established core is defined as a separate core; however, no additions of adjacent authorities are allowed.

The criterion for inclusion as part of the metropolitan ring of an urban core is straightforward: a local authority area is so classified if over fifteen percent of its resident and economically active population works in the corresponding labor core. Those local authorities classified as part of the same ring must be contiguous, either to each other or to the core. The final criterion for inclusion as an SMLA is that the combined population of the core and ring must exceed 70,000.

The metropolitan labour market areas (MELA) are more spatially extensive than the SMLA's. They are created by the addition to the SMLA of an "outer metropolitan ring"

Figure 3a. Standard Metropolitan Labour Areas, 1971 (from Drewett, Goddard, and Spence, 1974).

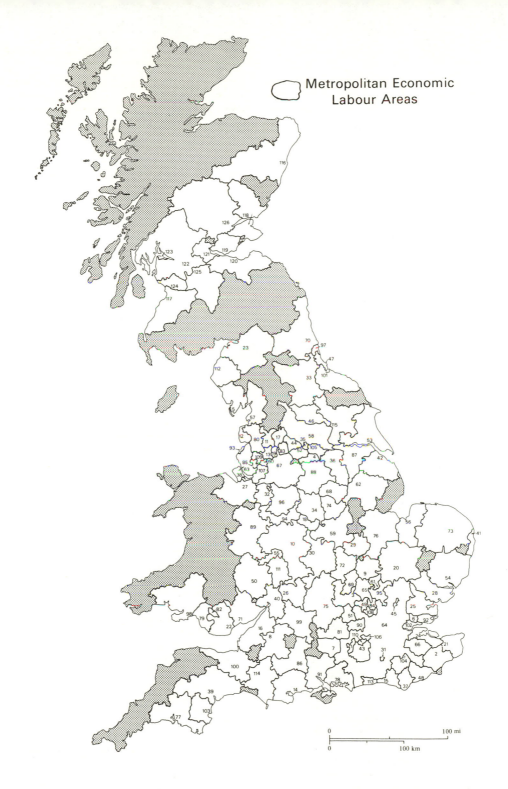

Figure 3b. Metropolitan Economic Labour Areas (from Drewett, Goddard, and Spence, 1974).

of local authorities less strongly integrated with the core. Any authority sending commuters to one or more labor cores is allocated to the outer ring of the contiguous core to which it sends its largest number of commuters. In most instances the outer ring completely encloses the SMLA, but in some more densely populated areas of the country the commuting fields overlap extensively and the outer rings may be incomplete or nonexistent.

## SOME FINAL COMMENTS

Official data agencies clearly play an important role in shaping our views of national development patterns and particularly of our urban systems. Every decade a new wave of census material forces us to reconstruct our picture of urban and regional patterns, development problems, and social trends. Predictably we are spending the 1970s trying to comprehend the changes that took place in the 1960s and we will likely spend the 1980s reviewing the 1970s.

For the most part, census enumerators tend to be conservative in their approach to defining urban areas. They cherish the boundaries of local municipalities, because these municipalities are major data users as well as the source of much political power, and steer clear of the controversies and technical difficulties that attend more experimental aggregations. Recent technical advances in computing systems and in techniques of geocoding have made it possible, however, for researchers to apply their own definitional criteria and to create their own aggregations of urban units from census tapes.

It is important that we test the sensitivity of our descriptions of urban systems against alternate data units. The experimentation of Berry and his associates and of the PEP group may in themselves lead to a new view of urban America and urban Britain, respectively, and to produce new images of growth, prosperity, and change. Similar outcomes may appear from such comparative international analyses as those being done by the European Common Market (EEC, 1975), the International Insti-

tute for Applied Systems Analysis (Hall, Hansen, and Swain, 1975), and other international groups. The spatial units used in urban systems analysis are that important.

## REFERENCES

Berry, B.J.L. 1973. *Growth Centers in the American Urban System*. Vol. 1. Cambridge, Mass.: Ballinger.

_____, Goheen, P. G. and Goldstein, H. 1968. *Metropolitan Area Definition: Reevaluation of Concept and Statistical Practice*. Working Paper No. 28. Washington: United States Bureau of the Census.

_____, and Horton, F., eds. 1970. *Geographical Perspectives on Urban Systems*. Englewood Cliffs, N.J.: Prentice-Hall.

_____, and Lamb, R. 1974. "The Delineation of Urban Spheres of Influence: Evaluation of an Interaction Model." *Regional Studies*, vol. 8, pp. 185–190.

Cameron, D., Emerson, D. L., and Lithwick, N. H. 1974. "The Foundations of Canadian Regionalism." *Discussion Paper 11*. Ottawa: Economic Council of Canada.

Clawson, M. and Hall, P. 1973. *Planning and Urban Growth*. Baltimore: Johns Hopkins University Press.

Drewett, R., Goddard, J., and Spence, N. 1974. "Urban Change in Britain: 1966–71." *Working Paper No. 1*. London: London School of Economics and Political Science, Department of Geography.

European Economic Community. 1975. "European Communities Urban Research Programme." Report of meeting, Dec. 3–5, 1975, Brussels.

Goddard, J. and Spence, N. 1976. "British Cities: Urban Population and Employment Trends 1951–71." London: Department of Environment Research Report No. 10.

Hall, P. *et al.* 1973. *The Containment of Urban England*. Vol. 1. London: Allen and Unwin.

_____, Hansen, N. and Swain, H. 1975. "Urban Systems: A Comparative Analysis of Structure, Change and Public Policy," *Research Memorandum RM-75-35*. Laxenburg, Austria: International Institute for Applied Systems Analysis.

Huff, D. 1973. "The Delineation of a National System of Regions on the Basis of Urban

Spheres of Influence." *Regional Studies,* vol. 7, pp. 323–329.

International Urban Research. 1959. *The World's Metropolitan Areas.* Los Angeles: University of California Press.

Lankford, Philip M. 1972. *Regional Incomes in the United States, 1929–1967.* Research Paper No. 145. Chicago: University of Chicago, Department of Geography.

Linge, G.J.R. 1965. *The Delimitation of Urban Boundaries.* Canberra: Australian National University.

Phillips, P. D. 1976. "The Changing Standard Metropolitan Statistical Area." *Journal of Geography,* vol. 75, pp. 165–173.

Ricour-Singh, F. 1972. "Census Metropolitan Areas: Revision of the Concept, Criteria and Delineations for the 1971 Census." Ottawa: Statistics Canada (mimeo).

Schwind, P. J. 1971. *Migration and Regional Development in the United States.* Research Paper No. 133. Chicago: University of Chicago, Department of Geography.

Simmons, J. W. Forthcoming. *The Canadian Urban System.* Toronto: University of Toronto.

Thompson, G. 1975. "United States Census County Divisions as a Geographical Data Base." *Professional Geographer,* vol. 27, pp. 467–469.

# The Urban Field as Human Habitat

JOHN FRIEDMANN

My purpose in this paper is to draw attention to a new form of the human habitat that I believe to be emerging. This form, which I shall call the urban field, is more extensive in its spatial dimensions than any concept we have previously had of the city.[1] Planners refer to it disparagingly as peripheral sprawl, and public policy has roundly ignored it. Yet the urban field continues to expand and develop. More than 90 percent of the American people are residing within its boundaries. The urban field has become our home. We are born there, we live there, we are buried there.

The urban field may be described as a vast multi-centered region having relatively low density, whose form evolves from a finely articulated network of social and economic linkages. Its many centers are set in large areas of open space of which much is given over to agricultural and recreational use. The core city from which the urban field evolved is beginning to lose its traditional dominance: it is becomming merely one of many specialized centers in a region.

The urban field thus represents the latest in a series of continually expanding concepts of the city. Beginning with the urban nucleus of preindustrial society, the city steadily grew as a physical entity, enroaching upon existing urban places on its periphery and incorporating them into its physical structure. The urbanized area—meaning the continually built-up area of the city—eventually gave place to the city region as an area whose economy was closely integrated with the old center.[2] But this enlarged region, in turn, yielded to the urban field which differs from preceding concepts of the city by stressing the uses made by urban populations of their environment. Spatially constrained by distance to the core from which it grew, it is also the physically most extensive concept. The urban field may be regarded as the basic territorial unit of post-industrial society.[3]

At the present stage of our knowledge, a formal definition of the urban field is a hazardous undertaking. The following three-dimensional definition is proposed as a basis for further discussion:

(1) *as a territorial subsystem of society,* the urban field is characterized by a spatially extended pattern of functional interaction and a multi-centric form of spatial organization. Its outer limits are defined by periodic recreational uses on the part of its resident population;

(2) as a *density configuration,* the urban field is

---

1. The concept of the urban field was first proposed by the author, in collaboration with John Miller, in "The Urban Field," *Journal of the American Institute of Planners*, Vol. 31, No. 4 (November 1965), pp. 312–320. For a related discussion, see Kevin Lynch, "The Pattern of the Metropolis," in William H. Leahy, David L. McKee, and Robert Dean, eds., *Urban Economics*. New York: The Free Press, 1970, Ch. 2.

2. John Friedmann, "The Concept of a Planning Region," *Land Economics*, Vol. 32, No. 1 (February 1956), pp. 1–13.
3. For a critical evaluation of current metropolitan concepts, see Brian J. L. Berry, *Metropolitan Area Definition: A Re-Evaluation of Concept and Statistical Practice*, U.S. Department of Commerce, Bureau of the Census.

From S.P. Snow, ed. *The Place of Planning* (Auburn, Ala.: Auburn University, 1973). Reprinted in revised form by permission.

characterized by the spatial dispersion of its population into high density activity clusters, surrounded by low-density open spaces that are related to each other by a complex network of transport, communication, and energy flows;

(3) as a *physical environment,* the urban field is characterized by permanent as well as periodic uses of land-extensive environmental resources for activities such as outdoor recreation, intermixed with spatially segregated but permanent and land-intensive uses for residential, economic, cultural, and political activity.

This vast new urban complex can no longer be visualized as a whole. Nor can it be directly experienced except in its parts and sequentially. The central city which gave birth to it no longer dominates its life, yet the field which surrounds the mother city is held together by a tight pattern of interconnected activities and land uses. If we center the urban field on a city of intermediate metropolitan size, its physical reach would extend for roughly two hours' driving distance from this center—and less where adjacent urban fields contain it—encompassing an area of as much as 9,000 to 15,000 square miles, or roughly two to three times the size of Connecticut. By this measure, the 100-odd urban fields we have today would cover approximately one-third of the total land surface of the continental United States.[4] Most of our lives unfold within their boundaries. No longer drawn to a single center of commerce, industry, and political power, we use the urban field by traveling along its many arteries in all directions. Suburban fingers reach out into it; second and mobile home areas spring up along its major throughways and on its outer fringes; its open spaces—lakeshores, beaches, and forests—are used intensively for recreation. The total population of the urban field may be as small as half a million and as large as twenty.[5]

In many parts of the country, urban fields

are clustered into "galaxies" of which Megalopolis along the northeastern seaboard of the United States was the first to be recognized. A recent study identifies twelve emerging urban galaxies. Using a more conservative criterion than the one I am proposing here, the author estimates that by the year 2000 fully 70 percent of the American people will come to live in them. Their population densities will range from a low of 250 per square mile to over 1000, covering an area that is only 10 percent of the nation. The remaining 90 percent of the land area is projected to a density of only 33 people per square mile (Map 1).[6]

This expansion of our living space into the physical peripheries of large core cities is occurring at a time when the total population growth rate of the country is declining, and the excess supply of rural labor has all but vanished.[7] Henceforth, rural populations will amount to only a small and rapidly dwindling fraction of the total migrant stream.[8] Adding the growth of population over all urban fields, we find it to be nearly equal to the average population increase in the nation. It follows, if we discount immigration from abroad, that population gains above the average which are scored by any urban field will necessarily imply a loss of population for some other field.[9] This conclusion is strengthened, if we

4. Urban fields begin to be significant features in settlement geography for core areas of about 300,000 population.

5. The recognition that a radically new settlement pattern is emerging in the United States is coming to be recognized in such works as Wilfred Owen's *The Accessible City* (Washington, D.C.: The Brookings Institution, 1972).

6. Jerome P. Pickard, "Trends and Projections of Future Population Growth in the United States, with Special Data on Large Urban Regions and Major Metropolitan Areas, for the Period 1970-2000," presented to the Ad Hoc Subcommittee on Urban Growth, Committee on Banking and Currency, U.S. House of Representatives, July 22, 1969. See also Jerome P. Pickard, *Dimensions of Metropolitanism.* Research Monograph 14. Washington, D.C.: The Urban Land Institute, 1967.

7. In 1971, the natural rate of increase of the American population was down to 0.81 percent, but foreign immigration raised the net population increase to 1.2 percent. At the same time, farm population was only 4.8 percent of the total, or 9.7 million in 1970. (*Report on National Growth 1972.* Washington, D.C.: USGPO, 1972, Ch. 1). Agricultural labor force, on the other hand, was only 3.8 million in 1968 and has been projected to 2.8 million by 1980. (U.S. Department of Labor, Bureau of Labor Statistics, *Patterns of U.S. Economic Growth.* Washington, D.C.: USGPO, 1970).

8. Paul J. Schwind, *Migration and Regional Development in the United States—1950-1960.* Research Paper No. 133. The University of Chicago, Department of Geography, 1971.

9. This is an extrapolation of an argument developed by William Alonso. According to Alonso, "Migration from non-metropolitan areas and from abroad plays a shrinking role in metropolitan growth. The rate of migration to all metropolitan

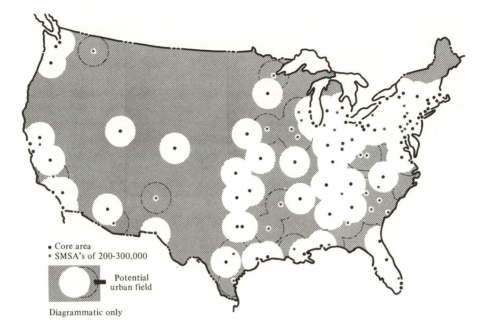

Map 1. The Urban Field.

recall that a substantial proportion of well-to-do commercial farmers are also residents of urban fields. The remnants of the population who live off relatively unproductive land, in villages and towns of the intermetropolitan periphery, beyond the reach of urban fields, will either move to them or else grow old in museums of a way of life no longer known to most of us.

My purpose here is to take a closer look at the structural changes occurring inside this new form of the human habitat. As people move further and further away from the mother city, they do not leave the urban field behind; they merely extend its radius until they push against the edges of adjacent fields. And there may come a time, not far away, when we shall suddenly become aware that escape from pervasive urbanism is no longer possible. Already the majority of those in search of open space are carrying their home amenities with them like snails.[10]

It is quite likely that the urban field has already reached its maximum physical dimensions which are set, in part, by the willingness of people to spend part of their waking hours in travel. Most people are unwilling to spend more than two hours of a 16-hour day in the journey-to-work, and two hours of commuting time would amount to a one-way travel distance of 40 to 50 miles.[11]

areas has declined from 21 per 1000 inhabitants per year in the first decade of the century to less than 5 in 1960–1965. Migration's share of total metropolitan growth declined over this same period from 70 percent to less than 30 percent, and it is now apparently about 20 percent. In other words, the intermetropolitan population system has become more closed, and changes in the structure will accordingly respond more to its internal dynamics and less to external forces." ("The System of Intermetropolitan Population Flows," Working Paper No. 155, Institute of Urban and Regional Development, University of California, Berkeley, August 1971, p. 2).

10. Ecologists Edgy Over Boom in Motor Homes," *Los Angeles Times,* (February 28, 1972).
11. This is a maximum distance. *Average* time spent in work trips varies from 68 minutes in the New York region to about 43 minutes in smaller metropolitan areas. This is equivalent to a one-way travel distance of between 15 and 25 miles. (See James M. Morgan, *et al., Productive Americans.* Ann Arbor, University of Michigan Institute for Social Research, Research Center Monograph 42, 1966, Table S-3, p. 80.)

Weekend commuting to second home communities and prepared recreational areas would extend the boundaries to between 75 and 100 miles. Given the spacing of potential core cities, this would appear to be the furthest reach of the urban field. In many places, especially the eastern United States, distances will be less than this because urban fields are bounded there by other urban fields at higher densities than elsewhere.[12]

The urban field is an artifical environment. Farms and forests are interspersed with clustered urban settlements and centers of productive work. But the land is no longer primeval: in a fundamental way, whether its use is in agriculture or not, it has become "urbanized." Architects call it a "plug-in city," by which they mean that anywhere within the urban field one can connect his home to an intricate and, for the most part, efficiently managed network of freeways, telephones, radio and television outlets, and electric energy and water supply systems.

## The Desire for Increased Environmental Control

This change to an enlarged living space has crept upon us silently. It is the unanticipated collective outcome of countless individual decisions to leave the city for the countryside. Different reasons have been propounded to account for this drive into the open spaces beyond the mother city, among them the steadily rising incomes, physical mobility, and leisure of middle class Americans. I would like to suggest a more fundamental reason, however. The occupance of the urban field is an attempt on the part of a growing number of people to secure for themselves a measure of effective control over their immediate surroundings. Life in the older parts of the city is relentlessly encroaching upon

personal space.[13] The protective shelter of one's environment is becoming thinner and thinner as strangers who follow life styles different from one's own move into established neighborhoods; as crime rates soar, endangering physical safety; as declines in land values threaten personal savings; as new traffic routes destroy the integrity of old neighborhoods; as air pollution lays down a blanket of smog over the city.[14]

Psychological stress increases with the city's pressure on the protective layers of personal space. As John Cassel has pointed out, people are no longer able to elicit anticipated responses to what were once appropriate cues, and one's neighbors can no longer be relied upon to conform with traditional values.[15] Accelerated urbanization is disrupting the character and strength of the group supports of individual lives.

And, therefore, those who can afford it, pack up their things and leave, first for the suburbs and then, as even the suburbs are invaded by the perceived menace of urban life, for the dales of ex-urbia. Out there, among their own kind, in maximum security communities, they hope to build a haven for themselves. Environmental control seems so easy to purchase: one has merely to opt for it by moving away from the chaos of central locations to the rustic calm that is assumed to lie beyond.

12. These distances are calculated on the basis of central commuting. Although central commuting is declining in relative importance, it remains a useful criterion for delimiting the outer boundaries of the urban field which, because of their historical evolution, seem to bear a continuing relationship to the location of the core city.

13. The best treatment of the concept of personal space is found in Robert Sommer's *Personal Space. The Behavioral Basis of Design*, Englewood Cliffs, New Jersey: Prentice-Hall, 1969. Personal space, according to Sommers, is a "portable territory" that involves the emotionally charged zone around individuals that may regulate spacing and is also concerned with the process of marking and personalizing space. For a recent assessment of this concept in terms of geography, see Edward W. Soja, *The Political Organization of Space*. Association of American Geographers, Commission on College Geography, Resource Paper No. 8, Washington, D.C., 1971.

14. In a recent study of the environmental preferences of New York City college students, safety was found to be of critical importance. See Mark Hinshaw and Kathryn Allot, "Environmental Preferences of Future Housing Consumers," *Journal of the American Institute of Planners*, Vol. XXXVIII, No. 2 (March 1972), pp. 102–107.

15. John Cassel, "The Relation of Urban Environment to Health: Towards a Conceptual Frame and Research Strategy." Typescript, 1972. Empirical evidence on this point is presented by Gerald D. Suttles, *The Social Order of the Slum*. Ethnicity and Territory in the Inner City. Chicago: University of Chicago Press, 1968.

All this is made easier by an accommodating government that provides not only low-cost lines of credit but also the necessary comforts for an increasingly dispersed environment for living. The social costs of this accommodation are enormous, but substantial savings accrue from letting the core city run down.[16] Expressways permit the recent urban refugees to draw on the resources of their vastly expanded living space: jobs, services, outdoor recreation. The city they have left behind has been pushed to the periphery of their cognitive map; its existence continues to be recognized chiefly because residences can relocate more swiftly than jobs, and there is still central commuting. Those who are left behind hang on because they cannot afford the price or rent of a suburban home or, in the case of the black population, are not permitted in suburbia. For these people, the city is rapidly turning into what Richard Sennett has appropriately called a survival community in which accommodation, constant watchfulness, and the erection of complex protective devices is the price of individual survival.[17]

## Clustering: Affinity Environments and Metrocenters

We are reenacting the great American drama. Suburbanites are going homesteading. The healthy and vigorous life, they imagine, can be pursued on the urban frontier. But homesteading in the nineteen-seventies is not what it used to be on the prairies of Nebraska a century ago. The early pioneers of this country set out to start a new life that they would make themselves. No one would ask them where they came from; each man and woman would test himself against the harshness of the wilderness; the past was left behind. But the modern pioneers of suburbia do not wish for a

new life; they wish to reestablish an order of life that recalls the simplicities of an earlier day. They wish to protect their personal space.

In this, they behave very much like other human beings. If allowed to choose, people prefer living in social environments that are compatible with their own tastes. Give children an opportunity to design and build a model city, and they invent a city meant for children.[18] Others prefer the bustling street life of ethnic neighborhoods.[19] The city is a system of ordered spatial diversity; its fabric is woven into a rich pattern of affinity environments.

An affinity environment may be defined as a spatially bounded social environment that is based on voluntary residential choice and characterized by a shared preference for salient attributes such as ethnicity, life style, income, occupation, age, family status, and religion. Suttles calls the resulting socio-spatial pattern a system of ordered segmentation.[20] Other things being equal, affinity environments minimize the psychological stress of urban living at the same time that they maximize access to specific social amenities desired by the population, such as specialized food markets, religious schools and places of worship, social clubs, a certain housing style and density pattern, and educational and recreational facilities which evolve (or are created) in response to sizeable aggregations of populations with a shared environmental preference. Affinity environments are supportive of group life.[21]

16. I am not arguing that to "permit" the steady physical deterioration of the core city was at any time a conscious decision. If anything, the available evidence shows a rising concern with the physical condition of core cities. But it is hard to be persuaded that deterioration was not a result of an *implicit* policy to invest in the outward expression of urban populations at the expense of the core city. The costs and benefits of this policy have never been studied.

17. Richard Sennett, *The Uses of Disorder*. Personal Identity and City Life. New York: Alfred A. Knopf, 1970.
18. A model of the Venice Community in Los Angeles built by third and fourth graders is on display in UCLA's School of Architecture. It is a marvellous example of how children project their imagination upon the city to create a truly magical place for themselves.
19. Jane Jacobs, *The Death and Life of Great American Cities*. New York: Random House, 1967.
20. Gerald D. Suttles, *op. cit.*, Ch. 2.
21. According to Gerald D. Suttles, the local urban community is "the defended neighborhood which segregates people to avoid danger, insult, and impairment of status claims." This he considers to be a sufficient basis for explaining community differentiation. In addition, however, "the local community attracts to itself . . . hopes for the expression of self and sentiment. The desire to find a social setting in which one can give rein to an

A spatial pattern of ordered segmentation is not unique to the American city. It is also found in older European and Islamic cities famous for their "quarters"; we meet with it again in the contemporary African city with its tribal enclaves in which traditional modes of social life are maintained at the same time that customary behavior undergoes a transformation toward an intertribal model more adaptive to urban living.[22] The tribal enclave is a way of coping with the shock of first encounter with the city. Like any affinity environment, it serves to reduce mental stress.

A philosophical propensity to think more in terms of individuals than collectives has led many planners to overlook or minimize this essentially social patterning of urban space.[23] Where we find affinity environments, we tend to think of them as temporary historical residues rather than as the collective outcome of individual choice. Yet, the evidence is overwhelming. People prefer affinity environments because they seek to reduce the psychological cost of urban living to a (subjectively) optimal level, because they like to feel "at home" in the city.

I do not wish to be misunderstood. The black and Puerto Rican and Chicano ghettos of our large cities did not result from voluntary residential choice. They are not affinity environments in the present sense. The urban ghetto exists because of racial prejudice and economic necessity. On the other hand, it would be unrealistic to think that affinity environments based on ethnicity and race would vanish if the gates to the urban field were to be thrown wide open. For some ghetto inhabitants, affinities based on criteria other

than ethnicity would undoubtedly weigh more heavily in residential choice than spatial proximity to members of their own subcultures. But for many others, shared ethnic background and cultural expectations would continue to be the decisive criterion.

The push into the urban field is, therefore, likely to replicate the ordered segmentation of the core city, even though the existing diversity of affinity environments within the urban field is very much narrower than what it may become in the future.[24] The changing character of American society will eventually produce different "affinities" from those to which we have become accustomed, and questions of life style may loom more importantly than they have in the past.

The new community movement in the United States has largely obscured this shift to life-style environments. The federal government is striving to achieve a mixture of income-graded housing in the new towns it chooses to subsidize.[25] What is not generally recognized, however, is that people who move into new communities wish to pursue precisely the kind of life that new communities make possible. Developers carefully design a variety of living environments in new communities with an eye to the market and popular tastes.

## Freedom and Flexibility of Movement

Two kinds of demand are giving form to urban fields. The first is for increased personal control over one's immediate environment. It is met by private developers who build affinity environments to the taste of their customers and join in the construction of tightly designed metrocenters. These high-density clusters are built—or can be built—on a pedestrian scale. The second is a demand for

authentic version of oneself and see other people as they really are is not some unanalyzable human needs but the most fundamental way in which people are reassured of their own reality as well as that of other people." (*The Social Construction of Communities*. Chicago: The University of Chicago Press, 1972, p. 264). For a strongly supportive view, see Robert Dorfman, "The Functions of the City," in Anthony H. Paschal, ed., *Thinking About Cities*. New Perspectives on Urban Problems. Belmont, California: Dickenson Publishing Co., 1970.
22. William John Hanna and Judith Lynne Hanna, *Urban Dynamics in Black Africa*. Chicago: Aldine, 1971, Ch. 6.
23. Herbert J. Gans, "Planning for People, not Buildings," *Environment and Planning*, Vol. I (1969), pp. 33–46.

24. The strongest evidence for this statement comes from Herbert J. Gans's studies of the social patterning of suburban America. (*People and Plans*. New York: Basic Books, 1968, Ch. 4.)
25. To date (June 1972), ten communities with a projected peak population of 680,000 have been funded. All of them are within 50 miles of a metropolitan area.

diversity of choice among jobs, shopping, services, and recreation. Under conditions of overall low density in urban fields—which we may estimate at less than 1000 persons per square mile—this call for increasing diversity of choice can only be met by substituting mobility for place. It is extremely unlikely that, in a multi-centered system, the necessary mobility can be provided in any way other than by automobile expressways: the urban field depends on individual facility of movement.[26]

In his excellent new book, *The Accessible City,* Wilfred Owen argues that the redesign of the urban habitat is an essential condition for overcoming mounting problems of traffic congestion.[27]

Mobility depends on how thoughtfully space has been allocated and how efficiently activities have been arranged. The great delusion is that building more capacity will somehow lead to a congestion-free environment, with all the desired urban advantages.... Planned communities, by rejecting the outdated concept of separating urban life into compartments by zoning, have demonstrated that the transportation problem can be contained by focusing on non-transportation solutions that emphasize accessibility rather than movement.

His proposed solution is the regional city—comparable in all respects to the urban field,[28]

which combines urban densities with close-by country living. The regional city is made up of interconnected clusters surrounded by low-density uses, where the special benefits of concentration can be enjoyed without succumbing to a continuous urban buildup unrelated to the countryside. The multi-centered city offers a compromise between undesirably high density and the destructive side effects of indiscriminate sprawl.

Owen's regional city presupposes continued reliance on the automobile as the major

mode of transportation. He, as others in America have done, bows to the inevitablity of private motor transportation.[29]

## Environmental Quality: A Function of Resource Management

I do not wish to imply that the automobile does not contribute its share of problems to the urban environment. The massive invasion of the far reaches of large cities by a population that is mobile, well-to-do, and has a taste for outdoor recreation is putting increasing pressures on the available resources for urban living.

The issue is a subtle one. A simplistic approach would argue that, in order to save these resources from ultimate destruction, demand for them will have to be reduced. Increased intensity of use, however, does not inevitably have negative effects. Throughout history, the conversion of deserts and prairies into farmland has generally improved the quality of the original resource. A rigorous regime of resources development would raise the productivity of land over its unspoiled state. Breakdowns would occur only when, because of ignorance or negligence, management failed. This would then lead to over-grazing, over-cutting, soil erosion, siltation, floods, and ultimate abandonment.

In the occupance of urban fields, the major problem affecting environmental quality lies in the threatened destruction of key amenity resources. This has two aspects, the first relating to the temporary but recurring and intensive uses of desirable open lands for recreation, the second to the aesthetics of the natural landscape.[30]

The failure to perceive both open land and landscape quality as *limited* resources helps to account for the still widespread apathy toward questions of resource management in the urban environment. This apathy is changing to concern as we become aware that nearly all

---

26. An important corollary to this statement is that a severe restriction on the availability and use of automobiles would quickly curtail the settlement of urban fields. This, however, I do not consider to be a realistic alternative in the foreseeable future.
27. Wilfred Owen, *op. cit.,* p. 134.
28. *Ibid.,* p. 112.

29. *Ibid.,* p. 21.
30. I have chosen to ignore the problem of air pollution, chiefly because I believe this problem amenable to a technological solution.

of our lives will have to be spent within the boundaries of urban fields. Accepting the growing scarcity of urban field resources requires a drastic re-evaluation of our attitudes toward the bounded environment.[31]

The crucial discovery has been that the supply of available land in parks, beaches, lakeshores, and riverbanks, no less than scenic beauty, is extraordinarily limited in relation to potential demand, and that the very quality for which these resources are valued may be destroyed through excessive, unregulated use. This problem is exacerbated by holding to a democratic ideology which insists on equality of individual access to these resources. The tranquility of wooded areas, fields, and streams used to be regarded as the exclusive privilege of the wealthy. Lower user densities and the responsibilities of perpetual ownership ensured the practice of good management on this land. But the rapid democratization of the urban field has brought with it enormous problems.

## The Decline of Civic Consciousness

The spatial structure of the urban field grows out of the aggregate of individual demands for psychic security, mobility, and open space. It is assumed that government will somehow provide the guidance necessary to ensure that the countless, self-serving decisions of individuals will work to the benefit of all the people or at least will have neutral effects on the larger community. But this assumption has little basis in fact. Government, like business in this country, neither leads nor guides; it follows consumer demand. Indeed, it makes a virtue of following.[32]

A policy of allowing unrestrained consumer choice to determine urban form leads to collective disaster. There are no quick solutions to problems that have been gathering

over the decades. And when the crisis can no longer be avoided, government intervention is fragmented, too little, and too late.

Most people are unaware that by acting as individual consumers of space they do not get what they would want as members of the commonwealth that sustains them. As citizens of urban fields, they get what they ask for, affinity environments and metrocenters. But these private goods are purchased at great cost. Amenity resources of the urban field will be impaired until they cease to be attractive. More seriously, the diligent search for consumer satisfactions and security of private space on the periphery has led to the massive exodus of whites from central cities. Minority populations have occupied the vacant homes they left behind, but not in numbers sufficient to avoid the virtual abandonment of many residential areas.[33] According to one study, approximately 7 percent of New York's housing stock may be vacated over the next six years.[34] One frequently cited estimate asserts that in New York City alone, 52,000 housing units are being abandoned each year. In certain sections of St. Louis, 16 percent of the housing structures have been left to deteriorate, and in the Woodlawn and Lawndale areas of Chicago, 15 to 20 percent of the units ten years old or older have been demolished, are boarded up, or stand vacant and vandalized. The story is much the same in other large cities.

31. Harvey S. Perloff, "A Framework for Dealing with the Urban Environment," in Harvey S. Perloff, ed., *The Quality of the Urban Environment*. Baltimore: The Johns Hopkins University Press, 1969.
32. Edward C. Banfield, *Political Influence*. The Free Press of Glencoe, 1961.
33. In SMSA's of 500,000 or more, 13 percent (13.3 million) of the total population is black (1970). In the central cities of these areas, the black population was nearly double this ratio, or 23.7 percent (10.8 million). An estimated 200,000 middle class blacks are moving to surburban areas each year, most of them to inner ring black communities. This represents 2 percent of central city black populations and barely compensates for the natural increase of these populations. As a result, the proportion of black people in central cities has been gaining steadily from in-migration, even though the total number of in-migrants has been *less* than the number of both whites and blacks who are resettling on the fringes of core cities. (Data are from Weissbourd, *op. cit.*, chart 1 and from Lawrence Elliott Susskind, "Guidelines for State Involvement in the Development of New Communities in Massachusetts: Toward a State Urban Growth Policy," in *Papers on National Land Use Policy Issues*. Prepared for the Committee on Interior and Insular Affairs, United States Senate, Washington, D.C., 1971, p. 29).
34. Robert Powell Sangster, "Abandonment of Inner City Properties," Federal Home Loan Bank Board, *Journal*, Vol. 5, No. 2 (February 1972), p. 14.

## Toward New Forms of Governance

A realistic look at the future of the urban habitat is bound to terminate in a mood of glum resignation. But at least we have succeeded in identifying one of the major problems which lies at the root of our despair. This is the governance of urban fields.

The fundamental issue is whether the urban field can and should acquire the essential characteristics of a regional city, a true *civitas*. Given the present lack of civic concern with the urban field as a whole—a lack that partly reflects the invisibility of its network of functional relationships—suggests that the most probable outcome for governance is a gradual evolution of power from local communities upwards to state and federal levels. The failure (or unwillingness) to come to grips with the governance of urban fields thus implies the continued emasculation of territorial governments below the level of the state.

Increasingly within recent decades, local citizens in the United States behaved as if they were the casual residents of a hotel. They took for granted the adequate provision of services they had come to expect and were content to be "managed" by professionals and experts so long as their particular demands were gratified. When this was not the case, they usually moved on to another hotel. "The fact remains," Oliver William asserts, "that most urban dwellers vote by moving van, not by ballot box and that coalitions, not communities, are the characteristic urban collectivity.[35] If this is true, however, as I believe it is, one is left to wonder whether a "managed" society is ultimately preferable to one that is self-governing.

Technical experts have only an arbitrary calculus for weighing the costs and benefits of their decisions as they impinge on different collectivities. Except for consulting their own souls, they have no way of knowing which decisions would enact the public good. To turn over the governance of urban fields to technical experts means therefore to relinquish our right to have a voice in the distribution of costs and benefits. So long as the urban frontier was open, exit rather than voice was frequently chosen as a solution to situations that become insufferable.[36] But the urban frontier has finally been closed. Exit is no longer possible.

If we accept this interpretation of the urban condition, the conclusion is forced upon us that the exclusion of politics from the management of urban fields is no longer an acceptable alternative. Voice must replace exit in the exercise of our right as local citizens. This, however, leaves the question unanswered of how the new political game is to be arranged. One alternative would be to invest the state with greater powers of planning for and control over the settlement of urban fields. In view of the present incapacity of local governments to cope with their own problems, *this is the most probable alternative in view*.[37] But the solution is seriously deficient. Not only do many urban fields overlap state boundaries, but the individuality, scale, and complexity of urban fields require more attention to detail, quicker responses, and greater responsiveness to problem situations than state governments are likely to manage. The end result would be a vastly expanded and cumbersome state bureaucracy which, like its federal counterpart, would be incapable of subtle and speedy intervention.

A second alternative would be to transform existing Councils of Governments into multi-purpose regional governments with an elected legislative body and jurisdiction over a wider area than at present. Such governments might emerge as part of a larger solution that would involve major readjustments at all levels of territorial governance. At present, though, the outlook for

35. Oliver P. Williams, *Metropolitan Political Analysis. A Social Access Approach*. New York: The Free Press, 1971, p. 18.

36. Albert O. Hirschman, *Exit, Voice, and Loyalty. Responses to Decline in Firms, Organizations, and States*. Cambridge: Harvard University Press, 1970.
37. Strengthening the role of State governments in urban field governance is forcefully advocated by Anthony Downs, "Alternative Forms of Future Urban Growth in the United States," *Journal of the American Institute of Planners*, Vol. XXXVI, No. 1 (January 1970), pp. 1–11.

elected and politically responsible governments at the scale of urban fields is not very promising.

The third and final alternative envisions a tiered hierarchy of multi-purpose governments arranged according to a principle of territorial specialization. At the neighborhood level, elected community assemblies would address themselves to those issues of local governance which are of most direct concern to residents within affinity environments and which could be effectively internalized at that level. Day-care centers, elementary schools, public libraries, local parks, health care, local policing, internal traffic control, and zoning might be among their major projects. At the next higher level, elected representatives from among the membership of several community assemblies might meet in district assemblies at a metro-center to deal with such problems as high schools, public health, large-scale recreational facilities, and solid waste disposal. Members of district assemblies would, in turn, be elected to join in a regional assembly for the entire urban field to consider major internal circulation problems, justice, open space controls, anti-pollution measures, public utilities, economic development, and higher education. At the state level, finally, government would set general standards, guidelines, and policies, exercise a reviewing function over local planning, and concern itself with the management of interregional systems and, particularly, with the question of resource allocation among urban fields.[38]

The cellular system of governance for urban fields I have described seeks to return a measure of effective control to the local community without imposing closure upon the provincialism that is latent in the concept of neighborhood government. Territorial power in America has gradually been drifting upwards, leaving the bulk of the population with little more to do than to pursue their private pleasures, fend off unwanted neighbors, engage in generally futile remonstrances against shadowy external forces and, in the case of the poor, struggle for individual survival. Yet the all-too-apparent vacuum of power at the local level is not completely filled by state and federal governments. As a result, the quality of the physical environment is to a large extent an outcome of the ungoverned interplay of individual, utilitarian interest that, even though they may occasionally cluster into territorial or sectoral coalitions, rarely combine to advance the common good. Despite much rhetoric on the opposing side, a community perspective does not enjoy legitimacy in American society. In fact, a recent magisterial study of community organization sustains the thesis that fear of one's neighbors is the principal variable accounting for the territorial integrity of territorial communities.[39]

Over the past decade, the phrase "community of limited liability" has frequently been used to describe the fact that local residents do not "dissolve" into the communal soul but reserve important interests for other engagements. But, as I have tried to suggest, even the limited claims of the local community may turn out to be quite substantial. Some needs of local residents are best met locally; others require more general, system-wide forms of governance. Without the former, however, the latter would remain an empty gesture. The transformation of the urban field into a true *civitas* must begin with a radical restructuring of community organization and political power.

To appreciate the role of the federal government in this system, it is necessary to step back for a moment and consider the probable behavior of urban-regional development in a national perspective. In the future, most interregional migration will take place between and among urban fields. We have arrived at a stage where the development of urban fields has become a zero-sum game. It is no longer possible for everyone to win a part in the national sweepstakes. The winners in this

---

38. This territorial division of tasks represents an elaboration of a distinction first proposed by Oliver Williams between life style and system maintenance policies. See Oliver P. Williams, *op. cit.*, pp. 88ff.

39. Gerald D. Suttles, *The Social Construction of Communities, op. cit.*, Ch. 9.

game are likely to be urban fields which have attractive environments and high levels of public services. Economic differences are declining as a factor in the locational decisions of families.[40]

If this picture is correct, questions of equality in the distribution of life chances are going to acquire increasing importance in national life, and the federal government will have to devote a good deal more attention to these questions than it has done. In situations where population gains in favored urban fields must be compensated by losses in other urban fields, a situation of great instability is created. In the losing regions, private investment becomes riskier and, consequently, more costly. If sustained over a period of time, this investment behavior will further reduce the attractiveness of the losing area and accelerate population decline, raising the per capita costs of public services and allowing physical deterioration to continue. Once such a process has been started, it becomes extremely difficult to reverse it. To avert an outcome that is likely to affect a growing number of urban fields, the federal government may have to undertake huge subsidy programs to counteract the disinclination of private business to invest in declining areas or to seek such other measures as may effectively reduce the rate of inter-regional migration. Since neither policy can be guided by objective or even widely accepted criteria of right and wrong, urban politics in America is bound to become increasingly acrimonious.

Two centuries of spectacular and steady urban growth are drawing to a rapid and ignoble close. We, who have been raised on a belief in individualism and minimal government, find ourselves challenged by the necessity to evolve a public philosophy capable of countering the disruptive consequences of our pioneering heritage. The invisible hand not only is invisible; it never existed. We are beginning to learn at great pain how to live with this reality.

---

40. For persuasive evidence on this point for as early as the 1950's, see Paul J. Schwind, *op. cit.* and Section V.

# 1.3

# Megalopolitan Systems Around the World

JEAN GOTTMANN

The concept of megalopolis applies to very large polynuclear urbanized systems endowed with enough continuity and internal interconnections for each of them to be considered a system in itself. A megalopolis must also be separated by less urbanized broad spaces from any other large urban network that it does not encompass. In most cases the density of population, or urban activities and of interweaving internal networks within a megalopolitan region is such as to make it substantially different from surrounding areas that do not possess the same mass and density of population and a comparable intensity of urbanization.

Before we can list the existing megalopolitan systems, it is necessary to agree on a minimum size for the phenomenon. A number of works published on the concept and occurrences of megalopolis set a concentration of 10 million inhabitants within the area as the minimum size. This is much below the figure I have long advocated and would still prefer to propose; I would set the minimum at 25 million. If we accept this figure, the list of megalopolitan systems will be much shorter and every case will be endowed with certain characteristics which I believe are common to the whole lot and basic to the concept. There are, indeed, six cases of such, over 25 million each, megalopolitan occurrences in the present world: first, the American Northeastern Megalopolis, the study of which has served as the prototype of the concept; then the Great Lakes

Megalopolis, described by C. A. Doxiadis and by Alexander Leman; the Tokaido Megalopolis in Japan, which has been carefully studied under the direction of Eiichi Isomura; the megalopolis in England which has been identified and analyzed by the team directed by Peter Hall; the megalopolis of northwestern Europe, extending from Amsterdam to the Ruhr and to the French northern industrial conglomeration, described by I.B.F. Kormoss and now being studied by an international team at The Hague; and a sixth case of which we yet know relatively little, the Urban Constellation in Mainland China centered on Shanghai.

To these six cases we may soon be able to add three others, located on different continents; in each of these cases, the different parts seem to be coalescing fast enough to be considered megalopolitan systems in their own right, and the populations of each seem close to my proposed minimum of 25 million inhabitants: one consists of two big nuclei that are growing fast and are being linked by a narrow corridor, that is, the Rio de Janeior-São Paulo complex in Brazil; another, differently shaped megalopolis is forming in northern Italy, centered on the Milan-Turin-Genoa triangle and extending arms along the Mediterranean seashore southward to Pisa and Florence and westward to Marseilles and Avignon. The third case will probably be in California, centered on Los Angeles, extending northward to the San Francisco Bay area and encompassing urban centers along both

From *Ekistics*, vol. 243, February 1976, pp. 109–13. Reprinted by permission.

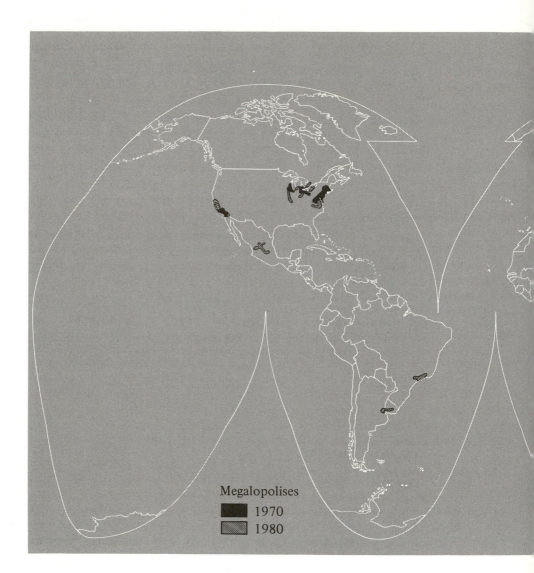

Figure 1.  World Distribution of Megalopolitan Areas. The six megalopolises with more than 2.5 million are in bold: the three developing megalopolises are in standard type (adapted from C.A. Doxiadis and J. G. Papaioannou, *Ecumenopolis, the Inevitable City of the Future* (Athens: Athens Publishing Center, 1974), pp. 144-45).

sides of the Californian-Mexican border. There may also be some formation of megalopolitan size and structure in India, but I have as yet no clear information on that part of the world.

If we lower the minimum size of population to 10 million, the number of megalopolitan systems would rise rapidly and in a disputable fashion; on the one hand, many mononuclear urban agglomerations could be identified at

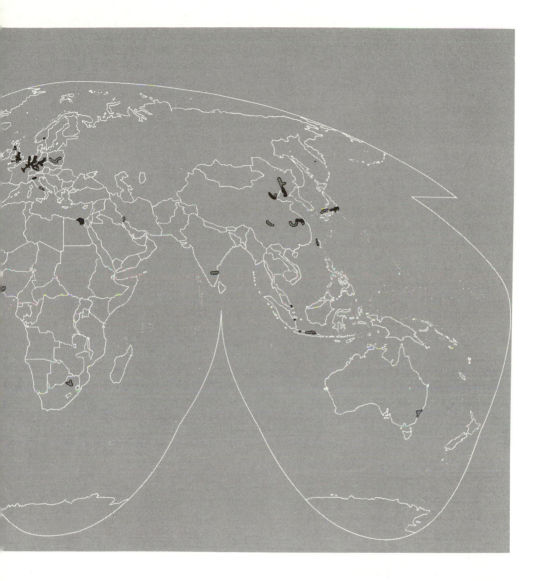

about the 10 million size, for instance, around Paris, Buenos Aires, Calcutta, Bombay, perhaps Moscow, etc; on the other hand, by accepting the 10 million gauge, we would be justified in breaking up the larger megalopolitan systems, some of which could then be considered independently of the adjacent and interconnected parts, so that Greater New York would be considered a megalopolis on its own, as would be London, with its southeastern crown; the Ruhr-Cologne complex, the Tokyo-Yokohama and Osaka-Kobe metropolitan regions, etc. The Great Lakes Megalopolis could then be dissected into several sections, each in the 10 to 15 million size: one around Chicago and Milwaukee, another in the Detroit-Cleveland sector, and still another in Canada from Hamilton to Quebec.

The general view of the interconnected vaster system would be lost. The important idea to keep in mind is that megalopolis is *not* simply an overgrown metropolitan area. It is not only another step on the quantitative scale. It is a phenomenon of specific qualities of a different nature.

## HINGES OF DEVELOPMENT

The megalopolitan systems have arisen along *polynuclear,* rather elongated axes. Sometimes the system takes on an irregular or a triangular shape, as has happened in Europe, but there is always a major axis of traffic and communication, and the nuclei strewn along it have a national and international function. For my original American Megalopolis, I used the metaphor of the "continent's economic hinge" to describe its major function throughout history. All megalopolitan regions have been *hinges* in terms of trade, and cultural, technological and population exchanges between the countries they belonged to and the outside world they participated in. This is obviously true of the past and present functions of the systems that have grown along an axis such as Boston-New York-Washington, or Tokyo-Osaka, or London-Liverpool, or Amsterdam-Antwerp-Brussels-Cologne, or Montreal-Toronto-Detroit-Chicago.

It seems that a necessary condition of a megalopolis is a hinge articulating two or more networks, one of them a national internal network, and another an international and overseas network. Hence the importance of the seaport function of some of the major bolts forming the hinge. It may be noteworthy that of the large megalopolitan systems, the axis of only one is not directly related to a seaboard, and that is the Great Lakes Megalopolis. Still this extends along a system of navigable waterways forming an international boundary.

Water transport and peripheral location were especially important in the past, when all transport went by surface means, when ships were by far the cheapest mode of transport, and when the essential breaking points in the networks of transport and communications were located on the shores of the land masses. Water and especially sea transport still preserves some importance owing to the greater ease and lower cost of shipping large cargoes by water. A large concentration of population and industry consumes huge quantities of goods. Megalopolitan growth occurs in highly developed countries where the per capita consumption of goods and services is much larger than average. Hence the intricate web of networks to carry goods, people and messages within and around a megalopolis. Looking at the various maps of means of transport and communications and of traffic flows around the world, one is impressed by the extent to which the existing webs enveloping our planet converge on the main hubs of the megalopolitan systems.

The convergence is increased by the part played by the hinge in the handling of an enormous volume of *transactional activities* resulting from the linkages in the networks connected by the hinge. The expansion in the volume of the transactions, and in the personnel they occupy, explains the rise of the megaloplitan system and its relations to other parts of the world. The recent evolution of technology and society, that transferred large numbers of people from the work of producing or processing material goods to work in the services producing or processing information, is largely responsible for the megalopolitan phenomenon.

## CHARACTERISTICS OF MEGALOPOLISES

The first characteristic of a megalopolitan region is its density of settlement. The megalopolis concentrates a larger proportion of a country's population, at least one-fifth, on a small fraction of the land area. This results in relatively high densities of over 250 per square kilometer on the average, and a great density of nuclei of a particularly urban character—of towns and cities in which the population density is still much higher than the average in the megalopolitan region. This pattern of a thick network of towns and cities within megalopolis is a very important characteristic: it entails more proximity between the constituent parts and, therefore, a more intertwined web of relationships between a variety of distinct urban centers. The web of relationships is expressed partly in a physical infrastructure consisting of highways, railways, waterways, telephone lines, pipelines, water supply and sewage systems criss-crossing the whole area, and partly in more fluid networks, some of them visible and measurable, such as the flows of traffic, the movement of people and goods, the flows of telephone calls, of mail and of financial instruments. The same web includes other networks of a more abstract and rather invisible nature, such as common interests and concerns, rivalries or cooperation, exchanges of information and the human relations that make for community life.

The superimposed networks of linkages help make the region more united and more intricately intertwined, creating the interdependence of the various components within the megalopolis. But this fact should not overshadow the diversity and complexity existing in the megalopolitan structure. The sizes and specializations of the various spatial components are extremely varied, as demonstrated by the diverse characteristics of the cities, towns, villages, suburban and rural areas that form the vast system. In each sector along a megalopolitan axis that may be endowed with some greater unity because of its dependence on one or two major metropolitan centers, there is still great diversity in the land use, in the people, in the occupations and interests. No megalopolitan region is as yet completely and fully urbanized in the sense of being totally covered with buildings at a thick density. There are interstitial spaces, some reserved for recreation, some for other special uses (such as water reservoirs, for instance), some for agriculture of a specialized and usually very intensive kind, and some are wooded.

In my study on the American Megalopolis, published in 1961, I reported that in the mid-1950s 48 percent of its area was under commercial forest cover. A recent enquiry made by another research project of the Twentieth Century Fund has shown in the late 1960s, within the limits I had assigned to that megalopolis, 49 percent of the total area was under forest of commercial value. In the intervening 15 years the population in megalopolis and the suburban sprawl had substantially expanded; however, there has been apparently enough abandonment of tilled land or pastures, which were turned into woods, to cause a small increase in the total area of commercial forest. These trends will not continue for ever; they reflect a complex interplay of economic and social processes. The role that forest and agricultural land play in spatial terms within the megalopolitan structure involves not only land use but various aspects of the region's way of life, its resources in terms of amenities and supplies of certain goods. This is true of the megalopolis on the American northeastern seaboard; it is also true, and to an even greater extent, of the Great Lakes Megalopolis. The concept of megalopolis must include the green fringe of the densely built-up corridors. It should not be made into an image of hopeless crowding, of a hell of cement, steel, brick, and motorcars. The appearance of megalopolitan systems coincides in time and in space with societies blessed with more leisure time, more outdoor recreation, more physical and social mobility. The spatial framework of the system incorporates the resources available in the environing areas for the needs of high density. New constraints appear, new regulations are desirable. They must be considered in the proper staging, on an adequate scale.

## EVOLUTIONARY LAYERS

Within the urban centers, diversity has not been only one of size and site, but it has been compounded by the history of past growth which deposited several layers of economic and technological evolution one on top of another. To an earlier stage of settlement, when cities and towns were chiefly centers of administration, trade and servicing of surrounding rural areas, a layer of industrial revolution was added, piling up manufacturing plants, warehouses and all the attendant infrastructure. Today, it is agreed that, in the better developed regions, a third stage has set in. The instruments of heavy manufacturing are gradually moved outside the major metropolitan centers. Now offices cluster in the central business districts of most cities, attracting the institutions that service the new transactional way of life. The evolution of a large sector of the labor force towards the white collar employment and quaternary work processing various forms of information has given a new allure to many cities within megalopolis. It is certainly exploding in the landscape of central Chicago or the skylines of Montreal and Toronto, and even more so in the recent growth of the metropolitan complex of Ottawa. These trends have been recognized in most large urban agglomerations, but they originated and have taken more spectacular shape in the megalopolitan groupings.

The diversity is again increased by the variety of the population. The process of growth and concentration of so many millions of inhabitants on a relatively narrow strip of land has involved many different waves of in-migration. Migrants came into megalopolitan areas from the surrounding regions but also and especially because of the hinge function, many came from afar. Ethnic and linguistic pluralism must be added to the gamut of occupations, levels of incomce and social variation that exist in every megalopolitan system; some of this spectrum is found even in the most homogeneous of them, which is certainly the Tokaido Megalopolis

A megalopolitan system must be described and understood as a huge *social and economic mosaic*. This term has been, I believe, recently used and accepted in Canada to describe the national structure. It expresses both an indisputable reality resulting from the great fluidity and diversity of the modern world and also rare wisdom in the assessment of human organization. The megalopolitan structure is particularly well described by the term mosaic, because both the land use and the population are formed by an immense number of places of great variety tightly put together and all interdependent. The diversity of the constituent elements remains well apparent even when one admires the unity of the whole design.

The *mosaic* is physical, economic and social; it is also political and governmental. The density and fragmentation of the system causes an extremely intricate lacework of administrative and political limits to be woven over the megalopolitan land. This can be clearly seen on a map of units of local government but it also appears strikingly in the distribution of governmental and political divisions on higer levels. It is not a simple accident that the older megalopolitan systems arose along axes which extended across boundaries between states, whether those were some of the original states in the American Federal Republic or the national states that divided among themselves the northwestern corner of the European continent. This political plurality may be both cause and effect of the lively competition between the major cities along a megalopolitan axis as they play their part in the operation of the hinge function. Similar economic competition may have obtained between large cities and industrial centers under the unified rule of one nation under the conditions of a rapidly developing Industrial Revolution, especially within the geographical constraints of an insular kingdom, as at different historical periods must have been the case in Great Britain and in Japan. Whatever the difference in the individual cases, it remains that the mass, density and plurality of a megalopolitan mosaic make such a region particularly difficult to manage by governments.

Studies of the megalopolitan phenomenon cannot get away from the extraordinary complexity and ensuing difficulties arising in such a region. But it is necessary to strive for solutions even in such environments. Accepting that the complexity, the diversity and the complementarity between all the pieces of the mosaic resulted from the process of growth and concentration, it should be possible to establish solutions on the foundations of plurality and complementarity.

## AN INCUBATOR

Modern economic theory and analysis has come to recognize that, in the process of economic development, social stability or change, the social, political and institutional trends and forces are more decisive than the purely physical, economic and technological factors. Any regional development of megalopolitan or submegalopolitan scale and nature cannot be understood without acknowledging a special convergence of social, political and cultural forces. It is in these fields that the answers needed will be found or the causes will be lost. The pressures arising in megalopolitan circumstances affect both the physical environment, in its natural and man-made elements, and the people in their modes of life. Megalopolitan systems have been the framework and location in which have developed many recent trends shaping our ways of life. Megalopolis is an incubator of new trends. Change occurs there at a faster and more intensified pace than in a more stabilized and homogeneous area experiencing less pressures and problems.

To the characteristics of megalopolis as a hinge and a mosaic, must be added its function as *an incubator*. This function is a threat to habit and stability, because it introduces change. It compounds the difficulties of local governments and of national and international administrations. However, it is their mix of functions and their great dynamism that have made the megalopolitan regions so important in the present world and have bestowed upon them so large a share of the general direction of contemporary economic prosperity and of the general advance of civilization.

## DILEMMAS

The growth of megalopolitan structures and the importance they have assumed testifies to the capacity of these regions and their people to accommodate concentrated and even congested development, and to withstand the pressures these very processes cause within the system. But a few words of caution must be uttered in conclusion.

First, the pressures have reached danger level on many occasions and at times it has seemed that megalopolitan regions are becoming unmanageable.

Secondly, the size and intensity of such concentrations of wealth and power have been resented by other regions of the countries in which megalopolitan systems have arisen. The other regions claim a more equal share in the sum total of the country's population, wealth and power. A too-large portion of these seems held in the megalopolitan areas. There is a basic ethical and political problem inherent in geographical concentration on such a scale.

Thirdly, the resulting spatial imbalances cause concern for the future fate of the vaster spaces gradually thinned out, especially for nations with large territories.

Fourthly, the very large urban structures are accused of generating an environment that crushes the individual and debases the human condition.

Finally, the concerns thus aroused, though largely political in nature, also entail moral dilemmas and I would like to give two examples of these. In the much studied decisions on the reapportionment by the United States Supreme Court, of June 15 1964, a minority opinion opposed the strict application of the ''one man, one vote'' principle to both houses of the Legislature of New York State, arguing that it would leave the inhabitants of large upstate areas at the mercy of the interests and decisions of a megalopolis. To this legal argument may be added a theological one. Twelve years ago in Vancouver I was asked to comment on a statement made by a bishop in that city that Vancouver's growth should be restricted because very large cities were inordinately sinful.

These concerns stem from long-standing dislikes and distrust of large, dominant cities.

They remind us of the ancient invectives against Nineveh, Babylon and even Rome. In our egalitarian times flagrant inequalities in the distribution of population and of economic weights, created by modern urbanization, come under fire and suspicion. In the more congested parts of megalopolitan systems, indeed, the problems pile up and methods are not incubated fast enough to cope with them in adequate fashion.

But, if megalopolitan growth arouses so much worry and protest, how is it that it has developed on such a scale? Despite all the stress, strain and unpleasantness it may cause, urban growth on a huge scale continues. Despite the endeavors of national and state or provincial governments to spread population and economic opportunity more evenly, the large agglomerations, as a rule, have not shown signs of dissolving. As a longer-term trend, the large urban agglomerations continue to attract very large numbers of migrants, and of course they also grow because of local natural demographic increase. The peripheral hinges of the continents continue to gather activities of a transactional nature in an era of worldwide economic and political interdependence and complementarity.

Some redistribution in space is, however, occurring either as a result of concerted planning or under the pressure of social and market forces. The formation of megalopolitan, more-or-less continuous axes and networks is in itself the product of deconcentration from the main original nuclei. Older categories of industries are gradually scattering away from the larger and more congested metropolitan centers. Some students of urban affairs even believe that the diffusion of the functions and trends that originated in megalopolitan systems disperses them rapidly to a multitude of other widely scattered towns and cities, particularly in the United States and Western Europe. In these countries, and in Canada, the migration off the farms will soon be almost completed and reduced to a trickle. Ultimately, megalopolitan systems will mainly grow through natural increase and international immigration, if allowed.

While diffusion, delegation and decentralization are certainly developing in many respects and on a vast scale, it does not seem, however, from recent trends of migration and population change, that megalopolitan systems are doomed and dissolving. Careful observation of what happens around the world indicates that, within the framework of expanding and generalizing urbanization, the old megalopolitan structures still prosper, and that new ones arise.

Twenty years ago, the patterns of urbanization along the Great Lakes did not yet seem to be truly comparable in density and functions with the Northeastern Seaboard Megalopolis. A vast chain of metropolitan regions was forming there especially on the American side of the Lakes, but with a looser structure and a specialization in manufacturing production rather than in quaternary activities. Now a rapid evolution has taken place modifying the picture, and I am much inclined, even in my strict interpretation of the megalopolitan concept, to recognize its rise here.

Megalopolis is a spectacular and fascinating phenomenon. Facts so huge and so stubborn can only be caused by the convergence of powerful and sustained forces. As a produce of the twentieth century, it arose with mechanization and automation on the farms, in the mines and lately in the manufacturing plants. It took shape as the people of the more advanced countries obtained more freedom from constraining work, more leisure time, more means to consume goods and services, more mobility and more education. It is not simply urban growth on a bigger scale; it is rather a new order in the organization of space and in the division of labor within society, a more diversified and complex order, allowing for more variety and freedom.

# The Organization of the Urban System

JAMES W. SIMMONS

In its narrowest and most traditional sense, the urban system refers to the set of cities in a region or nation and their attributes. The system is simply the aggregate of cities; no attempt is made to identify relationships among them. But when the concept is developed more fully, the urban system can embrace the totality of activities in a nation, account for the observed relationships among regions, and provide a model for the analysis of spatial variations of growth and change in the system.

The urban system, in this broader sense, is still based on urban nodes, that is, on spatial concentrations of people and activities within the region or nation, but it also includes the relationships of the nodes to their surrounding areas and particularly the linkages among nodes. What are the patterns of connections and flows among cities and how do they cumulate into growth impulses to be transmitted through the system?

In this essay, then, we are concerned with the description of the organization of a nation's territory and how it evolves over time. This spatial organization has three main components (see Figure 1): 1) a set of attributes, or *attribute matrix,* which describes the structural characteristics (size, economic structure, social properties) of each urban region, and which in aggregate comprise the nation; 2) a *behavior matrix,* which indicates the patterns of interaction among the urban regions in terms of movements of people, data, goods, and money; and 3) the *interdependency matrix,* which indicates how any city or location in the system responds to a change in any or all other cities. This interdependence, among and between sectors and locations, defines what we term the "space economy." How, for example, is growth in a port, an automobile manufacturing center, or a pulp and paper town transmitted to other economic activities and other locations?

The focus throughout this discussion is on the urban system as a whole. How can the urban system as a complex entity be described? How does it work as a unit? What parameters best describe it in its entirety? The approach here is holistic and operates on the premise that the system is more than an aggregate of cities and that individual elements can only be examined in relation to other elements. The *distribution* of attributes of cities in the system—their average values and variability—are of paramount interest, as is the covariation among different attributes. When examining a particular city those properties held in common with other cities are the object of principal concern.

Many different principles (or forces) combine to determine the spatial organization of an urban system. The military, the church, or the process of public administration each creates its own pattern of structure, flow, and growth. In Canada, for example, each primary industrial activity has its own distinct pattern of economic relations, its own geography. As other industrial activities are added, they transform the inputs (coming from primary products) and outputs (going to markets) to alter the interdependency matrix. The expansion of public-sector activities further modifies the growth relationships by translating part of the growth of the national economy into growth at certain specific locations, such as a military base or a new prison. The urban system helps to integrate all or at least most of these diverse processes.

When the process of spatial organization (or urbanization) is examined over the long run, it becomes evident that the context provided by one organizing principle (e.g., the fur trade) inevitably affects the distribution of

From "Canada as an Urban System," *The Canadian Urban System.* Forthcoming.

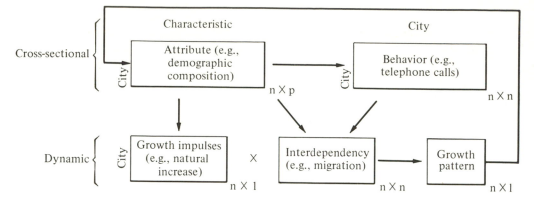

Figure 1. Urban Systems Components.

elements of those that follow (the timber trade and the railway, for example). This effect is cumulative over a succession of organizing principles until what was initially an economic sector-specific spatial system becomes a complex, multi-purpose urban system, coordinating flows among many different economic sectors and affecting social relationships as well. As the range in size of urban regions increases and the limiting effects of distance and the local resource base decline, the urban system becomes more and more the dominant factor in the location and growth of any new economic or social activity—a principle of spatial organization in its own right.

Another area of concern is the relationship between the urban system and the rest of the world. That is, how open or closed is the national urban system? At what points do the external contacts occur, and in what sectors, with what impacts? The future of an urban system, particularly in countries with small populations, such as Australia, Sweden, or Canada, depends very much on these exogenously derived inputs. The future is essentially as unpredictable as these inputs are. The variety of external influences is endless. Inflation, trading patterns, immigration, and preferences for environmental amenities, or attitudes against pollution are just a few examples of such influences. An historical example of this importance is provided by Thomas (1972), who uses international migration and capital movements to link the

inverse economic cycles of Britain and North America in the 19th century. When the system is defined on a world scale, the cycles of growth or decline become explicable; when treated from the viewpoint of one nation, they often seem random.

## MODELS OF SYSTEM ORGANIZATION

Numerous commentators have described and discussed the development process of national urban systems. Depending on their discipline, and the scale in time and space on which they focus, these researchers have drawn on different interpretive themes. These themes contain implicit models of system organization, such as the size, spacing, interaction, and particularly the growth focus in the system. The latter is the major taxonomic criterion used below. For present purposes we focus on the North American example where at least four models can be recognized:

(1) *The Frontier:* the growth of cities is initiated externally by investment decisions from a previously developed urban subsystem.

(2) *Staple Export:* the growth of cities depends on the growth of primary activities in the areas they serve.

(3) *Industrial Specialization:* The growth of cities depends on the growth of the national economy and the relative strength of the cities' sector of economic specialization.

(4) *Social Change:* the growth of cities is

largely unpredictable in the face of rapid social and technological change.

Most discussions of national urban systems as complex as those in North America contain some elements of each model, but for the most part they focus on one or two. A summary of each model is given in Table 1 and in Figure 2.

Each model has its own era and location of particular relevance. Hence the tendency of those writers who are concerned with the rise of cities in Britain or the U.S. manufacturing belt in the 19th century to stress factors of industrial advantage and to draw from their studies an emphasis on system stability and stages of urban growth within an essentially closed system. More recent commentators are impressed with the volatility of the system and its increasing response to consumption preferences rather than to production characteristics.

## The Frontier-Mercantile Model

The frontier has long been a fundamental theme in American history (Turner, 1894; Mikesell, 1960; Innis, as discussed by Neill, 1972), but its explicit relationship to the urban system has, until recently, received less attention (Gras, 1922; Careless, 1954; Wade, 1959, Vance, 1970; Pred, 1973). At the continental level urban growth in the U.S. has occurred in a regular spatial pattern, begin-

Table 1. Models of Urban-System Organization

|  | Frontier-Mercantile | Staple Export | Industrial Specialization | Social Change |
|---|---|---|---|---|
| *Location* | Edge of growing periphery | Periphery | Heartland | Universal |
| *Period of Greatest Relevance in North America* | 1740–1910 | 1700 to the present | 1840–1920 | 1880 to the present |
| *Source of Growth* | Growth of core region | Resource base, External markets | Agglomeration advantages | Technology, Labor supply |
| *Degree of Openness* | High. Depends on capital and labor transfer. | High. Depends on external demand | Low | High. Responds to information and technological change |
| *City Size Distribution* | Primate (single, very large city) | Rank size rule | Not specified | May change rapidly |
| *Economic Specialization* | Little, except by scale. Cities are service centers | All cities share the same staple specialization | High | Specialization evolves over time |
| *Interaction Patterns* | Links to core region dominate | Hierarchical, modified by staple | Highly linked | Varies with mode |
| *Settlement Pattern* | A long frontier arc | Dispersed, but depends on staple | Clusters, Agglomerations, Transport sensitive | Corridors or nodes specified by leading edge of economy |
| *System Characteristics.* | Investments by older centers send stimuli down to frontier area | Growth stimuli move up the hierarchy. (The central place system.) | Complex market linkages diffuse growth throughout | Growth responds to the removal of technical/physical constraints |
| *Examples* | Colonial America, prairie settlement | Southern U.S., British Columbia | Manufacturing belt to World War II | U.S. at present |
| *Authors* | Taaffe, Morrill and Gould (1963); Lukermann (1966); Pred (1973) | North (1961); Christaller (1933); Innis (1957) | Lampard (1955); Thompson (1965); Pred (1967) | Borchert (1967); Berry and Neils (1969); Dunn (1971) |

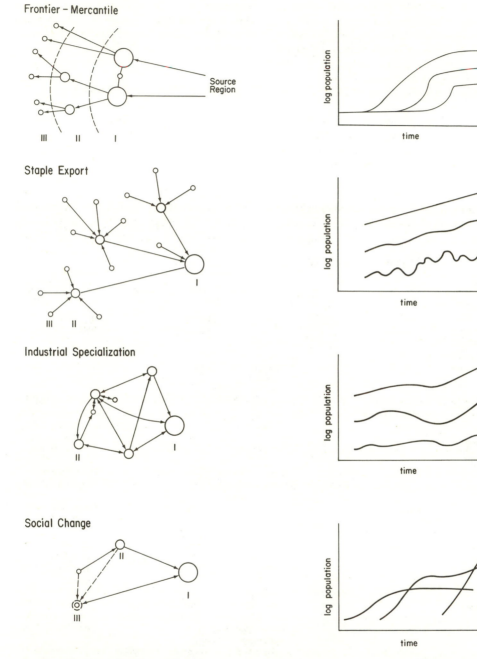

Figure 2.  Models of Urban System Organization: Spatial Structure and Paths of Growth (I, II, and III are levels in the urban hierarchy).

ning in the northeast and moving inland in regular rings of change over time. Lukermann (1966) points out that the "urban frontier" must be defined carefully. It is only partly identified by growth rates since older cities supplying higer-order services to the new frontier may grow rapidly as well. It is measured better by the generation of new cities (those crossing the urban-size threshold) and particularly by the geographic pattern of increases (or decreases) in the rank ordering of cities during any time period.

The growth wave of cities follows the settlement frontier and ties each new regional urban subsystem into the existing national system, with the nature of this linkage having important implications for the older cities. To what eastern U.S. cities will the Midwest be linked, for instance? Over a long period of time the extension of the frontier creates a continual tension between the older, high-order urban places and the newer subsystems. The former attempt to maintain their economic control and to extract income for the supply of services; the latter strive for economic, political, and social independence. This power struggle has been described by later authors as the "core-periphery relationship" (Friedmann, 1966), or the "heartland-hinterland pattern" (Ray, 1972). It implies economic differentiation between the frontier and older areas, with the former producing staples and the latter largely industrial goods and services.

The frontier depends on growth, since it is characterized by relatively high levels of capital investment and in-migration. Its rate of expansion is determined by a complex of forces. The rate of growth in the national or international economy is obviously a driving factor in the expansion of the frontier as a whole, determining such conditions in the source areas as employment, wage levels, rates of natural population increase, outmigration, etc. Yet the operation of the international market in staple products, the development of new modes of transportation, and the conflicts among nations are also important at various times for various frontiers.

When frontier expansion takes place on a broad front, as it did in North America, the spatial sequence of expansion, hence of initial advantage in urban development, requires an intricate model of the development process (for example, Meinig, 1972). Relative differences in current states of information or knowledge (Pred, 1973) regarding accessibility to source areas, political conditions, and the resource base (e.g., gold) often determined the growth response at any one time. Wade's (1959) comparison of the early growth of cities in the U.S. Midwest portrays the moment-to-moment evolution of a city's changing growth prospects. The timing of growth or specific entrepreneurial decisions become as important as the spatial situation.

Out of this kind of micro analysis, however conducted, emerges an urban subsystem which has considerable stability, even as the entire region evolves in its role, and which has a cumulative impact on the urban system as a whole through its pattern of linkages to the earlier system and its degree of interdependence (i.e., whether that subsystem is economically specialized and in what way). A less transient version of the frontier model but one using the same set of forces to explain the location of growth is the mercantile model described by Vance (1970) and Pred (1973). Urban growth in this model is determined by accessibility to the sources of merchandise, information, and new technology, and it specifically responds to capital-investment decisions and transportation improvements.

## The Staple Export Model

The staple export model describes the pattern of regional growth and organization in certain peripheral regions of the continent—the South, the Pacific Northwest and, in particular, Canada—where expansion is determined by external demands for primary products or staples. The urban system supplies goods and services in response to the growth and prosperity of the region. There is some evidence (see Neill, 1972) that the staple theory is essentially a reinterpretation of the frontier model where external market demands and technological conditions governed the pattern of exploitation of the wilderness, but the staple theory is better viewed as a framework that describes the mechanism driving a continuing and stable economy, growing perhaps, but not necessarily expanding in space. It can be conceived of as a static equilibrium model, and may be valid for large portions of the nonwestern world.

The difference between the frontier model and the staple model then rests largely in the interpretation of the dynamics of the process involved. The former requires expansion of a core area, and the process is governed by investment decisions and expectations; the latter is governed by year-to-year fluctuations in productivity. Compare, for example, the California gold rush with the growth of the corn belt. Also, a staple economy is driven by external markets while the frontier economy depends on development decisions made in the source region.

Watkins (1963) makes the basic assumption of the staple export theory: "Staple exports are the leading sector of the economy and set the pace for economic growth." The spatial distribution of a resource and its production function in turn determine the location of its impact; the character of the staple production determines the distribution of the income it generates and the rewards to factors of production; and its bulk and perishability account for the linkages it shows with the rest of the economy.

Several types of linkages can be defined. Backward linkages are inputs from other industrial sectors required for production of the staple, such as the purchase of mining machinery. Forward linkages are the outputs from production of the staple when those outputs are used by other firms, such as the conversion of iron ore to pig iron and steel. Final-demand linkages trace the impacts on other sectors of the staple income, creating a tertiary economy in the form of a local system of central places.

North (1961) employs the same resource-based ("staple" is the Canadian term) argument to explain the growth of the United States economy from 1790 to 1860. During the first thirty years the significant resource was New England shipping. The merchant marine provided the main source of external revenue, but its prosperity was initially controlled by foreign legislation and by European and domestic wars. After 1820 peace brought about an enormous surge in world trade, with the key contribution from the U.S. being cotton. Very rapidly a three-region system emerged: the South became specialized in cotton production, having backward linkages to the Midwest in order to provide food for the increasingly labor-intensive (slave) production while the cities of the northeast provided final-demand linkages to both regions. The latter linkages were very complex, including high-order goods and services for consumption, as well as business services, such as capital, shipping, insurance, and the organization of trade. Finally, forward linkages developed between the South and the North as the textile mills of New England expanded with the capital and entrepreneurship of the New England merchants. During the period prior to the Civil War, North shows how closely national growth and prosperity were linked to the balance between external demand and the internal production of cotton. Approximately twenty-year growth cycles developed, based on surges of expansion of the cotton belt.

Tangentially, North (1961) also mentions the role of the urban system in this expanding economy. The major urban functions of finance, trade and service, transportation, and manufacturing went to the northeast. Despite the great surge of growth in the South virtually no urbanization (except for New Orleans) took place. The production of cotton was intensely rural, even hostile to the growth of cities (see Wade, 1964). The contrast with the West was notable. There, a broad agricultural base rapidly developed a complete urban subsystem, with a full range of service linkages. By 1870 there were four cities west of the Alleghenies with populations greater than 100,000.

Lampard (1960) carries the theme of the regional economic base through to the present, although his interpretation is not that of a staple theory in the sense used by Watkins (1963). No regional economy is assumed to be entirely dependent on a single staple and its production function, but the significance of primary products (one or more, in sequence or simultaneously), for regional growth is evident. Repeated examples show how a local resource development transforms and reshapes the economic and social basis of a region. One such example is the Pacific northwest, which has undergone the staple sequence of furs, fish, and timber.

Because most U.S. primary production is marketed within the nation a certain stability emerges. Market demands depend primarily on the national growth rate, and each region competes with other regions in the country for a share of that growth. Market shares can be protected by legislation or by transporation preferences. Some analysts treat primary resource specialization at this level as another form of industrial specialization.

The major differences between the Canadian and American discussions of staple theory arise from the implications of specialization in a staple product for growth and prosperity. North (1961) suggests that dependence on an export base can only bring a temporary prosperity and that the boom must eventually collapse as the staple market declines or the resource is over-exploited. He notes: "Regions which remain tied to a single export staple almost inevitably fail to achieve sustained expansion" (p. 3). In his view a more complex economic base is required to sustain growth. The logic is similar to discussions of the dangers of extreme economic specialization among cities. The Canadian literature, however, is more optimistic. A history of sustained national growth over 150 years stimulated largely by a succession of staples suggests that a viable economy and a stable urban society is possible (though possibly not preferable) under these conditions.

## The Industrial Specialization Model

The industrial specialization of the 19th century undoubtedly dominates most discussions of urbanization and the evolution of urban systems, overwhelming most students of the U.S. urban experience (e.g., Lampard, 1968; Pred, 1967; Thompson, 1965). They tend to equate the urbanization process with industri-alization and to associate urban growth with industrial growth. Certainly this period and these processes did create the basic outline of the North American urban system. First, New England and the growth of the great coastal ports occurred, and then the giant industrial cities of the Midwest—Pittsburgh, Cleveland, Detroit, Chicago, and St. Louis—emerged. In each case a city's position as a regional leader was converted into national metropolitan status by the development of a powerful and integrated industrial economy. At the same time scores of smaller places suddenly grew several times in size as a direct result of the location of factories within their borders. The ability of industry to impose a whole new urban pattern on top of the existing structure was indeed impressive, although the specific location of manufacturing activities within any given region is not readily explained.

Studies of urban growth based on the theme of industrialization, however, tend to be aspatial. There are occasional references to the regional resource base which differentiates the industrial structure of cities, such as St. Louis in leather goods, Minneapolis-St. Paul in grain milling, and Pittsburgh and its coal-based economy. Harris (1954), for example, has demonstrated the close relationship between the extent of the manufacturing belt and access to the national market. For the most part, however, analysis is focused on a particular urban place. It is usually assumed that growth in industrial production (serving a national market of infinite capacity) is primarily due to characteristics peculiar to that city. The role of "initial advantage" and "circular and cumulative growth" (Pred, 1967) are posited, which can be tied to other concepts such as economies of scale, agglomeration and urbanization, the growth pole, and the industrial complex. Entrepreneurial competence, the structure of capital investment, and the ability to innovate and to adopt innovations have also been suggested as local factors explaining urban growth. In this American framework every individual, every firm, every city has the potential for success, if only the will is there.

The industrial model of the organization

and evolution of urban systems stresses size, internal industrial structure, and recent growth trends (momentum) rather than regional linkages, hierarchic level, and relative location within the national system. However determined, the resultant linkages among cities are complex, cutting across size hierarchies, and they emphasize scale but not distance. This model has its own form of evolution as well. Thompson (1965) has described the process by which the oldest (hence highest-order) cities lose their older and less technically innovative activities to smaller and more peripheral places as a "trickledown" process. The movement of textile firms from New England to the South is an obvious example. The old firms are replaced in New England by new growth industries requiring high skills, risk capital, and research capacity, as Perloff *et al.* (1960) have documented.

In fact the urban system emerging from the 19th century was quite complex. Duncan and Lieberson (1971) stress the dual structure of closely linked manufacturing cities with weak hierarchic relationships such as Pittsburgh and Cleveland, coexisting with a commercial-financial urban system operating very much on central-place principles of the range and threshold of a good or service. In their words, "Large scale manufacturing became an alternative to commerce as a city-building activity. The graded order of commercial centres was no longer adequate to account for the role and sizes of cities in the national economy."

## The Social Change Model

Those authors whose analyses of the city are firmly rooted in mid-twentieth century phenomena (e.g., Borchert, 1967, 1972; Berry and Neils, 1969; Berry, 1974; Meier, 1962) see the growth of an urban system primarily as a reflection of a complex and evolving society in which an urban place plays many roles simultaneously and operates under a wide variety of interwoven forces. In their view one must add to the evolving economic forces the characteristics of an evolv-

ing society with increasingly higher incomes and levels of education, new preferences for places to live, and new life styles. Both the national economy and these cultural variables operate on and through the urban system, often through intermediaries that are themselves subject to change, such as the technology of communication, transportation and production processes, and the institutional infrastructure (political systems and legislation, educational and research procedures, service-delivery systems and the like). Social change becomes a determinant rather than a consequence of other changes.

The advocates of this approach treat the urban system as open in the fullest sense. For them, it is open not only to commodity and financial input and output from abroad, but also to forces of change and evolution whose affects are largely unpredictable at any point in time. The temporal (and spatial) path of the urban system is comprehensible only *ex post*. The diagram from Borchert (1967) in Section II (page 00) indicates the many waves and frequencies of change-generating innovations. When, in addition both the spatial implications and the interaction effects among such forces are considered, the growth or decline of an urban region becomes almost a random event.

This latter view of the American urban system has clearly been reinforced by the events of the last two decades. Examples are numerous: the stimulation of urban growth in selected areas by amenity (climate, recreation) factors (Ullman, 1954); the impact of the massive federal investment in space and defence programs on peripheral areas with no observable location logic (Berry, 1973); the tendency of further investments in transportation and communication facilities increasingly to channel social contacts rather than to diffuse them; and the largely unanticipated decay of the central cores of many large urban areas. Urbanologists monitoring such current phenomena turn for explanations to the past and observe the impact of new technologies such as steamboats, railroads, and canals. They note the inability of statistical models of any kind to predict consistently variations in urban growth rates and they conclude that the evolution of the urban system is virtually unknowable.

# REFERENCES

Berry, B.J.L. 1973. "Contemporary Urbanization Processes," in *Geographical Perspectives on Urban Problems*. Washington: National Academy of Sciences, pp. 94–107.

———, and Neils, E. 1969. "The Urban Environment Writ Large," in H. S. Perloff, ed., *The Quality of the Urban Environment*. Baltimore: Johns Hopkins Press.

Borchert, J. 1967. "American Metropolitan Evolution." *Geographical Review*, vol. 57 (July), pp. 301–322.

———. 1972. "America's Changing Metropolitan Regions." *Annals of the Association of American Geographers*, vol. 62 (June), pp. 352–373.

Careless, J.M.S. 1954. "Frontierism, Metropolitanism and Canadian History." *Canadian Historical Review*, vol. 35 (March), pp. 1–21.

Christaller, W. 1933; rpt. 1966. *Central Places in Southern Germany*. Translated by C.W. Baskin. Englewood Cliffs, N.J.: Prentice-Hall.

Duncan, B. and Leiberson, S. 1970. *Metropolis and Region Revisited*. Los Angeles: Sage Publications.

Duncan, O. D. *et al.* 1960. *Metropolis and Region*. Baltimore: Johns Hopkins Press.

Dunn, E. L. 1971. *Economic and Social Development: A Process of Social Learning*. Baltimore: Johns Hopkins Press.

Gras, N.S.B. 1922. *An Intoduction to Economic History*. New York: Harper.

Harris, C. D. 1954. "The Market as a Factor in the Localization of Industry in the United States." *Annals of the Association of American Geographers*, vol. 44, pp. 315–348.

Innis, H. 1957. *Essays in Canadian Economic History*. Toronto: University of Toronto Press.

Lampard, E. E. 1960. "Regional Economic Development, 1870–1950," in H. S. Perloff *et al.*, *Regions, Resources and Economic Growth*. Baltimore: Johns Hopkins Press, pp. 109–292.

———. 1968. "The Evolving System of Cities in the United States," in H. S. Perloff and L. Wingo, eds., *Issues in Urban Economics*. Baltimore: Johns Hopkins Press, pp. 81–140.

Lösch, A. 1937; rpt. 1954. *The Economics of Location*. Translated by W. H. Woglom and W. A. Stolper. New Haven: Yale University Press.

Lukermann, F. 1966. "Empirical Expressions of Nodality and Hierarchy in a Circulation Manifold." *East Lakes Geographer*, vol. 2, pp. 17–44.

Meier, R. L. 1962. *A Communications Theory of Urban Growth*. Cambridge, Mass.: M.I.T. Press.

Meinig, D. W. 1972. "American Wests: Preface to a Geographical Introduction." *Annals of the Association of American Geographers*, vol. 62 (June), pp. 159–184.

Mikesell, M. W. 1966. "Comparative Studies in Frontier History." *Annals of the Association of American Geographers*, vol. 50 (March), pp. 62–73.

Neill, R. 1972. *A New Theory of Value: The Canadian Economics of Harold Innis*. Toronto: University of Toronto Press.

North, D. C. 1961. *The Economic Growth of the United States, 1790–1860*. Englewood Cliffs, N.J.: Prentice-Hall.

Perloff, H. S. *et. al.* 1960. *Regions, Resources and Economic Growth*. Baltimore: Johns Hopkins Press.

Pred, A. 1967. *The Spatial Dynamics of U.S. Urban and Industrial Growth*. Cambridge, Mass.: M.I.T. Press.

———. 1973. *Urban Growth and the Circulation of Information: The United States System of Cities, 1790–1840*. Cambridge, Mass.: Harvard University Press.

Ray, D. M. 1972. "The Economy." Chap. 3 in L. Gentilcore, ed. *Ontario*. Studies in Canadian Geography. Toronto: University of Toronto Press, pp. 45–63.

Taaffe, E. J., Morrill, R. L. and Gould, P. R. 1963. "Transport Expansion in Underdeveloped Countries: A Comparative Analysis." *Geographical Review*, vol. 53, pp. 503–529.

Thompson, W. R. 1965. *A Preface to Urban Economics*. Baltimore: Johns Hopkins Press.

Turner, F. J. 1894. *The Frontier in American History*. New York: Henry Holt.

Ullman, E. L. 1954. "Amenities as a Factor in Regional Growth." *Geographical Review*, vol. 44, pp. 119–132.

Vance, J. E., Jr. 1970. *The Merchant's World: The Geography of Wholesaling*. Englewood Cliffs, N.J.: Prentice-Hall.

Wade, R. C. 1959. *The Urban Frontier*. Chicago: University of Chicago Press.

———. 1964. *Slavery in the Cities*. New York: Oxford University Press.

Watkins, M. H. 1963. "A Staple Theory of Economic Growth." *Canadian Journal of Economic and Political Science*, vol. 24 (May), pp. 141–158.

# The Role of Cities in National Development

JOHN FRIEDMANN

## THE MEANING OF NATIONAL DEVELOPMENT

The idea of national development is tantalizingly ambiguous; precisely for this reason, it has become one of the germinal ideas of our time. Its ambiguity arises from a value judgment: development is widely regarded as a social good. The onlookers—the students of development—may be of different minds when they are pressed for closer definitions. Each will envelope the term in an aura of ideology, but all are likely to agree that development, whatever its historically specific meaning, is a desirable achievement.

To be developing is good; stagnation is bad; indifference is inadmissible. There can be little doubt that national development displays this and many other features of a genuine social movement. It is taken for granted that national societies have a historical commitment to the idea of continuous and cumulative change.

This assumption is not quite exact, however. All national societies, it is true, may harbor elites that wish to enter such commitments, but effective power often rests with authorities that see development essentially as threatening their privilege and power. As if this were not enough, many societies are national in little more than name, lacking a genuine sovereignty, torn by antagonistic interests, and having yet to achieve a substan-

tial measure of territorial integration. Development as a social movement may thus extend to something less than the entire world. But even nations that reject development must face prevailing international opinion that acts as if a moral obligation attached to the idea.

This essentially ethical view of development is not invoked for any particular set of policy prescriptions. It is agreed that nations differ in their historical conditions, and that every nation has a right autonomously to determine its own future.[1] Yet even granting this, no nation can entirely escape the moral imperative to "develop" and to continuously transform itself. These clashing views are somehow merged. The historically concrete is wedded to a universal expectation.[2]

There is, moreover, a growing conviction that the individual destinies of national societies are converging on a common path, and that the ultimate level of integration is a global one.[3] This belief has given rise to the

1. This is the ideal. In practice, large-scale intervention is often found, spheres of influence are carved out by contending powers, and national options are limited by the criteria governing international assistance.

2. This probably explains why many American observers admire Communist China's staggering effort to lead a population of 800 million into the twentieth century (despite possible disagreement with the methods used), and why they hold right-wing (but pro-American) dictatorships, from Portugal to Paraguay, in contempt for failing to do likewise. Moral imperatives are stronger than political philosophy.

3. According to Gideon Sjoberg, "industrial cities over the

This excerpt from "The Role of Cities in National Development," by John Friedmann is reprinted from *Urbanization, Planning and National Development* © 1973, pp. 21–34 by permission of the Publisher, Sage Publications, Inc.

distinction between underdeveloped (U) and developed (D) societies. The language suggests that the latter are passing through a phase in their historical unfolding that has not yet been reached by the former. Both types of society may be "developing," but, as late arrivals, the underdeveloped are obliged, in varying degree, to follow in the footsteps of the "developed" nations.

The argument can be properly understood only if we introduce two levels of abstraction. On the first, U-countries must, it is believed, acquire certain traits that are common to D-countries in order to survive in a developing world system. On a second, more specific level, each country must itself invent the concrete social forms and institutions corresponding to its actual condition.[4]

To give a simple illustration: all developing societies are faced with the necessity of steadily increasing the productivity of labor and of altering the composition of industrial employment. But it is left for each country to decide not only the pace at which these changes will be introduced, but also the rate at which different industrial sectors will increase their share of employment, the division of the means of production between public and private ownership, and the forms and methods of distributing the national product.

The bifurcation of the world into U- and D-countries is rudimentary. Nonetheless, it suggests that U-countries will hold in common certain comprehensive aims that, at an earlier period, were typical for the presently "developed" nations. These aims include:

(1) *an increase in the autonomy of national society,* by gaining effective sovereignty, increasing its military strength, enlarging the number and range of available choices, and acquiring a sense of national dignity;

(2) *an increase in the levels of living of the population,* by increasing production at faster rates than population growth, maintaining monetary stability, redistributing income in favor of the poorer segments of the population, and granting the rights of the people to certain basic claims of creature comfort;

(3) *an increase in social integration,* by promoting a wider and more effective participation of all the adult population in the decision processes of the society;

(4) *an increase in modernization,* by creating an institutional framework adapted to the requirements of generating and adjusting to continuous change and promoting those activities, especially in science and artistic creation, which will permit the country to share more fully in an emerging global culture;

(5) *an increase in spatial integration,* by articulating the development process across the entire settled space of the nation through a balanced system of human settlements.

Although these aims are sufficiently general so that they will, to some extent, be present also in the developed countries, the idea of national development is not confined to them. After a critical point is reached in the evolution of a national society, the former aims may lose their urgency, while other social goals will rise to take their place. Contemporary D-countries appear to have shifted their attention to the uses of wealth and leisure, the problems of mass culture, the progress of science, and the conquest of space. These new aims of national development appear to be so remote from the perceived realities of U-countries, that they are thought to be of little relevance for them. The idea of development thus undergoes a radical change in content as we pass on to D-countries. The historical meaning is new; what remains is the driving ethical imperative.

world are becoming alike in many aspects of their social structure.... Implicit in our analysis is another hypothesis: as technology becomes increasingly complex, a significant number of structural imperatives become more narrowly defined.... Cultural values induce stylistic differences among industrial cities that cannot be ignored. However, a value system cannot modify structural arrangements in an infinite variety of ways. Industrial cities share certain values because of their dependence on scientific method and modern technology. Overemphasis of cultural values as an independent variable leads to historicism and a denial of the possibility of making cross-cultural generalizations" ("Cities in Developing and Industrial Societies: A Cross-Cultural Analysis," in Philip M. Hauser and Leo F. Schnore, eds., *The Study of Urbanization.* New York: John Wiley and Sons, 1965, pp. 249–250). To the extent that development implies the spread of industrial culture, the thesis of cultural convergence may be maintained with a certain logic.

4. See Reinhart Bendix, "Tradition and Modernity Reconsidered," *Comparative Studies in Society and History,* Vol. 9 (April 1967), pp. 292–346, for a subtle elaboration of this argument.

Aims, however, are the governing criteria, and the performance of societies is judged in terms of them. Where it is satisfactory, no unusual measures need be taken. But implicit in the idea of development is the preparedness of a society to take responsibility for its performance and to intervene in the normal processes of change where the results expected from them fail to be produced. Development has the connotation of an *intended* good: it is a process endowed with moral purpose for which developing societies assume responsibility, and almost always this involves attempts at guided change or planning.[5]

## THE SETTLEMENT SYSTEM

The main task of this essay is to show, by way of introduction, the various modes of interaction between cities and national development.

As a form of human settlement, the city is a social system located in geographic space that occupies a precise position in a system of interconnected settlements, extending from hamlet to megalopolis.[6] National development occurs within this social interaction network stretched out over the landscape. But its occurrence in the spatial system is neither uniform nor simultaneous. Impulses for development originate at certain localities and are relayed to other localities in a definite sequence. The pattern of settlements creates a structure of potentials for development that will eventually be registered in indices of regional performance and will condition the evolving character of the society.

Since the goals of national development differ between U- and D-countries, each set of countries must be separately studied. In both,

the spatial pattern of settlement will bear a close relation to the key events of national development, but the specific role of cities will be different in each.

These summary observations may be better understood if we look at a few salient features of the settlement system of a nation.

(1) The system of settlements is differentiated according to the functions performed by every subsystem within it.

(2) Each subsystem stands at the node of a communications network that originates, absorbs, and transmits impulses of change to the other subsystems.

(3) Each subsystem stands at the node of a field of forces that acts upon and influences the location of activities and population.

(4) Each subsystem serves as an agent of change for populations living in dependent areas.

(5) The development options of each subsystem are limited partly by its position within a complex system of dependency relations.

(6) The development options of each subsystem are partly determined by its internal capacity to respond to exogenous impulses for change.

(7) A change in the relative position of one of the subsystems in the hierarchy of dependency relations signifies a change in the structure of the system as a whole.

(8) A change in the relative position of one of the subsystems in the hierarchy of dependency relations can result from a disproportionate increase (or decrease) in subsystem size, from changes in its social and political organization, or from a change in its functions for the system as a whole.

If, as is claimed, the pattern of spatial dependency relations is a controlling one for national development, it is reasonable to focus attention on those subsystems that display a greater-than-average capacity for autonomous transformation and consequently for sustained innovation. The development capacity of the system as a whole will, therefore, come directly to depend on the performance of these centers or *core regions*. For each core region, one or more dependent

5. The literature on development planning has grown impressively in recent years. For a comprehensive account of national development planning in practice, see Albert Waterson, *Development Planning: Lessons of Experience*. Baltimore: Johns Hopkins Press, 1965.

6. Differences in urban social systems do not concern us for the moment. Later, when we return to consider this question, it will be shown that only a few, but important features are relevant for national development.

*peripheral regions* may be defined, bearing in mind that lower-order cores may fall within the periphery of, and be dependent on, one or several higher-ranking cores. Core regions can thus be arranged into a hierarchy according to their relative autonomy in developing decisions. Peripheral areas, on the other hand, may be divided into upward- and downward-transitional regions in keeping with their estimated potentials for development. Finally, on core regions' peripheries, new settlement areas or *resource frontiers* may come into being.

The entire settlement space of the nation will thus be spanned by an array of regions that is articulated through a system of nodes and connecting channels of communication. This polarized space will display systematic variances in the capacity for development of given areas. Later comment will make the reasons for these differences more explicit. Here it is only necessary to point out that core regions possess the means for limiting and controlling the development of their peripheries and for extracting from them the resources that will contribute to their own accelerated growth. This imbalance of power between core and periphery, which displays a strong tendency to increase over substantial segments of the development path, will naturally lead to social and political tensions. Where these tensions cannot be held down to tolerable levels, they eventually undermine the stability of the system and its ability to generate further development.

Many appropriate examples come to mind. A striking account of the dangers inherent in this conflict between cores and their peripheries is given by Eric Wolfe in his description of the collapse of Theocratic society in Mesoamerica during the seventh and eighth centuries of our era.[7]

The web of Theocratic society contained another fatal flaw: a built-in imbalance between holy town and hinterland, between city and provinces. Ulti-

mately, the towns grew wealthy and splendid, because the countryside labored and produced. Not that some of the wealth did not flow back into the rural area. Some benefits must be returned to the ruled in any complex society. Undoubtedly the Theocratic society forged its own chain of command with the final links in the villages and hamlets; some men in the countryside must have acted as messengers of the gods and received rewards commensurate with the utility of their services. The growing gap between center and hinterland was not based on an absolute enrichment of the center while the countryside remained absolutely impoverished. Both grew in their involvement with each other; but the centers grew more quickly, more opulently, and—more obviously.

Spatial integration—which appears as a major development objective for U-countries—thus requires action that will increase the autonomy of peripheral regions with respect to their controlling cores, diminish one of the important sources of conflict between them, and assure the stability of the system during its period of transition.

## URBANIZATION AND THE DEVELOPMENT PROCESS IN U-COUNTRIES

City growth appears as an irrepressible accompaniment of modern development experience in U-countries. The statistical evidence leaves little question on this score.[8] The data for nearly all of the developing U-countries also show that large cities tend to grow at faster rates than smaller ones and that the national capital complex is particularly favored. But statistical associations constitute no proof of a causal relation. It is to this question of causality that we shall therefore turn by examining three fundamental forces in the process of development: the passage from

7. Eric Wolfe, *Sons of the Shaking Earth: The People of Mexico and Guatemala*. Chicago: University of Chicago Press, 1962, pp. 168–169.

8. A good recent summary of data is found in Gerald Breese, *Urbanization in Newly Developing Countries*. Englewood Cliffs, N.J.: Prentice Hall, 1966. For a sophisticated comparative analysis of urban population trends in one of the world's major underdeveloped regions, see Lowdon Wingo, Jr., "Recent Patterns of Urbanization Among Latin American Countries," *Urban Affairs Quarterly*, Vol. 2 (March 1967), pp. 81–109.

tradition to innovation, from a limited culture to one of constantly expanding opportunities, and from an elitist to a mass political system striving for national integration.

## Innovation and Urbanization

Invention must be distinguished from innovation. The former consists in the creation of something new out of a rearrangement of already existing elements, while the latter may be viewed as the transformation of inventions into historical fact. Both terms may be applied to tangible and intangible objects.[9]

The term "invention" for anthropology does not mean only the deliberate creation of a machine, of any type of mechanism, or of any other material achievement of a culture, an achievement in the nature of a radical innovation, but also new ideas, new concepts or patterns in social, political or religious organization, as well as new economic systems which play such an important role in the entire historical evolution. Man's inventive mind and the cultural process which ensues from it do not act exclusively upon elements of culture that are in some way tangible, but certainly also upon its universal life.

Accepting this broad interpretation, we may then say that comprehensive development occurs when single innovations—large and small—are linked into innovative clusters and systems. Since innovations arise out of an established traditional matrix, their integration into larger systems occurs as an asynchronic process, pitting new forces against an already established order.

We can now assert a first hypothesis: *the frequency of inventions is positively correlated with a high potential for interaction, that is, a high probability of information exchange or communication.* The probabilities of communication over a given surface can be plotted on a map so as to yield a landscape of communication potentials or communication fields. Cities, especially

large cities, appear as peaks in this landscape. It is the large city where the frequency of new idea combinations is generally greatest.[10]

A second and related hypothesis will say, first, *that urbanization will positively vary with the probability of communication at any given locality*—city growth is related to increases in potential communication, and, second, *as cities are joined into systems*—as the channels for transmitting information expand among cities—*the probability of information exchange among them will increase.* The growth of a single subsystem and expansion of intercity linkages are, to a large degree, substitutes for one another.

When we pass from invention to innovation, a third hypothesis may be stated, according to which *the frequency of innovation in a given locality is a function of its internal structure of social power.* A tightly controlled, rigid, hierarchical system of power will be less permissive of innovations than an open, horizontal, nonbureaucratic system of dispersed power. We should expect to find significant variations in the structure of social power among cities. But speaking generally, it is possible to assert that increasing size creates conditions that will bring the city's power structure into greater conformity with our second model.[11]

We are now in a position to ask whether a high probability for information exchange is causally related to certain forms of social and political organization. The answer, presumably, would be affirmative. If so, a fourth hypothesis may be stated: *increases in the level of urbanization will lead to an increasing openness of the system of social power and hence to an increase in the frequency of innovation.* This, then, may be regarded as the first positive contribution of urbanization

9. Gonzalo Aguirre Beltrán, "Confluence of Culture in Anthropology," *Diogenes,* No. 47 (Fall 1964), pp. 4–5.

10. An early but, nonetheless, excellent reference on the origins of innovation is H. G. Barnett, *Innovation: The Basis of Culture Change.* New York: McGraw-Hill, 1953.
11. The two alternatives describe extreme situations. Optimal innovative systems may result from some combination of authoritarian and democratic power structures. As ideal types, however, the two polar models of social organization may still be useful as a heuristic device. See T. Burns and G. M. Stahler, *The Management of Innovation.* Chicago: Quadrangle Books, 1962, pp. 119–125.

to national development. It will transform traditional society into an innovative system.

## Opportunity and Urbanization

George M. Foster describes peasant societies in terms of what he calls "an image of the limited good."[12] In such a society, the interests of one person can be advanced only, it is believed, by depriving someone else of the coveted benefits. The result is a brutally egocentric, defensive society whose members behave in accordance with this rule: "Maximize the material short-run advantage of the nuclear family; assume that all others will do likewise."[13]

The image of the limited good—a kind of zero-sum game—tends to be associated with isolated peasant societies. But contemporary urbanization is based on the opposite image of constantly expanding opportunities.[14] Cities undergoing development tend to transform the bitter little zero-sum games of peasant society into competitive nonzero-sum games. We should expect this image of the "unlimited" good to vary a good deal with both the rate of increase in employment and with city size. Both variables will increase economic choice and multiply the upward channels of mobility available to individuals.

Of course, image and experience do not always coincide. Expectations are not always bartered for the real thing. The older residents of the city, having pressed against the very real obstacles to opportunity that exist, may think society a fraud. Their political behavior will reflect a growing frustration with the social order. It is the recent migrant to the city—comparing his present condition to a dismal rural past—who looks upon his new environment with hope.[15] Return migration to the countryside is rare.[16]

What we may call the culture of the "unlimited" good is, on the whole, less tooth-and-claw, more given to accommodation, than societies organized around the opposite cultural image. Urban, in contrast to rural, society in U-countries tends to be more tolerant and generous towards the other, reinforcing the achievement impulses of large numbers of people. Continuous expansion of the urban system will tend to lower the level of interpersonal friction that might otherwise be expected.[17] The modern notion that development involves unceasing, positively valued change has grown out of urban experience. This, then, is the second contribution of urban to national development: *the city has*

12. George M. Foster, "Peasant Society and the Image of the Limited Good," *American Anthropologist*, Vol. 67 (April 1965), pp. 293–315.

13. Edward C. Banfield and Laura Pasano Banfield, *The Moral Basis of a Backward Society*. New York: The Free Press, 1958, p. 85.

14. This is illustrated by abundant data in a study carried out by the Centro de Estudios del Desarrollo of the Universidad Central de Venezuela (*Estudio del Conflicto y Consenso*. Serie de Resultados Parciales, Vols. 1–3. Caracas, 1965). This Venezuelan survey shows a surprisingly high incidence of hope among urban population samples, In this connection, it is worth noting that Oscar Lewis considers the "wide range of alternatives for individuals in most aspects of life . . . one of the most distinctive characteristics of cities, whether industrial or pre-industrial" (op. cit., p. 499). It is therefore those population sectors that fail to gain access to some or all of these alternatives for improving their condition that are "marginal" to urban society.

15. Myron Weiner, "Urbanization and Political Protest," *Civilisations*, Vol. 17, Nos. 1–2 (1967), pp. 44–52. Weiner's findings concerning voting behavior, that recent migrants to the city vote more conservatively than those who have established longer residence, may be interpreted in terms of the theory of "marginality" mentioned in note 14. The recent rural migrant to the city is initially absorbed into the "marginal" population sector where he can follow his customary life-style with only minimal adjustments. But for rural populations, this style includes a profoundly conservative outlook. It is, therefore, not especially surprising to discover that the voting behavior of recent migrants to the city is also conservative.

16. Richard D. Lambert, op. cit., pp. 135–136.

17. This, of course, is still a relatively unorthodox view. More commonly, rural arcadia is contrasted with urban violence and anomie. There are no definitive studies on this subject, but the evidence on rural violence is steadily accumulating. Irving Louis Horowitz, for instance, cites data on the positive rank correlation of deaths from group violence and numbers of people in farming ("Electoral Politics, Urbanization, and Social Development in Latin America," *Urban Affairs Quarterly*, Vol. 2 (March 1967), Table 7). At the same time, he notes an inverse correlation between the urbanization process and these causes of death. There are, however, significant exceptions at very high levels of urbanization. This suggests that one should perhaps distinguish between two forms of violent conflict: the urban form, tending to be goal-oriented and limited in time and purpose (e.g., a strike or a street demonstration), even though the frequency of such incidents in the total population may be high; and the rural variety, geared to a culture of the "limited good," which is characterized by "bitterness and hostility between factions." According to G. M. Foster (*Traditional Cultures and the Impact of Technological Change*. New York: Harper, 1962, p. 102), "the length to which people will go to humiliate their rivals (in small peasant societies) is difficult to believe."

*not only invented the concept of unlimited opportunity, but also made it possible and finally internalized it as the basis for its own unique form of culture.*

## Political Transformations and Urbanization

Industrialization and urbanization are not always parallel phenomena. Migration to cities in U-countries generally takes place at faster rates than the absorption of new labor force into employment of high productivity. Accelerated urbanization in this sense will inevitably lead to the formation of a massive urban proletariat whose members, lacking special skills, are only partially within the labor market, if at all, and for this reason are excluded from most of the material—and spiritual— benefits of the developing, participant society. The political significance of this situation derives from a heightened visibility of the city proletariat that, being looked at and looking at the world from which it is excluded in any but the strictest functional sense, may acquire a keen sense of its own "marginal" condition and become potentially available as a potent political force to whatever leadership is capable of capturing its confidence.

The second result for political development is the emergence in cities of innovative groups that pose a challenge to the established powers in their attempt to legitimize new claims and create a social climate favorable to further innovation, insofar, at least, as this would be consistent with their own schedule of values. In this endeavor, innovative counter-elites may seek alliances among successively larger, more inclusive sectors of the population: the upper-middle class, the lower-middle strata, the workers, the urban proletariat, and eventually also the excluded rural proletariat of the periphery. As their base for political action expands and the masses become politicized, the politics of innovation first turn populist, and later integrationist, on a national scale.[18] Strongly doctrinaire and

ideological during the struggle for power with the established elites, innovative groups will tend to become open to compromise once they have risen to power.[19] Political parties may consequently become transformed into giant bartering systems striving to aggregate ever widening circles of multiple and overlapping interests.

This outcome is not inevitable; it is merely possible. We may, therefore, wish to test the following hypothesis: *the resistance of the "established" powers to innovative counter-elites diminishes with the acceleration of the urbanization process.* This may be regarded as the third main contribution of the city to national development: *accelerated urbanization hastens the coming of a national mass politics based on bargaining and compromise among competing interest groups.*[20]

## Summary

We have tried to suggest that the three basic processes of national development—innovation, social, and political transformation—are closely linked to yet another process, that of urbanization, which tends to reinforce the latent predispositions to developmental change through increasing communication potential and a change in the pattern of social organization from Euclidean hierarchies to Einsteinian systems existing in

*America*. New York: Oxford University Press, 1965, pp. 47–73; and Kalman H. Silvert, ed., *Expectant Peoples: Nationalism and Development*. New York: Random House, 1963.
19. John Friedmann, *Venezuela: From Doctrine to Dialogue*. Syracuse: Syracuse University Press, 1965; and Fred D. Levy, Jr., "Economic Planning in Venezuela," *Yale Economic Essays*, Vol. 7 (Spring 1967), pp. 273–321.
20. Francine F. Rabinovitz, *Urban Development and Political Development in Latin America*. Occasional Paper. Bloomington, Ill.: Comparative Administration Group, 1967. An opposite interpretation of the same set of facts is found in Shanti Tangri, "Urbanization, Political Stability, and Economic Growth," in Roy Turner, op. cit. The reason for this difference in interpretation is given by Tangri's implicit belief that economic development can be successfully pursued without major structural change in the political system. Our own position is that conservative, rural-based political structures are incapable of bringing development about and must be changed to achieve development objectives in U-countries. In this connection, it may be observed that rural societies tend to be more prone to totalitarian appeals than highly urbanized societies, though the evidence on this point is admittedly still inconclusive (see S. M. Lipset, *Political Man*. Garden City, N.Y.: Doubleday, 1963).

18. Torcuato Di Tella, "Populism and Reform in Latin America," in Claudio Veliz, ed., *Obstacles to Change in Latin*

time. We have further tried to show that large cities are more effective in promoting these changes than small cities, and that the linkage of cities into urban systems has an effect analogous to increasing city size. It is also probably true that these variables— urbanization, city size, and expanding urban systems—are positively correlated with conflict. Urban society is a conflict society, but this conflict is only the external and highly visible accompaniment of more creative processes beneath the surface. Where conflict is absent, we can be certain that development does not occur.[21]

## THE DEVELOPMENT PROCESS AND CHANGES IN SPATIAL ORGANIZATION

In the preceding sections, we have described the development process as if it extended uniformly across a nation, except for a sharp intensification—and acceleration—at a small number of core regions. Superimposed upon a uniform development "surface," core regions polarize surrounding space and set up fields of tensions between themselves and their peripheries. If we now examine this surface more closely, we discover that it is finely articulated by a system of settlements which, subject to change itself, ends by completely transforming the structure of spatial relations in the social economy. The form in which this spatial transformation occurs exerts a decisive effect on the ability of a nation to achieve a satisfactory development of its internal resources.

Two pervasive forces underlie a change in spatial organization. The first is a steady improvement in the overall accessibility of the system that comes as a direct result of the five universal characteristics of modern development:

(1) a progressive expansion of transport and communication capacity over larger areas,

(2) an increase in the number of possible interconnections within the system,

(3) a reduction in the unit cost of transportation and communication,

(4) a rise in real incomes per capita, and

(5) an increase in the speed and efficiency of the transport and communication system.

Changes in the location propensities of firms and households is the second force determining the path of spatial transformation. The tendencies will differ with the experience of each country, but among the more significant changes in the location propensities of industrial and commercial firms—as development proceeds—will be shifts from a predominant resource to a market orientation, from single to multiple firm corporations, from an emphasis on the presence of economic to social infrastructure, from small to large firms (in employment), and from isolated firms to clusters of related enterprise.

During the early and intermediate phases of development, the location of households tends to be determined by the geographic pattern of emerging economic opportunities, but gradually this grim determinism will be relaxed as the classical formula of "labor follows industry" is reversed, and the natural and social amenities of different community environments come to exert a growing influence on where people decide to settle.

### The Transformation from Simple to Complex Structures[22]

The spatial structure of U-countries is, by comparison to later periods, a very simple one. Regional economies show relatively little specialization, since most of the population obtains its living from agriculture. Farming activities may be grouped into broad

21. The problem of controlling urban conflict is to guide it towards constructive ends while keeping rapidly changing social systems from disintegrating. See Lewis Coser, *The Functions of Social Conflict*. New York: The Free Press, 1956.

22. The following paragraph is based on Brian J. L. Berry, *Geography of Market Centers and Retail Distribution*. Englewood Cliffs, N.J.: Prentice-Hall, 1967; John Friedmann and John Miller, "The Urban Field," *Journal of the American Institute of Planner*, Vol. 31 (November 1965), pp. 312–320; and J. R. Lasuén, "Urbanization Hypotheses and Spain's Cities System Evolution." Paper presented at the Workshop on Regional Development. Institute of Social Studies, The Hague, October 1967 (mimeo).

ecological or production zones, but the cities that organize the national economy show only minor functional distinctions. One or two of them, however, will eventually stand out from the rest, evolving to the point where they can be unambiguously identified as core regions that will reduce the rest of the country's economy to a peripheral status. As core-region development proceeds, this simple structure is gradually filled out: territorial specialization occurs and urban functional hierarchies—following a modified Christaller pattern for all but the largest centers—become established. The new system will be coordinated—it would be wrong to speak here of direction—through spatial aggregates at the top of the hierarchy whose internal complexity is so great that new terms have had to be invented to describe them: metropolis, urban field, development corridor, megalopolis. Development comes to be concentrated in these potent spatial forms through which the former national peripheries are reorganized into elaborate patterns of interdependency. As larger and larger areas are brought into the structure of core regions, the national periphery is trimmed to a vestigial status. Most of the population comes eventually to live within these new foci of development.

## Transformation from Imbalanced to Balanced Structures

The initial spatial imbalance may be observed not only in the pronounced core-periphery structure of U-countries, but also in the relationship of population size to rank of cities in the system. According to a widely accepted rule, the size of each city in a fully developed system is determined by its rank, so that by dividing the size of the largest city, by the rank of any city, we obtain its population size.[23] There is a second rule that connects the size and function of cities with regional income. This states that the number of central functions of a city will increase with regional per capita income—holding size constant—but will also increase with an increase in city size, for constant income.[24] Combining these two rules with what has been said about growing functional specialization in the preceding paragraph, it may be asserted that, whatever the initial structure, continued development will be accompanied by an increase in the rank-size ordering of cities.[25] If we now extend the posited relationship horizontally across the settled space of a nation, the result of a process of increasing rank size will be a fully developed, hierarchically ordered spatial system, in which all places have approximately equal access to similar urban functions.[26] The system minimizes distances and is a stable one in its overall configuration, even though it may continue to evolve internally. Thus, lower-order functions may be recombined in larger centers, thereby eliminating the smaller places in the hierarchy, while, at the top, entirely new urban forms come into being.

## Transformation from Narrow Impact of Urban Life-Styles to Total Immersion in Urbanism

The spread of urban life-styles is not coincident with the pattern of cities, though it is strongly influenced by it. Initially, the gradients of urban influence are very sharp: urbanism is typically a large-city phenomenon, but the population affected by it will tend to live in very close proximity and constant interaction with the center.[27] Development, however, acting through the forces of equalizing access and location propensities, will work to reduce these gradients and to introduce elements of urban life-styles into the

23. Brian J. L. Berry, "City Size Distributions and Economic Development," in John Friedmann and William Alonso, eds., *Regional Development and Planning. A Reader*. Cambridge, Mass.: The M.I.T. Press, 1964.

24. J. R. Lasuén, op. cit.
25. J. R. Lasuén et al., "City Size Distribution and Economic Growth: Spain," *Ekistics*, Vol. 24 (August 1967), pp. 221–226.
26. Brian J. L. Berry, *The Geography of Market Centers and Retail Distribution*, op. cit., pp. 76–79.
27. Richard A. Ellefsen, "City-Hinterland Relations in India," in Roy Turner, op. cit., pp. 94–116.

remotest corners of the nation. Vast zones of an engulfing urbanism thus appear as the large city penetrates smaller towns and even the countryside with mass information media and modern forms of large-scale organization (e.g., commercialization of agriculture, unionization of farm labor, and industrial production). Since urban life-styles may set up expectations that cannot always be fulfilled in the locality, massive population readjustments occur as migrant streams move from peripheral areas lightly touched by urbanism to the more thoroughly urbanized development regions of the country.[28]

## Transformation from Partial to Complete Regional Integration

Each of the preceding three transformations of spatial systems—functional specialization of areas, increasing urban balance, and incorporation of most of the population into the culture of urbanism—contributes to the full regional integration of the nation. They do so not only by forging multiple and stronger linkages among all parts of the country, but also by encouraging greater geographical mobility of labor, capital, and commodities in expanding national and regional markets. At this point, the classical economic law of equal factor remuneration comes into full force, allocating resources in an efficient way according to the returns expected in each case.[29]

But regional integration has an even more basic meaning. It suggests the transformation of an entire nation into an innovative system with great capacity for self-renewal, the integration of most of the population into a social realm of constantly expanding opportunities, and the creation of a truly national polity whose individual members have roughly equal access to decision-making centers.

These results will also tend to lead to less authoritarian patterns of social organization and to a society held together by force of innumerable strands of criss-crossing communications, producing a "new man."[30]

The system of cities thus appears as a dynamic agent of development, not only generating but also mediating development impulses—an agent subject to change no less than changing, whose structural elements may be arranged in optimal ways to facilitate the process of national transformation.

## NOTES ON URBANIZATION AND NATIONAL DEVELOPMENT IN D-COUNTRIES

Sometime during the course of spatial transformation just described, a country will pass, quietly and unnoticed, from U to D, from a condition of underdevelopment to one of development. The exact timing of this changeover is somewhat arbitrary, for the process of transition is a relatively smooth one, and precisely where one elects to place the magical barrier that divides these different worlds is a matter on which experts may differ. Moreover, admission to the select company of D-countries signifies neither that all internal phenomena will automatically be consistent with each other—the oxcart coexists with the jet engine—nor that the process of development will increase. On the contrary, election of D-status means that a country has pushed forward into a period of self-reinforcing and continuous change, based, as in the past, on invention and innovation. Inevitably, therefore, discrepancies arise among the elements of which developing societies are made. Development appears as an asynchronic process.[31]

28. Aníbal Quijano Obregón, "La Urbanización dela Sociedad in Latinoamerica," Santiago: United Nations Economic Commission for Latin America, Division of Social Affairs, 1967 (mimeo).

29. In calculating investment returns, social considerations may, of course, lead one to assign values that are different from those of individual enterprise operating in a freely competitive market.

30. Karl Mannheim was among the first to realize the importance of psychological adaptation to the new conditions of an industrializing society (Freedom, Power, and Democratic Planning. New York: Oxford University Press, 1950. Part 3: "New Man—New Values"). David Riesman's concern with "other-directed" personality types is a more recent example.

31. The following analysis of Japan's development is to the point: "The attempt to evaluate Japan's place in the scale of economic development reveals a paradox. In terms of a set of

Nevertheless, in taking stock of the changes that have occurred, students of development will discover that the general situation of a D-country differs radically from earlier periods. For our purposes, the most important change to have occurred is the substitution of time for place. Expressed in different language, this means:

(1) increased freedom from economic constraints in location decisions,

(2) increased geographic mobility of population and productive resources,

(3) larger networks of social interchange,

(4) larger number of decision-making centers, and

(5) easier communication among centers.

The substitution of time for place also means a substantial reduction in the so-called friction of distance that will enlarge the options for locational choice and make the real time of reaching other places in the system a more decisive fact than out-of-pocket costs of movement. Eventually, even time may cease to be important. As the time for covering a certain distance shrinks, a situation of approximately equal access is eventually approached. This will extend to the entire space of the nation the salient traits of a core region.

Modern development tends to push these changes farther in the same direction. This does not mean, however, that location decisions will henceforward be treated with whimsy. For even in postindustrial societies, the past bears heavily upon the present. Old centers persist in having strong attractive power, roughly in the same proportions as over decades past, though activities may spill out into urban fields, enlarging the concept of city and constituting a new unit of spatial integration.[32] On the other hand, the reconcentration of communication-oriented services and industries into broad zones will tend to influence the location choices of those firms that still perceive an advantage in being physically near to the means of interchange.

If the substitution of time for place reduces economic constraints on location decisions, the city ceases to be a propulsive force of development. Spatial patterns of development were primordial national concerns of an underdeveloped society seeking greater autonomy, higher living levels, more social integration, greater world participation, and a more complete integration of its territory. They cease to be so for countries that are rapidly slipping into the postindustrial era.[33] The new salient interests in leisure, mass consumption, and science are no longer dependent on an urban focus—they may be called trans-urban. Nor is the city—in its traditional meaning—any longer an important instrument for their fulfillment.

This is not to claim total irrelevance of the settlement pattern for development in these societies. Problems of transition will continue to command the attention of policy makers.[34] Pockets of peripheral poverty remain, dramatic changes in the internal ecology of meta-urban units call for difficult adjustments; the poor are too handicapped to take advantage of the new location freedom; massive transportation problems demand urgent solutions. In addition, the policy of linking national economies into supranational systems, such as a common market, will pose problems of spatial reintegration similar to those familiar to U-countries and amenable to a similar treatment. In both cases, the urban pattern will play a major role.

The problem of urban form, however, remains an open one where the dominant social concerns fall more in the realm of culture than of politics or economics. For locational freedom imposes a special kind of responsibility:

variables for which data have been presented by Ginsburg, Japan is in many respects among the most developed countries in the world. On the other hand, in terms of the criteria of backwardness described by Leibenstein, Japan may be classified as a backward country. Specifically, Japan is backward as measured by the criterion of per capita national income" (Leon Hollerman, "Japan's Place in the Scale of Economic Development," *Economic Development and Cultural Change,* Vol. 12 (January 1964), p. 139).

32. John Friedmann and John Miller, op. cit.

33. Daniel Bell, "Notes on the Post-industrial Society," *Public Interest,* Vol. 6 (Winter 1967), pp. 24–35 and Vol. 7 (Spring 1968), pp. 102–118.

34. U.S. Department of Commerce, Area Redevelopment Administration, *Area Redevelopment Policies in Britain and the Countries of the Common Market.* Washington, D.C. Government Printing Office, 1965.

freedom for what? The forms of urban settlement are therefore not indifferent to postindustrial societies.

Which patterns are optimal for this new phase of development? In attempting to answer this question, we trespass on unknown territory. U-countries, after all, have the example of the more developed societies as a guide, and we are able to study the regularities and phases of succession in spatial organization. But on what model may D-countries pattern *their* development? We are only now beginning to know postindustrial society and are still missing a full vision of its potentialities.

The study of urban development has never been approached in quite this way. The perspective is normative; the ultimate aim is prescription. The analysis appropriate to this objective is cast in terms of a dynamic systems model in which the relevant aspects of economics, sociology, political science, and geography are brought together. Combined with this is an unfamiliar emphasis on the spatial aspects of development. We are therefore conscious of making a first reconnaissance in difficult terrain.

**2**

# HISTORICAL GROWTH AND THE EVOLUTION OF URBAN SYSTEMS

# Introduction

Despite the incredible rates of urban growth witnessed in most countries in recent times, combined with massive migrations and increases in the speed of transportation and communication, certain aspects of urban systems have been remarkably stable. Lasuén (1973), for example, has demonstrated that the relative rankings of cities by population size do not change greatly over several decades. The reason is that basic patterns of accessibility, as determined by geography and the transportation network, tend to maintain the locational advantages of one city relative to all others.

The outlines of most present-day urban systems were thus clearly visible in the maps and census statistics of a century ago. Going further into the past, Pounds (1969) and Russell (1960) describe urban systems in the classical period and in early post-classical Europe, respectively, which share many of the characteristics of size distributions and interactions of modern urban systems.

Urban historical writers are skilled at representing the inexorability of the present, given the past. The advantages of centrality and the economic and social benefits of agglomeration seem so powerful that smaller and peripherally located places have little or no chance in the competition for growth. They seem eternally doomed to relative obscurity, poverty, and even cultural oppression. And yet, how do we account for the rapid rise in importance of Los Angeles, Dallas, or São Paulo? Or the prosperity of many smaller and less accessible centers? Over the long run, as we search for systematic patterns of urban growth and change over decades and centuries, we must somehow incorporate these apparent exceptions into a more general theory. In a period of one hundred years, wars, boundary changes, and varying rates of demographic increase, as well as shifts in income and technology become important sources altering the evolution of urban systems. These external influences cannot, as some theorists suggest, be assumed as constant.

The readings in this section were selected to display the continuing tension between the forces maintaining stability within an urban system and those often external forces that act to alter its growth path. Our emphasis here is of necessity limited to recent history, at most the last century. Robson, for instance, in a study of 19th-century England and Wales, emphasizes the regularities of growth patterns and processes, which operate on a large number of places to maintain a stable, hierarchic structure of city sizes. Borchert, on the other hand, in examining American metropolitan growth stresses the differing historical and technological contexts to which the urban system of any country must adjust. In addition to making this point, Borchert also provides us with a superb overview of urban development in America (see also Borchert, 1972), as well as the historical spread of settlement across the country, which created, simultaneously, areas of boom and areas of decline. The two essays nicely complement each other in methodology and in context.

In another provocative study, unfortunately far too long to reproduce here, Thomas (1972) has attempted to render long-run changes in urban growth patterns more regular by examining historical urban growth within a framework of international interaction and interdependence. Growth appears to move from one national urban system to another in a regular sequence through the extraordinary mobility of labor and capital. He stresses movements of capital and immigrants across the Atlantic, particularly those which took place toward the end of the 19th century. Long-term cycles of development tend to be complementary, reaching a peak in one country while at a low in others. Urban growth in England, for example, was slowed by movements of the settlers and capital necessary to fuel urban growth in the U.S. and Canada.

## THE RISE OF THE URBAN SYSTEM

Perhaps the most profound pattern of long-term change in our economic and population structures has been the rise in importance of a national urban system. At the end of the 18th century, urban places made up only a small minority—from ten to twenty percent—of the population of most countries, with most people engaged in spatially extensive, near subsistence farming and fishing activities. Since then most Western nations have witnessed a massive urban transformation, including the concentration of national population into one hundred or so high-density nodes reflecting the economy's reorganization, for commercial if not social purposes, into specialized activities. These activities require an intricate organization of transportation and communication facilities to link urban regions. Kingsley Davis documents the present-day continuation of this process of concentration on a global scale. Although the world as a whole remains largely rural, the rapid urban transformation of Third World countries will soon reverse this dominance.

A city grows, prospers, and specializes in accordance with its role within the urban system. At one time the prosperity of a region depended on the fertility of the land and the vitality of its culture, as modified by the occasional plague or invasion. Now, as Friedmann argues in Section I, it increasingly reflects the extent and organization of the urban system and the allocation of growth or income to each component or city. New York and Washington tend to determine the prosperity of Dubuque and Lexington by defining the *operating rules* for the urban system to which they belong. This urban transformation of nations has spawned hundreds of books and articles (see Lampard, 1968 and the review articles in Hauser and Schnore, 1965; and Jakobson and Prakash, 1971) precisely because of the fundamental social and economic changes to which it is obviously linked (Vance, 1976).

Urbanization still varies in completeness from one national urban system to the next, but there is also a process of convergence. Urbanization tends to diffuse from one nation to another, along with new technology, international capital, and political imperialism. Often, because of high rates of consumption of material goods, those countries that lead in this diffusion process are forced to *export urbanization* (and the services it both requires and provides) to other countries in order to obtain the necessary raw materials. This, however, is the subject of discussion later in this introduction and in Section VI.

While certain aspects of the urbanization process are repeated in country after country, such as high urban growth rates and wide variations in city sizes and economic structure, considerable latitude exists in the actual form and spatial organization of the urban system. In his overview, *The Human Consequences of Urbanization* (1973) Berry describes a threefold pattern. First, the market-responsive Western nation (as described in most of the articles in this book) evinces an interaction of economics and public policy that creates basic similarities in urban systems. Second, in less developed countries, such as India, or much of Africa, the urban system is still emerging. Here the dual economy outlined in the both the development and geographical literature (see Brookfield, 1975; Chang, 1976; Abu-Lughod and Hay, 1977) is the model. In this model a highly developed urban subsystem, complete with high-speed transportation systems and highly specialized export activities, is superimposed on a predominantly rural society. This society may be touched relatively little by the urbanization process, or it may be slowly destroyed.

The urban systems of socialist nations (the third pattern), are less clearly identifiable. The spatial distribution of urban activities is determined largely by the state, just as growth is allocated to various economic sectors. Efficient production is the dominant goal, and differences in patterns of consumption or in life-styles are not explicitly acknowledged or encouraged. The elaboration of regional urban subsystems is encouraged (Kansky, 1976). The U.S.S.R., for example, has developed a number of new industrial and resource-based cities as part of its program to decentralize growth away from Moscow, while also directing growth to existing medium-sized centers (Harris, 1970). At the same time Moscow continues to grow more rapidly than was planned, and extra incentives are required to attract workers to remote areas. However, policy statements often differ more widely in these countries from those of Western nations than do their results.

## TRENDS IN URBAN-SYSTEM EVOLUTION

Are there universal patterns of change in urban systems—or, if you prefer, distinct stages in urban-system evolution? Probably not. Urban systems, as stressed above, are too varied, too complex, and too open to external forces to permit such generalizations. Nonetheless, the close links between the growth of an urban system and other processes, such as economic development, demographic change, and technological innovation, suggest some underlying trends, which, at least for most nations in recent history, appear valid. Friedmann (1972) has attempted to document such urban-system changes in formal statements.

The predominant characteristic of most urban systems is continued population growth throughout the system by natural increase. These growth rates respond to even the most rudimentary improvements in sanitation and in health care, as well as to improvements in national productivity. An increase in the total national product may or may not lead to improvements in product per capita, but some form of economic growth will usually accompany demographic growth. At the most basic level this is due to the additional input of labor to the production process, but more likely it reflects the reorganization of the urban system.

Improved transportation and communication facilities are also critical. They permit greater interregional trade, specialization of the means of production, and higher levels of production throughout a country. The ability of labor and capital to shift toward the most productive activity or location further increases the growth in productivity. Economies of agglomeration and increasing returns to scale tend to concentrate production and consumption in the largest urban areas. Rural population densities, however, remain relatively unchanged; the effect of new population growth is largely concentrated in cities. As the cities assume different production roles they become more closely interlinked. And as development continues, regional differences in levels of income, technology, and culture tend initially to rise and then at later stages to fall as the polarization effects of economic growth are modified by interregional migration and improved access to technology and culture on the part of residents of peripheral regions. Herein lies one of the fundamental dilemmas of urbanization. Massive urbanization is both an initial cause and eventually a possible solution to the problem of regional and social disparities (see the excellent summary by Williamson, 1965).

The external forces acting on a national urban system in turn increase; or at least shift away from acts of God towards the *premediated incursions* of foreign governments and multinational corporations. Every urban system is affected by the marketing practices of organizations such as Pepsi-Cola and IBM or the resource explorations of Standard Oil and Shell-BP. In developed and developing countries alike they impose their own hierarchical distribution systems, establish marketing centers, and build transportation networks for imports and exports. In the process, they alter the rates of inflation, political change, and patterns of regional growth.

It is not technology so much as it is "technique" (a term Ellul coined) that creates urban systems. It is not the gadgets, but the host of design engineers, management experts, accountants, financial systems,—in other words, the whole production and consumption apparatus, which shape the development process. The size and the number of cities grow and the interactions among them increase. These cities produce increasingly different goods, but their patterns of consumption become more and more alike. The fate of any one city, or subsystem, or national system then becomes inexorably linked to the next higher-order urban system, as Boulding makes so clear in his article in this section.

## THE PREDICTABILITY OF CHANGE IN URBAN SYSTEMS

Complex social systems, as previously defined, resist unexpected change. Galbraith (1968, 1974) describes in great detail how the large modern enterprises, which make up an increasingly large share of our urban and production activities, require long planning horizons and regular rates of change in order to survive and prosper. Complex social systems, therefore, have considerable inertia because of these same attributes and because of their diffused decision-making structure and internal complexity. As in any large organization, the many components that must be adjusted if change is to occur ensure that change is slow. These systems are, in short, resilient. At the same time they are frequently able to "internalize" external factors, which otherwise would be beyond their control, and thus to absorb many kinds of localized shocks with little effect, shocks which might devastate smaller and less-integrated systems. They often can, for example, effectively compensate for a flood, a crop failure, a change in government, or the uncertainty of a supplier or service by diversifying their operations and investments.

This increasing integration of an urban system changes the importance attached to different planning horizons. There is now very little possibility of a localized famine due to crop failure in developed countries. In the U.S., relief agencies, food stamps, and the entire agribusiness are designed, at least in part, to cope with such problems.

At the same time it is also possible for every facet of the American economy and its geography to be affected by a Vietnam War and its resulting social unrest and inflation. While localized, short-term difficulties may be reduced through greater interdependence, in the process we may leave ourselves more exposed to the larger and less frequent events that alter life across the whole urban system. In other words, as the short-term predictability of such systems increases, longer-run trends may become less certain.[1]

As an urban system matures, the intensity of integration among places makes all locations respond increasingly to common problems—the Depression, the Korean

---

1. For an interesting discussion of the question of efficiency and related issues in planning, see M. A. Goldberg (1975).

War, the energy crisis, climatic change are just a few examples. Each event is spread throughout the urban system by various means, such as taxes, prices, and industrial linkages, and through a common cultural response enforced by powerful national institutions and the communications media. Consequently, as suggested in our introductory remarks in Section I, terms like "urban" and "rural," or the "South" and the "Midwest," can begin to lose their meaning as integration leads to greater cultural homogeneity. All news comes from news services such as the Associated Press; all beer from a few national breweries, and most of our lettuce from the same two or three valleys run by the Jolly Green Giant and his friends.

These trends are now so well advanced that significant counter movements have been established to resist further integration. The essence of these movements is the establishment of greater consumer sovereignty and local community independence in planning and in decision making. Consumer protection associations, self-help groups, and the trend to greater autonomy of home rule in urban-policy formulation are obvious examples. Although the odds are strongly against most of these movements, whatever the outcomes might be they will be expressed in increasing conflicts within the urban system.

## THE FORCES OF CHANGE IN THE URBAN SYSTEM

How then do we describe and analyze these broad and very complex macro influences, which may alter the entire urban system? In part one plans for flexibility and in part one simply accepts living with uncertainty. We cannot hope to anticipate the directions of technological change even if we were able to translate the implications of rockets, satellites, transitors, and computers for the urban system. We will never be able to predict the flow of international relations that alters political boundaries, trading blocs, defense expenditures, and resource supplies. Nor is our record particularly good in anticipating social change and the diffusion of new ideas.

Our concept of the urban system, however, at least guides us to ask particularly specific and appropriate questions about these changes. Most studies of urban systems neglect or downplay the impact of forces and relationships arising outside national boundaries. For example, foreign countries are important sources of raw materials and markets for any developed economy. These ingredients affect the accessibility patterns within an urban system, now and in the past, and their role shifts continually through time. The same is true of the movements of other components of the production process: capital, labor, and technological innovation.

The important changes to observe are those that alter the operation of the urban system as a whole. Does an innovation—be it the coaxial communication cable proposed for the "wired" city of the future or the industrial conglomerate—tend to integrate the urban system more closely or to relax the linkages among cities? Does new legislation create local autonomy in some planning role or shift power to some central agency? Does a large-scale business merger alter the organization of the urban system by linking urban subsystems that were once largely independent? Does a series of major economic developments in one region alter the balance of the urban system as a whole, creating an irreversible shift of power, say from Philadelphia to New York or from San Francisco to Los Angeles?

## CONCLUDING REMARKS

Over time the emphasis in these questions will change as the origin of the dominant forces affecting urban systems shifts increasingly from natural to man-made, from private to public, and from internal to external sources. The prosperity of the farmer in North Dakota or Western Australia, for instance, depends not so much on the weather but on the price of wheat, which is set not just by the market but also by public fiat, which in turn is determined not only by national needs but by world politics. The classical location theory of Lösch (1937) and Ohlin (1933) must give way to the political economy of Galbraith (1974) and Friedmann (1972 and see Section IV) and to the cultural geography of Vance (1977) in attempting to understand the historical evolution of cities and systems of cities.

## REFERENCES

Abu-Lughod, J. and Hay, R. Jr., eds. 1977. *Third World Urbanization*. Chicago: Maaroufa Press.

Berry, B.J.L. 1973. *The Human Consequences of Urbanisation*. London: Macmillan & Co.

Borchert, J. 1972. "America's Changing Metropolitan Regions." *Annals, Association of American Geographers*, vol. 62, pp. 352–373.

Brookfield, H. 1975. *Interdependent Development*. London: Methuen.

Chang, Sen-Dou. 1976. "The Changing System of Chinese Cities." *Annals, Association of American Geographers*, vol. 66, pp. 398–415.

Dwyer, D. J., ed. 1972. *The City as a Centre of Change in Asia*. Hong Kong: The University Press.

Ellul, J. 1964. *The Technological Society*. Translated by John Wilkinson. New York: Random House.

Friedmann, J. 1972. "A General Theory of Polarized Development," in N. Hansen, ed. *Growth Centers in Regional Economic Development*. New York: The Free Press, pp. 82–107.

Galbraith, J. K. 1969. *The New Industrial State*. New York: Harper & Row.

——. 1974. *Economics and the Public Purpose*. New York: Harper & Row.

Goldberg, M. A. 1975. "On the Inefficiency of Being Efficient," *Environment and Planning A*, vol. 7, pp. 921–939.

Harris, C. D. 1970. *Cities of the Soviet Union*. Chicago: University of Chicago Press.

Hauser, P. M. and Schnore, L. F., eds. 1965. *The Study of Urbanization*. New York: John Wiley and Sons.

Jakobson, L. and Prakash, V., eds. 1971. *Urbanization and Economic Development*. Beverly Hills: Sage Publications.

Kansky, K. 1976. *Urbanization Under Socialism*. New York: Praeger.

Lampard, E. 1968. "The Evolving System of Cities in the United States: Urbanization and Economic Development," in H. S. Perloff and L. Wingo, Jr., eds. *Issues in Urban Economics*. Washington: Resources for the Future Inc.

Lasuén, J. R. 1973. "Urbanization and Development: The Temporal Interaction Between Geographic Clusters." *Urban Studies*, vol. 10, pp. 163–188.

Lösch, A. 1937. *The Economics of Location*.

Translated by W. H. Woglom and W. A. Stolper. New Haven: Yale University Press, 1954.

Ohlin, B. 1933. *Interregional and International Trade*. Cambridge, Mass.: Harvard University Press.

Pounds, N.J.G. 1969. "The Urbanization of the Classical World." *Annals, American Association of Geographers*, vol. 59, pp. 135–157.

Russell, J. C. 1960. "Metropolitan Regions in the Middle Ages." *Journal of Regional Science*, vol. 2, pp. 55–70.

Thomas, B. 1972. *Migration and Urban Development: A Reappraisal of British and American Long Cycles*. London: Methuen.

Vance, J., Jr. 1976. "Cities in the Shaping of the American Nation." *Journal of Geography*, vol. 76, pp. 41–52.

_____. 1977. *This Scene of Man: The Role and Structure of the City in the Geography of Western Civilization*. New York: Harper's College Press.

Weber, A. F. 1899. *The Growth of Cities in the Nineteenth Century*. New York: Macmillan.

Williamson, J. G. 1965. "Regional Inequality and the Process of National Development: A Description of the Patterns." *Economic Development and Cultural Change*, vol. 13, pp. 3–45.

# World Urbanization, 1950–70

KINGSLEY DAVIS

By 1970 the world's total population had reached approximately 3.6 billion people. Of these, about 1.4 billion, or nearly 39 per cent, lived in urban places, and the rest (2.2 billion, or 61 per cent) lived in rural areas. Among those living in urban places, approximately 864 million, representing 23.8 per cent of the earth's people, were in urban places having 100,000 or more inhabitants.

Clearly, by the standards of a highly industrial nation, the world is not yet extremely urbanized. The United States, for example, has about 75 per cent of its population in urban places, and 56 per cent in places (urbanized areas) of more than 100,000. Australia and Great Britain are even more urbanized than that, with around four-fifths in urban places and close to three-fifths in urban agglomerations. Compared to such advanced countries, the entire globe, with six-tenths of its people classified as rural and more than three-fourths living in places of less than 100,000, is still in a predominantly agrarian condition.

Yet it is worth noting that the present degree of world urbanization is both very recent and totally unprecedented. Prior to 1850 no country, no matter how advanced, was as urbanized as the world is today. It was not until just after 1850 that the United Kingdom, the first country to industrialize, became as urbanized as the world was in 1970, and not until around 1900 that urbanization reached this level in the United States. In other words, although the world as a whole is just entering the twentieth century with respect to urbanization, it is not far behind the most advanced countries and is certainly a long way from the Middle Ages. Furthermore, as we shall see in the next chapter, the global level of urbanization is rising rapidly. In 1950 the proportion urban was only 28.2 per cent, in contrast to probably 38.6 per cent in 1970. Barring some great reversal in the process of change, it will not be long before the world as a whole is as urbanized as even the most advanced nations are today.

The 1970 proportions given here are based on the B projections made at IPUR.[1] These will be discussed further in a moment, and their difference from the A projections described. The 1950 and 1960 proportions are based on data for all countries in the world published in Volume I of this study.[2] The definition of "urban" is usually that of the country itself (modified only when necessary), and the definition of "city" is, whenever possible, the urbanized area (or urban agglomeration) rather than the city proper. The term "city" is reserved for places

1. International Population and Urban Research. See Chapter 1 in original text.
2. Davis, *World Urbanization 1950–1970*, Volume I. This volume has four chapters and eight explanatory sections describing the definitions used and the methods of compilation and estimation employed. It gives data for the 1970(A) projection, but not, except incidentally, for the 1970(B) projection.

From "World Urbanization 1950–1970: The Urban Situation in the World as a Whole," *World Urbanization*, Population Monograph Series No. 9 (Berkeley: University of California, 1972). Reprinted by permission.

of 100,000 or more inhabitants; places of less than 100,000, if they are urban, are referred to here as "towns."

## Rural-Urban Distribution of World's Population

The numbers of the earth's rural and urban inhabitants, and the proportions they constitute of the world's total population, are shown in Table 1. It will be seen that in 1970 the 1.4 billion people living in places classified as urban are more than matched by the 2.2 billion still living in places calssified as rural. Since the overwhelming majority of this huge rural population are dependent on agriculture for a living, the immensity of the figures shows the extent to which the human species, for all its vaunted science and technology, is still devoting its labor to meeting the elementary needs for food and natural fibers. *Homo sapiens* as a whole is still far from leading a synthetic life in the city and far from using simply brains and pushbuttons to satisfy his needs.

Even the people classified as urban are not all in cities; almost four-tenths of them live in towns of less than 100,000. Sometimes observers are so mesmerized by rates of change that they overlook how backward the world continues to be. Although the future may eventually bring advanced urbanization to the entire world, the actual situation is still predominantly one of rural villages and small towns. It must be remembered that, of the two projections for 1970 in Table 1, Projection A, which represents a summation of the projections we made for all countries of the world, is the more conservative. The other one, Projection B, which assumes that the world's urbanization proceeded in 1960–70 as it did in 1950–60—that is, that the total population, and the urban and city populations, all grew at the same rate as in 1950–60—is slightly less conservative, but it too may understate the actual situation in 1970. If so, it is more likely to do so with respect to the urban and the city populations than with respect to the total

population. I am confident that the B projection is nearer to reality than the uncorrected A projection, at least with respect to the urban population, but I include both projections in Table 1 to show that the two different methods yield results that diverge only slightly.

## The Town and City Populations

In delineating the degree of world urbanization, we need not be confined to the rural-urban dichotomy. Our data enable us to make finer distinctions. For instance, the urban population can itself be dichotomized by separating it into the city population (100,000 or more) and the town population (urban places under 100,000), the latter being obtained by subtraction of the city population from the total urban population.

Table 1 confirms my statement that the town category accounts for a substantial share of the world's urban dwellers (43 per cent in 1950 and 38 per cent in 1970). When the town population is added to the rural, the two together account for 76 per cent of the world's population in 1970. Clearly, big-city life is by no means the general norm.

Of course, the social and economic importance of cities is far greater than the ratio of their inhabitants to the total population. The reason for this is that influence or power is determined not only by the number of people but also by their skills and organization, and the city population is generally better trained and organized than the rural population. However, since numbers do exercise an influence in their own right, one must know what proportion of the population lives in cities before one can accurately understand their role. The numerical proportion of city inhabitants in the world today, approximately one-fourth, is certainly enough to give them a dominant position. This can be shown in many ways, but one way in which our data reveal it is the fact that a disproportionate share of the world's city inhabitants are to be found in the highly developed countries,

Table 1. World's Town and City Population: 1950–1970.

|  | 1950 | 1960 | Projected[1] | |
|---|---|---|---|---|
|  |  |  | 1970(A) | 1970(B) |
| POPULATION (000's) |  |  |  |  |
| World total | 2,501,894 | 3,012,659 | 3,604,518 | 3,628,000 |
| *Urban* | 706,383 | 993,718 | 1,371,378 | 1,399,000 |
| Town | 300,365 | 401,490 | 524,034 | 535,136 |
| City | 406,018 | 592,228 | 847,344[2] | 863,864 |
| PERCENTAGES |  |  |  |  |
| *Urban* | 100.0 | 100.0 | 100.0 | 100.0 |
| Town | 42.5 | 40.4 | 38.2 | 38.3 |
| City | 57.5 | 59.6 | 61.8 | 61.7 |
| *World* | 100.0 | 100.0 | 100.0 |  |
| Town | 12.0 | 13.3 | 14.5 | 14.8 |
| City | 16.2 | 19.7 | 23.5 | 23.8 |
| Rural | 71.8 | 67.0 | 62.0 | 61.4 |

[1]The difference between the two projections is explained in the original text.
[2]Owing to our difficulty in locating all the towns likely to become cities between 1960 and 1970, Projection A underestimates the population in cities. If a correction is made for this misallocation (without changing the world population estimate), the proportions come out higher than in Projection B.

which are of course the countries that exercise the greatest influence.

Whenever we speak of the city population, one must remember that our data do not refer to units defined in strictly comparable terms. Some of our cities are Cities Proper (CP's)—with suburbs, if any, omitted because of lack of information—while others are units variously known as Urbanized Areas (UA's), Urban Agglomerations, or Metropolitan Areas (MA's), in which the suburbs are included. Had we been able to find or estimate the population of the urbanized area for *all* places of 100,000 or more, we would have found a higher figure for the total population in such places than the one we have. The difference, however, would not have been large, because the great majority of our cities of 100,000+ are delimited in an approximately adequate way, and these contain more than eight-tenths of the total population in places of that size. For simplicity, we refer to all urban places of 100,000+ as "cities," regardless of whether they are, out of necessity, defined as Cities Proper or, when possible, as some unit more broadly conceived.

## The World's Cities Classified by Size

Having split the earth's urban inhabitants into two groups (towns and cities), we can now subdivide each group according to finer size categories. The task is easy with respect to cities, because we have the populations of individual places of 100,000 or more; but it is difficult for towns, because we have data only for the class as a whole and not for the individual places. The town classes, therefore, have to be estimated. I shall discuss the city classes first, and then deal with the towns.

Since we have information on individual cities, we can classify them according to whatever size categories we wish. In Tables 2 and 3 they are grouped in eight classes, but the class boundaries are different. In both tables, for reasons to be explained in a moment, the principle of classification is that of having the upper boundary of each class equal to twice the lower boundary. If this principle is followed consistently, beginning with 100,000 at the lower end of the scale (which is the lower boundary of our city category as a

Table 2. Cities Classified by Size, 1950, 1960, 1970: Log-equal Scale.

| | | | | | | Projected[1] | | |
|---|---|---|---|---|---|---|---|---|
| | 1950 | | 1960 | | 1970(A) | | 1970(B) | |
| Size-Class | Number of Cities | Per Cent | Number of Cities | Per Cent | Number of Cities | Per Cent | Number of Cities | Per Cent |
| *All Cities* | *962* | *100.0* | *1,300* | *100.0* | *1,644* | *100.0* | *1,777* | *100.0* |
| 12,800,000+ | — | — | 1 | 0.1 | 1 | 0.1 | 1 | 0.1 |
| 6,400,000 | 2 | 0.2 | 6 | 0.5 | 14 | 0.9 | 14 | 0.8 |
| 3,200,000 | 10 | 1.0 | 14 | 1.1 | 18 | 1.1 | 18 | 1.0 |
| 1,600,000 | 29 | 3.0 | 42 | 3.2 | 61 | 3.7 | 61 | 3.4 |
| 800,000 | 59 | 6.1 | 93 | 7.2 | 128 | 7.8 | 128 | 7.2 |
| 400,000 | 127 | 13.2 | 163 | 12.5 | 232 | 14.1 | 232 | 13.1 |
| 200,000 | 251 | 26.1 | 340 | 26.2 | 479 | 29.1 | 479 | 27.0 |
| 100,000 | 484 | 50.3 | 641 | 49.3 | 711 | 43.2 | 844 | 47.5 |

[1]See footnote 2 in Table 3. In the present table all extra cities in the 1970(B) projection are in the 100,000–200,000 class.

whole), the resulting class boundaries are those of Table 2. These boundaries have the inconvenience of not falling on even millions at any point. Accordingly, I have grouped the cities another way in Table 3 by starting the doubling at 125,000 instead of 100,000. This arrangement has the disadvantage of producing, at the bottom of the city distribution, a lame-duck class (100,000–125,000) that does not conform to the doubling principle, but on the other hand it has the convenience of producing class intervals that fall on even fractions or whole numbers of millions.

The reason for employing class intervals in

Table 3. Cities Classified by Size, 1950, 1960, 1970: Conventional Scale.

| | | | | | | Projected | | |
|---|---|---|---|---|---|---|---|---|
| | 1950 | | 1960 | | 1970(A) | | 1970(B)[2] | |
| Size-Class | Number of Cities | Per Cent | Number of Cities | Per Cent | Number of Cities | Per Cent | Number of Cities | Per Cent |
| *All Cities* | *962* | *100.0* | *1,300* | *100.0* | *1,644* | *100.0* | *1,777* | *100.0* |
| 8,000,000+ | 2 | 0.2 | 3 | 0.2 | 10 | 0.6 | 10 | 0.6 |
| 4,000,000 | 9 | 0.9 | 13 | 1.0 | 17 | 1.0 | 17 | 1.0 |
| 2,000,000 | 15 | 1.6 | 27 | 2.1 | 43 | 2.6 | 43 | 2.4 |
| 1,000,000 | 53 | 5.5 | 71 | 5.5 | 104 | 6.3 | 104 | 5.9 |
| 500,000 | 108 | 11.2 | 138 | 10.6 | 179 | 10.9 | 179 | 10.1 |
| 250,000 | 189 | 19.6 | 268 | 20.6 | 384 | 23.4 | 384 | 21.6 |
| 125,000 | 381 | 39.6 | 551 | 42.4 | 679 | 41.3 | 731 | 41.1 |
| 100,000[1] | 205 | 21.3 | 229 | 17.6 | 228 | 13.9 | 309 | 17.4 |

[1]This class is not formed in the same manner as the others, because its upper boundary is not twice the lower boundary. Furthermore, it is under-represented in the 1970(A) projection because not enough towns could be found which were likely to reach 100,000 or more by 1970.
[2]In the 1970(B) projection, the number of cities in each class is taken to be the same as in the 1970(A) projection, except for the lowest two classes.

which the lower boundary is half the upper one is twofold.[3] First, when the logs of the boundaries are taken, the class intervals under this arrangement are equal. Second, this mode of classification brings out some intriguing regularities in the distribution of the number and populations of cities by size. It is these regularities that I wish to consider now. The best procedure is to deal first with the distribution of cities themselves by size-class and then discuss the distribution of the city population.

*Number of cities in each class.* It will be noticed in Tables 2 and 3 that the number of cities in each class is approximately twice the number in the next higher class. This regularity is especially observable in the classes between 100,000 and 6,400,000 in Table 2 and between 125,000 and 8,000,000 in Table 3. The apparent exceptions to the rule (as distinct from minor variations) are understandable. They include the lame-duck class at the bottom of the scale in Table 3, the open-ended classes at the top of the scale in both tables, and the lowest size-classes, known to be deficient, in the 1970(A) projection. These apparent exceptions do not invalidate the rule. Ignoring the inapplicable classes and using only the 1970(B) projection, we have, for the three dates combined in Table 3, 19 classes and 16 comparisons with which the degree of regularity of the rule can be tested. For these the mean ratio between classes (dividing the number of cities in each class by the number in the next higher class) is 2.13. The mean deviation around this mean is .32, or 15 per cent of the mean. In view of the fact that the data are subject to various kinds of error, refer to two kinds of units (Urbanized Areas and Cities Proper), and cover the entire world, the degree of interclass regularity is impressive.

Stated more precisely, the rule is that the number of cities is inversely proportional to their size. When the class boundaries are determined by a multiplier of 2, we have (looking *down* the class scale) the following

3. I am indebted to Mark H. Skolnick, formerly on the staff of International Population and Urban Research, for suggesting this arrangement of the city classes.

equation for the relation of the boundaries of any two classes:

$$a_i = a_{i+n}(2^n) \qquad (1)$$

where $a_i$ is the lower limit of class i, and $a_{i+n}$ is the lower limit of the $n^{th}$ class down the scale. With respect to the number of cities in any two classes (still looking *down* the scale), we have the following:

$$f_i = f_{i+n}\frac{1}{2^n} \qquad (2)$$

where $f_i$ is the number of cities in class i, and $f_{i+n}$ is the number in the $n^{th}$ class below.

Let us illustrate the approximate fit of equation (2) by reference to Table 2. Suppose we have given the number of cities between 1.6 and 3.2 million in size, and we wish to estimate the number between 100,000 and 200,000. The $n = 4$, and either the lower or the upper boundaries are, by definition, related according to equation (1). In 1950 the number of cities in the 1.6 to 3.2 million class was 29; hence by equation (2) the estimated number of cities in the bottom class would be $29(2^4)$, or 464. The actual number of cities recorded in the bottom class in 1950 was 484. The estimate is thus only 4 per cent short of the actual number.

If one looks *up* instead of *down* the city size scale, the expression in parentheses is of course exchanged between equations (1) and (2). It will become clear in a moment that the two equations taken together explain the constancy of population from one city class to another.

The $2^n$ rule holds approximately in the case of individual countries provided of course that the number of cities is large enough to represent a fair test. Among the 153 urbanized areas of the United States in 1960, the successive classes from 100,000–200,000 to 6,400,000–12,800,000 had an average inter-class ratio of 1.97. Furthermore, the fit of the United States cities in 1890 and 1900, on the one hand, with the world data in 1950 and 1960 respectively, on the other hand, is quite close, as determined by $\chi^2$ test. Comparison with the United States in 1960 and

1970 is more adequate, because by that time the nation had more cities. Using an index, we can see that the world distribution in Table 3 is very similar to that in the United States (below).

| Size-Class | Index of Number of Cities (Each Class as Per Cent of Next Lower Class) | | | | |
|---|---|---|---|---|---|
| | United States | | World | | |
| | 1960 | 1970 | 1950 | 1960 | 1970(B) |
| 4,000,000–8,000,000 | 50.0 | 50.0 | 60.0 | 48.1 | 58.8 |
| 2,000,000–4,000,000 | 44.4 | 23.5 | 28.3 | 38.0 | 39.5 |
| 1,000,000–2,000,000 | 40.9 | 81.0 | 49.1 | 51.4 | 41.3 |
| 500,000–1,000,000 | 73.3 | 60.0 | 57.1 | 51.5 | 58.1 |
| 250,000– 500,000 | 49.2 | 48.6 | 49.6 | 48.6 | 46.6 |
| 125,000– 250,000 | — | — | — | — | — |
| *Mean* | 51.6 | 52.6 | 48.8 | 47.6 | 48.9 |

There appears to be a slight tendency for the 500,000–1,000,000 class to be over-represented, and for one or two classes next above it to be under-represented. The 2,000,000–4,000,000 class, in particular, has fewer cities than it should have. We cannot follow the scale on down because the cities, as we are defining them, do not include urban places of less than 100,000 and hence do not provide us with the bottom part of the distribution of urban places by size.

Because of the close approximation to the $2^n$ principle, the distribution of cities by size has the shape of a steep pyramid. This is illustrated for the world's cities in 1960 in Figure 1. The steepness of the pyramid means that the bottom two classes have most of the cities.

*Where Does the Average City-Dweller Live?* So far, this discussion of the distribution of cities by size has shown that the number of cities in the higher brackets is relatively few but that the population living in them is huge. This fact makes it clear why the size of the *average city* (which was given in the section on the number of cities in each size-class) is different from the size of *city in which the average city-dweller lives* (a subject

now to be discussed). Whereas the mean size of city is obtained by dividing the number of cities into the total city population, the size of city in which the mean city-dweller lives is found by weighting each city by its population. Since the size of a city is also determined by its population, this weighting means multiplying each city's population by its population. Summing the products and dividing by the total city population, we have the size of city which, on the average, city-dwellers live in. In symbols, the calculation is as follows:

$$\bar{c}_c = \frac{\sum C_i^2}{\sum C_i}$$

where $\bar{c}_c$ is the city size of the average city-dweller, and $C_i$ is the population of the city of size i.[4] The index can be approximated by multiplying the mean population of each size-class by the population of that class and dividing by the total city population.

In similar fashion, whereas the *median city* is found by finding the *mid-city* in the distribution of cities by size, the size of *city in which the median city-dweller lives* is found by locating the *mid-individual* in the distribution of city-dwellers by size of place. At present, although the number of cities with a million or more inhabitants is less than 10 per cent of all cities in the world, the population they contain, as mentioned above, is 53 per cent of all city-dwellers. It follows that the size of city in which the median city-dweller lives is more than a million. The following are the city sizes of the mean and median city-dweller at three dates:

| | CITY SIZE | | |
|---|---|---|---|
| | 1950 | 1960 | 1970(B) |
| Mean City-Dweller | 1,933,000 | 2,182,000 | 2,533,000 |
| Median City-Dweller | 777,000 | 932,000 | 1,100,000 |

4. This type of index was developed by Eduardo E. Arriaga, a member of the staff at International Population and Urban Research. See his "Methodological Note on Urbanization Indices, with Applications," *Proceedings of the Conference of the International Union for the Scientific Study of Population,* Sydney, Australia, August 1967.

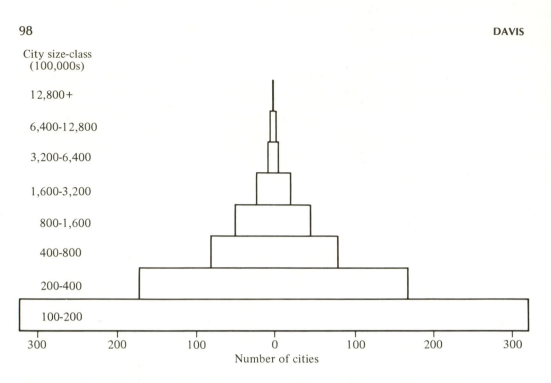

City size-class
(100,000s)

12,800+

6,400-12,800

3,200-6,400

1,600-3,200

800-1,600

400-800

200-400

100-200

| 300 | 200 | 100 | 0 | 100 | 200 | 300 |

Number of cities

Figure 1. Pyramid of Number of Cities in the World According to City Size: 1960 (Data from Table 2.)

It should be stressed that these averages, like the ones given in the section on the number of cities by size, pertain only to cities and to the city population. I have not yet spoken of averages with respect to *all* urban places or with respect to the whole urban population. To do that, one must know the distribution of towns (urban places below 100,000). As already indicated, the basic tables in the present study do not have data on individual towns.

## All Places and All People in the World, by Size of Place

The findings just described apply only to *urban* places and to the *urban* population. As noted above, we know the size of the *rural* population, even though we do not know the number of rural places. This fact enables us to estimate how much of the world still lives on farms, in villages, or in small towns. Because of the preponderance of the rural population, the estimate turns out to be high indeed. If any

urban place with fewer than 12,500 inhabitants is defined as a small town, our data lead to the conclusion that in 1970 almost 66 per cent of the earth's population lived in rural places or small towns. If the definition is made more rigorous—that is, if only places under 10,000 are defined as small towns— then the proportion is still almost 65 per cent. Here are the figures for the three dates under study:

| | Per Cent of World's Population in Rural Areas and Small Towns | | |
|---|---|---|---|
| | 1950 | 1960 | 1970(B) |
| In Places under 12,500 | 75.8 | 71.4 | 65.8 |
| In Places under 10,000 | 74.8 | 70.3 | 64.7 |

The conclusion is clear: the world is still overwhelmingly a rural and village affair.

This fact necessarily affects various kinds of averages that can be calculated, but it affects them to different degrees. For in-

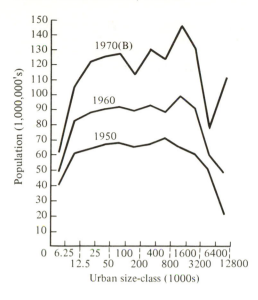

Figure 2. World's Urban Population by Size of Place: 1950, 1960, and 1970 (B)[1].

stance, the preponderance of small towns and rural villages necessarily means that the average size of place (combining all rural and urban places) is quite small. Unfortunately, no one can say how small because global information is lacking on the number and size of rural villages and the number of farmers living on isolated farmsteads. It would be hazardous to try to supply these missing data by estimation. One can *assume* an average size of rural place, but this makes the result a hypothetical finding rather than an estimate. For instance, an arbitrarily low guess would be to suppose that the average rural place (or neighborhood, when farmers are living on isolated farmsteads) has 300 inhabitants. An arbitrarily high guess would be to suppose that the average rural place has 1,000 inhabitants, taking the world as a whole.

|  | Mean Population per Place | | |
| --- | --- | --- | --- |
|  | 1950 | 1960 | 1970(B) |
| Assuming Rural Mean = 300 | 416 | 446 | 486 |
| Assuming Rural Mean = 1,000 | 1,375 | 1,469 | 1,599 |

Since it seems unlikely that in reality the average rural area has a population falling outside these limits, the mean place in the world is clearly quite small, although no one knows exactly how small. Doubtless, the *median* place is substantially smaller, because it has to be a rural place, and there are probably more small rural places than larger ones.

However, as we have seen already with respect to cities and with respect to all urban places, the size of places *in which the average person lives* is quite different from the average size of place. This is because, in the calculation of the mean size of place per person, the bigger cities are weighted by their population and thus exercise a powerful influence on the mean. It is like computing an average height in a community in which the bulk of the population is around five feet tall but some people are ten to a hundred miles tall. Computed on that basis, the size of place in which the average person in the world lives turns out to be a city, although not a very big one. Here are the results when the mean size of rural place is assumed to be 300 or 1,000:

|  | Size of Place in Which Mean Person Lives | | |
| --- | --- | --- | --- |
|  | 1950 | 1960 | 1970(B) |
| Assuming Rural Mean = 300 | 318,000 | 434,000 | 608,000 |
| Assuming Rural Mean = 1,000 | 318,000 | 434,000 | 608,000 |

The influence of cities and large towns on this mean is so great that the contrasting assumptions about the size of rural places make no difference in the result, at least none that is not ironed out in rounding.

However, the opposite is true about the *median* person. We know that he does not live in an urban place at all; he lives in a rural village. He is a farmer, but he probably does not live on a separate farmstead because most farmers in the world live in hamlets and villages. Although it cannot be calculated exactly, it is this median rather than the particular mean calculated above that helps to demonstrate, as the other figures have done, that the human species is still overwhelmingly a small settlement animal, living on the average in communities with far fewer members than most ant and termite nests have.

At the same time our data abundantly demonstrate that the human species is capable of living in giant communities as well. Millions are moving swiftly in the direction of ever more gigantic agglomerations.

# American Metropolitan Evolution

JOHN R. BORCHERT

The landscapes of any American city reflect countless decisions and actions from the time of settlement to the present. The results are apparent not only in differences in land use but in the kaleidoscopic variety of building facades, street patterns, and lot sizes. Early actions precluded or frustrated many later locational decisions. The metropolitan physical plant has accumulated through various historical epochs, and clearly those epochs were distinguished from one another by different ideas and technologies. Increasingly, in proportion to its size and age, the metropolis is becoming a complicated puzzle of heterogeneous and anachronistic features.

The evolutionary nature of the metropolitan anatomy is, of course, widely recognized, and this fact is reflected in a wealth of studies of the historical-geographical development of individual cities and of the anachronistic legacies that make up much of the urban physical plant. Yet research on systems of cities, cities as central places, cities and transportation networks, internal spatial structure of cities, and rank-size distributions has lacked a general historical context.[1] A structured urban history of the country or of its major regions, which would help to bring order to the mixture of historical-locational forces that generate the urban landscape,[2] has not yet appeared. Meanwhile, future populations are projected, and increasingly massive clearance and redevelopment proceed in the old central areas of metropolises without a fully developed theory of metropolitan growth and form.[3] Stages of urban economic growth and social evolution have been postulated. Wilbur Thompson has observed that these are "highly impressionistic generalizations" and "leave much too strong a feeling of the inevitability of growth and development." And he has asked, "What are some of the dampening and restraining forces that surely must exist? We see all about us evidence of local economic stagnation and decay and even demise."[4]

Central questions relate to the factors that have influenced the location of relative growth and decline, the relationship of anachronistic regions within cities to the evolution of the national pattern of urban growth, the threads that run consistently through the evolutionary process, and the nature of future change as suggested by experience to date.

1. See the excellent summary by Brian J. L. Berry, "Research Frontiers in Urban Geography," in "The Study of Urbanization" (edited by Philip M. Hauser and Leo F. Schnore; New York, London, Sydney, 1965), pp. 403–430. For further comment see Fred Lukermann: Empirical Expressions of Nodality and Hierarchy in a Circulation Manifold, *East Lakes Geographer*, Vol. 2, 1966, pp. 17–44. A notable exception is the work of Allan Pred: Industrialization, Initial Advantage, and American Metropolitan Growth, *Geogr. Rev.*, Vol. 55, 1963, pp. 158–185.

2. This is the thesis of a detailed review of the literature of United States urban history by Charles N. Glaab; "The Historian and the American City: A Bibliographic Survey," in "The Study of Urbanization," pp. 53–80.
3. William Alonso: The Historic and the Structural Theories of Urban Form: Their Implications for Urban Renewal, *Land Economics*, Vol. 40, 1964, pp. 227–231.
4. Wilbur R. Thompson: "Urban Economic Growth and Development in a National System of Cities," in "The Study of Urbanization," pp. 431–490; reference on pp. 438–439. See also his "A Preface to Urban Economics" (Baltimore, 1965), pp. 12–17.

From *Geographical Review*, vol. 57, no. 3, July 1967, pp. 301–32. Reprinted by permission.

These questions can be illuminated by examining the evolution of the present pattern of standard metropolitan statistical areas through a series of historical epochs, from the first census, in 1790, to the most recent, in 1960.

## MAJOR INNOVATIONS AND EPOCHS

Most American metropolitan areas, throughout much of their history, have functioned chiefly as collectors, processors, and distributors of raw materials and goods. Consequently, it might be expected that changes in their growth rates would have been particularly sensitive to changes in (1) the size and resource base of the hinterland and (2) the technology of transport and industrial energy for the processing of primary resources. These two sets of variables are interrelated. The technology partly defines the resource base, and the transportation technology, in particular, strongly affects the size, and therefore the resources, of a city's hinterland. There is, of course, no implication that the technological changes have been independent variables or basic causes of growth. The presumptions are, rather, that within the given framework of values and institutions they were stimulated by the economic growth and geographical expansion of the nation and that they in turn not only further stimulated growth but also helped to differentiate it geographically.[5]

Among many possibilities, this essay emphasizes three relatively brief periods since the 1790 census in which major innovations appeared in the technology of transport and industrial energy.

## THE INNOVATIONS

### Steamboat and "Iron Horse"

The first of the innovations was the use of the steam engine in water and land transportation.

The census year selected is 1830. To be sure, the early steamboats in America preceded that date, but the real buildup of steamboat tonnage on the Ohio-Mississippi-Missouri system began in the 1830's (Fig. 1),[6] and the main period of increase in the tonnage of general-cargo vessels on the Great Lakes also began in the 1830's and 1840's. Rail mileage, likewise, grew rapidly after initial development in 1829. By the end of the decade "the major mechanical features of the American locomotive were established," boxcars had been introduced, regular mail routes were in operation on the railroads, and the first transatlantic steamer had arrived in New York.[7]

The introduction of steam power created major transportation corridors on the western rivers and the Great Lakes and resulted in enlargement of the hinterlands of ports on both the inland waterways and the Atlantic. It made possible the development of a national transportation system through the integration of these major waterways and regional rail webs. These changes favored the growth of ports with relatively large harbors and proximity to important resource concentrations. Simultaneously, however, they hurt the economy of nearby smaller ports.

Steam power was also applied in manufacturing, but its impact was apparently more localized because of the impracticality of long hauls of coal or other bulk commodities with the comparatively light equipment and iron rails of the time. As a result, local waterpower sites continued to influence industrial location. By 1870 waterwheels were still providing roughly half of the inanimate energy for manufacturing, especially in the major manufacturing region. About half of the entire inanimate power for industry was in the five states of Massachusetts, Connecticut, New York, Pennsylvania, and Ohio. Oliver observes that steam "was not universally used in cotton mills until the railroads were sufficiently developed to transport coal

---

5. For an excellent summary of the operation of contingent, interrelated variables in the growth process see Robert W. Fogel:

"Railroads and American Economic Growth" (Baltimore, 1964), pp. 234–237 (section on Implications for the Theory of Economic Growth).
6. John W. Oliver: "History of American Technology" (New York, 1956), pp. 192–193 and 202.
7. *Ibid.*, pp. 184–185, 189, and 202.

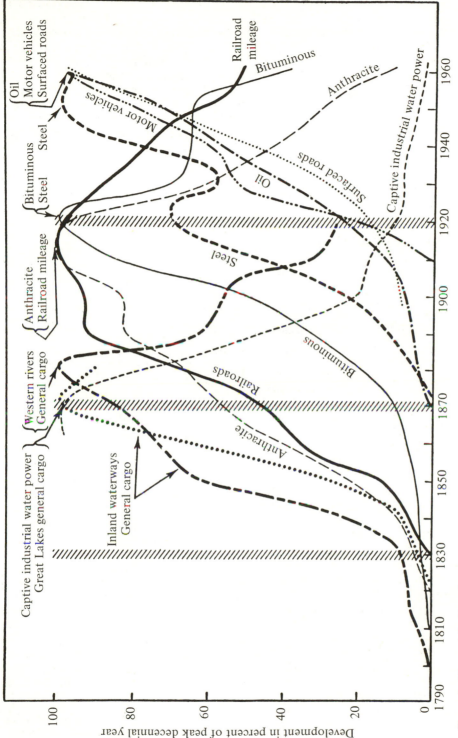

Figure 1. Rise and decline of ten indicators of the technology of transport and industrial energy. Peak values of past years concentrate around 1870 and 1920. Sources: "Historical Statistics of the United States," pp. 416–417, 427–429, 446, and 458; *Statistical Abstract of the United States 1965*, pp. 561, 569, 718, 729, and 811 (see text footnote 24 for both); and "A Compendium of the Ninth Census," (U.S. Bureau of the Census, 1872), p. 706.

cheaply.''[8] That ability came generally in the 1870's.

## Steel Rails and Electric Power

The second major innovation was the appearance of abundant, and hence low-priced, steel. The census year chosen for this is 1870. The preceding decade had seen the first commercial output of Bessemer steel in America, and by the mid-1870's American steel products were breaking into the world market (Fig. 1).

A number of related events, each with geographical ramifications of great importance, occurred in dramatic sequence in the decade of the 1870's. Steel rails replaced iron on both newly built and existing lines. Heavier equipment and more powerful locomotives permitted increased speed and the long haul of bulk goods. Rail gauge and freight-car parts were standardized[9] (there had been eleven gauges among the northern systems in 1860), so that interline exchange and coast-to-coast shipment were possible. Refrigerated cars made their entry, ushering in a new era of regional specialization in agriculture and centralization of the packing industry at major rail nodes. Other ramifications favored industrial, hence urban, centralization. The practical length of coal haul was extended and the cost reduced. The effort was to open vast central Appalachian bituminous deposits and to facilitate the movement of coal to the great ports whose growth had been launched four decades earlier. The greater availability of coal was soon supplemented by the availability of central-

station electric power, which followed in the 1880's.

For the first time massive forces were arrayed favoring market orientation of industry and the metropolitanization of America. At the same time there were negative impacts. The long rail haul spelled the doom of most passenger traffic and cargo movement on the inland waterways, especially the rivers. Small river ports were destined to become virtual museums. It is noteworthy that general-cargo shipping capacity on the western rivers peaked not on the eve of the Civil War but in the 1870's; thereafter it fell precipitously for half a century (Fig. 1). The easier availability of coal and central-station electricity doomed the small waterpower sites. Most small industrial cities retained their function; many were rail nodes large and important enough to continue to grow with the national economy. But for subsequent decisions the decentralizing factor of many small waterpower sites had yielded to the centralizing force of the metropolitan rail centers, their giant markets, and their superior accessibility.[10]

## Internal-Combustion Engine and Shift to Services

The third major innovation, and probably the least debatable, was the introduction of the internal-combustion engine in transportation and related technology. The census date chosen is 1920. To be sure, the automobile had entered the American scene in the 1890's, but motor-vehicle registration was insignificant before 1910, and road surfacing and petroleum production began their steep climb in the 1920's (Fig. 1). The need for a national system of highways was recognized in 1916 with the first federal aid for road construction.

The impact of the internal-combustion engine on the geography of American cities needs little review. But some of the most

8. Oliver, op. cit., p. 160.
9. The urgency of rebuilding existing lines with steel rails at standard gauge in the 1870's is related in Robert J. Casey and W.A.S. Douglas: "The Lackawanna Story" (New York, 1951), pp. 92–94. The impact of the introduction of the long haul on the geography of an existing system is described in Louis Jackson: "A Brief History of the Chicago, Milwaukee, and St. Paul Railway" (1900), pp. 6–8. See also Harlan W. Gilmore: "Transportation and the Growth of Cities" (Glencoe, Ill., 1953), p. 51. For a full account of the beginning of the steel era in the United States and for further references see Oliver, op. cit., pp. 319–425, especially pp. 416–425.

10. Allan Pred has developed at length the fact that the period from the Civil War to World War I saw the major growth of large cities as industrial centers (op. cit., pp. 161–162).

profound changes affecting the city occurred in agriculture.[11] True, the new technology put the farmer in an automobile and thus encouraged the centralization of urban growth at the larger, diversified centers in all the commercial farming regions. But also, by putting the farmer on a tractor, it multiplied the land area he could work alone, initiated a revolution in family farm size, and sped the urbanization of much of rural America. In addition, air passenger transport helped to encourage centralization of the national business management function in a few cities,[12] and the auto stimulated the decentralization of most metropolitan functions. The internal-combustion engine had a profound and happy impact on the growth prospects of cities in the oil fields, but the opposite effect on cities in the coal fields and at railroad division points.

Another change, of overriding importance, coincided with the beginning of the auto-air age. Throughout the nation's history the primary (agriculture, forests, fisheries, mining) and secondary (manufacturing) sectors of the economy had dominated the employment picture. Their share of total employment had been gradually diminishing, but in 1920 they still accounted for 56 percent. Since 1920, however, the share has been less than half and has been falling rapidly (Fig. 2). The trend is, of course, a reflection of the combined technological advances that have been leading the nation gradually toward an era of automation.

When employment was mainly in resource and processing industries, it was fair to look on cities mainly as assemblers and processors of the nation's resources. It was appropriate to assume that changes in the technology of transport and industrial energy would be crucial for the growth or decline of cities. In the auto-air age, when primary and secondary employment occupies only a decreasing minority of the labor force, such technological changes are of declining importance in the

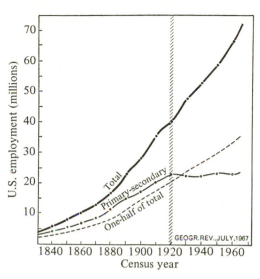

Figure 2. The changing relationship of employment in primary and secondary industries to total employment in the United States. Sources: "Historical Statistics of the United States," p. 74; *Statistical Abstract of the United States 1965*, p. 220 (see text footnote 24 for both).

life and death of cities. Two new factors have come to the fore. One is the increase in service employment. With a fast-growing majority of new jobs since 1920 in the least mechanized and least automated part of our economy—the personal and professional services—the most likely locations for new employment growth have been the places where there were already large concentrations of people to be served. Hence in the auto-air age, even more than in the preceding epoch, growth breeds growth. The second factor is the large and growing amount of leisure time available. As Ullman pointed out some years ago, this has led to the great importance of amenities as an urban location factor, both for commuting workers and for retired people.[13] It has also led to an increase in the time available for, and, presumably, the need of, formal education. Hence educational centers as well as high-amenity locations have been blessed by the

11. See Chauncy D. Harris: Agricultural Production in the United States: The Past Fifty Years and the Next, *Geogr. Rev.*, Vol. 47, 1957, pp. 175–193.

12. See William Goodwin: The Management Center in the United States, *Geogr. Rev.*, Vol. 55, 1965, pp. 1–16.

13. Edward L. Ullman: Amenities as a Factor in Regional Growth, *Geogr. Rev.*, Vol. 44, 1954, pp. 119–132.

fruits of changing technology in this present age.

## THE EPOCHS

In short, four epochs in American history can be identified that have been characterized by changes in technology crucial in the location of urban growth and development: (1) Sail-Wagon, 1790–1830; (2) Iron Horse, 1830–1870; (3) Steel Rail, 1870–1920; (4) Auto-Air-Amenity, 1920–.[14]

Although emphasis here is on factors affecting the differential growth of American cities as entities, these periods are differentiated also by internal features of urban geography and morphology.[15] The railroad had many impacts on the structure and location of industrial and central business districts, and these districts changed with the entry of steel and the long haul. The coming of steel and electric power made possible the skyscraper and rapid transit. The auto and coincident developments in electronics need no elaboration. Each innovation brought major changes in land-use patterns, densities, lot sizes, nodality of the central business district, and other intraurban variables.

Reservations and qualifications apply, of course, to this fourfold historical division. The periods are not homogeneous. Even if they should stand up as useful divisions for the description and study of American metropolitan evolution, they contain many subdivisions, which vary from one region to another.

Furthermore, the boundaries between the epochs, although characterized by the near simultaneity of important innovations, are nevertheless complex transition periods. Some of the features of transition constitute little epochs of their own; examples might be the canal epoch (*ca.* 1810's to 1840's) and the electric interurban railway epoch (*ca.* 1900's to 1930's). Oliver[16] observes, "The canal was at best a temporary and an inadequate answer to the need for inland transportation." In a sense, it represented an attempt to adapt the technology of water transportation to the quickly growing need for tapping inland resources as the frontier advanced. Likewise, the rash of interurban electric rail lines that appeared about the turn of the present century may be viewed as a "temporary and inadequate" attempt to adapt rail-transport technology to the growing need for a flexible, rapid linkage between farm, small town, and city as the populations of large regions became commercialized and urban-oriented.[17]

Finally, throughout virtually all the first three epochs the settled area of the United States was expanding westward. The rate, timing, and direction of advance of the settlement frontier were in many ways quite independent of the major technological innovations that opened each of these epochs. On the other hand, the westward expansion helped to press the need for these innovations. More important from the viewpoint of this essay, cities were needed and built as new lands were opened. Hence the land pioneered during each of these epochs constitutes a region within which all city sites were chosen,

14. This differentiation is somewhat related to Eric Lampard's formulation of three critical periods in the regional economic development of the United States up to 1910: (1) a period of initial resource exploitation in the historic eastern base region, from colonial time through the Civil War; (2) a period of "extension of accessibility" from the eastern base region to the rest of the country associated with an enlargement of the resource hinterland of the eastern base, from the Civil War to World War I; and (3) the era of "nationalization" of the economy, utilizing and improving on a virtually fully developed transportation system since World War I. See Eric E. Lampard: Regional Economic Development, 1870–1950, *in* "Regions, Resources, and Economic Growth" (by Harvey S. Perloff, Edgar S. Dunn, Jr., Eric E. Lampard, and Richard F. Muth; Baltimore, 1960), pp. 107–292 (Part 3). See also Constance McLaughlin Green: "American Cities in the Growth of the Nation" (New York 1957), Chap. 10, and the works cited by Sjoberg in connection with his discussion of the Technological School (Gideon Sjoberg: "Theory and Research in Urban Sociology," *in* "The Study of Urbanization," pp. 157–189; reference on pp. 170–171).

15. For an extensive discussion of urban evolution in relation to transportation technology and development in specific metropolitan areas see James E. Vance, Jr.: Labor-shed, Employment Field, and Dynamic Analysis in Urban Geography, *Econ. Geogr.*, Vol. 36, 1960, pp. 189–220, and his "Geography and Urban Evolution in the San Francisco Bay Area" (Berkeley, 1964).

16. *Op. cit.,* p. 180.

17. See Mildred M. Walmsley: The Bygone Electric Interurban Railway System, *Professional Geographer,* Vol. 17, No. 3, 1965, pp. 1–6; and the detailed maps and descriptive data in G. W. Hilton and J. F. Due: "The Electric Interurban Railways in America" (Stanford, Calif., 1960).

and subsequent investments made, under a particular sequence of technological considerations.

## METROPOLITAN SIZE CLASSES

In order to compare sizes and growth rates during the four historical epochs postulated here, American cities were divided into five population size categories. First, the 212 standard metropolitan statistical areas of the 1960 census were reduced to 178 by combining some and dropping those under 80,000 population. The 178 were then ordered by size. A smoothed curve joining them in rank-size distribution is shown in Figure 3. A change in slope is noticeable at four points—at populations of about 250,000, 820,000, 3,000,000, and 8,000,000. Above each of these critical points lies a group of cities whose growth at some period in their history has been accelerated as compared with the places below the critical point. These division points break the 1960 SMSA's into five groups, which may be labeled as follows: first order, more than 8,000,000 (New York); second order, 2,300,000 to 8,000,000; third order, 820,000 to 2,300,000; fourth order, 250,000 to 820,000; and fifth order, less than 250,000. Although the divisions are somewhat arbitrary, they seem to identify significantly different groups of cities. The New York metropolis is, of course, in a class by itself no matter how the SMSA's are divided. The second and third groups appear as clusters on the graph that portrays Jerome Pickard's population and functional size orders (Fig. 4).[18] The fifth group seems to match the primary wholesale-retail category identified, by the analysis of business functions, at the top level below Minneapolis-St. Paul in a regional hierarchy of trade centers in the northern Midwest and Great Plains.[19]

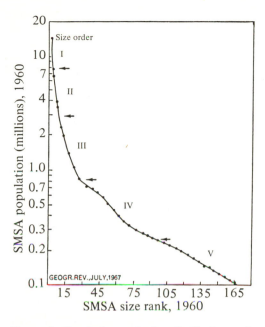

Figure 3. Population rank-size distribution and size-order limits for SMSA's in 1960. Except for the three largest metropolitan areas, dots represent only every fifth place in the sequence. The basis for this graph and for subsequent maps is a list of all 1960 SMSA's, with populations for the same counties or groups of counties for 1790, 1830, 1870, 1920, and 1960. The 212 census SMSA's on the list have been reduced to 178 by dropping areas with fewer than 80,000 inhabitants in 1960 and combining certain others, mainly in New England and several large multicentered urban complexes. Where SMSA's on the list differ in definition from those in the census, the differences are specified. Copies of the list are available from the author.

For the earlier census years two definitions had to be formulated before the procedure could be applied. First, it was necessary to define "SMSA" for those years. In the 1960 census an SMSA by definition had to contain, in effect, a central city of at least 50,000 population. For the present study the minimum size of the central city was reduced to be commensurate with the smaller total

18. Jerome P. Pickard: Metropolitanization of the United States, *Urban Land Inst. Research Menograph 2,* Washington, D. C., 1959, Figure 21 (p. 67).
19. John R. Borchert and Russell B. Adams: Trade Centers and Trade Areas of the Upper Midwest, *Upper Midwest Economic*

*Study Urban Rept. No. 3,* Minneapolis, 1963, pp. 36–39 and Figures 1 (p. 4), 8 (p. 25), and 9 (p. 27).

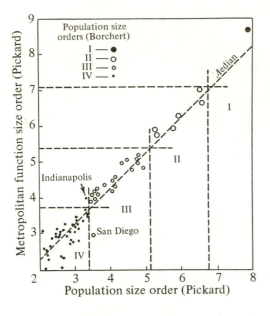

Figure 4. The 26 SMSA's defined as I, II, or III order in Figure 3 shown in their positions on Pickard's combined population and metropolitan-function scales. With only two exceptions, places that fall within the top three population size orders in Figure 3 also form discrete groups on the basis of metropolitan functions. "Metropolitan functions" in this case include measures of bank deposits, wholesale trade, Sunday newspaper circulation, federal-government employment, and manufacturing employment. The exceptions are San Diego, a third-order city based on population but weak in its metropolitan functions, and Indianapolis, a fourth-order city in Figure 3 (1960 SMSA definition of Indianapolis SMSA) but with exceptional metropolitan strength. Graph modified from Pickard, Metropolitanization of the United States (see text footnote 18 for reference), Figure 21.

population of the United States in the earlier census years. Hence the minimum-sized central city for an "emerging SMSA" in 1920 was 29,500; in 1870, 11,100; in 1830, 3600; and in 1790, 1100. The population of the county was used at each point in the time series. Where a county was split during the series, appropriate adjustments were made. But each SMSA or emerging SMSA that appears at any point in the time series is always defined by the same county or counties. To be sure, this is only one way of achieving a measure of consistency in dealing with a problem for which there is no entirely satisfactory solution at present.[20] Few of these counties in the early epochs were "metropolitan" in any modern sense. But they included the forty to fifty largest places in 1790 and 1830; and the definition identified, then as now, the nation's principal population clusters.

Second, it was necessary to define for the earlier census years the limits of the five size orders defined above for 1960. Again, each of the size-order limits was reduced to be commensurate with the smaller national population in the earlier years. These values, however, were then adjusted upward to account for the smaller proportion of a given "metropolitan" county covered by the smaller central city of earlier times.[21] The result was the set of limits shown in Table 1.

Thus five size orders and four historical epochs were established. By comparing the numbers of newcomers, dropouts, and shifts in size order through the series of epochs it is possible to observe the evolution of the modern array of metropolitan areas. It is also possible to observe the impact of several

20. See Karl Gustav Grytzell: The Demarcation of Compatable City Areas by Means of Population Density, *Lund Studies in Geography*, Ser. B, Human Geography, No. 25, 1963, especially pp. 5–9.

21. For the years before 1960 each size-order threshold, $T_y$, was first defined by the relationship $T_y = T_0(P_y-P_0)$, where $T_0$ is the threshold population in 1960, $P_0$ is the United States population in in 1960, and $P_y$ is the United States population in the earlier year. For thresholds under 100,000 "SMSA" population a further adjustment was made, using the relationship $T_r = T_y(F_y-F_0)$, where $T_y$ is the threshold defined for the earlier year by the initial adjustment, $T_r$ is the readjusted value, $F_0$ is the percentage of United States population that was rural in 1960, and $F_y$ is the percentage of United States population that was rural in the earlier year. Where the county population exceeded 100,000, it was assumed that rural (especially farm) population within the "SMSA" was negligible, and no second adjustment was made.

The net effect of this definition and procedure is to overstate the populations of urban areas in the earlier periods, especially before 1920 and especially in areas with populations under 100,000. Because of the second adjustment of threshold values, the size orders are roughly comparable throughout the series. Lukermann, *op. cit.*, approximated urban-area populations for the eastern and central United States 1790–1890. Comparison of his rank sizes and geographical patterns with those in this paper shows no significant discrepancies resulting from the different definitions.

Table 1. Limits of Size Orders for SMSA's in 1960 and Corresponding Areas in Earlier Years.*

| Size order | Population Threshold (*thousands*) | | | | |
| --- | --- | --- | --- | --- | --- |
| | 1790 | 1830 | 1870 | 1920 | 1960 |
| First | 180 | 530 | 1,300 | 4,750 | 8,000 |
| Second | 90 | 160 | 400 | 1,480 | 2,300 |
| Third | 40 | 90 | 130 | 470 | 820 |
| Fourth | 15 | 35 | 75 | 150 | 250 |
| Fifth | 5 | 15 | 30 | 60 | 80 |
| Central-city minimum | 1.1 | 3.6 | 11.1 | 29.5 | 50.0 |

*The fifth order is truncated by the lower size limits for an SMSA; a number of urban areas not large enough to be defined as SMSA's are fifth-order centers.

major changes in technology and the expansion of resource base and metropolitan hinterlands that accompanied the westward movement. Figure 5 shows all the places included in these five size orders during at least one of the four historical epochs.

## EVOLUTION OF THE PATTERN[22]

### Sail-Wagon Epoch, 1790–1830

At the time of the 1790 census almost all the major urban population clusters were ports on Atlantic bays or estuaries, or on the navigable reaches of the Connecticut, Hudson, Delaware, and Savannah Rivers, or on the Chesapeake Bay system (Fig. 6). Among the

22. This section is an attempt not to write history but to interpret briefly Figures 6 through 11 in the light of readily accessible secondary materials and historical census data. The regional framework and regional economic changes discussed are elaborated in Perloff and others (see footnote 14 above); in Ralph H. Brown: "Historical Geography of the United States" (New York, 1948); and in several standard regional geographies, notably J. Russell Smith: "North America" (New York, 1925); George J. Miller and Almon E. Parkins: "Geography of North America" (New York and London, 1928); and Harold Hull McCarty: "The Geographic Basis of American Economic Life" (New York and London, 1940). On the other hand, the detailed history and geography of specific cities within these regions, over time, are dispersed through myriad local studies. Important references appear in Harold M. Mayer: Urban Geography, *in* "American Geography: Inventory & Prospect" (edited by Preston E. James and Clarence F. Jones; Syracuse, N.Y., 1954), pp. 142–166; and in Glaab, *op. cit.*, pp. 73–80.

centers of third or high order, only Worcester, Massachusetts, was not a port, and only Worcester and Pittsburgh were not on the Atlantic waterway. Lower-order centers also were mainly Atlantic ports, though they included inland centers of agricultural trade and local industry. There was no primate city or national metropolis; the Boston, New York, and Philadelphia areas were of about equal size. Lukermann has observed that the entire family of Atlantic ports was characterized by small hinterlands and a primary orientation toward the sea and Europe and could in fact be considered part of the West European urban system.[23]

Change was modest during the epoch (Fig. 7). Virtually all places that rose in size order—that is, grew faster than the national growth rate—were in areas of westward expansion and accompanying development of new resources: the drift-filled valleys and drift-capped plateaus of western New York, the Ontario plain, the Great Valley, the Bluegrass, and the Nashville Basin. Other important resources lay within these new agricultural regions or adjacent to them—notably waterpower, the timber of the northern Appalachians and the Adirondacks, and the anthracite of northeastern Pennsylvania. The "boom" cities, those which rose two or more ranks, were mainly along the inland waterways that penetrated the new western

23. Lukermann, *op. cit.*

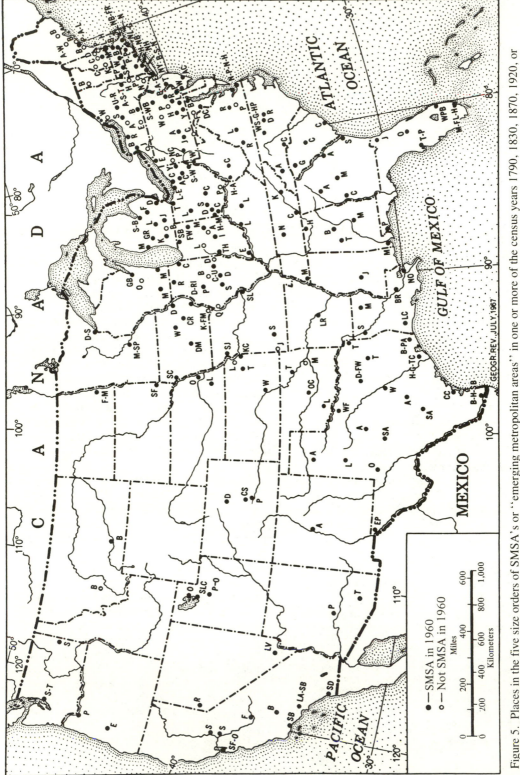

Figure 5. Places in the five size orders of SMSA's or "emerging metropolitan areas" in one or more of the census years 1790, 1830, 1870, 1920, or 1960. Names of the central cities are indicated by initials. Open circles represent the areas that were not SMSA's in 1960.

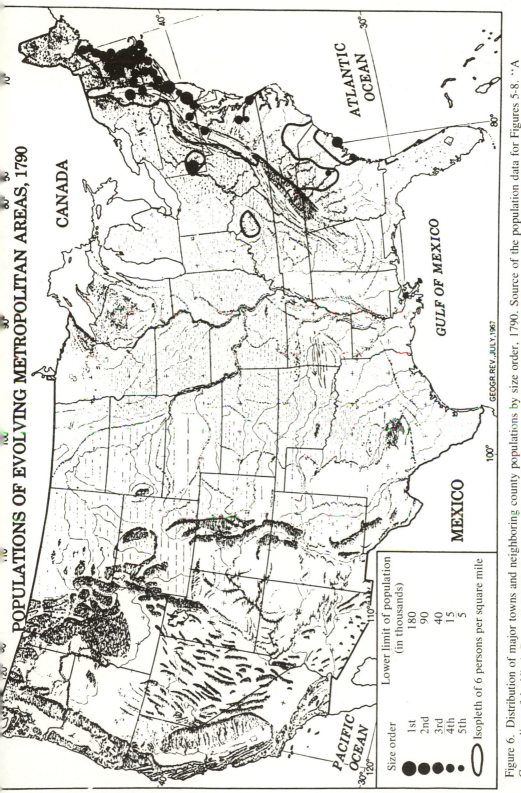

**POPULATIONS OF EVOLVING METROPOLITAN AREAS, 1790**

Size order | Lower limit of population (in thousands)
1st — 180
2nd — 90
3rd — 40
4th — 15
5th — 5

Isopleth of 6 persons per square mile

GEOGR. REV., JULY, 1967

Figure 6. Distribution of major towns and neighboring county populations by size order, 1790. Source of the population data for Figures 5-8. "A Compendium of the Ninth Census" (1872). Population-density isopleths generalized from Clifford L. Lord and Elizabeth H. Lord; *Historical Atlas of the United States* (New York 1953), p. 46. Base map in Figures 6-9 is A. K. Lobeck's *Physiographic Diagram of the United States* (courtesy C. S. Hammond & Co.).

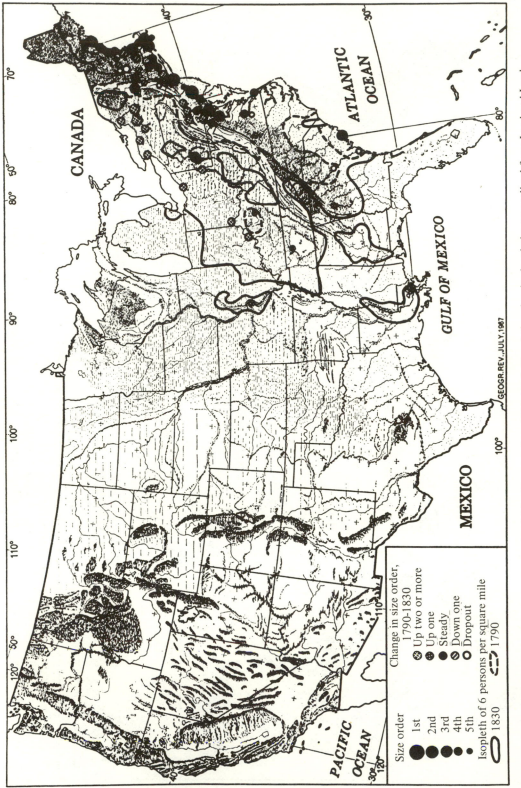

Figure 7. Changes in size order, major towns, and neighboring counties, 1790-1830. Population-density isopleths generalized from Lord and Lord, *op. cit.* (see Figure 6), pp. 46 and 49.

lands—the Erie Canal, the lower Great Lakes, and the Ohio River system. Exceptions were the Great Valley cities near the anthracite fields.

As agricultural settlement expanded in western New York there was a relative decline in growth rate, and a drop in size order, at a number of small ports and inland centers serving agricultural areas in eastern New York and New England. Meanwhile, although the struggle for deeper hinterlands had begun, the absence of any major change in the technology of land transport permitted most Atlantic ports to retain essentially the same functions through most of the epoch and to register neither relative increase nor relative decrease in size order up to 1830.

## Iron Horse Epoch, 1830–1870

At the beginning of this epoch all emerging metropolitan areas of third or higher order except Pittsburgh were east of the Appalachians or in western New York. The area of continuous settlement was spreading westward toward the Mississippi. But commercialization of the newly exploited land resources still awaited an effective network of transportation lines and cities.

The coming of the railroad brought drastic changes. A series of regional rail networks developed. The larger networks converged at critical port locations on the inland waterways that penetrated the vast agricultural land resource of the Interior Plains. Small networks or individual lines focused on the smaller ports. The emergence of these "great ports" of the Midwest accounted for most of the boom cities of the epoch (Fig. 8) and laid the metropolitan base for an important part of the market-oriented industrial growth of the Steel-Rail Epoch. Limitations of technology made the rail networks generally tributary to the water-transport system; they were built outward from major ports or to those ports from principal neighboring concentrations of farmland, mineral, or timber resources. In their initial effect they were therefore complementary to the waterways as long-haul general-freight carriers.

In the older settled areas of the North other important changes in the urban pattern emerged. Boom centers appeared in the anthracite fields, and Pittsburgh advanced to second order, where it would remain until the end of the Steel Rail Epoch. These changes reflected the accelerated demand for coal that came with the development of the railroad, the wider industrial application of steam, and accompanying changes in the iron industry. On the Atlantic seaboard New York became a first-order center; it had been about the same size as Philadelphia at the beginning of the epoch, it was twice as large at the close.

Thus the urban pattern of the United States was revolutionized by the development of a national system of transportation, albeit a crude one. The epoch saw not only the emergence of a first-order center but also the greatest increase, both relative and absolute, in the number of second- and third-order centers in the nation's history (Table 2).

The map for this epoch (Fig. 8) also reflects the aftermath of the Civil War and, probably more important, the slow rate of investment in urban, industrial, and transportation facilities in the South in the preceding decades. New Orleans was an exception. It was a critical point in the national transportation system that comprised the northern regional rail networks and the inland waterways. Before the Civil War it had risen to third order and largest city in the South. Meanwhile Charleston, despite pioneer railroad building into its comparatively static agricultural hinterland, dropped to fourth order and began a prolonged relative decline.

## Steel-Rail Epoch, 1870–1920

By 1870 major urban areas had arisen as far west as the Missouri River frontier, and one (Little Rock, Arkansas) had appeared west of the Mississippi in the South. Many resource concentrations remained unexploited pending further improvement of the land transportation system and creation of a network of urban centers in the West and South. By the beginning of the following epoch all these regions had been knit together by a standardized,

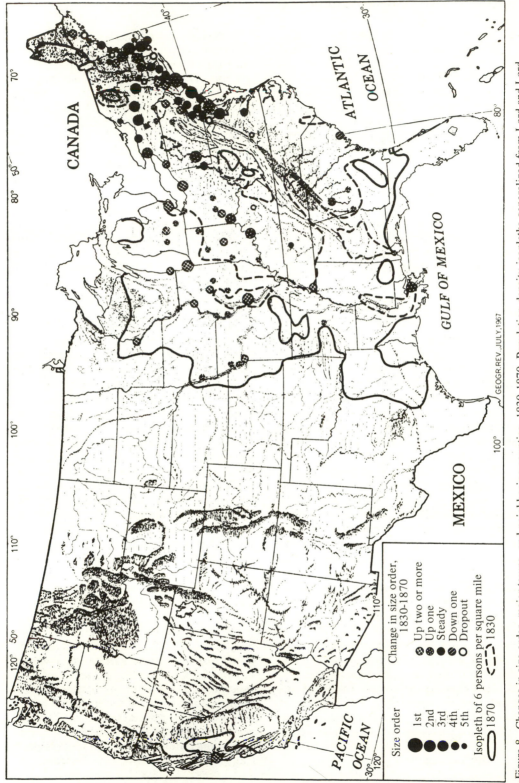

Figure 8. Changes in size order, major towns, and neighboring counties, 1830-1870. Population-density isopleths generalized from Lord and Lord, *op. cit.*, pp. 49 and 104.

GEOGR.REV.,JULY,1967

Table 2. Number of Centers and Total Population in Each Size Order.

| Size Order | 1790 | 1830 | 1870 | 1920 | 1960 |
|---|---|---|---|---|---|
| | | | Number of Centers | | |
| First | 0 | 0 | 1 | 1 | 1 |
| Second | 3 | 3 | 6 | 4 | 6 |
| Third | 8 | 8 | 14 | 16 | 19 |
| Fourth | 20 | 29 | 33 | 51 | 70 |
| Fifth | 8 | 12 | 37 | 75 | 82 |
| Total | 39 | 52 | 91 | 147 | 178 |
| | | | Total Population (*thousands*) | | |
| First | — | — | 2,171 | 8,490 | 14,760 |
| Second | 514 | 1,120 | 3,301 | 10,364 | 28,826 |
| Third | 499 | 784 | 3,627 | 13,918 | 26,493 |
| Fourth | 530 | 1,812 | 2,533 | 12,829 | 30,473 |
| Fifth | 95 | 300 | 1,826 | 6,972 | 12,647 |
| "SMSA" total | 1,638 | 4,016 | 13,458 | 52,573 | 113,199 |
| U.S. total | 3,929 | 12,866 | 39,818 | 105,711 | 179,323 |

nationwide system of rail lines, and the modern pattern of major urban centers was beginning to emerge (Fig. 9).

New urban centers reflected the opening or commercialization of the remaining important agricultural land resources of the West— the Texas and Oklahoma prairies, the Colorado piedmont, the Wasatch piedmont, the Central Valley and Southern California, the Puget Sound-Willamette lowland, and the Palouse. They also reflected the exploitation of thitherto isolated major mineral deposits, such as Butte copper, southwest Missouri lead and zinc, and Lake Superior iron ore, and of mineral and timber resources in the mountains adjoining the agricultural oases and valleys. Finally, they reflected the advance of the agriculture-timber-mineral frontier into Florida.

In the older settled areas the boom cities were associated mainly with the upward leap in the importance of coal—especially high-grade bituminous—that accompanied the growth of the modern iron and steel industry. A cluster of boom cities emerged on the western Pennsylvania coalfields and in the area between Pittsburgh and Lake Erie; and metropolitan Birmingham appeared on the map in the South. Other, but less spectacular, advances in rank occurred along the Norfolk-Toledo axis as long-haul technology opened the rich bituminous deposits of West Virginia and eastern Kentucky. Still others resulted from industrial growth based on the forest resources along the northern frontier of the agricultural Midwest and on the resources readily available for the hydroelectricity-based industrial development on the Piedmont in the South. Meantime, nearly all the great metropolitan commercial centers of the Midwest and Northeast, while establishing themselves as major industrial cities, retained their positions or advanced one level in the hierarchy.

Two groups of metropolitan areas accounted for most of the declines in size order in this epoch. The largest group comprised the towns along the Ohio-Mississippi-Missouri and principal tributaries. Smaller centers such as Dubuque and Quincy (Illinois) dropped out of the "metropolitan" ranks; St. Louis, Louisville, and Wheeling fell in the hierarchy, never to recover the relative positions they had held during the epoch of the steam packet and the iron horse. A second group consisted of a number of important industrial

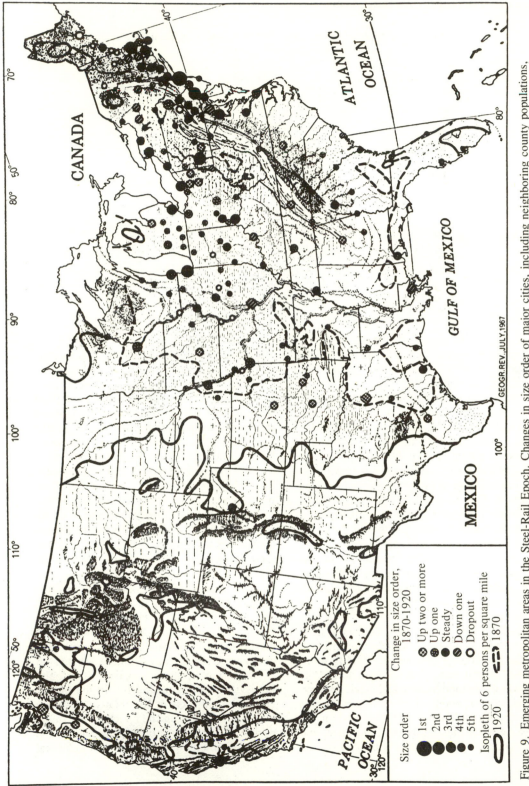

Figure 9. Emerging metropolitan areas in the Steel-Rail Epoch. Changes in size order of major cities, including neighboring county populations, 1870-1920. Population-density isopleths generalized from Lord and Lord, *op. cit.*, pp. 104 and 107-8. Sources of population data: "A Compendium of the Ninth Census" (1872) and "Abstract of the Fifteenth Census of the United States" (1933).

cities at historic waterpower sites along the Mohawk, the Merrimack, and the Blackstone and minor ports on the Hudson and the New England coast. None of these places was to regain the level it had held before the epoch of the steel rail and central-station electric power.

The main shifts during the epoch are summarized in Table 2. The new centralization of industry in major metropolitan areas was reflected in the growth of the five largest "SMSA's." That group increased its share of the national population faster than in any other epoch. The number of third- or higher-order centers, which had increased greatly in the Iron Horse Epoch, was stabilized, but their share of the nation's people rose sharply. The extension of national accessibility to isolated parts of the South and West augmented the number of lower-order metropolitan centers. The total number of fourth- and fifth-order cities registered its greatest growth in this epoch.

## Auto-Air-Amenity Epoch, 1920–

By 1920 the present pattern of settled areas had been established, and subsequent metropolitan changes have taken place within that pattern. Nevertheless, new resources and locations have been exploited and old ones abandoned (Figs. 10 and 11).

The much smaller labor force required per unit of production in the extractive industries is reflected on the map in the relative decline of Butte and Joplin and, along with the shift from steam to internal combustion, in the decline of coal and railroad centers in the Appalachians and across the Midwest. The shift to internal combustion is, of course, largely behind the outbreak of new or higher-order metropolitan areas in the oil fields from central Kansas to western Texas and the western Gulf Coast and in the concentration of growth in the SMSA's of southern Michigan.

Regional and metropolitan dispersal, inherent in the shift to auto and truck and in the development of a dense highway network, is reflected on Figures 10 and 11 in two principal ways. One is the entry into the metropolitan ranks of numerous "satellite" cities on the fringes of the historic Manufacturing Belt and within 100 to 150 miles of great metropolitan industrial centers. The other is the effect of suburban dispersal on the definition of a metropolitan area. In the Appalachians, for example, half a dozen "SMSA's" have dropped out because their central cities failed to maintain a population equal to, or larger than, that of other metropolitan centers. In these cases it is typical to find a central city crowded on a valley floor, blighted by obsolescent buildings, air pollution, narrow streets, and rusty rail lines, and exposed to flood risk. Population and commercial growth have dispersed to the uplands to exploit the resources of open space, a dense rural road net, panoramic views, and relatively clean air. The result is that the metropolitan area has grown and ceased to be "metropolitan" by definition, and the central city has declined and ceased to be "central" in fact.

This diffusion of metropolitan structure is also evidence of the increasing importance of amenities in determining the growth pattern of individual cities and regions. The location of the boom centers is further evidence of the force of amenity on a national scale. All are in Florida, the desert Southwest, and Southern California. The migration to the Southwest and Florida in the Auto-Air-Amenity Epoch has been as massive as any in the earlier westward movement. There was a net migration of 11.4 million persons to California, Arizona, and Florida from other regions between 1920 and 1960. This equaled the total population gain—and was probably double the immigration—for the twelve North Central States during the Iron Horse Epoch, 1830–1870.[24]

24. "Historical Statistics of the United States, Colonial Times to 1957" (U.S. Bureau of the Census, Washington, D.C., 1960), pp. 44–45 (1920–1960 migration data), p. 13 (1830–1870 population changes by states), and pp. 23–30 (early birth- and death-rate data); *Statistical Abstract of the United States 1965*, 86th edit., U.S. Bureau of the Census, Washington, D.C., 1965, p. 34.

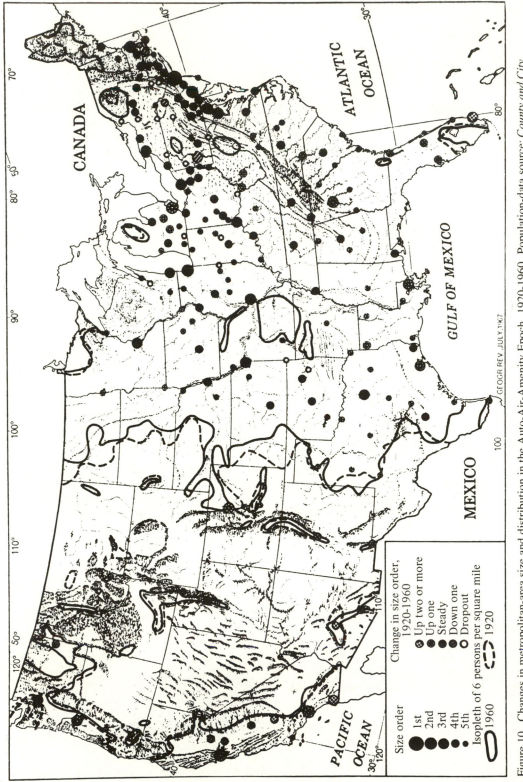

Figure 10. Changes in metropolitan-area size and distribution in the Auto-Air-Amenity Epoch, 1920–1960. Population-data source: *County and City Data Book, 1962,* U.S. Bureau of the Census. Population-density isopleths have been generalized from *Goode's World Atlas,* 12th ed., 1964, p. 58.

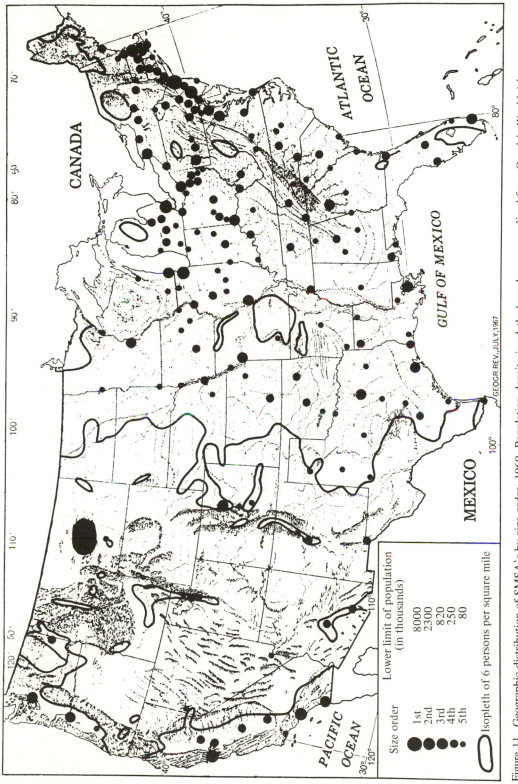

Figure 11. Geographic distribution of SMSA's by size order, 1960. Population-density isopleths have been generalized from *Goode's World Atlas*, 12th ed., 1964, p. 58.

Size order

- 1st ● 
- 2nd ●
- 3rd ●
- 4th ●
- 5th ●

Lower limit of population
(in thousands)

| 8000 |
| 2300 |
| 820 |
| 250 |
| 80 |

◯ Isopleth of 6 persons per square mile

GEOGR.REV.,JULY,1967

At the regional scale the increase in importance of educational centers, related in part to the growing importance of amenity, is illustrated by two pairs of Midwestern cities. The coal-rail center of Danville, Illinois, dropped out of the "metropolitan area" group, and the nearby university center of Champaign-Urbana entered it. Among the urban centers of the old eastern Indiana gas belt, the industrial city of Anderson dropped out, and neighboring Muncie, with both industrial and university functions, entered.

## EFFECTS OF TECHNOLOGICAL CHANGE

Throughout the evolution of the present pattern of American metropolitan areas two factors, great migrations and major changes in technology, have particularly influenced the location of relative growth and decline. Both factors have repeatedly been given specific geographical expression through their relationship to resource patterns. Major changes in technology have resulted in critically important changes in the evaluation or definition of particular resources on which the growth of certain urban regions had previously been based. Great migrations have sought to exploit resources—ranging from climate or coal to water or zinc—that were either newly appreciated or newly accessible within the national market. Usually, of course, the new appreciation of accessibility had come about, in turn, through some major technological innovation.

Nor can one see the end of these changes in locational advantage due to technological change and migration. Speculate, for instance, on the possible outcome of three changes, quite conceivable within the next half-century, whose seeds may well be lying in our midst at present. Assume the automation of, say, 80 percent of the office work heavily concentrated in the downtown skyscrapers of major metropolitan centers. Or assume the production of low-cost, mass-produced, single-family dwellings varied in style and superior in structure and maintenance to those now in use. Or assume the

introduction and success of a lightweight family vehicle that requires neither steel to build nor oil to power. Clearly, the process of urban growth in an open system is open-ended. To be sure, the rate of change from any point in time is constrained by the existing physical plant and institutions. But there is unlikely to be any "end product" of the process. Each epoch will simply be succeeded by another.

## VARYING PREDICTABILITY OF METROPOLITAN GROWTH

If metropolitan growth tends to be epochal and open-ended this suggests two probable characteristics of its predictability.

On the one hand, during any given epoch, similar conditions of paramount importance are likely to govern the rate and direction of growth over wide regions or types of location. Of course, countless short-term random effects are superimposed on the long-term trend. One might therefore expect the growth trend for a given metropolis during a given epoch to be regressive. That is, short-term spurts or declines will expectably be offset by succeeding short-term trends in the opposite direction. A regression line, fitted to the points representing these frequent ups and downs, describes the long-term trend. Thus the Upper Midwest Economic Study's urban research disclosed that past growth trends (during the automobile epoch) provided by far the most significant independent variable in a multiple regression equation to project 1950–1960 population growth rates of urban areas in its study region.[25]

On the other hand, when some basic component of the nation's society or economy or technology "turns a corner" and a new epoch opens, a new set of overriding and "long-term" forces goes into effect. Thereafter, one might expect past growth to cease to be a good predictor. At the least, its validity would have to be reestablished for a new set of conditions.

25. John R. Borchert and Russell B. Adams: Projected Urban Growth in the Upper Midwest: 1960–1975, *Upper Midwest Economic Study Urban Rept. No. 8*, Minneapolis, 1964, pp. 1–2 and Appendix.

The old regression line for a given metropolitan area would not necessarily represent the long-term growth trend in the new epoch. Short-term fluctuations would be less likely to regress toward the same line as in the preceding epoch (Fig. 12).

As the new epoch unfolds, a new pattern of "initial advantage" also emerges; for certain advantages are created that could not have existed before.[26] Business and civic institutions must reorganize to meet new challenges. This seems to have been done most effectively in the places least tied to natural-resource exploitation or secondary production, and with the largest and most diversified hinterlands, hence the most important centers of circulation and management. Even some of the high-order centers have had to make massive adjustments from one epoch to the next; St. Louis and Pittsburgh are probably the outstanding cases so far.

## INTERNAL DIFFERENTIATION OF METROPOLITAN AREAS

During each epoch a new increment of physical development has been added to each metropolitan area. Each increment is eventually differentiated from the adjoining ones not only by the age of its structures but also by their scale, design, use, degree of obsolescence, and, often, site or location. The successive increments form distinctive regions in the internal geography of any metropolitan area, and the regions have certain characteristics in common wherever they appear across the country.

26. This suggests a modification of Allan Pred's model of self-generating urban growth during a period of rapid industrialization (Pred, *op. cit.*). Innovation in a particular industry, because of its impact on the evaluation of a particular resource, may result in new or expanded industry at a place other than the one at which the innovation occurred. In that case, the flow of benefits may be diverted to a new location. The observed evolution also suggests that technological change may be considered an integral part of the basic process that generates an urban hierarchy. Although this was recognized by Walter Christaller in the section on "Dynamic Processes" in his "Central Places in Southern Germany" (translated by Carlisle W. Baskin; Englewood Cliffs, N. J., 1966, pp. 84–132), technological change has generally been handled as a secondary "modifier" of the basic model.

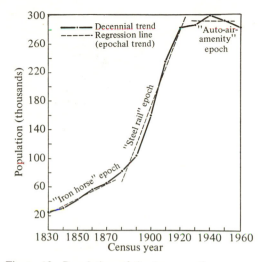

Figure 12. Population of the two counties comprising the Johnstown, Pa., SMSA (1960), by decades, 1830-1960. The depression of the 1930's, with its temporary decrease in mobility of a substantial economically "stranded" population, appears as a relatively short-term, low-amplitude event in the growth history in comparison with either the rise of the steel industry and dominance of steam-powered rail transportation or the advent of the internal-combustion engine.

But historically different increments tend to differentiate American cities at least as much as they tend to standardize them (Fig. 13), because cities differ profoundly in their epoch of initial settlement and in their periods of boom or decline. For example, it is possible that a Chicago or a Los Angeles metropolitan area will someday be as populous as the present metropolitan area of New York. But both are most unlikely to have a physical structure similar to New York's, even aside from the differences among the natural settings. Chicago's growth so far belongs 47 percent to the Steel-Rail Epoch and 45 percent to the Auto-Air-Amenity Epoch; corresponding percentages for Los Angeles are 15 and 85 (Table 3). Hence their historical increments have been markedly different, and their future increments will belong to a different technology from that which has built present-day New York.

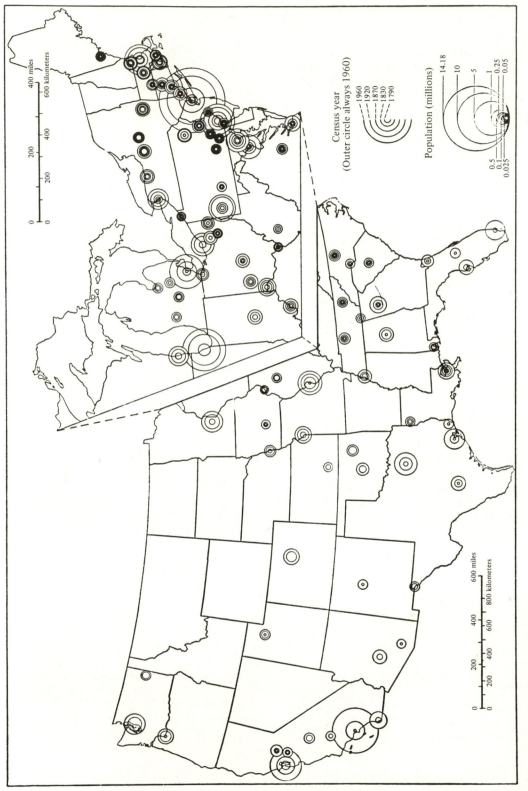

Figure 13. The varied historical layering of American SMSA's in 1960.

If the system is indeed evolving and open-ended, it is patently incorrect to consider either Los Angeles or Chicago illustrative of a stage en route to the development of another New York or, for that matter, to consider any American city to be at any stage in any rigid model of development.

## EXPLOITATION OF LAND

America's metropolitan centers grew initially on land whose sites and locations were regarded as advantageous, given the contemporary technology and migration pattern. Improvement and use of the land made redevelopment or restoration much more costly, if not impossible. At first the land was "improved"; but as the improvements aged and grew obsolete the land appeared instead to have been "despoiled." New technologies hastened obsolescence and transferred the locational and site advantages to other land. Men moved to this new land and began again the sequence of improvement and abandonment: they abandoned the obsolete buildings, locations, or cities to those who remained behind to adapt and abandon in their turn.

This sequence of land selection in the light of existing technology, development, use, despoliation, and abandonment has characterized in varying degree the past utilization of timber, soil, water, and mineral resources. It appears also to have characterized the use of land for urban purposes. The process can be visualized at three different scales on the accompanying maps. At the metropolitan scale it is illustrated by the partial abandonment of the central city for outlying areas during successive technological epochs; at the regional scale, by the shift of new development from mining towns to university towns, from railroad centers to recreational centers; at the national scale, by the shift from older cities in the Northeast to newer cities in the Southwest or Florida. It could be argued that, at any scale, the basic attitude toward the potential urban land resource has been exploitive. There is no general provision for

"recycling" the resource of developed land when the initial development has become obsolete.

The result is a gigantic, national "filter down" process with important geographical and historical dimensions. The nation's new construction has been concentrated, in any given epoch, not only in new neighborhoods and new suburbs but also in what have been, for all practical purposes, new cities (Table 3). The residue of obsolescent physical plant has also become concentrated, not only in certain districts of most cities but in virtually the entire area of some. Vast big-city cores and nearly the whole of some smaller metropolitan areas are approaching the condition of inhabited ruins, and the residue of old structures continues to expand, thanks to the lagging national rate of replacement. Analysis of available historical housing data indicates that the construction of new dwelling units over the first sixty years of the twentieth century was enough to replace, on the average, only 4 percent of the units standing at the end of each decade.[27] For later generations the legacy of buildings, like the earlier "natural" endowment, has become an exploitable physical resource.

On the one hand, the traditional exploitive development of the land resource for urban purposes is understandable in view of the abundance of undeveloped land, the high costs of acquiring and clearing used land, and the high replacement costs under prevailing conditions.[28] On the other hand, the growing accumulation and low level of maintenance of obsolescent districts and cities suggest the inadequacy of the present approach.

27. John R. Borchert, Paul E. Stewart, and Sherman S. Hasbrouch: Urban Renewal: Needs and Opportunities in the Upper Midwest, *Upper Midwest Economic Study Urban Rept. No. 5*, Minneapolis, 1963, pp. 1–4.
28. Louis F. Winnick (Housing and Urban Development: The Private Foundation's Role [The Ford Foundation, New York, 1965], p. 3) makes the following observations: "No other important consumer good has been as inflation-prone as housing. Over the past seventy years the cost of a unit of housing space has risen twice as fast as other costs." Also, Chauncy D. Harris has pointed out the very small fraction of the land resource required by cities (The Pressure of Residential-Industrial Land Use, *in* Man's Role in Changing the Face of the Earth [edited by William L. Thomas, Jr.; Chicago, 1956], pp. 881–895; reference on p. 889).

Table 3. Percentages of Populations of Selected 1960 SMSA's Attained in Major Historical Epochs.

| Size Order | SMSA[a] | Wagon-Sail Pre-1830 | Iron Horse 1830–1870 | Steel Rail 1870–1920 | Auto-Air-Amenity 1920–1960 |
|---|---|---|---|---|---|
| First | New York[b] | 3 | 11 | 44 | 42 |
| Second | Philadelphia | 9 | 15 | 38 | 38 |
| | Boston[c] | 9 | 18 | 48 | 25 |
| | Chicago[b] | 0 | 8 | 47 | 45 |
| | Detroit | 0 | 6 | 29 | 65 |
| | San Francisco-Oakland and San Jose | 0 | 7 | 27 | 66 |
| | Los Angeles | 0 | 0+ | 15 | 85 |
| Third | Washington | 5 | 5 | 19 | 71 |
| | Pittsburgh | 7 | 10 | 56 | 27 |
| | St. Louis | 2 | 21 | 34 | 43 |
| | New Orleans | 7 | 18 | 23 | 52 |
| | Seattle-Tacoma | 0 | 0+ | 42 | 58 |
| | Denver | 0 | 1 | 35 | 64 |
| | Dallas and Fort Worth | 0 | 3 | 30 | 67 |
| | Miami and Fort Lauderdale | 0 | 0 | 4 | 96 |
| Fourth | Albany-Schenectady-Troy | 23 | 25 | 23 | 29 |
| | New Bedford and Fall River | 13 | 12 | 65 | 10 |
| | Scranton and Wilkes-Barre-Hazelton | 4 | 20 | 63 | 13 |
| | Birmingham | 1 | 1 | 47 | 51 |
| | Omaha | 0 | 10 | 50 | 40 |
| | Flint | 0 | 7 | 27 | 66 |
| | Jacksonville | 0 | 3 | 22 | 75 |
| | Phoenix | 0 | 0 | 14 | 86 |
| Fifth | Corpus Christi | 0 | 2 | 8 | 90 |
| | Altoona | 0 | 21 | 72 | 7 |
| | Charleston, S.C. | 40 | 1 | 9 | 50 |
| | Lubbock | 0 | 0 | 7 | 93 |
| | Las Vegas | 0 | 0 | 4 | 96 |

[a]1960 SMSA except where noted to contrary.
[b]Standard Consolidated Area.
[c]Norfolk, Suffolk, and Middlesex Counties.

## ADAPTABILITY AND CONTROL

Two major problems seem to result from the nature of metropolitan evolution. First, long-term changes in size and physical character are highly uncertain. Second, the exploitation of new land and accompanying abandonment of old in successive periods lead to a gigantic accumulation of residual structures. This residue is a drag on both the improvement of the general health and welfare and the market for new, low-cost buildings.

It appears unlikely that the tendencies inherent in this evolutionary process will change significantly. To be sure, the fraction of the total number of metropolitan areas that

changed size order diminished during the Steel-Rail and Auto-Air-Amenity Epochs. Also, there have been fewer booms (Table 4). This increasing stabilization was to be expected as the national transportation network was completed and improved and nearly every part of the country raised its level of participation in the national economy.[29] Nevertheless, metropolitan areas continue to grow at differential rates. There has been virtually no decrease over the past two epochs in the number of places that advanced one rank in the size order, and only a slight decrease in the number that declined one

29. Lukermann, *op. cit.*

Table 4. Number of SMSA's and Emerging SMSA's Experiencing Shifts in Size Order

| Shift in Size Order | 1790–1830 | 1830–1870 | 1870–1920 | 1920–1960 |
|---|---|---|---|---|
| Up one rank | 7 | 37 | 66 | 65 |
| Up two ranks | 11 | 16 | 15 | 6 |
| Up three ranks | 2 | 4 | 3 | 1 |
| Up four ranks | 0 | 1 | 0 | 0 |
| Down one rank | 10 | 14 | 25 | 20 |
| Down two ranks | 2 | 2 | 2 | 0 |
| Steady | 26 | 24 | 49 | 103 |
| New entries | 19 | 47 | 69 | 48 |
| Dropouts | 6 | 8 | 13 | 17 |
| Net increase | 13 | 39 | 56 | 31 |

rank. At the beginning of each epoch a major change in technology registered its impact on the values of existing metropolitan locations and on the pattern of migration; and some new cities were also established. As long as America remains an open society, there will surely be unforeseen major changes affecting old cities and new alike—new rounds of initial advantage, reorganization, and adaptation, new reasons to exploit new land and abandon old.

Given the two problems of uncertainty and migration-abandonment, pressure is mounting to make the metropolitan settlement pattern more adaptable to change. For this purpose two types of development appear to be of great potential importance. One is the production, for the full range of urban functions, of soundly engineered and attractively designed structures that can be emplaced or removed at much lower costs than in the past.[30] The other is the improvement of information-education systems to increase the extent, accuracy, and currency of knowledge of the changing metropolis.[31] An important consequence of this

might be the development of a degree of public objectivity that would permit more rapid adaptation of institutions, notably local government.[32]

On the other hand, one might expect mounting pressure to create new institutions and shift values in order to retard the rate of change and thereby reduce the need for rapid and massive adaptation. For example, in some cases truly comprehensive, long-range planning could lower the permissible rate of technological change throughout an urban or regional system to that of the least tractable, slowest-changing component of the system, in the interest of preserving orderly development.

The mounting pressures for greater adaptability and greater control may often conflict. Where and how to compromise them seems likely to be an important and recurring issue in the future course of American metropolitan evolution. Furthermore, the issue is likely to be debated and resolved on many different grounds, since no one city is the evolutionary prototype for all others.

30. For a concise recent summary of one aspect of this topic see William K. Wittausch: New Concepts for the Housing Industry, *Urban Land,* Vol. 25, No. 5, 1966, pp. 11–12.
31. See Edward F. R. Hearle and Raymond J. Mason: A Data Processing System for State and Local Governments (Englewood Cliffs, N.J., 1963). Chapter 4 presents a long list of classes of data now generally noncomparable and incomplete in coverage that will inevitably be standardized and automated yet already form a vital body of information about the internal geography and other aspects of the structure of each metropolitan area. See also W. L. Garrison: Urban Transportation Planning Models in 1975,

*Journ. Amer. Inst. of Planners,* Vol. 31, 1965, pp. 156–158. This is an extension of the logic of Garrison's forecast of traffic planning that assumes more rapid adjustment to crises, through improved information systems and designs. See also Edward L. Ullman: The Nature of Cities Reconsidered, *Papers and Proc. Regional Science Assn.,* Vol. 9, 1962, pp. 7–23.
32. See Robert C. Wood: 1400 Governments (with Vladimir V. Almendinger; New York Metropolitan Region Study, Vol. 8; Cambridge, Mass., 1961), especially the introductory and concluding chapters.

# The Growth of Cities in England and Wales in the Nineteenth Century

BRIAN T. ROBSON

The various attempts to derive theoretical distributions of city size have worked from sets of assumptions about growth processes, but have not explored the extent to which their assumptions may be reasonable or may be met with in the real world. Such an examination seems long overdue, less for the light which it might throw on notions about rank-size curve, than in its own right as telling us something about the nature of urbanization. Here we shall look at data on the growth of towns in England and Wales in the nineteenth century to see to what extent empirical questions about the process of urbanization can be answered as well as to develop some more general ideas about urban growth.

First, a word might be said both about the time and the area to be studied. As to the period, it has already been argued that the nineteenth century—Giffen's "statistical century"—can be regarded as a most useful compromise period in Britain between the pre- and post-industrial periods. Not only does this mean that, so far as our individual units of observation are concerned (call them "objects" if one will), one can place greater confidence in the necessary assumption that each town is relatively more self-contained, and hence relatively more of a unit or object, than would be the case for twentieth-century cities, but it is also the earliest period for which one can have recourse to the demographic data of the censuses. Although the census data are very far from being entirely

reliable, they are much more so than any other comparable source and have the inestimable virtue of providing an almost complete coverage of urban places for a long period of time.[1] So far as the area of study is concerned, there are obvious limitations in using only England and Wales as an overall unit. It must be recognized, however, that whatever unit were to be selected, there would always be the problem of the lack of closure of the boundaries of the "system." England and Wales were much affected, in terms of their economic growth and the growth of their towns, by concurrent developments in Scotland and in Ireland—more obviously so in the case of the recurrent waves of immigration from the latter unfortunate country. Equally, developments in areas outside the British Isles would have their effects.

## Urban Populations

To measure the growth rates of individual towns, one needs to assemble population data for successive times for a number of defined urban areas. This immediately raises a number of the problems of definition which were earlier discussed in connection with what is meant by a "city." At what point does

1. The various local eighteenth-century surveys, from which much detailed demographic data can be derived, suffer both from the patchiness of their coverage as well as their lack of coincidence in time.

Adapted from B. T. Robson, *Urban Growth: An Approach*, pp. 47–89. (London: Methuen, 1973). Reprinted by permission.

a collection of people and buildings become a town; how can one define the areal extent of a given individual town? Such problems have long bedevilled any work which looks at changes in urban populations over time and they account for the uncertainty which must hang over any estimate of the relative sizes of urban and rural populations within any country, no matter how reliable its census information. A tentative definition of a city has already been made which suggested it as an area which contains a relatively large number of people, which is relatively densely settled and in which the majority of the population is involved in activities which are not agricultural. This provides at least guidelines to help resolve the difficulty of classifying urban and non-urban areas. The population data which are used have been taken from the mammoth recalculations of nineteenth-century census returns undertaken by Mr. C. M. Law and kindly made available by him. Law (1967) recalculated urban populations for urban areas which were more realistically defined than the administrative areas given in the census returns and, in defining towns for this purpose, he used three criteria which a place needed to meet to qualify as a "town": a minimum size of population; a minimum density; and a criterion of spatial clustering.

The minimum size is taken at 2,500; a threshold which is large enough to exclude many of the purely mining communities which sprang up in counties such as Durham during the later part of the century and also large enough to exclude most of the small market towns which never attracted industry to them, which relied almost wholly on supporting their tributary agricultural areas and which often suffered radical population decline in the later part of the century. It might be argued that, rather than taking a fixed population size as a criterion of qualifying as a town, a better yardstick might be a variable or sliding size-threshold, so that, as the century progressed, a successively larger figure would be used as a minimum size. This would certainly accord with the realistic argument that the scale of efficient size increases with time as technical and organizational expertise

improves and raises the level of scale economies and the lower threshold of efficient operation of units.[2] The use of such a sliding minimum would, however, have two main disadvantages. Not only would it be as difficult to justify the selection of any particular threshold at a given time as to select a constant threshold, but it would also introduce difficulties in handling towns whose population, even though remaining static or growing only slowly, would yet "die" out of the urban "system" as the threshold became progressively higher. As Friedlander comments with reference to just this problem of varying minimum size thresholds, "It seems that there are no simple or unique answers to these questions and there could probably be good arguments in favour of different approaches to such problems" (Friedlander 1970, p. 423).

Law's density criterion was fixed at a figure of one person per acre which, as he says, would be a very low figure for urban areas, but a very high figure for rural areas. It is thus a useful yardstick for deciding which of the parishes or areas surrounding an administrative urban area should be included in the total urban population or, indeed which administratively-defined non-urban areas should be regarded as towns. Since the censuses for England and Wales give population data for administrative units which are often seriously underbounded as descriptions of urban areas, it was this criterion which was used to define the basic areal extent of urban areas.[3]

---

2. A theme which forms the underpinnings of much of the argument of Social Area Analysis which has looked at changes in the internal structure of both cities and national economies (see, for example, Shevky and Bell 1955; Udry 1964; McElrath 1968).
3. In the United States, the Bureau of the Census—for long much more alive to the inadequacy of purely administrative definitions of urban areas than the British Census Office—began to experiment with more extensive definitions of urban aggregates as early as 1910 when statistics were given for "Metropolitan Districts." In 1950, data were reported both for "Urbanized Areas" and "Standard Metropolitan Areas." Subsequently, the "Standard Metropolitan Statistical Area" was added (for definitions, see U.S. Bureau of the Budget 1967 and, for the "Urbanized Area," Carter 1972, p. 24). The nearest British equivalent—the "conurbation"—falls between these two American definitions and suffers from the fact that it is still composed of administrative units.

Finally, the nucleation criterion takes account of the attempt to define towns as spatially continuous built-up areas. In a number of the parishes of England and Wales, even though the criteria of minimum population size and minimum density are met, the population is dispersed in a series of small communities over a relatively wide area and the several communities are not physically contiguous. In the nineteenth century, this was particularly the case of many settlements in South Wales and parts of northern England, where, most usually, mining communities were found scattered discretely throughout large parishes. In such cases these populations would not be regarded as a single urban area even though meeting the first two minima.[4]

Problems of definition of this sort are an inevitable conjunct of any work on urban growth. Despite such difficulties, and despite the variable quality of the census sources from which the populations have been recalculated, Law's figures provide as sensitive and accurate a set of estimates of urban populations as one could hope to derive.[5] Certainly in that they apply to areas which approximate as closely as possible to the actual and changing extent of the built-up area of nineteenth-century towns, they provide better estimates of urban populations than do the raw census data on which so many previous studies have had to be based—as, for example, in the figures given by Mitchell (1962, pp. 24–27) which have been widely quoted elsewhere (for example, Banks 1968).[6]

## The Numbers of Urban Places

If we look by way of introduction at the set of places which these definitions produce during

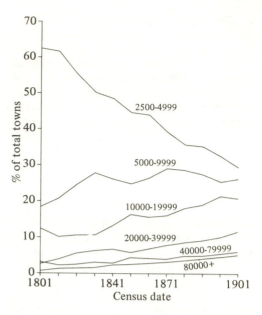

Figure 1. Percentages of towns in different size groups in England and Wales, 1801-1911. Details are given in Table 1.

the period 1801–1911, the easiest way to familiarize ourselves with the material is simply to look at the changing numbers of towns in each population size class over the whole span of the twelve dates. Table 1 shows the number of towns in each of nine size classes which have been selected so that each size class is a constant factor of twice that of the previous class. It can be seen first of all that the number of towns increases rapidly from a mere 256 in 1801 to as many as 923 in 1911. Secondly, within this increasing number of places, the proportional representation of each size class changes in a fairly systematic fashion. The percentage of towns in the size range 2,500–4,999 falls progressively from over 60 to under 30; that in the size range 5,000–9,999 rises from less than 20 to almost 30 and then falls to level off at about 25; percentages in the size ranges above 10,000

4. For a detailed description of data sources and definitions the reader is referred to the original text pp. 48–52.—Eds.
5. Only an impossibly laborious calculation based on the information contained in enumerators' books could provide a more sensitive set of populations and this source is, of course, available only for census dates between 1841 and 1871.
6. The same would be true of the heroic calculations of nineteenth-century commentators such as A. F. Weber (1899) and Welton (1900). In calculating percentages of the urban

population for England and Wales as a whole, Law (1967) compares the results based on his urban definition with the figures suggested by the census itself and by Price-Williams (1880), Welton (1900), A. F. Weber (1899), and Vince (1955).

Table 1. Numbers of towns in different size groups.

| Date | 2.5–4.9 | | 5–9.9 | | 10–19.9 | | 20–39.9 | | 40–79.9 | | 80–159.9 | | 160–319.9 | | 320–639.9 | | ≥640 | | Total |
| | No. | % | No. | % | No. | % | No. | % | No. | % | No. | % | No. | % | No. | % | No. | % | No. |
|---|---|---|---|---|---|---|---|---|---|---|---|---|---|---|---|---|---|---|---|
| 1801 | 160 | 62.50 | 47 | 18.36 | 32 | 12.50 | 7 | 2.73 | 8 | 3.13 | 1 | 0.39 | 0 | — | 0 | — | 1 | 0.39 | 256 |
| 1811 | 190 | 61.69 | 64 | 20.78 | 31 | 10.06 | 12 | 3.90 | 7 | 2.27 | 3 | 0.97 | 0 | — | 0 | — | 1 | 0.32 | 308 |
| 1821 | 200 | 55.40 | 89 | 24.65 | 38 | 10.53 | 20 | 5.54 | 9 | 2.49 | 3 | 0.83 | 1 | 0.28 | 0 | — | 1 | 0.28 | 361 |
| 1831 | 207 | 50.24 | 115 | 27.91 | 44 | 10.68 | 26 | 6.31 | 13 | 3.16 | 4 | 0.97 | 2 | 0.49 | 1 | 0.22 | 1 | 0.24 | 412 |
| 1841 | 226 | 48.60 | 121 | 26.02 | 62 | 13.33 | 32 | 6.88 | 13 | 2.80 | 7 | 1.51 | 2 | 0.43 | 2 | 0.38 | 1 | 0.22 | 465 |
| 1851 | 234 | 44.91 | 135 | 25.91 | 85 | 16.31 | 31 | 5.95 | 23 | 4.41 | 8 | 1.54 | 2 | 0.38 | 3 | 0.52 | 1 | 0.19 | 521 |
| 1861 | 255 | 43.97 | 153 | 26.38 | 91 | 15.69 | 40 | 6.90 | 24 | 4.14 | 9 | 1.55 | 4 | 0.69 | 2 | 0.29 | 1 | 0.17 | 580 |
| 1871 | 274 | 39.65 | 201 | 29.09 | 111 | 16.06 | 55 | 7.96 | 28 | 4.05 | 13 | 1.88 | 5 | 0.72 | 2 | 0.13 | 2 | 0.29 | 691 |
| 1881 | 270 | 36.00 | 215 | 28.67 | 135 | 18.00 | 65 | 8.67 | 37 | 4.93 | 17 | 2.27 | 7 | 0.93 | 2 | 0.24 | 3 | 0.40 | 750 |
| 1891 | 293 | 35.13 | 230 | 27.58 | 159 | 19.06 | 77 | 9.23 | 41 | 4.92 | 20 | 2.40 | 8 | 0.96 | 2 | 0.45 | 4 | 0.48 | 834 |
| 1901 | 290 | 32.77 | 225 | 25.42 | 190 | 21.47 | 89 | 10.06 | 49 | 5.54 | 23 | 2.60 | 11 | 1.24 | 4 | 0.45 | 4 | 0.45 | 885 |
| 1911 | 274 | 29.69 | 243 | 26.33 | 193 | 20.91 | 109 | 11.81 | 56 | 6.06 | 29 | 3.14 | 11 | 1.19 | 4 | 0.43 | 4 | 0.43 | 923 |

Size Group ('000s)

*Note*: Percentage figures are percentages of the total number of towns at each date.

tend almost universally to increase throughout the whole span of the period. Figure 1 traces these changes, showing the relatively greater rise in the numbers of large places at the expense of the smaller.

## Changes in Size

These are simple descriptive statistics which give some preliminary idea about the numbers of places which are to be studied and also suggest that there may be regularities in the changing sizes of those places which could lead to the development of hypotheses about urban growth. It is not, of course, the number of towns in which our interest lies, but the population changes of individual size groups of towns at successive decadal intervals. The first, and simplest, way in which this might be studied is to plot the movements of individual towns between the eight size classes during each pair of census dates. Table 2 gives transition matrices for three of the eleven successive periods. Each matrix shows the number of places which start the decade with populations in one size class and end the decade with populations either in the same or some different size class. The row entries show, for each size class, the classes in which towns ended the decade; the column entries show, for each size class at the end of the decade, in which size class the places had started the decade. In the first decade, for example, 160 places had populations in the size class 2,500–4,999 in 1801; by 1811, of these 160 places only 135 were still in that size group, twenty-four had increased their populations into the size group 5,000–9,999, one place had lost population so as no longer to qualify as a "town," and so forth. The totals of the rows and columns can be interpreted in the same way: the totals of the rows show the number of places in each size group in 1801; the totals of the columns show the numbers in each size group in 1811.

Attention might be drawn to four points in these matrices. First, the range of movement between categories is relatively small. This is very much a function of the large ranges of

population which are included in each size category. For a place to move from the midpoint of one size group to the mid-point of the next higher group, it would need to double its population during the course of the decade. It is therefore not surprising that there is only a minority of cases in which towns appear in cells more than one away from the diagonal. On the whole, such large movements tend to be restricted to the smallest range of town sizes which suggests that it is only in these towns that one might expect to find very high percentage growth rates. Second, it can be seen that the matrices are all "absorbing" matrices, that is to say that it is not possible for a town to move from one size class to every other of the size classes within the matrix—a requirement which would have to be met for the matrices to be "regular Markov matrices" (Kemeney and Snell 1960). For this to be possible, the rows would need to have entries in the cells both above and below the diagonal. Instead—and particularly in the higher population sizes—the pattern is for towns either to continue in the same size class or to move up into the next higher size class. Thus, if a given initial distribution of town sizes were to be powered up by successive multiplications by the transition probabilities,[7] all of the towns would eventually end up in the highest size class since, once above a certain population size, the probability of moving *down* into a lower size group becomes remote or non-existent. Third, the pattern of town "births" is of interest. These "births" are shown in the entries given in the "zero" row and which fall in columns other than the "zero" column—in other words, places which start a decade at populations below 2,500, but which end with populations greater than that figure. The rapid growth in the number of such new towns has already been noted, but here the pattern is shown much more clearly. The great majority is "born" in the lowest size category with popu-

7. The transition probabilities would be given simply as a weighting of the raw observations of the matrices. Thus, for each row, the probabilities would be the cell entries divided by the row total. These would give the probability of staying in the same size class or moving to another by the end of the decade.

Table 2. Transition Matrices: Numbers of Towns in Population Size Groups at Selected Dates.

| Size group | | No. in 1811 | | | | | | | | | Total |
|---|---|---|---|---|---|---|---|---|---|---|---|
| | | 0 | 1 | 2 | 3 | 4 | 5 | 6 | 7 | 8 | |
| | 0 | 625 | 53 | 0 | 0 | 0 | 0 | 0 | 0 | 0 | |
| No. | 1 | 1 | 135 | 24 | 0 | 0 | 0 | 0 | 0 | 0 | 160 |
| in | 2 | 0 | 2 | 40 | 5 | 0 | 0 | 0 | 0 | 0 | 47 |
| 1801 | 3 | 0 | 0 | 0 | 26 | 6 | 0 | 0 | 0 | 0 | 32 |
| | 4 | 0 | 0 | 0 | 0 | 6 | 1 | 0 | 0 | 0 | 7 |
| | 5 | 0 | 0 | 0 | 0 | 0 | 6 | 2 | 0 | 0 | 8 |
| | 6 | 0 | 0 | 0 | 0 | 0 | 0 | 1 | 0 | 0 | 1 |
| | 7 | 0 | 0 | 0 | 0 | 0 | 0 | 0 | 0 | 0 | 0 |
| | 8 | 0 | 0 | 0 | 0 | 0 | 0 | 0 | 0 | 1 | 1 |
| Total | | | 190 | 64 | 31 | 12 | 7 | 3 | 0 | 1 | 308/256 |

| Size group | | No. in 1861 | | | | | | | | | Total |
|---|---|---|---|---|---|---|---|---|---|---|---|
| | | 0 | 1 | 2 | 3 | 4 | 5 | 6 | 7 | 8 | |
| | 0 | 350 | 54 | 6 | 3 | 0 | 0 | 0 | 0 | 0 | |
| No. | 1 | 4 | 196 | 34 | 0 | 0 | 0 | 0 | 0 | 0 | 234 |
| in | 2 | 0 | 5 | 110 | 20 | 0 | 0 | 0 | 0 | 0 | 135 |
| 1851 | 3 | 0 | 0 | 3 | 68 | 14 | 0 | 0 | 0 | 0 | 85 |
| | 4 | 0 | 0 | 0 | 0 | 26 | 5 | 0 | 0 | 0 | 31 |
| | 5 | 0 | 0 | 0 | 0 | 0 | 19 | 4 | 0 | 0 | 23 |
| | 6 | 0 | 0 | 0 | 0 | 0 | 0 | 5 | 3 | 0 | 8 |
| | 7 | 0 | 0 | 0 | 0 | 0 | 0 | 0 | 1 | 1 | 2 |
| | 8 | 0 | 0 | 0 | 0 | 0 | 0 | 0 | 0 | 3 | 3 |
| Total | | | 255 | 153 | 91 | 40 | 24 | 9 | 4 | 4 | 580/521 |

| Size group | | No. in 1911 | | | | | | | | | Total |
|---|---|---|---|---|---|---|---|---|---|---|---|
| | | 0 | 1 | 2 | 3 | 4 | 5 | 6 | 7 | 8 | |
| | 0 | 7 | 34 | 7 | 1 | 0 | 0 | 0 | 0 | 0 | |
| No. | 1 | 4 | 238 | 43 | 5 | 0 | 0 | 0 | 0 | 0 | 290 |
| in | 2 | 0 | 2 | 191 | 31 | 1 | 0 | 0 | 0 | 0 | 225 |
| 1901 | 3 | 0 | 0 | 2 | 156 | 32 | 0 | 0 | 0 | 0 | 190 |
| | 4 | 0 | 0 | 0 | 0 | 76 | 13 | 0 | 0 | 0 | 89 |
| | 5 | 0 | 0 | 0 | 0 | 0 | 43 | 6 | 0 | 0 | 49 |
| | 6 | 0 | 0 | 0 | 0 | 0 | 0 | 23 | 0 | 0 | 23 |
| | 7 | 0 | 0 | 0 | 0 | 0 | 0 | 0 | 11 | 0 | 11 |
| | 8 | 0 | 0 | 0 | 0 | 0 | 0 | 0 | 0 | 8 | 8 |
| Total | | | 274 | 243 | 193 | 109 | 56 | 29 | 11 | 8 | 923/885 |

*Note:* Size groups are as follows:

0 <2,500
1 2,500–4,999
2 5,000–9,999
3 10,000–19,999
4 20,000–39,999
5 40,000–79,999
6 80,000–159,999
7 160,000–319,999
8 ≥320,000

131

lations between 2,500 and 4,999, but many are "born" in the later decades at figures well above this and it is some of these places whose early population figures are impossible to derive. Fourth, and conversely, the entries in the "zero" columns which do not fall in the "zero" rows show the pattern of "deaths" of towns—those places which fall below the threshold of 2,500. In most cases these represent places whose population hovered uncertainly around the threshold figure and declined below it for some of the twelve dates. They present far fewer operational problems in deriving population totals than do some of the places which were "born," however, not only because of the smaller number involved, but also because, when an administrative core had once been defined for such places, appropriate figures tend subsequently to be given in the census returns.

These are the main features of the transition matrices. In general they show that the great bulk of towns cluster along the diagonals of the tables, confirming in a very approximate way an expectation that urban growth would tend to occur at a rate common to the whole set of towns. A sharper focus is needed, however, before anything more precise or of greater interest than this general description might emerge.[8]

## Regression of Opening and Closing Sizes for Each Decade

One might hypothesize that towns grow by some common overall rate, but that the common rate is subject to fluctuations from one town to another. This hypothesis suggests a regression formulation of the following sort:

$$X_t = a + bX_{t-1} + \epsilon; \qquad (1)$$

where $X_t$ is the population of a town at time $t$; $a$ and $b$ are constants; and $\epsilon$ is a normally distributed error or disturbance term. If the

growth of the set of places were to conform to the law of proportionate growth, the value of $b$ would be expected to be 1.0 and the overall change produced by this growth within the total population of towns would be represented by the constant $a$ which would measure the vertical displacement of the curve. The variances in the growth rates of individual towns would be contained in the error term. The interest in this formulation is twofold: first in the extent to which real-world data do produce a value of $b$ which is not significantly different from 1.0; and second in the increasing concentration produced in the distribution of urban populations by the value of both the $b$ term and the disturbance term.

## Concentration of Urban Population

Before turning to the statistical regression, we might digress a little to expand on this latter point about the growing concentration of population. If it were to be found that empirical data on urban growth fitted a regression model in which the value of $b$ was greater than 1.0, this would mean that larger places tended to grow more rapidly than smaller places and the consequence on the size distribution of those places would be that the slope of the frequency curve would grow steeper as increasing proportions of the total population were contained within the larger cities at the expense of the smaller. There is, indeed, some evidence that the slopes of more developed countries tend in general to be somewhat steeper than those of less developed countries. Lopes (1972), for example, in criticizing the distinction between "lognormal" and "primate" size distributions, suggests that attention should instead be focused on the relationship between the degree of economic development of countries and the *slope* of their size-distribution curves.[9] He finds that the correlations between the slope coefficients and indices of economic development for a number of countries are posi-

---

8. The formal application of Markov methods to these matrices is excluded here. The reader is referred to the original text pp. 61–63.—Eds.

9. A suggestion which was advanced much earlier by Singer (1936) and Allen (1954).

| Time | Size of city | | | | | | | Total number of cities | % of total population in top 10 cities |
|------|-------|-------|-------|--------|--------|--------|--------|---------|---------|
|      | 7,110 | 7,900 | 9,000 | 10,000 | 11,000 | 12,100 | 13,310 |         |         |
| $t_1$ |       |       |       | 128    |        |        |        | 128     | 7.81    |
| $t_2$ |       |       | 32    | 64     | 32     |        |        | 128     | 8.59    |
| $t_3$ |       | 8     | 32    | 48     | 32     | 8      |        | 128     | 9.28    |
| $t_4$ | 2     | 12    | 30    | 40     | 30     | 12     | 2      | 128     | 11.53   |

tive and quite high and, while the calculation of slopes is very much dependent upon the lower threshold of size at which cities are selected, the results would tend to support the notion of increasing urban concentration over time. In practice, however, the great majority of studies of rank-size distribution curves has found that the curves at successive dates tend to be parallel with each other and tend to settle down at a slope of approximately 45°.[10] In the regression format of the closing size on the opening size of cities, if we find a $b$ value of 1.0, will this then explain the parallelism of size curves?

In fact, so long as there is a disturbance term around the common growth rate, even a value of $b$ equal to 1.0 will still produce increasing population concentration over time. The connection of concentration and the nature of urban growth is best seen with a simple example. Suppose one takes a set of 128 cities each of which has an identical population at some given time $t_1$—a situation perhaps representing an early stage of unspecialized development in which each place is relatively independent and serves only a small and relatively self-contained tributary area (a statistical parody, in fact, of the preindustrial city). Let us assume that each city has a population of 10,000; then a measure of concentration which might be used is the percentage of the total population contained in the ten largest places and this, at time $t_1$, would be 7.8. Obviously if each individual city were subsequently to grow by an identical

rate, the percentage of population contained in the ten largest places would remain unchanged no matter how many time periods were involved. However, if we assume that there is even a very slight random fluctuation of individual city growth around this common rate, the effect is very different. Let us assume that this fluctuation conforms to Simon's (1955) growth model, so that the disturbance term is identical within any band of city sizes. This fluctuation can be of the following order: within each size band, half of the cities will population which is found in the ten largest places increases progressively over time from 7.8 at time $t_1$, to 8.6 in $t_2$, 9.3 in $t_3$ and 11.5 in $t_4$. Despite the fact that there is a common overall rate of growth and that the fluctuation around that rate is the same for groups of larger and smaller places, the degree of concentration will increase. Only if there is *no* fluctuation whatsoever and a common rate of stay the same size, one-quarter will increase by 10 per cent, and one-quarter will decline by 10 per cent.[11] The progression of sizes will then be as follows: The percentage of the total growth, will concentration not occur. The greater the degree of fluctuation the more rapidly will concentration take place. Interest in the regression formulae should therefore be focused upon the size of the disturbance term as well as upon the closeness of the $b$ term to

10. The successive curves of city sizes in the United States demonstrate the point. (See original text, p. 30.)

11. By using size bands, this growth process conforms to an assumption discussed in the original text, pp. 31–32. It means that it is perfectly possible for any given city to increase consistently over successive decades. The percentage growth rates used in this instance should be regarded as departures from the overall average growth rate which is taken as being zero.

1.0. Only some form of countervailing tendency in the growth of cities will prevent increasing urban concentration from occurring.

This phenomenon of concentration was discussed very early by Galton who recognized the need for some form of "regression towards the mean"[12] if the growth of units was not to lead to growing concentration. In the study of business-firm growth, this requirement has been discussed by Kalecki (1945) and by Prais and Hart (1956) and a similar regression towards the mean has been recognized in the study of IQs of parents and children.[13] A somewhat parallel phenomenon can be seen in the discussion of positive and negative feedback effects in regional economic development.[14]

The need for some retarding element in order to maintain concentration at a constant level has briefly been noted in the case of urban growth (E. N. Thomas, 1967) and the suggestion of retardation in the growth rates of individual cities has been discussed most fully by Madden (1956b and 1958) and Williamson (1965b; Williamson and Swanson, 1966). It is by no means clear, however, that one can as yet reconcile the apparent stability of size-distribution curves with the inevitable tendency towards increasing concentration which is a concomitant of the urban growth process of proportionate effect which has so often been assumed in studies of urbanization.

## Regression Analysis of Nineteenth-Century Urban Growth

Bearing in mind the discussion about urban concentration, our regression formulation can now be re-expressed in the following terms:

$$X_t = a + (1 + c)X_{t-1} + \epsilon; \qquad (2)$$

where $c$ is Galton's constant—the negative weighting which is necessary to retard the growth of large places relative to small places by an amount which will maintain the level of concentration in the distribution under consideration. Obviously, this is directly the equivalent of equation (1) since the $c$ term equals the slope coefficient, $b$, minus 1.0. Equation (2) simply argues that, to produce a distribution whose component units grow while maintaining the overall stability of the distribution, the larger units have to grow more slowly than the smaller. The size of the negative weight, $c$, which is required for stability, will depend on the size of the disturbance term, $\epsilon$, since, as was shown above, concentration will tend to increase more quickly the larger the variance around the common growth.

Table 3 shows the regression coefficients of towns' opening and closing sizes for each of the eleven decadal periods between 1801–11 and 1901–11. Throughout, the natural logarithm of population sizes has been used in the calculations. There are two points of particular interest. First, it is apparent that the values of $b$, the slope coefficient, are in every case very close to 1.0 which suggests that the growth of these nineteenth-century cities is governed by an approximately constant proportion irrespective of city size. Second, however, it is not without significance that, with only one exception, all of the values are slightly higher than 1.0. If we subtract 1.0 from each of the values of $b$ (thus giving the value of $c$), it can be seen that it is only in the final decade that Galton's constant gives a negative weighting. Indeed, there would appear to be a pattern of some regularity in the

12. So as not to cause confusion between the statistical technique of linear regression and Galton's term "regression," the latter will be referred to as "regression to the mean."

13. On average, the children of parents with high IQ tend to have slightly lower IQs than their parents and children of parents with low IQ tend to have slightly higher IQs than their parents. The regression towards the mean level of IQ operates to prevent the distribution of IQs from becoming progressively distended.

14. Hirschman (1958), Myrdal (1957) and others argue that economic inequality is the product of cumulative growth which is

aided by "backwash" effects within a national economy and that, only at a later stage, is the level of inequality dampened by "spread" effects operating from growth centers as negative feedback replaces positive. In a study of a number of national economies over time, Williamson (1965a) supports this temporal progression. Some of the checks to cumulative growth which have been suggested for national growth centers could obviously be applied directly to the growth of large cities.

Table 3. Regression of Urban Populations: Closing Size on Opening Size of Towns at Successive Dates.

| Decade | No. of towns in calculation | Intercept (a) | Slope (b) | b − 1 (c) | Coeff. of determination (R²) | Standard error of estimate ($s_{X_t · X_{t-1}}$) |
|---|---|---|---|---|---|---|
| 1801–11 | 256 | 0.009 | 1.017 | 0.017 | 0.977 | 0.128 |
| 1811–21 | 308 | −0.047 | 1.028 | 0.028 | 0.980 | 0.127 |
| 1821–31 | 361 | −0.147 | 1.037 | 0.037 | 0.978 | 0.128 |
| 1831–41 | 412 | −0.159 | 1.035 | 0.035 | 0.970 | 0.160 |
| 1841–51 | 465 | −0.186 | 1.037 | 0.037 | 0.978 | 0.131 |
| 1851–61 | 521 | −0.086 | 1.024 | 0.024 | 0.968 | 0.166 |
| 1861–71 | 580 | 0.112 | 1.006 | 0.006 | 0.959 | 0.200 |
| 1871–81 | 691 | 0.049 | 1.013 | 0.013 | 0.967 | 0.183 |
| 1881–91 | 750 ´ | −0.012 | 1.015 | 0.015 | 0.975 | 0.166 |
| 1891–1901 | 834 | 0.065 | 1.008 | 0.008 | 0.974 | 0.166 |
| 1901–1911 | 885 | 0.148 | 0.998 | −0.002 | 0.978 | 0.159 |

Notes
1. All calculations are for $X_t = a + bX_{t-1} + \epsilon$, where $X_t$ is population at date $t$.
2. Values are for natural logarithms of town populations.

changes of the value of $c$. In the early decades it tends to increase in size, but in 1861–71 it falls markedly and stays at a low level until it actually falls to a negative value in the very last decade. If anything, therefore, the regression model of closing size on opening size suggests a weak positive relationship with the size of city for the early decades of the century, but that in the final quarter of the century and the first decade of the twentieth century this positive relationship was weaker and turned to a negative relationship in the decade immediately before the First World War. In all cases however, the relationship between size and growth rate is never strong.

The results of the regression approach might therefore suggest two conclusions. First that, at this aggregate level, the assumption that urban growth is a random proportion of existing population size does not appear to be unreasonable. Second that, since there is a marked disturbance term throughout and the variance of individual cities' growth rates is not compensated for by a negative $c$ term which would produce "regression to the mean," one would expect that the level of population concentration would have increased for all except possibly the final decade. The extent to which such growing concentration occurred during the nineteenth century is suggested in tables 4 and 5 which

show, for the whole period of 110 years, both the percentage of the total urban population which was contained in the top 10 per cent of the cities as well as the standard deviations of the whole array of cities. It is evident that both measures suggest similar conclusions; that the rate of concentration increased in the period up to 1861, but thereafter slowed down somewhat and that concentration decreased in the final part of the whole period.

We might try to draw together some of these apparently disparate forays on the body of data by developing the ideas inherent in the regression model. The results suggest that equation (2) provides a useful model by which to represent the growth of cities over successive dates. It argues that the population of a city at one date is some common proportion of its size at an earlier time irrespective of that size, but that there is a (log)normally-distributed fluctuation in the growth rates of individual cities which can be seen as a disturbance term common to the whole set of places. The empirical data which fit this model therefore provide, for nineteenth-century England and Wales, some support for the idea of a form of stochastic growth process which has been the underpinning of many of the theoretical models of city-size distributions. However, this is to ignore the generally positive value of the $c$ term which

Table 4. Concentration of the Urban Population: Percentage in the Largest Towns.

| Date | A<br>Total no. of towns<br>used in calculation | B<br>% of total urban population<br>in largest 10% of towns | C<br><br>Rate of change |
|------|------|------|------|
| 1801 | 250 | 61.63 | 1.006 |
| 1811 | 300 | 62.02 | 1.013 |
| 1821 | 360 | 62.81 | 1.024 |
| 1831 | 410 | 64.31 | 1.020 |
| 1841 | 460 | 65.57 | 1.020 |
| 1851 | 520 | 66.88 | 1.017 |
| 1861 | 580 | 68.02 | 0.994 |
| 1871 | 690 | 67.58 | 1.015 |
| 1881 | 740 | 68.37 | 1.012 |
| 1891 | 830 | 69.18 | 1.000 |
| 1901 | 880 | 69.18 | 0.987 |
| 1911 | 920 | 68.28 | |

*Note:* Column C gives the ratio of the percentages (column B) at time $t$ to those at time $t + 1$.

suggests that there is a deviation away from constant growth to one with a slightly positive relationship with the previous size of a city. This, and the variation in individual growth rates which is given by the $\epsilon$ term, suggest that the particular growth process operating in the nineteenth century would not lead to a stationary size distribution of cities, but rather one characterized by increasing concentration of population. Ideally, it would be of some interest to calculate the value of the $c$ term which, for a given value of $\epsilon$, would produce a distribution which would become neither more nor less concentrated over time. We know that a positive $c$ term will lead to greater concentration, but how large a negative term would be needed to halt the progress of concentration? The calculation of such a value

Table 5. Concentration of the Urban Population: Dispersion of Sizes.

| Set of towns | No. | Starting year | | | Closing year | | |
|------|------|------|------|------|------|------|------|
| | | Mean ($\bar{X}$) | Standard deviation(s) | Coefficient of variation (V) | Coefficient of variation (V) | Standard deviation(s) | Mean ($\bar{X}$) |
| 1801–11 | 256 | 8.608 | 0.801 | 9.308 | 9.408 | 0.824 | 8.763 |
| 1811–21 | 308 | 8.623 | 0.813 | 9.434 | 9.583 | 0.845 | 8.819 |
| 1821–31 | 361 | 8.694 | 0.840 | 9.665 | 9.935 | 0.881 | 8.872 |
| 1831–41 | 412 | 8.768 | 0.878 | 10.012 | 10.345 | 0.922 | 8.915 |
| 1841–51 | 465 | 8.816 | 0.915 | 10.373 | 10.708 | 0.959 | 8.957 |
| 1851–61 | 521 | 8.886 | 0.947 | 10.661 | 10.939 | 0.986 | 9.011 |
| 1861–71 | 580 | 8.923 | 0.976 | 10.939 | 11.030 | 1.002 | 9.086 |
| 1871–81 | 691 | 8.977 | 0.979 | 10.903 | 11.027 | 1.008 | 9.141 |
| 1881–91 | 750 | 9.061 | 1.014 | 11.187 | 11.342 | 1.042 | 9.188 |
| 1891–1901 | 834 | 9.096 | 1.037 | 11.398 | 11.468 | 1.059 | 9.236 |
| 1901–1911 | 885 | 9.170 | 1.065 | 11.610 | 11.553 | 1.074 | 9.299 |

Notes
1. Each set of towns is comprised of those which had populations $\geqslant 2,500$ at both the start and close of the decade shown.
2. Values are for natural logarithms of town populations.

Table 6. The Rate of Addition of New Towns.

| Decade | A Total no. of towns at start of decade | B No. of new towns at end of decade | C B as % of A |
|---|---|---|---|
| 1801–11 | 256 | 53 | 20.70 |
| 1811–21 | 308 | 53 | 17.21 |
| 1821–31 | 361 | 51 | 14.13 |
| 1831–41 | 412 | 54 | 13.11 |
| 1841–51 | 465 | 57 | 12.26 |
| 1851–61 | 521 | 63 | 12.09 |
| 1861–71 | 580 | 113 | 19.48 |
| 1871–81 | 691 | 59 | 8.54 |
| 1881–91 | 750 | 86 | 11.47 |
| 1891–1901 | 834 | 59 | 7.07 |
| 1901–1911 | 885 | 42 | 4.75 |

would be very easy were one dealing with a constant set of cities, but the fact that the set of places is increasing in number complicates its calculation unduly. Here is one of the further difficulties encountered in dealing both with the "birth" of new places and the "death" of declining places. It will be recalled that the second of Simon's assumptions about growth was that new places (or, in his case, new words) were added at a constant rate and that it was this rate which determined the closeness of the convergence parameter of $b$ to a value of 1.0 in the growth formula noted earlier.[15] The rate of addition of new places in nineteenth-century England and Wales, however, was far from constant. Table 6 shows the "births" of towns as a percentage of the total number of cities at the start of each decade and shows that this percentage declined from a "high" of over 20 down to almost 12 in 1851–61, then rose markedly almost to 20 once again in 1861–71, but thereafter fell drastically to figures of less than 10 in all but one of the following decades and ended with a "low" of under 5 in 1901–11. Such varying rates of addition to the set of places complicates our assessment of Galton's constant—the value of $c$ which would be required to maintain a stable distribution. For decades when the rate of entry of new places is high (assuming, as is the case, that the

majority of "births" was in the small size groups), the effect will be to increase the rate of concentration of population, whether measured in terms of the percentage of population found in the largest 10 per cent of the cities or in terms of dispersion. The opposite will apply when "births" are low so that the markedly lower ratio of "births" in the last quarter of the period would have the effect of increasing the concentration to a lesser extent so that the declining rates of concentration in that period must be seen as the product both of the falling value of $c$ and of the falling ratio of "births."[16]

There are therefore three types of function which influence the extent to which a size curve will be stable or will show increasing concentration over time. Where the variance of the growth rates, $\epsilon$, is high, concentration will proceed more rapidly; this concentration will be countered or exacerbated depending on the value of $c$—only where $c$ is of a "sufficiently" large negative value will concentration tend to be reversed; but in addition the rate of entry of new small towns has to be considered since it will tend to distend the tail of the lower end of the size distribution and it will do this to a greater extent when the rate is

15. See original text, p. 32.

16. Fuguitt (1965) draws a parallel conclusion in suggesting that much of the apparent decline of very small communities in the United States is more a product of the declining rate of incorporation of new small places than of the actual decline of existing small places.

high than when it is low, with the consequent effect of increasing the speed of concentration.

## Growth Rates

So that the individual growth rates of towns can be more readily comprehended, the actual populations, rather than the natural logarithms of populations, will be used here. Further, in estimating the actual growth rates of individual towns, a slightly more complex measure of growth has been used than is normally the case. In the overwhelming majority of the work which has studied growth rates, a simple rate of population increase has been calculated for each decade, given by the formula:

$$G_{t-1,t} = (P_t - P_{t-1}).P_{t-1}^{-1}. \qquad (3)$$

where $G_{t-1,t}$ is the growth rate between the times $t - 1$ and $t$; and $P$ is population. A more realistic estimate of the rate of growth and one which, as Gibbs (1961, p. 108) suggests, is a close approximation to a compound growth rate, is given by expressing the denominator of the equation not as the initial population of a place at $t - 1$, but as the mid-point population between the opening and closing dates. The calculation of growth is then given by the following:

$$G_{t-1,t} = (P_t - P_{t-1}). \left( \frac{P_t + P_{t-1}}{2} \right)^{-1} \qquad (4)$$

The use of this estimate of growth rates would seem to have two advantages. First, it is a more accurate assessment of growth since population change is a continuous not a discrete phenomenon and the estimated midpoint population is a closer approximation to the changing base from which increments to or decrements from the population occur during the course of a decade. Second, its use has the effect of altering the distribution of growth rates in such a way as to help counter the tendency of simple growth rates to be positively skewed.[17] This tendency has been widely noted (Madden 1956a; Lampard 1968, p. 128), but the fact that studies have produced sets of growth rates which have a long tail of very high values is partly the result of using simple rather than compound measures of growth. By comparison with a simple rate, equation (4) tends to compress the high positive growth rates and expand the negative rates. For example, a town which increased in population from 10,000 to 15,000 over the space of a decade would be considered, by using the simple growth rate of equation (3), to have a growth rate of 50 per cent; if it were to decrease in population to a figure of 5,000, it would be given a growth rate of −50 per cent. However, by using equation (4) which would involve denominators of 12,500 and 7,500 for the case of growth and decline respectively, its growth rates would be considered as 40 per cent in the case of expansion and −111 per cent in the case of decline. The tendency for positive skew in the distribution of growth rates is therefore counteracted to some extent by the use of this second estimate of growth and the assumption of normality which underlies parametric statistical tests will be more likely to hold true. The growth rates used in the following analysis are therefore all based on the somewhat modified form of equation (4) which approximates the compound rather than the simple growth-rate formula.

Growth rates for each town were calculated during each pair of successive census dates in which the town had a known population of over 2,500. The numbers of observations at each intercensal period are therefore comparable with the numbers used in the regression study: for the first decade there are 256 observations; for the final decade there are 885. The scatters of observations for three of the eleven decades are shown in fig. 2, which plots the growth rate against the population size of places on semi-logarithmic scales.

---

17. It was partly to correct the different and much more extreme skew of town sizes that natural logarithms of population size were used in the regression analysis above.

On casual inspection of these diagrams, the first clear impression is of the increasing number of observations during the whole period; the galaxies of dots become much denser in the later decades are more and more towns are "born" into the population. Second, if one squints sufficiently hard, discernible patterns can be seen. It is clearly true, as the earlier regression analysis suggested, that growth and size are virtually unrelated. If one visualizes lines representing the average growth rates across the whole span of city sizes during each decade, then the lines would be roughly horizontal, suggesting that the whole set of places can be characterized as having a common growth rate around which disturbance occurs. If these lines are horizontal, then their vertical shifts upwards and downwards from one decade to another represent differences in the overall growth rate during the different decades.[18] A third comment on the diagrams, however, must be that it is quite apparent that the scatter of observations around the imaginary average growth lines is not constant with increasing size of town. The disturbance appears to grow distinctly less as one moves from smaller to larger towns.

These latter two points are obviously of some importance in relation to our ideas about the overall growth rates of sets of cities and deserve a more detailed examination than the

18. The relationship between these scatters of growth rates on the one hand and the earlier regression analysis of equation (2) on the other is quite apparent. A horizontal line of average growth rates corresponds to a slope coefficient of $b = 1.0$ in the regression of closing on opening population sizes. The scatter around the line of growth rates equals the disturbance term, $\epsilon$.

Figure 2. Selected growth rates and town size in England and Wales, 1801-11; 1851-61; 1901-11. Note: A small number of places in the lower size ranges have growth rates greater than 70 per cent and are not shown in the scatter diagrams. The numbers involved, for all decades, are as follows: 1801-11, 1; 1811-21, 3; 1821-31, 3; 1831-41, 3; 1841-51, 3; 1851-61, 9; 1861-71, 13; 1871-81, 10; 1881-91, 6; 1891-1901, 11; 1901-11, 9.

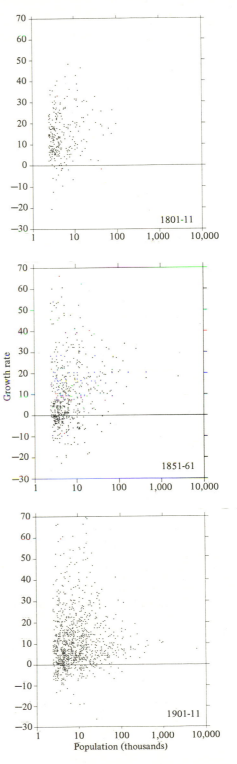

simple inspection of scatter diagrams. They are of importance because of their bearing on the stochastic growth models which have been widely assumed to apply to urban growth. Gibrat's law—or the law of proportionate effect—would state, as has been seen, that growth would be a common proportion of existing size and, as a strict and necessary version of the law, that the error term around this proportionate growth would be normally distributed. We therefore need to test whether or not these two properties are met in the empirical data of nineteenth-century growth in England and Wales.

One way in which this might be approached is, again, to use a regression model and table 7 gives the results of simple regressions of the following form:

$$G_{i.d} = a + b \log P_{i.t} + \epsilon; \qquad (5)$$

where $G$ and $P$ are respectively the growth rate and population of town $i$ during the decade $d$ which starts at time $t$.[19] The standard errors of these regressions formulations are, of course, very large, reflecting the expectedly low amount of explanation provided by the regression since the regression lines are virtually horizontal. Apart from the somewhat unreliable fact that the slopes of the relationship between size and growth rate are positive for all but the final decade, the regression approach is of little analytic value.

A more profitable approach is to test the means and variances of growth rates for subgroups of town sizes. Again, the size categories of 2,500–4,999, 5,000–9,999, and so forth, in which each group is twice that of the lower group, have been used. The values of the means and standard deviations for each of these size groups in each decade are given in table 8. The results are plotted in fig. 3 in which the means of each size group are joined by thick lines and thinner lines are drawn above and below them at one standard deviation from the means. These diagrams, and the

19. Equation (5) differs from the earlier regression equations of (1) and (2) in that it uses growth rate rather than closing population size as the dependent variable.

Table 7. Regression of Growth Rates on Town Size

| Decade | Intercept (a) | Slope (b) | Standard error of estimate ($^s$G.P) |
|---|---|---|---|
| 1801–11 | 0.71 | 3.94 | 12.11 |
| 1811–21 | −4.63 | 6.43 | 11.67 |
| 1821–31 | −14.63 | 8.53 | 12.59 |
| 1831–41 | −15.80 | 7.97 | 15.49 |
| 1841–51 | −18.59 | 8.49 | 13.81 |
| 1851–61 | −8.31 | 5.35 | 17.09 |
| 1861–71 | 10.26 | 1.47 | 18.98 |
| 1871–81 | 4.28 | 3.06 | 17.58 |
| 1881–91 | −1.83 | 3.67 | 15.91 |
| 1891–1901 | 7.25 | 1.72 | 16.45 |
| 1901–1911 | 14.95 | −0.54 | 15.52 |

*Notes:* Values are for the equation $G_{i.d} = a + b \log p_{i.t} + \epsilon$, where $G_{i.d}$ is the growth rate of town $i$ during decade $d$; and $P_{i.t}$ is the population of town $i$ at the start of the decade.

data of table 8 on which they are based, are simplified descriptions of the galaxies of points showing the growth rates of each individual town.

In testing the two properties of Gibrat's law, the evidence on the relationship of variance and population size is unambiguous. In virtually every case, the standard deviations and the coefficients of variation grow progressively smaller for the larger size groups. While the progression is not necessarily smooth, there is a tendency throughout for there to be a gradual fall in the size of the variance with successively larger city-size groups. The assumption of uniformly-distributed error around the line of proportionate growth is clearly not met.

On the second Gibrat property—the invariance of the means of different size groups—the conclusion is less immediately apparent. The regression analyses have both suggested slight positive relationships between growth and size. Here, with more disaggregated material, we can use more discriminating tests of whether this is or is not significant. In making comparisons between the mean growth rates of the different size groups allowance has to be made for the fact that the size groups have different variances as well as different num-

Table 8. Selected Means and Dispersions of Growth Rates of Towns in Different Size Groups.

| Period | | 2,500– | 5,000– | 10,000– | 20,000– | 40,000– | 80,000– | 160,000– | 320,000– |
|---|---|---|---|---|---|---|---|---|---|
| 1801–11 | $N$ | 160 | 47 | 32 | 7 | 10 | | | |
| | $\bar{X}$ | 14.5 | 14.3 | 20.7 | 18.6 | 17.5 | | | |
| | $s$ | 12.3 | 12.1 | 11.6 | 11.6 | 7.4 | | | |
| | $V\%$ | 85.0 | 84.9 | 55.8 | 62.5 | 42.2 | | | |
| 1821–31 | $N$ | 200 | 89 | 38 | 20 | 9 | 5 | | |
| | $\bar{X}$ | 15.3 | 17.9 | 20.0 | 27.8 | 24.6 | 29.6 | | |
| | $s$ | 12.0 | 13.6 | 13.1 | 12.4 | 10.5 | 7.5 | | |
| | $V\%$ | 78.6 | 75.9 | 65.5 | 44.5 | 42.7 | 25.5 | | |
| 1851–61 | $N$ | 231 | 135 | 85 | 31 | 23 | 8 | 5 | |
| | $\bar{X}$ | 10.3 | 11.6 | 15.6 | 14.8 | 16.2 | 20.6 | 21.8 | |
| | $s$ | 16.9 | 17.3 | 20.5 | 12.8 | 9.8 | 8.5 | 5.1 | |
| | $V\%$ | 163.6 | 148.9 | 131.5 | 86.4 | 60.6 | 41.1 | 23.5 | |
| 1881–91 | $N$ | 268 | 215 | 135 | 65 | 37 | 17 | 7 | 4 |
| | $\bar{X}$ | 11.0 | 11.9 | 14.2 | 14.6 | 16.5 | 17.3 | 16.6 | 13.3 |
| | $s$ | 17.8 | 15.6 | 15.9 | 13.8 | 10.4 | 8.5 | 4.4 | 3.7 |
| | $V\%$ | 161.3 | 131.3 | 112.0 | 94.8 | 62.9 | 49.0 | 26.2 | 28.1 |
| 1901–1911 | $N$ | 287 | 225 | 190 | 89 | 49 | 23 | 11 | 8 |
| | $\bar{X}$ | 12.4 | 12.9 | 14.5 | 13.1 | 10.0 | 10.5 | 9.4 | 8.6 |
| | $s$ | 18.5 | 13.6 | 15.8 | 14.5 | 8.5 | 8.2 | 4.6 | 2.6 |
| | $V\%$ | 149.1 | 105.4 | 108.8 | 111.1 | 85.2 | 77.8 | 49.3 | 29.9 |

Size group ('000s)

*Notes:* For each size group, observations are as follows: $N$ = number of towns, $\bar{X}$ = mean growth rate, $s$ = standard deviation of growth rates, $V\%$ = coefficient of variation (%) of growth rates.

bers of observations, and that the standard tests comparing means are consequently ruled out. However, an appropriate test which does take account of the different variances and numbers of the observations is that suggested by Aspin and Welch (1949; for its application to business firms, see Singh and Whittington 1968, pp. 75–80). Taking the 2.5 per cent confidence level, for example, it can be seen that, in the decade 1801–11, out of a possible total of ten comparisons between the means of size groups, only two are significantly different. In all of the eleven decades there is a total of 230 such comparisons in which no fewer than 58 shows that one mean is significantly higher than another at the 2.5 per cent confidence level.[20] There is a marked pattern in the distribution of these significant differences from one decade to another. The earlier decades show a much larger number of

20. The exact pattern of significant differences would, of course, depend upon the particular size groupings whose means are chosen for comparison, but the overall tendency in these sets of sizes over the eleven decades is relatively clear.

significant differences than do the later decades and in all cases the pattern of differences is one of higher mean growth rates being found in the larger city sizes. In the later decades, there are relatively few such significant differences and in the very final decade a completely different pattern emerges with larger cities tending to have significantly *lower* average growth rates than smaller cities. This changing pattern is clearly seen in fig. 3 in which differences between means which are significant at the 1.0 per cent level are shown by sets of arrows for selected decades.

This is a most interesting finding and one whose implications need to be spelled out both in terms of the theoretical notions of urban growth and in terms of the nature of the facts of the growth of towns in England and Wales in the nineteenth century.

First, in terms of Gibrat's law of proportionate effect, both the decreasing variance of growth rates with size and this relationship between average growth rate and population

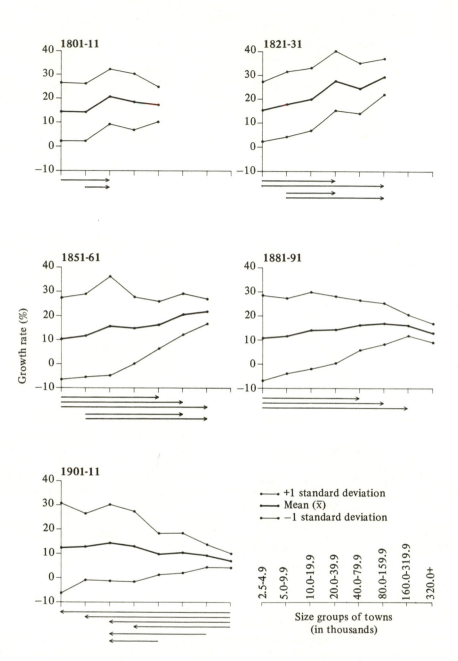

Figure 3. Growth rates and town size: selected means and dispersions. The diagrams summarize the data shown in Figure 2. Arrows below each plot show those size groups with mean growth rates significantly different at the 1.0 per cent confidence level, the arrow head points to that size group with the *higher* mean.

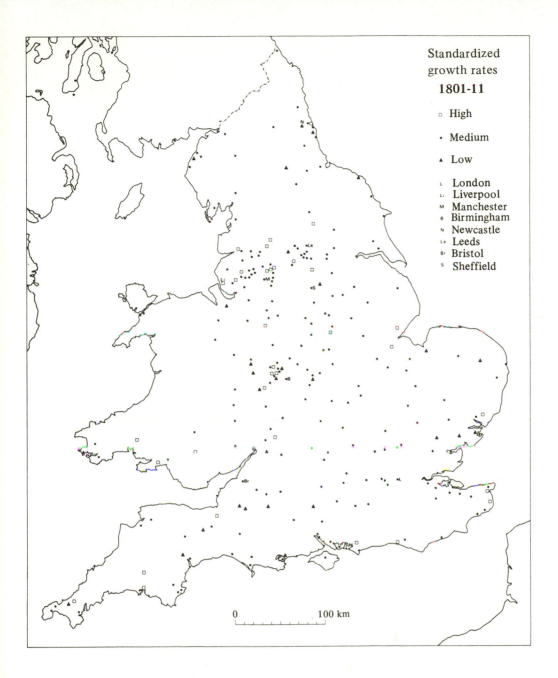

Figure 4(a). The spatial pattern of urban growth in England and Wales, 1801-11. Standardized growth rates are as follows: high = ≥ 1 standard deviation above the mean for the appropriate size group; low = ≤ 1 standard deviation below the mean for the appropriate size group; medium = between ± 1 standard deviation from the mean of the appropriate size group. Details of means and standard deviations for each size group are given in Table 8.

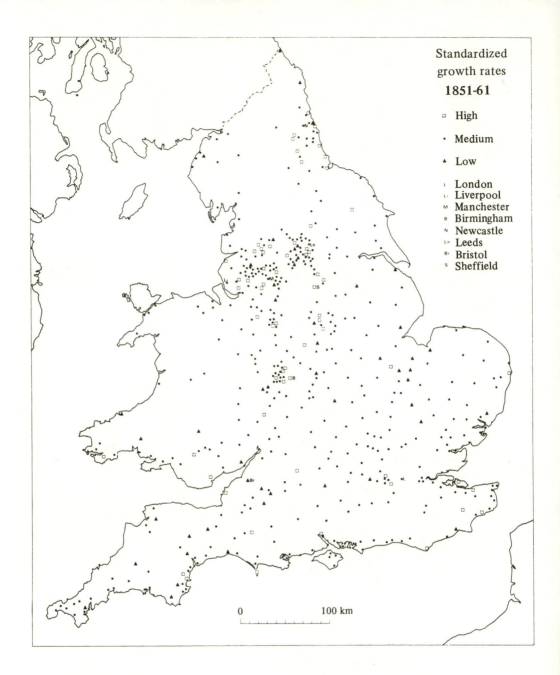

0          100 km

Figure 4(b). The spatial pattern of urban growth in England and Wales, 1851-61. For explanation, see Figure 4(a).

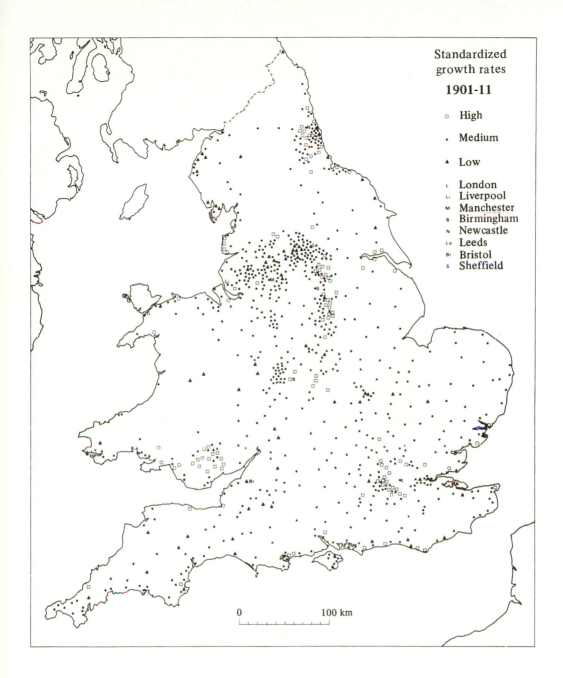

Figure 4(c). The spatial pattern of urban growth in England and Wales, 1901-11. For explanation, see Figure 4(a).

size suggest that neither property of Gibrat's law are met.[21] During all the decades, variance decreases with city size and in only some of the later decades are the mean rates of growth of larger size groups not significantly higher than smaller sizes. This finding adds considerable weight to our earlier observation that the regression of growth on size tended to be positive. Now that the suggestion of the regression analysis is complemented by the more rigorous finding of significantly higher growth in larger city-size groups, it can be said that a uniform urban growth rate cannot be proven for most of the decades of nineteenth-century England and Wales. Were our tests of stability in the didstribution of city sizes sufficiently powerful, the effects of this unequal growth could be demonstrated. The effect of higher average growth rates in larger towns would be to steepen the slope of plots of size against rank at successive decades as urban concentration progressed. If the average rate of growth grew progressively greater for larger towns, this would not necessarily have the effect of destroying an existing logarithmic-linear plot between rank and size, but it would certainly alter the overall shape of the distribution. In terms of an expectation that city sizes are distributed as the right-hand tail of a lognormal distribution, it would mean that the tail would become increasingly elongated as the degree of concentration of the population progressed. However, our second finding—that the variance of growth declines with city size—would tend to have a retarding

effect upon this rate of concentration. To expand this point, one need only think back to the earlier discussion about the effect of the disturbance term in the regression formulae of equations (1) and (2). The greater this term— the greater, that is, the variance in growth rates—the quicker will be the increase in concentration, assuming that the slope of the regression is held constant. In the regression model it was assumed that the disturbance term was both (log)normally distributed and was homoscedastic—in other words, that the variance was equal irrespective of size group. Since the disaggregated empirical data show that the variance is distinctly heteroscedastic and that it is the larger places which have smaller variance in their growth rates, the size of the disturbance term is lower for larger size groups and they will therefore tend to spread out in size less rapidly than will smaller places so that the overall rate of concentration of population will be less than would be suggested by the overall variance of the total set of places.[22] If this finding were to be fed back into the regression formulae to produce a model which might characterize the level of population concentration and the future sizes of sets of towns, the regression formulation would need to have added to it a vector of correcting factors given by the declining variances of larger groups of towns or it would need to be further partitioned into sets of equations of the following sort:

$$X_{t.s} = a + (1 + c) \cdot X_{t-1.s} + \epsilon_s; \quad (6)$$

where the subscript $s$ is a size group of cities and the $\epsilon_s$ term would become smaller for increasing values of $s$. Obviously this is a far less attractive form of growth model since it is less general than equation (2) and because, without calibrating it for particular sets of data, it is impossible to use it to generate expected plots of future city-size distributions.

A more general suggestion from our find-

21. No comparable formal tests of the applicability of both of the Gibrat properties to urban growth have been discovered. Thompson (1965b) has looked at the relationship of size and variance in his study of the growth rates of Standard Metropolitan Statistical Areas in the United States in the decade 1950–60 and finds the same pattern of declining variance amongst larger cities. His suggestion (Thompson 1965a, p. 22) on the relationship of growth and size is that, above a certain size of city, no cities decline in size and that there is a common growth rate. This he likens to an "urban ratchett": "at a certain range of urban scale, set by the degree of isolation of the urban place, the nature of its hinterland, the level of industrial development in the country, and various cultural factors, some growth mechanism, similar to a ratchett, comes into being, locking in past growth and preventing contraction." The reasons adduced for this ratchett-effect are the diversification of industry, the existence of political power, the huge fixed investments, the rich local market and the steady supply of industrial leadership and innovativeness which characterize large urban economies.

22. This would mean that any attempt at calculating the value of Galton's $c$ at which concentration would not occur would be even more complex than suggested above.

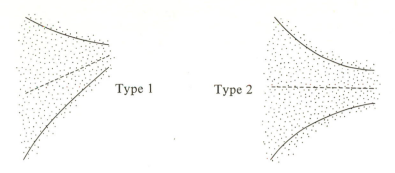

Figure 5. Two ideal types of growth in a set of towns.

ings, however, would be that there is great value in the more empirical historical study of sets of towns as against the more general theoretical growth models which draw on micro-economics and the behaviour of the firm. Lampard (1968, p. 95) suggests that there is a need "for a distinctive *developmental* perspective on the evolution of city-regions, a perspective that allows for greater disaggregation and, at the same time, yields generalizations of a somewhat lower order than those of formal theory"; and even the economist Thompson (1965a, p. 60) says, "It may be that a rigorous synthesis of many . . . case studies is needed to unlock the secrets of the urban growth process: the economic historian may have fully as much to contribute to urban growth theory as either the economic theorist or the econometrician." It is this view which has buttressed the present concern with a more historical and a less formal systems' approach to the study of urban growth.

## Two Questions

Two interesting puzzles are posed by our findings on the empirical data of nineteenth-century urban growth. The pattern of urban growth which is outlined by the analysis of the scatter of means and variances calls first for the development of ideas about how urban growth in a set of cities produces a pattern of declining variance with increasing city size and what factors might determine the varying slope of the relationship between growth rate and size. Second, since the relationship between growth rate and size appears to have changed during the course of the nineteenth century, how can this change be explained? There appear to be two types of pattern: on the one hand there is a scatter of urban growth in which average growth is positively related to city size; and on the other, a pattern in which growth and size are virtually unrelated so that the curve of average growth is not significantly different from horizontal.[23] In both cases the variance declines regularly about the average at larger city sizes. These two patterns are crudely represented in fig. 5. Can one specify the decade at which the change from the first to the second of these patterns occurred? Table 9 shows the percentages of the total number of observations in each decade in which the average growth rate was significantly different. It is clear, both from this and from the actual values of the means in table 8, that the proportion of significantly higher average growth rates is considerably lower in the decades after 1861 than in those before. The pattern of the first two decades is somewhat ambiguous, reflecting perhaps the greater imperfections in the census material, but they would both nevertheless appear to be closer to the first than the second of our ideal

23. These are, of course, idealized types. They ignore the pattern of the final decade in which the relationship is negative. Clearly, during the final quarter of the nineteenth century the once strongly positive relationship grew progressively less so until, by the final decade it had become negative.

Table 9. Percentage of Comparisons between Size Groups in Which Larger Towns have Mean Growth Rates Significantly Higher than Smaller Towns

|          | Level of significance | |
| -------- | --------------------- | --------- |
| Decade   | 1.0%                  | 5.0%      |
| 1801–11  | 20.0                  | 20.0      |
| 1811–21  | 6.7                   | 46.7      |
| 1821–31  | 26.7                  | 53.3      |
| 1831–41  | 20.0                  | 46.7      |
| 1841–51  | 38.1                  | 61.9      |
| 1851–61  | 23.8                  | 52.4      |
| 1861–71  | 14.3                  | 19.0      |
| 1871–81  | 7.1                   | 17.9      |
| 1881–91  | 10.7                  | 28.6      |
| 1891–1901| 0.0                   | 10.7      |
| 1901–1911| 21.4                  | 39.3      |

*Notes*
1. Calculated from Aspin-Welch tests.
2. For the final decade, 1901–11, the values show the percentage of comparisons in which large towns have significantly *lower* mean growth rates.

types. The third, fifth, and sixth decades however conform very closely to our first ideal pattern in which growth is positively related to size; the fourth decade is less clear. The decades from the seventh onwards—that is, from 1861–71—tend to grow increasingly close to the second pattern in which size and growth are virtually unrelated and this is especially clear in the decade 1891–1901. By 1901–11, the pattern has become the reverse of our first type with growth being lower for larger city sizes.

## REFERENCES

Allen, G. R. (1954) The 'courbes des populations': a further analysis, *Bull. Oxf. Univ. Inst. Statist.* 16, 179–89.

Aspin, A. C. and Welch, B. L. (1949) Tables for use in comparisons whose accuracy involves two variances, separately estimated, *Biometrika* 36, 290–6.

Banks, J. A. (1968) Population change and the Victorian city, *Victorian Stud.* 11, 277–89.

Carter, H. (1972) *The study of urban geography* (London).

Friedlander, D. (1970) The spread of urbanization in England and Wales, 1851–1951, *Popul. Stud.* 24, 423–43.

Fuguitt, G. W. (1965) The growth and decline of small towns as a probability process, *Am. Sociol. Rev.* 30, 403–11.

Gibbs, J. P. (ed) (1961) *Urban research methods* (New Jersey).

Gibrat, R. (1931) *Les Inégalités économiques* (Paris).

Hirschman, A. O. (1958) *The strategy of economic development* (New Haven, Conn.).

Kalecki, M. (1945) On the Gibrat distribution, *Econometrica* 13, 161–70.

Kemeney, J. G. and Snell, J. L. (1960) *Finite Markov chains* (Princeton, NJ).

Lampard, E. E. (1968) The evolving system of cities in the United States: urbanization and economic development, in Perloff, H. S. and Wingo, L. (eds), *Issues in urban economics* (Baltimore), pp. 81–139.

Law, C. M. (1967) The growth of urban population in England and Wales, 1801–1911, *Trans. Inst. Br. Geogr.* 41, 125–43.

Lopes, A. S. (1972) The economic functions of small towns and rural centres, *Unpublished Ph.D. Dissertation,* Univ. of Oxford.

McElrath, D. C. (1968) Societal scale and social differentiation: Accra, Ghana, in Greer, S. *et al.* (eds), *The new urbanization* (New York), pp. 33–52.

Madden, C. H. (1956a) On some indicators of stability in the growth of cities in the United States, *Econ. Dev. Cult. Change* 4, 236–52.

Madden, C. H. (1956b) Some spatial aspects of urban growth in the United States, *Econ. Dev. Cult, Change* 4, 371–87.

Madden, C. H. (1958) Some temporal aspects of the growth of cities in the United States, *Econ. Dev. Cult. Change* 6, 143–69.

Mitchell, B. R. (1962) *Abstract of British historical statistics* (Cambridge).

Myrdal, G. M. (1957) *Economic theory and under-developed regions* (London).

Prais, S. J. and Hart, P. E. (1956) The analysis of business concentration: a statistical approach, *Jl. R. Statist. Soc., Ser. A.* 119, 150–75.

Price-Williams, R. (1880) On the increase of population in England and Wales, *Jl. R. Statist. Soc.* 43, 462–96.

Shevky, E. and Bell, W. (1955) *Social area analysis: illustrative application and computational procedure* (Stanford, Calif.).

Simon, H. A. (1955) On a class of skew distribution functions, *Biometrika* 42, 425–40.

Singer, H. W. (1936) Courbes des populations: a parallel to Pareto's law, *Econ. J.* 46, 254–63.

Singh, A. and Whittington, G. (1968) Growth, profitability and valuation, *Occasional Pap.* No. 7, Dept. of Applied Econ., Univ. of Cambridge.

Thomas, E. N. (1967) Additional comments on population size relationships for sets of cities, in Garrison, W. L. and Marble, D. F. (eds), "Quantitative geography, Part I: economic and cultural topics," *N. West Univ. Stud. Geogr.* No. 13, 167–90.

Thompson, W. R. (1965a) *A preface to urban economics* (Baltimore).

Thompson, W. R. (1965b) The future of the Detroit Metropolitan Area, in Haber, W. (ed.), *Michigan in the 1970s: an economic forecast* (Ann Arbor, Mich.).

Udry, J. R. (1964) Increasing scale and spatial differentiation: new test of two theories from Shevky and Bell, *Social Forces* 42, 403–13.

Vince, S.W.E. (1955) The rural population of England and Wales, 1801–1951, *Unpublished Ph.D. Dissertation,* Univ. of London.

Weber, A. F. (1899) *The growth of cities in the nineteenth century: a study in statistics* (New York) (republished, Ithaca, NY, 1967).

Welton, T. A. (1900) The growth of population in England and Wales and its progress in the period of ninety years from 1801–91, *Jl. R. Statist. Soc.* 63, 527–89.

Williamson, J. G. (1965a) Regional inequality and the process of national development: a description of the patterns, *Econ. Dev. Cult. Change* 13, 3–45.

Williamson, J. G. (1965b) Antebellum urbanization in the American northeast, *J. Econ. Hist.* 25, 592–608.

Williamson, J. G. and Swanson, J. A. (1966) The growth of cities in the American north east, 1820–1870, *Explor. Entrepreneurial Hist.* 4, 44–67.

# The City as an Element in the International System

KENNETH E. BOULDING

An international system may be defined as a set of social organizations or organized groups of people whose relations are governed mainly by threat and the perception of threat. Defined this broadly, the international system goes back a long way in human experience, and the primitive international systems of the paleolithic era may seem to have little resemblance to the complex international system of today. Nevertheless, in social evolution something like an international system has nearly always been present and can be thought of as a segment of the total ecological system of mankind that is at least moderately recognizable and has something of an evolutionary pattern of its own.

In spite of the observation that even very primitive peoples have organized groups, the relations among which are governed by some kind of threat system, a case can be made for the proposition that the international system as we would recognize it today emerges only with the development of cities and civilization—civilization, of course, being what goes on in cities. The threat relations among paleolithic people seem to be sporadic and very casual. In any case, before the invention of agriculture man was too near the margin of subsistence in most places to have any surplus left over, either for more elaborate organization or for organized fighting.

The domestication of plants and animals seems to have led at first to a degree of relative affluence in which productive activity paid off better than predatory, and hence the threat system seems to have been fairly well muted. A great many neolithic villages seem to have been undefended.

As long as population was sparse in relation to agricultural land, this idyllic Garden of Eden could persist. The rise of cities may well have been associated with population pressure that made simple expansion of the old way of life impossible. The first cities seem to have been created by internal threat systems. In the early days, this appears to have been mainly a spiritual threat. A charismatic priesthood somehow persuades the farmer to hand over some of his surplus food, and with this food the priests, the artisans, and the builders of temples, houses, and walls are fed, but not much comes back to the farmer.

The simplest model both of the city-state and of the international system would suppose each city to have a small agricultural hinterland around it, from which the surplus of food flows into the city and which receives from the city primarily spiritual goods or threats. At this stage at any rate, the city would have little in the way of products to export. The spiritual threat of the priest is usually succeeded by the more material threat of the king who uses the food that he extracts from the farmers to feed soldiers who can extract the surplus that feeds them by material threat. An international system develops out of this because of the fundamental principle that threat capability and credibility diminish with dis-

Reprinted by permission of *Daedalus*, Journal of the American Academy of Arts and Sciences, Boston, Mass. Fall 1968, *The Conscience of the City*.

tance from the origin of the threat, since threat capability has a cost of transport. Consequently at a certain distance from the king or the city, its threat capability and credibility decline to the point where they can no longer control behavior. At this point, there is an opportunity for another king or city. Once the second city is established there comes to be a boundary of equal strength between the two cities, and we have an international system.

A model as simple as this, of course, could never have described a real situation, even in the earliest times. The system is always more complex than we have indicated. Even in the neolithic era, for instance, there seems to have been extensive trade covering thousands of miles. The development of metallurgy meant a quite early development, at least of specialized villages that exported metals in return for food. The development of pottery, jewelry, weaving, and crafts producing transportable articles led to the development of organized trade; and trading cities, such as Tyre, had economic structures very different from the simple exploitative city and also played a very different role in the international system. The threat capability of a trading city, for instance, may be used not so much simply for the extraction of commodities from unwilling producers, as for the monopolization of trade opportunities, as in the case of Venice.

The next stage of development of the city and the international system is empire, which begins when one city conquers another without destroying it. A system of city-states is only stable if what I have called the "loss of strength gradient"—that is, the decline in threat capability and (or credibility)[1] per mile of distance traveled away from its origin—is very high. Thus, for the system of city-states

to be stable, the threat capability of the city must be exhausted once it has covered an area that is capable of feeding the city from its food surplus. One city, then, cannot conquer another, for as it expands its threats beyond its own territory, it becomes too weak, and the other city becomes too strong.

The cost of transport of threat capability however, for instance in the shape of organized armies, soon fell below the critical limit that would permit the city-state to be stable. This happened first along the great river valleys simply because water transportation of anything, including threats, is very cheap. It is not surprising, therefore, that we get empires along the Nile, along the Tigris and the Euphrates, along the Indus, and along the Hoang-Ho. One of the puzzling questions of human history, incidentally, is why the pattern in America was so different, where the great river valleys like the Mississippi did not produce any early civilizations, but the wild mountains of Mexico and Peru did. The answer may be that a river had to flow through at least a semi-arid region in order to support an empire due to the extraordinary difficulties of transportation through forests. Certainly the desert plays something of the role of the sea in transportation. Just as the Roman Empire was the product of the Mediterranean and of sea transport, so the empires of the nomads of Central Asia were a product of relatively unobstructed land transportation in semi-arid regions. Forests grow faster than man, with primitive tools, can cut them down. He can only conquer the forested regions once the techniques of clearing have gone beyond a certain point. Even the arid lands cannot support an empire without something like a horse, which is probably why the incipient city-states of the Southwest Pueblos in the United States never developed into empires, having neither navigable rivers nor horses.

In the empire, there is a sharp distinction between the capital city and the provincial cities. The capital city is more purely exploitative, though the empire as a system usually involves the collection of surplus food by the provincial cities, some of which is retained and some of which is passed on to the

1. It is the credibility of the threat which really matters from the point of view of its ability to organize social systems. Credibility in very complex ways is related to capability. The relationship is closer in the case of material threat than in the case of spiritual threat where capability is hard to demonstrate, but where the threat often justifies itself: for example, the fear of Hell. Even in the case of material threat, credibility can remain long after capability has disappeared. Nevertheless, in the long run there must be a tendency for capability and credibility at least to run parallel.

capital city. There is probably more incentive, however, for the provincial cities to become producers of specialized manufactures and to begin to exchange these with food producers for food. Here the exchange system slowly develops and spreads as an alternative to the threat system. Finally, with the advent of the so-called Industrial Revolution and the rise of science-based technology, we begin to get virtually a-political cities like Birmingham (England) or Detroit, which grow up on a basis of pure production and exchange, usually outside the old political structures. These commercial and industrial cities play virtually no direct role in the international system though their indirect influence may be great in strengthening the power of the nation-state and the capital city to which they happen to be attached. Thus the rise of cities like Birmingham, Manchester, and Sheffield undoubtedly increased the power of Great Britain in the international system from the eighteenth century on. This increase in power, however, was largely accidental in the sense that it was not particularly planned by the central authorities and owed little to success or failure in war. What we had here was a quite independent dynamic of the exchange system that had a spillover effect on the international system.

The United States is an even more striking example of a country that has risen to power in the international system largely because of economic development through production and exchange. In the United States, the fact that the capital city of Washington was relatively insignificant over most of its history and even today is far from being the largest city symbolizes and illustrates the peculiar nature of this political organism. In the ideal type of national state, the capital city is the largest city in the country and dominates the life of the country, acting as a centralized focus for inputs of information and outputs of authority and, as the derivation of the word implies, as a ''head'' to the body of the rest of the country. One thinks of Paris, Rome, Madrid, Vienna, Warsaw, Copenhagen, Tokyo. The list could be extended. By contrast, Washington, Canberra, Ottawa, and, one

should no doubt add, Brazilia play a different role in their respective countries. These might almost be called ''economic'' as opposed to ''political'' countries in which the major centers, such as New York, Montreal, Sydney, São Paulo are commercial and industrial cities rather than administrative and military centers. In this connection, it is interesting to note that even the state capitals of many American states are relatively minor cities like Lansing, Springfield, and Sacramento, and it is highly significant that the capital of West Germany is Bonn. One feels that it is almost a pity that the capital of France did not remain permanently at Vichy!

Another important aspect of the city in the international system is its role in creating security against threats and violence. In classical civilization, human life was frequently more secure against violence in the city than it was in the country. Adam Smith observes, for instance, that ''order and good government, and along with them the liberty and security of individuals, were, in this manner, established in cities at a time when the occupiers of land in the country were exposed to every sort of violence.''[2] Even today, one sees the contrast between the landscape of France and England where the greater authority of the central power permitted men to live in open farmsteads in the country without undue fear of violence and the landscape of Germany where farmers still huddle together in villages and the countryside between villages is empty of habitation. In earlier times the city wall was a symbol of the security of the city's inhabitants. Like all forms of security, this tended to break down in the long run, and virtually all walled cities have been destroyed at some time or another. Nevertheless, in what children call the ''olden days,'' the inhabitant of the city did enjoy at least a temporary security frequently superior to that of his rural brother. Without this, indeed as Adam Smith again points out, the accumulation that went on in the cities, the increasing division of labor, and the improvement of technology would probably have been impossible, for unless the fruits

2. Adam Smith, *The Wealth of Nations*, Book 3, Ch. 3.

of accumulation are reasonably secure, people will not accumulate.

With the advent of aerial warfare and especially the nuclear weapon, the position of the city is radically changed. The city and the civilian who lives in it have now become hostages, and the civilian's chances of survival in a major war are much less than that of his rural brother or even that of a member of the Armed Forces. In the modern world, both the city and the civilian are expendable to the lust of the national state. This has created a complete reversal of the traditional pattern. Whereas in the earlier period the national state fostered the growth of nonpolitical cities by creating relatively large areas free from the threat of serious violence, today the national state is one of the greatest threats to its cities. Hiroshima and Nagasaki, after all, were commercial not political cities and were sacrificed to the senseless ambition of the national state. It would be very surprising if in the next "X" years Boston, Cleveland, Seattle, and so on are not similarly sacrificed on the altar of the present national system. The cities have become helpless pawns in an international system that is developing rapidly toward a major breakdown.

I have argued on another occasion that there are many reasons why the classical city, clearly bounded in space and organized from within by a strong sense of community, is incompatible with modern technology and is likely to survive only in special cases as a kind of anomaly.[3] The ecological structure of the classical city depended on a high resources cost, both of transportation and communication. The city was clustered and bounded; spatially it tended to have a ring structure centered around a market square, a cathedral, or some other civic center. Its population density was high, and there was usually a fairly sharp boundary that separated it from the countryside.

Both the economic and the political structures of the modern world are dominated by

the reduction in cost of transport of people, commodities, information, and violence. Clustering of any kind is a result of cost of transport of something. If cost of transport was zero, we would expect activity of all kinds to be uniformly spread over space. The lowering of cost of transport, therefore, inevitably reduces clustering and increases dispersion. We see this very clearly in what is happening to the cities. The central cities are decaying and disintegrating. The level of amenity in them has fallen, the level of violence has risen. The central cities may decay completely, and an urban structure may emerge that looks something like chicken wire; a network of ribbon development enclosing areas of country and rural settlement. The automobile, the telephone, the television, and the missile with a nuclear warhead—all move the ecological system in the same direction.

The critical question under these circumstances is what happens to the structure of community. Before the twentieth century, community was structured geographically in fairly well-defined ways. In his political role especially, a citizen belonged to a well-defined local community, whether village, town, or city, toward which he felt some attachment and some obligations. Beyond this were regional political organizations, such as counties and states, and beyond these again the national state. A great deal can be learned about the prevailing image of community by simply asking large numbers of people "Where do you live?" or "Where do you come from?" The answer, of course, depends somewhat on the context. If one is abroad, for instance, one would tend to respond by giving the name of one's national state. In the United States, one would be unlikely to respond by giving the name of one's county. A great many people probably do not even know it, for this is not a salient community. One suspects there might be almost an even chance of giving the name of a state or the name of a city. Some people would say "I come from Dedham," some might say "I come from Massachusetts." A person from Syracuse might even say "I

3. Kenneth E. Boulding, "The Death of the City: A Frightened Look at Post-civilization," in *The Historian and the City*, eds. Oscar Handlin and John Burchard (Cambridge, 1963), pp. 133–45.

come from upstate New York," thereby dissociating himself from the appendage at the lower end of the Hudson. On the other hand, a man may say "I come from Boston" when he actually lives in Concord, or "I come from New York" when he really lives in Scarsdale.

There can be little doubt that the impact of the modern world is to diminish allegiance to the local community and especially to the central city. The increase in mobility assures this. In the days when a man lived all his life in the place where he was born and where his forefathers had lived for generations, there was a strong tie to the local community. In the modern world, hardly anybody lives where he was born and a man changes his location many times during his life. Under these circumstances the sense of allegiance to the local community as something special declines, and if the local political community is to be run successfully, it must rely less and less on allegiances and sentiment. It will have to rely on professionalization and the use of exchange in order to attract the kind of support necessary. Everybody recognizes that the great problem of the central city today is that the people who make the decisions about it do not live there and do not feel themselves to be part of its community. They may live in the suburbs or in another part of the world altogether. Hence the city as a decision-making unit is really disintegrating. From being a social organism, it has declined to being a chance aggregation without even the organizational structure that permits the decisions to be made that will affect the local community. One sees this, for instance, in the field of banking, finance, and corporate management where decisions may be made that profoundly affect the future of a particular community by people who have never even seen it. We see this even more dramatically in the international system where the decision of a man in the White House consigns the people of cities on the other side of the world to the flames. We have passed from the stage where the cities nurtured civilization to a world in which the city is simply a victim of forces far beyond its own control, a sacrificial lamb on the altar of corporate or national ambition. The great danger here is that the sense of local community will be wholly eroded by the sense of impotence on the part of local people and local decision-makers. This can create a situation in which the cities almost literally fall apart. The city is something that nobody loves, and what nobody loves will die.

It is not surprising, therefore, that in the modern world the city is in deep crisis. It is an aggregation of humanity that has lost its sense of community and cannot, therefore, provide a human identity. St. Paul was able to say with pride that he was a citizen of no mean city. Would the same be said by a resident of Harlem or of any of our central cities? The cities of today that are not mean, like Venice, Florence, Kyoto, and one might almost add Williamsburg, are the fossil relics of a departed age. There are a great many things in our own age and in our society in which we can take great pride—the pictures of Mars, the conquest of disease, the great universities, even let me say with some trepidation, the middle-class suburbs with pleasant lawns, solid comforts, and relaxed neighborliness. The city, however, is not on this list, perhaps because it is really a survival from a past age, and we have not yet made the adjustments that can transform it into something worthy of the rest of our accomplishments.

The crux of the problem is that we cannot have community unless we have an aggregate of people with some decision-making power. The impotence of the city, perhaps its very inappropriateness as a unit, is leading to its decay. Its impotence arises, as I have suggested earlier, because it is becoming a mere pawn in economic, political, and military decision-making. The outlying suburb is actually in better shape. It is easier for a relatively small unit to have some sense of community, and the suburb at least has a little more control over its own destiny. It is somewhat less likely to be destroyed in war. Its economic base tends to be diversified as its residents commute over a wide area; hence its fate is not in the hands of a single decision-maker. Its local government, its school board, and other community agencies often are able to gather a considerable amount of support and interest from the people they serve.

It is not wholly absurd to ask whether we should not abolish the city altogether as a political organization. Let us divide Chicago and Detroit into thirty suburbs, small enough so that they have some chance of achieving a sense of local community and local responsibility for things that can be done locally. Then, of course, we would need "functional federalism"—metropolitan water boards covering a wide area, air-pollution agencies, educational finance institutions that would equalize local opportunities without destroying local initiative, police forces of different levels of size and function, and so on. Political scientists have often lamented about the multitude of political agencies in the United States, but the case against this may easily have arisen out of a prissy desire for tidiness. In terms of productivity, a multiplicity of agencies may be precisely what the times require. We seem quite incapable of expanding the central cities out into their suburban environment. Perhaps we should try reversing the recipe and move the suburbs into the city, building up around them a network of functional agencies.

The problem of integrating the city into the world community is much more difficult than the problem of reorganizing it locally. Nevertheless, the future of the city as an institution probably depends more on the future of the international system than it does on any other aspect of social life. More than any other aspect of the sociosphere, the international system is destroying the city, either physically by bombing or more critically by eroding its problem-solving capacity through the withdrawal of both intellectual and physical resources into the international system itself. The brain drain into the international system and the war industry is one of the principal reasons why the city receives so little attention and why what attention it has received in such efforts as urban renewal and public housing has been largely disastrous. The impact of urban renewal and of throughways on a city is

physically not unlike that of a small nuclear weapon, but with less damage to bodies and perhaps more damage to minds. Both urban renewal and nuclear destruction come from the national state. They are both thunderbolts hurled at the city from afar without regard to the tender ecological structure of its life and community. The cities by themselves, of course, cannot solve the problem of the world community, though one would think they might exercise a little bargaining power on it. The difficulty here is twofold. In the first place, the cities seem to have astonishingly little bargaining power in general. This is a puzzling phenomenon. One looks, for instance, in the United States at the extraordinary bargaining power of the agricultural interest, even at a time when it has shrunk to an almost insignificant proportion of the total electorate. By comparison with the apparent impotence of the cities, one sees the even more astonishing bargaining power of the military, who both starve and threaten the cities and eat high off the hog at a time when the cities have to be content with scraps. The second difficulty is that the international system is not really salient to the people who live in cities, even though it affects them so profoundly. The decision-makers in the international system are few, they are remote, and it all seems a long way from the experience of the ordinary citizen. Hence he is inclined to "leave this to father" even when the great White House father is dangerously incompetent in these matters. It is not the importance of a problem that determines how much attention will be paid to it, but its salience. Unfortunately, importance and salience are very loosely related, sometimes even negatively related.

All these difficulties resolve themselves into a single structural deficiency. There are virtually no channels in society or in the world at large by which the city as such can exercise bargaining power. One wonders what would happen if the cities were represented directly, as states, not only in the United States Senate, but in the United Nations. Could we envisage a new Hanseatic League of cities against the national state and the military establishments that are threatening to destroy them? All these suggestions, alas, sound like brainstorming and pipe dreams.

Nevertheless, what we face here is perhaps the most important single example of a much larger problem of political and social organization. The conflict in the world today—underlying the cold war at the international level, civil rights and the Black Power movement in the United States, and the inability of so many tropical countries to resolve their internal conflicts to the point where economic development becomes possible—is a conflict of two political concepts. The names "individualism" and "collectivism" are quite inadequate to describe these concepts, but these are probably the best words we have. On the one hand, there is the political ideal of the individual acting as an individual and independent person in a larger community, exchanging his capacities with other individuals in a social contract and in a market economy, expressing his political activity primarily by voting in elections on the one-man, one-vote basis. In political organization, this leads to what we might call "atomistic parliamentarism." In economic organization, it leads to capitalism and the free market. In religious organization, it leads to Protestantism and sectarianism; in family life, to the free choice of partners. It goes along with the life style of mobility and rootlessness, entrepreneurship, achieved rather than ascribed status, and so on. On the other side, we have the collective ideal stressing the notion that the identity of the individual is so bound up with the community with which he identifies that he can only become an individual as part of a community. His political activity here is exercised by activity influencing the decisions and the bargaining power of a series of concentric communities, rather than as an individual among other individuals. This leads toward a consensus-oriented society, totalitarianism, socialism, catholicism, monasticism, associationism, such things as trade unions and professional associations, collective rather than individual bargaining, and the corporate rather than the par-

liamentary state. Each of these philosophies has its own virtues and vices, and almost any political system is some sort of uneasy compromise between the two. Some lean toward one side, and some toward the other. At the present moment in history, the crisis of the cities has arisen because in *no* political structure is the city adequately represented. At the level of individualistic democracy, the city has lost its sovereignty and independence. It has become a pawn in the sense that its local autonomy has been destroyed. At the level of collective organization, the city is not organized as a bargaining unit. It does not bargain with the other agencies of society, such as the national state or the corporation, as effectively, shall we say, as the labor unions bargain with the employers. The city, therefore, gets the worst of both worlds. Its citizens as such are effective neither as political individuals nor as members of a bargaining collectivity.

Much of the same problem is seen in the Negro or other minority groups. The rise of the Black Power movement is in a sense a breakdown of individualistic democracy at this level. On the other hand, the Black Power solution is also likely to fail, because black power is not very great and the movement is likely to raise expectations that will probably be disastrously disappointed. One sees the same problem in the demands for "student power," which are simply not constructive, though occasionally they can be destructive, as in Latin America and Japan. Nevertheless, the student is not satisfied to be a mere individual and feels the need of identifying himself with a collectivity.

The synthesis and reconciliation in both structure and philosophy of the two political "modes," as they might be called, of individualism and collectivism perhaps represent the greatest single long-run problem of the human race at its present state of development. The city, or at least the urban collectivity, is one of the principal arenas in which this problem is or is not being worked out, as the case may be. Almost the only consideration that leads to any hopefulness about the future is that communication and aggregation foster the process of human learning. In the age of civilization, the concentration of people in cities unquestionably contributed to the fast growth of knowledge, simply because of the facilitation of communication that this concentration implied. Rural isolation leads to rural backwardness and cloddishness. The implications of the words "civilized," "civil," "urbane," and even "civilian," as over against "rustic" and "bucolic," suggest the values that have arisen from easy urban communication. The country may be the depository of traditional virtue, but new ideas come out of the wicked city. The city, therefore, historically has been the main source of change, both in the international system and in all aspects of the social system, as it has produced new ideas, new ideologies, new philosophies, and new technologies. The towns, as Adam Smith observes, improve the country. The decay of the city today does not represent a return to rural virtue or to rural ignorance. It is a symptom, if anything, of the urbanization of the whole world. The communications revolution has created, in effect, a world city, and this is why the local cities are in decay. It is to be hoped, therefore, that we can look forward to new knowledge, new ideas, and even a transformation of the international system that will give us security, arising out of the knowledge process of the world.

The essential key to this process may be the development of self-consciousness in the city dweller that he is a member of a city and indeed of the world city. One suspects that the unexploited bargaining power of the city is great simply because the city, disorganized as it is, is inevitably a focus or nodal point of the world network of communication. Airports are the synapses of the world communications network; so in a sense are the television stations and the newspapers of the city. So are its universities. It is a pretty fair generalization in the theory of location to say that the synapses, the gaps, or the switches in the communications and transportation network produce the city in the first place. This is why, for instance, so many cities have arisen at ports, at heads of navigation, and at points of transshipment. In a world in which the transportation of communication is beginning to overshadow the transportation of commodities, the city—because of its position in the communications network—has real power that is as yet unexploited, mainly because it is not self-conscious. If I can take a leaf out of the book of Karl Marx, and this is one occasion where the leaf may be better than the book, we may urge the rise of self-consciousness in the cities, a rise of their joint self-consciousness of the community as a world city representing the constructive and developmental forces of humanity as against the essentially backward-looking or destructive tendencies of the country and the military. Our motto, therefore, perhaps should be "Cities of the world unite, you have nothing to lose but your slums, your poverty, and your military expendability." On this note of modest long-run optimism, I had better conclude for fear that the pessimism of the short run catches up with us first.

**3**

# CITY SIZE, LOCATION, AND DIFFERENTIATION

# Introduction

This section and the next describe the basic properties of the contemporary urban system: the characteristics of sets of cities, their distribution by size and by location, and the interaction among them. Studies of city-size distributions and of differences in the economic role of cities are in fact the original materials that led to formulation of the concept of urban systems outlined in the previous sections; and the existence of systematic variations in these characteristics provides the basis for classifications of cities in this section and permits the exploration of analytical models that attempt to account for variations in growth rates in subsequent sections.[1]

This descriptive literature has evolved rapidly in the last two decades, and only very selective examples can be included here. Among those areas in which growth of the geographical literature has been pronounced, the following are represented: the application of urban-systems concepts to discussions of variations in city-size (scale) distributions and hierarchies; economic base and functional specialization (differentiation); the use of multivariate analyses to construct factorial ecologies (classifications) of urban systems; and the recent extension of such studies to include a wide range of political variables, social indicators, and the psychological images which people have of different cities or those which the cities attempt to present.

## THE VARIETIES OF VARIATION

Before we turn to generalizations on the structure of urban systems, it is worthwhile to remind ourselves of the very wide variations possible in the patterns of urbanization in individual nations. Substantial differences exist from country to country in the underlying distributions of population, in growth rates, in the degree of primacy (dominance) of a single urban core (often the capital city) or urbanized region, as well as in the importance of external forces in urban development. The result is a very different urban map for each country (see Figures 1a–h).

1. Examples of the systematic description of a national urban system's characteristics include Harris's (1970) book on the Soviet Union and a recent compilation of papers by Michael Ray et al. (1976), on the Canadian urban system.

In some ways the United States may be the antithesis of the archetypal urban system, at least compared with most European countries (Figures 1a–h). It has two dominant and strongly differentiated urban nodes, New York and Los Angeles, both of which are peripheral (in geographic location) to the rest of the nation. Australia, Canada, and many other former colonies (for example, Brazil), have two leading cities identical in some respects, complementary in others, and competitive in still others, but which are relatively close to each other in the very center of the national heartland (Ray, 1971; Bourne, 1974). Clearly, many different spatial forms of urban systems are possible and viable. Historical events, timing, physiographic barriers, and individual personalities all play a much larger role than many theorists care to admit.

The overall nature and form of the urban system are themselves of importance here. Very large and/or primitive urban systems, for example, are essentially independent. Countries that have these systems tend to devote only a small proportion of their national economy or GNP (gross national product) to foreign trade and produce internally nearly the full range of goods they require. Urban regions within these countries, then, may be largely self-sufficient (as in the Chinese model) or highly specialized in one or a few of many possible economic sectors (as in the U.S. model). In the former a typical provincial city might ship only fifteen percent of its production to outside markets, while Detroit might ship out over sixty percent. Those countries with sizable portions of their GNP attributable to foreign trade (the Denmark and Switzerland model) may be highly specialized in only a few export-oriented sectors.

The economic diversity of the national urban system as a whole, therefore, constrains the potential specialization of any one city in that system. The same holds true for variations in ethnicity, income levels, and so on. A homogeneous national culture effectively limits the range of social differences among cities. As we will see in the last two sections of this book, diversity is both a positive attribute (increasing the possible range of choice for individuals) and a negative one (complicating the policy goals of regional balance and social equality).

Over time, shifts in the composite characteristics of a nation will be reflected in changes in the internal distribution of population and economic activities, and in particular in the degree of spatial concentration. In terms of economic sectors, the increasing specialization among cities made possible by improved transportation networks and closer communication links is offset by the decline of locationally specialized primary and secondary activities relative to more widespread service activities.

## SCALE AND VARIATION

By far the most important aspect of a city is its population size. No other attribute varies so widely (from under 10,000 people to over 10 million) within an urban

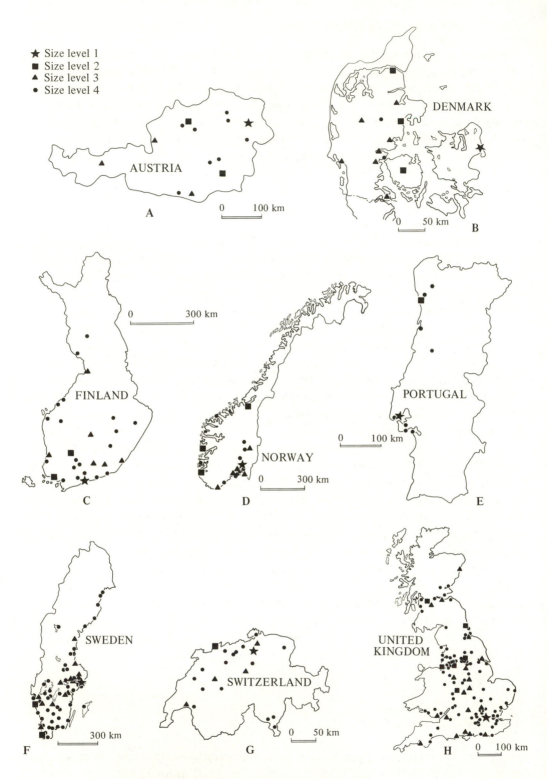

Figures 1a-h. Urban Maps of Selected Countries (from EFTA, 1973).

system. Simple population size is also related to almost every other measure of urbanization—to the number of cars, average income, industrialization, and the number of theaters. Through the concept of threshold, central-place studies use population size to estimate the mix of services and industries available in a town. A wide variety of other ratios—crime rates, ethnic composition, voting behavior, and service costs—can be related to city size as well (Hoch, 1972; Richardson, 1973; Stone, 1974).

If an urban region can be treated as an independent entity operating within an infinitely large market for its services, then discussions may focus on the advantages and disadvantages of economic scale (agglomeration benefits and disbenefits). This in turn leads to discussions of optimum city size. Mera's paper in Section VI is an excellent summary of the growing literature, largely in economics, on optimum city size, but that literature has its counterpart in political science, geography, and planning. Combined, this literature raises a number of interesting questions. How do lifestyles differ in larger cities? What new public services are required with increased city size, and at what levels of cost? What political forms are required to govern large urban regions? Is there a most efficient urban size in terms of production and of consumption?

The first two papers in this section provide comprehensive overviews of the basic literature on city size. In the first paper Richardson provides a thorough outline of both the theories and the debates on city-size distributions and of models employed to explain those distributions. Preston introduces classical central-place theory through a detailed case study of the now familiar ground of the state of Washington. Among the many recent extensions on the traditional form of central-place study, described in Preston but far too numerous to reprint here, include those incorporating explicit postulates on the behavior of consumers using the system of central places and more formal mathematical derivations of the city-size hierarchy, attempting to link central-place theory to that of regional growth, and attempting to make such models dynamic over space and time (see Rushton, 1970; Parr and Denike, 1970; Parr, 1973; Puryear, 1975; Dziewonski, 1975).

## ECONOMIC SPECIALIZATION

Another dimension to research on size (scale) and structural differences among cities is the measurement of their economic base and the degree of economic specialization. Innumerable approaches to measurement (Bahl, Firestone and Phares, 1971) and analysis (Smith and Morrison, 1975) are possible. In the next paper Crowley employs traditional shift-share analysis applied to changes in labor-force composition to differentiate the sources of economic growth in the Canadian urban system.[2] The results suggest which cities grow (or decline) because of their

2. The interested reader might also wish to refer to the debate surrounding Crowley's paper on measures of industrial diversification, which appeared in the journal *Urban Studies*. See Clemente and Sturgis (1971) and Crowley (1973). A much more detailed analysis of the economic specialization of Canadian cities is given in Hartwick and Crowley (1973).

particular economic structure or their share of sectors that are growing (or declining) at the national level.

The student of urban systems, on the other hand, is more likely to treat any given urban region as one of several competing locations within a national space economy. Growth and the economic role of one location are partly determined by the characteristics of alternative locations. The potential productivity of Omaha, for example, is neither infinite nor entirely locally determined: it serves what is essentially a finite hinterland, which produces for a specialized market. At the same time, factors of production, such as labor, capital, and fertilizers can and do move freely to other cities—Chicago, for instance.

The growth of a city within an urban system, then, is jointly determined by its internal resources and productivity and by the resources and productivity of all alternative locations. That is, the range of population sizes and growth rates for any given city is limited by the structural characteristics of the urban system as a whole and by its spatial organization. And for cities dependent on extensive space-using economic activities, such as agriculture, forestry, or mining, the very limited potential density of production at any location is an important consideration in understanding how that urban system evolved. Urbanization, in effect, describes how the population living off a particular economic base is organized in space.

## URBAN FACTORIAL ECOLOGY

Aside from population size there are an almost limitless number of measures that can be used to differentiate cities for varying purposes. Their relevance varies from one urban system to another and depends on the purpose of the analysis. Economic specialization is perhaps most widely studied, but the specific variables of interest and spatial scale of reference can shift from the modern-traditional continuum employed in studying a developing nation to the industrial-commercial differences appropriate to a diverse economy, such as the United States, to the variations within industrial sectors in highly industrial nations, such as Britain and West Germany.

In all systems, however, an attempt is usually made to identify the implications for other social concerns of differences in city size and economic role. The models are inductive, and the common technique is factor analysis. The technique was first applied in a large-scale fashion in a study entitled *British Towns* by Moser and Scott, published in 1961. A large number of measures, perhaps fifty to one hundred, are taken from a data source—usually the national census—and defined for appropriate units, such as cities or metropolitan areas. The structure of correlations among these variables is then examined as a basis for grouping the original measures into common factors. The scores of cities on these new factors or indices can be used to compare or to group urban regions in turn. Extensive reviews of this literature and the methods used are provided, for example, in Berry (1972).

Considerable differences appear in the results of factorial ecologies of urban systems because of fundamentally different variances among the variables themselves. Canada is a polarized cultural mosaic—French-speaking and English-speaking—which shows up in and dominates most analyses (Ray, 1971; Ray *et al.*, 1976). British towns have sharply varying class and occupational structures (Drewett, Goddard, and Spence, 1976). Nonetheless several regularities occur in all systems of cities. Population size is frequently linked to the presence of a diverse economic base and to a complex social structure. Population growth is linked to a youthful demographic structure and an overrepresentation of expanding occupational groups. Primary economic activities are linked to other heavy industrial activities but may also generate different educational and cultural mixtures as well.

While factorial ecology provides relatively easy and quick access to the basic patterns contained in large amounts of urban information, it is vulnerable to many of the analytic difficulties pointed out in earlier sections. The results are sensitive to the spatial units used and particularly to the number and mixture of variables selected. The inclusion of thirty different measures of economic activity will generate an apparently complex economic structure whether one exists or not. A major interpretative difficulty also emerges if one tries to use correlations based on aggregate data in a causal fashion, particularly in terms of drawing inferences on individual behavior. A close association between percent of blacks and percent of the housing stock in apartments among U.S. cities, for instance, is simply an observed correlation. One cannot infer that blacks live in apartments, or that apartments logically follow a black population. Two papers included in this section were chosen to illustrate the utilities and difficulties in using such techniques.

Probably no one has used the factorial ecology approach with greater skill and insight than Brian Berry. We include a brief example of his work in this section. The selection is actually a merger of two of his papers, designed to provide the reader with a clear and concise introduction to the technical and descriptive aspects of the approach as well as a simple illustration of its application. The technical introduction belongs to a much longer paper (Berry, 1972) that treated a particular empirical problem: the social and economic bases of urban municipalities in the U.S. Because the empirical results relate to politically defined cities and towns (1762 in total), which only represent parts of metropolitan areas, we chose instead to substitute the results reported in another paper (Berry and Neils, 1969). This analysis uses, for our purposes at least, more appropriate spatial units, that is, the standard metropolitan statistical areas of the U.S. (1960). Unfortunately no similarly suitable analysis of the 1970 data is available.

One of the questions raised in Berry's paper is: factorial ecology for what purpose? That is, how can one use a classification of cities? Berry himself provides one example: the development of a pollution-sensitive typology of U.S. regions, which offers a means of assessing the relationships between attributes of urban spatial structure and levels of pollution (Berry *et al.*, 1974). Another application of factorial-ecology methodology is included here in a paper by Knox. He attempts to measure variations in level of living, or well-being, among cities in England and Wales through the analysis of a range of different social and structural variables.


## SOCIAL INDICATORS

Knox's paper leads us into another area of growing interest: the development of more socially sensitive and policy-useful measures or indicators of social and economic status and change. Social indicators are usually measures of the quality of social environments. They attempt to tell us whether places are perceived of as being good or bad to live in, and how this perception changes depending on whether one is rich or poor, black or white.

Measures of well-being, as described in the paper above are examples of such indicators; and other studies have used various indices, such as crime, pollution, political participation, and social services (e.g., Flax, 1972; Smith, 1973; Strumpel, 1975; Knox, 1975; Campbell *et al.*, 1976). Their aim is to develop a sensitivity to the important noneconomic aspects of urban living and ultimately to develop a theory relating these indices to other aspects of urban-system growth, such as size and accessibility, and then to policy questions.

Research on social indicators is plagued by data difficulties, notably the unavailability of data for certain critical issues, such as social needs and aspirations, and the lack of agreement on uniform definitions of measures, for crime and health, for example. Often one finds that high levels of crime simply reflect high levels of police reporting and enforcement. High levels of medical care also tend to increase the apparent incidence of many diseases that formerly went unrecognized, and so on. The conceptual framework of social indicators also comes under attack from those who disagree on the interpretation of what is good or bad. Is the steadily increasing number of doctors in urban areas a good thing? Are certain forms of local government better than others? Do certain aspects of poverty reflect real inequalities between people and regions or simply unusual life styles? Should we expect incomes to be the same for every city?

Despite the complexity of these questions the identification of new variables for comparative urban studies is proceeding rapidly. Political scientists are increasingly concerned with the form and operation of municipal government (e.g., Kesselman, 1972); economists and planners are elaborating new measures of social productivity, returns to factors of production, and the quality of life (Wingo, 1973; Strumpel, 1975); and sociologists are trying to measure the relative alienation of individuals, social classes, and cultural groups.

A major source of inspiration in this regard is still the novelist or journalist who selects words, phrases, or images of different cities, building an impression of differences that reflect both historical attitudes and contemporary life-styles. We have included an excellent discussion of this *genre* in a fascinating paper by Tuan.

He describes the common images of various American cities and their symbolism in terms of landmarks or life-styles. These images frequently capture the role of that city in the nation's urbanization process. The study of imagery extends the possible descriptions of cities by several orders of magnitude, while at the same time it brings the largely theoretical discussions of previous papers back down closer to ground we all know.

## REFERENCES

Bahl, R. W., Firestone, R. and Phares, D. 1971. "Industrial Diversity in Urban Areas: Alternative Measures and Intermetropolitan Comparisons." *Economic Geography,* vol. 47, pp. 414–425.

Beckman, M. J. and McPherson, J. C. 1970. "City Size Distributions in a Central Place Hierarchy." *Journal of Regional Science,* vol. 10, pp. 25–33.

Berry, B.J.L., ed. 1972. *City Classification Handbook.* New York: Wiley Interscience.

——— et al. 1974. *Land Use, Urban Form and Environmental Quality.* Research Paper 155. Chicago: University of Chicago, Department of Geography.

Bourne, L. S. 1974. "Urban Systems in Australia and Canada: Comparative Notes and Research Questions." *Australian Geographical Studies,* vol. 12, pp. 152–172.

Campbell, A. *et al.* 1976. *The Quality of American Life. Perceptions, Evaluations and Satisfactions.* New York: Russell Sage Foundation.

Clemente, F. and Sturgis, R. 1971. "Population Size and Industrial Diversification." *Urban Studies,* vol. 8, pp. 65–68.

Crowley, R. W. 1973. "Reflections and Further Evidence on Population Size and Industrial Diversification." *Urban Studies,* vol. 10, pp. 91–94.

Drewett, R., Goddard, J., and Spence, N. 1976. "What's Happening in British Cities?" *Town and Country Planning,* vol. 44, pp. 14–24.

Dziewonski, K. 1970. "Specialization and Urban Systems." *Papers, Regional Science Association,* vol. 24, pp. 39–45.

———. 1975. "The Role and Significance of Statistical Distributions in Studies of Settlement Systems." *Papers, Regional Science Association,* vol. 34, pp. 145–155.

Evans, A. 1972. "The Pure Theory of City Size in an Industrial Economy" *Urban Studies,* vol. 9, pp. 49–77.

Flax, M. J. 1972. *A Study in Comparative Urban Indicators: Conditions in 18 Large Metropolitan Areas.* Washington: The Urban Institute.

Harris, C. D. 1970. *Cities of the Soviet Union.* Chicago: University of Chicago Press.

Hartwick, J. M. and Crowley, R. W. 1973. *Urban Economic Growth: The Canadian Case.* Working Paper A.73.5. Ottawa: Ministry of State for Urban Affairs.

Hoch, I. 1972. "Urban Scale and Environmental Quality," in R. G. Ridker, ed. *Population, Resources and the Environment.* Washington: Commission on Population Growth and the American Future.

Kesselmann, M. 1972. "Research Perspectives in Comparative Local Politics: Pitfalls and Prospects." *Comparative Urban Research,* vol. 1, pp. 10–31.

Knox, P. L. 1975. *Social Well-Being: A Spatial Perspective.* London: Oxford University Press.

Moser, C. A. and Scott, W. 1961. *British Towns.* London: Oliver and Boyd.

Parr, J. B. 1973. "Growth Poles, Regional Development and Central Place Theory." *Papers, Regional Science Association,* vol. 31, pp. 173–212.

———, and Denike, K. 1970. "Theoretical Problems in Central Place Analysis." *Economic Geography,* vol. 46, pp. 568–586.

Puryear, D. 1975. "A Programming Model of Central Place Theory." *Journal of Regional Science,* vol. 15, pp. 307–316.

Ray, D. M. 1971. *Dimensions of Canadian Regionalism.* Ottawa: Information Canada.

———et al., eds. 1976. *Canadian Urban Trends.* Toronto: Copp Clark.

Richardson, H. W. 1973. *The Economics of Urban Size.* London: D. C. Heath.

Rushton, G. 1971. "Postulates of Central Place Theory and the Properties of Central Place Systems." *Geographical Analysis,* vol. 3, pp. 140–156.

Smith, D. M. 1973. *The Geography of Social*

*Well-Being in the United States.* New York: McGraw-Hill.

Smith, D. M. 1977. *Human Geography: A Welfare Approach.* London: Arnold.

Smith, P. and Morrison, W. I. 1975. *Simulating the Urban Economy: Experiments with Input-Output Techniques.* New York: Academic Press.

Stone, P. A. 1974. *The Structure, Size and Costs of Urban Settlements.* Cambridge: The University Press.

Strumpel, B., ed. 1975. *Economic Means for Human Needs: Social Indicators of Well-Being*

*and Discontent.* Ann Arbor: University of Michigan, Institute for Social Research.

von Böventer, E. 1973. "City-Size Systems: Theoretical Issues, Empirical Regularities, and Planning Guides." *Urban Studies,* vol. 10, pp. 145–162.

Wilson, A., ed. 1972. *Patterns and Processes in Urban and Regional Systems.* London Papers in Regional Science, vol. 3. London: Pion.

Wingo, L. 1973. "The Quality of Life: Toward a Micro-Economic Definition." *Urban Studies,* vol. 10, pp. 3–27.

# Theory of the Distribution of City Sizes: Review and Prospects

HARRY W. RICHARDSON

## INTRODUCTION

How to explain the size distribution of cities is one of the most fascinating intellectual problems in urban and regional analysis. There are several reasons for this: the topic is relevant to all societies, regardless of their level of development, location or cultural background; it has attracted the attention of many social scientists—economists, geographers, sociologists and statisticians—and no one discipline has the monopoly of wisdom; despite past research, there is no widely acceptable theory and the problem remains a mystery. Tinbergen (1968, p. 65) has argued that "No scientific explanation worthy of that name has been advanced so far." The models examined in this paper suggest that this opinion is too harsh, but the theoretical challenges of the problem remain immense. First, Champernowne's (1953, p. 319) comments on the theory of income distribution apply with even more force to city size distributions: the forces "are so varied and complex, and interact and fluctuate so continuously, that any theoretical model must either be unrealistically simplified or hopelessly complicated." Second, it is difficult to sort out "good" theories from "bad" via empirical testing. The statistical functions of city size (see next section) are so similar that the differences between them are insufficiently sensitive for any single function to dominate as the "best" general relationship. It is impossible to favour one theory or another on the

basis of its predictions, since any one of the observed statistical relationships is compatible with several theories while many of the individual theories are consistent with more than one of the standard empirical distributions. The future for empirical testing lies in the evaluation of the underlying individual hypotheses and assumptions that underpin each model rather than in comparing predicted and actual city size distributions.

The objective of this paper is to survey a wide range of theories: to assess the standard explanations, to revive a few neglected contributions, to review some very recent suggestions, and to offer one or two new ideas. The aim is not to search for the one superior theory since some of the theories are complementary, nor to present any empirical evidence, but rather to comment on the current state of the theory, to promote interest in the problem and to offer some guidelines for future research. First, however, we must clear the ground by making some general observations on statistical relationships of city size distributions.

## LOGNORMAL, PARETO AND RANK-SIZE DISTRIBUTIONS

All city size distributions are strongly positively skewed to the right, i.e., there are many small but only a few very large cities with a tendency for the number of cities in each size class to decline as city size increases. This

From *Regional Studies*, vol. 7, 1973, pp. 239–51. Reprinted by permission.

rules out normal distributions. The three main candidates then become the lognormal distribution, the Pareto distribution and the rank-size rule. As we shall see, all three have close similarities. If the frequency distribution of city sizes is hump-shaped and positively skewed the lognormal distribution may yield a good fit, i.e.,

$$N = \log P \qquad (1)$$

where $N$ = cumulative percentage of cities and $P$ = city size.

The lognormal distribution attempts to represent the whole range of city sizes, and this differentiates it from the Pareto distribution which deals only with the upper tail (city sizes above a defined level, $\bar{P}$). However, the lognormal can be translated into Pareto distribution terms by either arbitrarily imposing a threshold city size or estimating it from the data using a three-parameter distribution (Aitchison and Brown, 1957).

The Pareto distribution is given by

$$N(\bar{P}) = AP^{-\alpha} \qquad (2)$$

where $N(\bar{P})$ = cumulative percentage of cities above the threshold level, $\bar{P}$
$A, \alpha$ = constants.
This can be expressed as

$$\log N(\bar{P}) = \log A - \alpha \log P \qquad (3)$$

which is similar to equation (1). If the data yield a good fit the city size distribution can be represented by a straight line with a slope of $-\alpha$.

The rank-size distribution is given by

$$R \cdot P^q = K \qquad (4)$$

where $R$ = city rank
$q, K$ = constants.
Rearranging, we obtain

$$R = KP^{-q} \qquad (5)$$

which is identical to the Pareto distribution except that rank of city is used instead of

cumulative percentage of number of cities. A special case of the rank-size distribution is obtained where $q = 1$. This is the so-called rank-size rule

$$R \cdot P = K = P_1 \qquad (6)$$

where $P_1$ = size of the largest city. Thus the product of city size and its rank is a constant, equal to the size of the leading city in the system. A frequent reason for the failure of this special case to hold is that $K \neq P_1$ (this inequality also has repercussions on the value of $q$), usually because $P_1$ is overdeveloped relative to the rest of the urban system. The tendency for the largest city to be "excessively" big with stunting effects on cities of nearby rank is the primate distribution case.[1]

The three distributions are so similar that it is difficult to choose between them. If we were concentrating on the upper tail there might be a preference for the Pareto or rank-size distributions, especially if data limitations impose a minimum urban place threshold as defined by Census data, or if a minimum critical size for a viable urban service centre is determined on theoretical grounds. The Pareto may also be preferred if the upper tail is highly skewed. On the other hand, if very disaggregated data are available and if the analyst is concerned with the whole range of city sizes, the lognormal may be more appealing. Distortions due to the minimum threshold and/or primacy may be handled by using the three- and/or four-parameter log-normal form. Yet despite the greater generality of the lognormal and its flexibility from a statistical point of view, most of the literature has concentrated on Pareto and rank-size distributions, especially the latter. Christaller (1966, p. 59 and n. 19) described the rank-size rule as "a most incredible law" which was "not much more than playing with numbers." This criticism is directed solely against the rule itself (i.e., the special case $q = 1$). Despite satisfactory fits in

1. The theory of primacy is another story, if a fascinating one. For some insights see Jefferson (1939), El Shaks (1965), Morse (1962), Mehta (1964), Linsky (1965) and Harris (1971).

some cases,[2] there is no reason for restricting analysis to the $q = 1$ case. The rank-size distribution may instead be interpreted as a very general model according to the value of the exponent. If $q = 1$ implies the rank-size rule, $q > 1$ represents metropolitan dominance while $q < 1$ stands for an urban system in which intermediate cities (such as regional capitals) are relatively large. The limiting cases, unknown in practice, are $q = \infty$ (only one city) and $q = 0$ (all cities of the same size). This interpretation gives some support for Parr's (1970) view that the rank-size distribution has "greater validity" than other models. Zipf (1949, p. 423) suggested that if the rank-frequency distribution were to include the *whole* population the curve would bend downward below the 2500 population mark, and that this could be interpreted economically "as an indication of a deficiency of smaller communities" and socially "as the demarcation between the traditional classes, *urban* and *rural*." This is analogous to the minimum threshold requirement of the Pareto distribution.

## HIERARCHY MODELS

Hierarchy models have received most emphasis in the literature. Whereas the earliest studies on city size distributions merely concentrated on trying to account for the shape and nature of the observed statistical functions, the central place model was the first deductive theory of the distribution of cities. No-one has pruned the structure of the model to a minimum set of assumptions more successfully than Beckman (Section 3(a)). However, other hierarchy models are feasible. The Tinbergen model (Section 3(b)) is more general in the sense that it can apply to manufacturing as well as service industries, though additional assumptions are needed to derive a determinate solution. It is also possible to construct a city size distribution model

in which administrative functions substitute for service functions.

## A Central Place Model

Beckmann (1958, 1968; Beckmann and McPherson, 1970) developed the key model relating central place and market area hierarchies to the distribution of city sizes, though the analysis stems directly from the Christaller-Lösch tradition. Cities of different size perform different functions because it is more efficient for some goods and services to be produced in small cities and others in larger centres. A city's prime economic functions are assumed to be to service its hinterland which, except for the smallest urban centre, encompasses smaller cities. Goods and services are ranked into higher and lower orders depending upon the demand *threshold* (i.e., the minimum viable level, in population and/or income, required to support the service) and the *range* (the outer limits of the market area) of each goods. The threshold and the range, reflecting economies of scale and transport costs, act as lower and upper bounds, stratifying cities into a hierarchy and determining the number and size of urban places in each level.

Starting from a homogeneous plain over which resources are uniformly distributed, Beckmann makes two crucial assumptions. First, city size is proportional to the population the city serves:

$$p_m = kP_m \qquad (7)$$

where $p_m$ = population of city of order $m$, $P_m$ = population served by this city and $k$ = proportionality factor.

This assumption implies simplistic production functions in which labour is the only input and the ratio of inputs to output is constant above the threshold level. Second, cities of each order have a fixed number ($s$) of satellite cities of the next lowest order,

$$P_m = p_m + sP_{m-1}. \qquad (8)$$

---

2. The most widely tested successful fit is with United States data (Zipf, 1949; Duncan and Reiss, 1956; Madden, 1956; Mills, 1972).

The smallest urban centre serves a basic rural population $(r_1)$ and itself; from this fact the population served by this centre may be derived

$$P_1 = r_1/1 - k. \tag{9}$$

Via substitution and rearrangement we obtain

$$P_m = \frac{ks^{m-1}r_1}{(1-k)^m} . \tag{10}$$

City size increases exponentially with the level of the city in the hierarchy.[3] The basic parameters of the model are $r_1$ (the rural population served by the smallest town), $k$ (the ratio of city size to population served) and $s$ (the number of satellites per city).

The model predicts that all cities of the same rank are of equal size, and this conflicts with observation. However, if we treat the city size multiplier, $s/1 - k$, as a random variable, the product after several multiplications will tend to lognormality. This transforms the discrete stepwise hierarchy into a more continuous distribution. Other modifications having a similar effect include the introduction of non-central place functions such as manufacturing, variations in production costs between cities, variable population densities and spatial differences in the impact of technology.

Many objections have been levelled against the model. However, these have been misdirected since the main object of attack has been the model's simplifying assumptions. The objections can usually be accommodated without affecting the theory's basic structure. For instance, some observers (e.g., Mills, 1972) have commented on the paradox of a theory of city size distribution built upon the foundations of a rural population $(r_1)$. However, though the model needs a minimum base this could easily be an urban nucleus representing the minimum efficient size for

urban functions. Others have argued that the assumption that cities only export down the hierarchy is wrong, but this can be dealt with via allowing $k$ to be a variable rather than a constant; the same relaxation allows local demand to vary with city size (Dacey, 1966). The number of satellite cities $(s)$ can also be permitted to vary between levels. These modifications make the mathematics more cumbersome, but do not destroy the rationale of the hierarchy model. Rather, by making it more flexible they transform it into a more general theory with a wider range of predictions compatible with more empirical examples.

Beckmann's version purges the hierarchy model of spatial elements. This has two defects. First, it ignores the fact that the relative size of cities is affected by distance between them. Deviations from the theoretical interurban distance may not account for major changes in ranks, but they distort the regularity of the hierarchy. Second, it ignores intra-urban space. High commuting costs and density functions such as congestion and pollution are diseconomies of urban scale that may limit city size independent of hierarchial effects.[4]

## A More General Urban Hierarchy Model

Tinbergen (1968) developed a hierarchy model of city size distributions, similar in some ways to the classical (Beckmann) model, but described in terms of income and initially assuming that each city exports only its highest order goods. Also, the model is more easily applied to manufacturing industry since it does not depend on central place functions.

He assumes a closed economy of regular shape evenly covered with farms except in cities. There are $H$ industries $(h = 0, 1, \ldots,$

---

3. The ratio $P_m/P_{m-1} = s/1 - k$. Since $s > 1$ and $0 \leqslant k \leqslant 1$, it follows that $(s/1 - k) > 1$. Thus, city size increases geometrically with $m$.

4. This argument suggests the desirability of allowing for both interurban and intra-urban phenomena within the same general model. Weiss (1961) and Berry (1964) make two modest steps in this direction.

$H$), where $h$ is called the rank of the industry (for agriculture $h = 0$). Each industry consists of firms of optimal size (defined by scale economies). Demand for product $h$ is satisfied by $n_h$ firms[5] and its total demand is $a_h Y$ where $Y =$ national income and $a_h =$ demand ratio for $h$. It is assumed that there is only one firm in the highest ranked industry ($n_H = 1$), and that the number of firms in each industry varies with its rank ($n_1 > n_2 > n_3 \ldots > n_H$). All income is spent, i.e., $\Sigma_h a_h = 1$. Rural income $Y_0$ is given by $a_0 Y$.

To obtain predictions about the size distribution of cities other assumptions are made that are also testable hypotheses. There are only $M$ orders of centre ($m = 1, \ldots, M$). In any centre of rank $m$ only the industries appear for which $h \leq m$. The number of firms in each industry in each centre is just sufficient to satisfy local demand for the industries of a rank lower than the centre's rank. The industry of rank $h$ in centre of rank $m$ satisfies both local demand and the demand for that product in lower rank centres, and exports down the hierarchy are equally distributed among all $m$ centres. The total income earned ($Y^m$) in all centres of a given rank can be derived from

$$Y = \Sigma_m Y^m = Y_0 + \Sigma_m \Sigma_h Y^m_h = \frac{a_0 Y}{1 - \Sigma_h a_h} \quad (11)$$

since total income can be calculated at any stage as we ascend the hierarchy, e.g.,

$$Y_0 + Y^1 + Y^2 = \frac{a_0 Y}{1 - (a_1 + a_2)} .$$

We may derive the number of centres of each rank ($n^m$) if we assume that there is always *only* one firm of the highest rank in each centre. This is given by the relationship

$$n^m = n_h \frac{a_0}{1 - \Sigma_h a_h} . \quad (12)$$

5. Of course, $n_h = Y_h / \bar{Y}_h$ where $\bar{Y}_h =$ optimal output of firm in industry $h$.

Equations (11) and (12) determine the size distribution of cities. This simple hierarchy model can be extended by introducing complications such as foreign trade, intermediate products, various transportation assumptions, uniquely located industries, and more complex interurban trade flow patterns (Bos, 1965).

## Administrative Hierarchy Models

The hierarchical structuring of administrative functions presents an alternative to central place models as a hierarchical theory of the distribution of city sizes. Although such an explanation is useful only as a special case, it may be valuable for interpreting the city size distributions observed in socialist economies. Service activities are so imperfectly developed in such countries (the share of service industries in employment is about 2½ times greater in the U.S.A. than in the U.S.S.R.) that central place models are unconvincing. In the Soviet economy highly developed administrative functions may substitute for underdeveloped service functions (Harris, 1970).

Christaller (1966) and Lösch (1954, p. 132) both emphasised the importance of administrative functions as a mechanism for stratifying the urban hierarchy, stressing "the administrative principle" where a city of a given rank controls seven cities—including itself—of the next lower rank. The nesting of seven cases is unnecessarily restrictive. A plausible city size distribution can be generated from two key assumptions: a constant number of cities under direct control of the next highest order city; a constant ratio of the populations of the controlled area to the control centre as we ascend the hierarchy.[6] Modifications to these assumptions can be made as in the central place hierarchy model; for instance, the number of controlled centres can be treated as a parameter. Even so, the higher the *average* number of controlled centres the more skewed the distribution of city sizes will be. Also spatial considerations, as reflected in transport and communication costs, are no less important in determining the efficiency of an administrative hierarchy as that of a central place hierarchy.[7]

Hierarchical structures of this kind are not necessarily limited to public administration. In the private sector there are size hierarchies of firms and size hierarchies of establishments within firms. Although these are not necessarily distributed among cities with size of firm directly correlated with city size,[8] Edel (1972) has argued that such a correlation may be very important in explaining the upper tail of the city size distribution. He draws attention to the fact that the largest cities invariably tend to be "corporate cities," i.e., cities that are locations for the headquarters of large business corporations.

## STOCHASTIC MODELS

Since the size of a city is the net outcome of a multiplicity of forces the individual contributions of which are difficult to identify, there is a temptation to resort to stochastic models which treat urban growth determinants as proportional to city size (proportionate effect) or the city size distribution as the probabilistically derived steady-state equilibrium (entropy).[9] Also, two of the models analysed in later sections of this paper contain substantial stochastic elements. Whereas the case in favour of including random variables in the theory of the distribution of city sizes is strong, it is implausible to exclude altogether systematic factors (such as central place concepts or agglomeration economies).

6. Lydall (1968) adopted a very similar model to explain the personal income distribution based on the assumption that large organizations—which dominate the upper tail of the income distribution—are organized on a hierarchical principle.
7. Both Christaller and Tinbergen (1968) suggest that a nesting of four is most efficient from a communications point of view.
8. The size distribution of firms between cities varies in the Tinbergen model for a different reason—the distribution of industries (each composed of firms of optimal size) among cities.
9. Vining (1955) suggested that the rank-size distribution is a time-dependent stochastic process according to which the distribution of city sizes maintains a high degree of stability (a kind of statistical equilibrium) despite a great deal of individual flux, e.g., changes in city populations, rank-jumping, births and deaths of towns.

## The Law of Proportionate Effect

Simon (1955) argued that the distribution of city sizes could be regarded as the steady-state equilibrium of a stochastic process, and approximately described by the Pareto distribution, equation (2) above. The particular stochastic process is *the law of proportionate effect* which implies that city growth is proportional to city size. Not every city needs to grow proportionately, provided that the probabilities of proportionate growth are spread symmetrically. Even if the initial distribution of city sizes were a normal distribution, subjecting that distribution to a stochastic process by applying a transitional probability matrix may, after $n$ operations, generate a steady-state Pareto distribution.

Simon suggested demographic forces as a possible explanation of why the law of proportionate effect might apply, e.g., if population growth was solely due to natural increase, and net growth was proportional to present population (either within each city or, less restrictively, within each size class). It is also possible to allow for migration if the net population change of individual cities *within any region* is proportional to city size. Another possibility is where rural-urban migration is determined by the "friends and relatives" effect (Greenwood, 1970) provided that the probability of having a friend in a city is proportionate to its size.[10] The model can also allow for new cities crossing the minimum size threshold ($\bar{P}$) provided that the probability of this remains constant (or that new cities account for a constant fraction of total urban population growth); on the other hand, declines can be accommodated only if offset by the growth of another city in the same size class. Also, non-demographic factors could have a role in this model if their random influence on city size were proportionate to city size. The main drawback of the model is its total reliance on random and neglect of systematic factors. For example, the existence of diseconomies of urban scale

10. For an alternative explanation see Ward (1963).

(Mills, 1972) could be a systematic influence that distorts its predictions.[11]

## A Market Opportunities Model

Following upon Simon's work, Ward (1963) also used the law of proportionate effect. However, he focuses directly on migration rather than natural increase and his model is based more on economic than statistical theory. It is assumed that *all* changes in city sizes are due to migration, that employment opportunities are the main stimulus to migration, that these opportunities arise because of expansion in the market or technical change, that in the long run the latter can be subsumed under market expansion factors, and that all opportunities can be aggregated (ignoring the differential effects of technical change, demand- and product-mix effects, and so on). The model is made endogenous by treating city population as a measure of market size so that market-expansion opportunities can be assumed to depend on city size. The probability of these opportunities occurring is proportionate to the size of the market (i.e., city size). This is the law of proportionate effect once again. To justify a Paretian distribution, Ward hypothesizes that below a certain size of city the probability of opportunities developing is very low, partly because small towns are neglected in the search process of entrepreneurs and migrants, partly because of economic efficiency thresholds for opportunity creation (e.g., supply of public services, labour market thresholds, etc.). It is possible to relax some of the model's restrictive assumptions, for example, by disaggregating opportunities to allow for industrial structure differentials among cities and by taking account of the fact that some cities have special locational advantages such as access to a unique natural resource. These introduce more realism without distorting the final result. A limitation of the model is that its emphasis on market opportunities could make it a culture-bound explanation applicable to market-oriented societies but much less plausible as an explanation of the similar empirical distributions of city sizes found in socialist and centrally planned economies.

## Entropy Maximization

Berry (1961, p. 587) argued that "when many forces act in many ways with none predominant a lognormal size distribution is found." This emphasis on a multiplicity of forces strengthens the case for treating city size distributions as the outcome of a stochastic process.[12] Curry (1964) developed an entropy maximization model which provides an alternative stochastic model to Simon's law of proportionate effect. The attractiveness of entropy models is increased for those who believe in the value of a general systems approach (e.g., Berry, 1964; Olsson, 1967).

Entropy (derived from the second law of thermodynamics) is a measure of the degree of equalization reached within a system, and is maximized when the system reaches equilibrium. The steady state equilibrium is the most probable state. Given $P$ individuals, the number of ways in which $N$ cities can be distributed among size bands is given by

$$\frac{N!}{\prod_{i=0}^{P} p_i!} \qquad (0 \leqslant i \leqslant P) \qquad (13)$$

where $p_i$ = city size class of $i$ individuals. In a large system entropy ($E$) may be defined as

$$E = N \log N - \Sigma p_i \log p_i. \qquad (14)$$

This is maximized when

$$p_i = (N/n)e^{-(i/n)} \qquad (15)$$

where $n$ = average city size ($P/N$).

---

11. Analogously, when the law of proportionate effect is used to explain the skewness of the size distribution of firms it is necessary to assume constant long-run average cost functions.

12. However, note the disparaging comment by Higgs (1970, p. 253): "Explanations hinging upon unnamed 'forces' which are 'many and act randomly' are not theories at all but rationalizations for the lack of a theory."

This may be rewritten as

$$p_i = p_1[1 - e^{-(i/n)}]$$    (16)

where $p_1$ = the primate city.
This is similar to the rank-size rule. A city size distribution obeying the rank-size rule is the most probable distribution and represents the steady state equilibrium in which entropy has been maximized.

The model achieves the most probable distribution of a random arrangement of a given number of people in a given number of cities. Randomness avoids too much concentration in large cities and ensures that population is spread (if unequally) among all cities. However, there is no reason why the most probable distribution should be either the observed or the optimal distribution (Richardson, 1972). As with other stochastic models, the chief drawback of the entropy-maximizing model is the absence of a role for systematic forces. However, it is possible to introduce structuring and order into the framework of an entropy model (Berry, 1964; Fano, 1969) by resorting to central place notions and to information theory.

## QUASI-ECONOMIC MODELS

The models in this section all rely upon deductive economic theory, though surprisingly two of them were not developed by economists.

### A Growth Theory Model

Davis and Swanson (1972) have recently developed a model that integrates growth theory with a stochastic process in order to generate a lognormal city size distribution. The model assumes Cobb-Douglas production functions. Each city is assumed to be constrained in its investment by local savings, assumed to be a constant fraction of output. Equilibrium in product markets is obtained via equality of savings and investment (i.e., no unintended savings or investment). The distribution of city sizes is changed over time by the differential growth of city labour forces (constant labour force participation rates are assumed). Each city enjoys a perfectly elastic supply of labour since workers can be drawn in from the hinterland by higher urban wages. Income is distributed according to the marginal products of factors.

The key to the model is an efficiency progress function, $\epsilon(t)$, in which technical progress is assumed disembodied and Hicks-neutral. It is specified as follows:

$$\epsilon(t) = \exp(\rho t + z)$$    (17)

where $\rho$ = a parameter, $t$ = time and $z$ = a random variable. This equation makes $\epsilon(t)$ also a random variable and its distribution over all cities can be described in two-parameter lognormal form. The economic reasoning here is that technical progress can either complement or detract from other attributes of each city such as natural resource endowment, amenities (e.g., climate), supply of entrepreneurs, and so on. It is assumed that, on the average, technical progress is complementary, but its random incidence may make for deviation in an individual city.

The simplifying assumptions of the growth theory enable the relative growth rates of city labour forces to be expressed as a function of the efficiency progress function

$$l(t) = \rho\beta + sc^{1-\beta}[\epsilon(t)]^\beta$$    (18)

where $l(t)$ = distribution of city labour force growth rates, $s$ = propensity to save in each city, $\beta = \alpha^{-1}$ where $\alpha$ = capital's share in output and $c = w(1 - \alpha)^{-1}$ where $w$ = constant real wage. The variable $l(t)$ is a three-parameter lognormal variable with the threshold parameter equal to $\rho\beta$.[13] The results still hold even when some of the restrictive assumptions are relaxed. For instance, we could allow rural wages to increase, the capital stock to depreciate and interurban capital flows to take place (provided they are linear

---

13. Alternatively, $[l(t) - \rho\beta]$ can be treated as a two-parameter lognormal variable.

homogeneous functions of output in the receiving cities). The virtue of this model is that it draws upon deductive economic theory to predict a lognormal distribution of city sizes consistent with empirical observation.

## A Neoclassical Equilibrium Model

Rashevsky (1943, 1947, 1951), a mathematical biologist, developed a theory of the distribution of city sizes based on the economic concept of neoclassical equilibrium. Migrants migrate between cities in pursuit of higher income, and if marginal productivity assumptions are made equilibrium is achieved when productivity per head $(\delta)$ is equalized between cities:

$$\delta_1 = \delta_2 = \delta_i = \bar{\delta}. \qquad (19)$$

Rashevsky suggests that the generalized production function takes the form

$$\delta_i = f(p_i, P_i) \qquad (20)$$

where $P_i$ = total number of people inhabiting all cities of size $p_i$. The total number of cities

$$N = \Sigma \frac{P_i}{p_i}. \qquad (21)$$

To solve the city size distribution problem the productivity function, equation (20), needs to be specified. Rashevsky took a simple form whereby urban productivity was expressed as a function of city size and of population distribution characteristics of the system as a whole (total national population, population of the size class and the total number of cities). This simple model yielded an equilibrium distribution of city sizes satisfying equation (21).

Apart from doubts about the appropriateness of neoclassical migration models, the key question is whether such a model generates a distribution of city sizes consistent with those observed in the real world. Since such a distribution is not generated directly, something else must be added to the model. The

most obvious solutions are: (1) to argue that urban production functions are lognormally distributed, either via an analogy between business firms and cities or, more plausibly, because several influences behind the urban production function combine together multiplicatively (as in the model below); or (2) within a multisector framework to distribute industries among cities hierarchically (e.g., as in Tinbergen's model).

## An Economies of Scale-Transport Costs Model

Zipf (1949) is justly famous for his empirical research on rank-size relationships, but his theoretical contribution has been neglected or misunderstood.[14] Zipf's analysis is based on a set of theoretical forces governing social organization in general. These "mainsprings of human behaviour" are the *Principle of Least Effort* and its major manifestations the *Force of Unification* and the *Force of Diversification*. Another force—the *Force of Innovation*—is also important, and shows itself as the *Economy of Specialization*. Although these concepts are elevated in Zipf's theories to the status of natural laws, and vary slightly in meaning according to their context, they have direct analogies in economics. The principle of least effort is, in effect, a dynamic interpretation of cost minimization which (under certain assumptions) is equivalent to utility maximization. The force of unification refers to economies of agglomeration while the force of diversification relates to the minimization of transport costs. The effect of the force of unification would be to concentrate all population, production and consumption in one big city. The effect of the force of diversification would be to split total population into a very large number of small, widely scattered and autarchic communities. The actual distribution of city sizes reflects the rela-

---

14. His theory of the distribution of city sizes can be expressed in economic terms. Zipf (1949, p. 13) himself pointed out that his main organizing principle—the principle of least effort—has a very close relationship to classical economics. In the brief exposition which follows I paraphrase Zipf freely.

tive impact of the two forces.[15] This is equivalent to the familiar hypothesis that the relative strength of concentration and dispersion in the space economy is explained by the comparative strengths of economies of scale and the need to save transport costs. The force of innovation introduces a dynamic element into the model. This reinforces the force of unification since scale economies make it cheaper for new goods and industries to be first introduced in large population centres. Their attraction as production centres is associated with increased attractiveness as consumption centres (e.g., they offer a more diversified supply of consumer goods).

Isard's (1956, p. 60) criticism that Zipf fails to establish a link between the empirical findings and his theory is a little harsh. When properly interpreted, his basic forces do shed light on the distribution of urban population among cities. However, the level of his analysis is so general that it would require considerable amplification to show why the net operation of his mutually offsetting forces generates a Pareto distribution of city sizes. For this reason, his empirical analysis has won wider acclaim than the theoretical framework that underpins it.

## Cities as Coalitions and Clubs

Evans (1972) has suggested an interesting theory of city size distribution that builds upon the economic theory of clubs. The idea is that business firms (and/or individuals)[16] are faced with alternative sizes of city. Each city can be treated as a coalition of firms (and/or individuals) offering a certain mix of costs and benefits. Each firm (or individual) tries to join the coalition, membership of which maximizes its own profits (or net benefits). Applying the theory of clubs, it can be

shown that under certain assumptions a stable hierarchy of city sizes results from this process. These assumptions include the variation of market opportunities and input costs with city size.

The defect of the model is that, as it stands, there is no mechanism for generating the kind of city size distribution observed empirically. Evans argued that the number of cities in a given size class will decrease as cities (coalitions) increase in size. This depends upon the number and size of firms (or households) seeking locations in cities of a particular size. Thus, there will be a large number of very small cities only if a much larger number of firms (or households) find their ideal locations in cities of this size. It is easy to substantiate this condition *ex post*, but there is no assumption in the model to ensure it theoretically. However, there is an easy solution in the households model.[17] The number of coalitions of size $p_i$ will be determined by the total population, $P_i$, seeking to join a coalition of that size. If we assume that the population wanting to join each size class is equal ($P_1 = P_2 = P_3 = \ldots = P_i = \bar{P}$),[18] a plausible city size distribution results. The number of cities at each hierarchical level ($1, 2, \ldots i$) will be equal to $\bar{P}/p_1, \bar{P}/p_2, \ldots, \bar{P}/p_i$, respectively. Thus, the number of cities increases as city size declines.

## ALLOMETRIC GROWTH AND GENERAL SYSTEMS THEORY

The law of allometric growth has occasionally been used to explain city size distributions. Frequently used in animal biology,[19] the law

15. The special case where the two forces exactly balance each other is the rank-size rule where $q = 1$ (or the Pareto distribution where $a = 1$).
16. This extends Tiebout's (1956) model in which individuals move between cities to associate with people having similar preferences for public goods and services and for tax-expenditure mix.

17. Additional complications arise from the need to achieve compatibility between the number of households wanting to join a city of a prescribed size and the number and size of firms choosing a location in cities of this size (von Böventer, 1970). One method of reconciliation is in the labour market via the supply of and demand for labour functions and the response of households and firms to changes in wages.
18. This assumption is equivalent to the EHP (equal hierarchical population) assumption discussed by Parr (1970) in his typology of central place hierarchies.
19. I am grateful to an anonymous referee for convincing me that the biological analogy, despite its popularity with some city size distribution theorists, is not a necessary component of allometric explanations of city sizes.

is used to describe the relationship between dimensions of individual organs and those of the whole body. This can be expressed as

$$y = bx^\alpha \qquad (22)$$

where $y$ stands for the relative growth of an organ and $x$ stands for the growth of the entire body.

It is doubtful whether this has much concrete value for city size distribution theory. Beckmann (1958, pp. 247–248) demonstrated the similarity between the allometric equation and the Pareto distribution when we identify the capital city with an organ and the total urban population with the organism. But this merely implies that the statistical functions are similar.[20] Beckmann (1968, pp. 120–121) later attempted to show a theoretical link. He argued that the diffusion of production establishments in new industries from large cities to small in a dynamic central place model implies that the growth process will be associated with decentralization of production, increased competition and the growth of intermediate cities. Beckmann suggests that this process can be described as allometric growth because the relative size of a city increases with the overall size of the economy but at a different rate. However, the process could be better described via an economic model of growth diffusion without introducing the allometry concept.

Interpreted broadly, allometric growth easily merges into general systems theory. The concept of the system of cities as a general system has been advanced in some quarters (e.g., Berry, 1964), but the results are unconvincing, apart from the self-evident fact that the size and growth of an individual city cannot be satisfactorily explained, independent of the wider urban system. Wilson (1969, p. 179) has put his finger on a major defect in analysing city size distributions in

terms of general systems theory—the fact that not *one* system but several sub-systems are involved.

## NEW SUGGESTIONS

Although Markov chain models have been suggested as providing a useful approach to city size distribution theory, their potential has not been developed. An attempt is made here to use a Markovian framework to analyse interurban migration and capital flows as determinants of city sizes. The second proposal draws upon the multiplicative form of the Central Limit Theorem, a concept which has been used before to explain the personal income distribution but never before suggested in a city size distribution context. These ideas are not introduced with any pretensions that they provide superior explanations to the earlier models, though they illustrate the fact that there is still scope for further theoretical work in the analysis of this complex phenomenon.

### Markov Chain Models

Fano (1969) has criticized Curry's entropy maximization approach for its excessive randomness and for its neglect of functional interconnections between cities and the fact that the urban system is indeed a system. Instead, there should be structural and ordering factors influencing the distribution of city sizes. There may be randomness, but it is a constrained randomness. A Markov model may be useful in this context[21] because it is "essentially a model of evolution providing for selection within systems and ultimate structuring of systems as wholes." (Fano, p. 32). An unconstrained Markov process with all transitions from one city size class to another equally probable at each step yields a solution equivalent to the maximum entropy case, but with a different result—each size class having the same probability of contain-

---

20. The stability of the $\alpha$ parameter in equation (22) above implies some kind of equilibrium between the growth of the whole body and individual organs, even though they do not grow at the same rate. Similarly, a stable Pareto exponent may imply the maintenance of equilibrium in city size distributions even though individual cities jump ranks.

21. Fano's argument was anticipated by Olsson (1967) a few years earlier.

ing an equal number of cities. To introduce an element of order we impose constraints by allowing different transitions to have different probabilities. For instance, growth takes so much time that cities cannot "leap-frog" size classes, competition for limited high-order metropolitan functions constrains the number of cities that can move into the higher size classes, and, conversely, the durability of urban capital prevents cities from declining very fast. If upper and lower bounds are imposed on size-class jumping by making the transitional probabilities $(p_{ij})$ inversely proportional to the difference between the size classes $(i - j)$, the equilibrium city size distribution becomes a Pareto distribution.[22]

An elaboration of this approach would be to make it less abstract and to deal directly with the dynamics of population change or the process of interurban capital flows. This merely requires adapting inter-regional Markov models of migration (Rogers, 1966) and capital flows (Richardson, 1973) to an interurban context. In the migration model a distribution of city sizes will be generated directly whereas the capital flows model needs an additional assumption such as

$$w_i = f(k_i) \qquad (23)$$

where $w_i$ = population of city $i$ and $k_i$ = capital stock of city $i$.

Rogers' migration model involves expressing the interurban migration flow matrix[23] in coefficient form in order to derive a transitional probability matrix, $P$. Death can be treated as the absorbing state in an absorbing Markov chain model, and if the initial vector of city size populations is $w^0$, we may write

$$\overline{w}^0 = w^0 Q \qquad (24)$$

where $\overline{w}^0 < w^0$ because of deaths during the

transition period and $Q$ is the non-absorbing sub-matrix.[24]

If we now add a vector of births $b$ we obtain

$$w^1 = \overline{w}^0 + b = w^0 Q + b. \qquad (25)$$

Repeating the process $n$ times yields

$$w^n = w^0 Q^n + b(I + Q + \ldots + Q^{n-1}). \qquad (26)$$

However, since $Q < 1$, as $n$ increases $Q^n \rightarrow 0$ while $(I + Q + \ldots + Q^{n-1}) \uparrow (I - Q)^{-1}$ we may write

$$w^e = \lim_{n \rightarrow \infty} w^n = b(I - Q)^{-1}. \qquad (27)$$

Over a long period of time, the initial population distribution fades out and the equilibrium distribution of city sizes becomes a function of births, deaths and migration.

In the capital flows model the Q matrix is the transitional probability matrix for interurban capital flows while the absorbing matrix $(\hat{R})$ is a diagonal matrix of intra-urban absorption directly into investment (i.e., $T = (I - Q)^{-1}$. $\hat{R}$). I have shown elsewhere (Richardson, 1973) that the distribution of urban capital stocks at time period $n$ is given by

$$k^n = k^0 (I + Z)^n \qquad (28)$$

where $k^0$ = initial distribution of urban capital stocks, and

$$Z = \hat{A} \hat{V}^{-1} (I - Q)^{-1} \hat{R} \qquad (29)$$

where $\hat{A}$ = diagonal matrix of urban propensities to save and $\hat{V}^{-1}$ = inverse of the

---

22. Champernowne's (1953) model of income distribution is very similar.
23. Rural-urban migration can be dealt with by adding one row and column to represent the rural sector.

24. Obtained by partitioning the $P$ matrix in the usual way

$$P \doteq \left( \begin{array}{c|c} Q & R \\ \hline O & I \end{array} \right).$$

The absorbing state is excluded because it is implicit in the fact that the rows of Q do not sum to unity.

diagonal matrix ($\hat{V}$) of urban capital-output ratios.

Taking a specific form of equation (23) the distribution of city sizes at period $n$ can be expressed as a function of the distribution of urban capital stocks:

$$w^n = \hat{G}k^n = \hat{G}k^0(I + Z)^n \qquad (30)$$

where $\hat{G}$ = diagonal matrix of population-capital stock ratios.

The $\hat{G}$ matrix reflects the fact that city populations require urban infrastructure (housing, roads, schools and hospitals, investment in buildings and plant to provide jobs) to sustain them. The $\hat{G}$ coefficients can be allowed to vary systematically. For example, they may first increase and later decrease as we ascend the hierarchy to reflect economies and ultimately diseconomies of scale. Moreover, the $\hat{G}$ matrix could change over time to reflect technical progress and other changes in efficiency. Finally, it should be noted that the city size distribution of this model is not necessarily an equilibrium distribution because the closed economy growth process (income → savings → capital → income) does not move towards a steady state except in a special case.

Both models are of a general nature in the sense that they may generate several alternative city size distributions depending on the assumptions made about the structure of the transitional probability matrix. For example, sufficiently strong polarization tendencies ($p_{i1} > p_{i2} > p_{i3}$, etc., where cities are ranked by size 1, 2, 3...) can lead to a primate distribution in which people and capital are sucked into the largest city. Alternatively, the coefficients could reflect a filtering process in which labour and capital flow to cities of similar size (i.e., adjacent size classes) rather than to much larger or much smaller cities. This would imply the Pareto distribution yet again. Moreover, the city size distribution can change radically over time as a result of changes in the Q matrix. This would be useful in formulating a developmental model of city size distributions (e.g., from primacy to log-normality). The value of the Markov chain models is that with constrained transitional probabilities they offer a simple method of combining random and systematic (ordering) influences on the distribution of city sizes.

## A Simultaneously Multiplicative Theory

Simon's stochastic model was conceived as a dynamic process through time. There is no reason why a similar analysis cannot be applied to several independent factors combining multiplicatively at a given moment of time. This idea has been applied to income distribution theory by Roy (1950), but its potential for the explanation of city size distributions has been ignored. The statistical theory supporting the idea is the Central Limit Theorem. If a random variable, $y$, is the sum of independent random variables, the distribution of $y$ approaches the normal distribution as the number of component variables increases, provided that no single variable dominates the others. Thus, if $y = \Sigma_{i=1}^n x_i$ then $y$ approaches the normal distribution as $n \to \infty$. A corollary is that if $y = \Pi_{i=1}^n x_i$ then, given the same assumptions, $y$ will approach a log-normal distribution. The distribution of $y$ will be skew and leptokurtic—characteristics typical of the city size distribution—even if the individual variable distributions are all symmetrical. Also, skewness increases with the number of variables, their coefficients of variation and the degree of correlation between the variables (Haldane, 1942).

How appropriate is this statistical theory as a basis for a theory of city size distribution? First, the advantages of an urban centre may arise from several sources (for instance, natural resource endowment, transportation advantages, the supply of entrepreneurs, high local savings, age of settlement, topography, amenities, degree of nodality), and these may explain why some cities become bigger than others. Second, multiplicative effects simply mean that any one factor exercises its effect proportionately to city size rather than by the same absolute amount. There is substantial empirical support for the view that impacts are proportionate rather than absolute (Duncan and Reiss, 1956). Third, it is possible that some aggregate variable such as the ''growth potential of a city'' could be a multiplicative function of a number of underlying factors, several of which are likely to be intercorrelated and therefore mutually reinforcing. Fourth, a major advantage of this approach is that it may be possible to test the theory directly by comparing the distribution of city sizes with the distribution of the product of key variables that influence size.

A problem as compared with Simon's model is that this theory assumes that the variables influence size at one point of time rather than over time. Since the size of an individual city at any moment of time reflects the combined influence of both current and past factors, and some of the latter are cumulative in their impact, the use of what is in effect a cross-sectional model is a substantial liability. However, this defect need not be critical. Some of the potential variables, e.g., age of settlement, industrial diversification, reflect factors that are built up over time. Other variables, e.g., mileage distance from other cities, are invariant with time. Perhaps most important of all, just as the size distribution of cities is itself stable over time, it is possible that the distribution of the size-inducing determinants is itself also stable.

## CONCLUDING REMARKS

It is improbable that any one of the above models would be universally acceptable. There are so many influences interacting to mould the relative size of cities that it would be too difficult to include them all within a single model. Strands and elements drawn from different models may be appealing as partial explanations. Certainly, the search for a monocausal explanation is a chimera, and the choice of one model rather than another must be based on a judgement as to whether the selected model concentrates on key phenomena. Most of the models in this paper are satisfactory in the sense that they generate

size distributions of cities that are consistent with those found in the real world. Since at least a dozen distinct theories were discussed, the appeal of one rather than another is likely to be based on the analyst's preference for stochastic or systematic mbdels, economic or statistical theories, hierarchy or non-hierarchy models, and so on.

If the theory is in an unsatisfactory state, the fault lies in the nature and complexity of the subject rather than in the poverty of the theories already developed. However, a few conclusions may be drawn as pointers for future research. First, a satisfactory explanation probably needs to draw on both systematic and random factors and the weaknesses of some of the theories stem from exclusive reliance on one rather than the other. The Markov chain models represent one reasonable attempt to deal with this problem, while Beckmann's suggestion of introducing random elements into a central place hierarchy model is another. One method of achieving the latter is to treat the size of manufacturing towns as random influences and the size of nodal service centres as systematic elements. The point is that manufacturing cities and towns may be of any size, and therefore have no systematic effect on the size distribution.[25]

Second, of all possible systematic influences on the distribution of city sizes, economic conditions may be the most important. The existence of cities *per se* may be justified on social, political and cultural grounds, but these criteria would not seem to demand cities of *different* size. The most plausible systematic explanations of why there is a *distribution* of city sizes are based on economic theory. For example, the number of highest order (national and supranational) functions is so limited that there is no scope for more than one or two cities to grow to the highest rank. In the interurban competition for big size there are few winners because there are so few prizes. Similarly, a tendency in some coun-

25. Of course, it is possible to give manufacturing a systematic influence by locating industries of a given rank in cities of given sizes as in the Tinbergen model.

tries for the tail of the Pareto distribution to curve downwards could still be explained via the law of proportionate effect if the chances of growth to a higher size class decline with increasing city size. Such a tendency might be accounted for in terms of congestion costs, urban land constraints and other economic restrictions on urban growth rates.

Third, as we have seen, some models of city size distributions have drawn upon ideas used in theories of the distribution of incomes and firm sizes (Champernowne, Lydall, Simon, Roy). There remains scope for further parallel research on these lines.

Finally, a neglected question is the relationship between urbanization and the distribution of city sizes. For example, in an interesting early empirical study, Madden (1958) showed that U.S. cities experienced retardation trends in their growth rates as they grew older. If city growth rates are a function of the age of the city, we might expect the size distribution of cities to be affected by such variables as the age of the economy since industrial take-off, the rate of population growth, the average age of cities and the pattern and rate of geographical expansion. Since the more obvious explanations of retardation trends are based on city rivalry within a growing urban system (competition for migrants and industry) and the time and space paths of technical progress (Pred, 1966), the relative growth rates of cities—and ultimately the distribution of city sizes—depend upon the stage of development at which new cities appear, the sequence in which they appear and how they cluster in time. In general terms, this is a manifestation of the fact that the size of any city at any point of time depends upon the size and location of all other cities, not only at that point in time but also historically. More particularly, it is feasible to devise a model based on the hypothesis that the size distribution of cities is a function of the age distribution of cities. This type of model could be of supplementary value in accounting for the variations in observed city size distributions from one country to another.

## REFERENCES

Aitchison, J. and Brown, J. A. C. (1957) *The Lognormal Distribution*. Cambridge University Press.

Beckmann, M. J. (1958) City hierarchies and the distribution of city sizes, *Econ. Dev. Cult. Change* 6, 243–248.

———. (1968) *Location Theory*. Random House, New York.

———. and McPherson, J. (1970) City size distributions in a central place hierarchy: An alternative approach, *J. reg. Sci.* 10, 25–33.

Berry, B. J. L. (1961) City size distributions and economic development, *Econ. Dev. Cult. Change* 9, 573–587.

———. (1964) Cities as systems within systems of cities, *Papers Proc. Reg. Sci. Assoc.* 13, 147–163.

Bos, H. C. (1965) *The Spatial Dispersion of Economic Activity*. North-Holland, Amsterdam.

Champernowne, D. G. (1953) A model of income distribution, *Econ. J.* 63, 318–351.

Christaller, W. (translated by Baskin, C. W.) (1966) *Central Places in Southern Germany*. Prentice-Hall, Englewood Cliffs, New Jersey.

Curry, L. (1964) The random spatial economy: An exploration in settlement theory, *Ann. Assoc. Am. Geogr.* 54, 138–146.

Dacey, M. F. (1966) Population of places in a central place hierarchy, *J. Reg. Sci.* 6, 27–33.

Davis, E. and Swanson, J. G. (1972) On the distribution of city growth rates in a theory of regional economic growth, *Econ. Dev. Cult. Change* 20, 495–503.

Duncan, O. D. and Reiss, A. J., Jr. (1956) *Social Characteristics of Urban and Rural Communities, 1950*. Wiley, New York.

Edel, M. (1972) Land values and the costs of urban congestion: Measurement and distribution, 61–90, in École Pratique des Hautes Études, VI<sup>e</sup> Section, *Political Economy of Environment: Problems of Method*. Mouton, The Hague.

El Shaks, S. (1965) Development, Primacy and the Structure of Cities. Unpublished Ph.D. dissertation, Harvard University.

Evans, A. W. (1972) The pure theory of city size in an industrial economy, *Urban Studies* 9, 49–77.

Fano, P. (1969) City size distributions and central places, *Papers Proc. Reg. Sci. Assoc.* 22, 29–38.

Greenwood, M. J. (1970) Lagged response in the decision to migrate, *J. Reg. Sci.* 10, 375–384.

Haldane, J. B. S. (1942) Moments of the distribution of powers and products of normal variates, *Biometrika* 32, 226.

Harris, C. D. (1970) *Cities in the Soviet Union: Studies in their Functions, Size, Density and Growth*. Rand McNally.

Harris, W. D. (1971) *The Growth of Latin American Cities*. Ohio University Press, Athens.

Higgs, R. (1970) Central place theory and regional urban hierarchies: An empirical note, *J. Reg. Sci.* 10, 253–255.

Isard, W. (1956) *Location and Space-Economy*. M.I.T. Press.

Jefferson, M. (1939) The law of the primate city, *Geogr. Rev.* 29, 226–232.

Kermack, K. A. and Haldane, J. B. S. (1950) Organic correlation and allometry, *Biometrika* 37, 30–41.

Linsky, A. S. (1965) Some generalizations concerning primate cities, *Ann. Assoc. Am. Geogr.* 55, 506–513.

Lösch, A. (1954) *The Economics of Location*. Yale University Press, New Haven.

Lydall, H. F. (1968) *The Structure of Earnings*. Clarendon Press, Oxford.

Madden, C. H. (1956) On some indications of stability in the growth of cities in the United States, *Econ. Dev. Cult. Change* 4, 236–252.

———. (1958) Some temporal aspects of the growth of cities in the United States, *Econ. Dev. Cult. Change* 6, 143–170.

Mehta, S. K. (1964) Some demographic and economic correlates of primate cities: A case for revaluation, *Demography* 1, 136–147.

Mills, E. S. (1972) *Urban Economics*. Scott, Foresman, Glenview, Illinois.

Morse, R. M. (1962) Latin American cities: Aspects of function and structure, *Comp. Studies Soc. History* 4, 473–493.

Olsson, G. (1967) Central place systems, spatial interaction and stochastic processes, *Papers Proc. Reg. Sci. Assoc.* 18, 13–45.

Parr, J. B. (1970) Models of city size in an urban system, *Papers Proc. Reg. Sci. Assoc.* 25, 221–253.

Pred, A. (1966) *The Spatial Dynamics of United States Urban-Industrial Growth, 1800–1914*. M.I.T. Press.

Rashevsky, N. (1943) Contribution to the theory of human relations: Outline of a mathematical theory of the size of cities, *Psychometrika* 8, 87–90.

———. (1947) *Mathematical Theory of Human Relations*. Principia Press, Bloomington.

———. (1951) *Mathematical Biology of Social Behaviour*. Chicago University Press.

Richardson, H. W. (1972) Optimality in city size, systems of cities and urban policy: A sceptic's view, *Urban Studies* 9, 29–48.

———. (1973) *Regional Growth Theory*. Macmillan, London.

Rogers, A. (1966) A Markovian policy model of interregional migration, *Papers Proc. Reg. Sci. Assoc.* 17, 205–224.

Roy, A. D. (1950) The distribution of earnings and individual output, *Econ. J.* 60, 489–505.

Simon, H. (1955) On a class of skew distribution functions, *Biometrika* 42, 425–440.

Thompson, W. R. (1972) The national system of cities as an object of public policy, *Urban Studies* 9, 99–116.

Tiebout, C. M. (1956) A pure theory of local expenditures, *J. pol. Econ.* 64, 416–424.

Tinbergen, J. (1968) The hierarchy model of the size distribution of centres, *Papers Proc. Reg. Sci. Assoc.* 20, 65–68.

Vining, R. (1955) A description of certain spatial aspects of an economic system, *Econ. Dev. Cult. Change* 3, 147–195.

Von Böventer, E. G. (1970) Optimal spatial structure and regional development, *Kyklos* 23, 903–924.

Ward, B. (1963) City structure and interdependence, *Papers Proc. Reg. Sci. Assoc.* 10, 207–221.

Weiss, H. K. (1961) The distribution of urban population and an application to a servicing problem, *Operations Res.* 9, 860–874.

Wilson, A. G. (1969) Notes on some concepts in social physics, *Papers Proc. Reg. Sci. Assoc.* 22, 159–193.

Zipf, G. K. (1949) *Human Behavior and the Principle of Least Effort*. Addison-Wesley, Cambridge, Mass.

# The Structure of Central Place Systems

RICHARD E. PRESTON

Central place theory has yet to be applied in its *classical* form.[1] Such is the case because workers have failed to operationalize the pivotal concept of "centrality" consistent with Christaller's original definitions. This inability has led to the use of proxy measures for centrality, and to its confusion with nodality, a related but far more inclusive concept. The meaning of this situation for empirical central place research is clear; it is quite conceivable that in studies completed thus far, the areal distribution of the central place function, in its classical sense, remains unidentified.

The purpose here is to provide application to Christaller's model. To that end, the system of central places in the Pacific Northwest in the early 1960s is identified and described. This is achieved by determining the relative size, class, and position in the area's central place structure of 164 places with 2,500 or more inhabitants, and by indicating the pattern of functional interdependence between all settlements by examining selected linkages. The approach closely parallels that offered by Christaller, and within that context, several of his arguments that are relevant to *application* of central place theory are further developed [10, pp. 137–68].

This study is organized so that its perti-

nence to central place research is established at the outset. Next, those elements of a central place system treated here, as well as selected operational definitions, are clarified. A centrality model is presented: centrality values are calculated for each place; the places are ranked, and the values are mapped. Then, the central places are classified and mapped, and the principal central place systems in the study area, are identified by reconstructing their nested hierarchies. After examining the central place structure of the study area, appropriate findings are considered in the light of current positions regarding classically defined central place systems.

In works that have become part of the permanent literature on central places, Ullman, and Berry and Garrison were the first to consider problems needing attention before Christaller's model could be verified. Ullman recognized thirty years ago that the concept of centrality would have to be operationalized if the areal distribution of the central place function was to be identified consistent with theory; he also noted the difficulty of measuring centrality and suggested possible solutions [29, pp. 858–59]. During the 1960s, Murphy, King, and others, pointed out that the problem of measuring centrality, in accordance with theoretical requirements, remained unsolved [21, pp. 74–84; 17, pp. 246–48; 13, pp. 61–63; 28, p. 144]. When the status of central place research was reviewed by Berry and Garrison in 1958, they concluded that evidence was available regarding

---

1. "Classical central place theory" refers to the contribution of Christaller [10]. Some feel that recent studies have produced a "modern central place theory." The modern version claims to have generalized, and thus broadened the applicability of Christaller's model [2].

From *Economic Geography*, vol. 47, no. 2, 1971, pp. 136–55. Reprinted by permission.

several theoretical implications: that larger centers are functionally more complex than smaller centers; that increasing functional complexity is accompanied by increasing size of the urban complementary region; and, that because of the differential provision of central functions, interdependence exists between urban centers in the distribution of central goods and services [6, p. 145]. Regarding the verification of these implications, Berry and his associates have brought forward additional evidence [2, pp. 10–40; 4; 5]. Berry and Garrison also concluded that satisfactory evidence had not been provided to verify the hierarchical class-system of centers postulated in theory. They did, however, offer findings supporting such a class-system, and Berry subsequently has confronted this controversial matter [6, pp. 146–54; 2, pp. 26–40; 4; 5].

This study offers evidence pertinent to the identification of central places; it supports the validity of the principal behavioral assumption underlying central place theory, the interdependence between centers in the provision of central goods and services, and the existence of hierarchical class-systems of central places.

## PROCEDURAL DEFINITIONS

Christaller took a central place system "to be a number of central places grouped around a central place (that is, the system-forming central place) according to given rules" [10, p. 164]. He identified the elements of such a system as: the system-forming central places; the central places grouped around them; the distances between central places; the positions in which the central places lie with regard to system-forming central places as well as other central places in the region; and, the area occupied by such a system, or the region of the system-forming central place [10, p. 164]. His spatial model called for seven orders of central places arranged in a nested hierarchy.

To facilitate the conceptual structure used

here, Christaller's view of a central place system is replaced by a more recent statement by Haggett. Haggett's view allows for greater precision in the analysis of urban systems, and at the same time is both more general in application and descriptively more complete. Nevertheless, it is in most respects in obvious harmony with Christaller's view; for Haggett's elements have at least an implicit counterpart in Christaller's conceptualization of a central place system. Haggett argued that the nearest equivalent to a general system in human geography is the nodal region, "in which the set of objects (towns, villages, farms, etc.) are related through circulating movements (money, migrants, freight, etc.) and the energy inputs come through biological and social needs of the community" [14, p. 17]. He pointed out that nodal regions can be broken-down into related elements; *movements* that flow over *networks* connecting *nodes* which are organized into a *hierarchy,* and that the interstitial zones can be integrated with the preceding four elements and treated as *surfaces* [14, pp. 17–19]. An attempt is made here to focus on nodes, hierarchies, movements, and complementary regions in an interrelated spatial context.

## Centrality and Classical Central Place Theory[2]

Haggett has stressed that one difficulty associated with studying an integrated regional system is that there is no obvious single point of entry [14, p. 31]. In the case of central place systems, for example, it is just as logical to begin with consideration of the central places themselves as with networks, movements, or complementary regions. Moreover, at some stage in every central

2. Only the operational definitions directly pertinent to this study are discussed below. For the full range of definitions supporting classical theory see Christaller [10], and consider the fact that the operational definitions presented in the "Theoretical Part" are termed incomplete at the end of the chapter on "Fundamental Meanings." It is thus necessary to synthesize the definitions as given on pp. 14–23 with their amplifications on pp. 139–51 to get their full meaning.

place inquiry, the central place importance of each settlement must be determined. A position taken here is that virtually all empirical studies attempting to develop and apply central place theory falter at this point. Such is the case because the basic distinctions between *centrality* and *nodality,* two essential concepts of classical central place theory, are not fully taken into account.

Nodality and centrality are related concepts that identify, respectively, the aggregate and relative importance of settlements, thus providing quite different concepts of settlement size or importance. It is clear, for example, that every settlement has a certain *importance* expressed rather inexactly by some index of its *size.* When studying the central place function, however, interest is not focused on size alone. It is focused on the relative importance of settlements as regional centers, that is, the settlements serve *as providers of goods and services in excess of those demanded by the center's own inhabitants.* Christaller argued that if central place importance was determined solely by aggregate measures of size, then part of the importance must be ascribed to the town itself as an agglomeration of population and another part to the town as a central place. He called the sum of these two parts *absolute importance,* and he considered *relative importance* to be that part attributable to a settlement's function as a source of goods and services for a surrounding region. Thus, only the relative importance shows the degree to which a settlement is a central place [*10,* pp. 17–18, 139–50]. To reduce ambiguity throughout the remainder of this paper, the term *nodality* will stand for the absolute measure and the term *centrality* will stand for the relative measure.

## A Centrality Model

The critical importance of the measurement of centrality was made clear by Christaller [*10,* pp. 143, 49]. Thus, implementation of a central place study along classical lines requires a model that satisfies the operational definitions

laid down by Christaller as well as the following specific definition of centrality:

$$C = N - L$$

where
$C = $ the surplus of importance, i.e., the relative importance of a place or centrality;
$N = $ the importance of a place plus its complementary region, i.e., absolute importance or nodality;
$L = $ the importance of a town as a unit consuming central goods and services, or local consumption.

The model presented here satisfies Christaller's operational definitions[3] and rests upon the following specific assumptions: families living in a central place purchase their central goods and services there (local consumption); each central place has a complementary region from which families come to purchase goods and services (complementary region consumption); and each central place provides some goods and services to persons living in neither the central place nor in its complementary region (irregular consumption). The sum of complementary region and irregular consumption equal centrality. With the exception of the concept of irregular consumption, a modification dictated by the increased mobility since Christaller's time, these assumptions are in conformance with the principal behavioral assumption underlying central place theory, namely, that consumers patronize the nearest center offering a particular good or service.

The next steps were to construct an operational model, collect pertinent data, and apply the model. In application the centrality model is

$$C = R + S - \alpha MF$$

where
$R = $ total sales of retail establishments;
$S = $ total sales in selected service establishments;

---

3. For a full discussion of this model and its operationalization, see Preston [*25*].

$\alpha$ = average percentage of median family income spent on retail items and selected services;

$M$ = median family income for a central place;

$F$ = total number of families in a central place.

In this model, $R + S$ provides an estimate of $N$ in the Christaller model, and $\alpha MF$ is an estimate of $L$. The difference is obviously $C$, or centrality. By comparison with Christaller's operational model (the well-known telephone index [10, pp. 139–47]),[4] the model used here eliminates the influence of the complementary region; instead, the fraction of nodality attributable to nonresidents is established specifically for each settlement. This improvement allows for direct identification and comparison of centrality values for particular places without indirect treatment of central places as comparative departures from regional averages. Here, with explicit consideration for retail trade and services, we satisfy Christaller's model more completely than did his own operational application.

## The Study Area

The Pacific Northwest—Washington, Oregon, Idaho, and the mountain counties of western Montana—is an area of strong and varied physical features. The Northwest is not an ideal laboratory for central place studies. Concern here, however, is not with spatially efficient geometries achievable only after an assumption of areal homogeneity; rather, interest lies in the spatial efficiency implicit in the overriding behavioral assumption identified above. If the assumption is correct, then some form of the central place system as well as basic patterns of spatial efficiency should be identifiable and measurable in any environment.

Especially important here are the populated

4. For a comparison of the telephone index and the model offered here, see Preston [25].

territories. Dominant among these are two urban-industrial concentrations: the Seattle-Tacoma complex and metropolitan Portland. Beyond the well-developed urban systems in those two lowlands, urban places are concentrated in two crescents. One is composed of a group of agriculturally oriented valleys that curves southeastward from Wenatchee through the Yakima Valley to the cities near the junction of the Columbia and Snake Rivers. The other crescent consists of three segments of the Snake River Plain in Idaho. From west to east the cities of Boise, Twin-Falls, and Idaho Falls-Pocatello each provide a focus for one section. Throughout the remainder of the study area cities do not tend to cluster. However, there are smaller but significant valleys scattered along the coast and throughout the highlands, and each has its urban node, for example, the Rogue River Basins and the valleys of northeastern Oregon and western Montana. A quite different situation is presented by the sparsely populated central plain and eastern border of the Columbia Basin, a vast area organized around Spokane. Each of the study area's populated territories should provide insights into the role of central places in the structure of different space economies.

## Measuring Centrality

To produce centrality values for specific places, the following data were collected: retail sales and selected service sales for each of 164 incorporated places which had 2,500 or more inhabitants in 1960 and were listed in the 1963 Census of Business [31, 32]; median income of families and unrelated individuals, and the number of families in each place from the 1960 Census of Population [30]; and, average annual expenditure patterns for urban families in 1960–1961 as reported by the Bureau of Labor Statistics [11].

Total sales in retail trade and selected services were summed for each of the places in the study area to produce an estimated nodality value for each place. Then, the numerous

Standard Industrial Classification entries used in the Census of Business were condensed into ten of the categories used in the income and expenditure reports. From these data the percentage of median family income spent for retail goods and selected services was estimated. This value, $\alpha$, (sixty percent) was then applied to the median family income for each place. The result is an estimation of expected local consumption, which, when subtracted from the nodality value for a place, yields an estimate of all nonlocal consumption, or centrality.

When ranked by their centrality values, 159 places (out of 164) show positive centrality values which range from $155,000 for Buckley, Washington, to $636,647,000 for Seattle. Support is thus offered for the position that all settlements are not automatically central places, a situation both recognized and operationalized by Christaller, but ignored by subsequent workers. It would appear that this seemingly elementary, but fundamental, finding would be impossible to establish when central place importance is determined by such nodality indexes as total population, retail sales, retail employees, key functions, or numbers of establishments or functions. The pyramidal nature of the centrality values is also clear: fifty-three percent of the places have centrality indexes of less than $10,000,000; sixty-nine percent less than $20,000,000; ninety percent less than $48,000,000; and ninety-six percent less than $100,000,000.

## Areal Distribution of the Central Place Function

In Figure 1, two values pertinent to an evaluation of an areal distribution of the central place function are revealed. On each figure, centrality indexes (in dollars) for each place are shown by circles, and the importance of each central place is further elucidated by patterns showing the ratio of centrality to nodality. These maps allow direct comparison of individual centralities both in terms of dollars and as a percentage of corresponding nodalities.

Several points become clear upon examination of the maps. Each population cluster is dominated by a place with a centrality value much greater than that of any other place in the respective cluster. It should be noted in this regard that only in the case of Eugene, Oregon, does a dominating central place also possess the highest centrality/nodality ratio. Throughout the entire study area, places with high centrality values tend to have smaller centrality/nodality ratios than places with low centralities. However, the relationship between centrality and nodality is clearly not a functional one; this emphasizes the need for recognizing central place importance on an individual basis.

## A Classification of Central Places

Attempting to solve the problem of how to classify the 159 central places meant also confronting the question of whether or not the hierarchical arrangement of central places called for in classical theory exists in the Pacific Northwest. In the past, hierarchies have often been produced on arbitrary grounds [6, pp. 146–48; 23, pp. 10–19; 12, pp. 51–65]. Even the powerful techniques presently used for grouping purposes fail to provide an analytic solution to the problem of how many groups exist in an array of spatial data [18, p. 199; 20, pp. 53–59].

The grouping technique used here is similar to the "moving average" commonly employed to detect trends in the study of time series [33, pp. 575–88; 34, p. 41]. The technique's strength lies in its ability to eliminate (or at least markedly reduce) random variations, and thereby aid in determining whether or not discrete groups of observations exist in a set of data. An attempt was thus made to capitalize on the smoothing effect of the moving average (the artificial stability introduced by the arithmetic of cumulation) through use of a "cumulative average of differences." Centrality values for 159 posi-

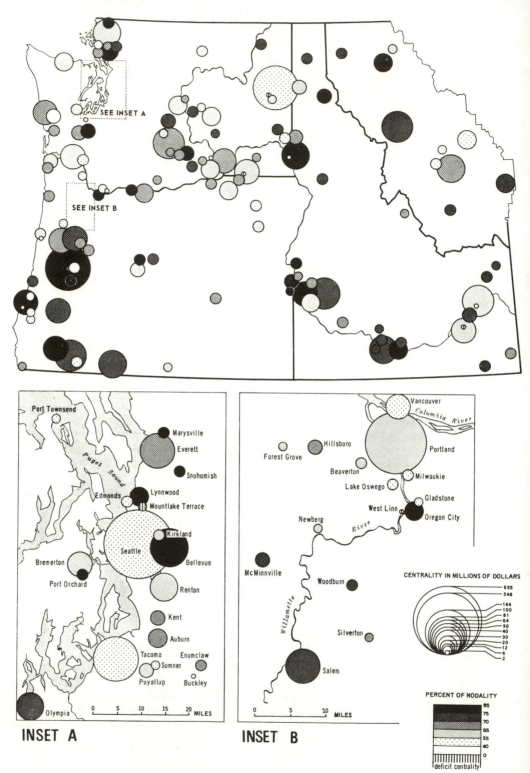

Fig. 1.   Centrality indexes for places with 2,500 or more inhabitants in 1960.

tive observations were ranked, differences between successively greater observations were determined, and a cumulative average of differences calculated. The logic of the technique is straightforward. If hierarchical conditions do not exist, the cumulative average of differences when graphed will assume a constant slope. For more than one group to be recognized, the graph must exhibit more than one slope. This can be achieved by displacement associated with the establishment of a second (though similar in attitude to the first) slope, or by a change in slope. If discrete groups of values do not exist in an array, marked displacements and slope changes will not appear. Bias is with the data rather than with the investigator. Results are shown in Figure 2.

## CENTRAL PLACES IN THE PACIFIC NORTHWEST

The regional central place hierarchy is considered briefly below. Then, the study area is analyzed by focusing in turn on downward linkages between: fourth and lower-order central places; third and lower-order places; and finally, between first and second-order central places and all lower-order centers.

### The Regional Hierarchy

The five-step central place hierarchy identified in Figure 2 is mapped in Figure 3. In Figure 3 the primacy of Seattle and Portland is emphasized by their rank and location relative to both the largest concentrations of population and the other central places. Seattle's centrality is greater than Portland's, but both have by far the greatest values in the study area. Spokane, Tacoma, and Eugene are the second-order central places, and all have similar centrality values. The third-order central places are Salem, Everett, Bellevue, Yakima, Boise, Idaho Falls, and Missoula, and are of two distinct locational types. Everett and Bellevue are secondary centers within Seattle's metropolitan area, while the others are the principal centers of the remaining significant population clusters in the study area. Each first-, second-, and third-order central place is surrounded by a cluster of smaller places; however, all higher-order central places are not surrounded by a complete range of lower-order places.

### The Nested Hierarchies

Marshall makes a strong case for the position that most central place studies have failed in

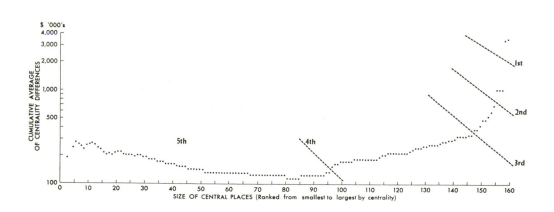

Fig. 2.   Orders of central places in the Pacific Northwest.

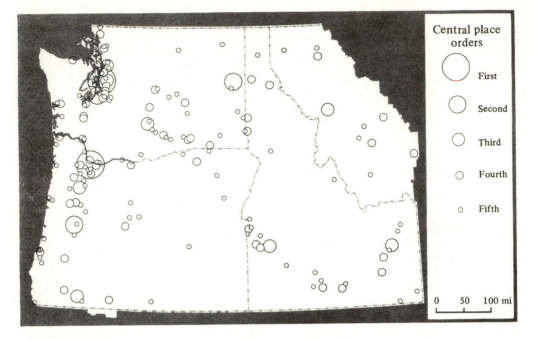

Figure 3. Central Place Hierarchy.

the sense that they do not identify, and thus do not consider, meaningful central place systems [20, pp. 23–24, 78–79]. An attempt is made here to examine the functional interdependence between settlements in the study area and thereby to identify such systems. The problem is twofold: first, to identify the areal extent and the pattern of functional interdependence that define the complementary regions of the system-forming central places of the first four orders; and second, to gain insight into the roles played in the study area's settlement structure by fifth-order central places and by places with fewer than 2,500 inhabitants. To achieve these ends, successively more general complementary regions were identified by plotting the following measures of spatial interaction: banking relationships, daily newspaper circulation, commuting patterns, Sunday newspaper circulation, and branch-firm distribution. In some instances supplementary interaction data were used as well.

An attempt was made to learn something of

the way fifth-order and smaller places were tied into the study area's central place structure, and to reveal some detailed information about functional interdependence. One type of available interaction data were banking relationships as revealed by the *Dun and Bradstreet Reference Book* (March, 1963).[5] Every place in the study area that contained one or more banks was identified, and banking towns were determined for every settlement of hamlet size and larger that did not have a bank. Figure 4 shows the resulting banking linkages for the area. Evidence is thus offered regarding the position of virtually all places not included in the Census of Business Reports in the hierarchical structure of the study area.

In order to identify as many complementary regions as possible for fourth- and higher-order central places, *daily newspaper circulation* was used as an index of functional

5. For an evaluation of the accuracy of Dun and Bradstreet information see Russwurm [27, pp. 271–73].

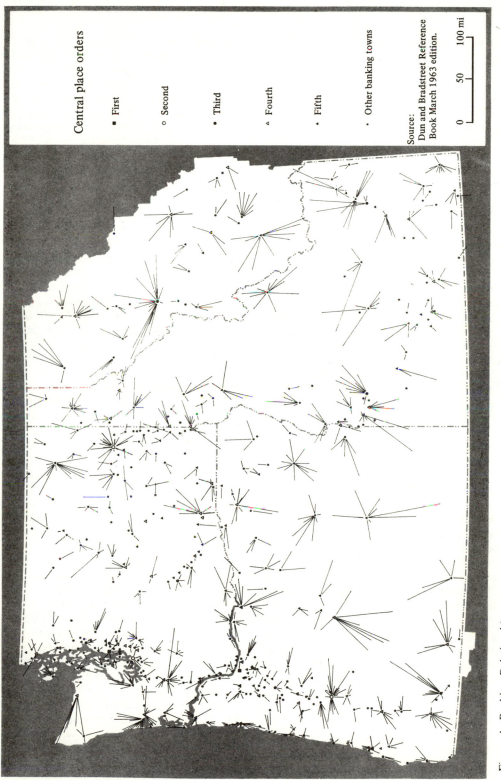

Figure 4.  Banking Relationships.

interdependence. *Ayer and Son's Directory of Newspapers and Periodicals* for 1963 indicated that the study area contained fifty-eight daily newspapers. Daily circulation data for 1963 were procured for forty-five of these at the Audit Bureau of Circulations [*1*].[6] Since the pattern of dominance in total daily newspaper circulation was sought, circulation data for *all* daily newspapers in the study area were mapped. Each settlement was assigned to the center from which it received the *most* daily papers (Figure 5). Only one requirement had to be met for a place to appear on the map. A place distributing a daily newspaper had to dominate at least one place beside itself; thus, four fifth-order places failed to qualify.

The pattern produced in Figure 5 was incomplete as ABC does not always report the number of papers delivered to places that receive less than twenty-five copies of a particular paper per delivery. In addition, the complementary regions revealed in Figure 5 were inadequate on three counts. First, one third-order and nine fourth-order places were not represented. Moreover, none of these ten places had daily newspapers. Rather than drop them from the analysis at this point, it was decided to attempt to get at least an indication of the extent of their complementary regions by seeking alternative interaction data. Weekly and semi-weekly newspaper circulation and one chamber of commerce estimate were used to establish the complementary regions for these ten places. The regions produced are probably not comparable with those determined by daily circulation patterns; however, weekly newspaper circulation does provide some indication of the role of these particular places in the study area's settlement structure.

A second inadequacy in Figure 5 consisted of blank areas in southeastern Idaho and in part of Lewis and Clark County in Montana. This suggested that complementary regional structure along the study area's borders should be examined. Necessary newspaper

circulation data were available from ABC, and analysis revealed that: no meaningful flow of daily newspapers crossed this part of the International Boundary between the United States and Canada; Great Falls, located outside the study area in Montana, dominated the northern part of Lewis and Clark County; Salt Lake City, Utah, dominated parts of southeastern Idaho; and Klamath Falls, Oregon, dominated several communities in northern California. These modifications were added to Figure 5 to arrive at its present form.

Centrality values were also calculated for Salt Lake City and Great Falls as their influence in the study area was apparent. Salt Lake City's centrality was $344,194,000, placing it between the first- and second-order central places, but closer to the first-order. Great Falls registered a centrality of $78,480,000 a value lying firmly in the third-order central places. Both cities were included in all subsequent analyses.

A third inadequacy in Figure 5 stemmed from the pattern of dominance revealed for Portland. On one hand, Portland newspapers dominated a county in the southwestern corner of Oregon, a distance of over 300 miles from Portland. On the other hand, Portland papers extended beyond the Cascade Mountains and dominated most of eastern Oregon as well as adjacent parts of Washington State. An unrealistic implication here was that frequent trips of from 85 to 400 miles one-way were made to Portland from these areas for central goods and services.

The problem was twofold: to correct for what would appear to be the excessive reach of Portland, and to unravel the actual central place structure of the areas in question. Figure 6 aids in resolving this and lesser problems, and constitutes a map of correction factors. Plotted first were the appropriate *commuting fields* of central cities developed by Berry [*3, 7*]. The outer boundaries of these commuting fields were then adapted to conform with the distribution of population in the study area in 1960 [*15*, pp. 14–15]. The assumption here was that such commuting fields provide a reasonable outer limit for areas within which

---

6. For a discussion of the methods used in the collection of newspaper circulation data, see Bennet [*8*]. On the use of newspapers as an index of urban dominance, see Lueck [*19*], Park and Newcomb [*24*], and Murphy [*21*, pp. 52–66].

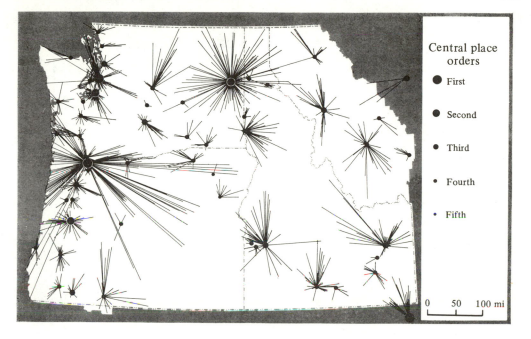

Figure 5. Patterns of Daily Newspaper Dominance.

frequent trips are made to particular central cities for central goods and services. Commuting fields were available for all first- and second-order centers, for seven of eight third-order, and for eleven fourth-order central places. When superimposed on Figure 5, the commuting fields were in general agreement with daily newspaper regions wherever both sets of data were available except in southwestern and eastern Oregon and in southwestern Idaho. The complementary regions in these three problem areas were resolved by consideration and analyses of "second-most-important" daily newspaper circulation, weekly newspaper circulation, and further examination of the banking relationships. Finally, a questionnaire was distributed to more than 100 postmasters which provided information to settle difficult assignments of boundaries.

Figure 7, "Complementary Regions of Fourth and Higher Order Central Places," was constructed as follows: (1) a dot map of population distribution in the study area in 1960 served as a base [15, pp. 14–15]; (2) Figure 5, "Patterns of Daily Newspaper Dominance" was superimposed on the population distribution to provide a primary interaction pattern upon which the initial delimitation of complementary regions was based; (3) Figure 6, "Other Movement Patterns" was superimposed on Figure 5 and aided in establishing outlines for all problem complementary regions; (4) Figure 4, "Banking Relationships" was then superimposed on the corrected complementary region map to insure that complete banking systems (the banking town of which was dominated by a particular fourth or higher-order central place) were included in the complementary region of a dominating central place; lastly, (5) to assure replication, and to serve as a base for making continuous complementary region population estimates, boundaries produced by the preceding four steps were adjusted to fit County Census Areas [9].

Figures 4, 5, and 7 clearly demonstrate the increase in size of fourth-order complemen-

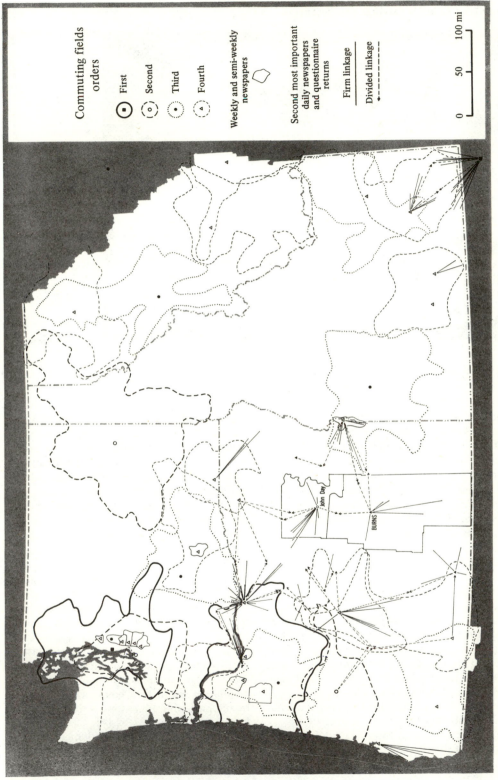

Figure 6. Other Movement Patterns.

Commuting fields
orders

First

Second

Third

Fourth

Weekly and semi-weekly
newspapers

Second most important
daily newspapers
and questionnaire
returns

Firm linkage

Divided linkage

100 mi

50

0

John Day

BURNS

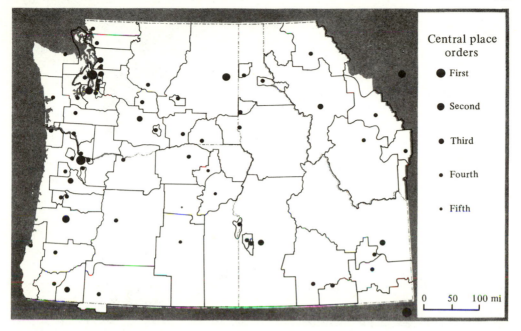

Figure 7. Complementary Regions of Fourth and Higher-Order Central Places.

tary regions with distance from the larger cities. This finding supports both Isard's earlier contention that market areas increase in size with distance from a city in any direction, and the superiority of his cartographic model of market areas over those offered by Christaller and Lösch [16, pp. 271–74; 20, pp. 39–40].

The next problem in tracing the nested hierarchical pattern in the study area was to determine complementary regions for third and higher-order central places. The index of spatial interaction used for this purpose was *Sunday newspaper circulation*. The assumption here was that Sunday newspaper distribution provides a meaningful summary index of metropolitan dominance [19; 24; 21, pp. 62–66]. Necessary data were acquired from ABC and are shown in Figure 8. Individual places were considered to be tied to the center from which they received the most Sunday newspapers. Figure 9 shows the third and higher-order complementary regions. In that context, Seattle dominated thirteen and one-

half fourth-order regions, and Portland dominated eighteen fourth-order regions, plus those of four fifth-order regions. Among the second-order centers, Spokane absorbed eight and one-half fourth-order regions, while the complementary regions of Tacoma and Eugene remained essentially unchanged from what they were in the fourth-order context. Salt Lake City dominated three fourth-order regions in southeastern Idaho. Among the third-order central places, Boise dominated three fourth-order fields while those of Yakima, Salem, Medford, and Idaho Falls changed little from what they were in the fourth-order situation. Great Falls expanded into a vacuum existing in the study area in southwestern Montana; and Everett and Bellevue were dominated completely by Seattle.

The final delimitation problem was to identify complementary regions for first and second-order central places. The measure of spatial interaction used here was the number of branches of firms located in first and second-order central places that are located in

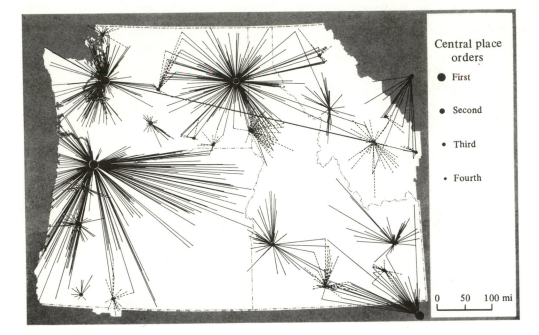

Figure 8. Patterns of Sunday Newspaper Dominance.

each third and higher-order complementary region. Necessary data were available in the *Dun and Bradstreet Reference Book* (March, 1963). Dominance in number of branch firms was the index used, so the number of branches of firms located in each of the first three orders of central places was calculated and plotted for every settlement in the study area listed in Dun and Bradstreet. Each place was awarded to the third or higher-order central place that provided it with the greatest number of branch firms. Then, the numbers of branch firms from each third and higher-order place were totaled for each third and higher-order complementary region. Finally, each complementary region was awarded to the third or higher-order central place represented by the largest number of branch firms. Regions determined on this basis are shown by a broken line in Figure 9.

The pattern of branch firm dominance is such that second and third-order central places fail to dominate any third and higher-

order complementary regions. In other words, second and third-order central places had fewer branch firms in their own complementary regions than there were branches of firms located in first-order centers. The study area thus contained two complete (Seattle and Portland) and one partial (Salt Lake City) nested hierarchies, and they exhibited the following nesting traits: (1) the second-order regions of Tacoma and Spokane along with those of third-order Yakima, Missoula, and Great Falls were dominated by Seattle;[7] (2) the second-order region of Eugene as well as the third-order regions of Salem and Medford were included in Portland's nested hierarchy; and (3) the third-order regions of Boise and Idaho Falls came under Salt Lake City. The nested hierarchies through those

7. The inclusion of the mountain counties of western Montana in Seattle's region was based on the fact that Seattle dominates Spokane and that Seattle and Spokane together dominate western Montana, and that Lueck found Seattle to dominate this area [*19*, p. 21].

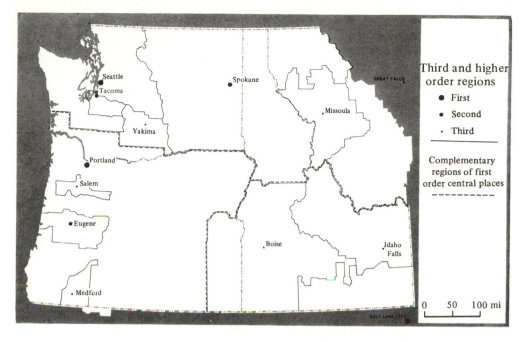

Figure 9. Complementary Regions of Higher-Order Central Places.

fifth-order places for which centrality values could be calculated are summarized in Figures 10, 11, and 12.

## IMPLICATIONS FOR RESEARCH

By reconstructing the nested hierarchies of Seattle and Portland as well as part of Salt Lake City's hierarchy, the central place system in the Pacific Northwest in the early 1960s was approximated. A start was thus made toward an eventual understanding of the urban system in that area. This was achieved by identifying the areal distribution of the central place function in the classical sense, establishing the central place hierarchy, and by identifying the nested hierarchical structure in terms of downward linkages between successively more general measures of functional interdependence. Empirical evidence presented here supports the explanatory power of central place theory in its classical form.

## The Identification of Central Places

In classical central place theory the mere presence of functions and a nucleated population does not automatically give a settlement status as a central place. This reality can now be taken into account in empirical studies. The model offered here identifies the relative importance of individual settlements as central places consistent with the requirements of classical theory, and should produce comparable descriptive and analytic findings for all places in the United States covered by the Census, or for any other place for which comparable data are available.

If it is true that not even all places with 2,500 or more inhabitants qualify as central places in the classical sense, then, what is the central place importance of settlements with

# NESTING RELATIONSHIPS OF HIGHER ORDER CENTRAL PLACES : SEATTLE

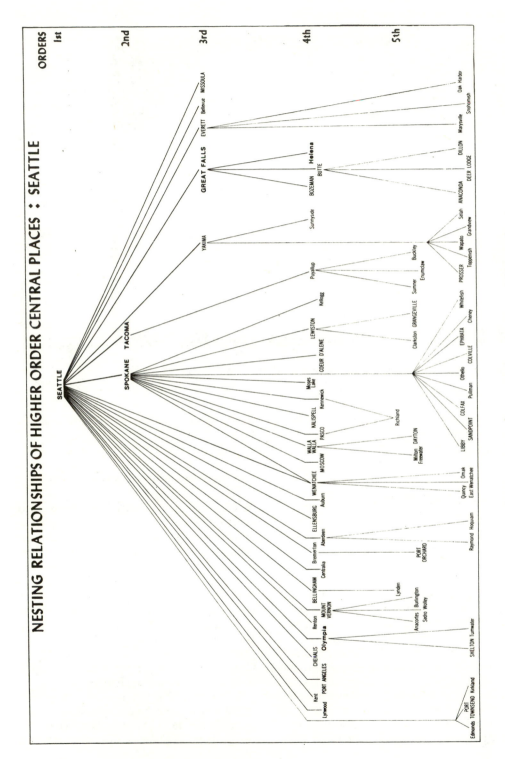

Figure 10. Nesting Relationships of Higher-Order Central Places: Seattle.

# NESTING RELATIONSHIPS OF HIGHER ORDER CENTRAL PLACES: PORTLAND

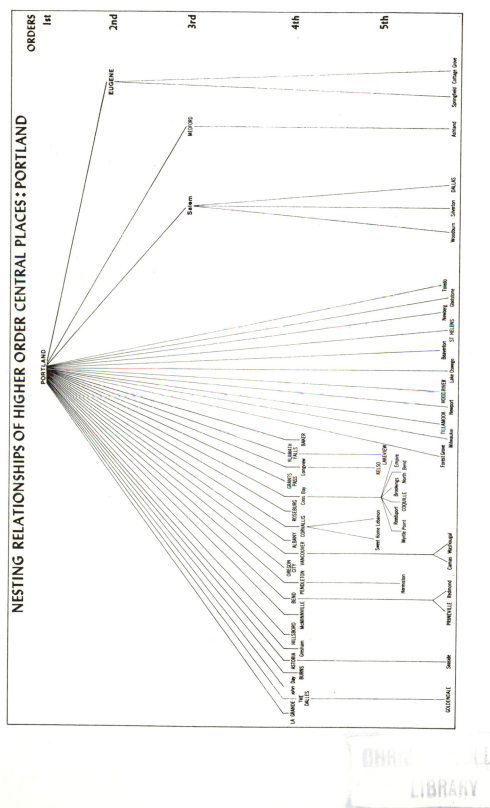

Figure 11. Nesting Relationships of Higher-Order Central Places: Portland.

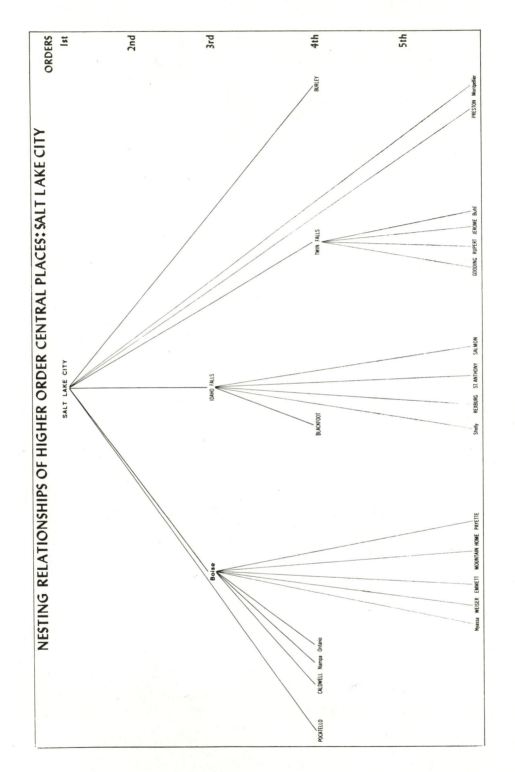

Figure 12. Nesting Relationships of Higher-Order Central Places: Salt Lake City.

fewer inhabitants? Are all such smaller places central places? Or do many of them fall under what Christaller classed as "dispersed places" (places of all types that are not central places), or as "auxiliary central places" (places with neither a significant surplus nor deficit of central place importance)? The overriding question for central place research, however, is: if the concept of centrality is not effectuated consistently with theoretical requirements, does the areal distribution of the central place function remain unidentified?

## The Functional Interdependence of Settlements

This analysis provides additional evidence regarding the functional interdependence of centers in the provision of goods and services. The existence of such interdependence was further verified and elucidated by identifying linkages: between hamlets and small towns for banking purposes; between small towns and their dependent banking systems and fourth- and higher-order central places for daily newspapers; between complementary regions defined by daily newspaper circulation and higher-order central places for Sunday newspapers; and lastly, between Sunday newspaper regions and the two main system-forming central places on the basis of branch firm dominance.

The measures of spatial interaction used here are readily available for virtually every center (hamlet through metropolis) in the United States and Canada. And, if it is true that any reasonable description of central place patterns must consider the matter of functional interdependence defined by flows, then the indexes examined here may prove to be useful measures of spatial interaction within central place structures.

## The Underlying Behavioral Assumption

It was stated above that if consumers do in fact patronize the nearest center offering a particular good or service, then the spatial efficiency implicit in that assumption should be identifiable and measurable in any environment. To at least partially examine this assumption in detail, the banking relations shown in Figure 4 were analyzed. If the assumption holds, then the overwhelming majority of centers without banks should be linked to the closest place where this service is available. In Figure 4, 400 banking towns and 970 banking linkages were identified. Airline distances between each linked pair revealed that 722 (74.5 percent) of the linkages connected settlements without banks to the closest available banking town. Three out of four seems more than a tendency. Moreover, this high percentage was achieved without taking into account the influence of accessibility, patterns of topography, road networks, or the location of state boundaries. Had these variables been considered, the percentage of places linked to the closest banking town would undoubtedly have been increased. Findings for this particular type of inter-settlement linkage thus provide additional support for the interpretative value of the original behavioral assumption.

## Central Place Hierarchy

The classification procedure used here appears to have produced at least three pertinent points. First, in at least one area there appears to exist a clear-cut central place hierarchy through five orders. As far as it goes, then, support is provided for an important and highly controversial component of central place theory. Second, not only does at least a five-step hierarchy appear to exist in the study area, but when the two nested hierarchies lying within the study area are isolated, strong hierarchical tendencies are also apparent (Figure 13).

These findings, though consistent with theory, are in partial conflict with what appears to be the presently accepted position; namely, that hierarchical patterns are clearly recognizable at subregional levels, but because of the greater social, physical, and economic heterogeneity of large areas, the inter and intra-area differences found in indi-

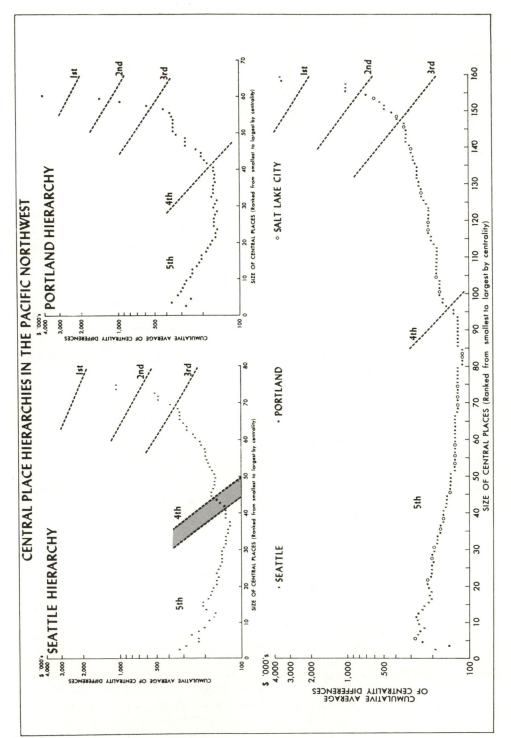

Figure 13. Central Place Hierarchies in the Pacific Northwest.

vidual subsystems are lost when they are aggregated, and thus produce a continuum [5, p. 35]. Lastly, evidence offered here keeps open the possibility that if the concept of centrality, in its classical sense, were operationalized for centers of all sizes, the full regional hierarchy called for in theory would emerge.

In summary, then, given the necessary updating of some of the original operational definitions to accommodate recent changes in both technology and life style, it would appear that Christaller's conceptual and procedural contributions to the investigation of the role of settlements in the structure and operation of particular space economies remains undiminished.

# REFERENCES

1. *ABC Membership List*. Chicago: Audit Bureau of Circulations, 1963.
2. Berry, B. J. L. *Geography of Market Centers and Retail Distribution*. Englewood Cliffs: Prentice-Hall, 1967.
3. ———. "Commuting Fields of Central Cities," a map prepared for the Social Science Research Council Committee on Areas for Social and Economic Statistics, in cooperation with the Bureau of the Census, U.S. Department of Commerce. Chicago: University of Chicago Center for Urban Studies, 1967.
4. ———. and H. G. Barnum, and R. J. Tennant. "Retail Location and Consumer Behavior," *Papers and Proceedings of the Regional Science Association*, 9 (1962), pp. 65–106.
5. ———. "Aggregate Relations and Elemental Components of Central Place Systems," *Journal of Regional Science*, 4 (Summer, 1962), pp. 35–68.
6. ———, and W. L. Garrison. "The Functional Bases of the Central-Place Hierarchy," *Economic Geography*, 34 (April, 1958), pp. 145–54.
7. ———, P. G. Goheen, and H. Goldstein. "Metropolitan Area Definition: A Reevaluation of Concept and Statistical Practice." Bureau of the Census Working Paper No. 28, Washington, D.C.: U.S. Department of Commerce, 1968.
8. Bennet, C. O. *Facts Without Opinion, First*

9. Borchert, J. R. and R. B. Adams. *Trade Centers and Trade Areas of the Upper Midwest*. Urban Report No. 3. Minneapolis: Upper Midwest Economic Study, 1963.
10. Christaller, W. *Central Places in Southern Germany*. Translated by C. W. Baskin. Englewood Cliffs: Prentice-Hall, 1966.
11. "Consumer Expenditures and Income: Total Western Region, Urban and Rural, 1961." BLS Report No. 237-92 (U.S.D.A. Report CES-14), May, 1965.
12. Davies, W. K. D. "The Ranking of Service Centers: A Critical Review," *Transactions and Papers of the Institute of British Geographers*, 40 (December, 1966), pp. 51–65.
13. ———. "Centrality and the Central Place Hierarchy," *Urban Studies*, 4 (February, 1967), pp. 61–79.
14. Haggett, P. *Locational Analysis in Human Geography*. New York: St. Martin's Press, 1966.
15. Highsmith, R. M., ed. *Atlas of the Pacific Northwest*. 3rd ed. Corvallis: Oregon State University Press, 1966.
16. Isard, W. *Location and Space-Economy*. New York: John Wiley and Sons, 1956.
17. King, L. J. "Central Place Theory and the Spacing of Towns in the United States," *Land and Livelihood*. Edited by M. McKaskill. Christchurch: New Zealand Geographical Society, 1962, pp. 238–54.
18. ———. *Statistical Analysis in Geography*. Englewood Cliffs: Prentice-Hall, 1969.
19. Lueck, V. "Hierarchy and Regionalization in U.S. Sunday Newspaper Circulation," *Minnesota Geographer*, 21 (1968–1969), pp. 10–23.
20. Marshall, J. U. "The Location of Service Towns." University of Toronto Department of Geography Research Publication No. 3. Toronto: University of Toronto Press, 1969.
21. Murphy, R. E. *The American City*. New York: McGraw-Hill, 1965.
22. Nystuen, J. D. and M. G. Dacey. "A Graph Theory Interpretation of Nodal Regions," *Papers and Proceedings of the Regional Science Association*, 7 (1961), pp. 29–42.
23. Palomäki, M. "The Functional Centers and Areas of South Bothnia, Finland," *Fennia*, 88 (1964), pp. 1–235.
24. Park, R. E. and C. Newcomb. "Newspaper

Circulation and Metropolitan Regions," R. E. McKenzie, chief author. *The Metropolitan Community*. New York: Mc-Graw Hill, 1933, pp. 98–110.

25. Preston, R. E. "Two Centrality Models," *Yearbook of the Association of Pacific Coast Geographers,* 32 (1970), pp. 59–78.

26. Rushton, G. *Spatial Pattern of Grocery Purchases by the Iowa Rural Population.* Studies in Business and Economics, New Series No. 9. Iowa City: University of Iowa Press, 1966.

27. Russwurm, L. H. *The Development of An Urban Corridor System, Toronto to Stratford Area: 1941–1966.* Waterloo: Department of Geography and Planning and Resources Institute, University of Waterloo, 1969.

28. Tarrant, J. R., "A Note Concerning the Definition of Groups of Settlements for a Central Place Hierarchy," *Economic Geography,* 44 (April, 1968), pp. 144–51.

29. Ullman, E. L. "A Theory of Location for Cities," *American Journal of Sociology,* 46 (May, 1941), pp. 853–64.

30. U.S. Bureau of Census. *United States Census of Population: 1960.* Vol. 1, *Characteristics of Population,* pts. 14, Idaho; 28, Montana; 39, Oregon; and 49, Washington.

31. ———. *Census of Business, 1963, Retail Trade.* Washington, D.C.: Government Printing Office, 1964.

32. ———. *Census of Business, 1963, Selected Services.* Washington, D.C.: Government Printing Office, 1965.

33. Wallis, W. A. and H. V. Roberts. *Statistics: A New Approach.* New York: The Free Press, 1963.

34. Walker, H. M. *Elementary Statistical Methods.* New York: Henry Holt and Co., 1943.

# Labor Force Growth and Specialization in Canadian Cities

RON W. CROWLEY

## INTRODUCTION

This paper is concerned with labor force growth and specialization in Canadian cities.[1] Specialization is, of course, a phenomenon well known to economists; Adam Smith's "discovery" of the pin-factory principle was the initial oil for the gears of the "dismal science." Recently, both economists and geographers have been interested in the structure of economic activity in a regional or national framework. While geographers (compared with economists) have emphasized the spatial dimension, this emphasis has been one of degree: the "tools" that have beem employed are similar.[2]

Unfortunately, much of the research in this area has been empirical without theory (except of a rudimentary sort), and even the empirical studies lead to diverging rather than converging results. The basis for these inconsistent results has not been examined in detail. The intention of this paper is: (1) to suggest a framework for evaluating some of the reasons for changes in labor force composition in the Canadian urban system; (2) to examine a number of alternative measures that have been used to provide a summary statement of this information; and (3) to assess the interrelationship of these measures and draw conclusions where possible. Since these results are preliminary, a number of questions will remain unanswered.

## DATA BASE AND COVERAGE

The 1951 and 1961 censuses provide the basis for this study.[3] Other studies attempting to compare 1951 and 1961 statistics have been hampered by the changes in the Standard Industrial Classification effected in 1960. We have used the Standard Industrial Classification of industries, but in modified form, to account for definitional changes.[4] Fifty-six industry groups have been delineated; the standarized groups, reflecting common production of a *range* of goods, are based on McInnis's work as well as unpublished disaggregated data obtained from the Dominion Bureau of Statistics (now Statistics Canada).[5]

All cities with a 1961 "urban area" population greater than 25,000 are examined. Only

1. I am greatly indebted to Stan McRoberts for carrying out the calculations for this paper and to Charles Grossner who codified the data in preparation for his M.A. thesis at Queen's University (Kingston, Ontario), "Specialization in Canadian Cities," 1970.
2. A review of this literature is contained in J. W. Maxwell, "The Functional Structure of Canadian Cities: A Classification of Cities," *Geographical Bulletin*, vol. 9, 1967, pp. 61–87.

3. Dominion Bureau of Statistics, *1951 Census of Canada, Labour Force, Occupations and Industries*, vol. 4, 1953; *1961 Census of Canada, Labour Force, Industries*, vol. 3, part 2; and *Occupations*, vol. 3, part 1, 1963–64, Ottawa.
4. Cf. R. M. McInnis, *A Consistent Industrial Classification of Canadian Work Force Statistics, 1911-61*, a report to the Department of Manpower and Immigration, Mimeo, May, 1969.
5. Unpublished data were required for industrial classifications of cities less than 30,000 since published data were too greatly aggregated.

From *Working Paper A-71-1* (Ottawa: Ministry of State for Urban Affairs, 1971). Reprinted by permission of the author and the Ministry of State for Urban Affairs.

for the ten cities classified as metropolitan in both 1951 and 1961 were metropolitan data employed; otherwise, component parts were aggregated to achieve consistency for the two census years. We thus have 1951 and 1961 data which are definitionally consistent with respect to industrial classification and geographical units.

Although these 1961 and 1951 data are generally comparable, it has not been possible to eliminate all problems.[6] Some of the remaining discrepancies are:

(1) Allocation of the unemployed is difficult since collected information is not market-based, but depends on the responders' willingness to volunteer information and on their perception of their would-be job.

(2) "Industry not stated" is a residual resulting from vague replies to the census enumerator's questions. Our choice to eliminate this category (rather than to prorate it) biases our results to the extent that (a) the proportion so identified varies among cities, and (b) the bias is systematic with respect to particular characteristics.

(3) In a few cases, sufficiently detailed data were unobtainable for some parts of an area (e.g., a township that was part of a metropolitan area); consequently, we may be dealing with only part of a larger urban area. For the most part, this is not a significant limitation.

(4) More important, the data are based on place of residence and hence reflect, to some extent, industries located outside metropolitan or urban boundaries. Similarly, those living outside but working inside the defined urban area are omitted.

(5) Minimum age of economic activity has changed: fifteen years in 1961, fourteen years in 1951 and 1941, ten years of age prior to 1941. Since it is primarily the agricultural sector affected, we assume that this is sufficiently insignificant to ignore for 1951.

(6) There is a range of other minor considerations that are not thought to significantly

affect our results, e.g., Indians were treated as a special group in 1951 but not in 1961.

## METHOD

The method we use to analyze urban labor force changes has been used elsewhere, though usually in the context of *regions* rather than *cities*. In particular, our analysis draws extensively on the work of Thirlwall and Cunningham in the United Kingdom.[7] Essentially, we pose the following question: "If a city has the same industry growth rates and the same industrial structure as all cities aggregated, its growth would also be the same as the aggregate. What, then, accounts for a city's growth different from aggregate? Is it a different initial industry structure? And/or is it different industry growth rates?

Following Thirlwall, we can thus distinguish (a) the growth effect and (b) the composition effect. The former is a measure of the extent to which differential growth results from higher than average growth of a city's industries; the latter relates the growth resulting from the particular industrial structure of a city. It is important to emphasize that the "difference" between a city's growth and some "average" or expected growth is what we are attempting to explain.

Once the two effects are defined, the general approach revolves about the assignment of appropriate weights to each factor. In fact, the primary methodological problem (largely unresolved and probably unresolvable) hinges on the "correct" weights to be applied, or, in other words the norm to be used for purposes of comparison. We might first define our terms with respect to "city weights":

---

6. Slight differences "in the reference period and in the form of the questions used are not considered to have greatly affected the comparability of the 1951 and 1961 census labour force statistics," *1961 Census*, Bul. 7, 1–12, p. 2.

7. See especially A. P. Thirlwall, "A Measure of the 'Proper Distribution of Industry,'" *Oxford Economic Papers*, March, 1967, pp. 46–58; N. J. Cunningham, "Note on the 'Proper Distribution of Industry,'" *OEP*, March, 1968, pp. 122–127; A. P. Thirlwall, "Weighting Systems and Regional Analysis: A Reply to Mr. Cunningham," *OEP*, March, 1969, pp. 128–133; D.B.S., *Growth Patterns in Manufacturing Employment by Counties and Census Divisions, 1949–1959* and *1961–1967*, D.B.S., 31–503, 31–505.

Let $N$ = Total labor force in all cities
$N_a$ = Total labor force in city $a$
$N_i$ = Total labor force in industry $i$ in all cities
$N_{ai}$ = Total labor force in industry $i$ in city $a$

The growth effect is:

$$g = \frac{dN_a}{N_a} - \sum_{i=1}^{n} \left(\frac{dN_i}{N_i}\right)\left(\frac{N_{ai}}{N_a}\right)$$

where $\dfrac{dN_a}{N_a}$ is the growth of the labor force in city $a$,

$\dfrac{dN_i}{N_i}$ is national growth in industry $i$,

and $\dfrac{N_{ai}}{N_a}$ is the proportion of industry $i$ in city $a$.

The composition effect is:

$$c = \sum_{i=1}^{n} \left(\frac{dN_i}{N_i}\right)\left(\frac{N_{ai}}{N_a}\right) - \frac{dN}{N}$$

where $\dfrac{dN}{N}$ is the growth of the national labor force,

and $\dfrac{dN_a}{N_a} - \dfrac{dN}{N} = c + g$

Using the data which we described earlier, Table 1 summarizes these effects for 46 cities.

The weighting system is essentially an arbitrary choice among a large set. Not only do the usual index number problems arise, but as well, the intricate question of the correct basis of comparison. The above formulation yields the effect of: (a) differences between a particular city and the all-city growth rates of particular industries; and (b) the difference between the respective industrial structures. The weighting system results in the calculation of a global growth *as if* all cities combined had the *same* industrial structure as the city in question. This is then compared with the city's growth and to actual global growth to derive the growth and composition effects.

The most obvious alternative is to compare a city's growth and global growth to the calculation of a growth rate *as if* the city had the same industrial structure as the global value.[8] We have called these $g'$ (growth effect) and $c'$ (composition effect) and their formulae are as follows:

$$g' = \sum_{i=1}^{n} \left(\frac{dN_{ai}}{N_{ai}}\right)\left(\frac{N_i}{N}\right) - \frac{dN}{N}$$

$$c' = \frac{dN_a}{N_a} - \sum_{i=1}^{n} \left(\frac{dN_{ai}}{N_{ai}}\right)\left(\frac{N_i}{N}\right)$$

The same condition as before holds:

$$\frac{dN_a}{N_a} - \frac{dN}{N} = c' + g'$$

On *a priori* grounds, neither approach is preferable. However, both yield information and one might argue, as does Cunningham, that a combination of effects such as $g'$ and $c$ provides more information than $g$ and $c$ or $g'$ and $c'$.[9] The reason for this is that once $g$ ($g'$) or $c$ ($c'$) is calculated, there exist no degrees of freedom; and the other parameter includes the residual factor, $r$, which is the interaction of $g$ and $c$. Thus,

$$\frac{dN_a}{N_a} - \frac{dN}{N} = c + g = c' + g'$$

$$g - g' = c' - c$$

$$= \frac{dN_a}{N_a} - \sum_{i=1}^{n}\left(\frac{dN_i}{N_i}\right)\left(\frac{N_{ai}}{N_a}\right) - \sum_{i=1}^{n}\left(\frac{dN_{ai}}{N_{ai}}\right)\left(\frac{N_i}{N}\right) + \frac{dN}{N}$$

Since

$$\frac{dN_a}{N_a} \equiv \sum_{i=1}^{n}\left(\frac{N_{ai}}{N_a}\right)\left(\frac{dN_{ai}}{N_{ai}}\right)$$

---

8. Or the equivalent, as if the industrial structure were the same as the all-city structure, but industry growth rates were those peculiar to the city. We also ran calculations based on *national* growth rates and structure but these were rejected because of the influence of "non-urban" industries.

9. Cunningham, p. 123.

Table 1. Total Labor Force Growth and Its Components Calculated by Two Methods for Canadian Cities with Population Greater than 25,000, 1951 to 1961.*

| City | (1)<br>Total<br>labor<br>force<br>growth | (2)<br>Growth<br>effect<br><br>$g$ | (3)<br>Compo-<br>sition<br>effect<br>$c$ | (4)<br>Growth<br>effect<br><br>$g'$ | (5)<br>Compo-<br>sition<br>effect<br>$c'$ | (6)<br>Inter-<br>action<br>effect<br>$r$ |
|---|---|---|---|---|---|---|
| 1. Montreal, Qué. | 37% | − 1% | − 2% | 2% | − 4% | − 3% |
| 2. Toronto, Ont. | 50 | 9 | 1 | 16 | − 5 | − 6 |
| 3. Vancouver, B.C. | 38 | − 5 | 3 | 4 | − 6 | − 9 |
| 4. Winnipeg, Man. | 26 | −13 | − 2 | − 5 | − 8 | − 7 |
| 5. Ottawa, Ont. | 44 | − 5 | 9 | 2 | 2 | − 7 |
| 6. Hamilton, Ont. | 33 | + 3 | − 9 | 14 | − 21 | − 11 |
| 7. Québec, Qué. | 25 | −22 | 7 | −15 | 1 | − 6 |
| 8. Edmonton, Alta. | 82 | 35 | 8 | 93 | − 50 | − 58 |
| 9. Calgary, Alta. | 83 | 38 | 5 | 83 | − 40 | − 44 |
| 10. Windsor, Ont. | 4 | −24 | −11 | − 3 | − 32 | − 21 |
| 11. London, Ont. | 61 | 22 | 0 | 60 | − 38 | − 38 |
| 12. Halifax, N.S. | 34 | −20 | 14 | − 9 | 4 | − 10 |
| 13. Kitchener, Ont. | 47 | 20 | −13 | 59 | − 51 | − 38 |
| 14. Regina, Sask. | 47 | − 3 | 10 | 53 | − 46 | − 56 |
| 15. Saskatoon, Sask. | 66 | 19 | 7 | 37 | − 11 | − 18 |
| 16. Port Arthur, Ont. | 32 | − 5 | − 2 | 17 | − 24 | − 21 |
| 17. St. Catharines, Ont. | 91 | 60 | − 8 | 107 | − 55 | − 47 |
| 18. Trois-Rivières, Qué. | 12 | −21 | − 6 | 14 | − 41 | − 35 |
| 19. Sudbury, Ont. | 73 | 31 | 3 | 61 | − 28 | − 31 |
| 20. Chicoutimi, Qué. | 24 | −19 | 4 | 4 | − 20 | − 24 |
| 21. Sydney, N.S. | − 4 | −45 | 1 | 90 | −133 | −134 |
| 22. Sherbrooke, Qué. | 16 | −17 | − 6 | − 8 | − 15 | − 9 |
| 23. St. John's, Nfld. | 14 | −29 | 4 | −10 | − 15 | − 19 |
| 24. Oshawa, Ont. | 31 | 7 | −15 | 94 | −102 | − 88 |
| 25. Brantford, Ont. | 34 | 8 | −13 | 54 | − 59 | − 46 |

*(continued)*

and

$$\frac{dN}{N} \equiv \sum_{i=1}^{n} \left(\frac{N_i}{N}\right)\left(\frac{dN_i}{N_i}\right)$$

$$c' - c = g - g' = \sum_{i=1}^{n} \left(\frac{N_i}{N} - \frac{N_{ai}}{N_a}\right)$$

$$\left(\frac{dN_i}{N_i} - \frac{dN_{ai}}{N_{ai}}\right) = r$$

The significance of $r$, the interaction effect, is "that it will be positive if the industries in which the city specializes . . . are also those whose . . . growth rates are relatively highest, compared with the growth rates of those same industries" for all cities combined.[10] It can be shown from the preceding that

$$\frac{dN_a}{N_a} - \frac{dN}{N} = c + g + r = c' + g' - r$$

Thus, $r$ is a residual term which, on the one hand is included in $g$ or $c$, and, on the other, in $g'$ or $c'$. Where it appears in each pair depends

10. Cunningham, p. 124.

Table 1 (continued)

| City | (1) Total labor force growth | (2) Growth effect $g$ | (3) Composition effect $c$ | (4) Growth effect $g'$ | (5) Composition effect $c'$ | (6) Interaction effect $r$ |
|------|------|------|------|------|------|------|
| 26. Saint John, N.B. | 2 | −42 | 5 | −35 | − 2 | − 7 |
| 27. Victoria, B.C. | − 2 | −55 | 13 | −48 | 6 | − 6 |
| 28. Kingston, Ont. | 42 | − 3 | 6 | 47 | − 44 | − 50 |
| 29. Sarnia, Ont. | 29 | − 9 | 2 | 13 | − 24 | − 22 |
| 30. Shawinigan Falls, Qué. | 9 | −28 | − 2 | 8 | − 39 | − 37 |
| 31. Peterborough, Ont. | 8 | −26 | − 5 | − 6 | − 26 | − 21 |
| 32. Moncton, N.B. | 41 | 6 | − 4 | 29 | − 27 | − 24 |
| 33. Conrwall,† Ont. | 108 | 78 | − 9 | 126 | − 57 | − 48 |
| 34. Sault Ste-Marie, Ont. | 24 | − 6 | − 9 | 10 | − 25 | − 15 |
| 35. Guelph, Ont. | 34 | 0 | − 5 | 21 | − 27 | − 22 |
| 36. Welland, Ont. | 93 | 67 | −14 | 127 | − 74 | − 60 |
| 37. Lethbridge, Alta. | 43 | − 1 | 5 | 21 | − 17 | − 22 |
| 38. Moose Jaw, Sask. | 25 | −14 | − 1 | 25 | − 39 | − 39 |
| 39. Granby, Qué. | 28 | 5 | −16 | 18 | − 29 | − 13 |
| 40. Belleville, Ont. | 38 | 1 | − 2 | 20 | − 21 | − 20 |
| 41. Chatham, Ont. | 28 | −10 | − 2 | 8 | − 20 | − 18 |
| 42. Timmins, Ont. | 3 | −39 | 2 | −26 | − 11 | − 13 |
| 43. Brandon, Man. | 31 | −12 | 4 | − 6 | − 2 | − 6 |
| 44. Drummondville, Qué. | 67 | 47 | −19 | 126 | − 98 | − 79 |
| 45. Valleyfield, Qué. | 5 | −20 | −14 | 19 | − 53 | − 39 |
| 46. St-Jean, Qué. | 14 | −23 | − 2 | 43 | − 68 | − 66 |
| All cities aggregate | 40 | | | | | |

*See text for explanation of terms.
†Involved large-scale annexation.

on which one is calculated first. The only way of calculating an independent $g$ and $c$ would be to apply *consistently* city or all-city weights. The interaction effect would be the same under the two weighting systems but with a different sign. So, when all-city weights are used the interaction effect is

$$r = \sum_{i=1}^{n} \left( \frac{N_i}{N} - \frac{N_{ai}}{N_a} \right) \left( \frac{dN_i}{N_i} - \frac{dN_{ai}}{N_{ai}} \right)$$

and when city weights are used, the interaction effect is

$$r' = \sum_{i=1}^{n} \left( \frac{N_{ai}}{N} - \frac{N_i}{N} \right) \left( \frac{dN_i}{N_i} - \frac{dN_{ai}}{N_{ai}} \right) = -r$$

As noted earlier, there is no *a priori* reason for preferring one method to the other. Hence, a reasonable approach to the approximation of the true growth and composition is to divide the residual equally between the growth and composition effects. However, since we are interested in the relative role of the two forces, this consideration is a problem specifically only when the information yielded by the two calculations is inconsistent. Unless

Table 2. Computed Values of Three Coefficients of Specialization, 1951 and 1961.*

| City | Percentage of labor force in three largest industries | | Gini coefficient | | Location quotients | |
|---|---|---|---|---|---|---|
| | 1951 | 1961 | 1951 | 1961 | 1951 | 1961 |
| 1. Montreal | 24.7 | 23.6 | .54 | .53 | .10 | .10 |
| 2. Toronto | 26.4 | 25.7 | .57 | .56 | .08 | .06 |
| 3. Vancouver | 28.5 | 28.1 | .60 | .59 | .51 | .35 |
| 4. Winnipeg | 31.1 | 28.5 | .62 | .61 | .19 | .14 |
| 5. Ottawa | 41.7 | 41.8 | .71 | .72 | 2.51 | 2.26 |
| 6. Hamilton | 30.3 | 29.5 | .60 | .60 | 1.40 | 1.30 |
| 7. Québec | 27.1 | 28.0 | .59 | .61 | .41 | .52 |
| 8. Edmonton | 35.4 | 31.9 | .67 | .71 | .21 | .16 |
| 9. Calgary | 33.5 | 32.4 | .65 | .65 | .23 | .40 |
| 10. Windsor | 49.3 | 37.6 | .74 | .69 | 5.87 | 2.81 |
| 11. London | 27.0 | 28.6 | .61 | .62 | .16 | .12 |
| 12. Halifax | 37.9 | 44.0 | .71 | .72 | 1.65 | 2.19 |
| 13. Kitchener | 28.4 | 25.6 | .65 | .61 | 2.68 | 1.18 |
| 14. Regina | 35.4 | 32.4 | .70 | .68 | .42 | .30 |
| 15. Saskatoon | 34.2 | 33.4 | .71 | .71 | .22 | .13 |
| 16. Port Arthur | 31.8 | 30.6 | .68 | .67 | 2.33 | 1.67 |
| 17. St. Catharines | 40.9 | 34.2 | .70 | .66 | 2.44 | 1.97 |
| 18. Trois-Rivières | 37.3 | 33.2 | .70 | .67 | 1.88 | 1.41 |
| 19. Sudbury | 54.6 | 48.6 | .80 | .77 | 14.86 | 10.07 |
| 20. Chicoutimi | 48.2 | 44.0 | .76 | .75 | 28.70 | 17.99 |
| 21. Sydney | 58.7 | 46.5 | .80 | .75 | 10.77 | 6.07 |
| 22. Sherbrooke | 33.2 | 30.2 | .68 | .66 | 1.64 | .89 |
| 23. St. John's | 32.8 | 34.9 | .69 | .70 | .62 | .49 |

*(continued)*

both of the sets (1) $c'$ and $g'$ and (2) $c$ and $g$ show one effect larger than the other, it is not possible to draw conclusions on the dominance of either effect.

Separate significance can be attached to the value of $r$.[11] (See column 5 of Table 1.) Consider the following:

(1) A usually positive value for $r$ is consistent with the interpretation that cities are specialized in those industries in which their growth prospects are best, i.e., a comparative advantage mechanism is working.

(2) A usually negative value for $r$ suggests that the industries in which a city is

specialized grow relatively less rapidly than other industries. This may be subject to a number of alternative interpretations, say, external diseconomies or the nature of industry itself.

These interpretations of $r$ are consistent with the properties usually assigned to coefficients of specialization, or more particularly, to location quotients.[12] There is a wide range of possible indices to measure specialization—the differences among them generally relate to the *basis* for comparison.

11. Cunningham, p. 124–125.

12. The relationship has been suggested, but not examined, elsewhere. Cf. David B. Houston, "The Shift and Share Analysis of Regional Growth: A Critique," *Southern Economic Journal*, April, 1967, p. 580.

Table 2. *(continued)*

| City | Percentage of labor force in three larg- est industries | | Gini coefficient | | Location quotients | |
|------|------|------|------|------|------|------|
| | 1951 | 1961 | 1951 | 1961 | 1951 | 1961 |
| 24. Oshawa | 61.2 | 52.5 | .80 | .76 | 9.85 | 9.79 |
| 25. Brantford | 36.9 | 28.9 | .67 | .61 | 7.14 | 3.03 |
| 26. Saint John | 29.0 | 31.5 | .65 | .66 | .53 | .53 |
| 27. Victoria | 32.0 | 35.5 | .67 | .70 | .73 | .86 |
| 28. Kingston | 33.8 | 33.6 | .71 | .71 | .63 | .60 |
| 29. Sarnia | 39.0 | 39.4 | .74 | .73 | 5.44 | 4.09 |
| 30. Shawinigan Falls | 37.6 | 35.0 | .72 | .68 | 2.47 | 2.16 |
| 31. Peterborough | 45.3 | 36.5 | .72 | .68 | 2.81 | 1.95 |
| 32. Moncton | 43.4 | 39.1 | .75 | .73 | .74 | .82 |
| 33. Cornwall | 51.3 | 37.0 | .77 | .72 | 4.13 | 2.02 |
| 34. Sault Ste-Marie | 56.8 | 49.2 | .79 | .76 | 13.81 | 9.39 |
| 35. Guelph | 38.2 | 30.2 | .70 | .66 | .92 | .57 |
| 36. Welland | 43.7 | 39.9 | .75 | .70 | 5.12 | 3.51 |
| 37. Lethbridge | 37.8 | 34.5 | .72 | .70 | .31 | .17 |
| 38. Moose Jaw | 38.6 | 36.2 | .73 | .71 | .59 | .39 |
| 39. Granby | 38.3 | 33.6 | .72 | .69 | 5.25 | 3.59 |
| 40. Belleville | 31.9 | 28.3 | .65 | .65 | .25 | .39 |
| 41. Chatham | 37.9 | 32.0 | .70 | .69 | 1.30 | .67 |
| 42. Timmins | 61.4 | 55.9 | .82 | .80 | 19.89 | 14.14 |
| 43. Brandon | 38.3 | 34.7 | .71 | .71 | .35 | .24 |
| 44. Drummondville | 57.6 | 48.4 | .79 | .73 | 8.79 | 7.12 |
| 45. Valleyfield | 56.7 | 42.3 | .81 | .73 | 8.49 | 3.79 |
| 46. St-Jean | 48.0 | 38.0 | .75 | .68 | 4.24 | 1.67 |

*See text for explanation of headings.

Specialization is "the extent to which the economic structure of a city or region differs from that of a benchmark economy, the nation being the usual benchmark."[13] The benchmark is critical and in this case our benchmark has been the characteristics of all Canadian cities in concert. Alternately, the index may be one of internal diversity or the extent to which a city's labor force is internally concentrated.[14] We have chosen to measure these dimensions as follows:

(1) Diversification/concentration
   (a) Proportion of labor force in three largest industries[15]
   (b) A Gini index[16]
(2) Specialization/relative concentration: location quotient indices[17]

13. P. S. Florence, *Industrial Location and Natural Resources,* Worthington: National Resources Planning Board, 1938, pp. 120–21.
14. John B. Parr, "Specialization, Diversification and Regional Development," *The Professional Geographer,* November, 1965, pp. 21–25.

15. A value of one indicates all the labor force of a city is concentrated in three or fewer industries.
16. See Herman P. Miller, *Income Distribution in the United States,* Washington, D.C.: U.S. Government Printing Office, 1966, pp. 220–21.
17. A value of zero suggests the city has the same or a smaller proportion of its labor force in each industry as all cities combined. For a general discussion of problems with location quotients as measures of specialization, see K. Dziewonski, "Specialization and Urban Systems," *Papers of the Regional Science Association,* vol. 24, 1970, pp. 39–45.

The value computed for 2 is the square of the excess of a city's percentage in a particular industry above the all-city percentage, divided by the latter times 100 and summed for all industries with location quotients greater than 1.[18] Symbolically,

$$\sum_{i=1}^{n} = \frac{1}{100} \left[ \frac{\left( \frac{N_{ai}}{N_a} - \frac{N_i}{N} \right)^2}{\frac{N_i}{N}} \right]$$

or all values of $i$ in which

$$\frac{N_{ai}}{N_a} \bigg/ \frac{N_i}{N} > 1 \text{ or } N_{ai}/N_a > N_i/N$$

This constraint is necessary since only where it holds is specialization extant. Table 2 relates these three measures for 1951 and 1961.

## INTERPRETATION

What do these data reveal? First, with respect to Table 1, the most interesting and conclusive feature is that the interaction effect, $r$, is negative for all cities without exception. This suggests either that concentrated industries tend to grow more slowly than dispersed industries and/or that cities are concentrated in those industries that are growing least rapidly (i.e., the apparent opposite of the theorem of comparative advantage). Causation, of course, cannot be suggested and alternative explanations have to be further explored.

Some alternative hypotheses might be:

(1) "New" or "innovative" industries and hence the fastest growing industries tend to be more competitive and subsequently more geographically dispersed in smaller units than are established industries.[19]

(2) There may be a "product diffusion" process occurring whereby new industries are associated with complete spatial specialization for a short period of time. As output expands (and the rate of growth of output), it may be possible to expand spatially as well; hence, industrial structures would then converge. The Vernon hypothesis with respect to trade among nations is similar; a country will initially produce and export a large proportion of world consumption of a good until other countries learn the technical processes. What we may be measuring is the equivalent of the diffused technology; for the most part, however, this is untestable.

(3) Since cities are not static, this result may arise due to dynamic adjustment.[20]

(4) The most plausible explanation is that what geographers call "ubiquitous" functions are prevalent; thus, some specialized functions may exist there but play a small overall role.[21] The relative role might in fact be expected to decrease as a city grew. It can be shown, for example, that the statistical relationship between city size and internal specialization is inverse.

Table 3 presents coefficients of rank correlation for the three specialization measures and city size. For specialization relative to other cities (i.e., location quotients) the relationship is not at all strong. This suggests that cities may be largely independent, rather than interdependent.[22]

---

18. This is similar to the measure used by E. L. Ullman and M. F. Dacey, "The Minimum Requirements Approach to the Urban Economic Base," *Papers of the Regional Science Association*, vol. 6, 1960, pp. 175–94; also see Bruce Gray, "Employment Structure and Population Size of Canadian Cities," unpublished M.A. thesis, Queen's University, 1969. There are a number of other possible location-quotient based indices. Some of these are as follows (the Spearman rank correlation with the measure we are using and Z-values are given in brackets): sum of squares of location quotients greater than 1 [.93(6.24)]; location quotients minus 1 and summed for all quotients greater than 1 [.87 (5.85)]; the sum of squares of percentages corresponding to location quotients greater than 1 [.704(4.68)].

19. Such industries would be fastest growing because in relative terms any change is compared with a smaller base.
20. Since the data classifications are "traditional," this may play a role in the results; for example, there may be fast growing segments of slow growing groups.
21. See Maxwell, pp. 67ff. There may be threshold sizes of cities or industries that affect these values.
22. Preliminary unpublished results of my colleague, John Hartwick, indicate that urban complexes centering on major Canadian cities are not integrated in the sense of producing complementary goods. See also Dziewonski, *op. cit.* and Wilbur Thompson, *A Preface to Urban Economics*, Baltimore, 1965, pp. 15–16.

Table 3. Coefficient of Rank Correlation between City Size and Measures of Specialization Canada, 1951 and 1961

| | Percentage of Labor Force in Three Largest Industries | | Gini Coefficients | | Location Coefficients | |
|---|---|---|---|---|---|---|
| | 1951 | 1961 | 1951 | 1961 | 1951 | 1961 |
| Population of City Units | −.56 (−3.78) | −.47 (−3.15) | −.60 (−4.00) | −.47 (−3.13) | −.38 (−2.52) | −.35 (−2.38) |
| Population of Aggregate Urban Area | −.52 (−3.51) | −.36 (−2.43) | −.57 (−3.79) | −.39 (−2.60) | −.33 (−2.23) | −.28 (−1.87) |
| Labor Force | −.57 (−3.86) | −.49 (−3.32) | −.63 (−4.21) | −.49 (−3.26) | −.41 (−2.78) | −.39 (−2.60) |

Source: Adapted from C. Grossner, *Specialization in Canadian Cities*, unpublished M.A. thesis, Queen's University, 1970, Table 13, pp. 78–81.

A separate but related matter is the relationship between other indices of specialization and our interaction effect ($r$). The results are not as neatly consistent; in the first place, of course, the three measures we have suggested do not measure the same value—the percentage of the labor force and the Gini coefficient evaluate specialization *within* a city while the location coefficient measures specialization relative to other cities. While specialization appears to have decreased from 1951 to 1961 in most cities, there is clear evidence that in some, specialization has actually increased. With the exception of two cities,[23] the first two indices consistently indicate those cities in which specialization has increased.[24] Of the nine cities indicated by one or both measures as having increased specialization, it is interesting indeed to note that seven are capitals of some jurisdiction (Ottawa, Québec, Edmonton, Halifax, St. John's, Saint John, Victoria—the others are London and Sarnia). A perusal of the data suggests that large increases in the labor force

did occur in provincial or in federal administration (including post office and defense) for the seven cities. In all of these cities, health and welfare services also increased considerably.

Inferences based on these measures are consistent with either an increase or decrease in location quotients. Our data suggest with respect to location quotients that increased specialization occurred only in Calgary, Halifax, Victoria, and Belleville. What differentiates these cities is at this stage not clear; however, it is probably relevant to note the location quotients for three of the four cities are quite small and a rather minor change could have produced the result.[25]

A third element that emerges from the data concerns the relative importance of the growth and composition effects. Contrary to what we might have hoped, the predominance of one or the other is not borne out. Of the forty-six cities, both measures consistently indicate that the growth effect is dominant in eighteen cities and the composition effect dominant in eight; for the remaining twenty cities, our calculations suggest neither effect

23. Sarnia and Edmonton. The change in Sarnia was small.
24. The Spearman coefficient of rank correlation between the two indices is .95 (6.37 Z-value) and .91 (6.12) for 1951 and 1961 respectively.

25. The process of squaring accentuates change, particularly increases.

dominates. Table 4 lists those cities in which both approaches suggest a dominant (consistently larger) growth *or* composition effect; the sign of the two effects is also noted.

If we apply all-city growth rates to the individual industrial structures ($g$ and $c$), the growth effect dominates the composition effect in a large proportion of the cases (thirty-four out of forty-six). On the other hand, if city growth rates are applied to the all-city industrial structure, the number dominated by the growth effect is much smaller (twenty-one out of forty-six). For the twenty-six cities in which both approaches suggest the same answer, eighteen are dominated by the growth effect.

Thus, a reasonable first conclusion is that the growth effect (i.e., faster growth or slower decline in a particular city compared with the all-city average) is generally more important in explaining change than is the composition effect (i.e., the type of industry characterizing a city).[26]

There appears to be no relationship between city size and the growth and composition effects; however, decomposing the cities into regions provides some interesting results. Disproportionately, cities in Ontario (and the West, to some extent) have experienced growth greater than average because of a dominant positive growth effect (see Table 5). In fact, even those Ontario cities that have experienced growth less than average, generally have a positive growth effect.[27] (Hence, the slower growth is explained *only* by an adverse industrial structure.) For cities outside Ontario, on the other hand, growth below the all-city average normally is associated with negative growth effects but positive composition effects.[28]

## CONCLUSIONS

In this paper, we have attempted to assess the two factors accounting for the differential growth of a city—the effect of industry growth and the effect of industry structure. In the process, we have examined a number of the relationships. Our findings might be summarized:

(1) There are a number of ways to define these two effects; the two major ones considered here do not always lead to consistent conclusions on the relative importance of the effects. When a consistent conclusion is suggested, the growth effect appears to be dominant in approximately two-thirds of the cities.

(2) Interpreting the residuals, and with corroborating evidence from specialization indices, we concluded that cities do not have labor forces concentrated in those industries that are growing most rapidly, relative to one another. Specialization of one city with respect to others appears to be decreasing generally; some cities (particularly those that are seats of government), however, have increasing *internal* specialization of their labor force.

(3) For Ontario cities, the growth effect is normally positive, whether the city grows slower or faster than other cities.[29] Thus, if an Ontario city grows less rapidly than "average," this can usually be attributed to an adverse industrial structure. However, for cities in other provinces, the opposite seems to be the case: slower than "average" growth is explained by relatively slow growing industries rather than an adverse composition.

If this finding is correct, it has particular ramifications for urban/regional development policies: policies to change the structural characteristics of cities, say in the Maritimes, do not attack the essence of the problem. If growth is desired in these areas, our evidence suggests that analysis should focus on the reasons why industries in these provinces do not expand as rapidly as does the average of all cities. Policy should then concentrate on ameliorating the factors accounting for this behavior. Attempting to attract only "new" (or "growth") industries is unlikely to have a significant effect in increasing the rate of growth.

26. Although those cities with relatively greater composition effects have higher *average* internal specialization indices, the variance is sufficiently great to preclude generalization.
27. The exception is Timmins.
28. The notable exception is Granby, Québec; the value of the effects for Montreal is similar.

29. For those eleven Ontario cities where information is consistent, the growth effect is positive in nine. Of those thirteen outside Ontario, only five are positive. See Table 4.

Table 4. Components of Growth for Cities in which Calculations are Consistent

| City | Differ-ential growth | Sign of growth effect | Sign of compo-sition effect | Consistently dominant growth or composition effect |
|---|---|---|---|---|
| 1. Montreal | − 3% | +/− | − | composition |
| 2. Toronto | +10 | + | +/− | growth |
| 3. Vancouver | | | | |
| 4. Winnipeg | | | | |
| 5. Ottawa | | | | |
| 6. Hamilton | − 7 | +/− | − | composition |
| 7. Québec | −15 | − | + | growth |
| 8. Edmonton | +42 | + | +/− | growth |
| 9. Calgary | +43 | + | +/− | growth |
| 10. Windsor | | | | |
| 11. London | +21 | + | − | growth |
| 12. Halifax | − 6 | − | | growth |
| 13. Kitchener | + 7 | + | − | growth |
| 14. Regina | | | | |
| 15. Saskatoon | +26 | + | +/− | growth |
| 16. Port Arthur | | | | |
| 17. St. Catharines | +51 | + | − | growth |
| 18. Trois-Rivières | | | | |
| 19. Sudbury | +33 | + | +/− | growth |
| 20. Chicoutimi | | | | |
| 21. Sydney | | | | |
| 22. Sherbrooke | | | | |
| 23. St. John's | | | | |
| 24. Oshawa | − 9 | + | − | composition |
| 25. Brantford | − 6 | + | − | composition |
| 26. Saint John | −38 | − | +/− | growth |
| 27. Victoria | −42 | − | + | growth |
| 28. Kingston | | | | |
| 29. Sarnia | | | | |
| 30. Shawinigan Falls | | | | |
| 31. Peterborough | | | | |
| 32. Moncton | + 1 | + | − | growth |
| 33. Cornwall | +68 | + | − | growth |
| 34. Sault Ste-Marie | −16 | +/− | − | composition |
| 35. Guelph | − 6 | + | − | composition |
| 36. Welland | +53 | + | − | growth |
| 37. Lethbridge | | | | |
| 38. Moose Jaw | | | | |
| 39. Granby | −12 | + | − | composition |
| 40. Belleville | − 2 | + | − | composition |
| 41. Chatham | | | | |
| 42. Timmins | −37 | − | +/− | growth |
| 43. Brandon | − 9 | − | +/− | growth |
| 44. Drummondville | +27 | + | − | growth |
| 45. Valleyfield | | | | |
| 46. St-Jean | | | | |

Table 5. Growth of Cities by Region and Dominant Effect

| Province (region) | Total | Number of cities | | Inconsistent under two weighting schemes |
| | | Dominant growth effect | Dominant composition effect | |
|---|---|---|---|---|
| (a) Growth above the all-city average | | | | |
| 1. Newfoundland, Nova Scotia, New Brunswick | 1 | 1 | 0 | 0 |
| 2. Québec | 1 | 1 | 0 | 0 |
| 3. Ontario | 9 | 7 | 0 | 2 |
| 4. Manitoba, Saskatchewan, Alberta, British Columbia | 5 | 3 | 0 | 2 |
| (b) Growth below the all-city average | | | | |
| 1. Newfoundland, Nova Scotia, New Brunswick | 4 | 2 | 0 | 2 |
| 2. Québec | 9 | 1 | 2 | 6 |
| 3. Ontario | 12 | 1 | 6 | 5 |
| 4. Manitoba, Saskatchewan, Alberta, British Columbia | 5 | 2 | 0 | 3 |
| Total | 46 | 18 | 8 | 20 |

Furthermore, the reasons for these findings may be related to the *scale* of industry, to external economies or diseconomies associated with different *mixes* of industry, to social overhead capital differences, or to a number of other factors.

REFERENCES

Ashby, L. D. 1968. "The Shift and Share Analysis: A Reply." *The Southern Economic Journal*, vol. 23, no. 3 (January), pp. 423–425.

Canada, Bureau of Statistics. 1971. "Growth Patterns in Manufacturing Employment by Counties and Census Divisions, 1961–1967." Ottawa. 138 pp. (DBS-31-505).

———. 1969. "Growth Patterns in Manufacturing Employment by Counties and Census Divisions,

1949–1959, 1961–1965." Ottawa. 146 pp. (DBS-31-503).

Cunningham, N. J. 1968. "Note on the 'Proper Distribution of Industry,'" *Oxford Economic Papers* (March), pp. 122–127.

Dunn, E. S. 1960. "A Statistical and Analytical Technique for Regional Analysis," *Papers of the Regional Science Association*, vol. 6, pp. 97–109.

Dziewonski, K. 1970. "Specialization and Urban Systems," *Papers of the Regional Science Association*, vol. 24, pp. 39–45.

Grossner, C. 1970. "Specialization in Canadian Cities." Unpublished M.A. thesis, Kingston, Ontario: Queen's University.

Hampton, P. 1968. "Regional Economic Development in New Zealand," *Journal of Regional Science*, vol. 8, No. 1 (Summer), pp. 41–55.

Houston, David B. 1967. "The Shift and Share

Analysis of Regional Growth: A Critique,'' *The Southern Economic Journal,* vol. 33, no. 4 (April), pp. 577–581.

Maxwell, J. W. 1967. ''The Functional Structure of Canadian Cities: A Classification of Cities,'' *Geographical Bulletin,* Vol. 9, No. 4, pp. 61–87.

Perloff, Harvey S., Dunn, Edgar S., Jr., Lampard, Eric E., and Muth, Richard F. 1960. *Regions, Resources, and Economic Growth,* Baltimore: Johns Hopkins Press.

# Latent Structure of Urban Systems: Research Methods and Findings

BRIAN J. L. BERRY

Cities differ in many ways. The literature is replete with efforts to reduce the complexity of the differences by classifying urban centers into relatively uniform types, in the belief that a typology aids in sampling and in generalization and prediction from sample evidence. Best known and most frequently used are the so-called functional classifications, developed from data on the economic specialties of cities.[1] Not unexpectedly each functional classification has ended up by differentiating between mining towns, manufacturing cities, service centers, college towns, and the like.

The cynic is inclined to say: "So what?" As Smith points out, the classifiers all too often fail to answer the question: "Classifica-tion for what purpose?"[2] To compound the brute empiricism of classification for clas-sification's sake, consumers often have used the resulting classifications uncritically. They have frequently sought explanation of some phenomenon of interest in *a priori* class differences, without asking whether similari-ties and differences between classes of cities have any relevance to the questions they want answered.

This essay was prepared in the belief that some rethinking of the city-classification problem would provide a framework within which the consumer might be induced to address the issue of theoretical relevance more directly. As such, the intent was to challenge, to provide an alternative point of departure, rather than to assert that there now exists some superior scheme for typifying the diverse elements in the American urban land-scape.

## METHODOLOGY

### The Classical Taxonomic Approach

The decision to place cities in the same class has usually been based on observed or "man-

1. The seminal contribution to functional classification was that of Harris. Chauncy D. Harris, "A Functional Classification of Cities in the United States," *Geographical Review*, Vol. 33, No. 1 (January 1943), pp. 86–99. More recent studies include the following: L. L. Pownall, "The Functions of New Zealand Towns," *Annals of the AAG*, Vol. 45, No. 4 (December 1953), pp. 332–350; Howard J. Nelson, "A Service Classification of American Cities," *Economic Geography*, Vol. 31, No. 3 (July 1955), pp. 189–210; John Fraser Hart, "Functions and Occupa-tional Structures of Cities of the American South," *Annals of the AAG*, Vol. 45, No. 3 (September 1955), pp. 269–286; William Steigenga, "A Comparative Analysis and Classification of Netherlands Towns," *Tijdschrift voor Economische en Sociale Geografie*, Vol. 46, No. 6/7 (June–July 1955), pp. 105–119; Victor Jones and Richard L. Forstall, "Economic and Social Classification of Metropolitan Areas," *The Municipal Year Book 1963* (Chicago: International City Managers' Association, 1963), pp. 31–44; Richard L. Forstall, "Economic Classification of Places Over 10,000, 1960–1963," *The Municipal Year Book 1967* (Chicago: International City Managers' Association, 1967), pp. 30–65.

2. R. H. T. Smith, "Method and Purpose in Functional Town Classification," *Annals of the AAG*, Vol. 55, No. 3 (September 1965), pp. 539–548, and "The Functions of Australian Towns," *Tijdschrift voor Economische en Sociale Geografie*, Vol. 56, No. 3 (May–June 1965), pp. 81–92.

From B.J.L. Berry, "Latent Structure of the American Urban System," *City Classification Handbook*, pp. 11–16, 49–57. Copyright © 1972 by John Wiley & Sons, Inc. Reprinted by permission. Extract from B.J.L. Berry and E. Neils, "Location, Size and Shape of Cities as Influenced by Environmental Factors," *The Quality of the Urban Environment* (Washington, D.C.: Resources for the Future, 1969), pp. 289–94. Reprinted by permission.

ifest'' similarities. To take an example, avoiding for the moment the most fundamental questions of *what* similarities for *which* units of observation, any one or a combination of the 66 variables used in this analysis could qualify as providing this manifest evidence when measured for such units of observation as the 212 standard metropolitan statistical areas (SMSA's) in the United States.

The traditional city classifier would approach the resulting 212 × 66 data matrix in a special way, developing a series of criteria for class membership and allocating cities to classes on their basis. Most frequently he would work with the variables one at a time, splitting the cities into relatively uniform subsets in a series of steps.

Consider a classification based on the percentages of the city's labor force in various sectors of the economy. After studying the frequency distributions of cities on each of the variables, the taxonomist might decide that it is important to separate towns with more than 20% of their workers employed in mining from those with less. Similarly he finds a 40% ''break'' in manufacturing and 25% in retailing employment ''significant.'' On reflection, he also decides that manufacturing is ''more important'' than mining, and mining is ''more important'' than retailing. Thus he first splits towns into subsets based on manufacturing, then on mining, and finally on retailing, so that his taxonomic ''tree'' takes the form illustrated in Figure 1. A relatively straightforward set of mutually exclusive types of town results.

## The Search for Latent Dimensions

Clearly the traditional approach will not suffice when a large number of variables are available. If 66 variables are each used to split cities into two groups, as in Figure 1, the number of classes possible is $2^{66}$. In practice, of course, many of the combinations will not be realized because many of the variables differentiate towns in the same ways. For example, high-income communities also have populations with high educational levels, large proportions of white-collar and

professional workers, and, more fundamentally, all of the outward symptoms of high social status. We might therefore postulate that the manifest similarities of cities are due to certain fundamental ''latent'' traits, tendencies, or progenitors like social status, resulting from basic cultural traits and processes, such as the aggressive pursuit of economic achievement and related ''success.'' A particular method of analysis, factor analysis, provides a means of searching for these causal factors, by separating and identifying clusters of closely interdependent variables whose interpretation is keyed to latent structure and processes.

Take the 212 × 66 city-data matrix $D$ and its 66 separate column vectors $d_1, d_2, d_3, \ldots, d_{66}$ (one for each variable). The fundamental hypothesis of factor analysis is that each of these columns is a product of different combinations of the same underlying factors or common causes and that these latent factors are substantially fewer than the manifest variables. To change the example for a moment, if a column of the $d$ terms were to represent the scores of 212 students on a test, one would be able to predict these scores on the basis of the underlying verbal and quantitative abilities of the students and the ''mixture'' of these latent abilities tested by the particular test, also taking into account a random-error term:

$$d_i = \Lambda \Theta_i + \Sigma_i$$

where $d_i$ is the manifest (test) vector (212 × 1), $\Lambda$ contains the coefficients measuring each student's latent verbal-ability and quantitative-ability scores (212 × 2), $\Theta_i$ identifies the verbal-quantitative ''mixture'' of test$_i$ (2 × 1), and $\Sigma_i$ is a vector of random errors and other ''disturbance'' terms for the test (212 × 1). Obviously $\Lambda$ is unchanged for different tests, but $\Theta_i$ and $\Sigma_i$ vary.

Educational psychologists determine the $\Lambda$ for students and the $\Theta_i$ for tests by factor analysis. In the same way, therefore, factor analysis of the 212 × 66 city-data matrix should produce *factor scores for cities* (coefficients measuring each city's rating on the latent urban dimensions) and *factor loadings*

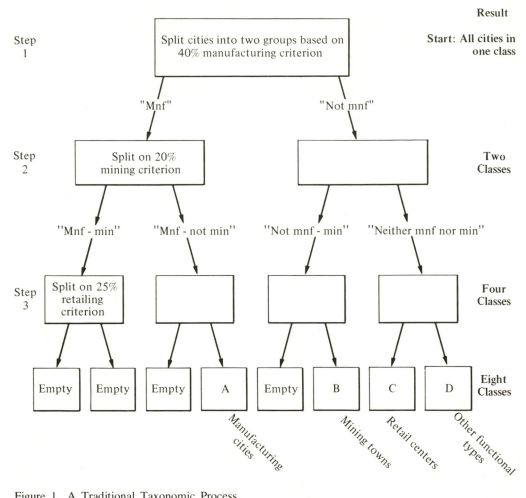

Figure 1. A Traditional Taxonomic Process.

*for manifest variables* (coefficients measuring the mixture of latent dimensions present in each manifest variable). This output should in turn enable the fundamental dimensions of the American urban system to be interpreted and new city classifications to be built *on the basis of those latent traits that bear usefully on the purpose for which the classifications are to be used.* The purposive orientation is critical.

Likewise the full output of scores of the 212 urban places on each of the latent dimensions should enable users[3] to focus more clearly on

the central issues in city classification as they bear on their subsequent analytic use:

(1) What dimensions of variation are relevant to the analysis, that is, which structural features are of explanatory significance?

(2) Are they of equal relevance, or should they receive different weights, that is, what is the relative explanatory power of the dimensions?

3. See Terry N. Clark, "Community Structure, Decision-Making, Budget Expenditures, and Urban Renewal in 51 American Communities," *American Sociological Review*, Vol. 33, No. 4 (August 1968), pp. 576–593. Robert C. Wood, *1400 Governments* (New York: Doubleday-Anchor, 1964).

4. Brian J.L. Berry, "A Method for Deriving Multi-Factor Uniform Regions," *Przeglad Geograficzny*, Vol. 33 (1961), pp. 263–279.

(3) How many classes, or types, of cities are needed?

When these questions have been satisfactorily answered, it is possible to prepare a classification that minimizes within-group differences, producing classes containing cities that are as much alike as possible.[4] The frame is then set for sampling, for cross-tabulation, or for covariance analysis and other forms of hypothesis-testing or estimation.

## AMERICAN URBAN DIMENSIONS, 1960

To provide output of the type described above principal-axis factor analysis was applied to the $212 \times 66$ data matrix after the 66 variables had been normalized by using logarithmic transformations. Only factors whose eigenvalues were greater than unity were extracted. Factor scores were produced after rotating the principal axes to orthogonal simple structure by using the normal varimax criterion.

The complete output of a factor analysis usually includes a correlation matrix for all variables, unrotated and varimax-rotated factor loadings indicating correlations of the primary variables with the latent dimensions, eigenvalues telling the amount of original variance accounted for by the underlying dimensions, and factor scores for each city on each dimension. Obviously not all of these can be presented here. Nor is it appropriate to divert attention from the substantive features of the urban dimensions by reviewing the method, which has been effectively described elsewhere.[5] Instead we focus on the 12 latent dimensions of variation of American SMSA's in 1960 that resulted from the analysis, presenting only those elements of the output that are necessary for purposes of illustration and identification.[6]

Earlier factors in this type of analysis span more of the variance than later ones, and each factor represents a complete *scale*. Table 1 summarizes the factor structure and provides the factor loadings (correlations of original variables and the factors). Thus, on factor 1—socioeconomic status (SES)—centers can be arrayed from those with the lowest (low incomes, housing values, educational levels, housing qualities) to those with the highest. Factor 2 scales cities by age, size, and their correlates. Factor 3 picks out differentiation according to population composition; factor 4 according to recent service-oriented growth, etc.

In a related study exploring urban pathologies, Maloney[7] has identified similar components, and related specific urban problems to them. For example, unemployment rises as the SES of a city drops (factor 1); governmental fragmentation, and per capita city service costs rise with size and age of city (factor 2); the crime rate is greatest in the largest and the most rapidly growing cities (factors 2 and 4); riot-prone cities are, on the other hand, the largest and oldest (factor 2) with the greatest Negro concentrations (inverse factor 7). There is much that is socially meaningful, therefore, in the typology.

Taken together, the twelve factors provide a "space" within which the similarities and differences of the metropolitan areas can be studied simultaneously, on the basis of the "distances" between centers located as points in this space. Use of numerical taxonomy then enables a meaningful typology of the metropolitan areas to be derived. (See Table 2.)

Apparently, within the twelve patterns of differentiation of the SMSA's, there are clear regional clusters arranged from the manufacturing belt heartland outwards to the periphery. Major contrasts are drawn between manufacturing and commercial cities. Rapid growth in the 1950–60 decade is largely at the periphery—in Florida, Texas and Arizona, and on the West Coast. (See Figure 2.)

Only the very briefest outline of the analytical results are displayed in the above maps

5. See, for example, D. Michael Ray and Brian J. L. Berry, "Multivariate Socioeconomic Regionalization: A Pilot Study in Central Canada," in S. Ostry and T. Rymes, eds., *Regional Statistical Studies* (Toronto: University of Toronto Press, 1965).
6. This study was undertaken by Harold M. Mayer, and is as yet unpublished. I am indebted to Professor Mayer for permitting me to draw on his results.

7. John C. Maloney, "Metropolitan Area Characteristics and Problems" (Working materials, Medill School of Journalism, Northwestern University, 1967).

Table 1. Factor Structure: U.S. Metropolitan Areas, (SMSA's) 1960*

Table 1 (continued)

| Factor | Variables represented by factor | Factor loading |
|---|---|---|
| Socioeconomic status | Median rent | 0.869 |
| | Value of homes | 0.784 |
| | Median family income | 0.907 |
| | Per cent white-collar workers | 0.567 |
| | Median school years | 0.754 |
| | Per cent with high school education | 0.720 |
| | Per cent families < $3,000 income | −0.821 |
| | Per cent families > $10,000 income | 0.881 |
| | Per cent homes with plumbing | 0.758 |
| Age and size | Population | 0.974 |
| | Age | 0.648 |
| | Per cent using public transportation | 0.643 |
| | Per cent population Jewish | 0.626 |
| | Proportion SMSA urbanized | 0.911 |
| | No. of railroad connections | 0.571 |
| | No. of airline passengers | 0.888 |
| | Tons waterborne commerce | 0.722 |
| | No. of vacant units | 0.911 |
| | Production workers in manufacturing | 0.954 |
| | Value added in manufacturing | 0.957 |
| Population composition and demography | Fertility rate | 0.627 |
| | Death rate | −0.644 |
| | Family size | 0.712 |
| | Median age | −0.857 |
| | Per cent population under 5 years | 0.891 |
| | Per cent population working age (21–64 years) | −0.602 |
| | Per cent population old (over 65 years) | −0.755 |
| | Population per housing unit | 0.852 |
| | Labor participation rate | −0.560 |

| Factor | Variables represented by factor | Factor loading |
|---|---|---|
| Growth 1950–1960 | Per cent homes built since 1950 | 0.867 |
| | Per cent homes with two cars | 0.538 |
| | Per cent population change 1950–60 | 0.837 |
| | Per cent population moved 1950–60 | 0.767 |
| | Per cent population migrated 1955–60 | 0.788 |
| | Distance to state capital | 0.591 |
| | Temperature range | −0.686 |
| | Mean annual temperature | 0.677 |
| | Per cent payroll from manufacturing | −0.550 |
| | Per cent labor force in manufacturing | −0.523 |
| Commercial vs. manufacturing orientation | Per cent workers white collar | 0.609 |
| | Manufacturing payroll, per cent | −0.550 |
| | Retail payroll, per cent | 0.659 |
| | Manufacturing labor force, per cent | −0.667 |
| | Trade labor force, per cent | 0.784 |
| | Transport (etc.) labor force | 0.666 |
| | Finance (etc.) labor force | 0.641 |
| Foreign-born population | Per cent foreign born | 0.867 |
| | Per cent of foreign parentage | 0.845 |
| | Per cent homes single family | −0.635 |
| | Per cent vote for Kennedy | 0.584 |
| Relative upland interior location | Per cent population non-white | −0.508 |
| | Average annual rainfall | −0.679 |
| | Elevation above sea level | 0.798 |

(continued)

(continued)

Table 1 *(continued)*

| Factor | Variables represented by factor | Factor loading |
|---|---|---|
| Institutional or military population | Per cent population living in group quarters | −0.853 |
| Location relative to SMSA | Distance to nearest SMSA | 0.893 |
| | Distance to nearest SMSA with 1 million population | 0.774 |
| Use of public transport | Per cent employees using public transport | 0.502 |
| | Per cent employees residing in another county | 0.597 |
| Low density | Per cent urban area in central county | 0.611 |
| | Average density of urbanized area. | −0.527 |

*Source: H. M. Mayer, unpublished paper, University of Chicago.

and tables. Such analyses generate mounds of further statistical information (correlation coefficients and factor scores), which can be used to directly compare the characteristics of pairs of cities, or to evaluate the contribution of new variables in differentiating between cities, or as inputs into models of growth and change within the urban system. Such community profiles also provide the basic data needed for analytically meaningful city classification, because the redundancies of overlapping variables have been eliminated by factor analysis. With such materials in hand, the questions to be answered by the user remain, to reiterate:

(1) Which of the structural dimensions are relevant to this study? Which afford explanation?

(2) Are they of equal relevance, or should they be weighted differentially, according to external criteria?

(3) How many classes of cities are needed?

## GENERALITY OF THE LATENT STRUCTURE

How general are the dimensions described above? Are they latent in systems of cities elsewhere? Have they been consistent through time? One author (Gerald Hodge) argues for complete universality:

1. Common structural features underlie the development of all centers within a region.

2. Structural features of centers tend to be the same from region to region regardless of the stage or character of regional development.

3. Urban structure may be defined in terms of a set of "independent" dimensions covering at least (a) size of population, (b) quality of physical development, (c) age structure of population, (d) education level of population, (e) economic base, (f) ethnic and/or religious orientation, (g) welfare, and (h) geographical situation.

4. Economic base of urban centers tends to act independently of other urban structural features.[8]

Clearly we need to review other studies that have been completed to see if Hodge's assertions are valid. If they are, considerable economy in urban studies is suggested, enabling the developing science to pass beyond the easily perceived structural entities of city classifications by supplementing and ultimately superseding them in attention by organizational and developmental ideas.

To move beyond morphology, however, one needs to be sure that there are certain time-constant aspects of the system, an enduring architecture whose physiology and organization, reversible changes in time, and adaptive or homeostatic adjustments to environmental pressure can be described and then explained by the development or evolution of the system—the irreversible secular changes that accumulate in time.

In effect we are only at the beginning of what must be a long-term effort to describe the processes giving rise to the structural organization and orderly functioning of urban

8. Gerald Hodge, "Urban Structure and Regional Development," paper presented at the 14th Annual Meeting of the Regional Science Association, Harvard University, 1967.

Table 2. Typology of SMSA's, 1960

A. *New England, eastern New York, and New Jersey cities*
　　Intermediate to higher SES, older and/or larger, slow growth 1950–60, substantial commercial orientation, foreign-born population, substantial use of public transport and cross-commuting.
　Aa.　*New England subgroups* (e.g., Fall River, New Bedford)
　　　Low status, older residual populations, crowding, etc.
　Ab.　*New York* (special case—modest status, old, large, commercial orientation, foreign born, public transport, etc.)

B. *Manufacturing belt cities*
　　Older and/or larger, industrial, slow growth 1950–60, high density, substantial foreign-born, use of public transport.

C. *Mining towns* (Pennsylvania, West Virginia, Duluth).
　　Low SES, older populations, substantial use of group quarters, public transportation.

D. *Cities of agricultural Midwest and Plains*
　　Younger populations, slow growth 1950–60, commercial orientation, relative isolation, little use made of public transport.
　Da.　*Chicago* (special case—older, larger, manufacturing)

E. *Smaller towns of Pennsylvania, Ohio, Southern Indiana and Border South*
　　Average or modest on all factors, few foreign-born, somewhat older population, weaker commercial bases.

F. *Larger Mason-Dixon line cities, plus Atlanta, Richmond, Roanoke*
　　Some manufacturing, younger populations, slower growth, fewer foreign born.

G. *Southern cities*
　　Low SES, young populations, growing, weak commerce, few foreign born, substantial Negro population.

H. *Florida*
　　Older populations, rapid growth, commercial, many foreign born, relatively isolated, low density.

I. *Texas and Arizona*
　Ia.　*Texas Gulf coast*
　　　Low density, substantial Negro populations and institutional or military base. Populations youngish, few foreign born.
　Ib.　*Mexican border towns*
　　　Very low SES, very young populations, commercial, many foreign-born, many institutional, military.
　Ic.　*West Texas and Arizona*
　　　Higher SES, younger populations, very rapid growth, automobile-oriented, low density.

J. *Mountain States cities*
　　Young cities, young populations, commercial, few Negroes, relatively distant.
　Ja.　*Denver and Colorado Springs*
　　　Same, except larger, growing more rapidly, more use of public transport.

K. *West Coast cities*
　　Higher SES, commercial, substantial military involvement.
　Ka.　*Los Angeles* (special case—older, larger, more rapid growth, less commerce, absence of public transport).

L. *Other groups*
　La.　Principal ''institutional'' metropolitan areas—Ann Arbor, Champaign-Urbana, Lawton.
　Lb.　Las Vegas
　Lc.　Midland-Odessa
　Ld.　Honolulu

Note: S.E.S. = socio-economic status

activities and the innovations giving rise to periodic transformations in the structural arrangements. A first step is to determine whether urban systems have common latent structures.

## Other Studies of the United States

There has been a long history of multivariate studies of American cities, largely overlooked until recently. These include Price's study of American metropolitan centers in 1930,[9] reanalyzed comparatively by Perle in 1960,[10] Hofstaetter's study (based on work by Thorndike) of American cities of 30,000 to 50,000 inhabitants in 1930,[11] Kaplan's 1950 study of 370 selected cities with populations exceeding 25,000,[12] and Hadden and Borgatta's equivalent 1960 investigation.[13]

Using 15 variables, Price found four dominant dimensions of metropolitan centers: size, nonservice occupational specialization, socioeconomic status, and trade-center orientation. Perle confirmed these factors for 1960, using the same set of input variables. Hofstaetter, using 23 variables that he thought indexed the quality of urban environments, found the principal dimensions to be socioeconomic status, degree of industrialization, and prevalence of slum conditions. Kaplan's factors in a 47-variable study were size, socioeconomic status, population stability and growth, relative ethnic and racial homogeneity, and age-sex structure (life cycle). Hadden and Borgatta, in a study closely corresponding to the one reported in this chap-

ter, produced 16 factors in all from data comprising 65 variables for 644 cities: socioeconomic status, nonwhite population, age composition, educational centers, residential mobility, population density, foreign-born concentration, total population, wholesale concentration, retail concentration, manufacturing concentration, durable manufacturing concentration, communication centers, public administration centers, high-school education, and transportation centers.

Clearly Hodge's generalizations hold in the United States for the period 1930–1960. Differences in the output of the various studies simply reflect differences in the subset of variables, and the larger scale Hadden-Borgatta work and ours embrace the data subsets and variety of results of the other research workers.

## Canada

The first multivariate studies of Canada were completed by King for the years 1951 and 1961.[14] Subsequently Ray et al.[15] restudied the Canadian urban scene in a broader framework of variables from the 1961 census and a wider interpretive context.

King (106 cities × 52 variables) found dimensions of socioeconomic status (related also to differences between English and French Canada), relative isolation with primary industry orientation, smaller specialized manufacturing towns, etc. Ray and his associates (113 cities × 95 variables) reiterated the basic socioeconomic significance of English-French contrasts in Canada and identified several functional types of city: mining service centers, manufacturing, and metropolitan growth poles.

A separate postwar growth pattern emerged, as did British Columbian and Prairie city types based on distinctive Asiatic

9. Daniel O. Price, "Factor Analysis in the Study of Urban Centers," *Social Forces,* Vol. 20 (1941–1942), pp. 449–461.
10. Sylvia M. Perle, "Factor Analysis of American Cities" (M.A. dissertation, University of Chicago, 1964).
11. Peter R. Hofstaetter, "Your City Revisited—A Factorial Ecology of Cultural Patterns," *American Catholic Sociological Review,* Vol. 13 (October 1952), pp. 159–168. Based on E. L. Thorndike, *Your City* (New York: Harcourt, Brace and Co., 1939).
12. Howard B. Kaplan, "An Empirical Typology for Urban Description" (Ph.D. dissertation, New York University, 1958).
13. J. K. Hadden and E. F. Borgatta, *American Cities: Their Social Characteristics* (Chicago: Rand McNally and Co., 1965), See also John E. Tropman, "Critical Dimensions of Community Structure. A Reexamination of the Hadden-Borgatta Findings," *Urban Affairs Quarterly,* Vol. 5, No. 2 (December 1969), pp. 215–232.

14. Leslie J. King, "Cross-Sectional Analysis of Canadian Urban Dimensions, 1951 and 1961," *Canadian Geographer,* Vol. 10 (1966), pp. 205–224.
15. D. Michael Ray et al. "The Socio-Economic Dimensions and Spatial Structure of Canadian Cities," unpublished paper, University of Waterloo, 1968.

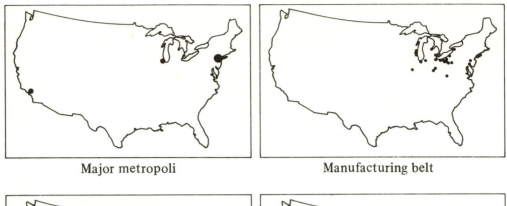

Major metropoli                    Manufacturing belt

Older New England              Service Centers of Midwest and Plains

New York, New Jersey, and New England        Smaller Border South Towns

Figure 2. Regional Patterns, SMSA Typology of 1960.

and Slavic culture components. From a comparison of our United States study and these Canadian materials,[16] all that need be said

here is that the similarities in latent structure are substantial.

### Britain

One of the best presentations of results of multivariate urban studies is *British Towns* by

16. See D. Michael Ray and R. A. Murdie, "Canadian and American Urban Dimensions," Chap. 6, pp. 181–210, in the same volume (Berry, 1972) from which the introduction in this paper was taken.—Eds.

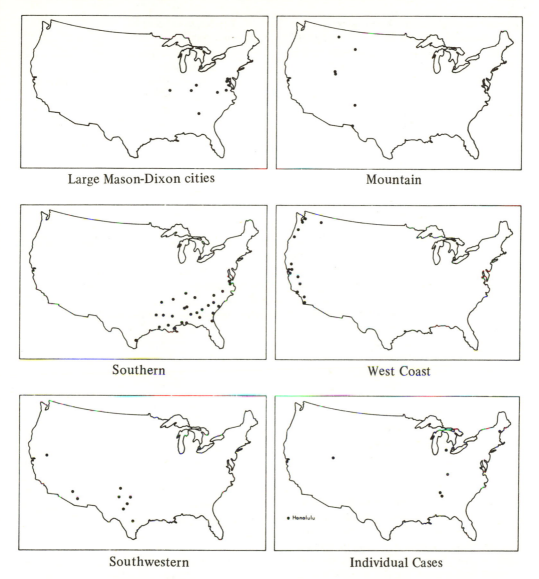

Large Mason-Dixon cities

Mountain

Southern

West Coast

Southwestern

Individual Cases

Moser and Scott.[17] In a path-breaking study the authors examined 157 towns in England and Wales with respect to 60 different var-

iables. The main object of their work was "to classify British towns into a few relatively homogeneous categories, or to see whether such a classification makes sense."[18] They used eight main categories of variables: popu-

17. C. A. Moser and Wolf Scott, *British Towns: A Statistical Study of Their Social and Economic Differences* (Edinburgh and London: Oliver and Boyd, 1961).

18. Moser and Scott, *British Towns*.

lation size and structure (7 variables), population change (8), households and housing (10), economic functions and employment characteristics (15), social class (4), voting behavior (7), health (7), and education (2).

Prior to classification the authors found it necessary to isolate the basic patterns according to which the towns varied, "because the many series that describe towns are not independent; they overlap in the story they tell.... Towns with a high proportion of heavy industry tend, on the whole, to have low 'social class' proportions, a substantial Labor vote, high infant mortality, and so on."[19] Four common factors were found to account for the correlations among the primary variables: social class, age of the area, including growth in 1931–1951, recent (1951–1958) growth, and housing conditions, including overcrowding.

Notable in these results is the correlation in the Moser and Scott "social status" dimension of North American socioeconomic status and age-structure elements. In Britain higher status is accompanied by higher proportions of older, smaller families, lower birth rates, etc. In turn the highest status communities represent a combination of resorts and retirement communities, exclusive residential suburbs, and professional administrative centers. The universal validity of factorial results postulated by Hodge is thus called into question.

Since the common factors summarized the essential differences among towns contained in the entire set of original primary variables, Moser and Scott could simplify the classification problem. Each town was given a score on each common factor, and towns were then allocated to groups on the basis of relative scores on the four factors. The 14 groups of towns that were identified fall into three major categories:

(1) Resort, administrative, and commercial centers
   (a) Seaside resorts
   (b) Spas; professional and administrative centers
   (c) Commercial centers
(2) Industrial towns
   (a) Railway centers
   (b) Ports
   (c) Textile centers of Yorkshire and Lancashire
   (d) Industrial centers of the northwest and Welsh mining towns
   (e) Metal-manufacturing centers
(3) Suburbs and suburban-type towns
   (a) Exclusive residential suburbs
   (b) Older mixed residential suburbs
   (c) Newer mixed residential suburbs
   (d) Light industrial suburbs, national defense centers, and towns within the influence of large metropolitan conurbations
   (e) Older working-class industrial suburbs
   (f) Newer industrial suburbs

In the grouping "the general aim [was] to minimize within-group [differences] and to maximize those between groups."[20]

## Yugoslavia

Moving beyond the North Atlantic context, Fisher,[21] using 1961 data, analyzed 55 selected urban centers in Yugoslavia with respect to 26 variables. He interpreted the most important latent dimension as comprising an index of relative development in which status and proportion of population in the economically active child-rearing age groups are highly related. This factor indicated a broad difference between the "developed" and the "underdeveloped" regions of Yugoslavia.

Fisher also found several functional types (construction and transportation; traditional culture, commercial, and administrative centers; industrial towns) and a factor identifying recent growth and change, but these he felt were secondary to the principal dimension.

19. Moser and Scott, *British Towns*.
20. Moser and Scott, *British Towns*.
21. Jack C. Fisher, *Yugoslavia. A Multinational State* (San Francisco: Chandler Publishing Co., 1966).

## Chile

Several analyses of Chilean data have been completed:[22] employment structure of 105 communes with populations exceeding 15,000 in both 1952 and 1960; 59 social, economic, political, and demographic variables for 80 urban communes in 1960; and exploration of data on transportation and traffic flows for 94 urban places in 1962–1965.

The principal factors in the first analysis were the functional sizes of centers in the urban hierarchy and a contrast between traditional towns of the agricultural heartland of the country and mining towns on the priphery. The larger analysis reiterated the factors of size and traditionalism versus modernism. The latter factor represented, as in Yugoslavia, a combination of socioeconomic status and age structure. In addition, separate factors were identified for recent growth, mineral exploitation, manufacturing, and certain elements of voting behavior.

## India

Ahmad's 102-city, 62-variable analysis of the largest Indian cities in 1966[23] identified as factors certain by now already familiar themes: size, recent change, and economic specialization (commercial, industrial). In addition, certain broad regional differences were also noted—between northern and southern India in the sex composition of cities and the position of women in the labor force, between eastern and western India in migration patterns, etc., each reflecting broad regional differences in India's cultures. Types of town were shown to be highly differentiated by region within the country.

## Nigeria and Ghana

Studies of the urban systems of Nigeria and Ghana have been completed by Mabogunge[24] and McNulty,[25] respectively.

McNulty found a principal factor differentiating urban populations according to age structures and sex ratios. This factor, he felt, reflected the migration of males in the active age groups to growing commercial and service centers, leaving behind high proportions of poorly educated young, old and females in areas of primary occupational specialization. A similar dimension was found by Mabogunge in Nigeria. These dimensions are not unlike Fisher's "modernism-traditionalism" scale for Yugoslavia.

A second factor found by McNulty related to functional type: highly specialized mining towns were distinguished from centers offering diversified employment in commerce, services, and manufacturing. Both McNulty and Mabogunge argued that these dimensions are structural correlates of the development process, particularly as overlaid on the countries by colonial capital, and that urban structural change, in turn, is attendant on development through the interrelated processes of migration and increasing economic diversification.

## CONCLUSIONS

Extending and modifying Hodge's arguments, several conclusions about the latent structure of urban systems follow:

1. The economic base of urban centers tends to act independently of other urban structural features (with the exception of

22. Brian J. L. Berry, "Relationships between Regional Economic Development and the Urban System: The Case of Chile," *Tijdschrift voor Economische en Sociale Geografie*, Vol. 60 (1969), pp. 283–307.

23. Qazi Ahmad, *Indian Cities: Characteristics and Correlates*, University of Chicago Department of Geography Research Paper No. 102 (1965).

24. Akin Mabogunge, "Economic Implications of the Pattern of Urbanization in Nigeria," *Nigerian Journal of Economic and Social Studies*, Vol. 7 (1965), pp. 9–30, and "Urbanization in Nigeria—A Constraint on Economic Development," *Economic Development and Cultural Change*, Vol. 13 (1965), pp. 413–438.

25. Michael L. McNulty, "Urban Structure and Development: The Urban System of Ghana," *Journal of Developing Areas*, in press; "Dimensions of Urban Structural Change in Chana: 1948–1960," unpublished manuscript, 1969.

hierarchical organization of market-oriented activities; see item 2 below), and, to the extent that there is geographic specialization based on locational factors other than market orientation, each broad economic function will lead to its own distinctive economic town type. Public activities—military bases, educational centers, public administration—act as any other specialized economic base.

2. Every urban system is organized system-wide into a hierarchy of centers based on aggregate economic power. The functional size of centers in an urban hierarchy is a universal latent dimension.

3. In every society the principal dimensions of socioeconomic differentiation are those of social status and age structure, or stage in life cycle. However, only at the highest levels of development do these factors appear to operate independently. At somewhat lower levels of welfare (Britain) there remains a correlation between income and family structure, and only the rich elderly can segregate themselves in retirement resorts and spas; at lower income levels there is a great mixture of family types in the same residential areas. Further down the scale still (Yugoslavia, Chile, West Africa), status and age-structure differences combine in broad regional patterns of development versus underdevelopment or modernism versus traditionalism, often expressed spatially in the differences between the national core region, or heartland, and the periphery, or hinterlands. In India, lacking a single heartland, the pattern is one of relative accessibility to the national metropolises of Bombay, Calcutta, Delhi, and Madras. In both the United States and Canada the factor of relative accessibility at the national level is independent of status and life-cycle variations but remains correlated with manufacturing as an economic specialization.

4. A culturally heterogeneous society will be characterized by separate ethnic or racial dimensions if the cultural groups are clustered in particular cities. If the groups occupy different status levels and have different family structures, the cultural differences may override other socioeconomic dimensions, as in the case of English-French contrasts in Canada.

5. Generally each new stage of growth will act independently of prior structural features if it is based on innovations giving rise to structural transformations. Thus distinct phases or stages of growth should each result in a separate latent dimension indexing a distinct pattern of variation of urban centers.

Such are the latent bases of manifest urban differences—the proximate underlying causes of distinctive town types. Their recognition and use can provide the much needed basis for a systematic comparative classification of cities.

# Spatial Variations in Level of Living in England and Wales

PAUL L. KNOX

National and regional well-being in western societies has traditionally been assessed by reference to income levels, together with rates of unemployment, demographic growth and industrial growth. Recently, however, there has been an increasing awareness that these indicators may reflect only some of the elements of prosperity, welfare and opportunity relevant to the quality of life in such societies, implying that any satisfactory examination of relative well-being should also consider aspects of socio-economic health and social welfare. Indicators of national social conditions are in fact currently being developed both in Britain and the United States, in an attempt to provide social statistics comparable in scope and accuracy with existing series of economic statistics. The ultimate aim is to develop a set of social indicators which could be related to national economic policy in much the same way as economic indicators such as the cost of living index have been developed in order to help guide national economic policy (Bauer, 1966; Moser, 1971). At the regional level, less progress has been made towards measuring variations in social conditions. In Britain, the examination of regional disparities was, until the mid-1960s, based largely on a consideration of the more immediately apparent variations in unemployment, migration, and money income (Holmans, 1965; Self, 1965; Thirlwall, 1966). Among the first to note more widespread socio-economic disparities were Coates and Rawstron (1966), who have recently emphasized the lack of an existing framework for the systematic measurement of socio-economic conditions within Britain (Coates and Rawstron, 1971). This desire for a greater knowledge of regional variations in social welfare (in its widest sense) is not without precedent. In 1970, for example, Chisholm suggested the compilation of a social atlas of Great Britain, dealing with subjects such as the availability of medical services, rates of crimes, educational provision and achievement, and the use of State and local authority welfare services (Chisholm, 1970).

In view of the widespread interest in the search for social indicators and a growing concern for the problems and injustices of regional disparities in social welfare, it is somewhat surprising that research workers in these fields have almost entirely overlooked the concept of level of living. Throughout a long doctrinal history in economics and sociology, level of living has been regarded as a convenient framework for the analysis of a large number of interrelated elements of social and economic well-being (Pipping, 1969) but the concept has never been used in an explicitly spatial context in Britain, despite the demonstration by Lewis (1968) of the utility of the concept in a regionalization of the north-eastern United States, an area which in many ways is similar to Britain. Thus, while it is clear that definite inequalities of opportunity and prosperity exist from place to place within Britain, little is known in detail of many important aspects of its social geog-

From *Transactions, Institute of British Geographers*, vol. 62 1974, pp. 1–15. Reprinted by permission.

raphy. In many cases only rather speculative suggestions have been made as to the relative performance of even broadly defined regions whilst even less is known of the spatial expression of unitary concepts, such as level of living, which involve multiple aspects of social welfare.

In the light of these considerations, the objectives of this paper are three-fold:

(1) to propose a definition of the concept of level of living relevant to contemporary conditions in England and Wales;

(2) to evaluate those indicators of level of living which best reflect the concept and its variations from place to place in England and Wales:

(3) to determine the most commonly occurring pattern or patterns of spatial variation displayed by these indicators.

Local authority areas are used as the areal framework since despite certain well-documented problems involved in using such units as bases for areal data collection (Duncan, Cuzzort and Duncan, 1961), local authorities contribute effectively towards standards of health, housing, education and law and order achieved by the communities within their jurisdiction, and are therefore of direct relevance to the study of many aspects of level of living.

## AN OPERATIONAL DEFINITION OF LEVEL OF LIVING

While several definitions of level of living have been suggested in the past (Hagood and Bowles, 1957; Rural Sociological Society, 1956; Waris, 1965) they have been formulated in relation to specific applications and none was regarded as completely acceptable for use in relation to the location, date and areal framework of this study. Nevertheless, some features are accepted as integral parts of any definition of level of living. In so far as it relates to the actual satisfaction of the needs and wants of the population, for example, the concept is not ambiguous. It is also clear that level of living should be regarded as more than just the equivalent of goods and services

relating to these needs and wants, since there are some important components of level of living which cannot be classed as consumers' goods and services (Drewnowski, 1970). Examples of these are afforded by many aspects of leisure and security. Finally, it is generally accepted that the concept can be disaggregated into a number of standard classes of needs and wants applicable to the population as a whole: housing, health, recreation and security, for example. Where level of living is considered in relation to large units of population, as in this study, there are additional factors to be considered. Certain aspects of demographic structure, physical environment and institutional organization are directly relevant to the ability or likelihood of satisfying the main classes of needs and wants. Physical environment, for example, has direct relevance to certain aspects of both health and recreation, whilst the movement of population between areas alters the relative local demand for, and supply of, labour, housing and public services. Level of living is therefore defined as follows:

The level of living of persons resident within a given spatial unit is constituted by the overall composition of housing, health, education, social status, employment, affluence, leisure, social security and social stability aggregately exhibited in that area, together with those aspects of demographic structure, general physical environment, and social institutions which have relevance to the question of the extent to which needs and desires relating to the foregoing constitutents of level of living can be, or are, met.

A thorough (but necessarily subjective) assessment of those indicators of housing, health, education and so on which are relevant to the study of level of living within England and Wales enables a list of variables to be drawn up which effectively represents the above definition and which therefore constitutes an operational definition of the concept.* No attempt has been made to ensure

*An appendix giving details of the 53 variables is not included here.—Eds.

that each variable is normative (in the sense that a move along a quantified scale in a particular direction can be said to be "good" or "bad"), since it is necessary to distinguish between the variables themselves and the context in which they are used. It is the latter which confers upon the variable any normative character that it assumes, and the same variable may have opposite normative characteristics in different circumstances (Moser, 1971). Within the context of level of living there are many variables about which there is no general consensus as to the direction of movement that is "good," but which nevertheless are generally agreed to form an important part of the information required for an understanding of certain aspects of level of living. An example is the proportion of persons aged sixty years or more (variable 03). Above-average proportions of such persons in an area may be considered "bad" because of the economic burden on the community and the social problems associated with old age, but equally there are many communities which are dependent upon the economic resources of wealthier retired persons. Moreover, it is the interconnections between variables which may be expected to be major parameters of spatial variation in level of living, just as they are more important than single variables in simply describing certain sections of society. So that, although old age is not strictly normative, its coincidence with low incomes, for example, provides a more detailed illustration of life-style than a wide range of single variables such as income. To be normative is thus a frequent but not a universal characteristic of the fifty-three variables selected to represent level of living.

It should also be noted that several important constituents of level of living are excluded from the operational definition because they are not subject to significant variations from person to person or from place to place within England and Wales. Most important of these are the basic human freedoms of expression, politics and religion, together with adequate basic standards of literacy, nutrition and clothing (United Nations Organization, 1961).

## A SYNTHESIS OF LEVEL LIVING

The magnitude and complexity of the matrix of raw data for the fifty-three variables (primary variables) and 145 administrative counties and county boroughs in England and Wales required several statistical procedures to be used for the sake of efficiency and parsimony. Correlation analysis was used as a first stage in both resolving the most commonly occurring patterns of spatial variation displayed by the primary variables and in evaluating those variables which might best reflect the concept as a whole. The zero-order correlation coefficients used are simple measures of the magnitude and direction of linear relationships between pairs of variables, but tend to understate the degree of the relationship where one of the variables exhibits a skewed frequency distribution, and so the data were first transformed where necessary to approximations of normal distributions. The correlation coefficients subsequently produced revealed a generally low order of interrelationship, with only 12 per cent of the 1378 unique coefficients in the correlation matrix exceeding $\pm$ 0.500 in value, although their average value (0.277) is greater than is required of an individual coefficient at the 0.01 per cent level of confidence. Closer examination of the correlation matrix showed that a number of variables (those relating to average occupational density, availability of a fixed bath, male manual workers, and male mortality rate from bronchitis, for example) had substantial average intercorrelations with the fifty-two other variables. Since these values were mostly derived from a large number of moderately high correlations rather than from a few very high correlations, it was concluded that some important general similarities in the spatial distributions of the variables did in fact exist.

In order to determine the structure of such sets of interrelated variables, principal components analysis was used. The mechanics and algebra of the method are described in detail by a number of authors (Kendall, 1957; Cooley and Lohnes, 1964; Harman, 1967). Table 1 shows the diminishing significance of

Table 1. Relative Importance of the First Ten
Components

| Component number | Eigenvalue | Cumulative per cent of total variance |
|---|---|---|
| I | 14.800 | 27.924 |
| II | 7.912 | 42.852 |
| III | 5.492 | 53.213 |
| IV | 2.607 | 58.133 |
| V | 2.524 | 62.894 |
| VI | 1.966 | 66.605 |
| VII | 1.608 | 69.673 |
| VIII | 1.347 | 72.179 |
| IX | 1.007 | 74.079 |
| X | 0.992 | 75.951 |

Table 2. The Component Loadings

*Component I*

| | |
|---|---|
| Male mortality from bronchitis | 0.870 |
| Manual workers | 0.866 |
| Average number of persons per acre | 0.851 |
| Average number of persons per room | 0.769 |
| Economically active persons | 0.765 |
| Vacant dwellings | −0.758 |
| Female activity rate | 0.747 |
| Early school leavers | 0.736 |
| Car ownership | −0.736 |
| Poll in local elections | 0.709 |

*Component II*

| | |
|---|---|
| Persons aged 0–14 | −0.704 |
| Female divorce rate | 0.685 |
| Illegitimate birth rate | 0.674 |
| Persons aged 60 and over | 0.664 |
| Dwellings with low rateable value | −0.567 |
| Persons aged 15–44 | −0.655 |
| Large households | −0.631 |
| Small households | 0.626 |

*Component III*

| | |
|---|---|
| Lack of fixed bath | −0.772 |
| Unemployment | −0.641 |
| Lack of hot water tap | −0.578 |
| New housing | 0.555 |
| Dwellings rented unfurnished | −0.555 |
| Low personal taxable incomes | −0.545 |
| Oversized junior school classes | 0.472 |
| Provision of cinemas | −0.456 |

*Component IV*

| | |
|---|---|
| Unemployment | 0.558 |
| Lack of hot water tap | −0.505 |
| High personal taxable incomes | −0.476 |
| Car ownership | −0.450 |
| Economically active persons | −0.397 |
| Male mortality from tuberculosis | 0.362 |

*Component V*

| | |
|---|---|
| Large households | 0.582 |
| Shared households | 0.554 |
| Dwellings with low rateable value | −0.451 |
| Early school leavers | −0.384 |

*Component VI*

| | |
|---|---|
| High personal taxable incomes | 0.475 |
| Dwellings owner-occupied | 0.454 |
| Extended secondary education | 0.425 |
| Persons accommodated by local authority welfare services | −0.327 |

the successive components produced in the present analysis. From an examination of this information, it was decided to examine the first six components in detail. These account for some two-thirds of the total variance, and represent a cut-off point of around 2.00 in terms of eigenvalues.

The character of the six components is indicated in Table 2, which shows the most important loadings for each component. The effect of using an unrotated principal components model can clearly be seen in that the first component is a "general" component, with high loadings on several constituents of level of living. In this sense, component I could be descriptively termed a "level of living" component. Social status, health, housing, employment and affluence are all represented strongly, whilst the high loading of the average number of persons per acre suggests a close association with urbanization. In general, the direction of the highest loadings on component I is such that high component scores will indicate generally lower levels of living. Other variables with high loadings (± 0.600 or more) on component I but not included in Table 2 are the infant mortality rate (positive loading) local authority expenditure on children's services (positive), new local authority housing (negative), the proportion of persons on general medical practitioners' lists of 3000 or more (positive), indictable offences (positive), the proportion of male pupils staying on at school (negative) the proportion of private households in unshared dwellings without exclusive use of a cold water tap (negative), and the proportion of unopposed seats in local government elections (negative). This list confirms both the generality and the character of the component as construed from Table 2. The one exception is the variable relating to the proportion of private households without exclusive use of a cold water tap, which has a loading contrary to the anticipated direction. The explanation is possibly to be found in connection with the urban character of the component: since there is little variability in the data for this variable (coefficient of variation = 4.16), the variation which does exist may be related to causes exclusive to extra-urban areas. One such cause may be the difficulty of providing piped water supplies to isolated rural dwellings.

The loadings of greatest magnitude on component II are most closely associated with age structure, social stability, and household size. Thus component II is associated with high divorce and illegitimacy rates, together with large proportions of elderly persons and a large proportion of single-person households and households sharing a dwelling. The connection between the three groups of variables may be the family life-cycle, which is regarded by some workers as more significant than social class in determining ways of life (Pahl, 1970), but because of the strong influence on the three variables relating to age structure, this component is nominally designated an "old age" component.

The third component is particularly interesting: it is closely related to a collection of variables which together suggest the effects of suburbanization. Thus Table 2 shows that as well as negative loadings on variables relating to the lack of household amenities such as a fixed bath, there are high negative loadings on the variables relating to privately rented unfurnished dwellings, single-person households, unemployment and the incidence of cinemas, whilst high positive loadings are found on the variables relating to the construction of new houses and overcrowded classes in junior schools. Such a combination of

factors may be expected to occur in areas of urban expansion beyond major urban centres. The nature of the five variables with moderate loadings (at least ± 0.400) on the component lends support to this idea: professional workers and persons on general practitioners' lists of 3000 or more are positively associated, whilst male mortality from tuberculosis, infant mortality and local authority housebuilding are negatively associated. For descriptive convenience, this component is called the "household amenity" component.

Component IV accounts for less than 5 per cent of the total variance, and is only moderately loaded (± 0.400 or more) on a few variables. The most outstanding of these is the proportion of economically active persons out of employment. It is not possible, however, to give a convenient descriptive or causal identity to the component because of its ambivalent nature. Table 2 shows only three variables with moderate loadings on component V, each related to some aspect of housing, whilst component VI is chiefly associated with income, together with housing and education variables. As with component IV, the structure of the component is such that it is difficult to coin useful titles, descriptive or otherwise.

Of the fifty-three primary variables, a surprisingly large number are heavily involved in the structure of the six components. As many as thirty-eight have communality coefficients of 0.60 or more, indicating that at least 60 per cent of their own variation is accounted for by the six components together. Several variables have particularly high values, the highest being that for the average number of persons per acre: 0.91. Other variables with high communality coefficients include those relating to manual workers (0.86), the lack of a fixed bath (0.86), car ownership (0.85), male mortality from bronchitis (0.85), and persons aged sixty and over (0.85). At the other extreme, only seven variables have less than 50 per cent of their variation accounted for by the six components: the migration balance (0.24), the provision of school dental officers (0.26), the incidence of good hotels (0.40), the incidence of cinemas (0.42), natural population change (0.46), local authority expenditure on children's services (0.46), and the ratio of pupils to teachers in senior schools (0.47).

These figures may be considered as an inverse measure of the uniqueness of the spatial distribution of each variable: the lower the value, the less the variable is spatially associated with the major dimensions of variation exhibited by the fifty-two other variables. One of the most striking features of the communality coefficients as a whole is the uniqueness of the variables directly related to the provision of local authority services: housing and housebuilding, school dental officers, welfare accommodation, children's services, police services and library staff. Each of these variables has a value well below the overall average of 0.66, suggesting that as far as can be measured by the six components, the provision of these services is at best only loosely related to the major socio-geographic patterns of England and Wales.

The spatial expression of the three most important components is portrayed by Figures 1–3, in which the component scores have been mapped by quintile divisions. Figure 1 shows the scores for component I, the "level of living" component, and amply confirms the urban character of the component suggested by its high positive loading with the average number of persons per acre. It also appears that, in general, areas which have been urbanized for the longest period of time have higher scores (and therefore lower levels of living) than more recently urbanized areas. Friedlander (1970) has pointed out that the earliest counties to be urbanized were London, from which urbanization has only spread outwards in the last fifty years or so; counties in the north-east and north-west, from which urbanization spread rapidly following the Industrial Revolution; and Glamorganshire and Monmouthshire in South Wales. These areas correspond to the areas with the highest scores on component I, and the connection between the two prompts the idea that the component may be related not only to urbanism, but also to the sequence of urbanization. It would also seem likely that such a pattern may be related

to the structure and sequence of industrialization, but both are propositions which need further investigation.

Figure 2 shows the spatial distribution of scores for component II, the "old age" component. Not unexpectedly, coastal resorts such as Bournemouth, Eastbourne, Hastings and Southport have high scores on this component, the reason being mainly the large numbers of elderly persons attracted to such areas for retirement. On the other hand, high scores for towns such as Blackburn and Rochdale are more likely to be caused by an out-migration of younger persons. The broad expression of the component is such that high scores dominate south-eastern England, whilst such scores are rare in the west Midlands, Wales, Yorkshire and northern England.

The scores for component III present a striking pattern of spatial variation, supporting the suggestion that this component reflects the influence of suburbanization (Fig. 3). The local authorities with the highest rank-values are the administrative counties encompassing the urbanized and industrialized part of England between Lancashire in the north-west, Hampshire in the south, and Kent in the south-east. These are areas which have attracted large numbers of persons because of their relative economic prosperity; conversely, people have been less willing or unable to establish new residences within the larger centres of population, especially Liverpool, Manchester, Nottingham, Leicester, the west Midlands conurbation and London. Thus within the area from the south and south-east to Lancashire, the majority of county boroughs fall within the lower quintiles. Those towns in this area with scores falling above the median class are towns such as Oxford, Reading, Coventry, and Northampton which have expanded in size relatively recently and which presumably had space for suburban expansion within their own boundaries. Outside this belt of high "suburbanization," rank-scores of administrative counties, as well as those of most county boroughs, decrease northwards, eastwards and westwards, with a concentration of

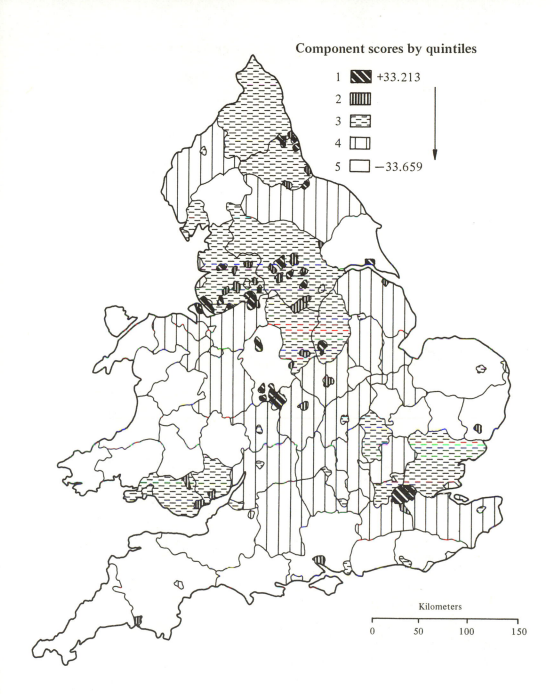

Component scores by quintiles

1  +33.213
2
3
4
5  −33.659

Kilometers

0    50    100    150

Figure 1. Component I: ''Level of Living.''

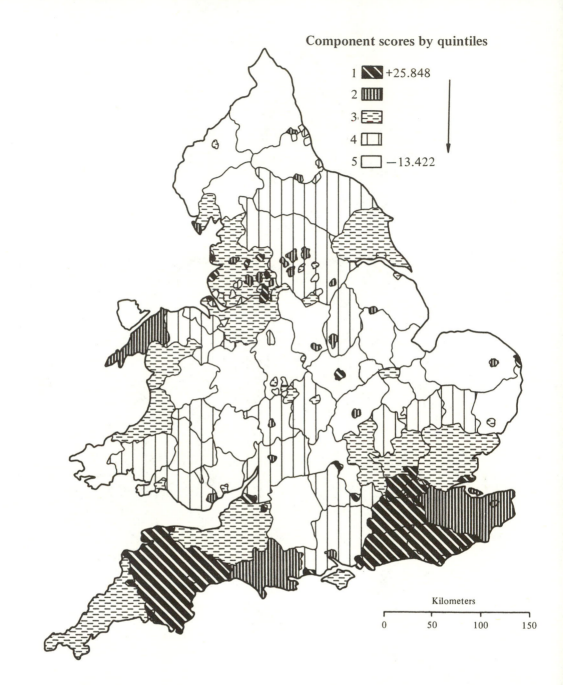

Component scores by quintiles

1 +25.848
2
3
4
5 −13.422

Kilometers

0    50    100    150

Figure 2. Component II: "Old Age."

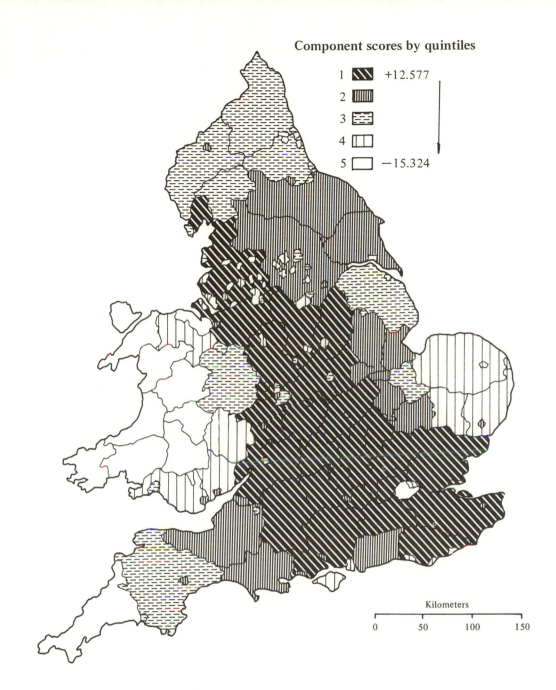

Figure 3. Component III: "Household Amenity."

the lowest scores in central and western Wales.

## AN OVERALL MEASURE

Inclusion of similar maps for components IV, V and VI would complete the presentation of the six principal, unrelated dimensions of spatial variation in level of living in England and Wales. But individual maps of component scores are not able to reveal the relative level of living of local authorities, groups of local authorities, or even "regions" in terms of the concept as a whole. Despite the relative importance and comprehensiveness of the first component, it is the first six components together which have been taken as representative of the spatial variation of the primary variables. To define spatial variations of level of living by scores on the first component only would therefore result in a considerable loss of information. On the other hand, six unrelated distributions of unequal importance are an unwieldy measure of a unitary concept, for which the construction of a single index is intuitively appealing. Since the component scores are themselves weighted indices of the association of each local authority with each component, they offer a potentially useful basis for an overall measure: a simple index could be derived from the summation of component scores or rank-scores over the six components for each local authority. This assumes, however, that high or low scores on each of the components can be regarded as "good" or "bad" or "high" or "low" in terms of level of living. This of course is not possible because a number of the primary variables are entirely non-normative in nature. Even where variables can be recognized as completely normative, variables with opposite normative characteristics often have high loadings on the same component. Component IV, for example, is associated with both high unemployment rates and low proportions of households without exclusive use of a hot water tap. Thus even the use of only normative variables in a study of this type would not preclude difficulties of this nature

occurring, a problem encountered recently by Gordon and Whittaker (1972) in their examination of indicators of local prosperity in south-west England.

In the absence of component scores as bases for an overall measure, it is possible to make use of the component structure by selecting a small number of "diagnostic" variables from the set of primary variables. In effect these diagnostic variables are taken to represent, between them, the character and composition of the first six components. The process of selection of the diagnostic variables is subjective, and only indirect measures of the efficiency of the resultant index are available. Nevertheless, it is possible to construct an index for which the complex relationships between the diagnostic variables and the rest of the primary variables have been clearly established. Diagnostic variables were selected such that each is highly associated with at least one of the components (with a loading of $\pm0.600$ or more) and has a large proportion (at least 75 per cent) of its variance involved in the component structure; that each is as normative as possible within the context of the character of the components; and that between them they reflect as broadly as possible the character and composition of all six components. In cases where direct alternatives remained after these requirements had been met, the diagnostic variables were selected with references to their utility and availability at other scales of measurement and to existing literature. In this way the resultant index represents an attempt to express the results of the components analysis as efficiently as possible and in such a way that the index may possibly be utilized in further studies.

The number of diagnostic variables used is necessarily arbitrary. Four were selected, after their utility had been roughly checked by comparing (by way of rank-correlations) the index values they produced with indexes derived from other combinations of various numbers of alternative diagnostic variables. The four which are used in the present study are the variables relating to the average number of persons per room (variable 07), lack of a fixed bath (22), unemployment (47), and the proportion of persons aged sixty or more (03). Index values were derived as follows:

$$I = 100 . \Sigma \left( \frac{R}{N.C} \right)$$

where $I$ is the index value,

$R$ is the individual rank-score,

$N$ is the number of diagnostic variables,

and $C$ is the number of cases.

In the computation of the index, local authorities have been ranked so that high index values are indicative of a low level of living. For this purpose, high scores on variable 03 have been regarded as "bad" in terms of the level of living of an area. This is because of the economic and social "burden of dependency" of the existence of a large proportion of older persons in a community (Brown, 1971), but it is clear that the presence of large proportions of older persons within an area does not necessarily have a depressing effect on the level of living of that area. Obvious examples are afforded by the concentration of relatively affluent retired persons in south coast resorts such as Eastbourne. However, this variable must be included because of the importance of component II, which strongly represents age structure and life-cycle, and it will be appreciated that a predominantly old age structure, in combination with other, wholly normative, diagnostic variables, can be a positive indicant of level of living. A large proportion of old persons, in association with an absence of household amenities and a high average occupational density for example, is clearly representative of a low level of living.

The index values produced from the analysis reveal a wide range of the data, from a value of 9.7 for Buckinghamshire (the best) to a value of 83.9 for Gateshead (the worst), whilst the overall amount of variation between local authorities is considerable. The coefficient of variation for the index values is 31.2, reflecting the diversity of the authorities which had been apparent at all stages of the analysis. In general the spatial distribution of the index values (Fig. 4) does not contradict or challenge accepted notions or assertions concerning the socio-economic geography of England and Wales: a high level of living index is associated with most of Wales, south-western and north-eastern England, Lancashire and East Anglia; whilst a low index is to be found chiefly amongst the counties of central and southern England and the Midlands. The most important exception to this generalization is the value recorded for the County of London, which has long been popularly regarded as relatively well-off in terms of opportunity and achievement in relation to many constituents of level of living. An index value as high as 70.1 applicable to more than 3.2 million people in the centre of the metropolis is therefore a considerable qualification to the above generalization. Clearly the overall level of living for the County of London does not match up to the availability of museums, libraries, theatres, hotels, restaurants, specialist retail stores, administrative headquarters, hospitals and department stores in central London upon which the percept of a socio-economically "healthy" London must largely be based.

On a regional basis, it is possible to distinguish an area of generally low index values (40.0 or less) extending from the Home Counties northwards as far as Nottinghamshire and westwards as far as Somerset in the south and Cheshire in the north. Within this area, the majority of county boroughs tend towards intermediate scores, but the most striking feature of the area as a whole is its contiguity. Only four authorities outside this area have values of less than 40.0: Westmorland, the North Riding of Yorkshire, York and Eastbourne. The lowest index values are found in administrative counties which both possess large areas of prosperous agricultural activity and contain many suburbs and satellite towns which are centred on the larger and more prosperous industrial and commercial cities. It is suggested therefore that the basic reasons for such low index values may be regarded as twofold: (a) economic structure, and (b) the urban process, particularly subur-

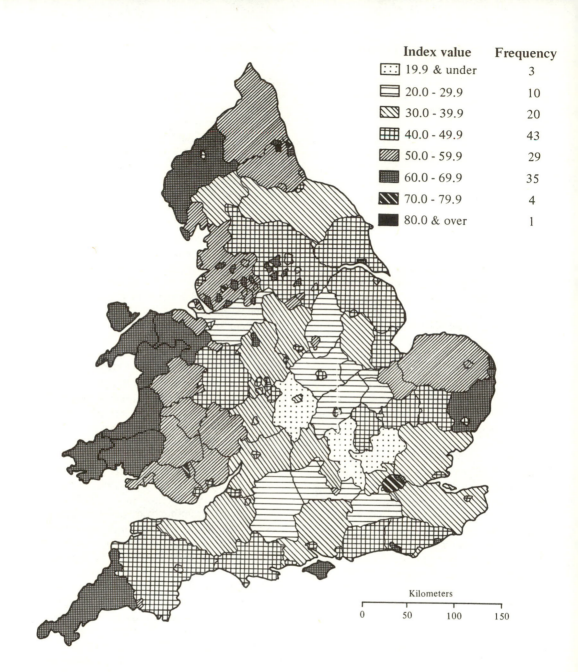

| Index value | Frequency |
|---|---|
| 19.9 & under | 3 |
| 20.0 - 29.9 | 10 |
| 30.0 - 39.9 | 20 |
| 40.0 - 49.9 | 43 |
| 50.0 - 59.9 | 29 |
| 60.0 - 69.9 | 35 |
| 70.0 - 79.9 | 4 |
| 80.0 & over | 1 |

Kilometers

0    50    100    150

Figure 4. An Index of Level of Living in England and Wales.

banization. The influence of both factors has already been noted in relation to the spatial expression of the components.

At the other extreme, two different sorts of area can be distinguished with high index values (60.0 or more). The most numerous of these are northern industrial county boroughs, amongst which the highest scores of all are recorded and in which the legacy of the inter-war depression combined with a continued decline in the coalmining, shipbuilding and textile industries are reflected in the index values. The second type of area is constituted by a group of administrative counties, in particular by those in western Wales, but including Cornwall and Cumberland. Several reasons may be postulated for high index values in such areas, amongst them remoteness and the cost of supplying services of all kinds to a small but dispersed population; economic dependence upon marginal agriculture; and the burden of dependency created by both the in-migration of retired persons to coastal areas and the out-migration of younger persons seeking a wider range of economic opportunities.

## CONCLUSIONS

The findings of this analysis must remain fairly tentative, since the success of the investigation hinges largely upon the availability of data and the selection of variables. Items for which data were not available, but which would be relevant within the context of level of living, include the possession of consumer durables such as television sets and washing machines, the provision of household power supplies, cooking facilities and garage space, and the incidence of mental ill-health. In addition, there are several aspects of level of living which would be difficult to quantify objectively. These include the quality of landscape and the general degree of satisfaction or contentment of the residents of a given local authority. Even if one accepts that it is not possible to measure some indicators of level of living, it must be admitted that some or all of the non-measurable indicators may be im-

portant in determining and describing spatial variations in level of living. The use of only measurable indicators in formulating an operational definition has therefore inevitably assumed that the correlation between the non-measurable and the measurable indicators is high enough to give validity to results based solely upon the latter.

Having said this, the principal components analysis must be regarded as successful in reducing the large and unwieldy set of available data to six components representing two-thirds of the total variation in the data. It is interesting that despite the use of an unrotated solution, the first three components are clearly identifiable with certain socio-geographic processes. The first and most important component is closely related to variables representative of many aspects of level of living, but, contrary to the findings of similar analysis of socio-geographic data at similar scales of measurement, they tend to reflect not social class but a broad set of socio-economic characteristics related to tte urban-rural dichotomy.

The second component is recognized as being most closely related to variables representing age structure, social stability and certain aspects of housing: a structure which is parallelled in most studies of the factorial ecology of cities, where this distinctive complex of associations is known as "Familism" or "life-cycle" (Timms, 1971). The third component, as with the first, is association with the process of urbanization, for the distribution of component scores and the structure of the component are clearly indicative of "suburbanism," although it should be stressed that this component may in fact owe its existence to the boundaries of the local authority areas as much as to anything else. Problems arising from the use of multivariate methods with such units have been widely discussed but remain largely unresolved. It should be emphasized that the results outlined here relate exclusively to the local authority areas used in the analysis. These cities and counties are large and heterogeneous and may conceal much greater internal variation in many of the indicators of level of living than is extant between them. The possibility clearly presents an important research problem.

The inevitably ambivalent nature of some of the components precludes the construction of either an index of level of living or a classification of local authorities based on component scores. The four diagnostic variables employed as alternatives facilitate the computation of an index which is useful in portraying the general spatial expression of level of living, but which must be regarded as being rather unsatisfactory in itself, since significant variations in the contribution of individual diagnostic variables are in many cases masked by the generality of the index. Thus despite the unitary character of the concept, it is desirable to supplement the index values with a consideration of disaggregated data.*

This paper has only been able to present some general ideas and findings but with an improved series of social statistics and more defined measures of the concept, level of living could well provide the conceptual framework for the close monitoring of the socio-economic geography of areas such as England and Wales. Without the information provided by such monitoring, "ignorance is bliss (and) spatial variations that are unjust, harmful and inefficient are accepted not only by those who govern both nationally and locally, but also by those who, did they but know it, suffer badly because they happen to live and work in particular areas" (Coates and Rawstron, 1971).

## REFERENCES

Bauer, R. A. (1966) *Social indicators*.

Brown, M. (1971) *An introduction to social administration in Britain*.

Chisholm, M. (1970) "Onwards from Barlow and Hunt: an agenda for research" (mimeographed paper given to the Annual Conference of the Institute of British Geographers, Belfast).

Coates, B. E. and E. M. Rawstron (1966) "Opportunity and affluence," *Geography*, 51, 1–15.

———. and E. M. Rawstron (1971) *Regional variations in Britain*.

Cooley, W. W. and P. R. Lohnes (1964) *Multivariate procedures for the behavioral sciences*.

Drewnowski, J. (1970) "Measuring the level of living" (paper delivered to the summer school of the Town and County Planning Association).

Duncan, O. D., Cuzzort, R. P. and B. Duncan (1961) *Statistical geography: problems in analysing areal data*.

Friedlander, D. (1970) "The spread of urbanization in England and Wales, 18511951," *Population Studies*, 24, 423–43.

Gordon, I. R. and R. M. Whittaker (1972) "Indicators of local prosperity in the South-West Region," *Regional Studies*, 6, 299–313.

Hagood, M. J. and G. K. Bowles (1957) "Farm operator level of living indexes for the United States," Part 7 of *Major Statistical Series of the United States Department of Agriculture: How they are constructed and used*, United States Department of Agriculture Handbook No. 118.

Harman, H. (1967) *Modern factor analysis*.

Holmans, A. E. (1965) "Inter-regional differences in income: are there "Two Nations" or one?" in Wilson, T. (ed.) "Papers on regional development," *Journal of Industrial Economics*, Supplement 2, 1–19.

Kendall, M. G. (1957) *A course in multivariate analysis*.

Lewis, G. M. (1968) "Levels of Living in the north-eastern United States *c*. 1960: a new approach to regional geography," *Trans. Inst. Br. Geogr*. 45, 11–37.

Mather, P. (1969) *Computer applications in the natural and social sciences: No. I: Cluster analysis*, University of Nottingham, Department of Geography.

Moser, C. A. (1971) "Social indicators: systems, methods and problems," *Central Statistical Office*.

Pahl, R. E. (1970) *Patterns of urban life*.

Pipping, H. E. (1969) *Standard of living: the concept and its place in economics* (Helsinki).

Rural Sociological Society (1956) "Sociological research into rural levels and standards of living," *Rural Sociology*, 21, 183–95.

Self, P. (1965) "North versus South," *Tijdschrift voor Economische en Sociale Geografie*, 56, 133–44.

---

*This analysis is undertaken in the original version of the paper but is not reprinted here.—Eds.

Thirlwall, A. P. (1966) "Migration and regional unemployment: some lessons for regional planning," *Westminster Bank Review,* November 1966, 34–38.

Timms, D. (1971) *The urban mosaic.*

United Nations Organization (1961) *Report on international definition and measurement of standards and levels of living: an interim guide.*

Waris, H. (1965) "Levels of living: theory and reality," *Proceedings of the Finnish Academy of Science and Letters,* 1963, 141–59.

# American Cities: Symbolism, Imagery, Perception

YI-FU TUAN

In great metropolises, no man can know well more than a small fragment of the total urban scene; nor is it necessary for him to have a mental map or imagery of the entire city in order to prosper in his corner of the world. Yet the city dweller seems to have a psychological need to possess an image of the total environment in order to place his own neighborhood. Knowledge of a city varies enormously from person to person. Most people are able to designate by name the two extremes of the urban scale, the city as a whole and the street they live on. Intermediate divisions are, by contrast, vaguely conceived to the extent that few people can readily recall the name of their district or neighborhood. The two ends of the scale appear to express a common human propensity to dwell on two widely disparate levels of thought: high abstraction and specific responses. On the level of high abstraction, the immense complexity of a city may be encapsulated in the name itself such as Rome, or to a monument (Eiffel Tower), or to a silhouette such as the famous skyline of New York, or to a slogan or nickname such as The Queen City of the West. On the level of specific responses are the rich images and attitudes that a person acquires from his immediate environment in the course of day-to-day living.

The ideal or symbolic aspect of a city is known to us through literary sources and from what we know of the people's religion and cosmology reflected, often, in the city's spatial organization and architecture. What people see in their urban environment, how they respond to it, cannot be known directly for cities of the past—nor, in fact, are they known for the bulk of the world's present-day metropolises—because surveys, interviews, and in-depth observations do not exist. However, something can be gleaned from the physical characteristics of that world and from the different life styles that have evolved in it.

## SYMBOLS AND METAPHORS

The dominant myths of America are nonurban. They are often antiurban: the image of paradisiac New World stands against the image of Europen sophistication and corruption. A later date saw the development of antinomic values within the New World itself, contrasting a virile, democratic West with an effete, autocratic, Mammon-worshipping East. The dominant spatial metaphors for American destiny, particularly in the nineteenth century, are the garden, the West, the frontier, and wilderness. The city, by contrast, stands for the world's temptations and iniquities. Beginning with Jefferson, the intellectuals, though they come largely from an urban background, have persistently enforced the agrarian myth to the detriment of the environment that nurtured their learning and elegance. The farmers

From Yi-Fu Tuan, *Topophilia: A Study of Environmental Perception, Attitudes, and Values,* pp. 193–206. Reprinted by permission of the author and Prentice-Hall, Inc., Englewood Cliffs, N.J.

themselves are understandably pleased. It has become an unthinking reflex for Americans to see the city as the farmer and the intellectual see it: Babylon-den of iniquity, atheistic and un-American, impersonal and destructive.

What has happened to the image of the city as the New Jerusalem, to the idea that the city in its monumentality and glory is a symbol for world society and cosmos? We have seen the importance of the idea of the city as a transcendental symbol in the Old World. Has none of it been transferred to the New? The idea did take root in America but its growth was, and continues to be, hampered by the pervasive agrarian myth. American towns acquired metropolitan stature and cosmopolitan traits in the nineteenth century, at a time when not only the transcendental symbolism of the city had long been buried in Europe but also the urban enthusiasms of such Enlightenment figures as Voltaire, Adam Smith, and Fichte. Romanticism, posing images of Gothic urban horror against the sunlit landscapes of the countryside, was regnant among the intellectuals. American Romantics in fact showed a greater respect for urban values than did their European counterparts.

The American urban vision borrowed from Old World sources, particularly the Bible; the works of Augustine, Dante, and Bunyan were also influential. To the Puritans the city served as metaphor for the ideal community, the New Jerusalem. As John Winthrop put it, "we must consider that we shall be as a City upon a Hill, the eyes of all people are upon us." Not only was the city to be a model community to which the eyes of the people could turn, but the Puritans intended it also as a community from which the saints could look down upon all the people; it was built not only to be an example to the world but a perspective on the world.[1] However, the Puritan's city did not aspire to cosmic symbolization. It made no effort to simulate the geometric order and mineral purity of the New Jerusalem of Revelations. Cosmic cities of antiquity shared

the cosmic faith of the countryside, but in the cities the faith was made brilliantly visible in monumental architecture and through the performance of royal-sacerdotal rites. This was not the ambition of the early Puritans nor of their town-founding descendants in the nineteenth century. From the beginning, the Puritan's "City on a Hill" shared the farmer's values and accepted his cosmos; and it was far from the Puritan's mind to translate these values into urban life styles and design.

Yet it is a mistake to think that the image of the city in America has been consistently bad. In the New World no less than in the Old, the city stood for the heroic achievements of man. Not all intellectuals have denounced it. Some poets and scholars have praised its vitality and creativeness. Moreover, the American city has had its share of extravagant boosterism, particularly in the middle portion of the nineteenth century when such places as Cincinnati, St. Louis, and Chicago competed with each other for settlers and grew with extraordinary rapidity.[2]

Whatever the image, cities have in fact played a vital role in the development of the United States since the founding of the nation. Indeed, as the historian Constance Green put it, "It was apprehension lest trade rivalries of city merchants of the eastern seaboard destroy the new states that led to the drafting of the federal Constitution and the formation of the federal Union."[3] As early as the seventeenth century, urban centers where men exchanged not only goods but ideas were emerging. The Revolution itself and the rise of the Confederation of thirteen independent states were nurtured in the cities of America. The cities were then very small and formed no more than three percent of the total population. In the nineteenth century, however, nonrural settlements grew rapidly. Rural and nonrural populations increased at a comparable rate

1. Michael S. Cowan, *City of the West: Emerson, America, and Urban Metaphor* (New Haven: Yale University Press, 1967), pp. 73–74.

2. Frank Freidel, "Boosters, Intellectuals, and the American City," in Oscar Handlin and John Burchard (eds.), *The Historian and The City* (Cambridge: M.I.T. Press, 1966), pp. 115–20; Arthur N. Schlesinger, "The City in American History," *Mississippi Valley Historical Review*, 27 (June 1940), 43–66.
3. Constance M. Green, *American Cities in the Growth of the Nation* (London: Athlone Press, 1957), p. 1.

only during the decade of 1810 and 1820. By 1880–1890 the cities acquired people at four times the rate of the countryside. Urban primacy was particularly impressive in the West where the city's economic and political substance tended to overshadow the weakly-developed personality of the state. For example, by 1880 Denver became the metropolis of a region much larger than Colorado. No other sizable town offered competition within a radius of 500 miles. Its hegemony showed that the city rather than the state was the key to the development of a new country.

As the object of allegiance the state appears to have declined in significance in the post-Civil War period. Two major causes were: the War itself which greatly heightened men's consciousness of America as a nation; and the rise of urban power in the last decades of the nineteenth century. Americans who reached adulthood before the Civil War had thought of themselves first as citizens of a state—South Carolina, Massachusetts, or Ohio—and only secondly as citizens of the United States. In the 1870s and 1880s they came to identify themselves first as Americans and secondly as Bostonians, Philadelphians, or Cincinnatians. Charlestonians and Chicagoans, it is true, had from the beginning marked themselves by their city. Until the mid-nineteenth century Charleston was South Carolina in essence, and a century later state officials still occasionally had difficulty in persuading elderly Charlestonians that their automobiles needed South Carolina licenses as well as Charleston plates.[4]

Writers of the first rank have often poured scorn on the city. It is easy to pick up comments such as that made by Hawthorne: "All towns should be made capable of purification by fire, or of decay, within each half-century." Or Whitman's indictment of New York and Brooklyn as "a sort of dry and flat Sahara." In fact the attitude of poets was characteristically ambivalent. Whitman, for example, did sometimes treat cities gazetteer-fashion but his better poems transformed them into ethereal visions, "gliding wonders." Manhattan nearly always ap-

peared to him as strangely evanescent ("heaven-cloud canopy my city with delicate haze . . ."). His indictments were offset with tributes. In one place, New York and Brooklyn might be likened to the Sahara and yet in another the poet would chant to the "Splendor, picturesqueness, and oceanic amplitude and rush of these great cities," which gave promise of a "sane and heroic life" (Democratic Vistas). Unlike bucolic poets, Whitman often reached lyrical heights when he affirmed man's links to both nature and the city. New York and the myriad people in it were on the scale of oceans and tides (Specimen Days). Hawthorne, too, saw an analogy between the city and nature. "The wild life of the streets has perhaps as unforgettable a charm, to those who have once thoroughly imbibed in it, as the life of the forest or of the prairie." Even Thoreau noted, somewhat mysteriously, that "Though the city is no more attractive to me than ever, yet I see less difference between a city and some dismallest swamp than formerly."[5]

The American dream is compounded of profoundly ambivalent and even contradictory elements. Nowhere is the dream's dichotomy more evident than in the desire to combine, in the nineteenth century, the antithetical images of an urban empire and an agrarian nation. Emerson's lament of 1844 epitomized a strain of deep malaise in American thought. "I wish," he wrote, "to have rural strength and religion for my children . . . and I wish city facility and polish. I find with chagrin that I cannot have both." Nonetheless, Emerson persistently sought to reconcile the idea of high civilization with the idea of untouched nature, empire with garden. His utopia aspired to amalgamate the best elements from diverse worlds. However, the city rather than nature assumed a central symbolic position in his larger utopia. Even in his youth Emerson recognized that the good people who lived in the woodlands of Connecticut did not esteem them; and that it was often the townsmen who were intoxicated with being in the country. Many years later he argued that

4. Green, *American Cities*, pp. 19, 142.

5. See David R. Weimer, *The City as Metaphor* (New York: Random House, 1966).

the "city boy" generally possessed a "finer perception" than "the owner of the wood-lots." The impulse toward the reconciliation of the rural and urban worlds was to come from the Western Cosmopolitan rather than from the Noble Savage. The master metaphor for Emerson was the City of the West, which combined urban and Western referents. Unlike the Puritan's exclusionist City on a Hill, Emerson's city was open—a place of radical equality and divine spaciousness. "O City of God! thy gates stand always open, free to all comers. . . ."

For the Puritans as for Emerson the term "city" stood primarily for the quality of the human community; the physical frame had only secondary importance. Emerson's vision of the physical frame was expansive in conformity with the spaciousness of the West itself. The vast hinterland offered the city scope to expand not only its boundaries but the scale of its internal components. Lecture tours enabled Emerson to visit many of the new and rapidly growing cities of the interior. He was impressed by St. Louis' "spacious squares and ample room to grow." He also praised the "magnificent" hotels of Cincinnati and Philadelphia and observed with pleasure the noble buildings and broad vistas of Washington. Vast urban scale pleased Emerson for what it could say about America. When he complained of the "miles of endless squares," he was not protesting against the spatial scale so much as man's failure to measure up to it.[6] Whitman, too, could glory in the work of man and yet find man wanting. His experience of New York made him realize "that not Nature alone is great in her fields of freedom and the open air . . . but in the artificial, the work of man too is equally great." This was how he felt, yet there remained the nagging question, "Are there, indeed, *men* here worthy of the name?"

## SPECIFIC URBAN SYMBOLS

The city itself can be a monument. Persepolis, the Round City of Baghdad, Palitana, and Peking are monuments. Their physical layout, their geometry and hierarchical ordering of forms, are architectural means to express an ideal of cosmos and society. In the United States, Washington, D.C., was conceived to symbolize an ideal. Not the cosmos but an image of national greatness inspired its founding and design. Pierre l'Enfant, the planner, sought to create a city of beauty and magnificence. His plan of 1791 emphasized the monumental and the symbolic. It allowed five grand fountains and three major monuments. Of the latter, one was to be an equestrian statue of Washington at the intersection of the axes from the Capitol and the President's house; another, a Naval Itinerary Column, was to stand on an open space facing the Potomac, and the third was to be an historic Column from which all distances of places through the Continent were to be calculated.[7] Such grand motifs of design were conceived to magnify the glory of despotic kings. Historians have often commented on the irony of applying them to a nation founded on democratic principles, but the irony apparently escaped the leaders of the young nation who were intoxicated with the sense of republican grandeur. Even Jefferson did not object. His agrarian and democratic beliefs seemed not to conflict with his ambitions for the capital. The urban scale of Washington, D.C. owed much to Jefferson. "It was he who appointed Benjamin Henry Latrobe, one of the greatest early architects, to be supervisor of public buildings; it was he who retained the services of Giuseppi Franzoni, an Italian sculptor, to work on the Capitol; it was he who persuaded Congress to appropriate moneys for the improvement of the city and spent a third of it in laying out Pennsylvania Avenue in the manner of a Paris boulevard."[8]

Washington is the exception. Most cities in the United States owe their morphology to the convenience of the survey grid and to the economics of growth along lines of transportation. Religious and civic aspirations take visible shape as discrete architectural ele-

6. Cowan, *City of the West*, p. 215.

7. John W. Reps, *Monumental Washington* (Princeton, N.J.: Princeton University Press, 1967), pp. 18–20.
8. Christopher Tunnard and H. H. Reed, *American Skyline* (New York: New American Library, 1956), p. 28.

ments in the urban scene. Until the last quarter of the nineteenth century church steeples were prominent, if not dominant, features of the skyline even in the largest cities. The spire of Trinity Church towered over lower Manhattan and it was only in the 1890s that skyscrapers rising at the head of Wall Street threatened the church with obscurity. Houses of God were so numerous in New York City that a whole section, Brooklyn, was known as the "Borough of Churches." In the 1830s Cincinnati had twenty-four churches, Philadelphia ninety-six and New York a hundred, in each case a house of God to every thousand people. Of churches in New York, James Fenimore Cooper wrote: "I saw more than a dozen in the process of construction, and there is scarce a street of any magnitude that does not possess one."[9] Until the 1940s, church spires dominated Charleston's skyline, and even in the second half of the twentieth century they are often the most assertive architectural element in the smaller communities throughout America.

Besides churches American cities possess another prominent architectural symbol for the country's noneconomic aspiration: this is the "temple of government." Government buildings have taken the form of public palaces, built often in the grand American-Roman style. Of course Washington, D.C. has the most magnificent public palaces but imposing specimens can be found in state capitals and even in some county seats of very modest size. As two architectural historians put it:

It is largely through these public palaces that Americans have expressed their desire for splendor, and the visitor to our cities must go to the state houses, post offices and court houses to find the mural painting, sculpture and ornament that are missing elsewhere. If it were not for government patronage of the arts, admittedly spasmodic and casual, our communities would be much farther from satisfying the need for symbols of civic and national pride, which the people of a republic

demand—and ours have demanded—no less than kings and popes.[10]

An urban symbol may be a functional structure like a bridge, a nonutilitarian edifice like the St. Louis arch, or a piece of land like the Boston Common. The bridge is simultaneously a utilitarian fact and a symbol for connectness or transition from one place to the next, from one world to another. *Pons* is the common Latin root for bridge and priest. Of American bridges perhaps the best known is Brooklyn bridge. From the beginning it commanded a degree of public interest that exceeded its function as a convenience of transportation. Physical dimensions contributed to the bridge's legend. Its 1,600-foot span, held up by a gauze of graceful cables, seemed to defy the heaviness of earth. Until skyscrapers went up in Manhattan in the 1890s the bridge's Gothic towers dominated the skyline. The fact that it was heavily used from the start also helped to impose its image on the public consciousness. When the bridge was opened officially in 1883, each of the two cities it joined already had about one million people. Legends surrounded the architect John Roebling, who was a philosopher-engineer and a Hegelian. He saw in his work the embodiment of the American ideal of westward movement and the linking of East and West. It is not surprising that the Union Pacific Railroad was hailed as the last link in the course westward to India that began with Columbus's vision; but Brooklyn bridge received similar acclaim. The opening ceremony was a public drama attended by the president of the United States, and designed to symbolize the union of the people with their leaders in their joint pride of achievement. For many Americans in 1883, Brooklyn bridge also proved the nation to be healed of its wounds of civil war and again on its true course, which was the peaceful mastery of nature. Effusions over the structure did not end with the closing of the ceremonies. The translation of Brooklyn bridge from fact to symbol continued in the experiences of the

---

9. Quoted in Christopher Tunnard, *The City of Man* (New York: Scribner's 1953), p. 13.

10. Tunnard and Reed, *American Skyline*, p. 29.

people who used it or moved in its ambiance, in the response of journalists and architectural historians, and in the works of the mythmakers—painters and poets. In 1964 Brooklyn bridge was declared a National Monument.[11]

The bridge is a fact that may or may not turn into a symbol. A monument like St. Louis' arch is designed expressly as a symbol—the outward sign of an inward grace, which in this instance is the city's historic role as the gateway to the West. In 1933 plans already existed to convert the site of the original village of St. Louis into a park, commemorating the Lousiana Purchase which enlarged the vision of America from the boundary at the Mississippi River westward to the Pacific. President Truman dedicated the site in 1950, but it was not until 1965 that the memorial's central showpiece, the Gateway Arch, was completed. This gleaming curve of stainless steel plating soars with catenary grace to a height of 630 feet, that is, 75 feet higher than the Washington Monument, as tourist guides and local residents are proud to point out. The meaning of the arch derives from ancient tradition: like the dome it symbolizes heaven, the limbs leading the eye upward to the round curve at the apex; and in analogy to the monumental portal that opens into the city or palace it regally beckons the traveler to enter the promised land. Historically, travel to the new frontiers began at St. Louis. The city's commerce had its beginnings in the supply of guns, saddles, wagons, tools, building material, medicine, and food to western travelers, and in marketing the furs that the mountain men sent back. Today officials at the center gently urge the tourists to go further west along the Santa Fe and Oregon trails and experience the environment, if not the hardship, of their forebears. The memorial is administered by the National Park Service which sees fit to remind the public that "Because the Gateway Arch is a National Memorial equal in dignity and grandeur to other great memorials and is becoming a symbol of

St. Louis, it should be utilized in advertizing, displays, cartoons, etc., with restraint." In making use of the arch, one should ask, "Is the proposed use frivolous or ostentatious? . . . Is the Gateway Arch displayed in its proportionate scale to other structures? It should not be displayed in a subordinate role to other structures since not only is it the dominant physical feature of the Memorial but also it is the dominant physical feature within the City of St. Louis."[12] It seems clear that, if not to the local citizenry then to the country at large, the outstanding symbol for St. Louis will not be such old landmarks as Eads Bridge or the Old Courthouse but the soaring arch built to serve no utilitarian ends.

The Gateway Arch is designed specifically to capture a widely-shared historical sentiment. Its success depends not only on the aptness of the symbol but also, to a large degree, on its ability to capture the public's imagination through novelty and sheer size. The green areas of Washington, D.C. contain some of the nation's greatest monuments: they are deliberately created sacred places. In contrast to these self-conscious symbols which must depend to some extent on bravura for success, Boston Common owes its status not to any intrinsic physical attribute but to its effectiveness in articulating and symbolizing the genuine historical sentiments of a significant portion of the community. Walter Firey has clearly shown how the spatial symbolism of Boston Common has exerted a marked influence on the ecological organization of the rest of the city. The Common is a 48-acre tract of land wedged directly into the heart of the business district, cramping it severely.

Unlike the spacious department stores of most cities, those in Boston are frequently compressed within narrow confines and have had to extend in devious patterns through rear and adjoining buildings. Traffic in downtown Boston has literally reached the saturation point. . . . The American Road Builders' Association has estimated that

11. Alan Trachtenberg, *Brooklyn Bridge: Fact and Symbol* (New York: Oxford University Press, 1965), pp. 8–9.

12. From a mimeographed sheet of the United States Department of the Interior, National Park Service, Jefferson National Expansion Memorial, May 25, 1970.

there is a loss of $81,000 per day in Boston as a result of traffic delay.[13]

Many proposals have been made to relieve the congestion by extending a through arterial across the Common; however, economic rationale could not contend with the sentimental values that influential Bostonians and people throughout the State have vested in that tract of land. The Common has become a "sacred" object. Its integrity has a number of legal guarantees. The city charter forbids Boston in perpetuity to dispose of the Common or any portion of it. State legislation further prohibits the city from building upon the Common, except within narrow limits.

## BOOSTER IMAGERY—CITY NICKNAMES

Civic pride and economic competitiveness have often combined to give cities labels (nicknames or epithets) that claim to capture their unique distinction. The nickname may complement the visual symbol: thus Florence is the Duomo or the Piazza della Signoria but it is also *la Fiorente*. New York is its famous skyline but also the Empire City and several dozen other competing epithets.

Cities in the United States are exceptionally rich in nicknames. The luxuriance is the result of competition among relatively young settlements which sense the need to advertize their individuality and unique virtues against the claims of rivals. Chambers of Commerce, civic leaders and businessmen, journalists and artists have all sought to bolster the reputation of their hometown with some striking image. Laudations are occasionally combined with the critical voices of disillusioned artists and visitors from rival towns. The result is a rich mix of incompatible images. Even where they all originate from some favorable source unforseen contradictions and ironies may occur. Fort Worth, for example, is the Cow Town, the Panther City, as well as the Arsenal of Democracy. New York is a gallimufry of conflicting labels: it is the Big Apple, the Front Office of American Business, the Vacation City, the Babylonian Bedlam, the Capital of the World, and many others. Nicknames also change as the character of the city changes: thus Chicago was once the Garden City, generating an image of sylvan elegance that was not far from the truth before the great fire. Subsequent growth and prosperity transformed Chicago into the City of Big Shoulders and the Crime Capital.

The pell-mell of nicknames that accrues to a city in the course of time is a forceful reminder of metropolitan complexity. In any large urban center, multifarious interests exist and each will push for a label that suits its purpose. Crude epithets bear little resemblance to the poet's distilled metaphors, but they may be truer to the rhetoric of the man in the street. Joseph Kane and Gerard Alexander have compiled a list of American cities and their nicknames. Although the list cannot claim to be systematic or exhaustive, it provides sufficient information to show a geography of urban labels used in boosterism.[14]

Despite the fact that all large cities have many nicknames and that similar ones appear with monotonous regularity, regional differences are clearly discernible. To illustrate, of the four cities with the largest number of nicknames New York boasts its world status, Washington, D.C. its political supremacy; Chicago projects virility and San Francisco elegance. The images of Chicago and San Francisco reveal noteworthy similarities and differences. Both lay claim to the geographical location "West." Chicago is the Metropolis of the West, San Francisco the Queen City of the West. Both recognize the distinctiveness of their metropolitan setting. Chicago is the City by the Lake, the Gem of the Prairies; San Francisco is the Bay City, the City of a Hundred Hills. San Francisco asserts its cosmopolitanism and elegance: it is the Queen City, the Paris of America, the City Cosmopolitan. Chicago emphasizes by con-

13. Walter Firey, *Land Use in Central Boston* (Cambridge, Mass.: Harvard University Press, 1947), p. 151.

14. This section on city nicknames is based on the data in J. N. Kane and G. L. Alexander, *Nicknames of Cities and States of the United States* (New York: Scarecrow Press, 1965).

trast its ties with the wealth of the region and its centrality within the nation: it is the Hogopolis, the Cornopolis, the Hub of American Merchandising and the Country's Greatest Rail Center. Although Chicago was known as the Garden City and the Gem of the Prairies, reflecting the earlier claim to gentility, the image of Chicago as an aggressive place where the men work hard and things get done has come to be far more prominent. Chicago makes no special pretension to elegance; indeed the City of Big Shoulders cannot also aspire to being the Queen City.

Geographical settings are recognized in the urban label if they are especially distinctive and attractive. For a small place like Carlsbad in New Mexico the limestone caves are its only title to fame: it is *the* Cavern City. For the big places the topographic attribute is of minor importance. Some cities acknowledge the presence of "hill," "lake," "bluff," or "mountain." San Francisco is of course the Bay City and Houston the Bayou City. If, however, the geographical setting seems undesirable it is ignored. In Kane and Alexander's list of nicknames of American cities, the word "desert" appears only six times. Palm Springs and Indio in California are exceptional in that they actually exploit their desert setting. Indio calls itself the Desert Wonderland or Southern California's Desert Playground. Palm Springs claims to be America's Foremost Desert Resort or the Oasis in the Desert. Nevada and Arizona do not have any water problem to speak of, if we give credence to the self-bestowed images of their cities. Each state (in the Kane-Alexander listing) has only one city where the word "desert" appears—surrounded and all but lost in the welter of effusive epithets. Las Vegas is the Broadway of the Desert. But scarcity of any kind is not implied, for Las Vegas is also the City That Has Everything for Everyone—Anytime, and the Town Blessed By An Ideal Year-Round Climate.

City nicknames reflect and exaggerate the basic values and myths of America. In a nation that takes pride in its industrial prowess, it is not surprising that numerous places seek identification with their industries and products. We find Auto City, Beer City, Cash Register City, Pretzel City, Insurance City, and Shoe City among others. On the other hand there exist (although in far smaller number than the first group) botanical and pastoral epithets like camellia, lawn, oak, bower, palm, and sycamore. The great epic of American history is the westward migration. In Kane and Alexander's lists, no less than 183 cities boast the title "Gate" or "Gateway." A few do not use the specific word "gate" but they nonetheless emphasize their character as passageways or routes. Modesto in California, for example, is advertized as the "City that is only two hours to the Sierras or the sea." Some of the smaller towns use the word "gate" merely to draw attention to a local tourist attraction or a scenic area; thus Grand Portage, Minnesota, is the Gateway to Isle Royal National Park. There are nine "Gateways to the West," four "Gateways to the South," but none to the north or east. Naturally, if one goes westward far enough one reaches the East. Hence San Francisco is the Gateway to the Far East. Beyond the Golden Gate lies Paradise, as Hawaii calls itself. But the course of empire no longer points westward. A place like Titusville (Florida) hopes to cash in on the future by claiming to be the Gateway to the Galaxies.

We normally think of cities as centers of convergence. To motorists moving across the continent, however, cities are not necessarily destinations; they may merely be places to refuel, eat, or obtain a night's rest. Even local residents proudly declare their hometown to be a "gateway," as though it were just a place to pass through. But this apparent show of modesty is countered by the citizens' desire to advertize their town as, in some sense, the world's center. So, if there are 183 "gateways," there are at least 240 variants of nicknames in which the word "capital" appears; and the number rises several fold if we include also the "Hub," the "Home," the "Center," the "Heart," the "Cradle," the "Crossroads," and the "Birthplace." Many cities stress both their centrality—a standing that is supposedly derived from their achievement and geographical advantages—

and their position as gateway, which promises the future. St. Louis is the Hub of American Inland Navigation as well as the Gateway to the West.

## IMAGEABILITY

Boosterism aims to create a favorable image and has little respect for complex truth. But to be effective the image must have some grounding in fact. A strong trait is made to stand for the whole personality. What this is, we have seen, varies not only with the real differences among and within the cities, but with the specialized concerns of the groups that wish to draw the public's attention to a particular attribute. An epithet or catch phrase provides the image. It cannot, however, project a clear visual image even when it tries to be descriptive as in the designations the Garden City, the City of Bridges, the Windy City, the Broadway of the Desert, and so on. Often the designations are more abstract as, for example, the Queen City of the West. Differing in approach, though not in aim, are the attempts to capture the character of a place by a specific scene or picture. Again we can point to the effectiveness of Manhattan's skyline as the emblem of New York. Anselm Strauss points out that for a film to establish its locale in New York the famous skyscraper profile needs to be flashed on the screen for only a second.[15] Many European cities have visual emblems of comparable power. London is easily recognized from a scene of Picadilly Circus or a view of the Houses of Parliament by the Thames River, Paris from the bookstalls along the Seine, Moscow from the Red Square in winter. American cities lack visual identity. Egregious exceptions like New York, San Francisco, or New Orleans remind us all the more of the visual greyness of most other metropolises. Yet even small cities sell postcards, revealing a faith in the worthiness of their main street, parks, and monuments. Postcards depict as-

pects of the town that are believed to do it credit. Occasionally a typical street scene is shown, but more often postcards stress the highlights—the parts that capture the attention, that have high imageability.

Postcards tell us something about imageability. They probably reflect the values of the local businessmen. Until Kevin Lynch's book *The Image of the City* appeared in 1960, little was known about the mental maps of city dwellers. Lynch presents us with the public image of the central districts of three cities, Boston, Jersey City, and Los Angeles.[16] Members of the professional and managerial class, for the purpose of the study, constitute the public. In Boston and Jersey City the sample tested and interviewed reside in the central district; in Los Angeles so few members of the middle class live in the central district that the sample has to be made up of people who work downtown but have their homes elsewhere. Anyone who has a passing acquaintance of these cities will probably say of Boston that it has a fairly strong visual personality; of downtown Los Angeles that it shows less character, and of Jersey City that it is nondescript. Such impressions are confirmed by the local residents. Their perceptions are naturally more specific: even Jersey City has more shape and pattern than a casual visitor might think, as indeed it must to be liveable.

To most of the people that Lynch interviewed, Boston is a historical and rather dirty city of distinctive locales, red-brick buildings and crooked, confusing paths. The favorite views are usually the distant panoramas that give a sense of water and space. Residents have a good grasp of the broad spatial structure of Boston, aided by the clear edge of the Charles River and the parallel streets of the adjoining Back Bay area that lead eastward into the Common and the shopping district. Away from the edge of the river the city seems to lose precision. The regular grid of Back Bay, a common enough pattern of American cities, takes on extra visibility in Boston by

15. Anselm L. Strauss, *Images of the American City* (New York: Free Press, 1961), p. 9.

16. Kevin Lynch, *The Image of the City* (Cambridge, Mass.: M.I.T. Press, 1964).

contrast with the irregular grid in other parts of the city. Places that strike most people as particularly vivid are the Common, Beacon Hill, the Charles River, and Commonwealth Avenue. For many they form the core of their image of central Boston.

Jersey City lies between Newark and New York City and is criscrossed by railroads and elevated highways. Competition has etiolated its central functions. It looks more like a place to pass through than to live in. "To the usual formlessness of space and heterogeneity of structure that mark the blighted area of any American city is added the complete confusion of an uncoordinated street system."[17] Residents can think of few landmarks; their mental map of Jersey City is fragmented and has large blank areas. To the question of effective symbols the most common response is to point to the New York skyline across the river rather than to anything within the city. A characteristic judgment is that Jersey City is merely a place on the fringe of something else. One resident claims that his two symbols are the skyline of New York, on the one side, and the Pulaski Skyway, standing for Newark, on the other. Jersey Citians appear indifferent to their physical setting. Streets look so much alike that the choice as to which one to use is reduced to arbitrariness when saving time is not important.

As the core of a metropolis, central Los Angeles is charged with meaning and activity. It has large imposing buildings and a fairly regular pattern of streets. Regional orientation in the metropolis seems not too difficult, being aided by mountains and hills on the one side and ocean on the other, by well-known regions such as the San Fernando Valley and Beverly Hills, by the major freeways and boulevards, and, finally, by recognizable differences in the architectural style and in the condition of the structures that mark the successive rings of growth. The distinc-

tive vegetation, too, gives central Los Angeles character. Yet its image is less sharp than that of Boston. One reason is that the title "downtown" is used of central Los Angeles largely as a matter of habit and courtesy, for several other cores compete with it in the intensity of shopping and in the volume of business. Another reason is that the central activities are spatially extended and shifting, thus, diluting their impact. But central Los Angeles is far from being another Jersey City. Mental maps formed of Los Angeles are more precise and detailed. Their composite image reveals a structure centered on Pershing Square nestling in the crook of the L formed by two shopping avenues, Broadway and 7th Street. Other prominent features are the Civic Center at the end of Broadway and the historical node of the Plaza-Olvera Street. Several architectural landmarks are recognized but only two in any detail: the black and gold Richfield Building and the pyramidal top of the City Hall. The degree of attachment to the old parts of Los Angeles, particularly to the tiny Plaza-Olvera Street node, is unexpectedly strong. To judge from the few interviews, it is even stronger than the attachment of conservative Bostonians toward what is old in their city. The middle-class people in Los Angeles that Lynch interviewed are commuters. They have a vivid impression of their own residential districts, and they continue to be aware of streets, the finer houses, and flower gardens as they drive away from their home areas; but sensitivity to the urban setting declines as they approach downtown so that on the mental maps of these commuters central Los Angeles is a sort of visual island surrounded by grey spaces. An instructive conclusion of this type of study is that experience does not necessarily increase the store of urban images of motorists.[18] The regular commuter and the occasional passenger respond to roughly the same set of visual cues.

17. Lynch, *Image of the City*, p. 25.

18. Stephen Carr and Dale Schissler, "The City as a Trip," *Environment and Behavior*, 1, No. 1 (1969), 24.

**4**

*BEHAVIOR: INTERCITY LINKAGES,*
*DIFFUSION, AND CONFLICT*

# Introduction

The essence of the urban-systems concept is regular contact among the different urban regions in that system. This contact can take many different forms and each may have a different purpose and impact. Flows of goods and commodities, for example, permit economic specialization to develop among regions; flows of information act both to regulate and to stimulate the growth of new urban activities; and actual movements of capital and households lead to variations in rates of growth from place to place (see Section V).

These patterns of continuing interaction we refer to here as measuring the *behavior* of the urban system. Although at first glance these patterns may appear almost infinite and chaotic, they are at least as structured and orderly as are the variations in city size and economic structure with which we are more familiar (see Section III). In fact contact patterns between cities are inextricably tied to variations in these attributes. Interregional trade and commodity flows are linked to the level of economic specialization, both of which in turn are clearly intertwined, though in many complex ways, with labor-force migration, city size, and rates of population growth. The composite pattern of these regular or recurring interactions reflects what Simmons defined in his paper in Section I as the "organization" of the urban system.

Given these complexities, it is not surprising that the behavior of the urban system as expressed in interactions among cities is the least explored component of the subject matter of this volume. Data inadequacies, conceptual vagueness, and analytical difficulties have thus far permitted us to make only fragmentary descriptions and even fewer explanations of interurban interaction patterns. We know little, for example, about the stability of industrial linkages and commodity flow patterns over time, or about their relationships to industrialization, urban growth, and social change. In some instances we find it difficult to identify even the relevant origins and destinations of various interactions.

The discussion below elaborates on these problems under three headings: first, recurring contact patterns, which include the full range of continuous interactions among cities—trade, travel, and information movements, for example. These in turn provide the basis for our second concept, that of integration within urban systems, which also links our concern for spatial structure with the political science interest in political integration. Third, the relation between short-term and more permanent or long-term flows are discussed. When and how, for example, does long-distance commuting to work lead to household relocation and thus to migration? Do trading patterns lead to increased economic specialization or to the spatial relocation of industries?

The readings in this section demonstrate several of these concerns. They are, on the whole, impressive papers. In the first paper Board, Davies, and Fair attempt a comprehensive description of the South African space economy in terms of a wide range of contacts within the urban system. Their study is one of the most thorough empirical examples of interaction that we know of, and the country itself clearly offers an unusual (and changing) case study of intercity contacts. In the second paper, Pred examines the increasing role of large multi-locational organizations, particularly in the advanced economies of North America and Sweden, in structuring interdependencies among cities. Contacts among such firms may cut across the usual hierarchical form of interaction in which ideas and goods filter down from large to small cities (Berry, 1972).

Growth and change in any economy involves exchange and the movement or diffusion of new ideas and technologies. There is now in fact a substantial literature in geography on diffusion from which we can draw (Hudson, 1972; Brown, 1974 and 1975). The importance of diffusion in the evolution of urban systems in one part of the developing world is described in the Pedersen paper. He sees the movement or diffusion of innovations within Chile and between countries of South America as jointly determined by an urban system whose spatial structure is largely inherited from the colonial period and by the truncated organizational relationships among cities. In poorer countries, the diffusion of ideas and technology seldom reaches down the hierarchy to small towns and rural areas, at least not for some time. The result is an increasing polarization of the urban system into developed and undeveloped regions (see Mountjoy's paper in Section VI).

Finally, John Friedmann, in what is now a classic paper, discusses the importance of patterns of economic exchange and power in forming political groupings and social attitudes within a nation. He looks at the implications of different kinds of power relationships for the form of the urban system and for the types of spatial interaction that take place within a country; we begin to see the direct link between political integration and socioeconomic change.


## RECURRING CONTACT PATTERNS

The importance and difficulty of identifying repetitive contact patterns in the study of urban systems emerges when we envision the variety of possible connections. A set of $n$ urban regions can generate $n^2$ flows, linking each pair of regions in two directions. For most kinds of flows, such as telephone calls or freight shipments, both of which are usually measured over a relatively brief period of time, less than ten percent of these $n^2$ possible connections may actually be completed. Many of the smaller places in an urban system—Iowa City and Spokane, for example—may have no direct connections with each other. Either the physical links for communication do not exist or they may not be utilized. The highly skewed distribution of city sizes typical of most nations has a multiplicative effect in producing an even more skewed distribution of intercity flows. The single link between New York and Washington, for instance, may account for as much as five percent of the total volume of movement in an urban system containing 1000 cities and thus having one million ($1000^2$) possible links.

A number of regularities do exist in any table of flow data, however, which can and must be generalized if we are to understand how urban systems behave. *Scale* is usually the most important factor. Larger and more populous regions offer more origins and destinations for flows of all kinds. For some types of commodities, on the other hand, patterns of *economic specialization* may override simple scale variations. A map of the shipments of tractors, for example, would show links between a small number of tractor plants and a large number of agricultural regions differentiated by the intensity of farm production. An input-output matrix of interindustry linkages between regions and cities is usually dominated by differences in industrial structure between those regions (Richardson, 1972). A third factor, *distance,* is important in spatially extensive urban systems, but is less important in compact ones. Scale and distance are both included in the simplest concept of an urban hierarchy, a concept which insists that each urban region be tightly linked to a series of larger urban nodes in order to obtain the services it cannot produce for itself.

The existence of an urban hierarchy and the network of transportation and communication facilities that serve it are probably the most powerful restrictions on the number of actual connections between urban places. In order to economize on transportation investments, as well as on marketing and distribution costs, usually only a restricted number of intercity links are constructed. The result is a *channelling* effect. To go from Madison, Wisconsin to New Haven, Connecticut by public transportation requires one to pass through both Chicago and New York. And as the number and range of direct connections between the large cities increase, the same restriction becomes true even for small cities that lie between the larger centers, such as South Bend and Albany.

The overall effect of the properties of the *intercity linkage matrix* is to define the accessibility of a node in relation to the rest of the system. Is one urban region more central than another in the sense that it is more easily reached by the people it serves? Accessibility itself may then be translated into a comparative advantage in production through a reduction in transportation and information costs, which in turn may lead to higher wages and profit levels and thus to increased rates of growth in the future.

At the outset, the major determinant of a place's accessibility, however, is our definition of the urban system it serves. Once you have established boundaries for that system, for example, to limit consideration to the southeast of England or the deep South of the U.S., the most accessible location follows logically from the existing pattern of population distribution and the present transportation infrastructure within the area. The place attracting and generating the most flows need not be spatially central, however. Iowa City clearly cannot displace New York. The gradual historical evolution of the urban system described in Section II, in which accessibility conditions at any one time influence subsequent location decisions by households and firms, and decisions regarding transportation network development, tends to reinforce the contact patterns of earlier periods. Many of these patterns were decided by events external to the country during Colonial times. Nonetheless, changes can and do take place—witness the growing importance of Atlanta, Miami, and Phoenix in airline connections—but changes tend to come slowly and to elaborate rather than replace the existing hierarchical structure of flows.

## INTEGRATION

The basic distribution of economic activities, the location of physiographic barriers, and the structure of transportation networks combine to determine the overall level of integration in any system, that is, the intensity of overall contacts among locations. We can contrast a highly integrated urban system such as that in England, where relatively short distances, high population densities, and a long-established industrialized economy create close ties among all regions with a partially integrated urban system such as that in Australia or Canada, where distance, physical or cultural barriers, and specialized export economies lead to profound regional differences and conflicts.

Any study of integration in an urban system must consider the consistency of interaction patterns for different transport modes (rail, air) and for different phenomena (telephone calls, coal shipments, and so on). Are the flow patterns the same? Do the same urban subsystems, hierarchies, and dominant centers emerge? Is there a consistent structure to the organization of the urban system? If so then these relationships should provide the basis for models of urban growth (via migration) and change (via diffusion). They may also suggest ongoing patterns of regional cooperation linked to strong social ties, or else political conflict due to economic or cultural barriers or to one-sided trading relations.

The extensive literature on political integration (Deutsch, 1963; Jacob and Toscano, 1964; Lindberg and Scheingold, 1971; Miller, 1975), is also relevant here. Much of this literature is based on a series of assumptions about interregional linkages: for example, the assumptions that structured contact patterns exist; that these patterns are strongly correlated with each other; that they are stable or at least evolve regularly over time; and that they help us to understand and to predict political relationships among urban regions. Most urban systems encounter, if they do not generate, internal tensions due to their hierarchical organization (between the larger and smaller cities). Since the smaller places are frequently peripherally located as well, the result is the core-periphery conflict suggested by Friedmann (1966). Additional conflicts may reflect economic differences, such as between industrial and commercial centers, or between primary and industrial regions, and between cultural groups (the French and the Flemish in Belgium, the English and French in Canada, and the Catholics and Protestants in Northern Ireland).

An interesting example of the potential for intrasystem conflict, arising from the effect of spatial variations in growth, comes from recent research by Conzen (1975, 1977). He traces the flows of capital through the emerging urban system of the American Midwest. The conflict there arose from the needs of rapidly growing frontier regions to import capital and the desire of slow growth regions to retain capital. The former regions wanted more integration in the form of a national banking system that could readily relocate capital; the latter regions resisted further integration, preferring independent and locally oriented banks.

Another form of urban and interregional integration, almost invisible to either the casual observer or even to the urban researcher, is that involving the activities of national and *international corporations*. Such organizations now account for the majority of economic production and wealth in most Western capitalist countries. They link together diverse activities in many locations through their headquarters, branch offices, manufacturing plants, distribution centers, and sales outlets, often in a markedly hierarchical fashion. We cannot see or easily evaluate the intraorganizational flows linking, for example, the General Motors head offices in Detroit to assembly plants in Ohio, California, Canada, Germany, or England, but we know that auto parts, money, information, personnel, and investment decisions pass along these routes.

As a result of these corporate connections, economic prosperity (or decline) at one location is intimately linked to prosperity (or decline) at other places. For instance, in the most recent recession in North American automobile sales, production levels at each location reflected not the productivity of the workers, but rather the product assigned to that plant by the head office. Certain kinds of larger General Motors cars declined sharply in sales, resulting in substantial layoffs; other smaller makes of cars maintained or increased their projected demand, and job openings grew in those locations.

Integration of this kind occurs over a wide range of activities: in retailing, from Woolworth's to Bonwit Teller's; in finance, from Lloyd's of London to Merrill Lynch, the stock brokers; and in public transportation, tourist facilities, and so on. The rules of location behavior for such enterprises are aptly described by Galbraith (1968), Törnqvist (1970), Goddard (1975), and Pred, in his article on pp. 292. Production and administrative functions are increasingly separated. Local interests become subservient to those of the organization. Vertical integration of such organizations allows for, or in fact may require, the subsidy of certain enterprises in order to maintain a market share at that location and to retain a complete network of nodes. The Holiday Inn chain, for example, may construct a large hotel complex in a very small town. In the short run it loses money; in the long run, and viewed over the whole system of hotels, this small-town hotel may complete an integrated nationwide set of services, which can be very profitable.

While in this case the small town may benefit, in other cases the results of such integration may be the reverse. A decline in the fortunes of the organization as a whole often results in the contraction or closing of plants in small and peripheral locations. In such a case, the system subsidizes the head office rather than the reverse. In either case the results often conflict with government efforts at more balanced regional development and a more equitable distribution of income.

## SHORT-TERM AND LONG-TERM FLOWS

Without anticipating too much the discussion in the sections to follow, some of the implications of day-to-day linkages for permanent changes in the urban system can now be outlined. Pedersen's paper on spatial diffusion within urban systems represents an example of a large and growing body of research on these topics, most of which follow the basic themes outlined initially by Hägerstrand (1953). The movement of new innovations, and therefore social change, follows well-worn paths of regular contact. Communication ties among people, advertising in newspapers and on television, and networks of dealerships or stores are necessary to get people to accept a new piece of technology—be it a threshing machine or the birth-control pill—and ultimately to carry that acceptance from one place to another. We also know that technological change is still the preeminent source of economic growth. The spatial organization of the urban system is thus the most logical device to explain differentiations in rates of growth and change among cities and regions.

The relationships are more complex, though, for other growth phenomena like the movements of capital and migration, both of which move in two directions simultaneously. Although gross flows, or the total number of migrants between, for example, Kansas City and New Orleans, may reflect the existing pattern of social contacts and the availability of transportation facilities between the two cities, we are not often able to predict the direction of net flow. Will New Orleans or Kansas City grow at the expense of the other? Capital movements are even more difficult to assess, in part because the commodity is often invisible and pertinent statistics are seldom available.

Net movements are the object of most interest in any urban-growth model. Specifically, the relationship of net flows to gross flows operates as a constraint on overall rates of change. A highly integrated urban system, with high levels of flows of both migrants and capital (as well as of entrepreneurs and of firms), always has the potential for rapid spatial change and redistribution simply because the flows are so large and so fluid. A steady stream of out-movement is generated, which may or may not be replaced or which may be over-replaced by in-movement from other locations. Contrast this with an urban system exhibiting a low level of integration or with the experience of a single region in an isolated location. In the latter case to achieve rapid growth requires a profound modification of existing flow patterns in order to overcome real barriers to the movement of individuals and firms. Thus, schemes for the stimulation of growth centers or population decentralization in such regions necessitate a substantial investment in new transportation facilities to encourage higher levels of interaction.

Despite this complexity, perhaps the most important thing to remember about interactions in urban systems is that they tend to be reciprocal. For every one hundred people moving to Los Angeles, probably seventy-five or eighty move back to Oklahoma City or to Dayton. For every $100,000,000 invested in Houston, another $60,000,000 is invested by Houston residents in General Motors, in A.T.&T., or in Canadian Arctic oil. Any investigation of how cities grow must clearly consider these regular reciprocal relationships between places, recognizing of course that the origins and destinations of these flows and their impacts will vary over both space and time. The magnitudes and stability of intercity contacts—the urban system organization—permit growth and change in the urban system to be managed in an orderly fashion.

## REFERENCES

Berry, B.J.L. 1972. "Hierarchical Diffusion: The Basis of Developmental Filtering and Spread in a System of Growth Centers," in N. Hansen, ed. *Growth Centers in Regional Economic Development*. New York: The Free Press, pp. 108–138.

Brown, L. A., ed. 1974. "Studies in Spatial Diffusion Processes: I. Empirical." Special issue of *Economic Geography*, vol. 50, no. 4.

———. ed. 1975. "Studies in Spatial Diffusion Processes: II. Conceptual." Special issue of *Economic Geography*, vol. 51, no. 3.

Conzen, M. P. 1975. "Capital Flows and the Developing Urban Hierarchy." *Economic Geography*, vol. 51, pp. 321–338.

———. 1977. "The Maturing Urban System in the United States, 1840–1910." *Annals of the Association of American Geographers*, vol. 67, pp. 88–108.

Deutsch, K. W. 1963. *Nerves of Government: Models of Political Communication and Control*. Glencoe, Ill.: The Free Press.

Fair, T.J.D. 1976. "Polarization, Dispersion and Decentralization in the South African Space Economy." *South African Geographical Journal*, vol. 58, pp. 40–56.

Friedmann, J. 1966. *Regional Development Policy: A Case Study of Venezuela*. Cambridge, Mass.: M.I.T. Press.

Galbraith, J. K. 1968. *The New Industrial State*. New York: Harper & Row.

Goddard, J. 1975. "Organizational Information Flows and the Urban System," in H. Swain and R. D. MacKinnon, eds. *Issues in the Management of Urban Systems*. Laxenburg, Austria: International Institute for Applied Systems Analysis, pp. 180–225.

Hägerstrand, T. 1953. *Innovation Diffusion as a Spatial Process*. Translated by Allan Pred. Chicago: University of Chicago Press, 1967.

Hudson, J. C. 1972. *Geographical Diffusion Theory*. Northwestern University Publications in Geography No. 19, Evanston, Ill.: Northwestern University.

Jacob, P. E. and Toscano, J. V., eds. 1964. *The Integration of Political Communities*. Philadelphia: Lippincott.

Lindberg, L. and Scheingold, S., eds. 1971. *Regional Integration*. Cambridge, Mass.: Harvard University Press.

Miller, D. C. 1975. *Leadership and Power in the Bos-Wash Megalopolis*. New York: Wiley.

Richardson, H. 1972. *Input-Output and Regional Economics*. New York: Wiley.

Soja, E. W. 1968. "Communications and Territorial Integration in East Africa: An Introduction to Transaction Flow Analysis." *East Lakes Geographer*, vol. 4, pp. 39–57.

Törnqvist, G. 1970. *Contact Systems and Regional Development*. Lund Studies in Geography, Series B, No. 35. Lund, Sweden: University of Lund.

# The Structure of the South African Space Economy: An Integrated Approach*

CHRISTOPHER BOARD, RONALD J. DAVIES and T. J. DENIS FAIR

## INTRODUCTION

In stating that "there is no understanding of the spatial organization of the United States economy that compares with our understanding of the static patterns, no functional regionalization to match the uniform," Berry (1964) has called for systems approach to the definition and understanding of the space economy of that country. A number of authors (Ackerman, 1963; Berry, 1968; Friedmann, 1966; Haggett, 1965; Philbrick, 1957) are pressing the need for and demonstrating the possibilities of such an approach. Moreover, attempts to view the space economy in integrative spatial terms are also being supplemented by the development of models of spatial organization over time (Friedmann, 1966).

In the applied field the approach imposes upon governments the need to view their planning efforts in nation-wide integrated spatial terms, as the processes generating the problems are themselves interconnected and national and even international in scale.

Our objective is to present an interconnected view of the South African space economy of the early 1960s. We concentrate upon the contemporary national and sub-national structure in terms of *surfaces* of differing economic character and strength representa-

tive of the underlying formal regional landscape; the status, character and economic level of *nodes;* the flows and *networks* of telephone calls, of road, rail and air traffic and of labour, all three elements together yielding a spatial structure that is both formal and functional in character.

## THE ECONOMY

Despite considerable ethnic differences, variations in geographic distribution and economic level among its racial groups and the presence of African reserves with strong traditional characteristics, the South African population, numbering 16 million in 1960 of whom 3.1 million are white, belongs to a single economic system. Movement of the non-whites into the South African economy has been such that 80 per cent of the labour force is non-white, mainly semi-skilled and unskilled workers. This trend is associated with the considerable rate of growth of the economy over the past thirty years, marked especially by a substantial rise in manufacturing (Table 1) and in part stimulated by an increase in mining, especially of gold, since World War II.

Spatially, the growth of the economy and changes in population distribution have proceeded at different rates in different areas—most rapidly in the expanding cities and new mining centres and least, if at all in some instances, in the still partly subsistent African

*Figures 1, 16, and 19, and the Appendix "Notes on Data and Methods," have been deleted from the original version of the paper.—Eds.

Table 1.    Gross Domestic Product (in Millions of Rands)

| Year | Total | % | Agric. | % | Mining | % | Manufg. | % | Services | % |
|------|-------|-----|--------|-----|--------|-----|---------|-----|----------|-----|
| 1936 | 756 | 100 | 107 | 14 | 143 | 19 | 118 | 16 | 389 | 51 |
| 1950 | 2429 | 100 | 432 | 17 | 236 | 13 | 539 | 22 | 1195 | 48 |
| 1960 | 4813 | 100 | 588 | 12 | 656 | 14 | 1160 | 24 | 2409 | 50 |
| 1965 | 7226 | 100 | 735 | 10 | 884 | 12 | 2038 | 28 | 3571 | 49 |

reserves. This disparity between advanced and less advanced areas and between urban and rural in general has generated considerable movements of capital and people which have had a marked effect upon the pattern of the space economy and upon its character and strength from place to place. It is to this economic landscape in terms of its major contrasts in a formal regional sense that we now turn.

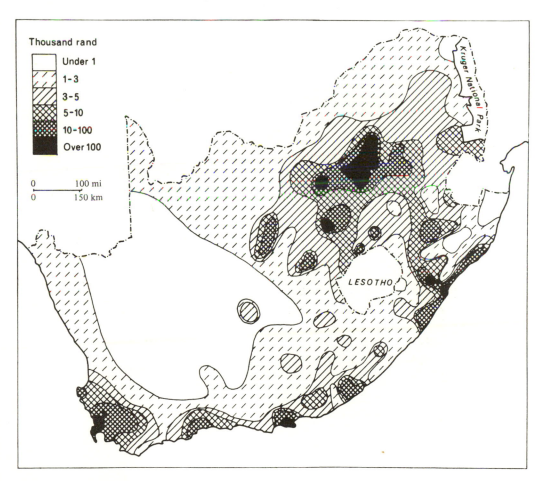

Figure 1. Gross Domestic Product per Square Mile, 1960.

## ECONOMIC SURFACES

In mapping economic surfaces criteria representative of both volume and welfare aspects of economic development have been used (Perloff *et al.* 1960, pp. 55–57). "Volume" has been mapped in terms of gross domestic product (g.d.p.) per square mile for each magisterial district, the latter being the standard areal unit for statistical purposes (Fig. 1). "Welfare" aspects involve income and g.d.p. *per capita* and the quality of the population in terms of education, age and employment characteristics. A measure of "welfare," due to its multivariate character, was

obtained from a principal components analysis performed upon fifteen variables. This yielded a first component, out of four extracted, which accounted for nearly 41 per cent of the variance. "Welfare" variables loaded highly on this component as did the proportion of the district's population engaged in manufacturing. The map (Fig. 2) is derived by plotting the scores for Component 1 for each magisterial district. The scores are standardized to zero mean and unit variance. On both maps values are represented as isopleths and then combined in Fig. 3 to give a pattern of economic surfaces.

Figure 1 indicates that South Africa's eco-

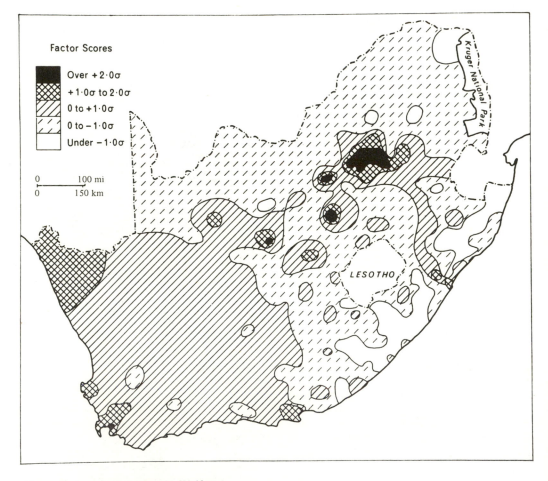

Figure 2. Level of Economic Welfare.

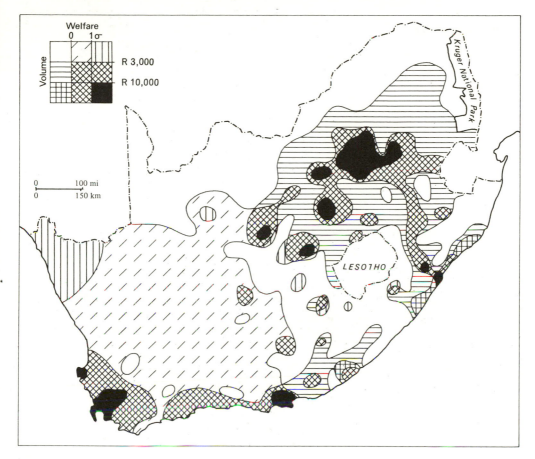

Figure 3. Socio-economic Surfaces.

nomic wealth lies mainly in the north and east with an intensity of output building up to over R100,000 per square mile (national average R10,140) in a comparatively few areas on the central plateau and at the coast. In the south and west, by contrast, areas of high intensity are few and are confined to the coast, while the semi-arid interior displays a very low intensity of economic activity.

Figure 2 emphasizes that high levels of "welfare" are also associated primarily with major poles of intensive economic activity but important differences in other respects now appear. Over wide areas of the pastoral west values are above the national mean while substantial parts of the eastern half of the country, where occurs the bulk of the population, mainly African and non-white (Fig. 4), have values below the mean and particularly so in those areas coincident with the African reserves. The average g.d.p. generated in those reserves which comprise whole magisterial districts, especially in the Transkei and Natal, was R19.29 per head of the total population in 1959–1960 compared with R298.80 for the country as a whole.

The economic landscape represented by Fig. 3 may be regarded as analogous to a series of topographic surfaces each varying both in economic level and character and with gradients of varying steepness between them. At the same time these surfaces represent

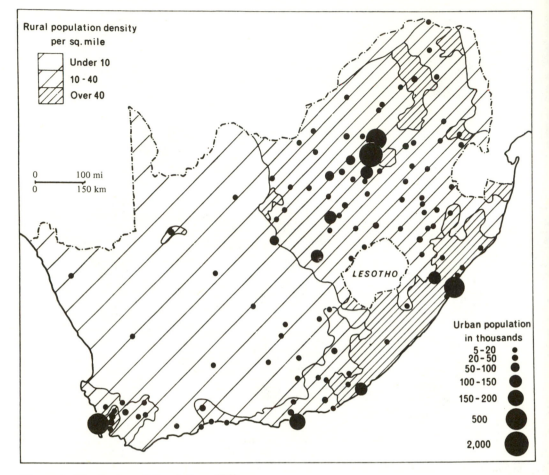

Figure 4. Distribution of Population, 1960.

types of economic space, each homogeneous but not necessarily contiguous, rather than continuous and homogeneous economic regions (Boudeville, 1966, p. 3).

*Surface 1 (High).* Both volume and welfare levels are highest on these "summits" (Table 2). They coincide with the major metropolitan, industrial and mining areas, occur preponderantly in the north-east and account for 71.9 per cent of the g.d.p. generated in the country as a whole. Of this 45.1 per cent is accounted for by the Southern Transvaal and its environs, and another 24.1 per cent by the three coastal representatives, *viz.,* Capetown and its environs, Port Elizabeth-Uitenhage, and Durban-Pietermaritzburg.

*Surface 2 (Upper).* Both volume and welfare levels are still satisfactory on national standards and the surface occurs (a) as isolated minor uplands of economic activity, (b) as areas circumferential to the summits and (c) as belts or ridges between them, notably between the Southern Transvaal and Durban, on the one hand, and along the Cape south coast, on the other. Together, surfaces 1 and 2, covering only 14.8 per cent of the area of South Africa, account for 82.4 per cent of its g.d.p., a degree of concentration manifested also by other aspects of the space economy.

*Surfaces 3 and 4 (Medium).* These represent the bulk of rural South Africa and are indicative of the country's environmental and

Table 2. Economic Surfaces by Gross Domestic Product and Area

| | Contribution to gross domestic product | | Area | |
|---|---|---|---|---|
| Surface | R000 | % of S.A. total | square miles | % of S.A. total |
| 1. *High* | | | | |
| S. Transvaal and environs | 1,828,698 | 38.24 | 7515 | 1.59 |
| W. Transvaal | 146,386 | 3.06 | | |
| N. Orange Free State | 180,060 | 3.77 | | |
| S.W. Cape | 581,068 | 12.16 | | |
| Durban-Pietermaritzburg | 392,577 | 8.21 | 8339 | 1.77 |
| Port Elizabeth-Uitenhage | 184,566 | 3.86 | | |
| Bloemfontein | 65,786 | 1.38 | | |
| Kimberley | 57,724 | 1.21 | | |
| Total | 3,436,865 | 71.87 | 15,854 | 3.36 |
| 2. *Upper* | 504,704 | 10.55 | 53,858 | 11.42 |
| 3. *Medium* | | | | |
| (a) | 63,945 | 1.33 | | |
| (b) | 418,294 | 8.75 | | |
| Total | 482,239 | 10.08 | | |
| 4. *Medium* | | | 401,733 | 85.22 |
| (a) | 31,199 | 0.65 | | |
| (b) | 115,063 | 2.41 | | |
| Total | 146,262 | 3.06 | | |
| 5. *Low* | 211,713 | 4.43 | | |
| *South Africa* Total | 4,781,783 | 100.00 | 471,445 | 100.00 |

human contrasts—on the one hand, a dry, sparsely-settled pastoral west but with a comparatively high productivity per head, and on the other, a wetter eastern sector far more heavily settled and intensively worked but far less productive in terms of output per head. Environmental handicaps in the former and a high degree of underemployment in the latter are responsible for these two areas together producing only 13.1 per cent of the nation's g.d.p.

*Surface 5 (Low)*. These handicaps combine in this surface to produce the "valleys" in the country's economic topography, a large area generally heavily settled in the south-east but generating only 4.4 per cent of the g.d.p.

It is clearly coincident in the first instance with the crescent of African reserves from the Ciskei and Transkei in the eastern Cape, through much of the more rugged parts of Natal, and the drier bush-clad country of the northern and north-western Transvaal and the northern Cape Province, in all of which low levels of agriculture, most of it non-commercial, combine with a lack of both manufacturing and urban development. In addition, this surface includes much of the European-owned farming land of the eastern Cape and southern and eastern Orange Free State, areas transitional between the drier and wetter halves of the country and between its more heavily and more sparsely settled parts.

Table 3. The South African Nodal Service Hierarchy

| Order | Title | Number of places | $k = 3$ |
|---|---|---|---|
| 1 | Principal metropolitan centre | 1 | 1 |
| 2 | Major metropolitan centres | 3 | 2 |
| 3 | Metropolitan centres | 8 | 6 |
| 4 | Major country towns | 19 | 18 |
| 5 | Country towns | 57 | 54 |
| 6a | Minor country towns (upper tier) | 173 | 162 |
| 6b | Minor country towns (lower tier) | | |
| 7 | Local and low order service centres | 340 | 86 |

*Note:* A Student's *t*-test employed in measuring the statistical significance of breaks in levels of centrality revealed two significant breaks either of which could serve as class limits between Order 6 and 7 nodes. The use here of the lower limit to distinguish Orders 6 and 7 suggests the division of Order 6 into upper and lower tier cases (i.e., Order 6a and 6b) (Davies and Cook, 1968).

The Christaller $k = 3$ model suggests eight orders of places. No significant break, however, was detected in the lower order places to distinguish an eighth order in the South African hierarchy.

Differentiation in level between the surfaces is far greater in the eastern half of the country than in the west. Consequently gradients between summits and upper levels, on the one hand, and the valleys in the economic topography on the other, are comparatively steep especially in Natal. Conceptually the structure suggests that there are certain elements present of a centre/periphery model—an abstract pattern of core areas surrounded by surfaces of progressively decreasing economic intensity and health. But the details of this structure will become clearer in the succeeding analysis.

## THE NODAL SYSTEM

### Hierarchical Structures

Fundamentally the nodal structure which underpins the space economy at the national level is that of a principal metropolitan centre supported by a graded system of sub-national metropolitan cities resting upon tiers of cities of lower orders.

The city system possesses a rank-size distribution which is nearer to log-normal than primate (Davies, 1968). The relationship between city rank and city size in South Africa produces a pattern in which cities with populations less than 50,000 are log-normally distributed but smaller than would be expected according to the rank-size rule. On the other hand, cities with populations greater than 50,000 are larger than would be expected. The level of national primacy is 53 per cent which is near the world average of 55 per cent (Berry, 1961, p. 581). The concentration of economic activity and the associated concentration of urban population on the Witwatersrand and in the major port cities is largely responsible for the degree of primacy present in the system. Thus, although the structure of the city system is reasonably balanced, it is headed by a set of nodally-dominant metropolitan centres of varying size which are duplicative rather than complementary—a pattern not dissimilar to that found in Australia, New Zealand and Canada. This intermediate distribution suggests a structure characteristic of states in which the city system has evolved over a considerable period of time and has been influenced by a complex of economic and social forces (Berry, 1961, pp. 583–584).

The Witwatersrand complex of economically integrated cities with overlapping and common service hinterlands focussed upon Johannesburg is the largest of the metropolitan nodes. It is followed by Cape Town, Durban, Pretoria, Port Elizabeth, East Lon-

Table 4. Relationship between Nodal Service Hierarchy and Volume of Economic Activity

| Order | Title | Volume groupings | | | | Total |
|-------|-------|---|---|---|---|-------|
| | | 1 | 2 | 3 | 4 | |
| 4 | Major towns | 14 | 5 | 0 | 0 | 19 |
| 5 | Towns | 0 | 12 | 38 | 0 | 50 |
| 6a | Minor towns (upper tier) | 0 | 0 | 18 | 39 | 57 |
| 6b | Minor towns (lower tier) | 0 | 0 | 1 | 83 | 84 |
| Total | | 14 | 17 | 57 | 122 | 210* |

*Two places, Klerksdorp and Vereeniging, have been classified as metropolitan centres.

don, Bloemfontein, Pietermaritzburg, Kimberley, Vereeniging, Klerksdorp, and the Orange Free State Goldfields metropolitan area.

Size of place and rank in a service hierarchy in the South African city system are highly correlated.[1] Thus the balanced form of the rank-size distribution is confirmed by a graded service hierarchy which conforms most closely to the Christaller $k = 3$ model (marketing principle). The hierarchy is headed by the principal metropolitan centre, the Witwatersrand, and possesses in addition two levels of metropolitan cities and four orders of lower ranking nodes. The hierarchical orders are functionally distinct (Davies and Cook, 1968, p. 119).

Rank-size and service hierarchy analyses provide two distinct structural measures of the city system. An additional dimension is added by the extraction of four rotated components in a principal components analysis of 212 places in the system. Components 1 and 2 are measures of volume of economic activity and are the components pertinent to this discussion. The components are distinguished by high loadings on variables such as total population, number of central services, rateable value of property, employment in services

and the number of units of electricity sold per head. They account for 40 per cent of the variance.[2]

While the components may be considered independently it is convenient to obtain a summary assessment of volume by plotting Component 1 against Component 2. This procedure identifies four major groupings of nodes:

(1) Nodes with high volume on Component 1 ($+1.5\sigma$ to $+4.0\sigma$) and moderate volume on Component 2 (0 to $+1.0\sigma$).

(2) Nodes with moderate volume on Components 1 and 2 (0 to $+1.5\sigma$).

(3) Nodes with moderate volume on either Component 1 or Component 2 (0 to $+1.0\sigma$) but with low volume on one component (0 to $-1.0\sigma$).

(4) Nodes without volume on either component (0 to $-1.0\sigma$).

Relating volume of economic activity to service hierarchy rank results in the findings illustrated in Table 4.

Relatively few nodes of high ranking service order possess high volumes of economic activity on both components but most Major Towns (Order 4) have high volume on Component 1 and moderate volume on Component

1. $r = 0.94$ in a correlation of total population and number of central services. Bivariate correlation coefficient derived from a principal components analysis of 212 urban places. See also Davies (1967).

2. Due to a lack of comparable data the principal components analysis is confined to levels of cities below the Metropolitan centres. Analyses of volume of economic development and of economic welfare in the identification of economic surfaces have shown, however, that the metropolitan areas emerge as poles of economic volume and welfare.

2. The majority of nodes of Minor Town status have low volumes of economic activity. Nodes in the intermediate order of Towns (Order 5) tend to have volume on one but not both components. The findings emphasize the significance of Major Towns and Towns (Orders 4 and 5) as foci of economic development and economic concentration in levels below the metropolitan centres.

### The Spatial Expression of the Urban Hierarchy

The country as a whole is served by a balanced hierarchical structure headed by a sys-tem of metropolitan cities of which the Wit-watersrand city complex is undoubtedly the most significant (Fig. 5).

The distribution of metropolitan cities is sufficiently balanced such that 59 per cent of the country lies within 150 miles of any of these centres. However, in those areas falling beyond this distance nodes of a lower order are the main urban foci and assume roles more important than their hierarchical level may suggest. Nodes of this type may occur singly or in small city systems. Examples of these are the George-Oudtshoorn and Nelspruit-Barberton systems together with Upington, Pietersburg, Beaufort West, De Aar, and Middleburg (Cape).

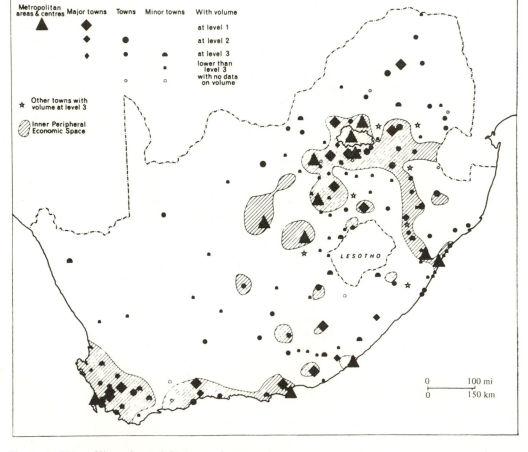

Figure 5. Urban Hierarchy and Volume of Economic Activity Related to Socio-Economic Surfaces.

Of the total of 21 cities with populations greater than 50,000 persons, 13 are located within the Southern Transvaal (Pretoria-Witwatersrand-Vereeniging area) city region. Ten of these cities form part of the Witwatersrand Principal Metropolitan Centre. This agglomeration of larger cities, on the one hand, introduces a measure of spatial imbalance in the city system ignored by formal rank-size analysis. On the other hand, it creates an economic environment of city interdependence and integration of considerable strength which is reflected in the summit of surfaces of economic volume and welfare forming the principal focus of the national space economy.

The national focus is supported by a distribution of nodes of higher population, service rank and volume of economic activity (Fig. 5) which collectively constitute a *primary urban mesh*. The mesh, which is near rank-size in distribution, includes the metropolitan centres of the Southern Transvaal together with Durban, the Orange Free State Goldfields, Bloemfontein, Pietermaritzburg, Kimberley, Vereeniging and Klerksdorp.

On the upper surfaces of economic volume and welfare the maximum distances separating nodes within the mesh at the level of Order 6a is 60 miles. In other words, the mesh on these surfaces has a "cellular distance" equal to or less than 60 miles and the mean distance

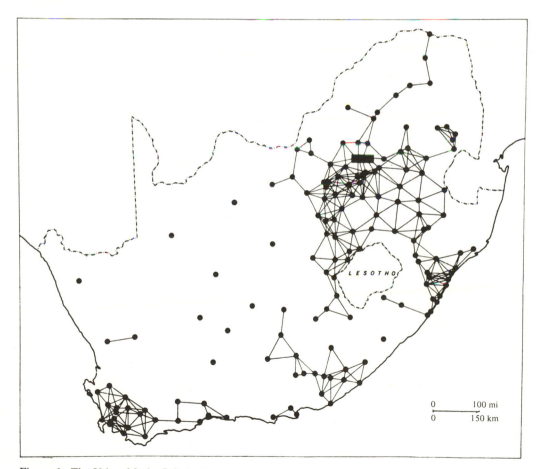

Figure 6. The Urban Mesh: Cellular Distances of 60 Miles between all Cities and Towns down to and Including the Upper Tier of Minor Towns.

to nearest neighbour at the Order 6a level is 26 miles (Figs. 6 and 7).

The parts of the primary mesh beyond surfaces 1 and 2 are less strongly developed. Northwards it is isolated in a single chain of higher ranking nodes. Southwards and westwards the nodal structure is characterized by a higher incidence of low-ranking nodes becoming progressively less dense with distance from the Witwatersrand so much so that in the vicinity of Bloemfontein and Kimberley higher order functions are focussed only in these metropolitan cities.

The primary mesh is supported by urban economies in which manufacturing and commerce play dominant roles (Fig. 8). The former function correlates significantly with urban growth (Davies, 1967).

A highly localized *secondary mesh* occupies the south-west Cape and is orientated about the metropolitan node of Cape Town. While not possessing a rank-size distribution, the mesh is closely knit and comprises a system of higher ranking nodes with relatively high populations and volumes of economic activity. The mesh is closely correlated to levels of areal economic welfare and intensity of production and has a maximum cellular distance measured at the Order 6a level of 40 miles. The mean distance to nearest

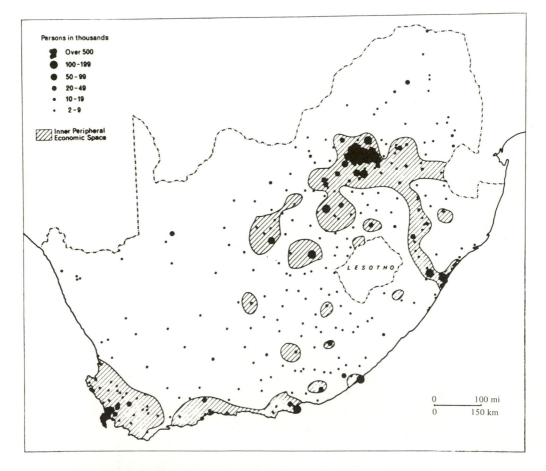

Figure 7. Population of Towns and Cities in Relation to Socio-Economic Surfaces.

neighbour at the Order 6a level is 25 miles. Urban economies with high levels of manufacturing and commerce reinforce the nodal strength of the mesh. At its margins the mesh declines steeply in level and density.

Smaller localized systems without a metropolitan focus have previously been identified marginal to the zone of metropolitan accessibility in the Southern Cape and Eastern Transvaal (George-Oudtshoorn, Nelspruit-Barberton, respectively).

A weak urban mesh commensurate with the sparsely populated pastoral areas deriving wealth from a rural rather than an urban economy is characteristic of the semi-arid western Cape Province. In areas dominated by African reserves no urban mesh of any quality emerges.

## NETWORKS AND FLOWS

The discovery of minerals produced a reorientation of the communications network. Until this discovery there had been several separate transportation and communication networks oriented about the coastal ports where the earliest phase of more intensive development had taken place. The discovery of diamonds on the site of Kimberley in the

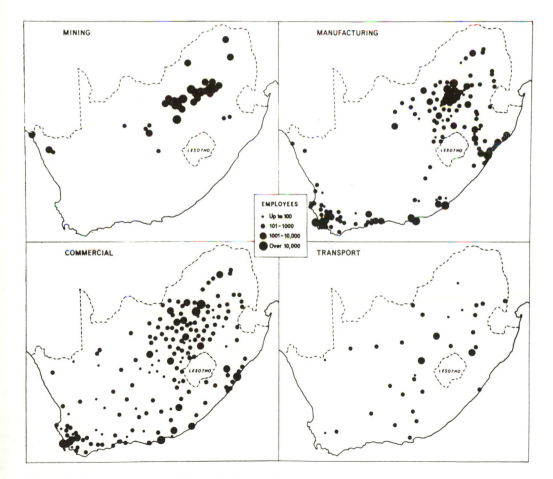

Figure 8. Economic Bases of Urban Nodes, 1960.

late 1860s provided a goal for the then short railways beginning to tap the agricultural hinterlands of Cape Town and Durban, but when gold was discovered on the Witwatersrand in 1886 a re-orientation of the railway system became inevitable with Johannesburg providing a much more powerful magnet for transportation and communications. For the past eighty years the pattern of communications has been focussed upon a single node with radiating axes stretching throughout South Africa, indeed into countries to the north.

Today the hierarchical city system is integrated and articulated by hierarchical networks of transportation and communications.

For example the road system, because of its flexibility in effectively linking all places, should be regarded as a set of nested sub-systems each performing successively higher order functions, carrying local, medium and long-distance traffic. In order, therefore, for the networks and flows to be keyed into the hierarchical pattern of nodes and to relate to different scales of area being integrated they will be treated as a series of interrelated systems of linkage at different levels. These will be (1) at the national level articulated on metropolitan nodes, (2) at the sub-national level articulated on metropolitan nodes and the highest ranking country towns (order 4

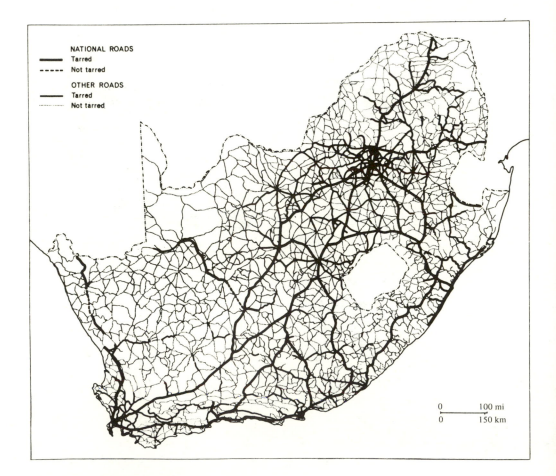

Figure 9. Road Pattern about 1963.

places), (3) at the local level articulated on all nodes with a rank of order 5 (minor country towns) and above and in some cases order 6 nodes where there are strong grounds for their inclusion (Fig. 9).

## The National Level

Evidence of a national system of linkages is given by the movement of passengers on the domestic airlines (Fig. 10). Two routes stand out above all others: the Johannesburg-Cape Town and the Johannesburg-Durban axes. The apices of this system handled over three-

quarters of the inland air passengers in 1965. Less important connections follow the coast from Durban to Cape Town, some including the intermediate centres of East London and Port Elizabeth. This movement is reinforced by coastwise traffic of freight and passengers.

Rail freight movements (Fig. 11) and the national trunk road system confirm the importance of the radial flows between the Witwatersrand and the ports of Durban and Cape Town and add a further dimension manifest in significant flows to Lourenço Marques and Port Elizabeth but not to East London. Certain road and rail routes have international significance and enhance the focal position of the

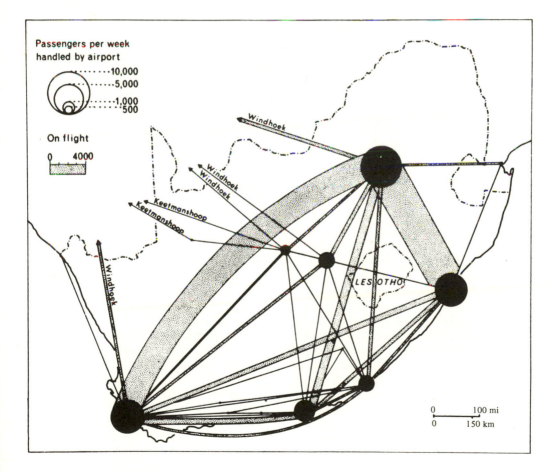

Figure 10. Passenger Traffic on Domestic Airlines, 1966.

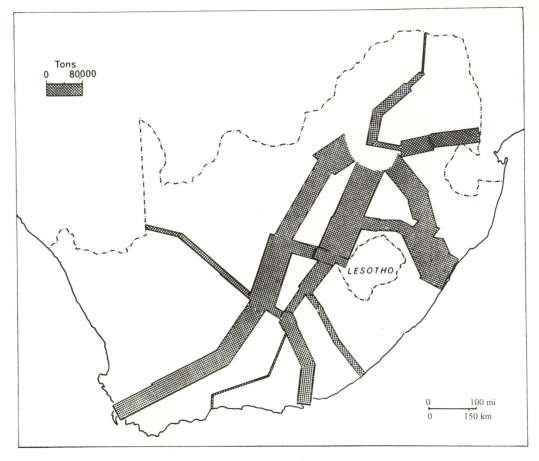

Figure 11. Volume of Rail Freight on Main Lines, 1965.

Witwatersrand. In addition, the relative completeness of the national road system provides a degree of connectivity, superior to the rail network, between all metropolitan centres and especially between those along the coast.

Inter-metropolitan telephone traffic which amounts to about 7 per cent of the total sample discloses much the same radial pattern and, in addition, identifies more clearly the degree of association within the national frame. On the one hand, the network closely integrates the northern metropolitan nodes and joins the system to Cape Town, through Johannesburg, the national focus; on the other, Port Elizabeth and East London are isolated in a secondary and peripheral nodal system.

## The Sub-National Level

Metropolitan centres in the national system of linkages tend to be central foci of individual systems at the sub-national level. These systems are defined by nodal flows of telephone traffic, newspaper circulation and road traffic (see Figs. 13 and 14). They reflect the comparatively balanced hierarchical nodal structure of the country and the absence of an unbalanced primate-city structure. There is, too, no truly national newspaper and the main metropolitan dailies indicate strongly localized circulations within their nodal systems.

Whereas the Cape, Port Elizabeth and East

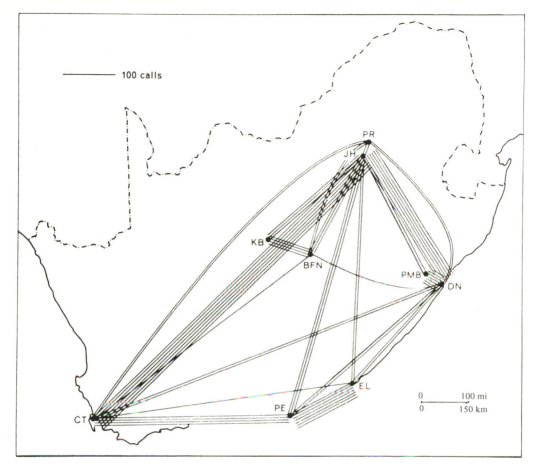

Figure 12. Volume of Trunk Telephone Traffic between Metropolitan Centres, 1963.

London systems focus on these individual metropolitan nodes, the system focused upon the Witwatersrand, however, comprises a composite and integrated set of systems which individually focus upon Durban, Pretoria, Bloemfontein and Kimberley, with Klerksdorp an interesting independent "inlier." The evidence lies clearly in the map of telephone traffic (Fig. 12 and is suggested also by the ganglion of roads with high traffic volumes centred upon the Southern Transvaal and dominating the whole of the northern part of the country. At the same time, however, a salient flows transaction analysis of telephone traffic shows within the composite system a distinct concentration upon Durban commensurate with its size, status and distance from the Witwatersrand.

Marginal location and a weak urban mesh on the peripheries of the nodal system gave rise to independent networks of nodal telephone traffic focussed upon George, Upington and Pietersburg, previously identified as outlying centres with distinctive roles. De Aar stands in a peculiar indeterminate relation to the network systems, on the one hand linked to Kimberley, as measured by telephone traffic, and on the other to Cape Town, Port Elizabeth, Bloemfontein and Kimberley, as measured by newspaper circulation. George,

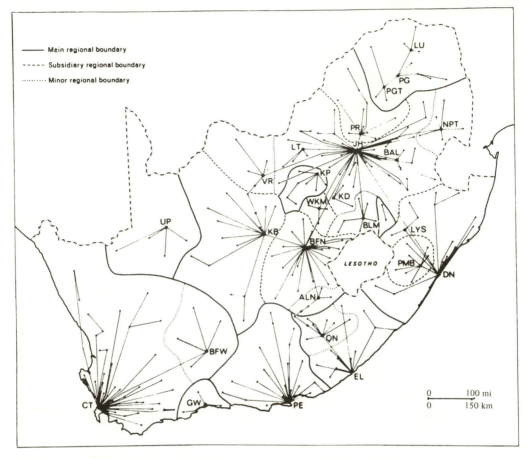

Figure 13. Nodal Flows of Trunk Telephone Traffic between All Centres, 1963.

similarly, occupies an indeterminate position between Port Elizabeth and Cape Town.

Flows of another kind, arising out of regional imbalance, are those of the temporary and permanent movement of Africans between areas of unequal economic opportunity.[3]

Transaction flow analysis (Fig. 15) discloses three systems of saliency. These are a large northern area from the northern Cape to

3. The African population was enumerated by region and also given was their region of permanent residence, "domicile" or "home." No indication is given of the precise meaning of permanent residence, but it may be assumed that the numbers reflect movements away from areas of permanent residence at some stage in the life of the individuals enumerated. No other data on internal migration are available.

the Natal border, a Natal system directed mainly towards Durban and a southern Cape system. Regions with substantial areas of African reserves are the main contributors whilst the zones of greatest economic activity provide the attraction. Indeed these are seen to be the upper and the high surfaces of the economic landscape whereas areas of supply lie in the low level economic surface. In the southern Cape connexions are maintained over long distances because with the exception of Port Elizabeth, Uitenhage and East London, the areas of opportunity lie in the south-western Cape some 800 miles from the Transkei, one of the most important sources of migrants. The intervening George-Mossel

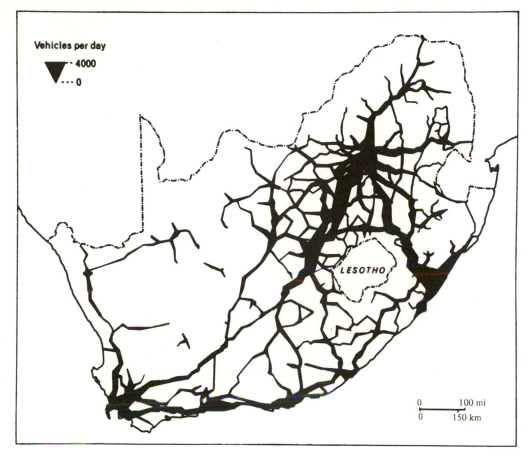

Figure 14. Road Traffic, 1965-1967.

Bay region plays a negligible part in these links. Long-distance migration is not only a feature of the southern Cape since it is also clear that movements from the south-eastern coastal rim have been directed towards the most important nodal regions in the northern system, particularly to mining areas. The links from the Transkei are particularly strong with Johannesburg, the West Rand, Klerksdorp and the Orange Free State Goldfields. Close ties also exist between East Griqualand, Pondoland and the Natal interior, and the Witwatersrand.

A significant characteristic of the migrations is that a smaller proportion of residents of the northern areas (mainly Transvaal)

moved to distant destinations than did those residents of the areas stretching from northern Natal south-westwards to the Cape province. In the former area desirable work on mines and on agricultural and forestry estates, especially in the northern and eastern Transvaal, is available locally whereas in the latter there are fewer opportunities for local employment, except in the areas of high economic intensity immediately north and south of Durban. The volume of African in-migration represented on Fig. 16 shows that areas of attraction are extremely limited. The Southern Transvaal is once again supreme in serving as a magnet for labour migration to the extent that 507,000 temporary African residents were enumerated

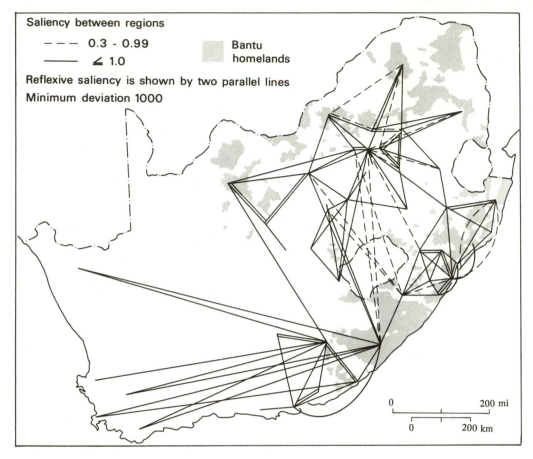

Figure 15. Labour Migration. Salient Flows of African Population.

there. Elsewhere, only the coastal nodes and their associated belts of upper economic surfaces provide comparable opportunities for large volumes of migrant labour.

## THE ORGANIZATIONAL STRUCTURE

The foregoing analysis of nodes and networks now provides us with a basis for understanding the organizational structure of the space economy. In the first instance the space economy is organized about its metropolitan nodes, one of which dominates all others. A composite picture of air passenger traffic, rail freight flow and inter-metropolitan telephone calls shows that interaction is greatest between the dominant national core (the Southern Transvaal city region) and the two major coastal nodes, Durban and Cape Town. Other interaction between metropolitan centres is relatively less significant. Thus, the dominant linkages are, unlike the Australian or South American patterns which are of roughly the same order of economic development, centripetal rather than circumferential.

Secondly, in the light of telephone traffic and newspaper circulation, each metropolitan node plays a significant part in organizing the economic space surrounding it. Thus three

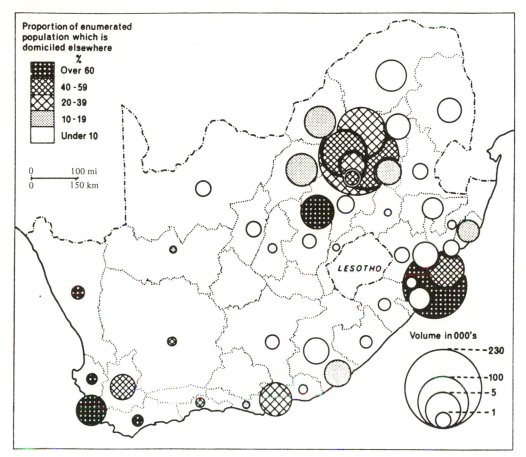

Figure 16. African In-Migrants.

distinct regions are organized about Cape Town, Port Elizabeth and East London. But the dominance of the national core is such that it draws into its sphere of organization a system of nodal systems covering the northern two-thirds of the country. This is termed the *Principal* region. Only its northern and western extremities display a lesser degree of integration with the core.

In the total national structure two indeterminate sub-systems emerge. De Aar at the junction of the Principal region and the Cape Town and Port Elizabeth regions; and George-Oudtshoorn, besides possessing this two-way linkage also enjoys a measure of organizational independence through the possession of the minor port of Mossel Bay.

## THE STRUCTURE OF THE SPACE ECONOMY

We are now in a position to establish the basic pattern of the contemporary space economy which is represented on Fig. 17. This combines the formal and functional elements of the space economy emphasizing their interdependence in a single system. By so doing it

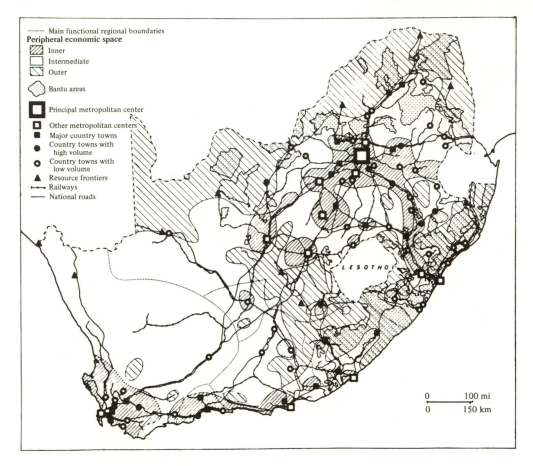

Figure 17. The Structure of the South African Space-Economy.

not only discloses which elements of the space economy are related but also how they are related in terms of human organization of area, and the degree to which this varies from region to region. It is this varying character and degree of spatial organization which forms the basis for regional division.

The *Principal region* represents the largest, the richest, the most complex, and the most highly organized segment of the South African space economy. It encompasses some two-thirds of the national area, contains all but three of its metropolitan nodes and generates 74.8 per cent of the country's g.d.p. This degree of integration results from:

(1) a relatively dense and closely interconnected pattern of nodes of graded size and importance;

(2) strong radial axes of movement in association with chains of higher order urban centres and belts of high economic intensity, and

(3) the comparatively large area of inner and intermediate peripheral economic space indicative of high level of economic development.

However, levels of economic activity and spatial integration progressively decline away from the main nodes and the belts of inner peripheral economic space. Thus the integration of the outer peripheral economic space with the rest of the region remains incomplete, as testified by the special positions of Pietersburg and Upington, on the one hand, and the weak networks and nodal mesh in this zone, on the other. What linkage does exist, mainly in the form of flows of Bantu labour to the major nodes, serves rather to drain the outer periphery of its men of working age than to distribute capital and skills to this zone in return. So powerful is the attraction of the areas of opportunity in the Principal region that substantial flows of African labour are drawn from beyond its borders, notably from the Transkei in the East London region.

Some degree of spatial integration of periphery with core is nevertheless being gradually fostered by the development of isolated resource outposts of mining and intensive irrigation agriculture.

The remaining regions have repeatedly emerged during the analysis as less complex and, therefore, less integrated nodal systems. Of these the *Western Cape* focusses upon a single major node and a high degree of spatial integration is confined to a small, well-organized and economically-healthy inner surface, comprising a tightly-knit cluster of high-order towns. In view of steep environmental gradients and the essentially rural base of the greater part of the region, there is a sharp concomitant discontinuity in the degree of spatial organization. Thus much of the peripheral economic space is only weakly integrated with the core. But, unlike the Principal region, it displays no strong radial structure, and no development corridor associated with a national axis has evolved.

The third and fourth regions are given a measure of unity by virtue of their historical association in an area popularly termed the Eastern Province. Rennie (1945) has shown, however, that area is essentially transitional both physically and culturally. First, there is a gradual passage towards semi-arid conditions in the west and, secondly, a change from the dominantly African land-ownership in the Transkei, through the mixed African reserves and white-owned farmland of the Border to the principally white-owned areas of the Cape Midlands. But as Rennie points out, distinct Midlands and Border[4] regions are "in process of achieving some degree of economic unity in relation to their respective ports and their interests" (p. 25).

The present analysis confirms this dual organization of the Eastern Province. But the nodal systems centred upon *Port Elizabeth* and *East London* lack the cohesion and continuity of organization beyond the immediate environs of the nodes. This is attributable mainly to their marginal location with respect to the three major cores (Witwatersrand, Cape Town, Durban) around which the national space economy is chiefly organized. Secondly, this is attributable to the weakness of the respective hinterlands, largely African reserves in the case of East London, and the predominance of pastoral areas of low economic intensity in the case of Port Elizabeth.

Marginal areas common to more than one nodal system are characteristic of most space economies and the distinctive situations of De Aar and George-Oudtshoorn have been referred to.

## CONCLUSIONS

While fuller understanding of the form and function of the South African space economy must await an analysis of the dynamic aspects of its past and future growth, the present study nevertheless provides an initial framework of interrelationships at the national and subnational levels within which more confident analyses of the country's macro- and microspatial structure can be made.

Level of economic development in a formal sense is brought into association with varying degrees of spatial integration as manifested by nodal systems and their networks. As Boudeville (1966, p. 38) points out, "the appearance, development and *integration* of polarized regions is synonymous with the

---

4. The Border includes part of the Transkei served by the Cape Eastern railway system.

progress of industrialization and market economy." The regions delimited in this study emphasize rather the varying degrees of spatial integration across the country than the differences of formal pattern place to place.

Thus, the Principal region emerges as the most advanced area of human organization in South Africa. It is that part of the national space economy which most nearly conforms to Friedmann's industrial stage (Friedmann, 1966, p. 36) in which the space economy is represented by a single national centre supported by strong peripheral sub-centres. The periphery is reduced to smaller, more manageable proportions as important resources are brought into the productive cycle of the economy. Growth prospects for the region for the nation are enhanced, but problems of poverty and cultural backwardness persist in inter-metropolitan peripheries, represented mainly by the African reserves. The remaining three regions are less advanced and lie somewhere between this stage and Friedmann's preceding transitional phase which in his model is represented by a single strong centre and a stagnating periphery. None is representative of the stage of transition, all having advanced beyond that phase, but all three, nevertheless, show strong regional primacy and the East London region approaches most nearly the pattern of an associated downward transitional periphery.

But in the final analysis the South African space economy must be looked at as a whole—as a system, i.e., as "a totality of relations amongst and including [the] parts" (Association of American Geographers, 1968, p. 2). In this sense the connexions between the parts have been stressed in the form not only of networks but also of the rank size, the hierarchical levels and the nesting of nodal centres, so that cores and their peripheries have meaning only in terms of the degree of integration between them. The regions delimited are thus open systems requiring a supply of energy for their maintenance and preservation. Viewed nationally they are, of course, sub-systems with recognizable kinds and degrees of interaction within the larger system or environment to which they belong. Similarly, the national system is an open system and is subject to the external influences of its own environment, i.e., the Southern African (Green and Fair, 1962) and world environment of which it is a part.

Finally, the flows and connexions characterizing the space economy are "usually initiated by human decision" (Association of American Geographers, 1968, p. 3). Decision-making processes will govern the spatial allocation of people, money, energy and goods to various parts of the system and "changes in one part [will be] felt throughout the framework" (Association of American Geographers, 1968, p. 2) as the degree of information in the system varies. Impact upon the system of the decision-making process, embodied in the first instance in government policy, must therefore also be gauged as, in turn, must the effects of the behaviour of the system on the framing of policy (i.e., feedback) be assessed. Elaboration of these aspects of the analysis remains to be done.

## REFERENCES

Ackerman E. A. (1963) Where is a research frontier? *Ann. Ass. Am. Geogr.* 53, 429–440.

Alexandersson G. (1956) *The Industrial Structure of American Cities,* Lincoln, Nebraska.

Association of American Geographers (1968) A systems analytic approach to economic geography, Commission on College Geography, Publication No. 8, Washington, D.C.

Berry B.J.L. (1961) City size distributions and economic development, *Econ. Develop. and Cultural Change,* 9, 573–588.

———. (1964) Approaches to regional analysis: a synthesis, *Ann. Ass. Am. Geogr.* 54, 2–11.

———. (1968) A synthesis of formal and functional regions using a general field theory of spatial behaviour, in *Spatial Analysis* (Edited by B.J.L. Berry and D. F. Marble), pp. 419–428, Prentice-Hall, Englewood Cliffs, N.J.

———. and Garrison W. L. (1958) Functional bases of the central place hierarchy, *Econ. Geogr.* 34, 145–154.

Boudeville J. R. (1966) *Problems of Regional Economic Planning,* Edinburgh University Press.

Brams S. J. (1966) Transaction flows in the international system, *Am. Polit, Sci. Rev.* 60, 880–898.

Davies R. J. (1967) South African town growth correlates, Jubilee Conference Proceedings, S. Afr. Geogrl. Soc. 173–197.

––––––. (1968) Resultants of urbanisation in South Africa: a nodal region analysis of urban demographic structure. *Proceedings of the Conference on Focus on Cities,* Durban, University of Natal, Institute for Social Research.

––––––. and Cook G. P. (1968) Re-appraisal of the South African urban hierarchy, *S. Afr. Geogrl J.* 50, 166–132.

––––––. and Young B. S. (1969) Economic structure of South African cities, *S. Afr. Geogrl. J.* 51, 19–37.

Fair T.J.D. (1957) Regions for planning in South Africa, *S. Afr. Geogrl. J.* 39, 26–50.

Friedmann J. (1966) *Regional Development Policy,* M.I.T. Press, Cambridge, Mass.

Green L. P. and Fair T.J.D. (1962) *Development in Africa,* Witwatersrand University Press, Johannesburg.

Haggett P. (1965) *Locational Analysis in Human Geography,* Arnold, London.

Nel P. A. and De Coning C. (1965) The regional distribution of purchasing power in the Republic of South Africa, Research Report No. 10, Bureau of Marketing Research, Pretoria, University of South Africa.

Nystuen J. D. and Dacey M. F. (1961) A graph theory interpretation of nodal regions, *Pap. Reg. Sci. Ass.* 7, 29–42.

Perloff H. *et al.* (1960) *Regions, Resources and Economic Growth,* Johns Hopkins Press, Baltimore.

Rennie J.V.L. (1945) The Eastern Province as a geographical region, *S. Afr. Geogrl. J.* 27, 1–27.

Soja E. W. (1968) Communication and territorial integration in East Africa—an introduction to transaction flow analysis, *East Lakes Geogr.* 4, 39–57.

South Africa, Bureau of Statistics. (1960a) *Population Census,* Vol. 1, *Geographical distribution of the population,* Government Printer, Pretoria.

––––––. (1960b) *Population Census, Special Tabulation of the industries of the population by urban places with more than 2000 persons,* Pretoria.

South Africa, Department of Planning (1967) *Development Atlas,* Government Printer, Pretoria.

United Municipal Executive of South Africa (1960–1961), *Official South African Municipal Yearbook,* Pretoria.

Winklé F. F. (1961) Economic regions of the Republic of South Africa for statistical and business purposes, Research Report No. 2, Bureau of Marketing Research, Pretoria, University of South Africa.

# 4.2

# On the Spatial Structure of Organizations and the Complexity of Metropolitan Interdependence

ALLAN PRED

In the United States and other highly industrialized, or postindustrial, countries the economy is dominated by large private-sector and government organizations that are normally composed of a number of functionally differentiated and spatially separated units. A variety of statistics indicates that the relative and absolute economic power of such organizations has been rapidly expanding in recent decades (Pred, 1974). Insofar as these organizations dominate the economy they are the most important generators of flows of goods, services, information, and capital. In other words, in an economically advanced system of cities large multilocational organizations are the major source of intermetropolitan and interurban interdependencies. Despite this fact, relatively little is known of the spatial characteristics of the city-system interdependencies created by the intraorganizational and interorganizational relationships of major business corporations and government activities.

The aims of this article are twofold:*

(1) To conceptually outline the characteristics of metropolitan interdependence arising from the spatial structure, or *intra*organizational linkages, of major job-providing organizations.

(2) To present empirical materials pertaining to the spatial pattern of intraorganizational and interorganizational interdependencies associated with specific metropolitan complexes and to ascertain whether or not these interdependencies are consistent with those assumed in the author's model of the process of city-system growth and development in advanced economies.

## SYNOPSIS OF AN ELSEWHERE-PRESENTED MODEL

A probabilistic model describing the means by which the interurban circulation of specialized information and the spatial structure of organizations supposedly feed back upon one another to influence the process of city-system growth and development in advanced economies has been tentatively presented at length elsewhere (Pred, 1971, 1974, 1975). In addition to the subprocess of locally propagated growth in each metropolitan complex and city, the model incorporates three interrelated subprocesses which function in a circular and cumulative manner (Fig. 1). These are the intraorganizational and interorganizational generation of nonlocal employment multipliers after each birth or large-scale expansion of an organizational unit, the diffusion of "growth-inducing" innovations from one metropolitan complex to another,[1] and

---

*A third section of the original paper, on regional planning implications, has been deleted.—Eds.

1. "Growth-inducing" innovations fall into three often interdependent broad categories: those that involve the provision of new goods or services; those that involve new production processes; and those that affect the structural relationships, operating procedures, or planning and policy-making procedures of organizations.

From *Papers, Regional Science Association*, vol. 35, 1975, pp. 115–31, 135–37, 140–42. Reprinted by permission.

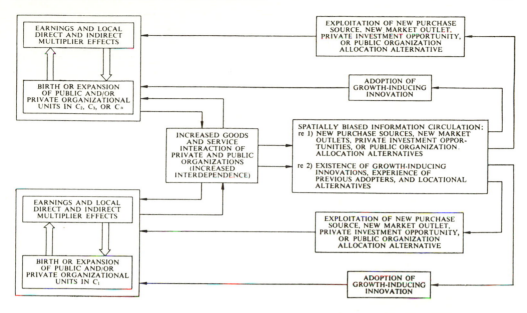

Figure 1. The Circular and Cumulative Feedback Process of Urban-Size Growth for Large Metropolitan Complexes ($C_1$, $C_2$, $C_3$, . . . $C_n$) in Advanced Economies.

the accumulation of "operational" decisions, which usually have an implicit rather than an explicit locational dimension.[2] When observing the national city-system as a whole—as opposed to the situation in Figure 1 where only a few large metropolitan complexes are considered—the entire process can be synopsized in the following admittedly oversimplified terms (Fig. 2).

The totality of intraorganizational and interorganizational linkages existing at a given date ($T_1$) creates a goods-and-service interaction matrix between the metropolitan complexes and lesser cities of the city-system in question. Each of the component linkages has a dual over which some form of specialized information flows (cf. Dunn, 1970). The totality of these specialized linkages can be visualized as a probability matrix that influ-

ences both the places to which new growth-inducing innovations diffuse and the places identified for the implementation of new operational decisions.[3] (In other words, because of limited search behavior, uncertainty-reducing behavior, and other factors, organizations tend to be greatly influenced by their existing network of market and other specialized information contacts when making explicit and implicit location decisions (cf. Lasuén, 1971, 1973). Each innovation adoption and operational decision either creates new intraorganizational and interorganizational linkages, or fortifies such existing linkages. Thus, by a later date ($T_1 + \Delta t$), a new slightly modified goods-and-services interaction matrix has emerged. The new counterpart specialized information flow probability matrix influences the loci of subsequent explicit and implicit location decisions until a later date ($T_1 + 2\Delta t$), when yet another

2. The "operational" decisions specified in Figure 1, as well as any other type of organizational decision involving the allocation of funds, always may be viewed as implicitly locational when they are not explicitly locational. This is so because, whatever the motivation, fund allocations involve the implementation of action in some place(s) as opposed to others.

3. For simple equations expressing the probabilities involved see Pred, 1973, pp. 34–35, 41.

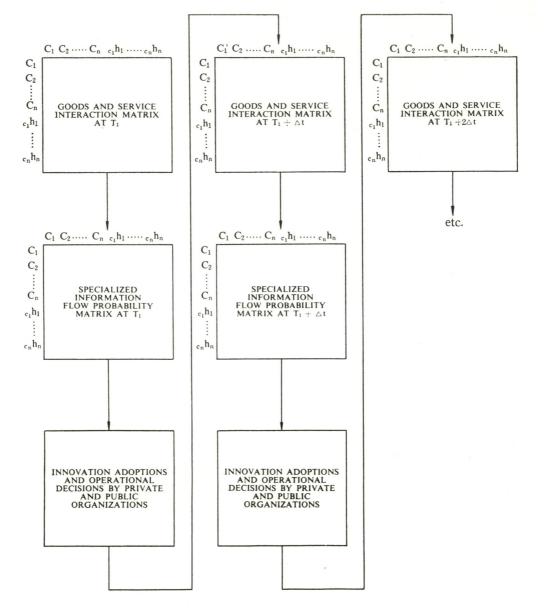

Figure 2. A Simplified Description of the Growth and Development Process for an Entire System of Cities in an Advanced Economy. ($C_1$, $C_2$, ...$C_n$) refer to large metropolitan complexes, $c_1h_1 \cdots c_nh_n$ refer to all medium- and small-sized cities within the regional "hinterlands" of large metropolitan complexes.

goods-and-service interaction matrix has evolved. And so on.

In developing the model, various pieces of very general and coarse-grained evidence suggested that:

(1) the most important nonlocal intraorganizational and interorganizational linkages within a city-system are those between large metropolitan centers; and

(2) intraorganizational and interorganiza-

tional city-system interdependencies are complex, since metropolitan centers of a given size may provide goods, services, and specialized information to nearby and distant larger metropolitan complexes, and since there exists an extensive criss-crossing of linkages between large metropolitan complexes on the one hand and medium- or small-sized metropolitan centers on the other. Thus, the assumed linkages and resulting probabilities are such that over time the rank-stability of the largest metropolitan complexes is either maintained or only slightly altered. This, of course, is consistent both with the considerable body of empirical evidence concerning long-term rank-stability among the largest units of national and regional systems of cities (for example, Pred, 1973b), and with the fact that in the United States, France, Great Britain, Canada, Sweden, and other advanced economies recent population and employment growth has been largely concentrated in previously large metropolitan complexes and their expanding peripheral areas, or urban fields (see Alonso and Medrich, 1972, Berry, 1973, Simmons, 1974, and Törnqvist, 1970). Also, in accordance with reality, the probabilistic qualities of the model are such that medium- or small-sized cities can occasionally make relatively rapid progress through the size ranks of a system of cities. This would occur when important explicit or implicit location decisions are implemented at organizational units in medium- or low-probability places. Progress would be accounted for by sizable and temporally concentrated local multipliers, increased interaction with other cities, and a higher probability of being associated with future explicit or implicit locational decisions.

## THE GROWING ROLE OF PRIVATE-SECTOR ORGANIZATIONS IN METROPOLITAN INTERDEPENDENCE

It is widely documented that since the end of World War II large multifunctional and multilocational organizations have been gaining an ever larger share of the economy in the United States and other postindustrial countries due to mergers, acquisitions, the expansion of existing units, and capital investment in new facilities (Blair, 1972, Reid, 1960). The almost frenzied pace of merger and acquisition activity, particularly during the late 1960s, was motivated primarily by a desire to spread risks in an era of high technological and economic instability and uncertainty, by the identification of personal management goals with organizational size and growth, and by "synergy," or the belief that the effectiveness of an enlarged corporation somehow becomes greater than that of the sum of its previously separately operating parts (Ansoff, 1965, Galbraith, 1973, Lorsch and Allen, 1973, and Reid, 1960). Only during the last year or so have government decisions, tight money, and lower stock prices really cut into the number of corporate acquisitions and mergers. (Each acquisition or merger, by definition, affects the spatial structure and intraorganizationally generated intermetropolitan linkages of the growing organization.) Nevertheless, there is ample evidence that large organizations are continuing to expand their economic dominance. For example, in 1969 the 500 largest industrial corporations in the United States[4] accounted for 74 percent of the profits of all such corporations, while in 1973 the profit share of the "top 500" had risen to 79 percent of the total. And, between 1972 and 1973 alone, the number of people employed by the 500 leading U.S. manufacturing corporations increased by almost 900,000 to over 15.5 million (*Fortune,* 1974).

Lacking any locational specificity, general statistics of the type just presented only provide suggestions as to the growing role of large private-sector organizations in metropolitan interdependence. More specific statistics referring to the growth and *location* of organizational activities are not readily accessible in the literature except in those headquarters-location studies based either on *Fortune*'s uncomprehensive annual directory

---

4. Industrial corporations include all those corporations deriving 50 or more percent of their sales from manufacturing and/or mining.

Table 1. Number of Jobs Controlled by Multilocational Private-sector Organizations in Selected
Metropolitan Complexes of the Western United States, 1959–1973

| Metropolitan Complex | Estimated Number of Employees Controlled by Locally Headquartered Multilocational Organizations[a] | | | Population | | |
|---|---|---|---|---|---|---|
| | 1959[b] | 1973 | % Increase 1959–73 | 1960 | 1970 | % Increase 1960–70 |
| Los Angeles[c] | 539,341 | 1,252,478 | 132.2 | 6,742,696 | 8,452,461 | 25.4 |
| San Francisco-Oakland-San Jose[d] | 572,101 | 892,451 | 56.0 | 3,291,077 | 4,174,235 | 26.8 |
| Seattle-Tacoma[e] | 165,210 | 204,411 | 23.7[g] | 1,428,803 | 1,832,896 | 28.3 |
| Portland SMSA | 55,732 | 146,234 | 162.4 | 821,897 | 1,009,129 | 22.8 |
| Phoenix SMSA | 18,625 | 123,182 | 561.4 | 663,510 | 967,522 | 45.8 |
| Honolulu SMSA | 18,885 | 93,492 | 395.1 | 500,409 | 629,176 | 25.7 |
| San Diego SMSA | 39,682 | 73,561 | 85.4 | 1,033,011 | 1,357,854 | 31.4 |
| Boise City SMSA | 12,702 | 66,891 | 426.5 | 93,460 | 112,230 | 20.1 |

Source: Dun and Bradstreet, 1974, U.S. Bureau of the Census, 1971, and a direct survey of Seattle-Tacoma organizations.
[a]Employment totals are based on units completely owned by corporations and firms with local headquarters. They do not include employment partially steered by locally present corporate divisional head offices. Both 1959 and 1973 totals are restricted to organizations with multilocational characteristics that employed at least 400 people as of 1973. Some no longer existing firms are included in the 1959 totals.
[b]Some of the organizations included in the 1959 totals did not provide Dun and Bradstreet with employment figures until subsequent years. In those cases figures from 1960 or later were substituted. Thus, the 1959 total for each of the eight metropolitan complexes is somewhat exaggerated and the percentage increases for 1959–73 are even greater than those indicated.
[c]Los Angeles-Long Beach SMSA + Anaheim-Santa Ana-Garden Grove SMSA.
[d]San Francisco-Oakland SMSA + San Jose SMSA.
[e]Seattle SMSA + Tacoma SMSA.
[f]1974 datum.
[g]See footnote 6.

of industrial and nonindustrial corporations, or on similar listings for other countries (e. g., Ahnström, 1973, Armstrong, 1972, Pred, 1974, Semple, 1973, Goddard, 1973, and Westaway, 1974). Thus, the data presented in Table 1 for selected western U.S. metropolitan units provides a picture of recent trends that, if still imperfect, is probably clearer than those elsewhere available.

Although somewhat different time spans are involved, it would seem quite apparent from Table 1 that, in most metropolitan complexes, the number of jobs associated with locally based multilocational business organizations has been growing at a rate of increase that far outstrips that of local population growth.[5] The only anomaly, Seattle-Tacoma, is attributable to the Boeing Company's unusual loss of almost 30,000 jobs between 1959 and 1973.[6] Even allowing that

5. Given the population of Boise, its 1959–73 job-control increase is remarkably high. However, without investing a considerable amount of time in compiling data for other U.S. metropolitan complexes with populations exceeding 500,000, there is no way of precisely determining the representativeness of the remaining data contained in Table 1. All the same, even if it is conceded that much of the job-control increases recorded for Los Angeles and Phoenix are the result of headquarters location shifts (e.g., the move of Greyhound Corporation from Chicago to Phoenix), other more crude data appearing in *Fortune* (Pred, 1974) provide reason to believe that during the 1960s extremely few U.S. metropolitan complexes had a population growth rate that surpassed the job-control growth rate of their multilocational private-sector organizations.
6. If the Boeing Company's employment is subtracted from both

some of the indicated employment increases have occurred at organizational units in foreign countries, there would appear to be little question that, at the very least, *there has been a significant burgeoning in those metropolitan and other city-system interdependencies which involve intraorganizational linkages between the headquarters offices of multilocational private-sector organizations and their subordinate domestic units.* If this is true, then it follows that *in many, perhaps most, metropolitan complexes and cities there has been a simultaneous absolute and relative increase in the number of local jobs controlled from elsewhere.*[7] Obviously, while lacking in detail, these observations hint at a mounting *complexity* of metropolitan interdependence arising from the intraorganizational linkages of multilocational business organizations.

The complexity of metropolitan interdependencies shaped by increasingly dominant multilocational business organizations stems from both the division of labor within such organizations and the more widely treated market-coordinated division of labor between all corporations and firms. On the intraorganizational side, the necessity of coping with environmental diversity and instability has required that large modern business (and governmental) organizations develop increasingly intricate links of interdependence between their component units, whether spatially proximate or dispersed (Lorsch and Allen, 1973). These links may involve the flow of various services and decision-making information, control information, or coordination information between a headquarters unit and other organizational units.[8] They may also subsume the flow of goods, ser-

vices, and information among two or more units without involving an organization's head offices. (Even when a multilocational business organization is not of the diversified conglomerate variety, there will be numerous functionally specialized units that must interact with one another. For example, large organizations whose sole or principal function is manufacturing usually are composed of some combination of main and branch plants in several product lines, management and administrative offices with different levels of authority, research and development units, and marketing, warehousing, and transportation facilities; cf. Parsons, 1972). On the interorganizational side, technological advances in production, transportation, and telecommunications have created an ever greater array of linkages between multilocational private-sector organizations. These ties take the familiar form of physical input-output relationships, financial and commercial service linkages, and other specialized backward and forward service linkages (cf. Wood, 1969). In particular: "Manufacturing has increasingly become a matter of teamwork within vast [*inter*organizational] production systems, in which work has been divided between a great number of component units specializing in one particular aspect of production" [or production-facilitating service provision] (Törnqvist, 1975).

## THE SPATIAL STRUCTURE OF MULTILOCATIONAL ORGANIZATIONS

### Hierarchical Structures in General

Whatever their particular multifunctional attributes, private (and public) multilocational organizations are usually spatially structured along intentional or *de facto* hierarchical lines.[9] Normally, the hierarchy consists of three or more tiers, with each unit at a successively higher tier serving a successively larger

---

the 1959 and 1974 Seattle-Tacoma totals, the resulting figures are 72,332 and 141,211. Thus, exclusive of the Boeing Company, the 1959–74 increase in employees controlled by multilocational business organizations headquartered in Seattle-Tacoma was no less than 95.2 percent.

7. There is ample documentation of such recent developments in Sweden (Godlund, 1972, Godlund *et al.*, 1973, and Nordström, 1974).

8. Apparently, the greater the volume of information specialized organizational units acquire from the environment, the greater their need to exchange information with their head office or other sister units (Persson, 1974).

9. The position taken in this section represents an elaboration and modification of the stance taken in Pred, 1973a, 1974.

area. Thus, when a nationally functioning organization purposefully assigns precisely outlined areas to its component units, or sets up geographical divisions, the hierarchy might take on the following appearance. At the peak of the hierarchy sits the controlling national headquarters. In most instances this coordinating and planning unit is situated in a metropolitan complex of national importance, but this need not invariably be so. At the next hierarchical level are the divisional offices, which are normally located either in metropolitan areas of regional significance, or in larger national level metropolitan complexes which also function as regional level foci. If the organization includes production units designed to serve the entire market area of each geographical division, they may be found in cities of varying size. However, if the plants in question either require several thousand workers, or are dependent on any of a variety of agglomeration economies, they also are apt to be located in populous metropolitan areas. Whether performing marketing, service, production, or low level administrative functions, the subregionally and locally oriented units at the bottom of the organizational hierarchy may have a wide spectrum of locations within the system of cities, ranging from small towns and cities to metropolitan areas of regional and national significance.

Most private-sector organizations are *not* explicitly or intentionally organized geographically. Instead, the individual units or multiunit divisions of private-sector organizations are typically coordinated along product or other functionally specialized lines.[10] Under these circumstances, in a nationwide organization the head offices, with their great demand for specialized nonroutine information, are also most likely to be found in a metropolitan complex of national stature. Despite quite different fundamental organizing principles, the subordinate components of these organizations as a matter of practice also

operate on a national, regional, or local scale, and are accordingly distributed among differently sized urban centers. Here too, those units having high information demands, large market thresholds, or sizable labor-force requirements are normally placed in large or very large metropolitan complexes, while other units tend to have a greater range of locations.

Since the most important private-sector organizations in advanced economies usually are either conglomerates with many more or less completely unrelated divisions (I.T.T., for example, contains some 200 divisions), or multidivisional corporations composed of semiautonomous and highly diversified vertically integrated divisions, it is important to distinguish between "polycentric" and "unitary" hierarchical spatial structures. In conglomerates and other large multidivisional organizations with great functional diversity, each division, or "profit center," is itself spatially structured along hierarchical lines with a quasi-independent divisional national headquarters unit at its peak. As a result of this, the hierarchical spatial structure of the organization as a whole is "polycentric," with the divisional headquarters serving as the second highest level of the organization's overall internal structure. The fact that an organization is "polycentric" does not preclude one or more of its divisional headquarters from having the same metropolitan location as that held by the organizationwide head office. Although the degree of divisional self-containment varies from case to case in the type of organization under discussion (Lorsch and Allen, 1973), there are virtually always important linkages between organizational headquarters on the one hand and divisional headquarters and other subunits on the other hand. Thus, while the multidivisional organization evolved largely because only a finite span of control over routine operational activities is possible,[11] head offices in organizations with "polycentric" spatial structures usually are still at the very least responsible for: determining and coor-

---

10. In some instances nationally functioning private-sector organizations have some of their units or divisions structured in geographically defined terms and other components or divisions based on functional specialization, with units that are implicitly local, regional, or national in purpose.

11. For comments on the development of multidivisional corporations see Chandler, 1962, Blair, 1972, and Reid, 1960.

dinating strategic objectives; general long-term planning; resolving conflicts; granting approval of capital and major expense projects; and the allocation of funds and resources among competing operating divisions and subunits (Williamson, 1970, Lorsch and Allen, 1973). From the standpoint of city-system growth, the last two frequently overlapping functions are crucial insofar as they directly and indirectly affect where new jobs will be created. In a nationally functioning "polycentric" organization the spatial distribution of new jobs determined by the head office over a given time period is very likely to be quite widespread, not only because of the nonlocal multiplier effects stemming from each birth or large-scale expansion of a unit, but also because units brought into an organization by merger or acquisition very often add to the scatter of the organization's existing locations. This is so since mergers and acquisitions are usually made on the basis of growth and other criteria, not locational criteria (cf. Chapman, 1974).

In organizations with few products, services, or functions, there is generally little discretionary authority delegated to subheadquarters units—even where routine operational activities are involved. This is also true of some organizations with many products, services, or functions. In both cases this centralization of authority requires that intraorganizational control be set up within a very strict hierarchical framework that is primarily based on chain-of-command principles rather than spatial designations. That framework in turn means that—regardless of the total number of subordinate organizational units—the management of all units is responsible to a *single* national level headquarters and that the linkages within the organization's intentional or *de facto* hierarchical spatial structure are very strong. Hence, such organizations may be described as having "unitary" hierarchical spatial structures.

## Hierarchical Structures at Different Scales

Thus far our discussion has been confined to nationally functioning organizations.

Private-sector organizations with hierarchical spatial structures exist at three other scales. First, there are multiunit retailing or service-providing organizations whose operations are restricted to a single metropolitan complex or urban field. Here the hierarchy is most often only two-tiered: headquarters and district or local outlets (furniture stores, specialty clothing stores, real estate offices, etc.). Obviously, these types of multilocational organizations may make nonlocal purchases, but for the most part they are of relatively little interest in terms of their impact on metropolitan interdependence and the process of city-system growth and development. Secondly, there are those regional-scale business organizations whose units are found either in a single state (such as banking organizations), or within the limits of a traditionally defined major metropolitan hinterland or multistate area. In these instances the structural hierachy typically is made up of regional, district, and local units. A similar three-level spatial structure is often found for state or provincial level government agencies. Hierarchical spatial structures at this scale can bring intermediate- and small-sized metropolitan areas into interdependent relationships with larger metropolitan complexes. Finally, in most cases very large nationally functioning business organizations simultaneously operate at a multinational scale. This condition adds an international tier to their hierarchical spatial structure. The metropolitan interdependencies propagated by this extra tier are of rapidly increasing importance. Little is said here of these interdependencies, partly because of my preoccupation with those interdependencies which are internal to national systems of cities and their regional subsystems, and partly because the topic merits extensive treatment on its own.

## Asymmetrial Organizational Spatial Structures and Metropolitan Interdependence

The spatial structure of nationally functioning multilocational organizations would be symmetrical if all organizationwide and national divisional headquarters were in the same metropolitan complex, and if the regional and local level units of each and every organization were present in the identical subset of cities. In addition, symmetry would require that any plant or other nonadministrative unit serving the entire nation also be located in the single metropolitan complex where all headquarters units were concentrated. Similarly, the spatial structure of multilocational organizations functioning in a given physically extensive region would be symmetrical if the regionwide, district (or subregional), and local units of each and every organization were distributed among the identical subset of cities.

Since this is quite clearly not the case, organizational spatial structures being *asymmetrical*,[12] one would expect *intra*organizationally based metropolitan and city-system interdependencies to be *complex*. More specifically, it is to be anticipated that the intraorganizational linkages of organizations with "polycentric" and "unitary" hierarchical spatial structures are synonymous with a high degree of interdependence among large metropolitan complexes. That is, it is to be expected that headquarters dominance and job-control linkages extend from large metropolitan complexes of national or regional significance to even larger metropolitan complexes, and not merely from the single largest metropolitan unit to less populous metropolitan complexes. Likewise, it is to be expected that headquarters dominance and job-control linkages run both between metropolitan areas of comparable size (regardless of population class) and even from metropolitan areas of small or intermediate size to much larger metropolitan complexes. Moreover, to the extent that multilocational organizations operate production units and various local-scale units throughout a country, one should find headquarters dominance and job-control linkages extending from metropolitan com-

plexes of varying size to smaller towns and cities within what are normally considered to be the hinterlands of other distant metropolitan complexes.

## Interdependencies: Asymmetrical Organizational Spatial Structures vs. Central-Place Theory

Conventionally, interdependencies within a system of cities are intentionally or unintentionally depicted in the hierarchical terminology of central-place theory, with the greatest emphasis being placed on the one-way dependence of cities of a given size upon cities of a larger size. As it has been demonstrated at length elsewhere (Pred, 1971, 1973a, 1973b) a literal central-place theory interpretation of city-system relationships logically eliminates any possibility of two-way interdependencies between large metropolitan complexes. (Rather general evidence presented by Borchert, 1972, Claval, 1973, Duncan and Leiberson, 1970, Pred, 1974, and others indicates that there is an intricate web of economic interdependence between large metropolitan complexes in advanced economies.) Furthermore, the other types of complex interdependencies just enumerated as being suggested by asymmetrical organizational spatial structures are not feasible under Christallerian or Löschian central-place theory. Actually, although it is infrequently stated, Löschian central place-theory does allow two-way interdependencies, interdependencies between comparably sized places, and the dependence of centers of a given size upon smaller places. However, these interdependencies *cannot* occur between the largest cities in a Löschian system and are limited to places within the same or adjacent 60° sectors of the economic landscape.[13]

Central-place theory stresses the conflux of consumers to supply points, or market-area and city-hinterland relationships, *and not either job-control and decision-making rela-*

---

12. See the discussion of headquarters location patterns and other evidence in Pred, 1974. Maps of the component units and linkages of individual Swedish business organizations (Godlund *et al.*, 1973) also succinctly capture the existence of asymmetrical organizational spatial structures.

13. For other comments on the limits of Löschian central-place theory see Parr, 1973.

*tionships, or interurban input-output rela-tionships.* Hence, it should come as no sur-prise that the interdependencies it generates are not fully compatible with those sup-posedly following from the asymmetry of organizational spatial structures. In light of the evidence about to be presented, and in light of the dominant role played in the econ-omy by multilocational business organiza-tions, it is contended that for planning and some other purposes the central-place theory image of city-system interdependencies must be displaced from its position of primacy.

## EMPIRICAL EVIDENCE ON THE COMPLEXITY OF METROPOLITAN INTERDEPENDENCE

Until recently, it has been possible only to partially portray the spatial pattern of *intra*or-ganizational linkages associated with any par-ticular U.S. metropolitan complex by falling back on materials last published for 1965 (Market Research Department of *Fortune,* 1966). This source revealed the headquarters location, plant locations, and plant-by-plant employment-size category for the 1,000 largest U.S. industrial corporations.[14] The metropolitan interdependence patterns dis-cernible from this source are highly incom-plete, in part because of the absence of data on organizations whose primary function was something other than manufacturing, and in part because no information is provided for marketing and other nonproduction units within the listed organizations. Here more recent and comprehensive pictures of intraor-ganizationally based interdependence are pre-sented in the form of job-control data for the Seattle-Tacoma metropolitan complex.* In addition, evidence on the complexity of *in-ter*organizationally based metropolitan inter-dependence is put forth in the form of flow data for Malmö and other Swedish cities.

14. See footnote 4, above. For summary data on specific met-ropolitan complexes based on this source see Pred, 1974, 1975. *A second example, of the Phoenix SMSA, has been deleted from this reprint.—Eds.

## Distribution of Jobs: Seattle-Tacoma Metropolitan Complex

As of spring 1974 over 204,000 jobs were under the jurisdiction of 53 multilocational business corporations and firms whose or-ganizationwide headquarters were located somewhere within the Seattle-Tacoma met-ropolitan complex (Table 1).[15] Through a mail survey and follow-up interviews, infor-mation was obtained on the location, em-ployment total, and functions of the U.S. and Canadian units[16] operated by these organiza-tions.[17] When viewed in summary form (Ta-bles 2–3, Figs. 3, 4, and 5), the acquired data presents at least four striking facets.

(1) The total array of *nonlocal* intraorgani-zational job-control linkages of private-sector organizations based in Seattle-Tacoma is dominated by ties with other metropolitan complexes. In fact, job-control linkages with other metropolitan complexes are almost three times as great as those with places located within what is traditionally regarded as the "hinterland" of Seattle-Tacoma.

15. In early 1974 almost another 44,000 jobs were associated with the Seattle-Tacoma divisional headquarters of elsewhere-based multidivisional corporations; that is, with the second-level nationwide administrative units of organizations with "polycen-tric" hierarchical spatial structures. Some additional nonlocal employment is controlled by small firms with less than 400 employees.
16. Data for Canadian units was requested because, despite the somewhat dampening effect the border between the United States and Canada has on metropolitan interaction (Simmons, 1974), the two countries may be regarded as having a single system of cities. This position is justified by the high *absolute* volume of interaction between Toronto, Montreal, and Vancouver and such U.S. metropolitan complexes as New York, Boston, Chicago, Detroit, and Los Angeles. The position is also supported by the fact that U.S. organizations own a larger share of the assets of all Canadian manufacturing, petroleum and natural gas, and mining and smelting activities than do organizations based in Canada itself.
17. As part of an ongoing project, similar information is being gathered for all the other metropolitan complexes listed in Table 1, plus Vancouver, British Columbia. The quality of the data provided by organizations based in Seattle-Tacoma was not uniform. In some cases it was necessary to make place-by-place employment estimates based on sales or other criteria. Con-sequently, there is a margin of error of 100 or more for some of the larger employment totals shown in Figures 3, 4, and 5. Likewise, because of the occasional use of estimating procedures it was not meaningful to precisely depict totals ranging from 1 to 49. Also, at this point it is not possible to make a complete functional breakdown of the jobs controlled from Seattle-Tacoma at the locations shown in Figures 3–5.

Table 2. Location by General Category: Jobs Controlled by
Multilocational Business Corporations and Firms Seattle-Tacoma, 1974

| Location | Estimated Number of Employees | Percentage of Total |
|---|---|---|
| Seattle-Tacoma[a] (local) | 90,551 | 44.5 |
| Metropolitan complexes | 63,310[b,c] | 31.1 |
| Non-"hinterland" smaller cities and towns | 23,607[d] | 11.6 |
| "Hinterland" | 21,287[e] | 10.4 |
| Including Alaska | 2,901[f] | 1.4 |
| Foreign, other than Canada | 5,841 | 2.9 |
| Total for all locations | 203,511[g] | 100.0 |

[a]Seattle SMSA + Tacoma SMSA.
[b]Including the Spokane SMSA (which is also included in the "hinterland" category described in note e) and Washington portion of the Portland SMSA, but not including the recently designated Anchorage, Richland-Kennewick, and Yakima SMSAs.
[c]Including 2,164 employees in seven Canadian metropolitan complexes.
[d]Including 2,661 employees in Canada.
[e]The Seattle-Tacoma "hinterland" is here defined, with the assistance of Borchert, 1972 and other sources, as encompassing all of the state of Washington (except Clark County, which belongs to the Portland SMSA), northern Idaho, and northeasternmost Oregon as well as Alaska. The "hinterland" subtotal includes 960 seasonal workers.
[f]Including 480 seasonal workers.
[g]Total for 52 corporations and firms. One firm with 900 employees refused to cooperate, hence the discrepancy with the figure of 204,411 in Table 1.

(2) The pattern of job-control linkages with no less than 141 other metropolitan complexes is scattered across the entire U.S.-Canadian economic landscape, and contains key elements that deviate from the relationships prescribed by distance-decay and gravity models. For example, largely but not entirely due to the Boeing Company, the most

Table 3. Location by Size of Metropolitan Complex: Jobs Controlled by
Multilocational Business Corporations and Firms Seattle-Tacoma, 1974

| Metropolitan Category | 1970 Population Range | Estimated Number of Employees | Percentage of Metropolitan Total |
|---|---|---|---|
| All metropolitan complexes | — | 63,310[a] | 100.0 |
| First-order national centers | ≥2,600,000 | 20,615 | 32.6 |
| Second-order national centers and regional metropolitan centers | 1,000,000 to 2,599,999 | 13,631 | 21.5 |
| Intermediate-sized metropolitan centers: | | | |
| A | 500,000 to 999,999 | 4,603 | 7.3 |
| B | 250,000 to 499,999 | 13,158 | 20.8 |
| Lesser metropolitan centers | <250,000 | 11,303 | 17.9 |

[a]See notes b and c in Table 2.

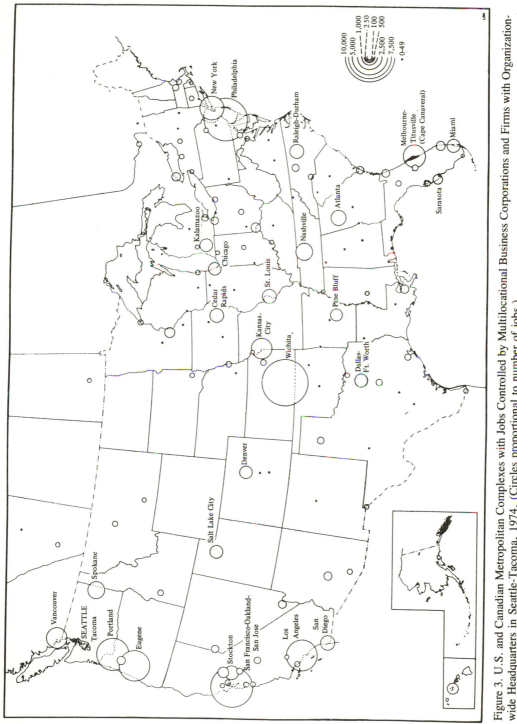

Figure 3. U.S. and Canadian Metropolitan Complexes with Jobs Controlled by Multilocational Business Corporations and Firms with Organization-wide Headquarters in Seattle-Tacoma, 1974. (Circles proportional to number of jobs.)

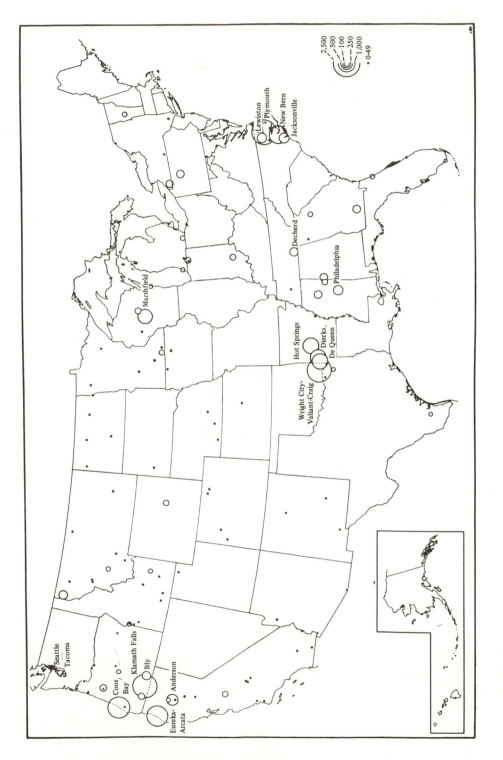

Figure 4. Jobs Controlled in Non-"hinterland" Smaller Cities and Towns by Multilocational Business Corporations and Firms with Organization-wide Headquarters in Seattle-Tacoma, 1974. (2,661 jobs scattered throughout Canada are not shown. Circles proportional to number of jobs.)

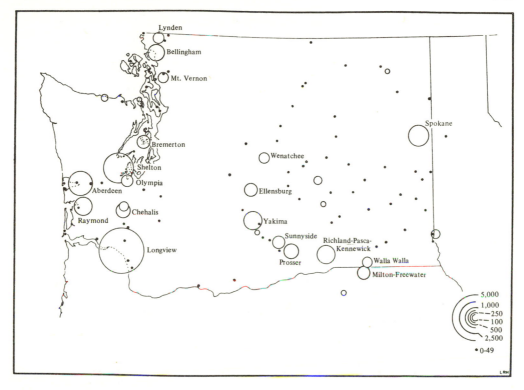

Figure 5. Jobs Controlled in "Hinterland" Locations by Multilocational Business Corporations and Firms with Organizationwide Headquarters in Seattle-Tacoma, 1974. (For "hinterland" definition see note e, Table 2. 2,901 jobs at Anchorage and 15 other Alaskan locations not shown. Circles proportional to number of jobs.

important job-control linkages are with the Philadelphia metropolitan complex and the Wichita SMSA, rather than with larger and more physically proximate metropolitan centers.[18] Likewise, the intraorganizationally generated interdependencies with places such as Nashville and Raleigh-Durham are more important than those either with the Chicago metropolitan complex, which is larger and closer, or centers such as Fresno and Tucson, which are both comparable in population to

18. The Philadelphia "metropolitan complex" consists of the Philadelphia SMSA plus the Wilmington, Delaware-New Jersey-Maryland SMSA. In addition to the Boeing Company, there are four other Seattle-Tacoma based organizations operating units in the Philadelphia metropolitan complex. The same is true of the Wichita SMSA.

the Tennessee and North Carolina metropolises and at much shorter distances from Seattle-Tacoma.

(3) Contrary to simple central-place hierarchy depictions of city-system interdependencies, over 54 percent of the job-control linkages with other metropolitan complexes occurs with centers that are either of the same size-order as Seattle-Tacoma, or of even larger population.

(4) The job-control linkages associated with smaller cities and towns located within the "hinterlands" of other major metropolitan complexes are greater in total than those associated with Seattle-Tacoma's own "hinterland." Significantly, a sizable fraction of the linkages with distant smaller towns and

cities involve retailing outlets, insurance offices, hospitals, and other nonmanufacturing activities.

It is of more than passing note that these generalizations are compatible with the findings of another recent, but less locationally specific, study of *inter*organizational interdependencies associated with the Seattle-Tacoma metropolitan complex. Using input-output techniques and three regional categories (local, other Washington, and other United States), Beyers (1974), found that on the whole the backward and forward linkages of 22 Seattle-Tacoma economic sectors are strongest with regions beyond the borders of the state of Washington.

## Intermetropolitan Flows and Interorganizationally Based Metropolitan Interdependence in Sweden

The complexity of metropolitan interdependence is also nicely captured by data on the economic flows generated by private-sector business organizational units located in Malmö and other Swedish cities.

Malmö, located across the Öresund from Copenhagen, is a metropolitan complex with a population of about 450,000. It is generally observed that, along with Stockholm (population about 1.4 million) and Göteborg (population about 700,000), this center dominates the smaller metropolitan centers and urban places within the Swedish system of cities. Table 4 partially summarizes the findings of a recently published study (Bylund and Ek, 1974) of the interdependence patterns created in 1970 by the flow of goods, services and information to and from national, regional, and local level organizational units located in Malmö. Aside from the category-to-category variations in the importance of local flows, at least four features stand out from this table.

(1) Private organizational units in Malmö sell substantial quantities of goods and services to the even larger metropolitan complexes of Stockholm and Göteborg. Goods and business service sales to Sweden's first-

and second-ranking metropolitan complexes clearly outstrip those to places within Malmö's own "hinterland."

(2) Malmö's interorganizational interdependencies are geographically widespread. This is partially reflected by the fact that more goods and business services are sold by Malmö's units to smaller metropolitan centers, cities, and towns outside its "hinterland" than to such places within its own "hinterland."

(3) Organizational units belonging to Malmö's private sector obtain a significant share of their physical inputs and business services not only from the larger complexes of Stockholm and Göteborg, but also from smaller metropolitan centers, cities, and towns. The physical goods purchased from smaller places include slightly processed raw materials as well as semifinished products, while those purchased from Stockholm and Göteborg are virtually entirely of the latter type.

(4) Based on a rather limited sample of the total number of studied Malmö organizations, there appears to be a reasonably close parallel between the pattern of goods and service flows and the flow pattern of specialized information contacts or exchanges.

Several other pieces of evidence resulting from recent Swedish flow studies testify to the importance and complexity of metropolitan interdependence. Here, only two are mentioned.

In the case of Borås, a metropolitan complex in west-central Sweden with a population of about 190,000, locally present industrial units sell a total of 58 percent of their outputs to the larger complexes of Stockholm (36 percent), Göteborg (18 percent), and Malmö (4 percent) (Bylund and Ek, 1974).

In the case of Skellefteå, a northern metropolitan area with a population of only about 85,000, paper and pulp mills and other locally occurring manufacturing facilities make roughly 25 percent of their *domestic* sales to organizational units in Stockholm (Erson, 1974). Approximately another 12 percent of domestic sales terminates in the Eskilstuna metropolitan area (population about 120,000) located just west of the Stockholm complex.

Table 4. Percentage Breakdown of Flows to and from Organizational Units Located in the Malmö Metropolitan Complex, 1970

| | Origin or Destination | | | | | |
| --- | --- | --- | --- | --- | --- | --- |
| Type of Flow | Local (within Malmö) | Stock-holm | Göte-borg | Smaller "Hinterland" Places | Other Smaller Metropolitan Centers, Cities, and Towns | Percentage Total |
| Outputs *sold* by Malmö manufacturing units | 34 | 27 | 9 | 11 | 19 | 100[a] |
| Services *sold* by Malmö business service units | 60 | 10 | 4 | 11 | 15 | 100[a] |
| Physical inputs *purchased* by Malmö manufacturing units | 32 | 12 | 5 | 15 | 35 | 100[a] |
| Business services *Purchased* by Malmö manufacturing units | 66 | 14 | 1 | 3 | 16 | 100[a] |
| All goods and service flows to and from the local units of ten selected Malmö organizatons | 47 | 20 | 7 | 9 | 18 | 100[a] |
| Information exchange of the local units of ten selected Malmö organizations | 45 | 17 | 4 | 8 | 26 | 100 |

Source: Bylund and Ek, 1974.
[a]Percentages based on monetary values.

## CONCLUDING OBSERVATIONS

If Seattle-Tacoma and Malmö are at all representative of metropolitan complexes in advanced economies, then some of the assumptions underlying the model of city-system growth and development outlined above would appear to be valid. In short, evidence for the two metropolitan complexes confirms that:

(1) The most important *nonlocal* linkages are not those between metropolis and "hinterland"—as in central-place theory—but those between large metropolitan complexes; and

(2) The overall pattern of metropolitan interdependence springing from the asymmetrical spatial structure of organizations is complex, both because metropolitan centers of a given size frequently provide job control and other links to nearby and distant larger metropolitan complexes, and because there is an extensive crisscrossing of economic ties between large metropolitan complexes on the one hand, and medium and small-sized metropolitan centers on the other.

The evidence also revealed a perhaps unexpected degree of complex interdependence between large metropolitan centers and smaller cities and towns in the "hinterlands" of other metropolitan centers. In addition, in accord with the model of city-system growth and development, rather limited evidence for Malmö seems to indicate that specialized information flows and goods and service flows follow parallel paths.

Of course, more conclusive statements cannot be made regarding the impact of organizational spatial structures on metropolitan interdependence until job-control statistics and other data are amassed for other metropolitan complexes. However, it is to be recognized that, if anything, the pattern of metropolitan interdependence is probably even more complex than indicated here. For one thing, Seattle-Tacoma has an unusually high percentage of "local" jobs associated with its locally headquartered corporations. Also, despite the tempo of foreign investments and acquisitions maintained by multinational corporations, international linkages have been ignored except for those between the United States and Canada. Moreover, no empirical consideration has been given to the interdependencies fashioned by the divisional headquarters within "polycentric" organizational spatial structures. Interdependencies growing from intraorganizational relationships that do not involve organizationwide or divisional headquarters have also been neglected. Finally, there has been no treatment of the interdependencies emerging either from joint ventures or from relationships between units belonging to large multilocational corporations and units belonging to their *partly owned* and *not fully controlled* subsidiaries.

# REFERENCES

Ahnström, L. *Styrande och ledande verksamhet i Västeuropa–en ekonomisk-geografisk studie*. Stockholm: Ekonomisk Forskningsinstitutet vid Handelshögskolan i Stockholm, 1973.

Alonso, W., and E. Medrich. "Spontaneous Growth Centers in Twentieth Century American Urbanization," in N. M. Hansen, ed., *Growth Centers in Regional Economic Development*. New York: The Free Press, 1972.

Ansoff, H. I. *Corporate Strategy*. New York: McGraw-Hill, 1965.

Armstrong, R. B. *The Office Industry: Patterns of Growth and Location*. Cambridge, Mass.: The M.I.T. Press, 1972.

Berry, B.J.L. *Growth Centers in the American Urban System*. 2 vols. Cambridge, Mass.: Ballinger Publishing Company, 1973.

Beyers, W. B. "On Geographical Properties of Growth Center Linkage Systems," *Economic Geography*, Vol. 50 (1974), pp. 203–218.

Blair, J. M. *Economic Concentration: Structure, Behavior and Public Policy*. New York: Harcourt, Brace & Jovanovich, 1972.

Borchert, J. "America's Changing Metropolitan Regions," *Annals of the Association of American Geographers*, Vol. 62 (1972), pp. 352–373.

Bylund, H. and T. Ek. "Regionala beroendeförhållanden—en studie av näringslivet i Malmö A-region," pp. 489–520, in *Produktionskostnader och regionala produktionssystem: Bilagedel II till Orter i regional samverkan*. Statens offentliga utredningar (SOU) 1974:3. Stockholm: Allmänna Förlaget, 1974.

Chandler, A. D., Jr. *Strategy and Structure*. Cambridge, Mass.: The M.I.T. Press, 1962.

Chapman, K. "Corporate Systems in the United Kingdom Petrochemical Industry," *Annals of the Association of American Geographers*, Vol. 64 (1974), pp. 126–137.

Claval, P. "Le Système urbain et les réseaux d'information," *Revue geographique de Montréal*, Vol. 27 (1973), pp. 5–15.

Dun and Bradstreet. *Million Dollar Directory*. New York: 1960–66, 1974.

Duncan, B., and S. Leiberson. *Metropolis and Region Revisited*. Los Angeles: Sage Publications, 1970.

Dunn, E. S. "A Flow Network Image of Urban Structures," *Urban Studies*, Vol. 7 (1970), pp. 239–258.

Erson, O. "Skellefteåregionen—företag och marknader," pp. 553–578, in *Produktionskostnader och regionala produktionssystem: Bilagedel II till Orter i regional samverkan*. Statens offentliga utredningar (SOU), 1974: 3. Stockholm: Allmänna Förlaget, 1974.

*Fortune*, Vol. 84, No. 5 (May, 1974).

Galbraith, J. K. *Economics and the Public Purpose*. Boston: Houghton Mifflin, 1973.

Goddard, J. B. *Office Linkages and Location: A Study of Communications and Spatial Patterns in Central London*. Progress in Planning, Vol. 1, Part 2, 1973.

Godlund, S. *Näringsliv och styrcentra, produktutveckling och trygghet: Förändringar beträffande struktur, ägande och sysselsättning inom industrin belysta med exempel från Norrköping*. Meddelanden från Göteborgs Universitets Geografiska Institutioner, Series B, No. 25 (1972), with abridged English translation.

———, L. Nordström, K. Godlund, and S. Lorentzon. *Örebro kommun: Utvecklingsmöj-*

*ligheter och handlingsprogram för en bättre struktur.* Göteborg: Regionkonsult AB, 1973 (mimeographed).

Lasuén, J. R. "Multi-regional Economic Development: An Open-system Approach," pp. 169–211, in T. Hägerstrand and A. Kuklinski, eds., *Information Systems for Regional Development—A Seminar.* Lund Studies in Geography, Series B, Human Geography, No. 37, 1971.

———. "Urbanization and Development—The Temporal Interaction between Geographical and Sectoral Clusters," *Urban Studies,* Vol. 10 (1973), pp. 163–188.

Lorsch, J. W., and S. A. Allen III. *Managing Diversity and Interdependence: An Organizational Study of Multidivisional Firms.* Boston: Harvard University Graduate School of Business Administration, Division of Research, 1973.

Market Research Department of *Fortune. 1966 Plant and Product Directory.* 2 vols. New York: Time-Life, Inc., 1966.

Nordström, L. "Mellanregionala beroenden— maktens regionala koncentration," pp. 345– 369, in *Produktionskostnader och regionala produktionssystem: Bilagedel II till Orter i regional samverkan.* Statens offentliga utredningar (SOU), 1974: 3. Stockholm: Allmänna Förlaget, 1974.

Parr, J. B. "Structure and Size in the Urban System of Lösch," *Economic Geography,* Vol. 49 (1973), pp. 185–212.

Parsons, G. F. "The Giant Manufacturing Corporations and Balanced Regional Growth," *Area,* Vol. 4 (1972), pp. 99–103.

Persson, C. *Kontaktarbete och framtida lokaliserings förändringar: Modellstudier med tillämpning på statlig förvaltning.* Meddelanden från Lunds Universitets Geografiska Institution, Avhandlingar 71, 1974.

Pred, A. R. "Large-city Interdependence and the Preelectronic Diffusion of Innovations in the U.S.," *Geographical Analysis,* Vol. 3 (1971), pp. 165–181.

———. "The Growth and Development of Systems of Cities in Advanced Economies," pp. 1–82, in A. R. Pred and G. E. Törnqvist, *Systems of Cities and Information Flows: Two Essays.* Urban Studies in Geography, Series B, Human Geography, No. 38, 1973.

———. *Urban Growth and the Circulation of Information: The United States System of Cities, 1790–1840.* Cambridge, Mass.: Harvard University Press, 1973.

———. *Major Job-providing Organizations and Systems of Cities.* Washington, D.C.: Association of American Geographers, Commission on College Geography, 1974.

———. "Diffusion, Organizational Spatial Structure, and City-system Development," *Economic Geography,* Vol. 51 (1975).

Reid, S. R. *Mergers, Managers and the Economy.* New York: McGraw-Hill, 1960.

Semple, R. K. "Recent Trends in the Spatial Concentration of Corporate Headquarters," *Economic Geography,* Vol. 49 (1973), pp. 309–318.

Simmons, J. W. *Canada As an Urban System: A Conceptual Framework.* University of Toronto Centre for Urban and Community Studies, Research Paper No. 62, 1974 (mimeographed).

Törnqvist, G. E. *Contact Systems and Regional Development.* Lund Studies in Geography, Series B, Human Geography, No. 35, 1970.

———. "Swedish Industry as a Spatial System," 1975, forthcoming.

U.S. Bureau of the Census. *1970 Census of Population: Number of Inhabitants, Final Report PC (1)-A1, United States Summary.* Washington, D.C.: U.S. Government Printing Office, 1971.

Westaway, J. "Contact Potential and the Occupational Structure of the British Urban System 1961–1966: An Empirical Study." *Regional Studies,* Vol. 8 (1974), pp. 57–73.

Williamson, O. E. *Corporate Control and Business Behavior: An Inquiry into the Effects of Organization Form on Enterprise Behavior.* Englewood Cliffs, N.J.: Prentice-Hall, 1970.

Wood, P. A. "Industrial Location and Linkage," *Area,* Vol. 1 (1969), pp. 32–39.

# Innovation Diffusion Within and Between National Urban Systems

POUL OVE PEDERSEN

It is characteristic of the development process in many of the less developed countries that, while new techniques, organizations, and ideas are accepted and adopted with relative ease in the capital cities, they do not spread to the lower levels of the urban hierarchy or to the rural areas. By contrast, investigations in the developed countries indicate that innovations spread rapidly down the urban hierarchy. It is the aim of the first part of this paper to investigate how the process of innovation diffusion functions in a less developed country, namely Chile.

Since the majority of the innovations which diffuse in an underdeveloped country most likely are first introduced by imitation from outside the country, rather than by local invention, the process of international innovation diffusion obviously will be important for the spread of economic development. Studies of international innovation diffusion are thus a logical continuation of studies of national innovation diffusion. The international diffusion process has recently been discussed in terms of economic theory (Blondel, 1966), but empirical studies of the international diffusion process are few. Apart from archeological studies of prehistoric innovation diffusion, the only example known to the author is that by Maddala and Knight (1967). In the second part of this paper, an empirical study of the diffusion of different innovations among the Latin American countries is described. Most diffusion studies agree that the speed of duffusion increases when the interac-

tion grows. The international innovation diffusion process, therefore, assumes special interest in the context of international integration, such as is taking place in Latin America. When realized, this integration will lead to increases and structural changes in the interaction among the Latin American countries and, hence, also to increased speed and structural changes in the innovation diffusion process.

## INNOVATION DIFFUSION IN A NATIONAL URBAN SYSTEM: THE CASE OF CHILE

Katz, Levin and Hamilton (1963) characterized the process of innovation diffusion as "acceptance over time of some specific item, idea or practice by individuals, groups or other adopting units (located in space, and) linked to specific channels of communication, to a social structure and to a given system of values or culture."[1]

No empirical study has yet taken the variability of all these factors into account simultaneously. Instead, different fields of study have emphasized different aspects of the diffusion process. This study concentrates on innovations impinging upon the urban popu-

1. Words in parentheses have been added by this author. Though Katz, Levin, and Hamilton discussed spatial aspects of diffusion to some length, they did not include it explicitly in their definition of innovation diffusion; and, since it is central to the present investigation, it has been added.

From *Geographical Analysis,* vol. 2, no. 3, July 1970, pp. 203–54. Reprinted in abridged form by permission. Copyright © 1970 by the Ohio State University Press.

lation of urbanized or urbanizing countries. It is hoped that first, some of the differences observed between the diffusion processes in countries at different levels of development can be explained, and that second, the interrelationships between the urbanization process and the process of innovation diffusion can be clarified.

## The Innovation Concept in the Context of an Urban System

*The innovation.* In the terminology of this paper an innovation is any new technique, organization, or idea which spreads. The word innovation is often used with an implicit positive evaluation which will be avoided here, with the exception that someone will need to evaluate an innovation positively if it really is to spread. For example, some planners might find the spread of the private automobile a negative innovation, but the people who buy the cars will evaluate the innovation positively. On the other hand, a government which initiates an agrarian reform often evaluates the reform positively, while those whose land will be expropriated as well as those who are to benefit from the reform might object to it.

The spreads of some innovations are limited to certain regions either because, as in the case of mining technology, they are tied to a specific natural resource or because, as in the case of irrigation techniques, they relate to a particular problem which only appears in specific regions. Such resource-oriented, regional-specific innovations will not be discussed here. Instead, we shall concentrate on the diffusion of innovations which are at least potentially acceptable to all or part of the population in any area. This does not mean that the percentage of the population which at any given time has accepted the innovation will be constant over the entire country; it will vary, for instance, with social and economic development, with relative location and with urban size. It is this variation which is the topic of this section of the paper.

*The Adoption unit.* We distinguish also, between two levels of innovations, *household*

and *entrepreneurial.* Household innovations are those which spread among private households or individuals and which might be accepted by all the population or by groups of the population having certain characteristics. Examples include the use of durable consumer goods (refrigerators, televisions, automobiles, etc.), installation of running water in dwellings, or membership in associations or cooperatives.

An entrepreneurial innovation is one which has direct consequences for people other than the adopter and his family. Depending on the type of innovation, the entrepreneur could be, for instance, local government, a committee of citizens, or a private businessman.

Many household innovations have a corresponding entrepreneurial innovation. Membership in a local association, for instance, requires that the association exist; installation of running water in a dwelling requires that a water supply system has been established in the community; and, though the spread of consumer goods in a community is not conditioned by the establishment of a shop for dealing with the particular good, the speed of adoption of the innovation by the households will be increased if a shop is established.

Just as many household innovations can only spread in a town when the corresponding entrepreneurial innovation has been adopted, so an entrepreneurial innovation can only be adopted in many cases when a number of households ready to adopt the related household innovation exists. This, however, is not always the case; new production techniques in already existing firms, or changes in local government administration procedures, need no direct household response in order to be adopted.

Three differences between entrepreneurial and household innovations are worth mentioning:

(1) Entrepreneurial innovation most often involves a higher risk, economically, socially, or politically, than the equivalent household innovation.

(2) While for the household innovation, each new adoption tends to increase the speed of diffusion, entrepreneurial innovation is competitive in the sense that its first adoption

in a town of a size about the threshold level for the innovation may block its further introduction. Only in towns of a size greater than the threshold level may repetitions be expected. The adoption of an entrepreneurial innovation can thus be conceived of as being an adoption by the town and might be called an urban innovation.

(3) With household innovation there is a large random element in the determination of the time and location of the individual adoption because an outsider, even in a remote village, might adopt a household innovation long before the village is ready to accept the innovation. Consequently, in studies of the diffusion of household innovations the date of adoption in a given area has generally been defined as the date at which some given proportion of all potential adoptors in the area has adopted. This procedure is not possible for entrepreneurial innovations which in many communities are only adopted once; and, furthermore, entrepreneurial innovation generally will require acceptance by at least part of the community before it can succeed.

Much of the literature on innovation diffusion has been concerned with diffusion of household innovations or agricultural innovations.[2] Such innovations have often been described as continuous wave phenomena. This analogy is possible partly because many adoptions are involved for each innovation and partly because such innovations most often have been studied as they diffuse from a central city over a continuously populated hinterland.

The entrepreneurial innovation, however, most often is not adopted at all in rural areas and small towns, but rather jumps from town to town in a discontinuous fashion. The wave analogy, therefore, is of doubtful value. This paper will be basically concerned with entrepreneurial innovations.

*Channels of communication and the social structure.* Many sociological diffusion

studies have been of innovation diffusion within communities; and, therefore, the channels of communication and the social structure have been treated as if they are identical (Coleman, Katz, and Menzel, 1957; Menzel, 1960). In this essay, which studies diffusion among towns, the physical communication structure is more important, and the communication channels are stressed in what follows.

The social structure aspect of the communication channels, however, is also important for the diffusion of entrepreneurial innovations in the urban system. First, it will influence the willingness of an urban center to adopt an innovation; that is, it will influence the level of information and persuasion necessary to get a town to adopt. Second, the geographic distribution of the national innovation-adopting elite is likely to be related to the urban hierarchy (for example, through the government beureaucracy and professional organizations with national and regional chapters).

In the model presented below it will be possible only to take the social structure into account implicitly.

*The value system.* This variable in the diffusion process is taken into account by distinguishing between innovation diffusion by spontaneous adoption and that by induced adoption. The model presented is principally concerned with the process of spontaneous adoption; but, on the basis of the model, an attempt is made to draw some conclusions about how diffusion of innovations can be facilitated in countries where the diffusion process does not function without friction.

## Initiation of the Diffusion Process

The first introduction of an innovation in a country can come about either by local invention or by imitation from outside innovation centers. In most of the less developed countries the last possibility is likely to be most frequent. But whatever is the origin, the innovation is likely to occur first in that city which has the highest exchange of ideas, people, and

2. Although agricultural innovation, in a sense, is an entrepreneurial innovation, the adopting unit is the rural household (except where the innovation involves cooperative action). According to the definition used here, it must thus be classified as a household innovation.

products with other cities in the country and with cities in other countries. This city most often will be the national capital; but in some instances large harbor cities or centers of massive immigration, distinct from the capital city, may rank as high as the capital on communication flows with foreign cities. This is clearly illustrated here by the Chilean innovations, of which five out of the seven were introduced first in Santiago and the remaining two were introduced in Valparaiso (Table 1).

In the following sections of the paper, it is assumed that the time and location of the first occurrence of an innovation are given; and on the basis of these, the mechanism by which the innovation spreads over the country is studied.

## Diffusion of Entrepreneurial Innovations: The Case of Chile

Earlier empirical studies such as Bowers (1937), McVoy (1940), Crain (1966), and Berry and Neils (1969), indicate that both urban size and distance from earlier adoptors are important factors in explaining the diffusion of innovations. These two relationships are the basis for the following empirical analysis of the diffusion throughout Chile of a number of entrepreneurial innovations.

*1. Urban size.* Figure 1 shows the relationship between the year of adoption and the size of town at the time of adoption, for the establishment of fire brigades in Chilean towns in different regions. The diagram shows a clear relationship between town-size and year of adoption but it differs from region to region. In the north the diffusion process has been much more rapid than in the other two regions (steeper slope of the line). This might be a result of a greater migration into and between the northern mining towns than is typical for towns in the rest of the country. In the south, on the other hand, much smaller towns adopted the innovation than was true for the rest of the country. This might be due partly to a tradition among German immigrants for solving problems by cooperative action and partly to a greater demand for fire brigades associated with greater frequency of wood construction.

For the diffusion of hospitals, waterworks, and radio stations, the picture is not nearly as clear. There is but little correlation apparent in the scatter diagrams, and no simple regionalization seems possible. If, however, diagrams for each province were shown, much better correlation would be obtained but with different regression lines for each province. The relationship between year of adoption and population size clearly is not a one-to-one relationship.

*2. Distance.* The distance over which an innovation must travel is also important. Table 2 shows that in 70-85% of all cases a town did not adopt before its nearest, larger

Table 1. Time and Location of First Adoption of Innovations

| Innovation* | Year of 1st Adoption | 1st City To Adopt |
|---|---|---|
| Hospitals (*Anuario Estadístico*, 1911, p. 3) | 1543 | Santiago |
| Newspapers | 1812 | Santiago |
| Fire brigades (*Anuario Estadístico*, 1911, p. 156) | 1851 | Valparaiso |
| Waterworks (*Anuario Estadístico*, 1912, pp. 98–99) | 1866 | Santiago |
| Rotary clubs (Ginouves, 1953) | 1923 | Valparaiso |
| Radio Stations | 1925 | Santiago |
| Supermarkets | 1952 | Santiago |

*Data sources given in brackets; otherwise based on unpublished materials.

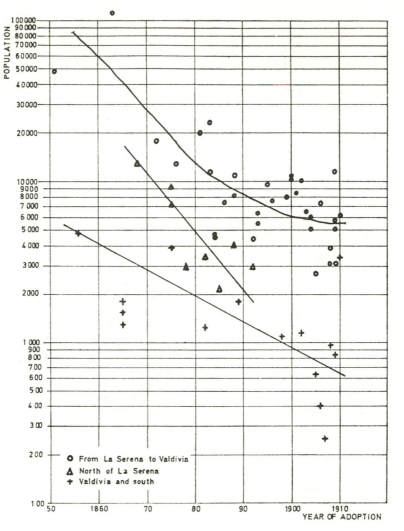

Figure 1. Diffusion of Fire Brigades in Chile (1851-1910).

Table 2. Percent Oases in Which a Town Adopted the Innovation

| Innovation | After Its Nearest Larger Neighbor | Before Its Nearest Larger Neighbor But after the Second-Nearest | Before Its 2 Nearest Larger Neighbors |
|---|---|---|---|
| Hospitals | 79.7 | 13.1 | 7.2 |
| Newspapers | 77.4 | 14.3 | 8.4 |
| Fire brigades | 84.9 | 13.2 | 1.9 |
| Waterworks | 71.7 | 17.9 | 11.4 |

Table 3.  Year of Adoption and Population of Towns for which Santiago Is the Nearest Larger Neighbor

| Town | Year | Pop. | Distance to Santiago (km) | Town | Year | Pop. | Distance to Santiago (km) |
|------|------|------|---------------------------|------|------|------|---------------------------|
| | | Hospitals | | | | Newspaper | |
| La Serena | 1745 | — | 470 | Valparaíso | 1827 | — | 140 |
| Valparaíso | 1772 | — | 140 | Talca | 1844 | — | 260 |
| Talca | 1807 | — | 260 | San Felipe | 1869 | 8,990 | 70 |
| Melipilla | 1841 | — | 67 | San Bernardo | 1895 | 4,160 | 18 |
| San Felipe | 1844 | — | 70 | Melipilla | 1896 | 4,490 | 67 |
| S. José de Maipo | 1879 | 1,250 | 50 | Rancagua | 1914 | 14,010 | 85 |
| Maipu | 1896 | 1,400 | 23 | | | | |
| San Bernardo | 1897 | 4,740 | 18 | | | | |
| | | Fire brigades | | | | Waterworks | |
| Talca | 1872 | 17,620 | 260 | Valparaíso | 1880 | 101,350 | 140 |
| San Felipe | 1883 | 11,300 | 70 | San Bernardo | 1882 | 4,840 | 18 |
| Concepción | 1883 | 23,000 | 525 | Talca | 1883 | 22,250 | 260 |
| San Bernardo | 1903 | 6,490 | 18 | Concepción | 1884 | 23,590 | 525 |
| Rancagua | 1909 | 11,420 | 85 | San Felipe | 1891 | 11,500 | 70 |
| Melipilla | 1910 | 6,260 | 67 | Melipilla | 1904 | 5,770 | 67 |
| | | | | Puente Alto | 1912 | 1,900 | 20 |

neighbor had adopted, and only in a few cases did a town adopt before its two nearest larger neighbors had adopted.

We conclude that there is a strong tendency for a town not to adopt an innovation before one of its nearest, larger neighbors has adopted it, but when two towns have the same nearest neighbor it might not necessarily be the largest which adopts first; often it will be the nearest (Table 3).

*3. The frequency of non-adopters.* Even when an innovation has reached out to all parts of the country and down to fairly small towns, there will still be some towns, however, which have not yet adopted it. The percent of non-adopters tends to decrease with increasing town size (Table 4).

*4. The diffusion time.* Studies have shown that the increase over time in the number of adopters can be described by an S-shaped,

Table 4.  Percent Adopters among Towns of Different Size

| Town Size | Fire Brigades 1910 | | | Newspapers 1885 | | | Newspapers 1930 | | |
|-----------|--------------------|--------------------|-------------|--------------------|--------------------|-------------|--------------------|--------------------|-------------|
| | No. of Adopt | Non-Adopt | % Adopt | No. of Adopt | Non-Adopt | % Adopt | No. of Adopt | Non-Adopt | % Adopt |
| 2–3,000 | 4 | 18 | 18.5 | 4 | 25 | 13.8 | 11 | 31 | 26.2 |
| 3–4,00 | 3 | 10 | 23.1 | 3 | 9 | 25.0 | 6 | 17 | 26.1 |
| 4–5,000 | 5 | 6 | 45.5 | 1 | 6 | 14.3 | 5 | 8 | 35.4 |
| 5–7,000 | 10 | 5 | 66.7 | 3 | 10 | 23.1 | 6 | 7 | 42.4 |
| 7–10000 | 5 | 3 | 62.5 | 1 | 8 | 11.1 | 12 | 4 | 75.0 |
| 10–15,000 | 10 | 1 | 91.0 | 1 | 1 | 50.0 | 9 | 1 | 90.0 |
| 15–30,000 | 6 | 0 | 100 | 4 | 1 | 80.0 | 11 | 1 | 91.6 |
| >30,000 | 7 | 0 | 100 | 2 | 0 | 100 | 9 | 0 | 100 |

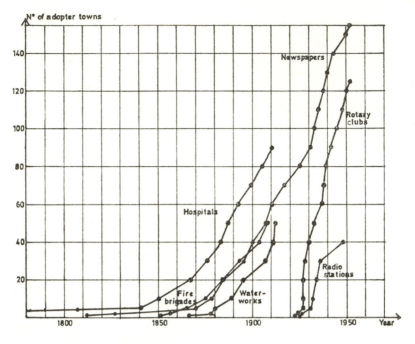

Figure 2. Diffusion Time for Six Innovations.

logistic curve (Bowers, 1937; Griliches, 1957; Hägerstrand, 1953; McVoy, 1940). This implies that the diffusion process is slow in the beginning but then increases in speed as more and more adopters are able to spread information about the innovation. After some time, when most of the potential adopters have adopted the innovation and the market is being saturated, the process slows down again; and complete diffusion may never be achieved.

The diffusion in time of the innovations studied here is shown in Figure 2. The diagram shows that, except for the diffusion of radio stations, none of the processes reached the point of inflexion (or at least not far beyond) within the study period. The diagram also shows that the two innovations initiated last, Rotary clubs and radio stations, spread at a much higher speed than the innovations initiated in the last century. This means that the period of time necessary for an innovation to be adopted by the first N towns has decreased over time.

This decreasing relationship between time of initiation and diffusion time until the Nth town adopts, is shown in Figure 3 for $N = 5$ and $N = 40$. The curves indicate that the diffusion period has decreased over time; and whereas hospitals required 305 years to spread from the first to the tenth town, radio stations were adopted by ten towns only seven years after the first station had been established.*

## Induced Innovation Diffusion

One of the main purposes of studying the spontaneous innovation diffusion process must be to find ways in which the process can be speeded up and guided by limited government action. Those findings of the above

*The mathematical model of innovation and its interaction with the growth of the urban system is omitted from this extract. The interested reader is referred to the original text, pp. 213–236.— Eds.

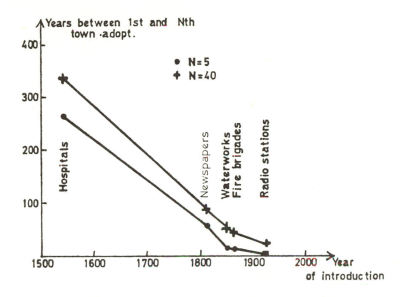

Figure 3. Changes in the Innovation Diffusion Time.

analysis which have relevance for this problem are now summarized.

The innovation diffusion process constitutes the greatest problem where the process is slow. This will be the case when the distance decay is strong, when the rate of population participation is low, where innovators are scarce, when threshold levels are high, or when the urban growth process is slow.

These are the factors which must be altered if the total diffusion time is to decrease. Thus, the action to be taken will be one or more of the following:

(1) Improve the accessibility for information flows of all types by improving transportation and communication. Both where the transportation and communication networks have developed from spontaneous growth and where their development has been due to planned central government action, they have tended to grow in response to the demand, rather than in advance of demand. This means that the largest cities or the closest neighbors will be the first to be connected by the networks. As a consequence, the diffusion of transport technology does not differ greatly from the diffusion of other innovations. Such

a growth of the network in response to, rather than in anticipation of, the demand in most cases probably is the only economically feasible course; but it might not be the one which results in the most rapid innovation diffusion process.

(2) Increase the number of centers for information diffusion by selecting some test towns for immediate government action. The selection of such towns usually seems to follow the general diffusion pattern, i.e., either big towns or towns close to the capital are selected. The reason for this probably is that it is likely to make central government guidance both easier and cheaper. Again, this selection, however, might not be the one which leads to the most rapid diffusion process.

(3) Increase the frequency of potential innovators. This can be done by improving the financial possibilities by high level educational programs or by reducing the risk, for instance, through government guarantees, loans, and tax concessions. In many countries, including Chile, this has been done in the form of industrial development programs for peripheral towns or regions.

(4) Reduce threshold levels by subsidies.

Table 5. Ten Innovation Waves in Latin America

| Country | Universities[1] | | Liberaton from the Spaniards[2] | | Postal Stamps[3] | | Railrds.[4] | | Housing Institu.[5] | | Rotary Clubs[6] | | Lion Clubs[7] | | Developm. Banks[8] | | Atomic Energy Comm.[9] | | TV[10] | |
|---|---|---|---|---|---|---|---|---|---|---|---|---|---|---|---|---|---|---|---|---|
| | Year | Rank | Year | Rank | Year | Rank | Year | Rank | Year | Rank | Year | Rank | Year | Rank | Year | Rank | Year | Rank | Year | Rank |
| Mexico | 1553 | 2.0 | 1821 | 9.0 | 1856 | 4.5 | 1872 | 13.0 | 1925 | 2.0 | 1920 | 4.0 | 1927 | 1.0 | 1934 | 2.0 | 1955 | 2.0 | 1950 | 1.5 |
| Guatemala | 1676 | 7.0 | 1821 | 9.0 | 1871 | 17.0 | 1873 | 14.5 | 1956 | 11.5 | 1925 | 8.0 | 1941 | 5.0 | 1948 | 9.0 | 1966 | 14.0 | 1956 | 7.5 |
| El Salvador | 1841 | 13.0 | 1821 | 9.0 | 1867 | 14.5 | 1851 | 3.0 | 1950 | 7.0 | 1927 | 12.0 | 1942 | 7.0 | 1955 | 16.0 | 1961 | 8.0 | 1956 | 7.5 |
| Honduras | 1847 | 15.0 | 1821 | 9.0 | 1865 | 12.5 | 1853 | 5.0 | 1957 | 13.5 | 1929 | 15.5 | 1942 | 7.0 | 1950 | 10.0 | 1963 | 9.0 | 1959 | 12.5 |
| Nicaragua | 1812 | 11.0 | 1821 | 9.0 | 1862 | 10.5 | 1880 | 17.5 | 1959 | 16.0 | 1929 | 15.5 | 1942 | 7.0 | 1953 | 13.5 | — | 16.5 | 1956 | 7.5 |
| Costa Rica | 1843 | 14.0 | 1821 | 9.0 | 1862 | 10.5 | 1880 | 17.5 | 1954 | 9.5 | 1927 | 12.0 | 1935 | 2.5 | 1952 | 11.5 | 1965 | 12.5 | 1960 | 14.5 |
| Panama | 1935 | 17.0 | 1821 | 9.0 | 1878 | 18.0 | 1850 | 1.0 | 1958 | 15.0 | 1919 | 2.5 | 1935 | 2.5 | 1953 | 13.5 | — | 16.5 | 1959 | 12.5 |
| Colombia | 1573 | 4.0 | 1819 | 5.0 | 1859 | 8.5 | 1857 | 7.5 | 1957 | 13.5 | 1926 | 9.0 | 1936 | 4.0 | 1931 | 1.0 | 1959 | 6.0 | 1954 | 5.0 |
| Venezuela | 1725 | 8.0 | 1823 | 15.0 | 1859 | 8.5 | 1864 | 10.0 | 1928 | 3.0 | 1937 | 17.0 | 1943 | 9.0 | 1946 | 8.0 | — | 16.5 | 1952 | 4.0 |
| Guayana | 1963 | 18.0 | 1966 | 18.0 | 1850 | 2.0 | 1865 | 11.5 | — | 18.0 | — | 18.0 | 1960 | 18.0 | 1954 | 15.0 | — | 16.5 | — | 18.0 |
| Ecuador | 1622 | 5.0 | 1822 | 13.5 | 1865 | 12.5 | 1879 | 16.0 | 1954 | 9.5 | 1927 | 12.0 | 1946 | 11.0 | 1944 | 6.5 | 1964 | 10.0 | 1960 | 14.5 |
| Peru | 1551 | 1.0 | 1824 | 16.0 | 1857 | 6.0 | 1851 | 3.0 | 1946 | 5.5 | 1921 | 5.0 | 1944 | 10.0 | 1936 | 3.0 | 1955 | 2.0 | 1958 | 10.5 |
| Bolivia | 1624 | 6.0 | 1825 | 17.0 | 1867 | 14.5 | 1873 | 14.5 | 1956 | 11.5 | 1927 | 12.0 | 1948 | 12.5 | 1942 | 5.0 | 1960 | 7.0 | 1961 | 16.0 |
| Brazil | 1808 | 10.0 | 1822 | 13.5 | 1843 | 1.0 | 1854 | 6.0 | 1946 | 5.5 | 1922 | 6.0 | 1952 | 15.5 | 1952 | 11.5 | 1956 | 4.5 | 1950 | 1.5 |
| Paraguay | 1890 | 16.0 | 1811 | 3.0 | 1870 | 16.0 | 1859 | 9.0 | 1962 | 17.0 | 1927 | 12.0 | 1952 | 15.5 | 1961 | 17.0 | 1965 | 12.0 | 1966 | 17.0 |
| Uruguay | 1833 | 12.0 | 1808 | 1.0 | 1856 | 4.5 | 1865 | 11.5 | 1937 | 4.0 | 1918 | 1.0 | 1951 | 14.0 | — | 18.0 | 1955 | 2.0 | 1956 | 7.5 |
| Argentina | 1613 | 3.0 | 1810 | 2.0 | 1858 | 7.0 | 1857 | 7.5 | 1886 | 1.0 | 1919 | 2.5 | 1954 | 17.0 | 1944 | 6.5 | 1956 | 4.5 | 1951 | 3.0 |
| Chile | 1738 | 9.0 | 1818 | 4.0 | 1853 | 3.0 | 1851 | 3.0 | 1953 | 8.0 | 1923 | 7.0 | 1948 | 12.5 | 1939 | 4.0 | 1965 | 12.0 | 1958 | 10.5 |
| Year of 1st adopt. | 1551 | | 1808 | | 1843 | | 1850 | | 1886 | | 1918 | | 1927 | | 1931 | | 1955 | | 1950 | |
| Year of 2nd adopt. | 1553 | | 1810 | | 1850 | | 1851 | | 1925 | | 1919 | | 1935 | | 1934 | | 1955 | | 1950 | |
| Diffusion time from 2nd to 17th adopt. | 382 | | 15 | | 21 | | 29 | | 37 | | 18 | | 17 | | 27 | | 10 | | 16 | |

[1] The World of Learning 1968-69.
[2] Kingsbury and Schneider. 1965.
[3] Catalogue de Timbres-Poste, 1959.
[4] Vicuna, 1927.
[5] Berry, 1958.
[6] Rotary Clubs, 1967.
[7] International Lions Club, 1967.
[8] International Bank, 1957.
[9] Atomic Energy Commission.
[10] Browning and Gibbs, 1961.

Introduction of many urban services, for instance, might only be economically feasible in peripheral low income regions if the cost of utilization is lowered by subsidies.

(5) Increase the population participation rate by increasing or redistributing income, by increased action in education and propaganda, or by improving transportation and communication.

(6) Speed up the urban growth process by an active urban development policy.

The above six points indicate that the structural differences between spontaneous and induced innovation diffusion in most cases will be small. While central government action will thus only lead to changes in the diffusion process if it is rigorously planned, it should be much easier to reduce the diffusion time without structural changes other than those inherent in the spontaneous diffusion process.

## INTERNATIONAL INNOVATION DIFFUSION—THE CASE OF LATIN AMERICA

An innovation in this section refers to any new technique, organization, or practice which spreads from country to country. We are interested in the way such innovations spread, i.e., the rank order of the Latin American countries according to the year the innovation was introduced in the country for the first time.

Unfortunately, reliable information about spread, especially of technical innovations, has proved difficult to obtain and is available

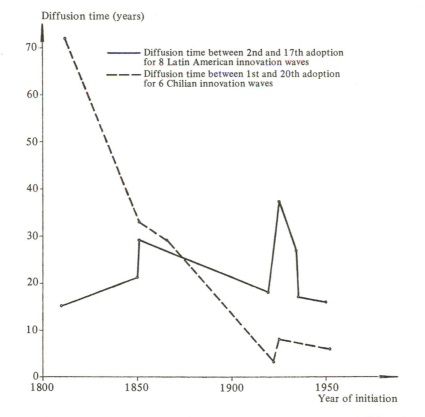

Figure 4. Development of the Innovation Diffusion Time for Latin American and Chilean Innovation Waves.

Table 6. Stable, Random and Actual Innovation Diffusion Processes

| No. of innovations adopted first in that of two neighboring countries which adopted first in 5 or more cases | Distribution of Pairs of Neighboring Countries | | | |
|---|---|---|---|---|
| | Stable process | Random process (binomial) | Actual processes | |
| | | | a* | b† |
| 10 | 29 | 0.06⎫ | 2⎫ | 2⎫ |
| 9 | 0 | 0.57⎬3.17 | 6⎬14 | 4⎬9 |
| 8 | 0 | 2.54⎭ | 6⎭ | 3⎭ |
| 7 | 0 | 6.80 | 7 | 5 |
| 6 | 0 | 11.89 | 6 | 7 |
| 5 | 0 | 7.14 | 2 | 8 |
| No. of pairs of neighboring countries | 29 | 29 | 29 | 29 |
| $\chi^2$ for deviation from random diffusion ($\chi^2_{.01} = 11.3$) | — | — | 43.6 | 13.3 |

*Innovations adopted in two neighboring countries in the same year have been distributed among the two neighbors such that the difference between the number of first-adoptions in the two countries becomes as big as possible.
†Innovations adopted in two neighboring countries in the same year have been distributed among the two neighbors such that the difference between the number of first-adoptions in the two countries becomes as small as possible.

for only 10 innovations, most of them organizational rather than technical (Table 5).

These innovations clearly cannot be claimed to be representative of innovations in Latin America; and though a quantitative analysis has been attempted, the conclusions presented are not comprehensive. With one exception all the innovations studied are urban-oriented and do not require any special natural conditions (resources, climate, etc.) to be adopted, but instead are potentially adoptable in all countries. The exception is the railroads, which in many Latin American countries were built by foreign companies for transporting minerals or other natural resources. Their adoption, therefore, was favored by the existence of these resources.[3]

3. The later factor analysis shows that the railroad is that innovation which deviates most from the common factor pattern created by the ten innovations together. The communality for the railroads' variate is only 0.20 (Table 7).

## Diffusion Time

Except for the universities, which in many cases were established just after colonization, the initiation of the innovation waves studied here covers a period of about 150 years, 1808–1955. This affords an opportunity to see how the diffusion times have changed over this period. The above analysis of innovation diffusion within Chile showed that the diffusion time has decreased steadily over the last 150 years; this is also what would be expected intuitively if innovation diffusion depends on interaction, as is most often assumed. The diffusion times for the international innovation diffusions shown in Table 5 and in Figure 4 do not confirm this pattern, however.

The diffusion times in Figure 4 vary from 10–30 years, but the variation does not seem related to the years of initiation of the diffusion processes. This, of course, may be due to insufficient data. For instance, it could be claimed that the innovations ought to be classified into groups according to different characteristics, and that the diffusion time then would decrease for innovations within each group, but that the picture would be disturbed when all innovations were mixed. The sample of innovations used in the international study, however, does not differ substantially from that which in the national study of Chile suggested a clear relationship between diffusion time and year of initiation.

If it is accepted that the diffusion time for the international innovation diffusions in Latin America does not decrease over time, then the question is how to explain this difference between the national and the international diffusion processes. One explanation might be that the introduction of an innovation in a country most often is due to the national elite, which has had few economic limits to its communication with other countries. This elite has been in frequent and continuing contact with Europe, the United States, and also, although perhaps to a lesser extent, with the other Latin American countries. On the other hand, within Chile the innovations had to diffuse from the national elite in the main city (cities) to a peripherical population for which the economic constraint to communication was serious. Correspondingly, the relative decrease in communication costs which has occurred over the last 150 years has resulted in increasing communication flows and decreasing diffusion times at the national level, but not at the international level.

## The Stability of the Spatial Innovation Diffusion Process

Theoretical as well as empirical diffusion studies indicate that many factors are at work shaping the spatial diffusion process. In fact, so many small unmeasurable factors might well be working that the outcome may appear random. If this were the case there should be no similarity between the diffusion processes for different innovations, and in the case of only two countries there should be a fifty-fifty chance that one country adopts before the other. Considering ten innovations and many pairs of neighboring countries, the distribution of the number of times (out of the ten) one country adopts before the other should follow a binomial distribution. Where the diffusion process is completely given, on the other hand, it would always be the same one out of any pair of neighbors who adopts first.

In this case there are 29 pairs of neighboring countries. The distributions of first adoptions corresponding to actual, random, and stable diffusion processes are shown in Table 6. It is clear from this table that the actual diffusion process is somewhere between the stable and the random processes.

Figure 5. Stable Elements in the Innovation Diffusion Process. (An arrow head in a country indicates that this country in eight or more of the ten innovations studied adopted later or in the same year as did its neighbor in which the arrow originates.)

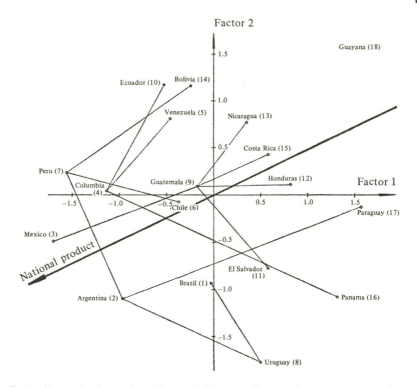

Figure 6. Factor Scores for Factor 1 and Factor 2. Numbers in parentheses represent ranks according to total national product in 1961 real prices (from Rosenstein-Rodan, 1961).

In Figure 5 are shown those pairs of neighbors which exhibit the most stable patterns. It shows that the small countries in South America that are neighbors of much bigger countries are late adopters, for instance, Bolivia, Ecuador, Guayana, and Paraguay. The map, however, also indicates that, except for a few fixed relations, different innovations spread in different ways. If there is any regularity to find in these empirical diffusion patterns, any common factors at work in shaping them, they should be discernible by using factor analysis.

### Factors in the Spatial Innovation Diffusion Processes

The basis for analysis of the common characteristics of the spatial diffusion processes is a matrix of the ranks of the 18 continental countries in Latin America according to year of adoption of each of the ten innovations. The method of analysis is a factor analysis, which extracts common factors (i.e. common diffusion patterns) from the ten empirical diffusion patterns.[4]

The most important common factor accounts for about one-third of the total variance in the ten diffusion processes, while five common factors are needed to account for two-thirds of the total variance. The first three factors, which have eigenvalues greater than one and each of which accounts for more than 10% of the total variance, are the only ones

4. The factor analysis was computed at the Northern European University Computing Center in Copenhagen, and the program used was the BMD 03 M factor analysis program which gives a varimax rotated principal factor solution (*BMD = Biomedical Computer Programs*, 1965).

considered here. Since the interest is with the spatial aspects of innovation diffusion, the factor scores are first analyzed. Study of each of the three factors independently did not result in any clear interpretation, and Figures 6 and 7 were drawn to show the relationship between factors one and two and one and three, respectively. A clearer picture emerges from these diagrams.

First, the hierarchical structure in Figure 6 suggests that factor one corresponds closely to the Spanish colonial administrative structure. Furthest to the left in the diagram are the two original viceroyalities, Mexico and Peru; then come the two vice-royalities which were established in the 18th century, Colombia and Argentina; next come the audiencias, Guatemala, Venezuela, Ecuador, Bolivia, and Chile; and finally, at the right of the

diagram are those countries which in the colonial era had no independent status in the administrative system. Uruguay, which throughout the colonial era was alternately under Argentinian and Brazilian rule, is shown linked to Brazil as well as to Argentina; and Brazil and Guayana, which were outside Spanish jurisdiction, are shown as independent.

Figure 6 also shows that factor 2 in combination with factor 1 gives an axis on which the countries rank much the same as on total national product. That the national product should be an important factor in determining the innovation diffusion process is easily understood because a large national product would make for easier adoption both of those innovations which require a large capital input and of those which require a large na-

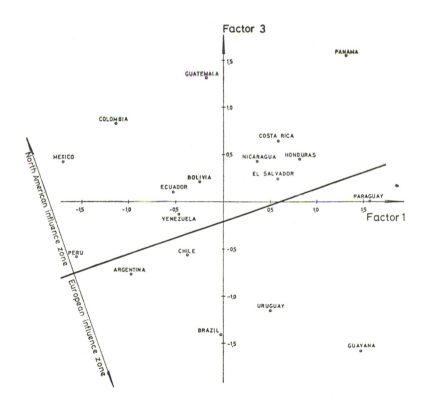

Figure 7. Factor Scores for Factor 1 and Factor 3.

tional market. It is interesting to note that the present-day national product in part is dependent on factor 1, the off colonial administrative system.

In Figure 7, factor 3 and factor 1 create a dichotomous axis on which positive values correspond to the North American influence field (Central America and Colombia) and negative values correspond to the European influence field (Guayana and the southern part of the continent). This factor corresponds to the distance dependence known from national innovation diffusion studies. In the diffusion study of Chile reported earlier, this distance dependence was assumed to result from distance decay in the information diffusion process. In the international case, information about many things spreads along with trade relations and Latin-American trade relations (Figure 8) replicate rather closely the pattern which factor 3 yields, namely that the southern part of the continent trades more with Europe than does the northern, which in

turn trades more with the United States than does the southern part.

It is thus possible to isolate three common factors which have influenced the spatial diffusion pattern for the ten innovations studied. They are the Spanish colonial administrative hierarchy, the total national product, and a dichotomous factor which differentiates between the European and the North American influence fields.

These factors are all acceptable in terms of the general theory behind most innovation diffusion studies, namely, that innovation diffusion is a function of information diffusion. The links in the colonial administrative hierarchy were channels of communication, and these probably did not disappear with the Spanish administration, though their importance decreased. A high national product generally will favor the spread of mass medias and will make the economic constraint to innovation adoption less important. Finally, the European-North American influence field

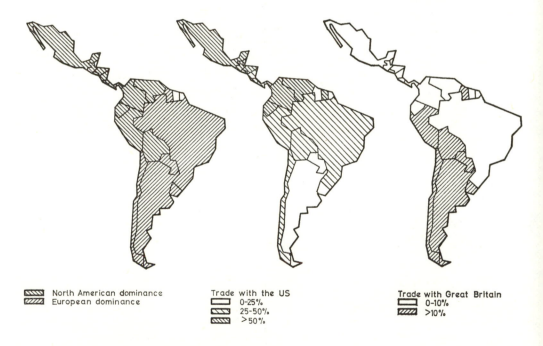

North American dominance
European dominance

Trade with the US
0-25%
25-50%
>50%

Trade with Great Britain
0-10%
>10%

Figure 8. Map on left shows European and North American Dominance fields according to Factor 3. The other two maps show Latin American foreign trade patterns (from Kingsbury and Schneider, 1965).

reflects the trade pattern and the interchange of information which occurs along with the trade.

## Past Changes in the Innovation Diffusion Processes

The innovation diffusion processes clearly have not been stable over the last two to three hundred years. The three common factors isolated from the ten innovation waves probably represent some average of what they actually have been at any particular points in this time span. For instance, in interpreting the graph of factors 1 and 2, the correlations with the 1961 national product were noted. Clearly, they should also have been correlated with some average of the national product over maybe 150 years. Similarly, it is to be expected that the importance of the factors has changed over time. It is unlikely that the Spanish administrative hierarchy is now as important for innovation diffusion as it was in colonial times. Again, it is very unlikely that the European-North American dominance fields became of great importance before very late in the colonial time, and after the liberation from the Spanish. When they did become important, they most likely reflected an initial orientation towards Europe and only later, when the world invention center moved from London to New York, did they change so as to emphasize the United States as the center of invention. Finally, it is probable that the second factor, national product, has been of increasing importance in recent years as scale and agglomeration economics and increased specialization have become more important.

This hypothesis about the changing importance of the factors should be verifiable by observing how factor weights for the innovations have changed from the earliest to the newest innovations (Table 7). Though the ten cases studied here are too few to allow for any firm conclusions, it is comforting that the data seem to support the hypothesis.

The colonial administrative hierarchy is important in explaining the spread of universities, the only one of the ten innovations which actually spread in colonial times. This factor also helps explain the spread of the development banks, which is less easily understood.

Factor 3, the European-North American influence field, explains the spread of postal stamps and Lions clubs. The first of these innovations spread in the middle of the 19th century and was European in origin, while the Lions clubs, which spread in this century, have a United States origin.

The total national product dimension, suggested by factors 1 and 2, explains the spread of three innovations—housing institutions, television, and atomic energy commissions—all of which are rather recent innovations. The remaining three innovations, liberation from the Spaniards, railroads, and Rotary clubs, are dominated by factor 2 alone, which could not be interpreted except in combination with factor 1.

## Future Changes in the Innovation Diffusion Processes

Assuming that the above hypothesis about the historical change of the factors in innovation diffusion holds true, the next question is how can the factors be expected to change in the future? The first of the factors, the colonial administrative hierarchy, is likely to disappear rapidly, if it has not done so already. The third factor, accessibility to the two world invention centers, has in recent years probably been biased more towards the United States. The increasing role of the United States in Latin America has been supported by the shift in emphasis from maritime shipping to air transport. For instance, the sail-route from London to Buenos Aires is only 8% longer than that from New York, while the air route from London is 32% longer than that from New York. These changes in accessibility are likely to result in greater disadvantages to the southern parts of the continent, which might be one of the reasons for the economic difficulties which both Argentina and Uruguay now seem to have.

When the Latin American common market becomes a reality, the second factor, total

Table 7. Factor Weights and Communalities

| Innovation | Year of 1st Adoption | Factor Weights | | | Most Important Factor | Communalities |
|---|---|---|---|---|---|---|
| | | Factor 1 | Factor 2 | Factor 3 | | |
| Universities | 1551 | 0.96 | −0.02 | −0.00 | Colonial Administr. | 0.91 |
| Liberation from the Spaniards | 1808 | −0.06 | 0.60 | −0.10 | ? | 0.38 |
| Postal stamps stamps | 1843 | 0.34 | 0.08 | 0.69 | From Europe | 0.60 |
| Railroads | 1850 | −0.03 | 0.44 | 0.09 | ? | 0.20 |
| Housing institutions | 1886 | 0.65 | 0.40 | 0.27 | National Product | 0.65 |
| Rotary clubs | 1918 | 0.36 | 0.71 | 0.03 | ? | 0.64 |
| Lion clubs | 1927 | 0.19 | 0.03 | −0.73 | From N. America | 0.57 |
| Development banks | 1931 | 0.85 | −0.22 | −0.14 | Colonial Administr. | 0.79 |
| Atomic energy commissions | 1955 | 0.57 | 0.43 | 0.28 | National Product | 0.59 |
| Television | 1950 | 0.59 | 0.46 | 0.05 | National Product | 0.56 |

national product, should decrease in importance. In this situation, international diffusion processes should approach the same structure which is found for national diffusion processes. This means that total national product as a determinant of the diffusion process is likely to be replaced by urban size and market potential. Such a change is likely to result in greater advantages for the areas in the Latin American core region stretching along the Atlantic coast from Rio de Janeiro to Buenos Aires. The creation of a Latin American common market thus might give back to Uruguay and Argentina some of what they lost when the world center moved from London to New York and maritime shipping was replaced for many purposes by air transport.

## REFERENCES

*Anuario Estadístico*, Vol. II. Beneficencia, Medicina e Higiene. Chile, 1911.

*Anuario Estadístico*, Vol. II. Higiene, Medicina y Beneficencia. Chile, 1912.

Atomic Energy Commissions. Unpublished materials, n.d.

Bell, G. "Change in City Size Distribution in Israel," *Ekistics,* 13 (1956), 98.

Berry, B.J.L. "City Size Distributions and Economic Development," *Economic Development and Cultural Change,* 9 (1958), 573–88.

_____. and E. Neils. "Location, Size and Shape of Cities as Influenced by Environmental Factors: The Urban Environment Writ Large," *The Quality of the Urban Environment*. Edited by H. S. Perloff. Baltimore: Resources for the Future, 1969.

Blondel, D. "Transmission International des Innovationes," *Revue Economic,* 17 (1966).

*BMD-Biomedical Computer Programs*. Los Angeles: Health Science Computing Facility, U.C.L.A. School of Medicine (1965).

Bowers, R. V. "The Direction of Intra-Societal Diffusion," *American Sociological Review,* 2 (1937), 826–36.

Browning, H. L. and J. P. Gibbs. "Some Measures of Demographic and Spatial Relationships among Cities," *Urban Research Methods*. Edited by J. P. Gibbs. Princeton, N.J.: D. Van Nostrand Co., 1961.

*Catalogue de Timbres-Poste*. Soizante-Troisième

Année, Tome III. Outre-Mer. Paris: Yvert y Tellier, 1959.

Coleman, J., E. Katz, and H. Menzel. "The Diffusion of an Innovation among Physicians," *Sociometry,* 20 (1957), 253–70.

Crain, R. L. "Fluoridation: The Diffusion of an Innovation Among Cities," *Social Forces,* 44 (1966), 467–76.

*Estadistica Chilena,* 17 (1944), 52–54.

Friedmann, J.R.P. "Economic Growth and Urban Structure in Venezuela," *Cuadernos de la Sociedad Venezolana de Planificación.* Special Issue, 1963.

Ginouves, E. G. *Treinta Años de Rotarismo en Chile.* Santiago, 1953.

Griliches, Z. "Hybrid Corn: Explorations in the Economics of Technological Change," *Econometrica,* 25 (1957), 501–22.

Hägerstrand, T. *Innovationsförloppet fur Korologisk Synspunkt,* Lund: Gleerup, 1953.

International Bank for Reconstruction and Development. *Report No. TA 5,* 1957.

International Lions Club. *Annual Report,* 1967.

Isard, W. "Gravity, Potential and Spatial Interaction Models," *Methods of Regional Analysis: An Introduction to Regional Science.* Edited by W. Isard. New York: John Wiley & Sons, 1960.

Katz, E., M. L. Levin, and H. Hamilton. "Traditions of Research in the Diffusion of Innovations." *American Sociological Review,* 28 (1963), 237–52.

Kingsbury, R. C. and R. M. Schneider. *An Atlas of Latin American Affairs.* New York: Frederick Praeger, 1965.

Koth, M. N., J. A. Silva, and A.G.H. Dietz. *Housing in Latin America.* Cambridge, Mass.: Department of Civil Engineering, M.I.T., 1964.

Lasuen, J. R., A. Lorca and J. Oria. "City-Size Distribution and Economic Growth," *Ekistics,* 24 (1967), 221–26.

———. *Urbanization Hypothesis and Spain's Cities System Evolution.* P. 168.

Mcvoy, E. C. "Patterns of Diffusion in the United States," *American Sociological Review,* 5 (1940), 219–27.

Maddala, G. S. and P. T. Knight. "International Diffusion of Technical Change—A Case Study of the Oxygen Steel Making Process," *The Economic Journal,* 77 (1967), 531–58.

Menzel, H. "Innovation, Integration and Marginality," *American Sociological Review,* 25 (1960), 704–13.

Morrill, R. L. "Waves of Spatial Diffusion," *Journal of Regional Science,* 18 (1968), 1–18.

Moore, F. T. "A Note on City-Size Distributions," *Economic Development and Cultural Change,* 7 (1959), 465–66.

Olsson, G. *Distance and Human Interaction.* Philadelphia: Regional Science Research Institute, 1965.

Pred, A. R. *Spatial Dynamics of U.S. Urban-Industrial Growth, 1800–1914.* Cambridge, Mass.: The MIT Press, 1966.

Rosenstein-Rodan, P. N. "International Aid for Underdeveloped Countries," *The Review of Economics and Statistics,* 43 (1961), 107–38.

Rotary Clubs. *Annual Report.* 1967.

Ruiz-Tagle, C. H. *Concentratión de Población y Desarrollo Económico, el Caso Chileno.* Santiago: Instituto de Economia, Universidad de Chile, 1966.

Stewart, C. T. Jr. "The Size and Spacing of Cities," *Geographical Review,* 48 (1958), 222–45.

*The South American Handbook.* London: Trade and Travel Publications Ltd., 1969.

*The World of Learning 1968–69.* 19th Ed. London: Europa Publications Ltd.

UNESCO. *World Communications. Press, Radio, Television and Film.* 1964.

Vicuna, S. M. *Politica Ferroviaria de la America.* Santiago: Imprenta Universitaria, 1927. P. 18.

Zipf, G. K. *Human Behavior and the Principle of Least Effort.* Cambridge, Mass.: Addison-Wesley Press, 1949.

# The Spatial Organization of Power in the Development of Urban Systems

JOHN FRIEDMANN

## Power, Exchange, and Spatial Integration

The study of urban systems in the context of national development is a relatively recent interest. Research has converged on two central questions: what variables account for the growth and development of urban systems? And, how is the growth and development of urban systems related to the more encompassing processes of national development? By "development of urban systems" I mean the structural growth of urban settlement measured by population and the volume of economic activities. "National development," on the other hand, is used here as a shorthand expression for the structural transformation of a national economy to industrialism. Although these questions are clearly not the only ones deserving consideration, they have so far received most of the attention.

The linkages between urban and national development are still inadequately understood. It has nevertheless become clear that their study must employ an explicit spatial framework for analysis. The emergence of modern industrial enclaves within the matrix of an agrarian economy has given rise to dramatic shifts in population and employment and has accelerated urbanization. At the same time, urbanization seems to have been generating its own dynamics, in partial autonomy of the development of modern industry. These complex changes, occurring over

the vastness of a national territory, have decisively affected the possibilities of national integration, by demanding new political loyalties, creating new patterns of transportation, giving birth to new social classes and elites, introducing new sets of "modernizing" values, and differentially affecting the well-being and life chances of every member of the population according not only to who he was but also where he lived.

Regarded in this perspective, the study of urban systems has become the study of national development in a spatial dimension. A key question that may, therefore, be put is how the development of an urban system will affect the character and evolution of spatial integration measured by political institutions, transactions, and social justice.[1]

Students of urbanization have tended to explore economic explanations, such as the distribution of natural resources, the location of transport routes, the organization of markets, and economies of scale and agglomeration. With but rare exception, they have ne-

1. Little agreement exists on what constitutes spatial integration. The term has come into recent usage by geographers who tend to use it in the sense of connectivity and who are likely to measure integration by functional linkages or transactions between places. This usage has much in common with that of Karl Deutsch and his associates. Political scientists have had a more long-standing concern with integration, particularly at the level of international relations. Current research has been brought together in a book edited by Lindberg and Scheingold (1971). For present purposes, the chapters by Ernst B. Haas and Fred M. Hayward are especially useful.

Published by permission of Transaction, Inc. from *Comparative Urban Research*, vol. 1, no. 2. Copyright © 1972 by Transaction, Inc.

glected political explanations and, more specifically, explanations given in terms of the spatial distribution of power.[2] The purpose of this paper is to suggest how the analysis of power relations in a national society may contribute to our understanding of the ways in which urban systems evolve. Exploratory in its intentions, it claims neither to give final answers nor to exhaust the range of possible insights. It will be deemed successful, should it persuade the reader that the spatial distribution of power is a theoretically significant variable in this context, capable of systematic empirical study.

The concept of *power* is one of the most elusive ones in the social sciences. Here, it will refer to the ability of organizational and institutional actors, located in geographic space, to mobilize and allocate resources (manpower, capital, and information) and intentially to structure the decision-field of others (i.e., to constrain the decisions of others to certain policies, rules, and commands). Both governmental and economic power will be considered. Both kinds of power, I will assume, have the capacity to influence the location decisions of firms and households, the quantity, location, and application of resources, and the flow of innovations. By acting on these variables and, in turn, by being acted upon by them, the spatial distribution of power influences the growth and development of urban systems and, at a higher level of synthesis, also the spatial patterns of integration of a national society.

Like capital, power refers to a stock of resources rather than to a flow of these resources in use. It will consequently be distributed either *symmetrically* (referring to the capacities of actors that are roughly equal with respect to a common decision area) or *asymmetrically*. The uses of power, on the other hand, involve exchange relations or transactions which may be either *reciprocal* (regarded as bringing roughly equal net-benefits to the actors involved) or *non-*

*reciprocal*. These distinctions allow us to construct a two-by-two matrix of power and exchange in urban systems (Fig. 1).[3] By shifting the argument to a consideration of urban systems, we are abstracting from the particular relations of power and exchange among actors distributed over the whole of a spatially integrated subsystem of society (a city) or an integrated system of cities.[4] The matrix, in fact, is intended to throw into relief the major forms of spatial integration across such systems.

According to this matrix, urban systems in Quadrants 1 and 2 are integrated on a basis of a rough equivalence of power; in Quadrants 3 and 4, they are integrated on a basis of inequality or dependence with respect to the urban system in Quadrant 1. Some homely analogies may help to clarify these relationships.

Under 1 (symmetry *cum* reciprocity), relations are like those between friends: neither dominates the other and the exchange between them will be in balance. Moreover, the rules governing their conduct with respect to each other are accepted as morally right: the costs and benefits of transactions between them are not closely calculated. This relationship is typical of actors within core regions comprising one or several rapidly growing cities that display strong and complexly interwoven patterns of transaction. Where several cities are so related, the form of the urban system will tend to be log-normal. Moreover, the laws and procedural rules under which transactions occur will not generally be open to challenge; their authority will be accepted as morally legitimate.

Under 2 (symmetry *cum* non-reciprocity), relations are like those between the owners of competing business firms: each transaction is separately negotiated in the hope of striking a bargain, so that commitments made in one period are not necessarily considered binding

---

2. See, for instance, Horowitz (1967) and Chapter 5 in Friedman (1972b).

3. The theoretical foundation for this matrix is in part derived from Blau (1964).
4. The systems approach to the study of cities was first formalized by Berry (1964) in his justly famous article, "Cities as Systems Within Systems of Cities."

| Power relations | Exchange relations | |
|---|---|---|
| | Reciprocal | Non-reciprocal |
| Symmetrical | [1]Fully integrated urban system: moral authority predominates | [2]Competitive urban system integrated on a basis of limited liability: utilitarian power predominates |
| Asymmetrical | [3]Active periphery of urban system integrated on a basis of protective dependency: utilitarian power predominates | [4]Passive periphery of urban system integrated on a basis of submissive dependence: coercive power predominates |

Figure 1. A Model of Power and Exchange Relations in Urban Systems.

on decisions in subsequent periods. Although each separate transaction may end up being reciprocal, it will be so to only a limited extent; the ultimate intention of each actor is to gain superiority over his competitor. This would be the case of a loose federation of states each having its own integrated urban system, as in Yugoslavia, where the conditions of every inter-system transaction may themselves become the object of intensive bargaining among would-be equals, with the goods offered in exchange serving as the principal counters in negotiation.

Under 3 (asymmetry *cum* reciprocity), relations are like those between superiors and subordinates in bureaucratic organizations: each stands in need of the other, but for quite different reasons. The former require subordinates to accomplish their intentions, but also to rise in general esteem and power, while the latter need the protective benevolence of their superiors and the guarantee of a job. With respect to the organization controlled by their superiors, subordinates have a contractual relationship that may be renegotiated from time to time, but whose legitimacy is generally not at issue. This is the situation typical of many border provinces, such as Magallanes and Tarapacá in Chile which use their exposed position vis-a-vis Argentina, on the one hand, and Peru and

Bolivia, on the other (an always threatened shift from 3 to 2), in bargaining for increased autonomy and economic benefits. (The relations of the Commonwealth of Puerto Rico to the United States is a similar instance; here the threat of national independence serves to strengthen the bargaining position of the Commonwealth.) Active peripheries are typically striving to build up one or more growth centers as core regions subordinate to the urban system in Quadrant 1. They do so in the hope—however much in the future—of ultimately being absorbed into the fully integrated core region itself.

Finally, under 4 (asymmetry *cum* non-reciprocity), relations are like those between master and slave: the master dominates his slave who, at least outwardly, gives evidence of properly submissive behavior but whose labors on behalf of his master are poorly rewarded. Occasional rebellion on the slave's part may invoke the full repressive power of the master. This is the case of regions under a regime of internal colonization (such as Bangladesh and many other backward parts of developing nations) which have few cities of any size and whose domination by the core region in Quadrant 1 gives rise to an urban system characterized by a pronounced condition of primacy. The latent capacity for rebellion by the passive periphery may induce the dominant interests in Quadrant 1 to invest heavily in the region and so to shift it eventually to Quadrant 3. Indeed, such measures may occasionally be taken for purely ideological reasons. On the other hand, the failure to invoke coercive power may result in little more than spreading anarchy without compensating economic benefit. This may be illustrated with reference to the apparent collapse of the agricultural system in Chile's southern provinces or the continued agitation of the extreme left-wing revolutionaries centered in the city of Concepción. Passive peripheries no longer fully dominated by the core in Quadrant 1 may come within the area of influence of the competing system in 2. They have little strength of their own to resist such advances, and their original oppressor may be equally incapacitated.

In the following four sections,* some of these relations of power and exchange in urban systems will be further analyzed. First, I shall try to show how the spatial distribution of governmental power influences the location decisions of entrepreneurs during the early phases of industrialization and how the growing interpenetration of governmental and private economic institutions channels the subsequent location decisions of individuals and households to locations of central power in excess of objective opportunities for productive employment. The resulting polarized pattern of urbanization tends to be self-perpetuating, whereas the eventual decentralization of productive activities into the passive periphery of major core regions tends to leave essential relations of power virtually unchanged.

The second example relates to the diffusion of innovations through the urban system. I will be concerned only with entrepreneurial innovations whose successful adoption translates into a relative increase in economic power to exploit specific resources in the environment. The diffusion of innovations will be considered in both space and time. The spatial diffusion of entrepreneurial innova-

tions tends to be hierarchical, leading to a steadily increasing concentration of power in the largest cities of the urban hierarchy, while the rate of diffusion, at least initially, gives special advantage to early over late adopters. The resulting growth pattern of cities tends to be allometric, implying invariant ratios in the rates of growth among individual urban units. Passive peripheries are thus "condemned" to a quasi-permanent condition of submissive dependence, though the active portions of the periphery may be able successfully to negotiate for growing autonomy in development decisions.

The third illustration concerns primarily the conflict patterns between competing economic and political elites, where the former are ethnically and/or culturally distinct from the latter and have primarily an urban base, while the latter's base of power tends to be in rural areas. Several options for resolving conflicting interests will be discussed, including cooptation, accommodation, open hostility, the creation of regional protectorates, and federative solutions, each of which will have different outcomes for the development of the relevant urban systems.

No effort will be made to synthesize these approaches to the study of power relations in urban systems. The paradigm presented in this section is intended to serve primarily as a source of hypotheses for testing in empirical settings. For this reason, too, I shall make no effort to append a section on policy options. At this stage in our knowledge, such an exercise would be fairly gratuitous. The only firm conclusion we may draw is that the process of national development and spatial integration is an eminently political one, involving fundamental relations of power and exchange and the resolution of resulting conflicts. Planning which fails to recognize this basic truth and proceeds as though the spatial allocation of resources were merely an exercise in applied rationality is bound to be disappointed in the results.[5]

*The fourth section, the empirical study of Chile, has been deleted from this reprinting—Eds.

5. The scientific bases for prescriptive policies of urban development are still weak. But even if they were stronger, it is unlikely that they would provide unambituous conclusions for

## Economic Location and the Spatial Distribution of Power

Economic location theory has traditionally addressed the question of how the location decisions of individual firms are affected by spatial variations in the costs of production and distribution. This emphasis reflects in part the observations of location theorists in industrially mature economies. In countries of incipient or early industrialization, however, non-economic influences appear to weigh more heavily in location decisions than considerations of relative cost. In these countries, *the choice of a location tends to be strongly influenced by a desire of management to gain direct access to the relevant centers of governmental power.*

In the following, I shall assume an industrializing country of moderate size whose government is unitary and whose population is culturally homogeneous. Subsequently, I shall relax this assumption, but for now it will serve as a necessary constraint. In such a country, economic enterprise is exceedingly dependent on the central bureaucracy and the corridors of legislative power. Licenses to import machinery must be secured; special subsidies and other favors are sought; a complex system of legislation pertaining to the conduct of business must be learned; and contributions of public capital and credit are expected. At the same time, economic interrelationships are relatively weak: an inter-industry matrix would show many empty boxes.

In themselves, these conditions would not prescribe a central location. They are reinforced by additional considerations that make the creation or survival of new enterprise in provincial districts highly improbable. Among them are (a) a still rudimentary system of transport and communication, (b) the great importance attached to personal, face-to-face relations in the conduct of business, (c) a high degree of bureaucratic centralism,

and (d) a superior infrastructure of economic and social facilities in the national capital, itself a reflection and symbol of accumulated (and steadily accumulating) power.

The resulting symbiosis between economic and governmental organizations creates a situation that consistently favors the nation's capital in subsequent business locations, though economic reasons, such as access to markets, undoubtedly contribute. Politicians, bureaucrats, and businessmen mingle in exclusive social clubs and the city's top restaurants, send their children to private schools (or the national university), and form tight social networks of their own. From this central location, an essentially passive periphery is organized into administrative and market areas following the principal routes of transport. Capital resources and surplus agricultural labor come to be withdrawn from these areas at an accelerating pace, adding to the reservoir of economic power in the center. In consequence, the urban pattern changes from one of low-level equilibrium (many small, equally-sized urban places) to one of growing primacy.[6]

With continuing development, however, certain changes in this spatial pattern may occur. Growing markets, the discovery of new natural resources, and a gradually improving system of transport and communications may render middle-sized cities in the periphery more attractive as possible business locations, a tendency that may be actively encouraged by explicit governmental policies for regional development. These changing circumstances, together with the growing organizational complexity of enterprise, make possible the physical separation of management from production units. With their vital decision functions thus removed, production units are released to locate according to economic criteria, while management components continue to be drawn to the center of

---

optimal courses of action. A brilliant review of the current state of knowledge in urban systems analysis, from a perspective of public policy, is Richardson (1972).

6. Much controversy has raged over the issue of whether the size distributions of cities is anything but an empirical curiosity. A great deal has been written specifically about the form of rank-size distributions and whether these are in any way related to conditions of economic development and integration. See Berry (1971).

governmental power. Even so, it is generally provincial administrative centers that are favored in the location of production units to facilitate the symbiotic decision process that governs the economic life of the nation.

Empirical evidence for this evolving pattern comes from a variety of country settings. For Latin America, the historian Richard M. Morse is quite emphatic. He writes:

In Latin America, it seems important that a city be a patrimonial center if it is to serve as a growth pole for economic development. Brasilia is already the classic case for a modern frontier zone. Or, if a capital is not actually transferred to a frontier, the central power may spin off an outlying city under its direct support and tutelage, as in the case of Ciudad Guayana. Without denying the regional economic and ecological justifications for this city, it is probably accurate to say that its ultimate legitimation derives from a process of patrimonial schizogenesis. Or again, if planners speak of decentralizing economic functions from a central corridor not to a frontier but to existing peripheral cities, it is usually implied that provincial capitals will be the beneficiaries. Thus it is no accident that the flourishing second-echelon growth centers (Monterrey, Guadalajara Cali, Medellín, Córdoba, Pôrto Alegre, Curitiba) are so frequently regional political capitals. When this is not the case, as with Chimbote, Peru, the city may face enormous obstacles in developing urban infrastructure for economic activity because of its weak political leverage (1971:194).

The second example refers to the Soviet Union and is reported by Harris.

The importance of administrative and related functions is expressed in the relatively rapid growth of *oblast* centers. In about 60 percent of the *oblasts,* the center grew more rapidly than other urban units within their boundaries (1971:360).

The third example comes from Riddell's study of the spatial dynamics of modernization in Sierra Leone.

Thus it is evident that the process of modernization, as summarized by the component analysis, is dominated and directed by the network and the (urban-administrative) hierarchy, which together define the spatial fabric of the country (1970:90–93).

The fourth example stems from Brazil, a country that has moved beyond the first thresholds of industrailization. The concentration of modern business enterprise in Brazil was initially confined to the two principal centers of economic power: Rio de Janeiro and São Paulo. By the time the political capital of the nation was shifted to Brasília in the latter part of the 1960's, industrialization had already established a powerful base in these two cities and, to a much smaller extent, in several of the more important state capitals (Belo Horizonte, Pôrto Alegre). Because economic power had now become more important than political power, the physical move of governmental functions to Brasília did not entail a similarly massive shift of corporate headquarters to the planalto of Goiás, though it did much to stimulate road building activity and cattle raising in the interior. By the same token, intensive government efforts to industrialize the traditionally backward regions in the North and Northeast of the country accomplished primarily the move of production units to these regions but failed to attract units of corporate management. With management remaining in the older centers, and attracting related business services, the "decapitated" production units in the periphery found themselves dependent on extra-territorial decisions. Business profits, in particular, were transferred to the "center" for reallocation.

The evidence for the pattern described is impressive. While political and economic decision-making power remain concentrated in the national capital, subsidiary growth centers spring up on the periphery, frequently paralleling the urban-administrative hierarchy. This process tends to induce a gradual filling out of the rank-size distribution of cities by encouraging the growth of intermediate urban centers. As a result, certain portions of the passive periphery may be activated sufficiently to bargain with central authorities for greater autonomy (e.g., the Northeast of Brazil). To the extent they are successful, the dependency relations of the remaining periphery may increasingly come to focus on these subsidiary, provincial centers.[7]

If we carry the analysis still further to include advanced industrial and post-industrial societies, the earlier pattern, though in a highly attenuated form, may still be discerned.[8] By this time, the extreme dependency of business on governmental power may have waned relative to the rapidly growing requirements for inter-industry contacts. Both market and supply areas will have become more diffused, and the transport and communications system will have made the relevant economic space more accessible from a larger number of central locations. Parts of the formerly active periphery may by now be effectively integrated into the principal core areas of the nation. Despite these new developments, however, certain nodal cities may still stand out as "control centers," experiencing rapid growth, even though the initial close linkage between centers of governmental power and business location will have been lessened.[9] The urban system will now tend toward a log-normal form in the distribution of its centers, and the passive periphery will be reduced to vestigial proportions.[10]

The foregoing description of the evolution of a spatial system is, of course, to some extent idealized. Small countries with only one or two major cities, very large countries such as the USSR, China, and India, countries with a federal structure of government, and countries with a cultural heterogeneous

and regionalized population may follow a different sequence of events. In actively federal systems, for example, central power will, to some degree, be shared so that several governmental centers may simultaneously compete for industry. By the same token, regions having politically powerful minorities may gain certain privileges, such as greater decision autonomy, sooner than would be predicted by the model. In these situations, the "idealized" spatial pattern may be distorted for the nation as a whole, though the pattern is likely to be replicated at the regional level.[11] Furthermore, once they are established, spatial patterns of urbanization tend to perpetuate themselves, casting a long shadow into the future.[12] The initial distribution of governmental power within a country will therefore tend to guide the subsequent evolution of the space economy.

## The Spatial Diffusion of Innovations in the Development of Urban Systems

Studies of the spatial diffusion of innovations have only recently begun to turn from an exclusive concern with questions relating to geographic theory to broader issues of socioeconomic development. These newer studies strongly suggest the possibility of interpreting the spatial dimensions of all facets of development, including urbanization, from a perspective of innovation diffusion. Although a parsimonious theory of the observed behavior is still some time away, its major contours are beginning to be seen.[13] An im-

7. Success in bargaining may depend on the strength of a number of variables, including the size of region, the ethnic/cultural composition of the region's population compared with that of core elites, the relative location of the region in terms of distance from the core and proximity to international frontiers, the unitary or federal structure of the government, and political finesse.

8. The most impressive evidence comes from a 1970 Swedish study by Törnqvist. For the United States, a statistical study of non-production personnel in manufacturing similarly suggests that locational separation between managerial and production functions exists, and that the former tend to be found in the larger, more rapidly growing metropolitan areas. See Uyehara (1972).

9. Empirical evidence supporting a concept of nodal city is found in Stanback and Knight (1970).

10. I am assuming a strong connection—still to be demonstrated mathematically—between Berry's model of the evolution of city size distributions and Williamson's model of the evolution of regional inequalities of income (1965: 3–45).

11. For India, Berry has found four core regions of approximately equal influence and through which India's space economy appears to be organized. They are based, respectively, on Bombay, Delhi, Calcutta, and Madras. See Figure 3 in Berry (1971:121).

12. The strongest case, both theoretically and empirically, for the stability of the spatial and size distributions of urban systems comes from Lasuén (1971). His findings are supported for the People's Republic of China by Wu (1967).

13. The starting point for the study of the spatial diffusion of innovations is Hägerstrand (1967). (Original in Swedish, 1953.) A comprehensive annotated bibliography of spatial innovation/diffusion studies through 1968 has been compiled by Brown (1968). The relation of the spatial diffusion processes to economic development is worked out by Pred (1969), Chapter 4, and by Friedmann (1972a). Lasuén's study (1971) is also relevant here, as is Dunn's pathbreaking study (1971). The basic reference for innovation diffusion studies generally is Rogers (1971).

portant link in such a theory is the relation of spatial diffusion to the distribution of economic power.

The basic thesis of this essay may be briefly stated at the outset. The adoption of innovations, and particularly of entrepreneurial innovations, *translates directly into an increase of power by the adopting unit over portions of its environment*. The firm adopting a corporate structure may push more traditionally organized competitors out of business; or the manufacturer introducing a piece of new machinery may improve the quality of his product (or lower his costs), capturing a larger share of the market. The cumulation of entrepreneurial innovations in a given city—the city being conceived as a spatially integrated subsystem of society—will therefore lead not only to its accelerated economic and demographic growth, but also to the consolidation of its hierarchical control over that portion of the urban system that has failed to adopt this particular set of innovations. Such a concentration of innovations in cities that have a high propensity to further innovation, produces the well-known phenomenon of core regions that extend their control over the dependent peripheries of the country. The basic relations in the spatial distribution of economic power are thus seen to be an immediate outcome of the diffusion of innovations. Only a concerted governmental effort to establish conditions favorable to accelerated innovation at selected points in the periphery is likely to produce a market reorganization of a growth pattern that, under normal conditions, displays remarkable stability. This stability, it turns out, is itself the result of innovation diffusion processes.

## Interregional Patterns of Conflict and Accommodation

Innovative entrepreneurial elites in urban areas are frequently found among foreign or national ethnic (or cultural) minorities. Although the entrepreneurial role of foreign "colonial" elites is generally recognized, national minorities which have gained control over significant portions of the modern eco-

nomic sector are equally important. The Jews in Western Europe were an early instance of such an elite. In the newly industrializing countries, the Chinese in Malaysia and Indonesia (McGee 1971:114–115; Geertz 1963; Goodman 1971:117–130), the Ibo in Nigeria, (Levine 1966), the Antioqueños in Colombia (Hagen 1962), and the Arabs, Italians, Germans, and Jews in Latin American countries (Lipset 1970), are frequently cited examples of urban innovative elites. (Other ethnic minorities whose entrepreneurial roles might be studied include English Canadians in Quebec, Arabs in Zanzibar, Indians in Burma, East Africa, Trinidad, and the Guayanas, Greeks in Egypt, Slovenes in Yugoslavia, and French settlers in Algeria.)

In nearly every instance, urban ethnic minorities operate in a political environment that is initially controlled by an agrarian-based governing elite whose members belong to a different cultural, ethnic, or religious group. This situation is dramatically illustrated by 1962–4 East African data. According to William and Judith Hanna, "In Kenya, 3 out of 100 residents are non-Africans, whereas in Nairobi the figure is 41 out of 100. Similarly, Uganda's population is just over 1 percent non-African, but for Kampala the percentage is 49. Comparable situations are found in Tanzania and Zambia (1971:109). And they continue: "With independence, some Africans moved to the top and, as a corollary, Asians and Middle Easterners have been left in a somewhat ambiguous position: subordinate to the new African elite, but on some measures superordinate to the African rank-and-file. The ambiguity arises because racial boundaries prevent Asians and Middle Easterners from entering a unilinear status hierarchy (1971:111). Many of these non-Africans were, in fact, born on the continent, but remain alien to the indigenous cultures.

Where innovative entrepreneurial elites are excluded from political power, a profound disjunction occurs between rural and urban development. Cities which have the largest concentration of innovative ethnic (cultural) minorities will experience the most rapid growth, while "native" centers, tied to the rural economy in the periphery, are likely to stagnate. Under conditions of rural/urban disjunction or *economic dualism*,[14] urban-generated surpluses tend not to be used for developing the rural sector (which contains a majority of the total population), but are accumulated, in part to build up the modern industrial-commercial complex at the core and, in part, to be expatriated to the home country of the intruding elite. By the same token, innovations will be contained largely within the core because contact networks and investment resources will also tend to be ethnically (and culturally) controlled. As a result, the remainder of the country will supply the urban core with food, raw materials, and labor and, in turn, provide a market outlet for certain core region products.

In situations of this sort, relations between innovative (urban-economic) and traditionalist (rural-governing) elites will be variously characterized by patterns of *co-optation, accommodation,* and *open hostility*.

Under *co-optation,* the governing elite is placed in a client relation to the entrepreneurial elite. This is typically the case where the latter is of foreign extraction and unassimilated to the national society (Americans in Venezuela under Peréz Jiménez, Japanese in occupied Korea, English in colonial Nigeria and Ghana, Russians in the former Baltic countries, Germans in Norway and France during World War II). For Spanish-speaking Latin America, it has been argued that foreign dependency and cooptation of national elites accounts for the extreme concentration of economic and political power in the national capital regions of countries such as Venezuela, Peru, Bolivia, Ecuador, and Chile.[15] Although this contention remains to be demonstrated, it is claimed that a more integrated form of spatial development will be achieved only if the governing elites regain a substantial measure of autonomy with respect to

foreign entrepreneurial elites (Hardoy 1970). In South America, these claims have been advanced primarily by intellectuals, equally hostile to foreign and traditional (co-opted) elites and eager to assume a major governing role themselves. (In Peru, the military forces appear to have made these claims effective, though the results for development of the urban system remain unclear [Hobsbawm 1970: 29ff.].) It is noteworthy that the national "counter-elite" of intellectuals is also the most receptive to modern technical and organizational innovation but sees its own aspirations for participation in governance thwarted by foreign powers and their national "lackeys."

An interesting case is that of Brazil, where the revolution which brought the military into absolute control of the country's governmental machinery may be interpreted, paradoxically, as the successful co-optation of the military—many of whose leading figures have strong provincial backgrounds by birth, education, and professional experience—by a national entrepreneurial establishment. Because unassimilated foreign elements constitute a relatively minor part of entrepreneurial groups in São Paulo and Rio de Janeiro, the military government has been able to pursue more nationalistic policies than would normally be expected under conditions of co-optation. These policies, however, have been directed more at problem areas that do not directly conflict with the central interests of the Brazilian business community, such as the building of trans-Brazilian highways and the colonization of new regions. Nationalistic efforts of this sort, as well as the absence of politics in the usual sense, have opened the door to the active collaboration of *tecnicos* and intellectuals with the government and have all but destroyed potential counter-elites in the country. The long-term spatial effects of these new policies are likely to be spectacular.[16] They will contribute to the spatial integration of the Brazilian territory under condi-

14. For an excellent recent discussion of dualism and its consequences for development, see Singer (1971: 23–31).

15. Quijano (1968b: 76–93). This article is not signed. However, it follows in general outline a paper by the same author, "Dependencia, Cambio Social, y Urbanización en Latinoamerica," *Cuadernos de Desarrollo Urbano-Regional,* No. 6 (March 1968), Santiago (CIDU, Universidad Católica de Chile).

16. See, for example, the extremely detailed study of new colonization along the Belém-Brasília Highway by Valverde and Dias (1967).

tions of internal dependency to the major core regions of the country.[17] But they will also uncover new possibilities for resources development, shift the gravitational field of the country's development away from coastal areas to the western frontier, and stimulate new urbanization along the major routes of interior penetration.

Under *accommodation,* a spheres-of-influence agreement of mutual non-interference may be tacitly reached according to which the management of the rural sector is left in the hands of the traditional governing elite, while the urban sector is "turned over" to the innovative minorities to develop as they see fit, essentially as an enclave within the larger national territory. Enclaves of this sort are likely to be related more to the international economy (i.e., to the international urban system) than to the rural areas within the country. In some cases, such as Singapore, urban enclaves may be politically separated as well (McGee 1971:114–115).

This process of accommodation has been analyzed by Marcos Mamalakis in his theory of sectoral clashes (1969:9–46). Although Mamalakis' theory is expressed primarily in terms of major economic sectors (industrial vs. agricultural) it is easily translatable into spatial (regional) terms as well. In pre-Allende Chile, where the theory of sectoral clashes appears to be most strongly supported by the empirical evidence—though supporting data also come from Mexico and Argentina—the urban elites contained a large proportion of national minority groups of Germans, English, Yugoslavs, Jews, and Levantines (in addition to foreign, predominantly American, nationals), whereas the governing elite (the rural-based "oligarchy") was primarily of Spanish and Basque origin. Sectoral conflicts, reflected in the formation of political parties, had therefore certain ethnic-cultural overtones as well.

Finally, under conditions of *open hostility,* events occur that lead to the disruption of existing relations of co-optation and/or accommodation. Conflict may assume a variety of forms, including *campaigns of national liberation* (Algeria), *the nationalization of foreign enterprise* (Cuba, Peru, Argentina, and Chile), *the elimination of ethnic minorities by their physical destruction* (Jews in German-dominated Europe, Chinese in Indonesia) or *by expulsion* (Indians from Kenya, French *colons* from Algeria), *economic pressure* (Chinese in Malaysia), *civil war* (Ibo in Nigeria), and *peaceful secession* (Singapore).

In some instances, the conclusion of hostilities has resulted in a renewed interest in rural development (involving the forceable transfer of resources from the core), with a consequent decline of growth in core areas and the concomitant renascence of small to medium-sized provincial centers as base points for agricultural development (Johnson 1970). Cuba provides perhaps the most clear-cut evidence on this point, though a similar shift in allocation has also been reported for Malaysia (Guyot 1969).

All of the situations discussed above relate to countries in which powerful innovative minorities in urban areas are *culturally distinct* from governing elites. But in other situations, such a split has not occurred and economic and political power is exercised conjointly from a dominant core region over ethnically and culturally varied populations (Northern Ireland, Soviet Union, Yugoslavia, Indonesia, Pakistan prior to Bangladesh, Rhodesia, South Africa).

Where this occurs, the dependent regions will often claim to be "oppressed" and generate political pressures for greater "national" (i.e., regional) autonomy, ranging from complete secession to a number of "protectionist" and "federalist" solutions, including demands for "preferential treatment" (Duchacek 1970).

Each of these solutions holds different implications for the development of urban systems. Some of them involve the massive transfer of populations (as has happened, most recently, in East Pakistan). Others lead to the isolation of the "protected" areas from

17. For one of the most concise statements on the "internal colonization" effects of the government's gigantic road building program, see Mendes (1971).

the "virus" of urbanization (South Africa) (Fair, Murdoch and Jones 1969; Green and Fair 1969). Still others produce vigorous urban-regional competition among federated states (Yugoslavia, India) with a consequent multiplication and strengthening of subsidiary core regions.[18] Occasionally, the mere threat of national independence or annexation to a neighboring country with similar ethnic traits may be sufficient to gain preferential status (Commonwealth of Puerto Rico, French Quebec, South Tyrol). These outcomes for urban systems may also be viewed from a perspective of (spatial) integration. The following table may help to recall the major patterns in this context. (The Roman numerals in the right-hand column refer to quadrants in Fig. 1; arrows indicate the principal direction of dominance.)

| Elite relationships | Urban system | Spatial integration |
|---|---|---|
| 1. co-optation | complete dominance of a passive periphery by the core: strong urban primacy; typical pattern of internal colonization, with strong linkages to international urban system | integration based on dependency relationships and the continued imbalance of major urbanization processes (I→IV) |
| 2. accommodation | spheres of influence agreement leading to regional dualism: small number of modern urban enclaves relatively independent of traditional rural areas and joined more closely to international urban system than to national territory. | weak integration on basis of economic dependency: rural migrants belonging to national majority groups are prevented from reaching controlling positions in the urban economy occupied by innovative ethnic minority groups (I→III) |
| 3. open hostility | if innovative urban minorities are effectively neutralized, the result may be a gradual transfer of resources from core to periphery, followed by accelerated rural development and the renascence of small and medium-size provincial centers; development of a "complete" urban hierarchy and attenuation of primacy | greater functional interdependency among regions and reduction of imbalances in urbanization: integration based on growing interdependency of urban centers (I→III) |
| 4. regional "protectorates" | policy of exclusion of urbanism from "protected" areas or rural enclaves: core region dominance | partial integration of urbanized (dominant) areas based on "protected" labor pools in stagnant rural enclaves: economic dualism (I→IV) |
| 5. federative solutions | preferential treatment and greater autonomy of "associated states" and federal territories: competition among urban areas: emergence of sub-cores within each region | although frequently a fragile political arrangement, this "solution" may eventually lead to a strong pattern of spatial integration based on urban-regional interdependency and the gradual attrition of peripheries: structured urban/regional competition (I↔II, I→III) |

## Final Comments

The influences on the development of urban systems are multiple and reciprocal. Governmental and economic power make up only one set of such influences, though I will argue that it is probably the most important set. In practice, of course, these influences are difficult to isolate, and it is still more difficult to measure their effects within a cybernetic framework of analysis. The customary two-variable regression models, dear to

18. For Yugoslavia, see Babarovic (1966). For India, the concept of regional competition emerges from a study by Berry (1966).

economists and sociologists, fail to yield the insights one would want. This suggests that we may have to choose between quantitative precision in research, leading to very restricted and possibly misleading insights, and a more comprehensive, qualitative approach which may have to sacrifice the elegance of mathematical formulations for a deeper historical and conceptual understanding. If we should opt for the second approach, formal models of the sort introduced at the start of this paper serve primarily a heuristic purpose. They fall short of theoretical constructs that purport to model complex causal relations in the development of urban systems. On the other hand, they focus the attention of researchers on critical variables and their interrelationships and help in posing questions that may eventually lead to significant insights into the workings of historical processes. They are preliminary to empirical research.

I have placed the emphasis in this paper on the spatial distribution of governmental and economic power. It could be argued, as William Alonso has done, that the degree to which all national policies have implications for urban growth, sectoral rather than spatial distributions of power are the critical variables. Most probably, both viewpoints are correct and complement each other. Whatever the conclusion, however, the model I have proposed points to a series of fascinating questions about the effect of power relations on the structural growth of hierarchical systems. It is with a view to clarifying these questions and setting the stage for a large-scale research effort that the present paper has been written.

# REFERENCES

Babarovic, Ivo. 1966. "Regional Development Policies in Socialist Yugoslavia." Unpublished Master's Thesis in Regional Planning, Department of City and Regional Planning, Harvard University.

Berry, Brian J. L. 1964. "Cities as Systems Within Systems of Cities," Chapter 6 in John Friedmann and William Alonso, eds., *Regional Development and Planning: A Reader*. Cambridge, Mass.: MIT Press.

———. 1966. *Essays on Commodity Flows and the Spatial Structure of the Indian Economy*. Department of Geography Research Paper No. 111, The University of Chicago.

———. 1971. "City Size and Economic Development: Conceptual Synthesis and Policy Problems, with Special Reference to South and Southeast Asia," chapter 5 in Leo Jacobson and Ved Prakash, eds., *Urbanization and National Development*. Beverly Hills: Sage.

Blau, Peter M. 1964. *Exchange and Power in Social Life*. London: John Wiley.

Brown, Lawrence A. 1968. *Diffusion Processes and Location: A Conceptual Framework and Bibliography*. (Bibliography Series No. 4.) Philadelphia: Regional Science Research Institute.

Duchacek, Ivo. D. 1970. *Comparative Federalism: The Territorial Dimension of Politics*. New York: Holt, Rinehart, and Winston.

Dunn, Edgar S. 1971. *Economic and Social Development: A Process of Social Learning*. Baltimore: Johns Hopkins Press.

Fair, T.J.D., G. Murdoch and H. M. Jones. 1969. *Development in Swaziland*. Johannesburg: Witwatersrand University Press.

Friedmann, John. 1972a. "A Generalized Theory of Polarized Development," in Niles Hansen, ed., *Growth Centers in Regional Economic Development*. New York: Free Press.

———. 1972b. *Urbanization, Planning, and National Development*. Beverley Hills: Sage.

Geertz, Clifford. 1963. *Peddlers and Princes: Social Change and Economic Modernization in Two Indonesian Towns*. Chicago: University of Chicago Press.

Goodman, Allen E. 1971. "The Political Implications of Urban Development in Southeast Asia: The 'Fragment' Hypothesis," *Economic Development And Cultural Change*, 20 (October): 117–130.

Green, L. P. and T.J.D. Fair. 1969. *Development in Africa: A Study in Regional Analysis with Special Reference to Southern Africa*. Johannesburg. Witwatersrand University Press.

Guyot, James F. 1969. "Creeping Urbanism in Malaysia," in Robert T. Daland, ed. *Comparative Urban Research: The Administration and Politics of Cities*. Beverly Hills: Sage.

Hagen, Everett E. 1962. *On the Theory of Social Change*. Homewood, Illinois. Dorsey Press.

Hägerstrand, Torsten. 1967. *Innovation Diffusion*

*as a Spatial Process.* Chicago, University of Chicago Press.

Hanna, William John and Judith Lynne Hanna. 1971. *Urban Dynamics in Black Africa: An Interdisciplinary Approach.* Chicago: Aldine-Atherton.

Hardoy, Jorge, 1970. "Urban Land Policies and Land Use Control Measures in Cuba," Report for the United Nations Centre for Housing, Building and Planning.

Harris, Chauncey D. 1971. "Urbanization and Population Growth in the Soviet Union: 1959–1970," *Ekistics,* 32 (November): 360.

Hobsbawm, Eric J. 1971. "Peru: The Peculiar 'Revolution,'" *The New York Review of Books.* (December) 29ff.

Horowitz, Irving Louis. 1967. "Electoral Politics, Urbanization and Social Development in Latin America," *Urban Affairs Quarterly,* 2:3–55.

Johnson, E.A.J. 1970. *The Organization of Space in Developing Countries.* Cambridge, Mass.: Harvard University Press.

Lasuén, J. R. 1971. "Multi-Regional Economic Development: An Open System Approach," in Torsten Hägerstrand and Antoni R. Kuklinski, eds., *Information Systems for Regional Development: A Seminar.* (Lund Studies in Geography, Ser. B. Human Geography, No. 37.) Lund: C.W.K. Gleerup.

Levine, Robert A. 1966. *Dreams and Deeds: Achievement Motivation in Nigeria.* Chicago: University of Chicago Press.

Lindberg, Leon N., and Stuart A. Scheingold, eds., 1971. *Regional Integration: Theory and Research.* Cambridge: Harvard University Press.

Lipset, Seymour Martin. 1970. *Revolution and Counter-Revolution.* New York: Anchor Books.

Mamalakis, Marcos J. 1969. "The Theory of Sectoral Clashes," *Latin American Research Review,* 4:9–46.

McGee, T. G. 1971. "Tetes de pont et eclaves. Le probleme urbain et le processus d'urbanisation dans l'Asie du Sud-Est depuis 1945," *Tiers Monde.* 12:114–115.

Mendes, Armando D. 1971. "Un Projecto Para a Amazonia," unpublished paper, Univ. Federal do Para.

Morse, Richard M. 1971. "Planning, History, Politics," in John Miller and Ralph A. Gakenheimer, eds., *Latin American Urban Policies and the Social Sciences.* Beverly Hills: Sage.

Pred, Allen. 1969. *Behavior and Location: Foundations for a Geographic and Dynamic Location Theory, Part II.* (Lund Studies in Geography, Ser. B. Human Geography, No. 28) Lund: C.W.K. Gleerup.

Quijano, Anibal. 1968a. "Dependencia, Cambio Social, y Urbanizacion en Latinoamerica," *Cuadernos de Desarrollo Urbano-Regional,* 6 (March), Santiago (CIDU, Universidad Catolica de Chile).

———. 1968b. "The Urbanization of Society in Latin America," *Economic Bulletin for Latin America.* 13:76–93.

Richardson, Harry W. 1972. "Optimality in City Size, Systems of Cities in Urban Policy: A Sceptic's View," Centre for Research in the Social Sciences, University of Kent at Canterbury (Reprint Series No. 18)

Riddell, J. Barry. 1970. *The Spatial Dynamics of Modernization in Sierra Leone.* Evanston: Northwestern University Press.

Rogers, Everett M. 1971. *Communication of Innovations: A Cross Cultural Approach.* Second Edition. New York: Free Press.

Singer, Hans W. 1971. "A New Approach to the Problems of the Dual Society in Developing Countries," *International Social Development Review.* 3:23–31.

Stanback, Thomas M., Jr., and Richard V. Knight. 1970. *The Metropolitan Economy.* New York: Columbia University Press.

Törnqvist, Gunnar, 1970. *Contact Systems and Regional Development.* (Lund Studies in Geography, Ser. B. Human Geography No. 35.) Lund: C.W.K. Gleerup.

Uyehara, Esther Emiko, 1972. "Production and Nonproduction Employment in Manufacturing: A Comparative Analysis of Metropolitan Areas. Master's Thesis, School of Architecture and Urban Planning, UCLA.

Valverde, Orlando, and Catharina Vergolino Dias. 1967. *A Rodovia Belem-Brasilia.* Rio de Janeiro: Fundacao IBGE.

Williamson, Jeffrey. 1965. "Regional Inequality and the Process of National Development," *Economic Development and Cultural Change,* Part II (July): 3–45.

Wu, Yuan-Li. 1967. *The Spatial Economy of Communist China: A Study of Industrial Location and Transportation.* New York: Frederick A. Praeger.

# 5

## URBAN SYSTEM GROWTH AND CHANGE

# Introduction

The papers in this section describe changes that occur within urban systems primarily during the period of a decade or less. They are, essentially, cross-sectional snapshots of short-term growth processes. They demonstrate that very different relationships exist among and between the components of growth, depending on the particular urban system, the data, and time period under study.

The processes involved are obviously complex. At one time the spatial distribution of economic activity within the system may be decentralizing; at other times it may be concentrating; while at other times both trends are apparent. In some periods it is production advantages, such as the introduction of new technologies translated into higher wage rates and profits, which explain variations in urban growth; while at other times consumption amenities, such as climate, offer the best explanation. Or perhaps the whole urban system is simply growing rapidly through natural increase alone; or maybe the spatial redistribution of population by net migration is the predominate process.

In fact, most empirical studies that have attempted to explain or predict differences in urban growth rates among cities have not been very successful (Richardson, 1974). Many, often diverse, processes of growth take place within an urban system over any one period of time. It is difficult to describe in one, two, or even a half-dozen maps, flow diagrams, or mathematical equations a phenomenon as complex as demographic change (Hägerstrand, *et al.,* 1974), the spread of inflation (Curry, 1976), the specific effects of an industrial boom (see Erickson below), a changing Defence Department procurement policy, or the effect of a national population that is simultaneously growing both older and wealthier. This extreme complexity of growth is augmented by such random events as earthquakes, an unexpected bankruptcy, or a decision to delay an expected public investment.

The first paper in this section, by Alonso and Medrich, exemplifies this complexity. The various regions of the United States when studied over the last seven decades demonstrate almost all the different varieties of urban population growth. Spontaneous growth centers have emerged in many locations, and have done so for very different reasons. Some show short-term growth while others show more sustained growth. The U.S. urban system is the summation of all of these growth impulses.

Equally complex is the process of urban economic growth. The extensive literature in this area can be subdivided conveniently, albeit rather arbitrarily, into two
broad groups. The first grew out of the concept of *the economic base* of a community. This concept treats an urban region, like a mining town, as locked into the
production of a particular good for a national or international market. Local growth
depends on that region maintaining its share of the growth in total demand for that
product. Labor and capital, as factors of production, are assumed to be universally
available. An alternative approach is to view an urban region as a set of productive
resources—notably labor and capital—which is able to produce a wide variety of
goods, like Philadelphia. Growth depends on the ability of the region to increase
this supply of resources, i.e., to attract new workers and capital. This can be
called the *labor-supply* approach.

Each approach has validity in some parts of any given country and at different
times. Kansas City, one could argue, depends for its growth on its existing economic base while Los Angeles seems able to develop new industrial specialties,
given the growth of its labor force and the markets that labor force creates.
Clearly, in all urban areas both kinds of growth occur simultaneously. Increased
demand for the local product creates more jobs and higher incomes. New workers
and higher wages create more local demand and attract new industries. The continuing debate as to which source of growth (demand or supply) is most important
has become something of a "chicken-and-egg" controversy (Muth, 1971).

## THE ECONOMIC-BASE ARGUMENT: JOBS BRING WORKERS

Economic-base analysis separates the economy of an urban region into two parts:
one which produces goods for export to the rest of the country, and the other
which produces goods and services for its own residents. A growth in demand for
the export good generates higher incomes per worker, and consequently more
workers are attracted into the export industries. These workers in turn create demands for more local services and thus local jobs, multiplying the effects of the
initial increase in export demand. This is one of the oldest theories to explain
urban growth (Tiebout, 1962). Exports are seen as the driving force in urban
growth, and thus are the community's economic base. Despite criticism of its
simplicity on the one hand and its operational difficulties on the other, economic-
base theory is still the basis for most urban-growth models, and it has been extensively refined and elaborated almost beyond recognition (Richardson, 1973).

The economic-base model is perhaps most effective for predicting urban growth
whenever the production patterns of urban regions are essentially fixed. This condition occurs in the very short run, when productive capacity is fixed and sufficient labor surplus exists to supply the needs of production, as well as when the
production of a region is limited to a small number of products, either because of
location, climate, or available natural resources. Many Canadian and Australian

cities, for example, fall into this latter group. They are dependent on world markets for iron, newsprint, or copper ore and have virtually no alternative for production. The economic-base approach treats an urban region as a very open subsystem, essentially dependent on its economic role within the larger urban system and often highly sensitive to demand or competition external to that urban system.

The economic-base model has frequently been applied to highly industrialized regions by studying regularities in the way cities respond to short-term economic impulses such as business cycles (Vining, 1946; King, Casetti, and Jeffrey, 1969; Haggett, 1971; Casetti, King, and Jeffrey, 1971; Pigozzi, 1975). This approach begins with a number of basic questions. How does growth spread through an urban system? Which cities or regions lead and which ones lag relative to the system-wide average? How do the growth impulses change over time?

Much of the recent literature in this area has emphasized employment change, not only because such data are more readily available than others, but because employment is a relatively sensitive economic indicator. Within a short time frame economic productivity adjustments are primarily made by changing the local unemployment rate. The essay by Jeffrey and Webb in this section, on regional fluctuations in the Australian urban system, illustrates some of the insights that one can gain from this type of analysis.[1] Variations in the speed, amplitude, and fidelity of the response of the local economy to national trends give the analyst a clearer picture of both the organization and intensity of integration of the urban system.

## THE LABOR-FORCE ARGUMENT: WORKERS CREATE JOBS

Over a longer period, however, or in a more complex and highly industrialized economy, it is not so easy to isolate the driving elements in the growth of a local urban economy. The industrial structure has greater flexibility over the longer term as firms can develop new products and alter capacity or markets. Growth in capital and the supply of labor then create jobs. An attractive area or community attracts new economic activities while others may lose the activities they do have. In this case the local economy can be treated either as a partially closed system, creating its own labor force and capital to produce for an infinite external market, or as a totally open system, able to attract factors of production in competition with other urban places.

Most of the available research relates to the movement of factors of production, that is, the spatial relocation of economic activity. In most instances, however, in the absence of data on the movement of capital or on the relocation of business firms, the emphasis has been on the labor force: usually in the form of

1. The reader is referred to a more recent but somewhat more technical paper by Jeffrey also treating growth in the Australian urban/regional system (see Jeffrey, 1975). Probably the most concise statements of the approach are given in earlier papers by King, Casetti, and Jeffrey (1969) and Haggett (1971).

population-migration studies. The numbers and composition of migrants lead to differences in the level of productive capacity and in consumer demand between regions. Net immigration increases both the work force and the income in a region. But individuals and firms move for many reasons that are difficult to devise models for: members moving to or within institutions, like colleges or the military; corporations rotating executives among plants and offices; social-security holders looking for a bit of sun; or returning migrants drawn from among the massive movements that occurred years ago (as with the "okies" who are now returning to the Ozarks from California).

Lowry (1966), Wertheimer (1970), and Greenwood (1973), among others, have attempted to show that intercity migration does follow a predominantly economic logic, as movers seek jobs, higher wages, and greater lifetime earnings. Schwind's paper in this section reviews the different hypotheses seeking to explain migration and evaluates them for the United States (see also, Schwind, 1975). Although he recognizes the importance of economic differentials, he also points out the growth of amenities as factors in migration. His paper, summarizing our knowledge in the late sixties, provides an interesting contrast to Morrison's paper in Section VI, which was written a few years later when the flight of population from large cities in the U.S. had become a flood, and interregional migration streams shifted substantially toward nonmetropolitan areas.

## THE COMPLEX GROWTH PROCESS

Other recent studies have attempted to merge the economic-base model and the labor-force change model (e.g., Richardson, 1973; von Böventer, 1975), trying to replicate the decisions of workers and entrepreneurs within a local labor market. What information triggers decisions that expand the number of jobs? What factors encourage workers to migrate in or out of a city?

Complex trade-offs exist in these decision-making processes, such as between high unemployment levels and the expectation of future jobs, between unemployment at home and jobs elsewhere, and between local wage levels and workers' expectations. These in turn are mediated by differences in the age, education, and occupation of the worker. Similarly, business organizations evaluate local wage rates, worker productivity, and transportation costs relative to other locations before making a decision to relocate. As one example of the merging of economic-base theory (labor markets) and migration behavior we include here a brief abstract from a paper by Cordey-Hayes.

Also adding complexity to the subject, what appears to be growth at one scale, measured either in space or time, may actually represent a decline at another. Urban-centered regions dominated by industries undergoing rapid technological change, such as some forms of agriculture, may display a rapid internal redistribution of population from the farms to urban settlements. A large part of the growth of Houston and Dallas, for example, has been at the expense of smaller communities within Texas. This change may occur with little overall growth in population, but with rapid increases in total income. Other areas, more specialized in service activities, either public or private, may have a much lower rate of job turnover and a more steady income growth. These long-term adjustments may partially or even completely override the effects of changes in demand, or of voluntary migration patterns.

The relationship between economic activity and the labor force is explicitly revealed by the calculation of indices such as the average wage level or the income per family (or per capita) both of which are also common measures of welfare. Foreshadowing sections to come, we see that policymakers are particularly concerned with per-capita income, its spatial distribution, and social incidence, as well as its relation to growth. This concern for income levels also introduces the need for new variables to measure the real cost of living, participation rates, wage levels, and education or occupational skills, all of which can affect the level of income. A rural area, for instance, can maintain high-income levels if productivity increases and high rates of rural out-migration are maintained. High rates of out-migration, however, may produce some degree of income disparity among those people remaining, at least in the short run. Industries (or regions) where gains in productivity are slow or nonexistent will tend to lag behind others in income growth.

One of the many expressions of growth and change within an urban system, difficult to visualize given the level of discussion in the above analyses, is the actual effect of massive growth (or decline) on specific urban regions. As a case study we have selected a recent paper by Erickson, which examines the sectoral and spatial impact of the rapid growth of the Boeing Company on the economy of Seattle (Puget Sound region) and the state of Washington in the mid-1960s. He notes, for example, that because of the strength of interregional and interurban linkages (as described in the paper by Pred in Section IV) among high-technology firms, such as Boeing and its suppliers, much of the impact of this growth on the industrial or manufacturing sector was felt outside the local region. In contrast, the impact of Boeing's growth on the service sector of the local region was both immediate and substantial. Local services, in such situations, became overloaded and prices often become inflated.

This differential effect, Erickson argues, necessitates a rethinking of conventional growth-center strategies designed to stimulate the development of depressed regions. Most of these strategies are based on the concept of introducing a "lead" firm into the region to generate sustained multiplier effects and in particular further industrialization within that region. However, if the dominant multiplier effect is interregional rather than intraregional this induced local growth will not materialize, at least not as envisaged initially. Hansen's paper in Section VI makes the same point.

## CONCLUDING REMARKS

At this broad scale of study we are only now becoming aware of the complexity of growth in urban systems and the almost intractable problems in analyzing that growth. Our theory is weak. Much of the necessary data is sparse. Those data that do exist are often of marginal relevance to the questions raised in this Introduction. Analytical models tend to be crude, simplistic, and partial, in that they specify only a small portion of this complexity. Policy recommendations for managing urban growth, partly as a consequence of these limitations of research and information, tend to be even more superficial and to lag rather than lead the trends they are supposed to influence. Moreover, public and political awareness of growth at this level have also been slow to develop, in part because the boundaries of urban systems and subsystems seldom conform to political jurisdictions.

Yet these interrelated problems of job creation, levels of income, forced and voluntary migration, and of the kind of economy or life-style an urban region will have are increasingly pressing concerns to many people. Public agencies have responded in varying ways to the pressures to "do something," but most of these responses are sufficiently recent that as yet we know little about the real impact of their actions and policies on different groups of people. Appalachian development proposals and plans, the New Towns in Britain, the restrictions on growth in Stockholm, London, and Moscow, and the redistribution of income among the provinces in Canada through transfer payments are well-known examples, but how much do they actually change patterns of urban and economic growth and prosperity? Who benefits and who loses by these policies? The debate continues.

In Section VI we examine aspects of this debate, and in the final section a range of alternative policies and strategies for managing urban systems is presented.

## REFERENCES

Batty, M. 1976. *Urban Modelling: Algorithms, Calibrations, Predictions.* Cambridge: The University Press.

Borts, G. H. and Stein, J. L. 1964. *Economic Growth in a Free Market.* New York: Columbia University Press.

Casetti, E., King, L. and Jeffrey, D. 1971. "Structural Imbalance in the U.S. Urban Economic System, 1960–65." *Geographical Analysis,* vol. 3, pp. 239–255.

Curry, L. 1976. "Fluctuation in the Random Spatial Economy and the Control of Inflation." *Geographical Analysis,* vol. 8, pp. 340–353.

Greenwood, M. J. 1973. "Urban Economic Growth and Migration: Their Interaction." *Environment and Planning A,* vol. 5, pp. 91–112.

Hägerstrand, T. *et al.* 1974. *The Biography of a People. Past and Future Population Changes in Sweden.* Stockholm: Royal Ministry for Foreign Affairs.

Haggett, P. 1971. "Leads and Lags in Interregional Systems: A Study of Cyclical Fluctuations in the South West Economy," in M. Chisholm and G. Manners, eds. *Spatial Policy Problems in the British Economy.* Cambridge: The University Press, pp. 69–95.

Harris, C. C., Jr. 1974. *Regional Economic Effects of Alternative Highway Systems.* Cambridge, Mass.: Ballinger Publishing Co.

Jeffrey, D. 1974. "Regional Fluctuations in Unemployment within the U.S. Urban Economic System: A Study of the Spatial Impact of Short

Term Economic Change." *Economic Geography,* vol. 50, pp. 111–123.

———. 1975. "Spatial Imbalance in the Australian Regional Economic System: Structural Unemployment, 1955–1970." *Australian Geographer,* vol. 13, pp. 146–154.

King, L., Casetti, E. and Jeffrey, D. 1969. "Economic Impulses in a Regional System of Cities: A Study of Spatial Interaction." *Regional Studies,* vol. 3, pp. 213–218.

———. 1972. "Cyclical Fluctuations in Unemployment Levels in U.S. Metropolitan Areas." *Tijdschrift voor Economische en Sociale Geografie,* vol. 63, pp. 345–352.

Lowry, I. P. 1966. *Migration and Metropolitan Growth: Two Analytical Models.* Los Angeles: University of California, Institute of Government and Public Affairs.

Muth, R. F. 1971. "Migration: Chicken or Egg." *Southern Economic Journal,* vol. 37, pp. 295–306.

Pigozzi, B. 1975. "The Spatial-Temporal Structure of Interurban Economic Impulses," *Tijdschrift voor Economische en Sociale Geografie,* vol. 66, pp. 272–276.

Richardson, H. W. 1973. *Regional Growth Theory.* London: Macmillan & Co.

———. 1974. "Empirical Aspects of Regional Growth in the United States." *Annals of Regional Science,* vol. 9, pp. 8–23.

Schwind, P. J. 1975. "A General Field Theory of Migration, United States, 1955–1960." *Economic Geography,* vol. 51, pp. 1–16.

Tiebout, C. 1962. *The Community Economic Base Study.* New York: Committee for Economic Development.

Vining, R. 1946. "The Region as a Concept in Business Cycle Analysis." *Econometrica,* vol. 14, pp. 201–218.

von Böventer, E. 1975. "Regional Growth Theory." *Urban Studies,* vol. 12, pp. 15–35.

Wertheimer, R. F. 1970. *The Monetary Rewards of Migration within the United States.* Washington, D.C.: The Urban Institute.

# Spontaneous Growth Centers in Twentieth-Century American Urbanization

WILLIAM ALONSO and ELLIOTT MEDRICH

Most discussion of growth centers concentrates on the where, the how, and the why of inducing growth in areas where by some criterion, development is lagging. In this the discussion reflects a concern with the equity or distributional objective of equalizing levels of welfare in different regions of the national territory. In developing nations, the concern is usually with countering the phenomenon of primacy as a manifestation of the duality of the economy. In most developed countries, as in the United States, the concern is rather that depressed or underdeveloped areas do not participate in the levels of social and economic welfare of most of the nation. Even those developed countries that want to diminish the concentration in their largest cities appear to consider their growth center efforts primarily as distributive ones.

It would seem that this view is too narrow for the formulation of national urbanization policies, that is to say, for policies to guide the growth of the national system of cities. Even a developed country is a developing country, and its development implies a structural evolution over time that will be reflected in the differential growth among territorial units as well as among economic sectors. In brief, development is not mere growth but also change. A national urbanization policy, as an element of a national urban policy, should address itself to the issues of efficiency or development, as manifested in growth centers that may be termed spontaneous, as well as to the questions of equity through inducing growth in centers where the overall functioning of the system is not producing it. A national urbanization policy should include developmental objectives for guiding the phenomenon of growth as well as equity considerations for dealing with retardation.

There are, then, two varieties of growth centers. Induced growth centers are those in which public policy is trying to promote growth. In this sense, the designation of a locality as a growth center is a normative one. Spontaneous growth centers are those that are growing without benefit of special assistance, or at least without benefit of conscious or explicit policy. In a lively socioeconomic system, there will always be a number of these centers, whose growth derives from the dynamics of the system. It would seem worthwhile to study the characteristics of such centers and the importance of their role in national urbanization, both for the lessons they may hold for inducing growth where it does not occur spontaneously and for their own sake as a valid subject of national developmental policy, since growth also has its problems.

Our aims are modest. We shall not try to analyze the reason for the development of spontaneous growth centers, nor shall we enter into the economic history of particular ones. Neither shall we try to suggest policy, except in the broadest outlines. We shall try to describe the magnitude of the role of spontaneous growth centers in the urbanization of the American population since the turn of the century and shall try to describe some of the shifts that have occurred. We shall limit ourselves to a consideration of time series of the numbers of people who lived between 1900 and 1965 in each of the 212 Standard Metropolitan Statistical Areas as defined territorially in 1960.[1] Estimates of net migration into all metropolitan areas (SMSAs) and into or out of each of them were constructed by assuming that they all followed the decade's rate of natural increase in the nation and that the difference in the observed population at the end of each decade from that which would have resulted from natural increase alone was attributable to migration.[2] Spontaneous growth centers were operationally defined as those which showed substantial in-migration.[3] Most of the presentation will use as a criterion for designating a metropolitan area as a growth center a rate of net in-migration twice that into the total set of SMSAs, but we have also looked at more stringent criteria. For convenience we will use 2M, 3M, and so on for twice, three times, and so on, the rate of migration into all metropolitan areas. We shall also use SGC at times as shorthand for Spontaneous Growth Centers. Thus, a 2M SGC is a metropolitan area that had a net rate of in-migration at least twice that into all metropolitan areas.

Several disclaimers are necessary as to the precision of our data. Estimates of natural increase in the early part of the century are not very reliable and neither are population esti-

mates for 1965, our last date.[4] Other problems arise. For instance, we assume nationwide rates of natural increase, but poorer and smaller areas tend to have higher rates of natural increase, as do fast growing areas whose population is heavily weighted toward the young. Our practice of using the 1960 SMSA territory implies, of course, that the early figures for many areas include farmers and villagers; but this effect may not be too serious, because, although it makes it harder for an area to qualify for the growth criterion by expanding the base on which growth is computed, the areas where the areal definition is most excessive in the early years must be those that experienced the most growth. In more recent years, two other problems arise. The first is that suburban and exurban diffusion are proceeding very rapidly, and many urban scholars think that the SMSA boundaries cut off substantial population that is functionally associated with the metropolis.[5] This effect is probably strongest for the larger metropolitan areas, and thus SMSA figures will tend to understate their most recent populations and their growth. The other problem is a more profound conceptual one. It is that, just as the single-centered nineteenth century city gave way to the multicentered metropolis, there are now recognizable congeries of metropolitan areas, sometimes called megalopolises, with strong interdependent functional relations. These are higher order systems that are inadequately recognized in our analysis, which is based on SMSA's; some glimmer of this effect is visible in the last of our maps in what we call "suburban metropolises." But for all these difficulties, we believe that the general outlines of our findings, if not the details, are reliable.

Figure 1 shows the share of all metropolitan growth accounted for by Spontaneous Growth Centers. In general, the share increases from the beginning of the century to the present,

1. Definitions of SMSAs from U.S. Bureau of the Budget, *Standard Metropolitan Statistical Areas* (1961) Population of individual SMSAs from *Eighteenth Decennial Census of the United States* (1960), Vol. 1-A, Table 31; *Sixteenth Census of the United States* (1940), Vol. 1, Table 4, *Fourteenth Census of the United States* (1920), Vol. I, Table 50; and U.S. Housing and Home Finance Administration, *Population Growth of Standard Metropolital Areas: 1900–1950* (December, 1953), Appendix, Table 2.
2. Based on Series C 88–114, *Historical Statistics of the United States: Colonial Times to 1957;* and Table 126, *Statistical Abstract of the United States* (1967).
3. Since the analysis is based solely on demographic data, we do not consider possible alternative modes of being a growth center, such as by increases in employment without increases in residentiary population (by drawing on a commuter shed), or economic growth without population growth, as may occur through capital-intensive industrialization.

4. 1965 estimates from *Statistical Abstract of the United States* (1967), Table 15.
5. See the map of commuting territories in B.J.L. Berry and E. Neils, "Location, Size, and Shape of Cities as Influenced by Environmental Factors: The Urban Environment Writ Large", in H. Perloff, *The Quality of the Urban Environment* (Baltimore: Johns Hopkins Press, 1969), pp. 276–77.

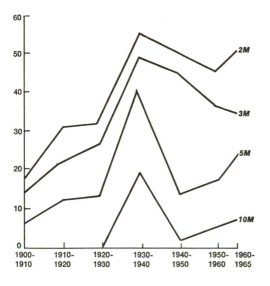

Figure 1. Percentage Share of Metropolitan Growth Accounted for by SGCs at 2M, 3M, 5M, and 10M, 1900-1965.

regardless of the criterion used, with a sharp temporary rise during the depression decade of 1930–1940. At the 2M level, SGC's account for nearly half of all metropolitan growth since 1940, while 3M centers, with a net in-migration at least triple that into all metropolitan areas, account for nearly one-third in the most recent period. Although the secular rise since 1900 is unmistakable, the 2M share shows no clear trend since 1940 and the 3M share has clearly declined slightly. But there has been a clear rise at the 5M level from 12.6 to 23.7 per cent and at the 10M level from 1.2 to 6.1 per cent. Thus, contrary to what might be imagined in a nation that has achieved our degree of economic maturity, rapidly growing cities account for an increasing rather than a decreasing share of total metropolitan growth, and this increase is most marked for the higher growth criteria.[6]

More detailed information is presented in

6. It is interesting to contrast the 1960–1965 shares of growth (which range from 48.6 per cent for 2M to 6.1 per cent for 10M) with the recent proposals of the National Committee on Urban Growth Policy, which suggested settling 20 per cent of the forthcoming urban growth in 100 new towns and in ten new cities. See D. Canty, *The New City* (New York: Frederick A. Praeger, Inc., 1969).

Table 1. The rate of growth of the metropolitan areas is remarkably stable from decade to decade (line 2), except for the high first decade (which resulted from a high rate of in-migration into metropolitan areas), the 1930–1940 decade (when both natural increase and in-migration were very low), and the most recent period (when again low natural increase and low in-migration combined to slow metropolitan growth). Migration's share of metropolitan growth (line 4) shows a marked decline over the period. Because of the increasing preponderance of vegetative growth for the metropolitan area set, it might be expected that growth rates would become more nearly equal among metropolitan areas, but we have seen that, in fact, the fast growers account for an increasing share of the total growth (line 7). Part of the explanation may be found in line 8, which shows that the SGCs account for a dramatically increasing share of all migration into the metropolitan set and currently receive as in-migrants a greater absolute number than all the SMSAs (including themselves) put together. This means that in the earlier decades migration from nonmetropolitan areas and from abroad was more evenly distributed among SMSAs, whereas in recent decades marked differences in growth rates have resulted from intermetropolitan migration. Illustrating this point, the number of SMSAs estimated to have been net exporters of population rose from eighteen in 1900–1910 to eighty-two in 1960–1965 (line 10).

Table 2 shows the shares of total SMSA growth contributed by SGCs of each size class and cumulatively. Disregarding the decade of the 1930s, which was anomalous in many ways and which will be discussed later, the main trends are apparent. SGCs below 200,000 population have contributed a declining share of all metropolitan growth since the beginning of the period. The fast-growers' increasing share of all metropolitan growth is the result of the emergence of larger SGCs. Since the 1940s, the population categories above the 300,000–500,000 bracket have each increased their shares while most of the lower categories have had declining shares. In

Table 1. Population, Growth, and Migration of Standard Metropolitan Statistical Areas (SMSAs) and of 2M Spontaneous Growth Centers (SGC), 1900–1965

| | 1900–1910 | 1910–1920 | 1920–1930 | 1930–1940 | 1940–1950 | 1950–1960 | 1960–1965 |
|---|---|---|---|---|---|---|---|
| 1) SMSA population at the beginning of the period (000) | 31,955 | 41,955 | 52,524 | 66,804 | 72,834 | 89,317 | 112,885 |
| 2) Decennial rate of SMSA population growth (%) | 31.4 | 25.2 | 27.2 | 9.0 | 22.6 | 26.4 | 17 .8[a] |
| 3) Decennial rate of migration into SMSAs (%) | 21.0 | 16.4 | 15.0 | 2.2 | 9.0 | 9.6 | 5.0[a] |
| 4) Migration as % of growth | 70 | 65 | 55 | 25 | 40 | 37 | 29 |
| 5) 2M criterion ((2) + (3)) (%) | 52.4 | 41.6 | 42.2 | 11.2 | 31.6 | 36.0 | 22.8[a] |
| 6) Share of SMSA population in 2M SGCs (%) | 5.5 | 10.3 | 11.1 | 20.4 | 21.4 | 19.7 | 25.1 |
| 7) Share of all SMSA growth accounted for by 2M SGCs (%) | 18.7 | 30.5 | 31.8 | 54.2 | 49.7 | 43.5 | 48.6 |
| 8) Share of net immigration into all SMSAs accounted for by 2M SGCs (%) | 24.5 | 41.3 | 48.8 | 157.3 | 92.2 | 85.0 | 109.1 |
| 9) Number of 2M SGCs | 40 | 40 | 48 | 87 | 69 | 52 | 60 |
| 10) Number of net out-migration | 18 | 31 | 52 | 77 | 50 | 60 | 82 |

[a]The 1960–1965 rates have been doubled to convert to the common decimal base.

that period, the share of growth of all SGCs under 300,000 has declined from just under one-fourth to just over one-tenth, while that of SGCs over 500,000 has increased from 22.3 per cent to 32.9 per cent. The relatively narrow categories in the table are somewhat unstable in their rates of change, but reading across the cumulative figures makes evident the overall shift toward larger urban sizes.

Because much present United States and foreign legislation and common practice in regard to induced growth centers focus on centers below 250,000 population, it is interesting to examine further the experience of

Table 2. Percent Share of All SMSA Growth Accounted for by 2M SGCs, by Size Class and Cumulatively, 1900–1965

| SGC size (000) | 1900–1910 (Cum.) | 1910–1920 (Cum.) | 1920–1930 (Cum.) | 1930–1940 (Cum.) | 1940–1950 (Cum.) | 1950–1960 (Cum.) | 1960–1965 (Cum.) |
|---|---|---|---|---|---|---|---|
| Under 50 | 5.6 ( 5.6) | 3.3 ( 3.3) | 3.6 ( 3.6) | 2.2 ( 2.2) | 1.2 ( 1.2) | 0.9 ( 0.9) | 0    ( 0 ) |
| 50–100 | 4.4 (10.0) | 5.8 ( 9.1) | 3.6 ( 7.2) | 8.8 (11.0) | 5.9 ( 7.1) | 3.2 ( 4.1) | 1.1 ( 1.1) |
| 100–150 | 3.8 (13.8) | 5.0 (14.1) | 4.2 (11.4) | 8.1 (19.1) | 3.9 (11.0) | 3.1 ( 7.2) | 3.3 ( 4.4) |
| 150–200 | 5.0 (18.7) | 2.5 (16.6) | 2.8 (14.2) | 4.6 (23.7) | 4.2 (15.2) | 2.0 ( 9.2) | 2.6 ( 7.0) |
| 200–250 | 0   (18.7) | 0   (16.6) | 2.3 (16.5) | 6.2 (29.9) | 1.1 (16.3) | 0.5 ( 9.7) | 3.7 (10.7) |
| 250–300 | 0   (18.7) | 0   (16.6) | 0   (16.5) | 1.4 (31.3) | 7.5 (23.8) | 3.8 (13.5) | 1.2 (11.9) |
| 300–500 | 0   (18.7) | 0   (16.6) | 0   (16.5) | 8.2 (39.5) | 3.6 (27.4) | 9.1 (22.6) | 3.8 (15.7) |
| 500–750 | 0   (18.7) | 13.9 (30.5) | 0   (16.5) | 4.9 (44.4) | 5.8 (33.2) | 6.8 (29.3) | 7.1 (22.8) |
| 750–1000 | 0   (18.7) | 0   (30.5) | 9.3 (25.7) | 0   (44.4) | 3.0 (36.2) | 1.9 (31.2) | 7.0 (29.8) |
| 1000–2000 | 0   (18.7) | 0   (30.5) | 6.1 (31.8) | 0   (44.4) | 4.7 (40.9) | 2.3 (33.5) | 6.6 (36.4) |
| 2000+ | 0   (18.7) | 0   (30.5) | 0   (31.8) | 9.8 (54.2) | 8.8 (49.7) | 10.1 (43.5) | 12.3 (48.6) |

areas between 50,000 and 250,000. Since the turn of the century, SGCs of this size have contributed a declining share of all metropolitan growth (from 18.7 per cent to 10.7 per cent); this, of course, reflects the declining share of all SMSA growth by all SMSAs in this size class (from 36.5 per cent to 16.1 per cent) and the decline of the share of all metropolitan population of metropolises in this class (from 33.8 to 11.7). Contrary to what might be thought, the decline does not stem from there being fewer such areas or fewer successful ones. The number of SMSAs of that size actually increased from 106 to 111. More surprisingly, their chances of success have increased markedly. Table 3 shows the percentage of SMSAs in each size category that qualified as 2M SGCs for each period. This percentage may be taken as a naive *a priori* expectation that a metropolis of that size will qualify as a 2M SGC.[7] This expectation was 12.3 per cent in 1900 for all SMSAs between 50,000 and 250,000 but rose by 1960 to 31.6 per cent, substantially above the 24.7 per cent expectation of larger areas. Further, the centers between 50,000 and 250,000 ac-

7. The percentage of fast-growers among centers below 50,000 is high throughout and rises steadily, but this derives from the self-selectivity of this group, which had to grow in order to qualify as an SMSA in 1960.

counted for 52 per cent of all 2M SGCs in 1950–1960 and 58 per cent in 1960–1965.

The sources of the declining national importance of these smaller metropolitan areas lie elsewhere. First, of course, there is the declining share of all metropolitan population in metropolitan centers of this size and the increasing share in larger centers. Second, there is the increasing probability of larger areas' being fast growers, which increased from nil (none of the twenty-one SMSAs greater than 250,000 qualified as a 2M SGC in 1900) to 24.7 per cent of 101 in 1960. Third and most important, there is the greater variability of growth rates for the smaller centers. Table 4 illustrates this point. The distribution of growth rates for larger centers is skewed to the right: with rare exceptions these centers grow either fast or at least steadily. Although some of the smaller centers grow faster than the larger ones, nearly one in ten is in fact losing population in absolute terms. This greater spread and symmetry in the distribution of smaller center growth rates means that the average rates of the smaller metropolitan size classes will be lower. Thus, information such as that in Table 5, although correct and frequently cited, must be accepted with some caution. It must not be thought that all smaller areas are growing slowly. Rather, smaller

Table 3. Percentage of SMSAs in Each Size Class That Were 2M SGCs

| SGC size (000) | 1900–1910 | 1910–1920 | 1920–1930 | 1930–1940 | 1940–1950 | 1950–1960 | 1960–1965 |
|---|---|---|---|---|---|---|---|
| Under 50 | 32.9 | 30.0 | 55.6 | 72.2 | 75.0 | 80.0 | 0 |
| 50–100 | 13.1 | 17.1 | 18.8 | 44.6 | 36.7 | 34.2 | 36.4 |
| 100–150 | 13.0 | 21.4 | 22.2 | 47.4 | 29.7 | 14.9 | 23.8 |
| 150–200 | 13.3 | 21.4 | 15.0 | 47.4 | 29.2 | 25.0 | 30.8 |
| 200–250 | 0 | 0 | 25.0 | 44.4 | 13.3 | 5.6 | 42.9 |
| 250–300 | 0 | 0 | 0 | 25.0 | 43.8 | 27.8 | 15.0 |
| 300–500 | 0 | 0 | 0 | 27.3 | 20.0 | 30.8 | 21.4 |
| 500–750 | 0 | 33.3 | 0 | 12.5 | 36.4 | 35.7 | 27.3 |
| 750–1000 | 0 | 0 | 20.0 | 0 | 20.0 | 14.3 | 71.4 |
| 1000–2000 | 0 | 0 | 20.0 | 0 | 20.0 | 14.3 | 21.4 |
| 2000+ | 0 | 0 | 0 | 14.3 | 14.3 | 12.5 | 20.0 |
| All SMSAs (212) | 18.9 | 18.9 | 22.6 | 41.1 | 32.6 | 24.5 | 28.3 |

metropolitan sizes are unstable, tending either to grow very fast into larger sizes or to lose ground.[8] But just what is meant by losing ground is not clear. There are as yet no instances of massive decline, such as has occurred in some towns and small cities, although many of the currently declining centers have been alternating absolute decline with insignificant growth for decades. It may be that policies and programs are needed in some cases not to induce growth but to facilitate and make decline less painful.

In brief, our discussion suggests that (1) smallish growth centers are possible and frequent, (2) smallish growth centers will not significantly affect national urbanization, although they may have great local regional importance, and (3) many successful smallish growth centers will grow to be far bigger because, as will be discussed below, spontaneous growth centers have considerable staying power.

Map 6 (1950–1960) and Map 7 (1960–1965) best illustrate the longevity of the SGCs. The numbers within the figures, which represent the number of decades each of the active SGCs has grown since 1900, make clear that most of the SGCs have had a long history of growth. It is harder to document this longevity statistically. For the 148 SMSAs that have met the 2M criterion at some point since 1900, the median number of years in the 2M category or higher is twenty-nine. But this would represent an underestimate of the typical growth period if one thinks of an S-curve of growth, since the sixty-five-year period would cut off portions of such curves before 1900 and, presumably, after 1965. The median number of growth years for the 1950–1960 2M centers was thirty-four years. Although this dropped to twenty-six years in 1960–1965, this drop was attributable to the rather large number (nine) of first-time centers. Looking at it another way, if a center had been growing in 1950–1960, its chances of growing at 2M in 1960–1965 were 61 per cent; if it had grown at 2M at any time since 1900, its chances of growing at this rate in 1960–1965 were 36.6 per cent. On the

8. Similar observations have been made recently by several authors. See E. Lampard, "The Evolving System of Cities in the U.S.," in H. S. Perloff and L. Wingo, eds., *Issues in Urban Economics* (Baltimore: Johns Hopkins Press, 1968), and W. R. Thompson, "The Future of the Detroit Metropolitan Area," in W. Haber *et al.*, eds., *Michigan in the 1970's: An Economic Forecast* (Ann Arbor: University of Michigan Graduate School of Business Administration, 1965). See also Berry and Neils, "Location, Size, and Shape of Cities," who base their argument on a break of the Pareto distribution.

Table 4. Number of SMSAs by Size and Growth Rates of Size Classes (1960–1965)

| Population Class (.000) | Less than −5% | −5 to 0% | 0–5% | 5–15% | 15–25% | 25–40% | 40+% | Avr. Gr.[a] |
|---|---|---|---|---|---|---|---|---|
| 50–100 | 0 | 2 | 4 | 11 | 2 | 0 | 0 | 6.8 |
| 100–150 | 1 | 3 | 11 | 18 | 1 | 1 | 0 | 6.0 |
| 150–200 | 0 | 2 | 10 | 8 | 7 | 0 | 1 | 9.4 |
| 200–250 | 0 | 3 | 3 | 10 | 1 | 0 | 2 | 11.4 |
| 250–300 | 0 | 3 | 8 | 9 | 6 | 0 | 0 | 7.6 |
| 300–500 | 0 | 1 | 8 | 17 | 3 | 1 | 0 | 8.8 |
| 500–750 | 0 | 0 | 5 | 12 | 1 | 0 | 0 | 8.4 |
| 750–1000 | 0 | 0 | 1 | 7 | 1 | 1 | 0 | 13.6 |
| 1000–2000 | 0 | 0 | 3 | 9 | 4 | 1 | 0 | 11.2 |
| 2000+ | 0 | 1 | 1 | 7 | 1 | 0 | 0 | 7.2 |

[a]Average of the growth rates of SMSAs in each size class.

other hand, a metropolitan area that had never been an SGC had only a 12.3 per cent chance of being a 2M SGC in 1960–1965.

The decade of the 1930s presents discontinuities in some of the trends and continuities in others. It was, of course, the decade of the Great Depression. It saw a proliferation of 2M SGCs and a great increase in the number of metropolitan areas that had net out-migration. In this it anticipated the most recent periods, in which SGCs accounted for increasing shares of all SMSA growth by intermetropolitan migration. Similarly, it anticipated the increasing share of the fastest growers (see Figure 1). However, it was an untypical regression to smaller places. Except for Washington, D.C. and one other, all SGCs were under 500,000 population, and nearly one-half of the SMSAs under 250,000 population qualified as 2M SGCs. Most of this growth was only a spurt, and the South and the Midwest in particular are crowded with centers that grew only in this decade because the trend toward bigger places resumed in the 1940s. On the one hand, this exhibits the weakness of demographic criteria for

Table 5. Population Change and Migration Rates for Metropolitan Areas 1960 to 1966, By Size in 1966

| Size Category | Number of Areas | Population 1966 (000) | Percentage of Change 1960–1966 | Net Migration 1960–1966 as Percentage of 1960 Population |
|---|---|---|---|---|
| All metropolitan areas | 221 | 132,160 | 10.8 | 2.4 |
| 2,000,000 and over | 11 | 49,223 | 8.7 | 1.2 |
| 1,000,000–2,000,000 | 19 | 25,192 | 14.3 | 5.2 |
| 500,000–1,000,000 | 36 | 24,572 | 11.5 | 2.9 |
| 200,000–500,000 | 76 | 22,757 | 11.9 | 2.7 |
| 100,000–200,000 | 61 | 8,858 | 9.4 | 0.3 |
| under 100,000 | 18 | 1,557 | 7.6 | −2.1 |

Source: Adapted from Table D, p. 5, U.S. Bureau of the Census, Series P-25 No. 427, "Estimates of the Population of Counties and Metropolitan Areas, July 1, 1966: A Summary Report" (Washington, D.C.: Government Printing Office, 1969).

socioeconomic purposes, for one may imagine the dismalness of these smaller metropolitan areas, crowded with impoverished farmers and with those who had given up on bigger cities. Such demographic growth under conditions of economic hardship can hardly be interpreted as development. The snuffing out of the growth of these centers with the return of economic vitality testifies to the pathology of this growth. On the other hand, for reasons that are unclear, the 1930s may have provided a boost to the viability of smaller centers, according to Table 3. In this table, the frequency or probability of high growth for the smaller centers may be viewed either as a long-run trend, or it may be viewed as an enduring effect of the 1930s, which pegged their growth levels to higher levels that are maintained even today. But there is no theoretical base for either interpretation, and although there appears to be pattern rather than randomness in these numbers (Table 3), a choice between these interpretations depends on squinting, preference, and numerology.

Maps 1 through 7 indicate several interesting features of the geographic distribution of SGCs. Perhaps the most striking is the antiquity of the growth in what may be called the "new regions": the older regions base their current growth on newer centers. The midwest's current SGCs are all new, and in fact there was a complete turnover of SGCs between the 1950s and the 1960s. The South, excepting Florida, experienced a flurry of growth in the 1930s, but the majority of these centers were quickly extinguished. There has been, however, sustained growth since then in centers in Virginia, the Carolinas, and Georgia. The Northeast presents most recently a flurry of quite recent centers, and these may be called "suburban metropolises." They include Brockton and Manchester in relation to Boston and a number of Connecticut areas in relation to New York. Such growth centers have a greater degree of

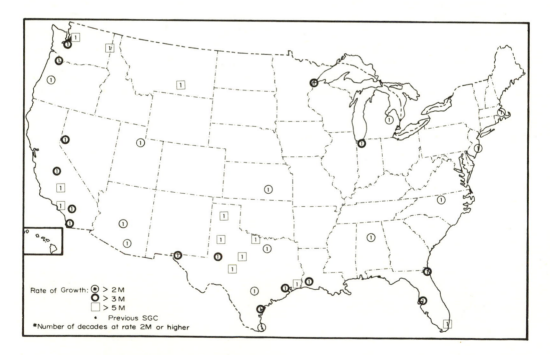

Map 1. Spontaneous Growth Centers, 1900-1910.

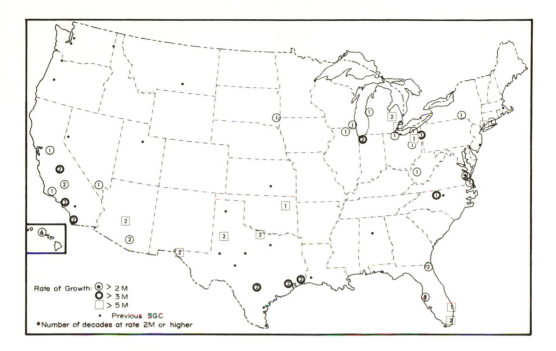

Map 2. Spontaneous Growth Centers, 1910-1920.

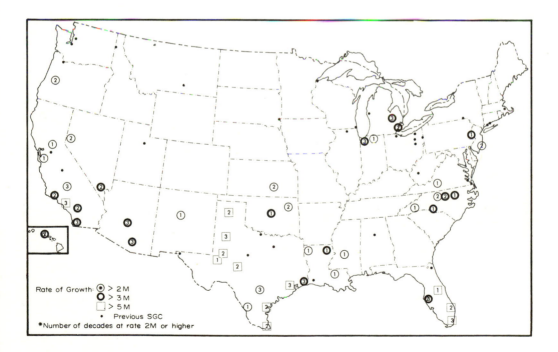

Map 3. Spontaneous Growth Centers, 1920-1930.

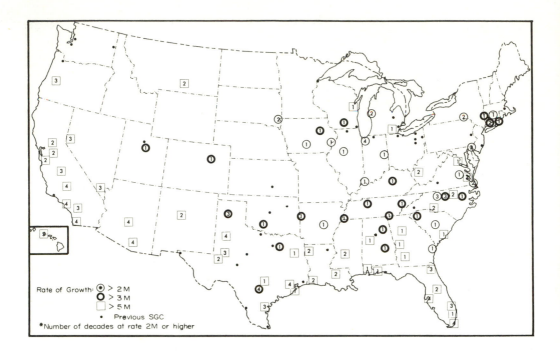

Map 4. Spontaneous Growth Centers, 1930-1940.

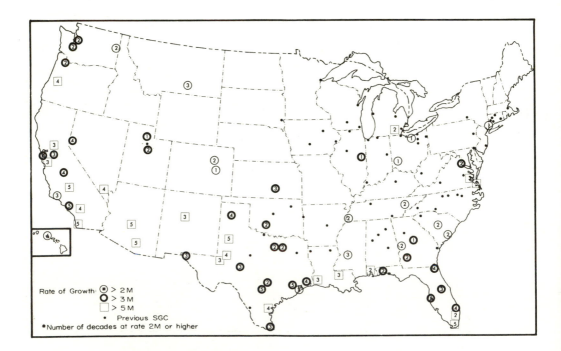

Map 5. Spontaneous Growth Centers, 1940-1950.

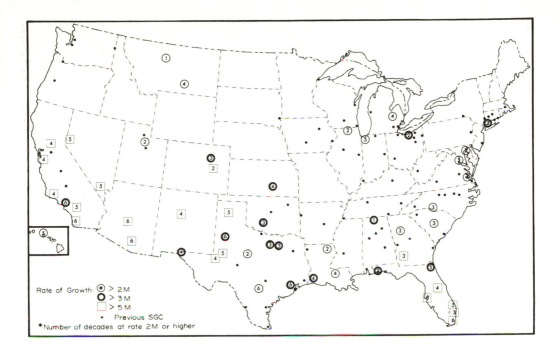

Map 6. Spontaneous Growth Centers, 1950-1960.

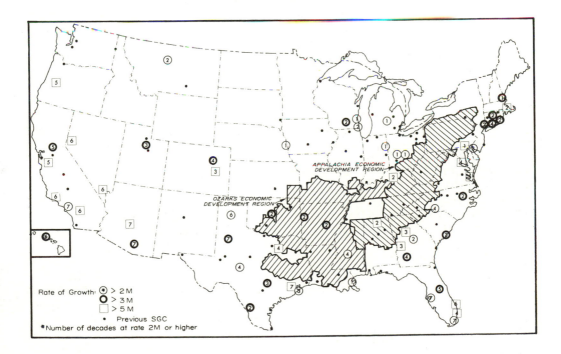

Map 7. Spontaneous Growth Centers, 1960-1965.

tional closure than an ordinary suburb, but they clearly owe their development to their adjacency to the larger centers. The phenomenon is not limited to the Northeast, as instanced by the continued growth of the San Jose area in relation to the San Francisco-Oakland metropolis. It is clear that in many cases and for many purposes the relevant unit for analysis is the complex of linked metropolitan areas, and that to deal with individual SMSAs in such cases may be as misleading as to work with data for a single municipality within a metropolitan area.[9]

The Appalachia Economic Development Region, shaded on Map 7, has had only one SGC since 1950. This is Huntsville, Alabama, and Huntsville owes its growth to the National Aeronautics and Space Administration activities. Other than this, Appalachia has had ten SGCs since 1900, but none has managed to grow for more than two decades; the majority of those in the southern half grew only in the 1930s, whereas most of those in the northern half grew only in the 1910s. It is not surprising that a region defined by its economic difficulties should be rather light in spontaneous growth, but the barrenness of this record is striking. In contrast, just to the east of southern Appalachia, a file of metropolitan areas in Virginia, North and South Carolina, and Georgia are exhibiting sustained growth with a median of twenty-seven years at 2M.

A Southwest depressed region, shown on Map 7, consisting of the Ozarks Economic Development Region plus all the contiguous authorized districts, presents a slightly better aspect. It has had seven SGCs since 1900 and has three current ones, as it had three in the 1950s. Curiously, the three in the 1960s are not the same as those of the earlier decade, so

that there have been six SGCs in the area since 1950.

CONCLUSION

Since the beginning of the century (and presumably earlier), a very large share of American metropolitan growth and a far larger share of the net in-migration into metropolitan areas have been absorbed by those metropolises that grew substantially faster than the metropolitan set. This share has been increasing recently, in spite of the declining importance of metropolitan in-migration, as a result of a more active and selective intermetropolitan migration. As the number of areas with substantial net in-migration has increased, so has the number of metropolises that are net exporters of people.

Although at any one time there are many metropolises putting on a spurt of growth that is not sustained, fast growth is more typically a long-run, sustained phenomenon, adding novae to the constellation of metropolitan areas. The metropolitan population of America continues to increase by means of these novae as well as by means of vegetative growth. At the same time, some of the new fast-growers are suburban metropolises in close relation to lower-growth, large metropolitan areas, suggesting that, as the metropolis transcended the city, new clusters of metropolitan areas are emerging as functional systems. But spontaneous growth centers are few and thus far episodic in areas of economic retardation such as Appalachia and the Ozarks.

Explicit American urbanization or urban growth policy has tended to limit itself to the question of induced growth centers in areas of retarded development. But growth has its problems, too, and national policy should concern itself with guiding the social, physical, institutional, and economic development of the emerging novae and of the evolving clusters of interdependent metropolises. On the other hand, growth might not be possible in some backward areas or not desirable in terms of the alternatives, and there national

9. The term *megalopolis* has sometimes been used for similar concepts, but it has some value connotations and is predicated on physical adjacency and geographic continuity of conurbation rather than on functional interdependence. *Megalopolis* means a very big city, and from medical usage, *megalo* implies abnormally big. Our meaning of a functional cluster of metropolitan areas would be better rendered by *genopolis*, meaning a tribe of cities.

policy should concern itself with welfare rather than developmental considerations. More generally, such a national policy should be framed in terms of guiding the development of the system of urban areas in accordance with national objectives. Within this more general system perspective, particular programs and policies, whether focused on the problems of growth or the lack of it, would be more intelligent and effective.

# Economic Fluctuations in the Australian Regional System

DOUGLAS JEFFREY and D. J. WEBB

Within the field of geography a well established research theme has been concerned with the description and explanation of spatial patterns of economic interaction within regional systems (see for example Berry, 1966; Ullman, 1957). Unfortunately these geographic studies have been limited in scope as regards the economy with which they purport to deal. Central place studies, for example, have concerned themselves exclusively with economic interaction in the tertiary sector. Those studies focusing specifically on patterns of spatial interaction have, for the most part, been concerned solely with "tangible" flows to the exclusion of "intangible" industrial and financial linkages (for example, Berry, 1966; and in an Australian context Smith, 1961, 1963). In addition to their limited scope the studies have generally been cross sectional and static in nature. The economic base and shift analysis studies (Fuchs, 1962; Perloff, 1960) illustrate the cross sectional approach to regional economic change. This paper provides a first airing of results obtained from a research project concerned with the identification of patterns of economic interaction in the Australian regional system. As such it falls within the well established geographic tradition of interaction studies. However the project will attempt to extend the scope of most previous work by focusing on the way in which entire regional economies interact within a dynamic framework. A significant portion of this interaction will be via the intangible industrial and financial linkages so long ignored by geographers.

A conceptual framework is first outlined structuring the way in which national, state and regional economic impulses may impinge upon a regional system. From this a model is developed for the quantitative separation of the local impact of both national and regional economic impulses. Using monthly unemployment rates as an index of local economic activity over time, the model is fitted to 73 local areas in Australia for the time period July, 1955 to December, 1970. Each local time series is decomposed into 3 components; a structural component, attributable to long term, non cyclical features of the local economy; a national cyclical component, attributable to national cyclical impulses; and a regional component reflecting the impact of purely regional cyclical impulses. It is postulated that regions displaying similar fluctuations in their regional components will be exposed to similar economic forces and may be characterised by a high degree of economic interaction. It is through the analysis of the regional cyclical components, from which the effects of long term and national cyclical forces have been removed, that patterns of regional economic interaction may be identified. However, such an analysis is not presented in this paper which contains only a discussion of the basic parameters of the

From *Australian Geographical Studies*, vol. 10, October 1972, pp. 141–60. Reprinted by permission.

model. Detailed analyses of the national, structural and regional components are reserved for subsequent publication.

## THE CONCEPTUAL FRAMEWORK

Consider a system of regions in an economically developed country. The regions are ordered in terms of population size and economic complexity. Amongst the regions there are variations in industrial mix and export base characteristics. The structural linkages between economic activities within the system result in spatial linkages between regions specialising in complementary activities. Now assume that short term economic impulses are introduced into the system. The literature on regional business cycles suggests that these impulses will be of two types (see Isard, 1960). On the one hand there are national impulses resulting from the impact of national cyclical forces on the levels of regional economic activity. Included among such forces would be changes in national monetary and fiscal policy, trends in consumer saving as opposed to spending, changes in business psychology with respect to investment, and international fluctuations in demand. All regions will not be affected equally by such forces but the differing regional reaction will be solely a function of the structural characteristics of the regional economy. The impact of national cyclical impulses will be experienced in an approximately uniform manner over space, though not in a uniform manner over different segments of the economy. The second type of impulse results from purely regional forces. Originating with certain regions, these impulses are transmitted through the regional system via a series of import-export ties. The causes of such regional impulses are numerous. They may result from the nature of regional response to national cyclical forces. For example, a region which responds in a distinctly different way to national business conditions may transmit this cyclical pattern to other regions with which it is strongly

linked. They may also result from purely regional phenomena. A series of plant closures, a local strike, or a natural disaster may be sufficient to generate regional cyclical impulses. With regard to the nature and intensity of regional impulses transmitted to and from it, the relative location of the region is crucial. They will spread through the system from their point of origin but in the process their impact will be dampened by the friction of space. The political economy of Australia operating as it does within a federal system of government would suggest a third or "intermediate" type of cyclical impulse which may result from the operation of state-wide economic forces. Within a given state political unit, such forces would act in a spatially uniform manner and this impact will be transmitted to other states via import-export ties. These so called "intermediate" forces would be expected to operate in Australia, for example, in so far as industrial and urban development and housing policies are state responsibilities.

In Figure 1 an attempt is made to structure the interaction of national, state and regional impulses and their impact on the local economy. Exogenous national forces produce national cyclical fluctuations within the system. The extent to which a given regional economy is affected by these national fluctuations is dependent on its structural characteristics. The influence of industrial mix and export base characteristics has been fully discussed in the literature on regional business cycles (Isard, 1970; Thompson, 1965). Those regions specialising in industries having high income elasticities of demand for their products will be more sensitive to national cyclical fluctuations. The growth performance and competitive advantage of a regional economy are also important in determining its degree of sensitivity to cyclical fluctuations. Cyclical instability tends to be associated with declining sectors of industry and is most pronounced where such sectors are concentrated locally (Mitchell, 1951). In a similar context Borts applies the concept of marginal production facilities to progressive and unprogres-

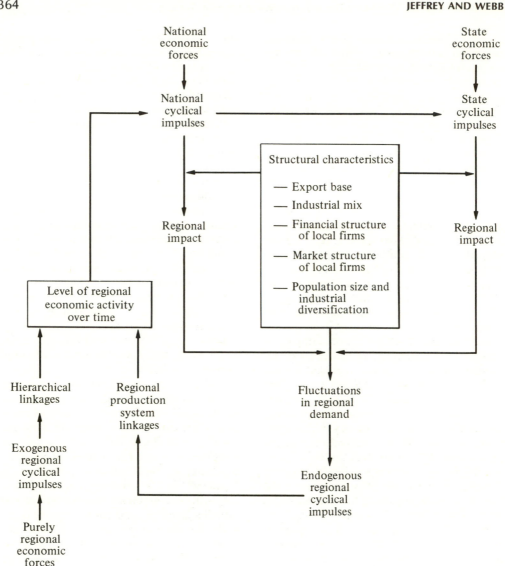

Figure 1. The Interaction of National, State, and Regional Impulses and Their Impact on the Local Economy.

sive firms in the same industry (Borts, 1960). He claims that a short run decline in demand consequent on a national recession might make production impossible for the unprogressive firms but allow progressive firms to stay in business and cover some portion of fixed costs. Where a region is dominated by unprogressive firms a greater degree of cyclical susceptibility is to be expected. This reasoning can be extended to cover interregional variations in production and transportation costs causing average and marginal cost curves to vary between firms in the same industry but in different regions. Regions might also vary in their cyclical susceptibility depending on the market structure of their major industries. As Thompson notes, if a region is dominated by smaller firms operating in a highly competitive market then price adjustments may lessen the impact on production and employment (Thompson, 1965). Conversely, if local firms are oligopolists administering their prices in collusion with a few non-price competitors then the full impact of demand fluctuations will be felt on production and employment levels. The financial structure of local firms may also affect the region's reaction to national business fluctuations. A high proportion of equity capital reduces the burden of fixed interest charges over a recession and increases the equity cushion making it easier to borrow in an emergency. The relationships between population size, industrial diversification and cyclical instability are also considered by Thompson. Increasing population size is usually associated with greater industrial diversification and diversification leads to a situation whereby national factors increase in relative importance with a regional cyclical response closely approximating the national pattern.

A more detailed discussion and testing of these relationships is reserved for a later paper. Here it is sufficient to note that national impulses, and impulses originating at the state level in a federal system, produce fluctuations in income and employment that vary in intensity, and possibly in timing, between regions. These in turn result in regional fluctuations in demand that differ in nature and intensity within the regional system (see Figure 1). Initially economic change will impinge most heavily upon certain industries located in certain regions. The changes brought about in these industries are transmitted to other industries and other regions where there is some degree of linkage. This transmission will be both direct and indirect. Directly, the effect will be felt through changes in expenditure on the exports of other regions. Indirectly the effect will be seen in changes in expenditures on residentiary industries, first in the regions themselves, then in all other regions in the

system. In addition to such endogenous regional impulses resulting from the nature of regional response to national forces there are also 'exogenous' regional impulses affecting regional levels of economic activity over time. Originating from purely local or regional factors, such as strikes, plant closures, natural disasters, the impact of these impulses will also be transmitted through the regional system.

Ultimately we are interested in the spatial manifestation of the regional cyclical interaction within the Australian regional economic system. Two distinct types of interaction might be initially hypothesised. If the lead of Vining is followed and central place notions are allied with the export base logic then it might be hypothesised that there exist regional sub-systems characterised by distinct cyclical patterns as a response to regional fluctuations transmitted through the sub-system via hierarchical linkages (Vining, 1956). It might also be hypothesised that regional impulses are transmitted via production system linkages existing between regions specialising in similar or complementary production activities.

## COMPONENTS OF REGIONAL UNEMPLOYMENT

In relation to this conceptual framework the initial problem is to achieve a quantitative separation of regional economic fluctuations which are attributable to national factors from those attributable to regional and local factors. Using regional unemployment rates over time as an index of the level of regional economic activity Brechling (1967) suggests a method whereby such a separation can be performed. He divides regional unemployment into three components, a national cyclical, a structural and a regional component.

The *national cyclical component* identifies that part of regional unemployment attributable to national levels of economic activity. If the national unemployment rate is taken as an index of the level of national economic activity then the national cyclical component of regional unemployment can be related to this index as follows:

$$N_{jt} = \alpha_j U_{t+n_j} \qquad (1)$$

where $N_{jt}$ = national cyclical component of unemployment in the $j$th region

$U$ = national unemployment rate

$t$ = time period $t$.

$n_j$ = length of lead or lag involved.

$\alpha_j$ = the sensitivity of $N_j$ to $U$.

The $\alpha_j$ parameter in the above equation provides a measure of the region's sensitivity to national cyclical fluctuations. If $\alpha_j = 1$ the region's cyclical fluctuations are as equally severe as the nation as a whole. If $\alpha_j > 1$ its cycles are more severe; conversely if $\alpha_j < 1$ its cycles are less severe than those of the nation.

In a recent study of cyclical fluctuations in the U.S. urban system Jeffrey reformulates this model in order to achieve a more precise separation of national cyclical effects (Jeffrey, 1970). It involves the use as a national index of a weighted national unemployment series defining the regional unemployment rate over time if each of the region's industries had the same unemployment rate as its national counterpart. However, since sufficiently disaggregated national unemployment rates by industry are not available for Australia, in this study the original Brechling formulation is employed.

Before the national cyclical component can be estimated the *structural component* of regional unemployment must be taken into account. Structural unemployment is caused by long term dislocations in labour market functioning which are brought about by structural shifts within the regional economic system (Gilpatrick, 1966; Casetti, King and Jeffrey, 1971). These shifts may result from changes in technology and final demand, the effects of which are concentrated locally. Alternatively, they may be related to changing locational patterns of industry and population. In either event, they act as destabilising forces producing long term structural imbalance within the system. At any point in time the degree of structural imbalance reflects the

rate at which structural shifts are occurring and the ability or willingness of the labour force to adjust. Following Brechling the structural component is assumed to conform to a quadratic time trend allowing it to be smoothly changing over time at an increasing or decreasing rate.

$$S_{jt} = c_j + b_j t + d_j t^2 \qquad (2)$$

where $S_{jt}$ = the structural component of regional unemployment at time $t$.

$c_j$ = $S_{jo}$ = the structural component at time zero.

$b_j, d_j$ = coefficients of the quadratic time trend.

The residuals from the national cyclical and structural components can be identified as the regional cyclical component $R_j$ attributable to regional cyclical impulses. If the residuals are positive the implication is that regional forces are operating to produce a higher rate of local unemployment than the level of economic activity in the nation would suggest. If the residuals are negative the reverse is the case. It should be noted, however, that where industries differ in national cyclical pattern and where the region differs significantly from the nation in its industrial mix then the regional component will contain an industrial mix component. However, this does not seriously affect the results discussed in this paper.

The level of unemployment in region $j$ at time $t$ is therefore made up of three additive components.

$$u_{jt} = S_{jt} + N_{jt} + R_{jt} \qquad (3)$$

Substituting for $S_j$ and $N_j$ from equations (1) and (2) then,

$$u_{jt} = c_j + b_j t + d_j t^2 + \alpha_j U_{t+n_j} + R_{jt} \qquad (4)$$

Given regional and national unemployment rates over time the parameters of equation 4 can be estimated by multiple regression techniques and $R_{jt}$ derived as a residual.

## DATA, REGIONS AND PARAMETER ESTIMATION

At this stage some justification for the use of unemployment data is called for. In any empirical study of regional economic fluctuations compromises must be made between the theoretically ideal and the data available. Three features of the present analysis suggest the appropriateness of unemployment data. Firstly, data are required for small regions over short time periods. Secondly, the study is concerned solely with the relative response of regional economies to cyclical impulses rather than with determining the absolute level of business activity over time. Finally, unemployment as an indicator reflects cyclical impulses because of its responsiveness to changes in aggregate demand.

Unemployment data were obtained from unpublished tabulations of the Department of Labour and National Service. These consisted of numbers of unemployed on a monthly basis for employment districts which in the aggregate comprise, although they are not coterminous with, the Local Government Areas as defined by the Bureau of Census and Statistics. The crude unemployment series were converted to unemployment rates using monthly estimates of the labour force for each employment area. The labour force estimates were obtained by extracting annual estimates of population by LGA which were aggregated to conform with the employment districts. A time trend was fitted to each series to obtain monthly estimates of local population. Labour force estimates were then derived by applying the labour force ratio which was obtained in the 1966 census. As a result of boundary changes the employment districts in this study are those as defined by the Department of Labour and National Service in July, 1955 (see Figure 2). There was therefore some aggregation of data where subdivision of employment districts had occurred over the study period from July, 1955 to December, 1970. Beginning at a national cyclical peak this period covers the recessions of 1956, 1961 and 1966 and subsequent recovery periods.

In the regression analyses to estimate the parameters of equation 4 dummy variables were introduced for seasonal adjustment and the following equation fitted for each area.

$$u_{jt} = c_j + b_j t + d_j t^2 + \alpha_j U_{t+n_i} + d_1 D_1 + d_2 D_2 + d_3 D_3 + d_4 D_4 + d_5 D_5 \quad (5)$$

where $d_{1,2,3,4,5}$ = the regression coefficients of the dummy variables for Jan/Feb, March/April, May/June, July/August, Sept/Oct respectively.

In order to determine the appropriate lead or lag (n) five different regression equations were run for each area with values of $n_j$ = −2, −1, 0, + 1 and + 2. In each case the lead or lag yielding the highest level of explained variance in $u_{jt}$ was adopted.*

## THE REGIONAL IMPACT OF NATIONAL CYCLICAL FLUCTUATIONS

Two parameters describe the relationships between national and regional cyclical fluctuations in unemployment. The coefficient $\alpha_j$ provides a measure of the sensitivity of regional unemployment to changes in national unemployment. Thus if $\alpha_j > 1$ the region's cyclical fluctuations are more severe than the nation's and if $\alpha_j < 1$ the reverse is the case. The $n_j$ parameter indicates the extent to which a regional economy leads or lags the nation in its response to national cyclical fluctuations. In addition the coefficient of determination $R^2$ indicates the importance of national factors in producing local cyclical unemployment fluctuations. The larger the $R^2$ value the greater the importance of national as opposed to regional cyclical forces.

The $R^2$ values are mapped in Figure 3. They range from a value of .89 for Brisbane to .08 for Longreach. A distinct regional pattern is apparent. In general those areas dominated by the larger urban centres have relatively high $R^2$ values implying that their economies are strongly influenced by fluctuations in the na-

*Table 1 in the original text, containing the seventy-three regression equations, was deleted from this paper.—Eds.

The numbers correspond to the
employment districts listed in
Table 1

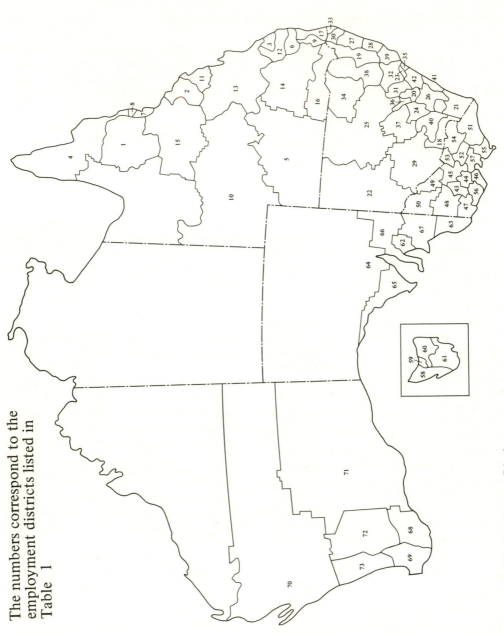

Figure 2. The Employment Districts.

The numbers correspond to the
employment districts listed in
Table 1

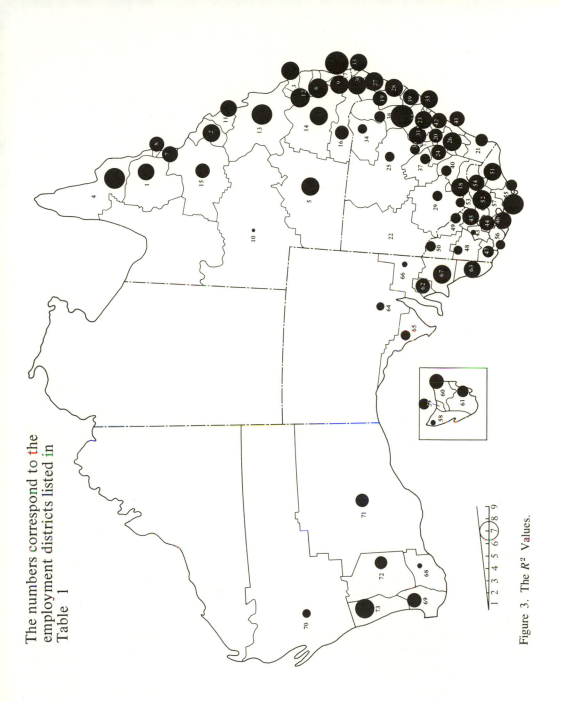

Figure 3. The $R^2$ Values.

tional economy. On the other hand those areas with economies dominated by rural activities have lower $R^2$ values implying a greater relative importance of regional factors. The high $R^2$ values for Perth (.80), Adelaide (.74), Melbourne (.86) and Brisbane (.89) and the extremely low values for the rural areas west of the Great Divide, for example, Longreach (.08), Narrabri (.44), Parkes (.42), Ararat (.20), Port Pirie (.22), Port Augusta (.37) and Albany (.20) support this generalisation. However the extremely high values for the employment areas of southeast Queensland and the Hunter Valley—Ipswich (.81), Gympie (.82), Toowoomba (.77), Cessnock (.72), Maitland (.86) and the relatively low values for Sydney (.65) and Wollongong (.64)—preclude a strict equation of the influence of national factors with population size. Clearly other factors such as industrial mix and export base characteristics play significant roles.

The values of $\alpha_j$ are mapped in Figure 4. They range from a high of 2.38 for Bundaberg to a low of .06 for Kerang, revealing considerable spatial variation in the intensity of national cyclical fluctuations. Again a rural/urban dichotomy is apparent, with cyclical sensitivity more characteristic of urban economies. This pattern, however, is much less clearly defined than with the $R^2$ values. Since the $U_t$ is merely an aggregate of the $u_{jt}$ it is not surprising that the major urban areas have a cyclical intensity closely approximating the national economy. However, Sydney (1.03) and Brisbane (1.09) display a greater degree of cyclical instability than the other capitals of Hobart (.96), Melbourne (.88), Adelaide (.82) and Perth (.66). Of particular interest is the extreme instability of the urban economies of Queensland and the Hunter Valley in New South Wales which contrasts with the relative cyclical stability of the rural areas of the eastern states and the whole of western Australia.

In interpreting the $n_j$ values displayed in Figure 5 it should be noted that positive values indicate that the region lags behind the nation and negative values indicate a lead. A marked spatial distribution of leads and lags is appar-

ent. Regional groups in South Australia and eastern Victoria (plus Bega, N.S.W.) consistently lead the nation. Others in the same category include Atherton, Kalgoorlie, Bunbury and Newcastle. Regions displaying no lead or lag include the major metropolitan areas, with the noticeable exception of Adelaide. In the same category are three major regional groupings comprising west-central Victoria, the area from south central New South Wales to Maryborough and a third extending from Mackay through to Cairns. The remaining regions of eastern Australia the economies of which are for the most part dominated by rural activities tend to lag the nation by one or two months.

## THE STRUCTURAL COMPONENTS OF REGIONAL UNEMPLOYMENT

As indicated earlier a structural component was introduced into the model to allow for long term structural unemployment. This was assumed to be a quadratic function of time (see equation 2). Since dummy variables were used for seasonal corrections the constant term $c_j$ must be obtained by averaging the five seasonal dummy constants and the regression constant. It ought to be noted that since $S_{jt}$ can be either positive or negative a strict equation of the structural component with the level of structural unemployment is not possible. The component merely measures the degree and direction of structural imbalance within a regional labour market in relation to the national norm. Nevertheless $S_{jt}$ can be equated with the incidence of structural imbalance in a relative sense in that the greater the $S_{jt}$ the greater the level of regional structural unemployment. The smaller the $S_{jt}$ the more likely is the region to experience pressure on its labour market in periods approaching full employment in the nation.

The $c_j$ values indicating the levels of regional structural imbalance in June 1955 ($S_{jo}$) are listed in Table 1. It is evident that few of the $S_{jo}$ values differ to any great extent from zero. Only Cairns (.85), Ingham (.77), Maryborough ($-.75$), Rockhampton (1.25),

The numbers correspond to the employment districts listed in Table 1

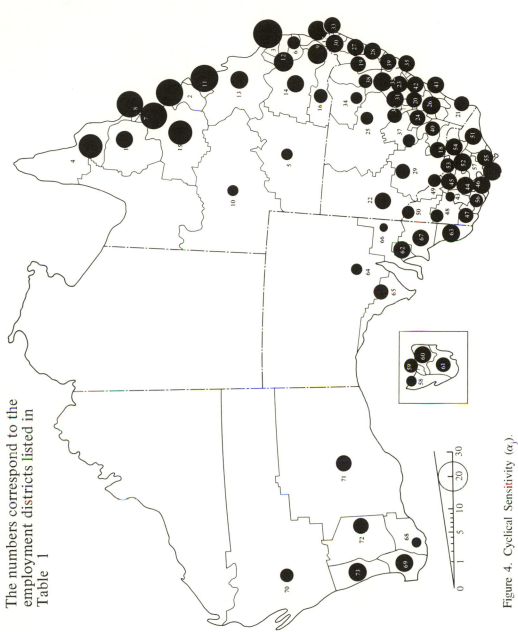

Figure 4. Cyclical Sensitivity ($\alpha_j$).

The numbers correspond to the employment districts listed in Table 1

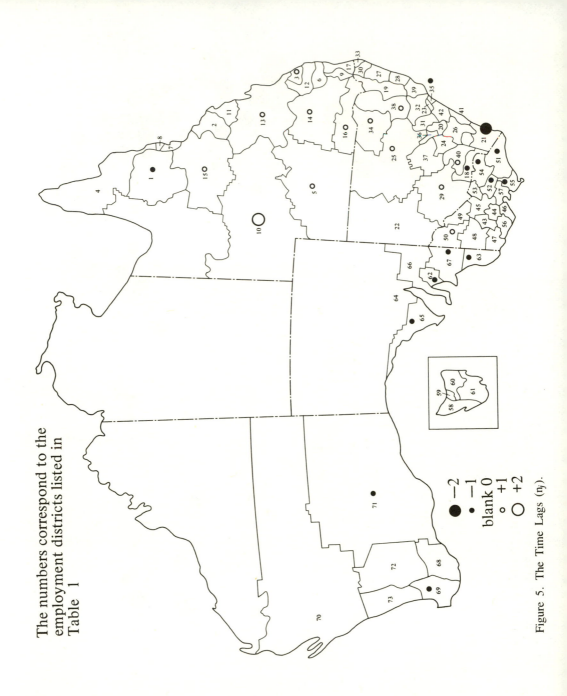

Figure 5. The Time Lags (n_j).

Table 1. Structural Components in Regional Unemployment June 1955 and Dec. 1970

| | $S_{jt}$ | | | | $S_{jt}$ | |
|---|---|---|---|---|---|---|
| | $t = 0$ | $t = 186$ | | | $t = 0$ | $t = 186$ |
| 1 Atherton | .38 | .64 | 38 Tamworth | | .23 | .41 |
| 2 Ayr | −.19 | 3.39 | 39 Taree | | −.46 | −.98 |
| 3 Bundaberg | .39 | 1.08 | 40 Wagga | | .22 | 1.30 |
| 4 Cairns | .85 | 1.96 | 41 Wollongong | | .01 | .26 |
| 5 Charleville | −.11 | .41 | 42 Sydney | | −.15 | −.57 |
| 6 Gympie | −.32 | 1.79 | 43 Ararat | | −.20 | .11 |
| 7 Ingham | .77 | .05 | 44 Ballarat | | −.08 | .58 |
| 8 Innisfail | .44 | .54 | 45 Bendigo | | .04 | .56 |
| 9 Ipswich | −.41 | −1.70 | 46 Geelong | | −.14 | .55 |
| 10 Longreach | .01 | .56 | 47 Hamilton | | .04 | .11 |
| 11 Mackay | .16 | .69 | 48 Horsham | | −.05 | .06 |
| 12 Maryborough | −.75 | .72 | 49 Kerang | | −.14 | .72 |
| 13 Rockhampton | 1.25 | .25 | 50 Mildura | | −.24 | .30 |
| 14 Toowoomba | −.38 | .69 | 51 Sale | | .05 | .89 |
| 15 Townsville | .22 | .80 | 52 Seymour | | −.34 | 1.94 |
| 16 Warwick | −.36 | .53 | 53 Shepparton | | −.14 | 1.47 |
| 17 Brisbane | −.04 | −.47 | 54 Wangaratta | | −.24 | .31 |
| 18 Albury | −.36 | .69 | 55 Warragul | | −.34 | .57 |
| 19 Armidale | .43 | −.33 | 56 Warrnambool | | −.06 | .15 |
| 20 Bathurst | .42 | .70 | 57 Melbourne | | −.08 | −.75 |
| 21 Bega | −.17 | .12 | 58 Burnie | | −.45 | .56 |
| 22 Broken Hill | −.41 | −.11 | 59 Devonport | | .39 | 1.71 |
| 23 Cessnock | −.08 | −1.17 | 60 Launceston | | −.51 | −.09 |
| 24 Cowra | .29 | .79 | 61 Hobart | | −.85 | −1.19 |
| 25 Dubbo | −.15 | .46 | 62 Gawler | | −.69 | .53 |
| 26 Goulburn | .03 | .32 | 63 Mt. Gambier | | −.26 | .57 |
| 27 Grafton | −.20 | .90 | 64 Pt. Augusta | | .07 | 1.15 |
| 28 Kempsey | .00 | .17 | 65 Pt. Lincoln | | −.14 | .56 |
| 29 Leeton | .08 | .49 | 66 Pt. Pirie | | .60 | 2.17 |
| 30 Lismore | .84 | 1.10 | 67 Adelaide | | −.34 | .55 |
| 31 Lithgow | .07 | −1.40 | 68 Albany | | .29 | .61 |
| 32 Maitland | .19 | −2.10 | 69 Bunbury | | −.32 | 2.41 |
| 33 Murwillumbah | .08 | .74 | 70 Geraldton | | .12 | 1.27 |
| 34 Narrabri | −.15 | .49 | 71 Kalgoorlie | | .57 | −.17 |
| 35 Newcastle | −.03 | −.48 | 72 Northam | | .14 | .34 |
| 36 Orange | .45 | 1.51 | 73 Perth | | .66 | −.98 |
| 37 Parkes | .17 | .23 | | | | |

Lismore (.84), Hobart (−.85), Gawler (−.69), Kalgoorlie (−.57) and Perth (.66) have absolute values greater than .50. The relatively uniform levels of the structural components recorded for the remaining regions (see Figure 6) implies that in the mid 1950s a labour market situation approximating a condition of long term spatial balance prevailed within the Australian regional economic system. This situation, however, altered significantly over the study period.

Figure 7 indicates the changes that occurred in the structural components of regional unemployment from June, 1955 to December, 1970. The significant feature of this map is that relatively few regions have been characterised by decreasing levels of structural unemployment. These correspond to the major metropolitan areas of Perth, Melbourne, Sydney, Brisbane and Hobart along with the provincial areas centred on Ingham, Rockhampton, Ipswich, Armidale,

The numbers correspond to the
employment districts listed in
Table 1

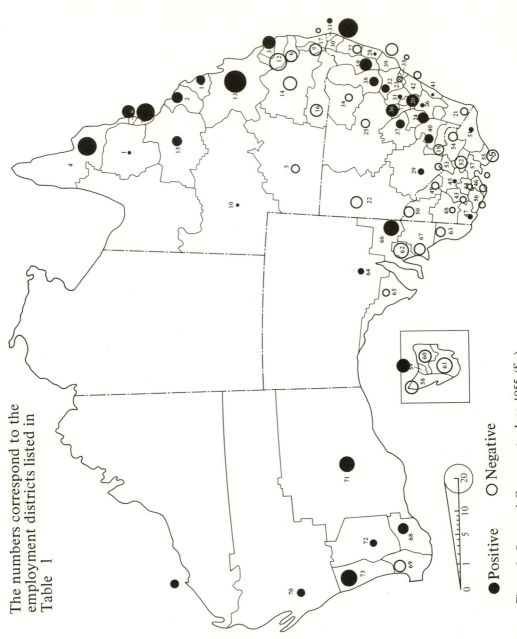

Figure 6. Structural Components, June 1955 ($S_{jo}$).

● Positive    ○ Negative

The numbers correspond to the
employment districts listed in
Table 1

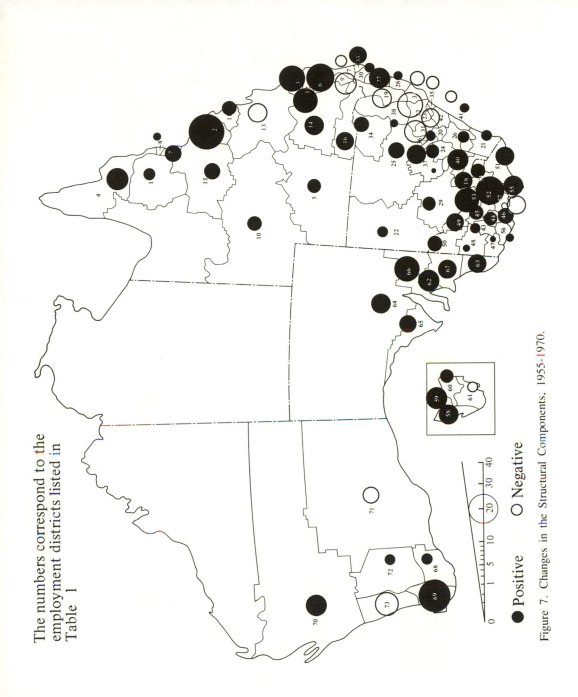

Figure 7. Changes in the Structural Components, 1955-1970.

The numbers correspond to the
employment districts listed in
Table 1

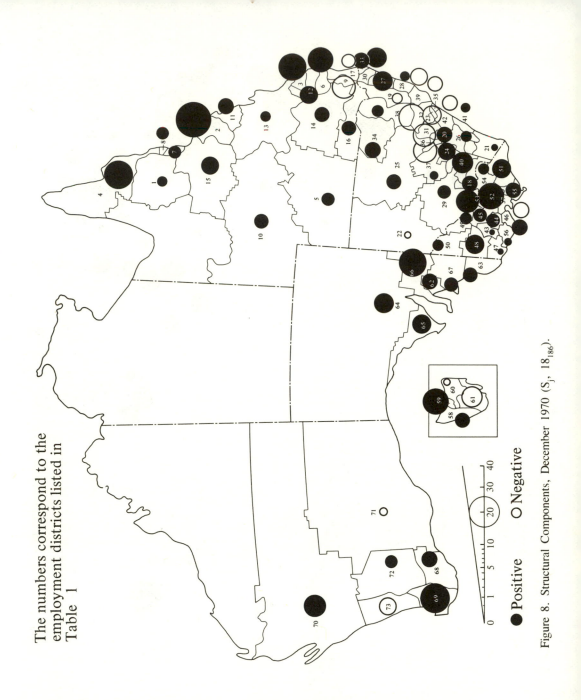

Figure 8. Structural Components, December 1970 ($S_j$, $18_{186}$).

and the Hunter Valley. All other regions have experienced increasing levels of structural unemployment. This trend has been particularly marked in the rural areas of northeastern Victoria and southeastern Queensland. The result is that by December, 1970 (see Figure 8) the Australian labour market is characterised by a marked regional pattern of structural imbalance. The major metropolitan areas, with the noticeable exception of Adelaide, along with the urban concentrations in the Hunter Valley plus Ipswich, Rockhampton, Broken Hill and Kalgoorlie have low levels of structural unemployment, possibly indicative of long term inflationary pressure on their regional labour markets. The remainder of rural Australia is characterised by high levels of structural unemployment, indicative of long term dislocation in labour market functioning. This is particularly noticeable in east-central Victoria, south-central New South Wales and coastal Queensland. Adelaide provides the only major exception to this rural urban-urban dichotomy.

## CONCLUSION

This paper must be placed within the context of a more extensive research project by the authors into cyclical fluctuations in the Australian regional-economic system. It merely provides the foundation on which this research is built. Only the basic parameters of the model have been presented and no attempt has been made at explanation. Nevertheless the results are of considerable interest in that they confirm the existence of a rural-urban dichotomy in the economic performance of regional economies in Australia.

A comparison of Figures 3 to 8 indicates that economies of regions dominated by major urban areas tend to be cyclically unstable, strongly influenced by national factors, approximate the national economy in the timing of their cyclical response and over the study period have experienced decreasing levels of structural unemployment. On the other hand regions dominated by rural activities tend to be cyclically stable, only weakly influenced by the national economy and have experienced increasing levels of long term structural unemployment. For the most part they tend to lag behind the nation in the timing of their cyclical response except for parts of rural South Australia and Victoria. Two major regional deviations from this generalisation are apparent. First, the employment areas of northern and southeastern Queensland combine their urban cyclical pattern with a long term deterioration in their labour market situations. Second, in South Australia increasing structural unemployment has occurred in both rural and urban regions. These insights provided into the differing response of rural and urban economies to long term structural shifts, and short term national business cycle fluctuations, have real relevance to the formulation of realistic regional planning policies.

## REFERENCES

Airov, J., 1963. The construction of interregional business cycle models, *J. Regional Science*, 10, 1–19.

Berry, B.J.L., 1966. *Essays in commodity flows and the spatial structure of the Indian economy*, (Chicago, The University of Chicago, Department of Geography Research Paper 111).

Borts, G. H., 1960. *Regional cycles of manufacturing employment in the United States, 1914–1953*, (New York, National Bureau of Economic Research).

Brechling, F., 1967. Trends and cycles in British regional unemployment, *Oxford Economic Papers*, 19, 1–21.

Casetti, E., King, L. and Jeffrey, D., 1971. Structural imbalance in the U.S. urban economic system, 1960–1965, *Geographical Analysis*, 3, 239–55.

Fuchs, V., 1962. *Changes in the location of manufacturing in the United States*, (New Haven and London, Yale University Press).

Gilpatrick, E. G., 1966. *Structural unemployment and aggregate demand*, (Baltimore, Johns Hopkins University Press).

Isard, W., 1960. *Methods of regional analysis*, (Cambridge, Mass., M.I.T. Press).

Jeffrey, D., 1970. *Economic impulses in an urban system* (Unpublished Ph.D dissertation, Ohio State University).

————., Casetti, E. and King, L. J., 1969. Economic fluctuations in a multiregional setting: a bi-factor analytic approach, *Regional Science,* 9, 397–404.

————. Economic impulses in a regional system of cities: a study of spatial interaction, *Regional Studies,* 3, 213–18.

Mitchell, W., 1951. *What happens during business cycles,* (New York, National Bureau of Economic Research).

Perloff, H. S. et al., 1960. *Regions, resources and economic growth* (Baltimore, Johns Hopkins University Press).

Smith, R.H.T., 1961. Methods in commodity flow studies, *Austr. Geogr.* 8, 73–7.

————. 1963. Railway commodity movements between N.S.W. and Victoria, *Austr. Geogr.,* 9, 88–96.

Suits, D. B., 1957. Use of dummy variables in regression equations, *J. Amer. Statistical Association,* 52, 548–51.

Thirlwall, A. P., 1966. Regional unemployment as a cyclical phenomenon, *Scottish J. Political Economy,* 13, 205–18.

————., 1968. Types of unemployment: With special reference to non demand-deficient unemployment in Great Britain, *Scottish J. Political Economy,* 15, 20–49.

Ullman, E. L., 1957. *American commodity flows: a geographic interpretation of rail and water traffic based on principles of spatial interchange* (Seattle, University of Washington Press).

Vining, R., 1946. The region as a concept in business cycle analysis, *Econometrica,* 14, 201–18.

————., 1949. The region as an economic entity and certain variations to be observed in the study of systems of regions, *Pap. Proc. American Economic Association,* 39, 89–104.

# The Spatial Structure of Migration Behavior

PAUL J. SCHWIND

In the context of regional development and growth, major spatial patterns of migration behavior need to be identified and related to the major dimensions of spatial structure. To this end, we require indices of regional attractiveness to migrants and salient measures of migration flows for incorporation in any analytical model. The analysis of migration and regional characteristics is constrained by demographic, temporal, and spatial aggregation problems, particularly in establishing connections between personal and group decision-making processes and observed migration patterns.

Migration is only one form of mobility experienced by the population. In addition to the spatial mobility category into which migration falls, there are the categories of (1) occupational mobility, involving the shifting of persons in the labor force between industrial or occupational categories of employment, or between individual or corporate employers; (2) social mobility, involving the change in status of persons as measured by a change in their income or educational attainment; and (3) life cycle mobility, involving the passage of individuals through stages of childhood, early adulthood, marriage, family raising, middle age, and old age and retirement. Analysis of any one of these closely interrelated forms of mobility can provide insights into the processes and patterns of the others, within the limitations of aggregated data.

## Aggregation Problems in Migration Analysis

Unless detailed population register data are available, we generally have insufficient information from Census sources to analyze simultaneously occupational, social, life cycle, and spatial mobility. The limitations are of three kinds. Demographically, detail on individual "migration units" (persons, families, households) or "population profiles" (groupings of individuals or households relatively uniform in terms of the mover-stayer decision)[1] is lost when only aggregate numbers of migrants in streams are recorded. Temporally, the effects of cyclical patterns, multiple and transient (short-term) moves, and mortality of migrants are increasingly obscured the longer the time interval for recording migration.[2] Spatially, increasing areal size and regularity of shape reduce the probability that individual random moves will be recorded and that small-scale effects on the distance and direction of migration will be detected.[3]

1. Julian Wolpert, "The Basis for Stability of Interregional Transactions," *Geographical Analysis*, I (April, 1969), 154.
2. See *ibid.*, pp. 175–76; and D. J. Bogue, H. S. Shryock, and S. A. Hoermann, *Streams of Migration Between Subregions*, (Oxford, Ohio: Scripps Foundation), pp. 4–5.
3. Spatial effects in migration analysis are well reviewed in E. S. Lee *et al.*, *Methodological Considerations and Reference Tables*, (Philadelphia, 1957) pp. 10–12; Allan Pred, *The External Relations of Cities During "Industrial Revolution,"* Department of Geography Research Paper No. 76 (Chicago: University of Chicago, 1962), pp. 67–68.

From *Migration and Regional Development in the United States* (Research Paper 133, Department of Geography, University of Chicago, 1971). Reprinted by permission.

This essay's investigation of the quantitative, locational, and directional aspects of migration flows among a large number of United States nodal regions must preclude consideration of age, sex, race, and occupation differentials among migrants, or of cyclical patterns prior to, within, or following the 1955–1960 period for which the migration stream data were recorded. However, some inferences regarding the aggregate spatial patterns of migration are possible from demographic and time-series analyses of occupational, social, and life cycle mobility in which spatial detail was suppressed, and from cross-sectional analyses of net migration-at-place. These inferences suggest variables for incorporation in a general model of the magnitude and net direction of migration.

## Personal Motivations and Group Mobility Behavior

A conscious desire for economic and social mobility seems directly or indirectly (through familial dependency) to provide the basic motivation for the majority of migrants, who seek better jobs, higher incomes, more education, and less social or racial discrimination.[4] What is most relevant in evaluating economic motivations for migration may be the fact that many migrants, particularly better educated

and informed individuals, migrate not so much for immediate gain in income as for the *prospect* of a more rewarding job opportunity (in terms not only of salary but of promotion, challenging tasks, pleasant working conditions, etc.) over an extended period of time.

The basic economic and social motivations to migration apparently do not apply equally to all individuals. A variety of studies have recorded the following migration differentials (relative rates of mobility) for occupation, income, age, sex, and race sub-groups of the United States population:[5]

(1) Professional workers and high-income, well-educated persons are more mobile over long distances than manufacturing, service, and trade workers and low-income, poorly educated persons. The latter, conversely, are more mobile over short distances. Unemployed persons in the labor force are more mobile than employed persons, who are more mobile than those not in the labor force at all (the very young, housewives, the very old and retired, and the least advantaged).

(2) Mobility rates peak between age 25 and 30, and fall off sharply for both younger and older migrants over all distances.

(3) Males are somewhat more mobile than females. Single persons are more mobile than married persons.

(4) Whites are more mobile than Negroes over long distances, while Negroes have greater rates of mobility for both short-distance (intra-urban) and lifetime (birthplace to present residence) moves, the latter clearly reflecting the substantial and continuing shift to northern and western cities of Negroes born in the South. Negroes seem to be less responsive than whites to local unemployment rates and to the present value of the income gain from migrating.[6]

The average socio-economic status of all migrants at their destinations has been found to be equal to or higher than that of non-migrant previous residents of the area, the

4. Only the rudiments exist of a theory of individual spatial decision-making related to migration. See: Julian Wolpert, "The Decision Process in Spatial Context," *Annals of the Association of American Geographers*, LIV (December, 1964), 537–58; *idem*, "Behavioral Aspects of the Decision to Migrate," *Papers of the Regional Science Association*, XV (1965), 159–69; Thomas R. Ford, "The Passing of Provincialism," and James S. Brown and George A. Hillery, Jr., "The Great Migration, 1940–1960," in *The Southern Appalachian Region: A Survey*, ed. Thomas R. Ford (Lexington: University of Kentucky Press, 1962), pp. 16–18 and 74–76; Roscoe Giffin, "Newcomers from the Southern Mountains," in *Institute on Cultural Patterns of Newcomers: Selected Papers* (Chicago: Welfare Council of Metropolitan Chicago, 1957), pp. 15–40; John Gulick, Charles E. Bowerman, and Kurt W. Back, "Newcomer Enculturation in the City: Attitudes and Participation," in *Urban Growth Dynamics in a Regional Cluster of Cities*, ed. F. Stuart Chapin and Shirley F. Weiss (New York: John Wiley and Sons, Inc., 1962), pp. 315–58; A. J. Fielding, "Internal Migration and Regional Economic Growth—A Case Study of France," *Urban Studies*, III (November, 1966), 200–14; and Russell B. Adams, *Population Mobility in the Upper Midwest*, Urban Report No. 6 (Minneapolis: Upper Midwest Economic Study, 1964).

5. Bogue, Shryock, and Hoermann, *Streams of Migration Between Subregions*, pp. 17–22, 46–63.
6. Warren F. Mazek, "Unemployment and the Efficacy of Migration: The Case of Laborers," *Journal of Regional Science*, IX (April, 1969), 101–7.

exceptions being migrants from non-metropolitan origins.[7] This reflects the predominantly intermetropolitan character of most migration, and the fact that a majority of migrants have had prior residential experience in urban areas.

It has been noted that migration seems not to increase the average earnings of migrants, at least not initially, but also that income is inconsistent in its relationship to mobility when compared with other indices of socio-economic status.[8] Thus the average status of migrants may be higher than that of non-migrant populations, despite negative migrant/non-migrant earnings differentials within specific occupational subgroups, simply because the younger and upper-status population groups tend to be the most mobile in general and over long distances in particular.

In summary, migration as spatial mobility is seen so far as a function of two orderly processes: occupational socio-economic mobility and movement through the family life cycle.[9] Thus educational status (as an index of occupational and socio-economic status) and age have been found to be, in combination, the two most efficient predictors of spatial mobility differentials.[10]

## Migration and Consumption Preferences

Part of the difficulty in assessing the causes and effects of population migration is that not all migrants are members of the labor force, nor are all migrants responding to strictly economic "signals" such as wage rates or per capita income differences, assuming these regional differences are even known to the majority of migrants. Migration decisions are generally influenced by consideration of en-

vironmental amenities (climate, housing quality, city "bright lights"). Migration is certainly directly affected by "changes in consumption associated with increasing per capita income and other features of modern economic growth."[11] Significant changes in consumption, which may directly induce migration, occur when a person retires from active participation in the labor force; when a person completes his education, particularly at the higher levels; and when a person contemplates changing high-income jobs, whereby the amenities and conditions of work and life associated with the job may be more important than its gross wage or salary. As the retired population grows, as higher education is extended to wider groups of the population, and as incomes from wages and salaries increase generally, we should expect consumption preferences to be increasingly influential in migration decisions.

## Regional Attractiveness Defined

"Attractive" regions are those experiencing positive net inmigration, with which the following broad characteristics are associated: relative concentrations of opportunities for occupational, financial, educational, and social mobility; relative concentrations of desirable environmental amenities; and relative concentrations of the young and well-educated—the most mobile groups. This interpretive definition is confirmed in the literature analyzing place-specific migration.

High values of the following variables have been found to be positively associated with net migration at regions: level of urbanization (per cent urban population), number of jobs and job vacancies (size of labor force), employment in professions and services (the growing sectors), per capita income, median education, and population "turnover" and/or "holding power."[12] Regions of "favorable" (warm and dry) climate and in reach of

7. Ronald Freedman, *Recent Migration to Chicago* (Chicago: University of Chicago Press, 1950), pp. 209–10.
8. Bogue, Shryock, and Hoermann, *Streams of Migration Between Subregions*, p. 22.
9. Jack Ladinsky, "Sources of Geographic Mobility among Professional Workers: A Multivariate Analysis," *Demography*, IV, No. 1 (1967), 293–309.
10. Wolpert, "Basis for Stability of Interregional Transactions," pp. 158–59.

11. S. Kuznets, "Introduction," *Selected Studies of Migration Since WWII* (New York: Millbank Fund, 1958), p. xxviii.
12. Adams, *Population Mobility in the Upper Midwest*, p. iv.

mountains and/or oceans are notably attractive, such that these amenities may be partly substitutable for monetary return to migration.[13] Variables such as employment in manufacturing (a relatively stagnant sector) and nonwhite population may be indeterminate in their effect on net migration depending on the scale of analysis.[14] Net migration is negatively associated with unemployment, per cent rural farm population (reflecting the declining agricultural sector), and median age of population.[15] Combined, the above variables constitute a set of positive and negative indices of regional attractiveness for incorporation in a model of net migration.

## Correlates of Net Migration

Assuming an initial condition of spatial disequilibrium, locational shifts of population may simultaneously increase individual welfare (by raising incomes and augmenting job opportunities for those who move) and reduce average regional disparities (by altering supply-demand relations, hence wage structures, in regional labor markets). If migration is properly performing this equilibrating function, economically motivated net migration may be poorly or even negatively associated with rising per capita income and declining unemployment as indices of regional attractiveness.

Sjaastad did find the change in state per capita income to be negatively correlated with state net migration rates of males.[16] Lowry

made equivalent findings for Standard Metropolitan Statistical Areas (SMSA), but was unable to interpret to his satisfaction the negative partial correlation coefficients of both median income and change in median income in his model to explain net migration rates.[17] The first coefficient may have resulted from the fact that recent migrants earn less than older migrants, or to the fact that high median incomes imply high living costs which migrants seek to avoid. The second coefficient may in fact have been due to the depressing effect on urban per capita income growth of employment structural shifts in favor of low-wage service industry jobs in expanding labor markets.[18]

Mueller reported that the rate of outmigration from counties during 1950–1960 was *positively* related to county per capita income and *negatively* related to county unemployment rates and duration, when 1960 statistics were employed, although outmigration rates for the period were highest for counties of roughly average 1950 per capita income.[19] Marsh found that at areas of high local unemployment rates, outmigration rates were not relatively increased, but rather inmigration rates were retarded.[20] The problem of negative net migration at relatively depressed areas is, then, not so much due to selective outmigration as to their failure to attract sufficient numbers of positively selected inmigrants.[21]

Interpretation of the above evidence is insufficient to establish the efficacy of migration as an independent equilibrating response of the population to regional disparities in income and unemployment.

13. Lay James Gibson, "The Amenities as a Factor in Arizona's Population Growth," *Annals of Regional Science,* III (June, 1969), 192–99.

14. Recently, von Böventer has found employment in manufacturing to be *negatively* associated with net migration to large German cities, though positively associated with migration to smaller cities. Edwin von Böventer, "Determinants of Migration into West German Cities, 1956–61, 1961–66," *Papers of the Regional Science Association,* XXIII (1969), 53–62.

15. Cicely Blanco, "Prospective Unemployment and Interstate Population Movements," *Review of Economics and Statistics,* XLVI (May, 1964), 221–22; and Larry A. Sjaastad, "The Relationship Between Migration and Income in the United States," *Papers and Proceedings of the Regional Science Association,* VI (1960), 37–64.

16. Sjaastad, "Relationship Between Migration and Income in the United States," pp. 37–64.

17. I. Lowry, *Migration and Metropolitan Growth,* (San Francisco: Chandler, 1966), pp. 50–52.

18. Between 1950 and 1962, employment opportunities declined in the high-wage manufacturing industries and increased in the low-wage trade, service, and clerical occupations. Lloyd Ullman, "Labor Mobility and the Industrial Wage Structure in the Postwar United States," *Quarterly Journal of Economics* (February, 1965), 73–93.

19. U.S. Department of Commerce, Area Redevelopment Administration, *Migration into and out of Depressed Areas,* by Eva Mueller *et al.* (Washington, D.C.: Government Printing Office, 1964), pp. 5–14.

20. Marsh, "Geographic Labor Mobility in the United States," pp. 17–20.

21. Lowry, *Migration and Metropolitan Growth,* pp. 30–33.

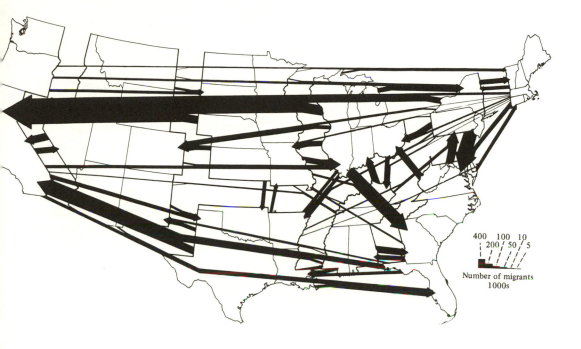

Figure 1. Interregional Migration, 1955-1960. Gross.

## Aggregate Migration Patterns

Several attempts have been made at descriptive generalization of the complex patterns of migration volumes and directions in the United States.[22] The observed patterns of mi-

22. C. Warren Thornthwaite, *Internal Migration in the United States,* Study of Population Redistribution, Bulletin No. 1 (Philadelphia: University of Pennsylvania Press, 1934); Bogue, Shryock, and Hoermann, *Streams of Migration Between Subregions,* pp. 75–76; Daniel O. Price, "Distance and Direction as Vectors of Internal Migration, 1935 to 1940," *Social Forces,* XXVII (October, 1948), 48–53; James D. Tarver, William R. Gurley, and Patrick M. Skees, "Vector Representation of Migration Streams among Selected State Economic Areas During 1955 to 1960," *Demography,* IV, No. 1 (1967), 1–18; Julian Wolpert, "Distance and Directional Bias in Inter-Urban Migratory Streams," *Annals of the Association of American Geographers,* LVII (September, 1967), 605–16; Richard Lycan, "Matrices of Inter-Regional Migration," *Proceedings of the Association of American Geographers,* I (1969), 89–95; Philip H. Vernon, "Distance Selectivity of U.S. Labor Force Migration, 1960–1963," *Proceedings of the Association of American Geographers,* I (1969), 153–56.

gration during the 1930–1960 period have been these:

(1) A general rural-to-urban shift, consisting of farm to nonfarm, small town to metropolis, and farm to metropolis components.

(2) A general westward shift of the population, particularly from the Midwest to the West Coast.

(3) Pronounced countervailing movements of whites from the Northeast to the Gulf South, particularly to Florida, and of Negroes from the South to northern metropolises.

(4) A general suburbanization process representing both turnover and transition of central city populations and the accommodation of urban population growth at the expanding edge of cities.

(5) A predominance of urban-to-urban (intermetropolitan) flows among a variety of flow types (rural-to-urban, rural-to-suburban, etc.).

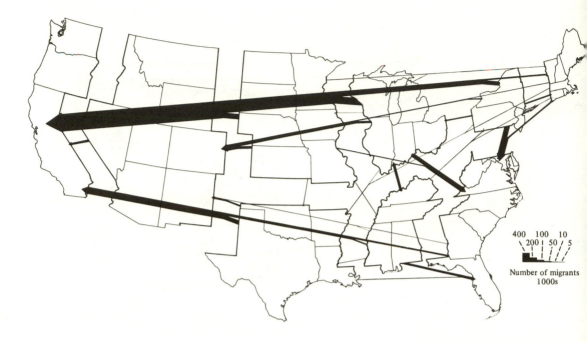

Figure 2. Interregional Migration, 1955-1960. Net.

The highly aggregated gross volume and net directional flow patterns shown in Figures 1 and 2[23] essentially document only the overall westward and southeastward drift of the population, and the fact that adjacent pairs of regions typically exchange more migrants than distant pairs. The scale of Census regions is too large to permit illustration of the other generalizations above. These must await the analysis of migration among metropolitan nodal regions.

## Passage to a General Model of Migration

The purpose of a migration model is to explain the present amount (magnitude) and distribution (net direction) of population movement or to predict future movement.

23. I am grateful to Russell B. Adams, University of Minnesota, for permission to reproduce Figures 1 and 2.

The typical migration model is a mathematical abstraction consisting of variables embedded in structural relations (equations) hypothesized as representative of the orderly process of population redistribution. We estimate numerical parameters defining the degree of association among variables in the model and between the structure of the model and the order (or lack of it) in real world data.

A common analytical procedure for estimating migration is to employ a single-equation linear multiple regression model. Two of the assumptions behind the use of this model, both of which are frequently violated, are that the effects of each explanatory variable on the dependent variable are (1) statistically independent and (2) additive. In standard multiple regression computational algorithms, each variable is entered in the equation in order of the explanatory power it contributes independently of the other variables. If intercorrelated data are used, only a few variables usually emerge as statistically significant, and the regression coefficients of even these are suspect due to the intercorrelations.[24] The additivity property of the model can be approximated by logarithmic transformation of the variables.[25]

## Net Migration: The Regional Attractiveness Component

Migrants do not simply flow unidirectionally from "negative" (undesirable) to "positive" (attractive) regions as in a "two-party" game like chess. Rather, the situation is a "multi-party" game like musical chairs in which every region both sends and receives migrants. The net outcome of the pairwise exchanges may be positive, negative, or zero at any given place, and is largely independent of size, although job vacancies (indexed by size of labor force) do constitute one attractive force.

Net volumes or rates of migration at regions are expressions of the marginal preferences of migrants in countervailing migration streams. These marginal preferences "may reveal themselves only by weak signals"[26] (low correlation coefficients of indices of attractiveness) in analyses of highly aggregated spatial and population data. Whether the attractive forces indexed by indices of attractiveness are essentially information effects[27] or are surrogates for other influences is of course debatable.

Models of net migration-at-place are particularly confronted with the statistical intercorrelation of most socio-economic indices of regional attractiveness.[28] The difficulty can be somewhat obscured, if not solved, by combining all the variables into a single attractiveness vector in the estimating model. Alternatively, the intercorrelated variables may be reduced to their principal components of variation, the latter being used to estimate the dependent net migration variable.[29]

When several variables are employed directly in a multiple regression model, the typical result is that net migration is best estimated by change in population, labor force, or total employment rather than by theoretically more satisfying indices of attractiveness. After allowing for natural increase and/or exogenous demand effects, these variables are virtually identical with net migration.[30] Such disturbing circularity inhibits the true explanatory power of an analytical model, no matter how well and parsimoniously the dependent variable is estimated statistically.

Several studies have estimated net migration in a properly specified multi-equation econometric model in which each of the endogenous explanatory variables is estimated in turn.[31] An excellent recent example is that of Muth.[32] He estimated net migration as both a dependent and an explanatory variable in a model to explain the differential growth of population, employment, and earnings

24. Regression coefficients are only good least-squares estimates of actual linear structural relationships when the explanatory variables are wholly exogenous to the model (are mutually independent). Leonid Hurwicz, "Prediction and Least Squares," in *Statistical Inference in Dynamic Economic Models*, ed. T. C. Koopmans (New York: John Wiley, 1950), pp. 271–73.

25. The form of the model affects the interpretation which may be given the regression coefficients. Coefficients in a non-logarithmic linear model may be interpreted as "elasticities" of change in the dependent variable with respect to each explanatory variable. In a log-linear model, coefficients must be seen as exponential powers to which values of explanatory variables are raised.

26. C. L. Leven, ed., *Design of a National System of Regional Accounts*, (St. Louis: Washington University, 1967), pp. 253–55.

27. Phillip Nelson, "Migration, Real Income and Information," *Journal of Regional Science*, I (Spring, 1959), 43–74.

28. In the studies reviewed in this essay, the major positive intercorrelations are among the per capita income, median education, and per cent urban variables, with which the per cent unemployed, per cent farm population, and per cent nonwhite population are generally significantly negatively correlated.

29. Theodore R. Anderson, "Intermetropolitan Migration: A Correlation Analysis," *American Journal of Sociology*, LXI (March, 1956), 459–62. Anderson tested the efficacy of four principal components (derived from a data matrix of fifteen variables) in explaining the variation in migration rates for 54 metropolitan subregions during 1935–1940.

30. Lowry, *Migration and Metropolitan Growth*, p. 78.

31. Shinichi Ichimura, "An Econometric Analysis of Domestic Migration and Regional Economy," *Papers of the Regional Science Association*, XVI (1966), 67–76; and Joseph J. Persky and John F. Kain, *Migration, Employment, and Race in the Deep South*, Program on Regional and Urban Economics, Discussion Paper No. 46 (Cambridge, Mass.: Harvard University, 1969).

32. Richard F. Muth, *Differential Growth among Large U.S. Cities*, Institute for Urban and Regional Studies, Working Paper CWR 15 (St. Louis: Washington University, 1968).

among 25 SMSA's from 1950 to 1960. He found that employment growth and labor force increase due to net migration simultaneously determine each other, but are actually relatively little affected by changes in wage rates. Wage rates, when caused to rise by an increase in demand for a city's exports, shift the composition of employment among the local and export sectors rather than the total amount of employment. The elasticity of employment change with respect to net migration is quite close to unity in Muth's model, regardless of the inclusion or exclusion of other variables in the equation or of certain SMSA's in the sample. The elasticity of migration with respect to employment change is, however, much more sensitive to the inclusion of other variables and to the SMSA's in the sample. If Muth's results are indicative, population change due to net migration may be relatively independent of the economic indices of regional attractiveness employed in most analytical models of migration.

Synthesizing from the mobility and migration studies reviewed, we hypothesize net shifts of population toward "attractive" urbanized regions of youthful, high income, and mobile population, concentration of nonagricultural (particularly tertiary and service) activity, and low unemployment; and away from "unattractive" rural regions of elderly, low income, immobile, and nonwhite population, concentration of agricultural activity, and high unemployment.

## Gross Migration: The Gravity Component

Equally as important as net population shift in a general model of migration is the estimation of gross population movement by magnitude and distance of flow. Empirically, sheer population size is the "dominant environmental influence" on volumes of migration.[33]

One of the principal means of generating an interregional flow structure and evaluating its magnitude and distance-decay aspects is the analog application of the gravity model from

Newtonian physics. The underlying assumption of the gravity model is that, everything else being equal, the volume of spatial interaction between two regions is in some way directly proportional to the two "masses" (usually populations) in question, and inversely proportional to the friction of intervening obstacles (usually physical distance) separating them.[34] Even Stouffer's "opportunities" model is essentially the gravity model, in which sums of inmigrants serve as both an attractive force at destinations and as a diverting force at intervening places.[35] In estimating interregional migration flows, the gravity model enjoys the same high degree of statistical success and suffers from a similar theoretical weakness as the economic models which estimate net migration from population change.

In an attempt to provide the gravity model with some social theoretical validity, Carrothers proposed the following scheme: (1) interaction requires communication, and is a function of it; (2) if all individuals generate equal amounts of communication influencing interaction, the sum of such communication is directly proportional to the potential destination area's population from which it emanates; and (3) the amount of communication (hence interaction) is inversely proportional to the difficulty of communicating, which difficulty is directly proportional to physical distance.[36] Thus communication and the

33. Leven, *Design of a National System of Regional Accounts*, p. 255.

34. W. Isard, *Methods of Regional Analysis*, (Cambridge, Mass.: M.I.T., 1960), pp. 493–568, especially pp. 493–504, 538–44. Another thorough discussion of the gravity model literature is Gunnar Olsson, *Distance and Human Interaction: A Review and Bibliography*, Bibliography Series No. 2 (Philadelphia: Regional Science Research Institute, 1965), pp. 43–70.

35. Samuel A. Stouffer, "Intervening Opportunities: A Theory Relating Mobility and Distance," *American Sociological Review*, V (December, 1940), 845–67; *idem*, "Intervening Opportunities and Competing Migrants," *Journal of Regional Science*, II (Spring, 1960), 1–26; Margaret J. Bright and Dorothy S. Thomas, "Interstate Migration and Intervening Opportunities," *American Sociological Review*, VI (December, 1941), 773–83; Fred Strodtbeck, "Equal Opportunity Intervals: A Contribution to the Method of Intervening Opportunity Analysis," *American Sociological Review*, XIV (August, 1949), 490–97; and Theodore R. Anderson, "Intermetropolitan Migration: A Comparison of the Hypotheses of Zipf and Stouffer," *American Sociological Review*, XX (June, 1955), 287–91.

36. Gerald A. P. Carrothers, "An Historical Review of the Gravity and Potential Concepts of Human Interaction," *Journal of the American Institute of Planners*, XX (Spring, 1956), 94–103.

amount of interaction it generates are directly proportional to population size and inversely proportional to distance. The difficulty with the physical gravity analog is that humans make decisions, while molecules in a mass cannot. Like the opportunities and consumption component of our migration model, the gravity component ideally requires information on aggregate decision-making behavior as a basis for specifying the amount of communication-generated interaction.

Recently an attempt has been made to reformulate the gravity model in terms of the economic principle of utility maximization, rather than from the "vague and irrelevant concepts of social physics."[37] In this reformulation, the total number of trips from origin $i$ to destination $j$ are (1) directly proportional to the total travel budgets of individuals at $i$, which are a function of aggregate money income and hence of total population at $i$; (2) directly proportional to the number of persons or things with which it is useful to interact at $j$, which is a function of total population at $j$; and (3) inversely proportional to the transport cost of covering the distance between $i$ and $j$. However rephrased in terms of specific variables, the general form of the gravity model of spatial interaction remains virtually intact.

The value of the gravity concept as a component of a model of interregional migration is its economy: its ability to account for large proportions of the variability of aggregate migration behavior with but two explanatory variables, demographic size and distance. We expect this fundamental orderly property of migration systems to be reconfirmed for metropolitan nodal regions.

With a few exceptions, migration streams have also been found to be positively associated with the degree of urbanization at both the origin and destination, and the income and education levels at the destination; and negatively associated with unemployment at both places and with income and education levels at the origin.[38] However,

these regional indices of attractiveness tend to add relatively little to the overall level of explanation of migration streams after the "gravity effect" has been removed. Individual ($i$ or $j$) regional indices were statistically insignificant in given analyses, although there is no general pattern to these events due to intercorrelation effects unique to each data set. Lowry had similarly poor results with combined ($j - i$) indices,[39] perhaps because migration streams are simultaneously responding to and alleviating regional differentials in income and unemployment.

Lycan had more consistent results using ($j - i$) difference statistics to estimate the net directional component of migration (pairwise differences in residuals from stream rates)[40] than other writers have had in estimating total streams, stream rates, or stream residuals using ($i$ and $j$) regional indices of attractiveness. His results compel formalization of the most salient measures of interregional migration for estimation in a general model.

## Spatial Equilibrium and Salient Measures of Flow

The supposition underlying the unmodified gravity model is that a condition of dynamic spatial equilibrium gives rise to equal countervailing migration streams between regions.[41] This supposition is tenable only under the assumption that all migrants are alike, and has two resultant difficulties: (1) if

37. J. H. Niedercorn and B. V. Bechdolt, Jr., "An Economic Derivation of the 'Gravity Law' of Spatial Interaction," *Journal of Regional Science,* IX (August, 1969), 273–82.
38. Recent empirical evidence includes that of Lowry, *Migration and Metropolitan Growth,* pp. 7–23; R. E. Beals, M. B.

Levy, and L. N. Moses, "Rationality and Migration in Ghana," *Review of Economics and Statistics,* XLIX (1967), 480–86; Michael J. Greenwood, "The Determinants of Labor Migration in Egypt," *Journal of Regional Science,* IX (August, 1969), 283–90; and Richard Lycan, "Interprovincial Migration in Canada: The Role of Spatial and Economic Factors," *Canadian Geographer,* XIII (Fall, 1969), 237–54.
39. Lowry, *Migration and Metropolitan Growth,* p. 13.
40. Lycan, "Interprovincial Migration in Canada," pp. 247–48.
41. Many students of migration, beginning with Ravenstein, have in fact noted that for every major migration stream, a counterstream develops, so that inmigration and outmigration tend to be quite predictable from each other. See E. G. Ravenstein, "The Laws of Migration," *Journal of the Royal Statistical Society,* XLVIII (June, 1885), 167–227; Everett S. Lee, "A Theory of Migration," *Demography,* III, No. 1 (1966), 47–57; and Esse Lövgren, "Mutual Relations Between Migration Fields: A Circulation Analysis," in *Migration in Sweden: A Symposium,* Lund Studies in Geogrpahy, Series B: Human Geography, No. 13 (Lund: C.W.K. Gleerup, Publishers, 1957), pp. 159–69.

all migrants were alike, there would be no logical reason except "wanderlust" for any of them to exchange places in purely random motion; (2) yet if all migrants were *not* alike, their exchange of places would clearly alter whatever equilibrium of regional demographic, social, and economic characteristics may have existed prior to the exchange. The *apparent* near-randomness of aggregate migration behavior is therefore the statistical result of observation of masses of individual moves about the motivations of which we have no knowledge, rather than the result of any collective irrationality of the population. As Vining put it, "the assumption is made that the results of millions of individuals making rational choices are substantially the same as though the individual movements were chance events."[42]

The equilibrium supposition underlying the gravity model is important not as a conclusion, but rather as a null hypothesis against which departures from expected values may be evaluated. Departures from equilibrium estimates of migration streams are of two kinds.[43]

(1) An individual stream or the sum of a pair of countervailing $(M_{i \to j}$ and $M_{j \to i})$ streams may differ in *magnitude* from the estimate, where the null expecation of magnitude is given by the product of the regional populations divided by distance $(P_i P_j / D_{ij})$.

(2) A pair of streams may also differ in *directionality* from the estimate, where under

the equilibrium supposition the null expectation of directionality is that the countervailing streams are equal, so that the net shift is zero $(M_{i \to j} - M_{j \to i} = 0)$.[44] It is clear that the two kinds of departures from expected flows are quite independent of each other.

Several writers have defined salient migration flows as residuals (actual minus expected values) greater than some specified threshold value, where the expected values may be determined from the gravity model, the indifference model, or the entropy model. Separate analysis of migration residuals would seem useful primarily when it is feasible to compute and inspect individual residuals from regression. When the number of regional observations $(n)$ is large, the number of dyadic observations $[(n^2 - n)/2]$ becomes unmanageable for this approach. In any event, the analysis of residuals does not necessarily distinguish between the two independent sources of deviation from expected migration stream values. Given equilibrium expected values, for example, the difference between the stream residuals will be identical to the difference between the actual countervailing streams.

In this essay, then, we are concerned not with salient individual flows but rather with salient measures of the independent magnitude and direction components of migration. The magnitude of gross dyadic migration can be most usefully expressed by the *sum* of countervailing streams $(M_{ij} = M_{i \to j} + M_{j \to i})$, which measure contains no information about the directionality of flow. The difference between countervailing streams $(\bar{M}_{ij} = M_{i \to j} - M_{j \to i})$ expresses directionality or the net shift of population, but as a cardinal variable is still partially a function of the magnitude of the streams. Therefore the independent measure of net directional dyadic migration must be the *ratio* of the stream-difference

42. Rutledge Vining, "An Outline of a Stochastic Model for the Study of the Spatial Structure and Development of a Human Population System," *Papers of the Regional Science Association,* XIII (1964), 39.

43. Equilibrium expected flow values may also be derived from the "indifference model" of transaction flow analysis as proportional to total inflows and/or outflows at the destination and/or origin, respectively. See I. Richard Savage and Karl W. Deutsch, "A Statistical Model of Gross Analysis of Transaction Flows," *Econometrica,* XXVIII (July, 1960), 551–72; and Leo A. Goodman, "Statistical Methods for the Preliminary Analysis of Transaction Flows," *Econometrica,* XXXI (January-April, 1963), 197–208. Similarly, expected flow values may be derived from the information theoretic assumption of a statistically most-probable state of *entropy* in a migration system. See Brian J. L. Berry and Paul J. Schwind, "Information and Entropy in Migrant Flows," *Geographical Analysis,* I (January, 1969), 5–14. In both cases, as with the gravity model, there are two sources of deviation from expectations: aggregate flow differential and lack of flow parity.

and stream-sum variables $(\bar{m}_{ij} = \dfrac{\bar{M}_{ij}}{M_{ij}})$. This

44. When the net pairwise shift is zero, the *efficiency* of population redistribution is likewise zero. Efficiency increases to a maximum value of one when the total dyadic interaction is contained in a single one-way stream.

ratio expresses the *efficiency* of pairwise net population redistribution.

## Spatial Structure of Development and Growth

A "regional factorial ecology" may be defined for the entire United States in terms of relatively few spatially and temporally independent dimensions: population size, population growth, stage in life cycle, socioeconomic status, race, agriculture, manufacturing, "urban" activity, labor force productivity, and unemployment. These dimensions correspond well to general expectations for regional structure,[45] to the results of prior factorial investigations of regional structure,[46] and to those dimensions identified in studies of urban factorial ecology.[47] Maps of factor scores on the structural dimensions[48] show three striking patterns (for agriculture, manufacturing, and non-white population) of convergence of major (declining) and lesser (growing) concentrations of the respective phenomena. Other dimensions (such as that of income levels and income change) show general evidence, however, of the divergence of economic development levels and growth rates between metropolitan core regions and rural periphery regions, in accordance with established theories of regional development.[49]

Both net migration-at-place and the net direction of migration between region-pairs are "correctly," but only weakly, associated with most of the indices of "attractiveness" of regions as defined in socio-economic terms. Population size by itself, moreover, is

indeterminate as an "attractive" regional characteristic for either net migration.

## Net Direction of Migration

The arrows in Figure 3 show only net dyadic flows in excess of 10,000 persons between "consolidated urban regions." It is presumed that these very largest net directional flows are representative of the majority of smaller net shifts. Their patterns correspond closely to the spatially much more aggregated net directional patterns in Figure 2.

Three kinds of net flow patterns are in evidence: (1) pronounced long-distance shifts from both metropolitan and nonmetropolitan regions throughout the country to southern California and southern Florida; (2) medium-distance shifts from rural hinterlands to regions of middle-sized metropolises, notably from: the Upper Midwest to Minneapolis-St. Paul; northern Appalachia to Cleveland-northern Ohio; central Appalachia to Cincinnati-southwestern Ohio; and eastern Texas to Dallas-Ft. Worth; and (3) short-distance shifts from the very largest megalopolitan areas to their "exurban" fringes: New York to southern New England, New Jersey, and eastern Pennsylvania, and Los Angeles to San Diego and Santa Barbara. In the Los Angeles case, outward shifts were also pronounced to the San Francisco Bay area and to Florida.

It seems that a combination of urban activity and climatic amenities, as found together primarily in the metropolitan regions with year-round warm temperatures in southern California and Florida, set a dominant pattern of United States net directional migration in the 1950–1960 decade.

Obviously, mere existence of a highly urbanized population or of warm winter temperatures and high percentage of possible sunshine is insufficient to allow or encourage rapid population and economic growth. Certain large cities tend to be foci for migration and economic growth because they possess the following general advantages: (1) a diversified mix of industries, in terms of both

45. H. S. Perloff and L. Wingo, Jr. "Natural Resource Endowment and Regional Economic Growth," in *National Resources and Economic Growth*, J. J. Spengler, ed. (Washington, R.F.F., 1961) pp. 191–212.

46. B.J.L. Berry, *Strategies, Models, and Economic Theories of Development in Rural Regions* (Washington, D.C.: U.S.D.A., 1967).

47. R. Murdie, *Factorial Ecology of Metropolitan Toronto.* Research Paper 116, Department of Geography, University of Chicago, 1969.

48. Not included in this paper.—Eds.

49. G. Myrdal, *Rich Lands and Poor* (New York: Harper & Row 1967).

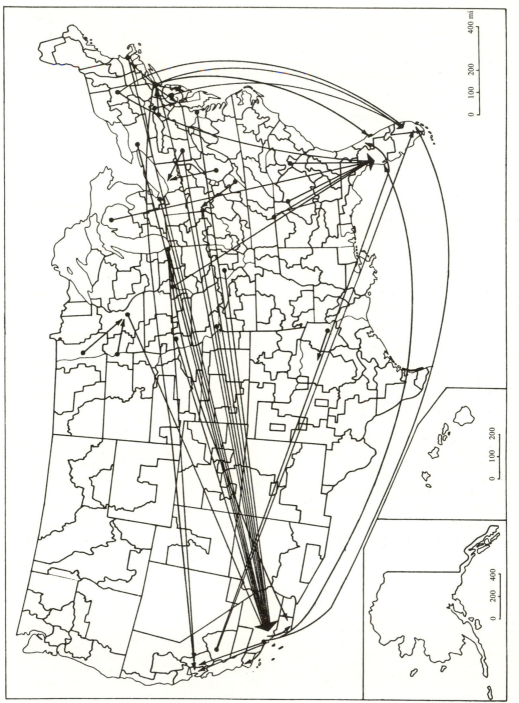

Figure 3. Net Directional Migration, 1955-1960: Streams Greater than 10,000 Persons.

income elasticities of demand for their (export) products, and age of industry; (2) a high capacity for innovation of new industries, product lines, technologies of production, etc.; (3) a large, varied, and relatively skilled labor force; (4) a long-term "infrastructural" economic base of service activities, educational and research facilities, etc.; and (5) chaper aggregate internal transportation and utilities. The major hindrance to economic growth ("external diseconomies") in very large cities is actually not their sheer size but the inadequacy of urban public management.[50] Two operational and non-circular indices of urban-regional growth potential, derivable from the above listing, would thus be a measure of industrial diversification, and the labor-force percentage in services, education, and research.

Net inmigration necessarily accompanies and contributes to employment and income growth at metropolitan destination regions. In fact, as other studies have implied, the economic growth variables (particularly employment growth) seem to be mutually determined with migration.[51]

It is perhaps too facile an assumption that an enveloping "unseen hand" of climatic preference is operating to guide a highly visible proportion of both individuals and "footloose" activities and firms—and hence much of the national economic growth—toward the locations of non-exportable amenity resources. Clearly, however, our understanding of urban-economic growth processes is imperfect if we rely too heavily on the commodity-export base concept of regional growth.[52] Given the large number of economically prosperous and growing metropolitan regions, and the overall levels of personal welfare and intermetropolitan mobility in the United States, it is perhaps reasonable to assume that labor-force migrants' marginal preferences for regions may be tipped in favor of broad amenity considerations such as climate, particularly if potential migrants possess little place-specific information on economic opportunities.

It is also clear that interregional population shifts involve the movement of persons not in the labor force, many of whom may be expected to be even less attentive than labor-force migrants to fine differences in regional income and employment levels.[53] In fact, in a recent survey, the majority (68 per cent) of family heads not in the labor force gave "only non-economic reasons" (family and community ties) for moving, whereas the majority (61 per cent) of family heads in the labor force gave "only economic reasons" (finding a new and/or better-paying job, or company transfer) for moving.[54] The categories of "reasons" for moving were vague and overlapping, however, and excluded any specific reference to climatic or other amenities of place. It is also difficult to know what proportion of the migrants in any given stream are in the labor force.

The general point to be made here is that a model of highly aggregated migration behavior should include only those variables which have a fairly uniform impact on all potential migrants, and about which the majority have at least some spatial perception. Per capita income and unemployment rate statistics probably do not meet these criteria, since like the net migration variable

50. Irving Hoch, *Progress in Urban Economics* (Washington, D.C.: Resources for the Future, 1969), pp. 29–30.
51. See R. Muth, *Differential Growth among Large U.S. Cities;* and David F. Bramhall, "A Projection Framework for State Planning," *Papers of the Regional Science Association,* XXI (1968), 139–55.
52. Recently an attempt to sketch the outlines of a broader approach, tracing the many lines of linkage in the "local industry-mix" affecting the level, distribution, and stability of urban-regional income and employment, has been made by Wilbur R. Thompson, "Internal and External Factors in the Development of Urban Economies," in *Issues in Urban Economics,* ed. Harvey S. Perloff and Lowdon Wingo, Jr. (Baltimore: Johns Hopkins Press, 1968), pp. 43–62; *idem, A Preface to Urban Economics* (Baltimore: Johns Hopkins Press, 1965).

53. E. Ullman, "Amenities as a Factor in Regional Growth," *Geographical Review,* XLIV (1954), pp. 119–32; and Gibson, "Amenities as a Factor in Arizona's Population Growth," pp. 192–99.
54. J. B. Lansing and E. Mueller, *Geographic Mobility of Labor,* (Ann Arbor: University of Michigan, 1967) pp. 57–88. Predictably, the proportion of respondents giving "economic reasons" for moving was highest for upper status individuals (based on income, education, and occupation). "Non-economic reasons" were more important to those under 35 and over 55 than to the middle-aged. This apparent age effect may reflect variation in labor force participation rates, which vary considerably by age and sex, and also show long-term changes. Lowry, *Migration and Metropolitan Growth,* p. 113.

they conceal innumerable, perhaps counter-vailing, individual characteristics, decisions, and actions. Induced inmigrants to an area respond to specific salary or job offers rather than median family income, whereas forced outmigrants from poverty areas may have little knowledge about alternative locations in the national job market. It may be that at the level of spatial, demographic, and temporal aggregation in this study of the United States, employment-related migration involving personal economic motivations is very nearly random motion. What appears to be environment-related migration, however, is clearly *not* random in pattern.

## Migration and Environmental Quality

Variables which comprise an overall image of environmental quality to which all individuals presumably respond include cost of living, ease of communication, quality of schools, climate, available recreational resources, pollution, crime, racial tension, etc. Accuracy of information on these matters may be highly variable and biased toward (or against) the most visible places: the largest, most "news-worthy" cities.[55] But inasmuch as each of these variables represents issues in the public discourse for which there is clear evidence of spatial variation, they represent the bases for area-specific (as opposed to job-specific or family-specific) comparisons which affect migration decisions, and ultimately the net direction of population redistribution.

It is therefore perhaps not as trite as it seems initially to suggest that inclusion of a sensitive indicator of regional climatic differences might significantly improve the explanation of net directional migration.[56] A climatic in-

55. Leven, *Design of a National System of Regional Accounts,* has suggested that variables such as the above tend to combine rather inaccurately in individuals' total perceptions of places, due to "halo effects."
56. An "annual percent sunshine" variable was used by Hirsch (personal communication, March 3, 1970) to reduce large residuals from estimated intermetropolitan migration to California and Florida. See Fred A. Hirsch, "Geographical Patterns of Inter-Metropolitan Migration in the United States, 1955 to 1960" (unpublished Ph.D. dissertation, Department of Geography, University of Washington, 1968).

dicator (such as mean January temperature) would have a rare and satisfying unidirectional causal relationship with demographic and economic variables. Even this presumption may be less valid than at one time, however, given man's capacity for despoiling the atmospheric and lithospheric environment so thoroughly that climatic modification at the micro and possibly also the macro scale seems a virtually certain result.

## Migration and Spatial Equilibrium

In addition to the distinctly climatic orientation of net directional migration, the net flows mapped in Figure 3 gives evidence of simultaneous centralization toward and dispersal from certain metropolitan centers. These conflicting patterns may reflect an indeterminate influence of regional population size and urbanization differences on net directional migration. The problem seems to be one of scale of the regional units, which are (deliberately) too large to reveal any but the most far-reaching suburbanization patterns, yet too small to enclose the handful of major hinterland-to-city migration systems which remained in the 1950's. The anomalous net flow patterns of this sort, however, along with the highly conspicuous climatic orientation of contemporary United States migration, only serve to emphasize to what extent the vast majority of population movements in the country are not rural-urban shifts or responses to severe interregional economic disequilibria.

The results of the present study, in line with those of previous works, are inconclusive with respect to the issue of regional income convergence. They suggest that the aggregate net interregional flow of population is weakly "rational" in terms of aggregate regional economic differences, but either contributes to or is overridden by more powerful factors (capital movements, natural increase, selectivity among migrants) producing regional income divergence. Neither the general evidence on regional income convergence, nor the evidence on the role of migration in this process, convincingly shows a trend toward regional income equilibrium in the United States. Much of the confusion may again lie in modifiable areal units effects, such that smaller regions show a trend toward income divergence, while larger regions (states, Census divisions) may show a trend toward income convergence due to rising urbanization and converging industrial structures.

## Implications for Regional Policy

A spatially elaborate estimation of regional descriptive dimensions and net directional migration patterns may seem to be little more than a geographic curiosity. Regional administrators and economic planners, concerned as they must be with questions of aggregate production capacity (employment) and personal welfare (income), may respond with a shrug of the shoulders to the information that "everyone is moving to California and Florida." Everyone is not, of course. But these findings may have implications for public policy, such as it exists, toward migration and regional development.

If the net direction of aggregate population movement in the contemporary United States is little affected by the economic characteristics of regions, then perhaps planned spatial economic incentives either to outmigration or inmigration may also not have sufficient desired net effects. Human beings, as the labor and entrepreneurial factors of production, may not be governed by the search for the highest rate of return to the extent that capital, the third traditional factor, is. It may be possible to justify an economically non-optimal capital investment (in an industrial plant, highway, etc.) if it coincides with and "exploits" revealed spatial preferences of the population, but not if it fails to do so. Conversely, an economically "optimal" capital investment may fail if its optimality of location is predicated on an invalid premise regarding the degree of human response to economic incentives.

Previous studies of motivations of migration may have found "economic reasons" to be dominant simply because the questions were posed so as to bring out that result. What is needed is a careful definition of the aspects of environmental quality to which migrants respond either positively or negatively; the degree to which potential migrants trade off one aspect against another (climate versus cost of living, for example); and the degree to which largely non-economic qualities of the environment may be substitutable for more strictly economic incentives such as wage rates.

In a situation in which large numbers of people have large numbers of choices of residence, some means may have to be found to discourage the piling up of population in climatically favored but constricted areas, and encourage (perhaps through selective positive development of non-climatic environmental qualities) the growth of population in presently less desirable regions. In a national system of regions, localized environmental benefits (climate) may have to be "spread" to the majority of the population desiring them only through short-term exposure (tourism), and compensation extracted from local residents by means of locally severe environmental costs (air pollution as in southern California, high prices as in Hawaii). To some extent, of course, the national economic system is already producing these compensatory effects in a self-regulating fashion.

# Migration Within a System of Post-Industrial Cities

MARTYN CORDEY-HAYES

## Tests of the Traditional Economic Approach

The traditional economic approach to interurban migration is summarised in figure 1. This theory is essentially based on a "push-pull" phenomenon that seems intuitively sensible: migration is motivated by poor employment conditions (low wages, high unemployment) and migrants are attracted to areas with high wages and low unemployment. Such a process is self-equilibrating since out-migration reduces the labour surplus and in-migration reduces the labour shortage. This equilibrating mechanism between labour supply and demand has been used to link the employment and demographic sectors of a number of regional models (for example, Rogers and Walz, 1972; Hamilton, 1969; Kadanoff, 1972). The basic hypotheses of the above push-pull theory are that in-migration is directly related to the economic attractiveness of an area, and that out-migration is inversely porportional to in-migration.

A great deal of research on migration was carried out in the 1960s. The general conclusion was that in-migration could be interpreted in terms of concepts of economic attractiveness; but several researchers, in particular Lowry (1966) and Lansing and Mueller (1967), conclude that *per capita* gross out-migration is independent of the economic characteristics of the generating region. This

means that the *per capita* rates of out-migration are similar for all regions irrespective of their economic character, and therefore out-migration is dependent only on the population characteristics within the region. Thus there are two rival hypotheses on the relationship between the directional components of migration. These are:

(1) the standard economic hypothesis that in- and out-migration are inversely related; and

(2) the empirically derived hypothesis that out-migration is independent of the economic characteristics of the area (and is therefore unrelated to in-migration, which is dependent on areal characteristics).

Cordey-Hayes and Gleave (1973) have tested these hypotheses by reference to city-region data from England and Wales, and found that neither hypothesis is correct; in fact, a strong direct correlation between the *per capita* rates of in-migration and out-migration was observed. (Similar results have been obtained by Miller (1967) and Stone (1971).) Areas with the highest in-migration rates also had the highest out-migration rates. Declining regions had the *lowest per capita* out-migration and minimal in-migration. These effects are clearly shown in figure 2, in which rates of in-migration and out-migration are plotted together. The 45° line indicates migration balance, points below this line indicate growing city regions, and points above

From "Migration and the Dynamics of Multiregional Population Systems," *Environment and Planning A: Special Issue,* Selected papers from IIASA conference on national settlement systems and strategies. © IIASA, Laxenburg, 1975, Vol. 7, pp. 793–814. Reprinted by permission.

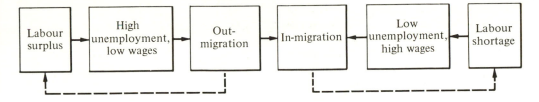

Figure 1. The Chain of Causality Implied in the Economic Theory of Migration.

indicate declining city regions. The growing areas (at the extreme right of the figure) have both the highest in- and out-migration *per capita,* whilst declining areas have the lowest values for both. This is clearly not in agreement with the hypothesis that in- and out-migration *per capita* are inversely related; it suggests that most migrants move from a position of economic strength rather than weakness, and consequently imposes significant reservations on push-pull approaches to migration. Decline should be associated with

the lack of a compensating flow of in-migrants, rather than with high out-migration. Similar results have been obtained for the USA, Canada, Germany, and France, but in all cases the correlation lies nearer to the 45° line, which indicates a slower rate of population restructuring amongst regions than is currently occurring in England and Wales.

This direct relationship between the directional components of migration has been explained by a dynamic mechanism which

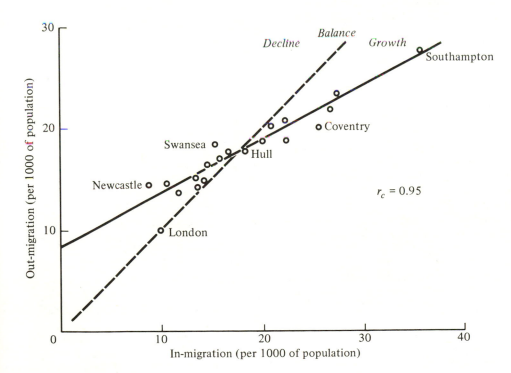

Figure 2. Graph of Out-Migration against In-Migration *per capita.*

associates regional out-migration with in-migrants from a previous time period (Cordey-Hayes and Gleave, 1973). That is, an intrinsic attractiveness concept was used to explain the differential attraction of migrants to specific destinations; then a positive-feedback mechanism was introduced such that recent migrants to an area were more likely to move on again than were the remainder of the resident population who had established a strong network of social and economic ties in the area. This feedback, based on a selective concentration of mobile population, satisfactorily explains the mechanism that relates the directional components of migration, but what is missing is an associated theory of labour mobility.

## Migration as an Extension of the Local Labour Market

Currently, a theory which looks on interurban migration as an extension of the local labour market is being developed and tested (Renshaw, 1972; Gleave and Cordey-Hayes, 1974), see figure 3. Here the probability of out-migration is hypothesized to depend on local employment conditions, the differential mobility of individuals within the region, and their knowledge/information of the opportunities outside their own region.

It is further hypothesized that a region with many job vacancies and low unemployment will generally have a rapid voluntary turnover of jobs: employees have a risk-free opportunity to change their jobs in an attempt to match their differential skills and tastes to a differentiated job market. This can be regarded as a stochastic learning process in which movers are acquiring new skills *and* gaining information, not only about the local labour market but also about a more extensive one. That is, conditions that favour local labour-market turnover are also those that induce occupational mobility and give a better knowledge of spatially more extensive labour markets. Both of these increase the likelihood of interurban migration, as indicated by the positive feedback arrows in the flow diagram.

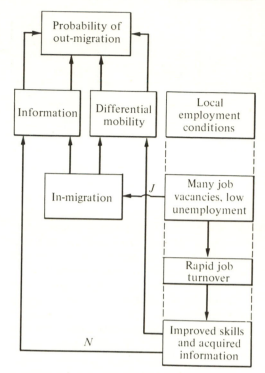

Figure 3. Positive Feedback Effects Relating Out-Migration to In-Migration.

A large number of job vacancies also attracts migrants, and therefore growth regions will be characterized by high in-migration and high out-migration. Conversely, low vacancies and high unemployment produce caution and overspecialization, and lead to a static local labour market with few people changing jobs. Individuals have no opportunity to take part in the learning process outlined above, and hence there is little occupational mobility and low out-migration.

These arguments are presented here simply to recast interurban migration in a way that has implications both for research and policy. Firstly, consider briefly the implications for research.

(1) The results suggest that the traditional demographic-economic linkage, based on migration as the equilibrating mechanism between labour supply and demand, is incor-

rect. Therefore, the results of regional and interregional models with this conceptual linkage should be treated with caution.

(2) It is of interest to compare the flow diagrams for the "standard economic theory" and the "mobility theory" sketched above. The former is based on a deterministic chain of monocausality, and is static. The latter is stochastic, with many feedback loops giving multicausality, and is dynamic. Whereas the concepts of the traditional economic approach are homogeneous labour, complete information, and perfect mobility, the approach presented here is based upon heterogeneous labour, partial information, and strong differential mobility. It considers that the labour market is a complex stochastic process involving interactions amongst many participants—and therefore should be modelled as such. One of the key variables in a stochastic linkage between the demographic and employment sectors is the dynamic concept of job vacancy. In a separate context (that of manpower planning) several labour-market models, based on a dynamic treatment of job vacancies, have been developed (Holt and David, 1966; White, 1970; Bartholomew, 1973), and these are currently being investigated in an attempt to link migration to a stochastic treatment of the components of employment change.

(3) More generally, the above research on migration suggests the need for a methodology which is capable of treating both occupational and geographical mobility within the same analytical framework. Potentially, the framework would be able to integrate spatial settlement systems with sociological concepts of relative opportunity, occupational mobility, and equity.

On the policy side, the differences amongst the three rival hypotheses have important implications. For example, the second implies that policies aimed at halting out-migration are likely to be ineffective, and the best that could be achieved is to steer out-migrants away from congested cities to selected growth areas. The results suggest that:

(1) A large part of interurban migration in developed countries is a spontaneous movement of individuals from economic "strength to strength," rather than a case of being "pushed" from economically weak regions. This suggests that a more subtle restructuring may be occurring other than simply the growth and decline of some regions. It also implies that a national settlement policy need not stimulate migration but simply channel it to selected growth areas. But these areas will be more successful if they have a wide range of job opportunities, which favour a voluntary job turnover and occupational mobility, rather than a highly specialized employment structure based on a few large plants.

(2) The results also suggest, inevitably, that each region loses a substantial proportion of its young, dynamic, and most mobile population each year, and therefore national settlement policy should recognize that new or expanding towns must continuously attract population in order to compensate for the large number of persons who will leave, irrespective of how successful the town may be.

## A Related Model

The conceptual framework given in figure 3 has been partially formalized into a model of migration movements and the differential growth of twenty city regions in England and Wales (Cordey-Hayes and Gleave, 1973). An outline of this model, which is part of the general research strategy, is now given.

(1) An accounting matrix, comprising migration transition probabilities obtained from observations on past behaviour, is constructed. It describes the migration process, through time, in a useful summary form and provides the basis for a number of simple probabilistic models (see section 5).

(2) These parameters must next be interpreted in terms of hypothesized causal relationships which represent the external forces.

(3) If we use these tested hypotheses for the particular form of migration transition probabilities, an analytical model can then give the future distribution of population over time, or at least the "behaviour modes" (approximate

time path) of that system of city regions. It should also contribute to the understanding necessary to implement policies for steering the system of city regions to some planned national settlement pattern.

The basic migration equation is

$$\rho_{ij} = \epsilon_i \mu_{ij} = \epsilon_i \frac{a_j P_j f(d_{ij})}{\sum_k a_k P_k f(d_{ik})}$$

where

$\rho_{ij}$ is the probability of an individual in city region $i$ migrating to $j$,

$\epsilon_i$ is the *per capita* rate of out-migration from $i$,

$\mu_{ij}$ is the conditional probability of a migrant from $i$ selecting city region $j$ as a destination.

$\alpha_j$ is a measure of the "intrinsic attractiveness" of city region $j$; the population, $P_j$, and the function, $f(d_{ij})$, weight this attraction in relation to its size and distance, $d_{ij}$, from the origin $i$.

This is a fairly conventional spatial-interaction model of migration, but in the simulation model considered here the migration equation is modified such that $\epsilon_i$ depends on the previous migration behaviour of the population (feedback $J$ in figure 3) and on the ease of occupational mobility within $i$ (feedback $N$).

Feedback $J$ is related to the concept of cumulative inertia (or more strictly its inverse). That is, a substantial amount of data indicates that the propensity to migrate decreases monotonically as length of residence increases (Taeuber, 1961; Land, 1969; Morrison, 1971). The model considered here uses the property that recent in-migrants to an area will, more probably, move again rather than those who have established strong social and economic ties through longer residence in the area. This process can be viewed in two ways: it may be that long residence strengthens one's ties to an area, thereby producing a decrease in one's propensity to migrate; alternatively, there may be a selective concentration of mobile and immobile

population in the sense that an individual has a long residence in an area because of an inherently lower propensity to migrate. In either case, the probability of moving decreases with increasing duration of residence, approximately as an exponential function; that is, the probability of moving after $d$ years of residence is $\exp(-ad)$, where $a$ is a constant related to the average time between moves. Then $\epsilon_i$ in the above equation is proportional to $\exp(-ad)$, weighted by the relative arrival rate of migrants and integrated over all arrival times. The equation system and flow diagram for this calculation of the dynamic mover pool is given in Cordey-Hayes and Gleave (1973).

Currently, feedback $N$ is regarded simply as a multiplier on the above process. That is, the selective concentration of mobile population, $J$, is the most important feedback in the short term but this process is enhanced by intraurban occupational mobility in the longer term. A more explicit inclusion of this second feedback is being developed in a Markovian model in which the transition elements are the

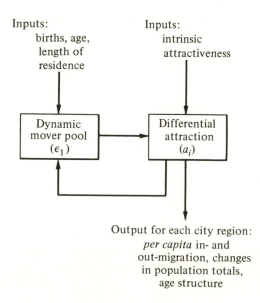

Inputs:
  births, age,
  length of
  residence

Inputs:
  intrinsic
  attractiveness

Dynamic mover pool ($\epsilon_1$)

Differential attraction ($a_i$)

Output for each city region:
*per capita* in- and out-migration, changes in population totals, age structure

Figure 4. The Dynamic Mover-Pool/Differential-Attraction Model.

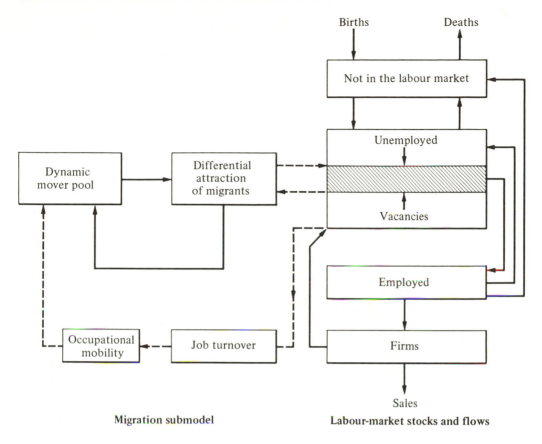

Figure 5. Interurban Migration and Flows in the Local Labour Market.

joint probabilities of job change and change of skill (see Bartholomew (1973) for related stochastic models of social processes).

The simulation model then integrates the concept of a dynamic mover pool with a differential-attraction submodel (figure 4).

The attraction component corresponds to the $a_j$ terms in the migration equation and is analyzed in terms of a dynamic concept of job vacancy. It is argued that the potential migrant is not attracted by the net employment growth of an area (as is considered in many models of migration) but, instead, perceives and reacts to job vacancies, and this is a stochastic variable that depends on many complex flows within the labour market.

Some of these flows are given in figure 5.

The model outlined above, and shown schematically in figure 4, has been used to reproduce the observed patterns of migration shown in figure 2; it will now be used to explore its effect on the multiregional population system of exogenous changes to the intrinsic-attraction variables. In the longer term it is possible to make the changes in vacancy rate endogenous by integrating the model with a stochastic labour-market model of the kind described by Holt and David (1966). An integrated model is illustrated in figure 5; the stocks and flows in the labour market determine job vacancies which, in turn, both attract migrants to an area and induce occupational mobility within the area, as described above.

## The Need for a Family of Models of National Settlement Systems

One of the aims of this paper was to take a perspective view of some of the difficulties of building disaggregated comprehensive models of national settlement systems. By taking migration as a focus for the discussion, it was suggested that the difficulties include a poor formal understanding both of the conceptual structure of the dynamics of multiregional growth and of the mechanisms involved in some key components of the process. For this reason it is important that analytical modelling of national settlement systems should be integrated into a structured learning process. It is of less value to focus research solely on the development of a single disaggregated comprehensive model, as if one were dealing with a well-structured engineering system. For poorly understood systems a strategy that integrates fundamental research on the structure and workings of the system, together with methodologies for analyzing the effects and repercussions of alternative policies should be adopted.

It is doubtful if this twin need, of advancing understanding and contributing to policy, can be accommodated within a single modelling style or level of approximation. Attempts to meet both requirements simultaneously can often (as in land-use-transportation modelling in the sixties) fail to do either effectively. A useful technique may be to develop a family of models that approach national settlement systems from differing conceptual viewpoints and at varying levels of approximation. The simplest of these should be able to give quick qualitative insights during the early stages of policy analysis, whilst more sophisticated techniques would be required in the detailed elaboration and evaluation of alternative strategies. The models discussed in this paper have been mostly of the latter kind.

## REFERENCES

Bartholomew, D. J., 1973, *Stochastic Models for Social Processes*, 2nd edition (John Wiley, New York).

Bergsman, J., Ehemann, C., 1974, "An econometric model of population and employment shifts among metropolitan areas," WP-74-3, The Urban Institute, Washington, D.C.

Cordey-Hayes, M., 1972, "Dynamic frameworks for spatial models," *Socio-Economic Planning Sciences*, 6, 365–385.

————., Gleave, D., 1973, "Migration movements and the differential growth of city regions in England and Wales," RP-1, Centre for Environmental Studies, London, England. Also published in *Papers of the Regional Science Association*, 33, 99–123.

————., Gleave, D., 1974, "Dynamic models of the interaction between migration and the differential growth of cities," RR-74-9, International Institute for Applied Systems Analysis, Laxenburg, Austria.

————., Wilson, A. G., 1971, "Spatial interaction," *Socio-Economic Planning Sciences*, 5, 73–95.

Gleave, D., Cordey-Hayes, M., 1974, "Interurban migration as an extension of the local labour market," WN-399, Centre for Environmental Studies, London, England.

Hamilton, H. R., Goldstone, S. E., Milliman, J. W., Pugh, A. C., Roberts, E. B., Zellner, A., 1969, *Systems Simulation in Regional Analysis* (M.I.T Press, Cambridge, Mass.).

Holt, C. C., David, M. H., 1966, "Concepts of job vacancies in a dynamic theory of the labour market," in *The Measurement and Interpretation of Job Vacancies* (National Bureau of Economic Research; distributed by Columbia University Press, New York).

Kadanoff, L. P., 1972, "From simulation model to public policy," *American Scientist*, 60, 74–79.

Land, K., 1969, "Duration of residence and prospective migration," *Demography*, 4, 293–309.

Lansing, J. B., Mueller, Eva, 1967, *The Geographical Mobility of Labour*, Survey Research Center, Institute for Social Research, Ann Arbor, Michigan.

Lowry, I. S., 1966, *Migration and Metropolitan Growth: Two Analytical Models* (Chandler, San Francisco).

Miller, A. R., 1967, "The migration of employed persons to and from metropolitan areas of the

United States," *Journal of the American Statistical Association,* 62, 1418–1432.

Morrison, P. A., 1971, "Chronic movers and future redistributions of population," *Demography,* 8, 171–184.

Renshaw, V., 1972, "Labour mobility, turnover and gross-migration," Working paper, Bureau of Business Research, University of Nebraska, Lincoln, Nebraska.

Rogers, A., Walz, R., 1972, "A multisectoral model of demographic and economic growth in West Virginia," WP-5, Technological Institute, Northwestern University, Evanston, Illinois.

Stone, L. O., 1971, "On the correlation between metropolitan area in- and out-migration by occupation," *Journal of the American Statistical Association,* 66, 693–701.

Taeuber, K. E., 1961, "Duration of residence analysis of internal migration in the United States," *The Millbank Memorial Quarterly,* 32, 143–147.

White, H., 1970, *Chains of Opportunity: System Models of Mobility in Organizations* (Harvard University Press, Cambridge, Mass.).

Wilson, A. G., 1971, "A family of spatial interaction models and associated developments," *Environment and Planning,* 3, 1–32.

# The Regional Impact of Growth Firms: The Case of Boeing, 1963–1968

RODNEY A. ERICKSON

Within the past two decades regional development planners have attempted to effect favorable changes in the economic well-being of problem regions. Theories of unbalanced economic growth, both sectoral and spatial, have been frequently used as sources of regional planning strategies.

Francois Perroux articulated his concept of sectorally unbalanced growth in the mid-1950s.[1] Perroux's conceptualization of economic growth postulated that expansion occurred in particular economic sectors or "poles of growth." He theorized that growth poles, through their structural interdependence linkages with other economic activities, were a driving force of economic growth.

In the mid-1960s growth poles came to be viewed, in the spatial context of a region, as towns or cities possessing a complex of propulsive growth firms or "lead firms."[2] The growth firm characteristics of lead firms were assumed to be responsible for the generation of significant growth in the regional economic environment. However, there has been a paucity of empirical analysis concerning the growth-inducing impacts of lead firms.

In this paper the mechanisms and extent of lead firm induced growth in a regional economy are examined. The empirical analysis focuses on the role of the Boeing Company as a lead firm in the Puget Sound and Washington State regions during the 1963–1968 period. This period of extremely rapid Boeing growth had dramatic impact upon the regional economy.

## THEORETICAL FRAMEWORK

The lead firm concept enunciates the principle that growth firms direct the nature and processes of regional economic growth.[3] Lead firms are generally considered to be large-scale and highly innovative production units. Rosenfeld has stated that such growth firms exhibit the following characteristics:[4] a higher rate of product growth than the average growth of the region's industrial output; a higher rate of productivity increase than the average productivity increase in the industry and the region; and an expanding share in the total product of the industry.

Lead firms, embodying rapid growth characteristics, exert growth-generating forces or lead effects (*effet d'entrainement*) on other elements of the regional economy.

1. Francois Perroux, "Note sur la notion de 'pole de croissance,'" *Economie Appliquée*, 1955, pp. 307–320.
2. Jacques Boudeville, *Problems of Regional Economic Planning* (Edinburgh, Scotland: Edinburgh University Press, 1966).
3. Rodney A. Erickson, "The 'Lead Firm' Concept: An Analysis of Theoretical Elements," *Tijdschrift voor Economische en Sociale Geografie*, November–December 1972, pp. 426–437.
4. Felix Rosenfeld, "L'industrie motrice dans la region et dans l'espace économique integre. L'exemple de l'industrie mécanique dans la province de Turin," *Economie Appliquée*, 1966, pp. 511–530.

From *Land Economics*, vol. 50, no. 2, May 1974, pp. 127–36. Reprinted by permission.

These induced growth effects are transferred to the regional economy through the structural interdependence linkage and income multiplier linkage networks. The analytical framework for examining lead firm induced growth focuses on three interrelated and interdependent systems of linkages: the technological system, the capital goods system, and the lateral-induced system.[5]

## Technological System

The technological system is based on the interindustry linkages which exist between a lead firm and other regional firms. This system is focused on induced growth arising from the direct and indirect effects of technological linkages. As a lead firm expands its output, forward- and backward-linked regional firms may be induced to increase their rate of output. The magnitude of directly induced economic growth in backward-linked supplying firms is conditioned by the net increase in the demand for inputs by the lead firm as determined by the output level and the form of the production function of the lead firm. In turn, expanding backward-linked firms have net increases in their demands for inputs which may be addressed to regional firms, thereby generating indirect economic growth.

The lead firm concept also has assumed that an expanding growth firm will generate external economies for forward-linked firms, leading to an expansion of output in existing regional firms and the establishment of new regional firms. These external economies purportedly arise from: (1) lead firm production cost reductions permitting relative or absolute input price reductions for forward-linked user firms; or (2) technologically superior inputs leading to a qualitatively superior product or linked firm production

cost reductions. Such external economies may induce forward-linked firms to increase their levels of output.[6]

## Capital Goods System

The capital goods system is based on the relationship which exists between lead firms and those firms which produce capital goods. As a lead firm experiences increased actual or potential demand for its products, it utilizes to the fullest possible extent its existing production plant and equipment, and/or constructs or purchases additional productive capacity. As articulated in investment theory, decisions to invest in additional productive capacity are, in the short run, a function of the level of sales in the previous period and the present level of capacity utilization. In the long run, the expected future profitability of a product or process innovation or a stream of innovations appears to be of importance.[7]

The lead firm's desire to expand its capital stock in relation to its anticipated output levels may lead to increased investment above and beyond the level needed for replacement purposes. The supply of investment capital within the firm and local economy, and the magnitude of capital imports from outside the region, also affect the level of lead firm investment which may be undertaken. The supply of exogenous capital is a critical factor where the local economy is incapable of providing the investment capital required by a large and rapidly expanding lead firm.

In the capital goods system, increased income and output is generated when the lead firm purchases capital goods from local industry sectors. Increased capital goods purchases from regional construction, materials, and industrial equipment sectors generate a higher level of output and income in directly affected

5. This framework was initially suggested by Morgan D. Thomas, "The Regional Problem, Structural Change, and Growth Pole Theory," in Antoni Kuklinski, editor, *Growth Poles and Growth Centres in Regional Planning* (The Hague, The Netherlands: Mouton Press, 1972), pp. 77–78.

6. Morgan D. Thomas, "Growth Pole Theory: An Examination of Some of Its Basic Concepts," Niles M. Hansen, ed., *Growth Centres in Regional Economic Development* (New York, N.Y.: The Free Press, 1972).

7. Edwin Mansfield, *Research and Innovation in the Modern Corporation* (New York, N.Y.: Norton, 1971).

industry sectors, and additional economic expansion through the technological and lateral-induced linkage systems focused on regional capital goods producers. Large lead firm capital investments can produce significant regional growth even where an expanding lead firm is not itself extensively technologically-linked within its regional economy. However, growth-leading firms must continue to expand their productive capacity or the growth-generating forces of the capital goods system will be expended in a relatively short period of time.

## Lateral-Induced System

The lateral-induced system is based upon the economic growth-generating influence of income multiplier linkages. Growth in this system is induced by the expansion of real income associated with the rise in the level of activity within the linkage system focused on the lead firm. If a perceived or actual expansion of real income occurs, causing regional firms, residents and local government to increase their purchases of goods and services from regional producers, further expansion can occur. Firms in the lateral-induced growth system have their own linkage networks through which expansion may proceed. A strong lateral-induced system is reflected in large magnitude lead firm income and employment multipliers. The flow structure of this multiplier effect is illustrated in Figure 1.

The lead firm as a rapid growth enterprise is a focus of expanding employment and real income. As workers and shareholders in the lead firms and technologically-linked enterprises increase their regional consumption purchases, the regional economy is stimulated, generating further income and employment.[8] Theoretically, a growth firm should be associated with greater than average income and employment multipliers, in

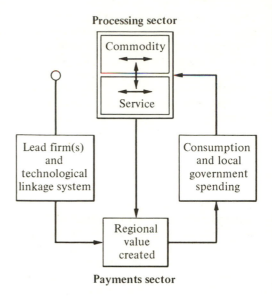

Figure 1. The Lateral-Induced System.

addition to the multipliers of the direct and indirect linkages in the technological system.[9] The economic impacts of the three linkage systems are differentially significant. Their identification and examination provide an indication of the workings and importance of these components arising from lead firm expansion.

## EMPIRICAL ANALYSIS[10]

The primary manufacturing activities of the Boeing Company include the production of jet aircraft, missiles and space vehicles, and research and development. Boeing output is of a comparatively homogeneous nature and the firm's operations and plants are heavily concentrated within the Puget Sound region.

8. The lateral-induced system describes the expansion of total income and output in the regional economy and therefore focuses on extensive economic growth.

9. Kevin Allen, "The Regional Multiplier—Some Problems in Estimation," in S. C. Orr and J. B. Cullingworth, editors, *Regional and Urban Studies* (Beverly Hills, Cal.: Sage, 1969), pp. 95–96.

10. The empirical analysis is based on, Rodney A. Erickson, "The 'Lead Firm' Concept and Regional Economic Growth: An Analysis of Boeing Expansion, 1963–1968," unpublished Ph.D. dissertation, University of Washington, Department of Geography, 1973, pp. 199–256.

Boeing's scale of operation has contributed to its dominant role in the economy of the Puget Sound region and its significant impact on Washington State.

During the 1963–1968 "rapid growth phase," Boeing possessed many of the theoretical characteristics of a lead firm.[11] During this period Boeing can be classified as a growth firm inasmuch as the company's output (shipments) increased, on the average, 11 percent annually. This output growth rate compared to 7.5 percent for all manufacturing industries in the nation and 5.4 percent for non-aerospace manufacturing in Washington State.[12] From 1963 to 1967, Boeing increased its total share of U.S. aerospace production from 7.7 percent to 9.5 percent as measured by value of shipments.[13] The firm's total employment (all divisions) rose from an annual average of 100,400 in 1963 to 142,400 in 1968. The cost of net additions to plant and equipment during the rapid growth phase totaled more than $500 million.[14]

Boeing innovations and related changes in the demands for the firm's products led to a different firm output mix. The changing nature of Boeing output during the growth phase is illustrated in Figure 2. Sales of jet aircraft to commercial air carriers covered the declines in Department of Defense and National Aeronautics and Space Administration sales and produced large annual increases in total corporate sales.

The changes which occurred in the Boeing output mix were favorable to the regional

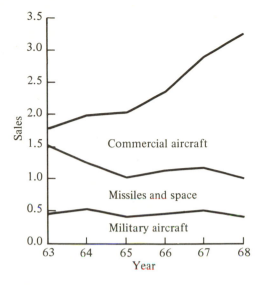

Figure 2. Boeing Sales, 1963-1968 (billions of dollars). Source: Boeing Company *Annual Report*, 1963-1968.

economy. The Seattle metropolitan area was the site of nearly all commercial aircraft production. In contrast, plants located outside Washington were involved primarily in production for defense and space markets. Extraregional localities therefore experienced the economic impacts of production cutbacks for the Department of Defense and the National Aeronautics and Space Administration.

## Technological Linkage Change

Boeing linkages to commercial air carriers represent flows of capital investment goods. These forward linkage flows tied the firm to (final demand) markets located outside the Puget Sound and Washington State regions, thereby preventing the generation of increased economic growth locally through forward interindustry linkage mechanisms. However, the output mix and the new technologies embodied therein produced changes in the kinds and levels of Boeing input purchases.

Inputs for Boeing are made up of inter-

11. Inasmuch as the Boeing Company ceased to exhibit the growth characteristics of a lead firm in mid-1969, the analysis of growth impacts is focused on the 1963–1968 period.
12. Boeing Company *Annual Reports*, 1963 through 1968; U.S. Department of Commerce, Bureau of the Census, *Statistical Abstract of the United States 1970*, Washington, D.C., U.S. Government Printing Office, 1970, pp. 701, 706; Philip J. Bourque and Eldon Weeks, *Detailed Input-Output Tables for Washington State, 1963*, Washington State University, Washington State Agricultural Experiment Station Circular 508, 1969; William B. Beyers, Philip J. Bourque, Warren Seyfried, and Eldon Weeks, *Input-Output Tables for the Washington Economy 1967*, University of Washington, Graduate School of Business Administration, 1970.
13. U.S. Department of Commerce, Bureau of the Census, *Census of Manufactures*, Washington, D.C., U.S. Government Printing Office, 1963 and 1967.
14. Boeing Company *Annual Reports*, 1963 through 1968.

Table 1. Boeing Company Processing Sector
Inputs by Principal Industry Source: 1963 and 1967
*(thousands of dollars)*

| Industry | 1963 | 1967 |
|---|---|---|
| Aerospace | 321,769 | 750,331 |
| Electrical Equipment | 37,074 | 316,519 |
| Business Services & Trade | 32,971 | 58,636 |
| Light Fabricated Metals | 15,841 | 39,705 |
| Printing & Publishing | 7,868 | 27,122 |
| Aluminum | 16,477 | 29,122 |
| Finished Plastics | 17,222 | 28,081 |
| Subtotal | 449,222 | 1,249,556 |
| Total Processing Sector Inputs | 520,264 | 1,370,307 |

Source: I. Hebner, "Input:Output Analysis of the Boeing Company—1963," unpublished M.B.A. Thesis, Dept. of Business Economics, University of Washington, 1965; also, M. Cox, "The Boeing Company (Washington): An Input-Output Study—1967," unpublished research report, Washington Interindustry Study, 1968.

mediate goods purchased from the processing sector and the services of households and government purchased from the payments sector. Rapid output growth and technological change within the firm were accompanied by increased demands for intermediate input supplies. Intermediate inputs as a share of total Boeing inputs increased substantially (9%) over the rapid growth phase. Accordingly, labor inputs as a percentage of total inputs decreased over the period, largely in response to the decreased relative requirements for labor in producing commercial aircraft.

Data for 1963 and 1967 (Table 1) indicate that Boeing processing sector input purchases more than doubled over the period.[15] The largest absolute linkage increase occurred in the aerospace sector, consisting primarily of aircraft engines and parts. The increase in aerospace inputs was closely followed by the electrical equipment sector, composed primarily of electronic components. Large

15. Lawrence C. Hebner, "Input-Output Analysis of the Boeing Company—1963," unpublished M.B.A. Thesis, Graduate School of Business Administration, University of Washington, 1965; Millicent Cox, "The Boeing Company (Washington): An Input-Output Study—1967," unpublished research report, Washington Interindustry Study, 1968.

absolute input increases were characteristic of the light fabricated metals, printing and publishing, and business services sectors, although the sectors' relative contribution of total inputs supplied was not significantly altered.

## Regional Impacts

Boeing has traditionally had limited technological linkages with industries in Washington State. While Boeing's regional operations grew rapidly during the 1963 through 1967 period, the region's relative contribution of processing sector inputs experienced limited increase from 11.2 percent to 12.0 percent, although an absolute increase of $105.7 million occurred (Table 2). (The region here refers to Washington State.)

Among the regional input sectors which experienced modest growth were aerospace, aluminum, and business services. In 1967 regional producers of aluminum and business services had become the principal sources of total Boeing input requirements from these sectors. The absolute regional input flow in these sectors amounted to $42 million above the 1963 level. The regional aerospace sector sales increase of $43 million to Boeing was the largest regional processing sector sales increase. The aerospace, aluminum and business services sectors together accounted for

Table 2. Boeing Company Regionally-Supplied
Processing Sector Inputs by Principal Industry
Source: 1963 and 1967
*(thousands of dollars)*

| Regional Industry | 1963 | 1967 |
|---|---|---|
| Aerospace | 13,388 | 56,629 |
| Aluminum | 1,858 | 19,879 |
| Business Services | 4,645 | 28,470 |
| Subtotal | 19,891 | 104,978 |
| Regionally-Supplied Processing Sector Inputs | 58,546 | 164,291 |
| Total Processing Sector Inputs | 520,264 | 1,370,307 |

Source: See footnote to Table 1.

Table 3. Aerospace Investment Expenditures for Capacity
Expansion in the Puget Sound Area: 1965–1968
(*millions of dollars*)

|  | 1965 | 1966 | 1967 | 1968 | Total |
|---|---|---|---|---|---|
| Land and Land Preparation | 5.2 | 7.5 | 2.6 | 0.1 | 15.4 |
| Land Installations | 3.1 | 24.9 | 16.8 | 17.9 | 62.7 |
| Buildings | 5.7 | 52.2 | 63.5 | | |
| Building | | | | 42.3 | 250.1 |
| Installations | 3.7 | 57.6 | 25.1 | | |
| Equipment | 22.5 | 66.5 | 110.6 | 62.4 | 262.0 |
| Total | 40.2 | 208.7 | 218.6 | 122.7 | 590.2 |

Source: Survey data.

80 percent of the increase in regional processing sector sales to Boeing.

While regional processing sector sales to Boeing increased during the rapid growth phase, regional producers captured only a small share of the total increase. Boeing's total domestic processing sector purchases in 1967 exceeded the 1963 level by $830 million, but regional producers contributed only 13 percent of the increased processing sector sales to Boeing. The region, therefore, did not fare particularly well in increasing its share of Boeing processing sector inputs produced over the rapid growth phase. In addition, the limited technological linkages with local producers precluded the development of significant regional economic growth generation through the indirect impacts of the technological linkage system. The direct and indirect effects output multiplier arising from aerospace sector technological linkages with other regional producers was 1.0604 in 1963 and 1.0785 in 1967.[16] That is, each dollar of aerospace output generated an additional output of 6.0 cents and 7.9 cents in 1963 and 1967, respectively, as a result of technological linkages with regional producers. Thus, the regional output generating impact of Boeing's backward technological linkages was relatively weak during the firm's rapid growth phase. However, because of the large magnitude of regional aerospace output, a significant increase in regional output occurred despite the small increase in the direct and indirect effects output multiplier.[17]

## Capacity Expansion in Boeing and the Puget Sound Aerospace Sector

The need for increased productive capacity in Boeing and the linked regional aerospace sector resulted in over $700 million in Puget Sound regional capital expansion projects during the 1963–1968 period.[18] From 1965 through 1968, aerospace capital goods expenditures on Puget Sound investment projects totaled $590.2 million (Table 3). The years of greatest capacity expansion (1966 and 1967) were primarily a result of Boeing capital investments in the Model 747 jetliner production facility at the Everett site.

Purchases of production equipment ($262.0 million) were directed almost entirely to firms located outside Washington State.[19] The production of capital equipment in the machinery sector of the Washington economy is highly specialized and serves both national and international markets. In 1967,

16. Over the study period, Boeing output comprised approximately 95 percent of the total Washington aerospace production. Philip J. Bourque, *et al.* (1969), *op. cit.;* William B. Beyers, *et al.* (1970), *op. cit.*

17. In 1967 an additional $45.6 million of regional output can be attributed to the increase in the direct and indirect effects output-multiplier for the aerospace sector.
18. Survey data.
19. Interviews with aerospace manufacturers.

output in the regional machinery sector totaled $332.3 million, of which only $17.8 million was sold to regional private capital investment, primarily to food and forest products sectors.[20]

Investment in buildings, building installations, and land installations (utilities and roads, etc.) totaled $312.8 million. Construction-related projects were contracted to various regional firms. The aerospace sector's purchases from the regional construction industry totaled approximately $300 million during the 1965–1968 period. These goods were purchased from the industrial and commercial construction subsector of the regional construction industry. Disaggregation of the construction sector is useful in estimating the regional economic growth generated through industrial subsector construction purchases.[21]

In 1967, aerospace expenditures on construction-oriented investments comprised 44 percent of the total output of the regional industrial and commercial construction subsector. The industrial construction subsector has strong backward linkage ties to regional industries, as indicated in Table 4. Backward linkage interdependence was comparatively strong, and if the 1967 multipliers were representative of other years 1965–1968, aerospace capital goods expansion would have generated over $850 million of increased regional output over the period.

The analysis therefore suggests that large capital goods expansions by lead firms are capable of generating substantial amounts of regional economic growth. Inasmuch as construction expenditures frequently comprise a large percentage of plant expansion, and local construction firms tend to be the primary contract participants, a large share of the capital goods expansion dollar remains within the regional economy. In addition, the strong construction sector linkage to the regional household sector and building materials sectors generates a comparatively high total multiplier effect. The empirical evidence pre-

Table 4. Industrial and Commercial Construction Input Purchases from Washington State: 1967 (*thousands of dollars*)

| Sector | 1967 |
|---|---|
| Heavy Metals | 23,600 |
| Cement and Clay | 18,500 |
| Business Services | 6,500 |
| Trade | 5,900 |
| Transportation | 4,100 |
| Other | 21,400 |
| Regional Processing Sector Purchases | 77,000 |
| Regional Payments Sector Purchases | 92,600 |
| Imports | 95,000 |
| Total Purchases | 264,600 |

Direct and Indirect Output Multiplier Effect–1.35
Direct, Indirect, and Household
   Supporting Output Multiplier Effect–2.86
Source: Construcon Sector Disaggregation compiled by W. Seyfried, W. Beyers, and S. Kwak, Washington Interindustry Study, University of Washington, 1970.

sented here suggests that the total growth impact of Boeing and linked aerospace capital goods expenditures in the region exceeded the level of growth generated through the technological linkage system over the Boeing rapid growth phase.

## Regional Income Generation in the Lateral-Induced System

Regional aerospace industry value created increased from $629 million in 1963 to $1089 million in 1967.[22] These value created figures include wages and salaries, local taxes, depreciation charges, and profits. Wages and salaries comprise by far the largest component of value created, and are re-spent by local residents for consumption purposes.[23]

20. William B. Beyers, *et al.* (1970), *op. cit.*
21. This disaggregation was compiled by Warren Seyfried, William B. Beyers, and Soo Kwak, University of Washington, 1970.

22. Boeing and other regional aerospace firms have consistently contributed 90–95 percent of the value created arising from the lead firm and the regional technological linkage system.
23. Washington State Department of Employment Security data indicate that wages and salaries comprised approximately 80 percent of value created in the regional aerospace sector during the 1963–1968 period.

Table 5. Income Multiplier Effects in the Washington State Aerospace Sector: 1963 and 1967

| Sector | Direct Income (1) | Direct & In- direct Income Change (2) | In- direct Income Change (3) | Direct In- direct and In- duced Income Change (4) | In- duced Income Change (5) |
|---|---|---|---|---|---|
| 1963 Aerospace | .520 | .558 | .038 | .989 | .431 |
| 1967 Aerospace | .429 | .471 | .042 | .816 | .345 |

Source: Computed from P. Bourque and E. Weeks, *Detailed Input-Output Tables for Washington State, 1963*, Washington State University, Washington State Agricultural Experiment Station Circular 508, 1969; W. Beyers, P. Bourque, W. Seyfried, and E. Weeks, *Input-Output Tables for the Washington Economy, 1967*, University of Washington, Graduate School of Business Administration, 1970.

These consumption expenditures are made primarily on service-related economic activities, which have in turn a high regional value created component. Thus, in the lateral-induced system the local service sector plays a crucial role in generating increased economic growth. Not only is local service sector development a function of the level of regional export industry, but it also influences the multiplier effects in the income-generating process of the local economy.

Data for 1963 and 1967 indicate that the Type II total income multiplier effect (direct, indirect, and household supporting) in the aerospace sector of the state's economy was 1.900 in 1963 and 1.901 in 1967.[24] These multipliers include the direct or initial income effect, the indirect effects arising from the technological linkage system, and the induced income effects arising from the lateral-induced system. Comparative calculations of indirect and induced income multiplier effects in the aerospace sector are given in Table 5.

Table 5 indicates that in 1963 each dollar of aerospace sales generated 52 cents in direct

income to regional residents as wages, salaries, profits, interest, etc., and to local governments as tax payments. The indirect impact generated through the technological linkage system was 3.8 cents, and the induced effect generated through the lateral-induced system was 43.1 cents, producing a total direct, indirect and induced income of 98.9 cents for each dollar of aerospace sales. In 1967 the appropriate direct, indirect and induced income effects per dollar of aerospace sales were 42.9 cents, 4.2 cents, and 34.5 cents, respectively, contributing to a total income of 81.6 cents of regional income per dollar of aerospace sales.

It is therefore evident that the income-generating capacity of the lateral-induced system focused on Boeing was considerably more important within the state economy than the income generation of the indirect effects of the technological linkage system. The ratio of induced effects to indirect effects was approximately 11:1 in 1963 and 8:1 in 1967. Furthermore, it appears that within the Puget Sound growth center, the relative role of induced income effects in the aerospace sector was also strong. Recent data developed by Beyers for 1967 indicate that indirect effects

24. Philip J. Bourque, *et al.* (1969), *op. cit.;* William B. Beyers, *et al.* (1970), *op. cit.*

in the Puget Sound Region were 3.5 cents while induced effects were 26.9 cents per dollar of aerospace sales.[25]

However, it is interesting to note that the magnitude of induced income effects (in the state economy) per dollar of aerospace sales declined over the 1963 to 1967 period. This change appears to be explained by the decrease in regional value created per dollar of aerospace sales, differences in structural interdependence, and by the expansion of imports in the regional economy.[26] Rapid expansion of Boeing and other exporting sectors in the 1963 through 1967 period probably increased the competition for regional resources and led to capital and labor shortages. While state exports in the 1967 period had increased by 51 percent over the 1963 level, regional industrial imports increased by 77 percent, thereby contributing to substantial leakages in the regional income stream.

Although the Boeing output level soared during the 1963 through 1968 period, the regional growth-generating impulses of the technological linkage system focused on Boeing were relatively weak. Evidence does not support the notion that a significant backward-linked industrial complex was developing during the firm's rapid growth phase. In contrast, the capital goods linkage system was shown to be a comparatively potent regional economic growth generative force, and the substantial value-created component and regional backward linkages of the construction industry generated a comparatively high multiplier effect in the local economy.

The principal generator of Boeing-related economic growth in the region was the lateral-induced system. Aerospace purchases from the value-created sector in 1967 were $460 million above the 1963 level. As indi-

Table 6. Aerospace Generated Output in the Washington Economy: 1967
*(millions of dollars)*

| Unit/System | Output |
|---|---|
| Boeing (Washington) | 2,406.3 |
| Regional Aerospace | 2,536.0 |
| Technological System | 197.1 |
| Lateral-Induced System | 3,329.8 |
| Capital Goods System | 301.4 |
| Estimated Total 1967 Aerospace Generated Output | 6,364.3 |

Source: Computed from previously determined multipliers.

cated in Table 6, the lateral-induced multiplier associated with the expansion of Boeing and technologically-linked regional firms produced by far the major part of the economic growth associated with the Boeing expansion.

Growth pole theory has traditionally focused attention on the technological linkage system as a generator of economic growth. Many growth center planning strategies have attempted to promote regional economic development by inducing expansion in the technological linkage system. Yet, the most significant finding of the analysis of the Boeing Company as a lead firm is the strong local growth-generating impact of the lateral-induced system. This system highlights the role of regional value created and the extent of local service sector development.

The significant growth-generating contribution of the lateral-induced system exemplified in the Boeing analysis may be typical of many contemporary growth firms located in metropolitan areas. Growth firms in many of the growth industries (e.g., electronics, pharmaceuticals, aerospace, etc.) do not appear to have been technologically-linked within their regional economies to the extent that older resource-oriented industries were linked. As a result of complex interregional procurement patterns, many of these growth firms generate substantial economic growth in extra-regional localities through their technological linkage systems. In contrast, the local concentration of service activi-

25. William B. Beyers, "Interregional Input-Output Tables for the Puget Sound Economy," unpublished data, Department of Geography, University of Washington, 1973.
26. Substantial increases in imports occurred in the regional private capital investment account and the construction sector, which was rapidly expanding during the 1963–1967 period. See, William B. Beyers, "On the Stability of Regional Interindustry Models: The Washington Data for 1963 and 1967," *Journal of Regional Science*, December 1972, pp. 363–374.

ties producing for the regional economy contributes to a substantial lateral-induced growth component. The growth-generating effects of the lateral-induced system need to be fully incorporated into growth center theory and planning, with a close examination of the income and employment multipliers which are associated with lead firms in alternative urban functional and regional settings.

# 6

# THE CONTROVERSY: ISSUES IN THE NATIONAL SETTLEMENT DEBATE

# Introduction

The debate on national settlement patterns has been sufficiently broad to include most of society's critical policy issues. In United Nations publications, as in the first paper in this section taken from Barbara Ward's report to the UN Habitat Conference in Vancouver and in her subsequent book (Ward, 1976), settlement problems include almost all aspects of man's use and occupancy of the earth's surface. The extreme breadth of this concern, however, makes it difficult to identify and to understand specific policy issues.

Our definition of the urban system focuses concern on a subset of these broad settlement problems. We cannot pretend that the social and economic problems created by the urban system are necessarily the most severe that bedevil mankind. After all, in the highly integrated urban systems typical of most developed nations the problems of quality of life, crime, and mental illness affect every city to a certain degree. Although there are significant differences in income level from one city or region to another, these differences pale next to the income inequalities among occupations, social classes, and age and ethnic groups.

Nonetheless conflicts among various elements of the urban system can and do occur, some of which are extreme. Most are expressed in social alienation, economic competition, and political tensions. The potential for conflict is greatest wherever sharp differentials—be they social, economic, or political—coincide in space or time with the two major dimensions of any urban system: the regional and the hierarchical dimensions. Regional conflicts emerge among very different urban subsystems, regardless of city size. The U.S. Civil War, for instance, pitted the South against the East and Midwest, reflecting both cultural and economic differences. And Scottish nationalism is based on both a cultural distinction and a sense of economic exploitation.

Other conflicts directly reflect the hierarchic structure of urban systems. That hierarchy tends to collect, shape, and then redistribute economic growth. The resulting conflicts between the largest city and the peripheral areas are often characterized in such expressions as Chicago versus "downstate" or London and "the provinces." Freidmann (1966; and in Section IV) has generalized this tension as the core-periphery problem, and it occurs in some form or other between any urban center and its surrounding service area. The root of the problem is usually differences in income, and in economic power and control, but it is frequently aggravated by differences in ethnic background, political allegiance, and social mores.

Of the many differences that might arise among different components of the urban system, at least four stand out as endemic to any system: 1) the quality of life and economic efficiency, 2) income disparity, 3) growth and stability and 4) the degree of political autonomy. The first issue addresses the problem of city size and urban agglomeration and their relation to economic efficiency and the good life in general; the second treats income variations among residents of different cities and regions; the third considers the question of what is an appropriate rate of growth; and the fourth asks who makes the decisions in an integrated economy. These issues are of course interdependent. A fifth issue, which we treat only briefly, concerns changes in the geometry or spatial distribution of national populations through urbanization and metropolitan concentration.

Although we have used a slightly different typology, Morrill provides an excellent overview of basically the same issues, in reference to American settlement patterns, in the second paper in this section. Together, the papers by Ward and Morrill serve as a broad basis for the debates in subsequent papers.

## THE QUALITY OF LIFE

One of the most pervasive, albeit unfocused, arguments for public intervention to modify the structure of an urban system is the sense that large cities are becoming increasingly unlivable. This view is not a recent one. A typical version of this attitude is given in a beautiful paper by an author signed simply "common sense," reprinted from the 1811 volume of the London *Monthly Magazine*. It reflects an attitude expressed daily in contemporary books, newspapers, talk shows, and government position papers (Hicks, 1975).

New York (read São Paulo, or Tokyo, or London, or Moscow, or Toronto, depending on your location) is too big, they argue. Such cities are ungovernable; their citizens are soulless atoms; traffic, servicing costs, building standards, and pollution are beyond control. Increasing crime and alienation are then seen as the inevitable responses by residents to an increasingly impersonal and stress-filled environment. Such themes are cited by residents of smaller places in referring to almost any larger place, and sometimes they are echoed by residents of the metropolitan centers themselves. In part, these attacks reflect the entire range of conflicts between cities of different sizes, including income inequalities and political autonomy; in part, they result from the different ways of life prevailing in communities of different sizes; and in part, they are real statements about urban problems, which increase with increased city size and which clearly tend to have an uneven impact on different social groups. There is no doubt that these large cities have severe problems; what we are asking in this book is that we recognize the differing sources and impacts of those problems.

Sometimes the issue of the quality of life is coupled with that of economic efficiency. Large cities, it is argued, are increasingly inefficient. Above a certain population size the social costs (per capita) of future growth begin to rise, soon exceeding the benefits of agglomeration. But as Mera (see pp. 000) and others have shown repeatedly, there is no optimal city size and no consistent limit beyond which cities are less or more productive (Hansen, 1975). Indeed theories of central place and industrial specialization suggest that a full range of city sizes is necessary for a viable urban system. Mera argues that higher levels of public expenditures in large cities are due more to the willingness of residents to pay for services than to diseconomies of scale. Yet the debate on agglomeration benefits and costs continues.[1]

The quality-of-life issue revolves, then, around cities as places to live and to work. Should governments intervene to slow down population growth in some of the largest centers and redirect that growth to other, usually smaller, communities? Would this reduce overall rates of pollution or crimes of violence or would it ease racial tensions or redistribute opportunities in the way people want? The honest answer is that we do not know. Issues of this kind are incredibly complex, as the earlier discussions on social indicators in Section III and on growth in Section V suggested. We are hardly able to even measure problems of this kind, let alone evaluate their relative importance.

We know that life in large cities is different from that in smaller centers, at least for certain people. Some can segregate themselves from the hustle and bustle and operate as "urban villagers" (see Gans, 1962). Others cannot. Even sophisticated economic and social measures of quality of life present mixed results (Andrews and Withey, 1976). Though unemployment may be more tolerable in smaller place, it is also more likely to occur there. The stress of social conflict in larger cities is, in theory, countered by greater opportunities for social mobility. Discussions of the quality of life and economic efficiency will likely diminish when the simple fact that there are and will always be *differences* between cities is accepted. Perhaps it is advantageous to maintain or even enlarge the choice of life-styles available by encouraging a wide range of city sizes, while ensuring that standards of social services are as high as possible and that access to job opportunities is everywhere the same (see Alonso, 1975; and Hägerstrand's paper in the following section).

## INCOME DISPARITIES

Income levels, on the other hand, are measurable. Despite data difficulties we do know that incomes vary systematically across the urban system and over time. In most urban systems that have been examined these variations are of considerable

---

1. For a criticism of the arguments in Mera's paper see Borukov (1975) and Mera's reply in the same journal. For further perspectives on this debate see Hansen (1975), Santos (1975) and the exchange between Gilbert (1976) and Richardson (1976).

magnitude (Williamson, 1965; Robinson, 1969; Morrill and Wohlenberg, 1971; Firestone, 1974; Benhayoun, 1976). Regional or urban subsystem differences in per-capita income may range from 75 to 140 around a national index of 100 in developed countries (see Figure 1 in Morrill's paper),[2] and may be many times that in the developing countries (see Cornelius and Trueblood, 1975; and Mountjoy's paper in this section).

In part these regional differences are simply due to variations in urban population size. In every nation for which we have data, income levels tend to increase directly with city size. The explanation for this relationship depends on one's ideology to a considerable extent. Economies of scale, the power of some regions and cities to exploit other regions, excess profits, the generally superior skills and education of the inhabitants of larger cities, and the effects of differential growth rates are all plausible explanations relevant both to capitalist and socialist societies. In traditional or neoclassical economic theory, social and spatial variations in income levels are necessary in order to guide the space-economy toward making the most efficient investment decisions. Traditional Marxian theory also argues that such variations in income are necessary, at least in capitalistic societies, in order to create the surplus capital essential for further growth and to ensure that labor is encouraged to strive for higher productivity. Both arguments are correct.

The issues become even more complex when one begins to weigh costs and benefits, that is to measure real or *effective income*. Residents of high-income cities like New York or Paris might argue that their incomes should be higher because the cost of living (especially housing) is higher and natural amenities are fewer. Two color televisions and wider access to cultural facilities in the larger cities may somehow compensate for congestion or the increased chance of contracting lung cancer or of being mugged. But cost-of-living indices almost never vary between cities as much as do income measures.

Income differentials among cities and regions remain, after all these explanations are explored, as a gnawing and divisive social issue. Poorer and less urbanized regions like Appalachia, or Newfoundland, or most of the developing world are unable to provide educational opportunities for workers or the infrastructure to create new jobs, and these areas show a steadily declining income, relative to other areas. Those who migrate to other more prosperous regions often obtain only the lowest paying jobs. And those left behind find that overall incomes of their region are reduced. All the imperfections of the labor market become visible. The lack of training, the lack of information on job opportunities (and job problems), as well as the costs of movement to other regions become severe barriers to achievement for anyone unfortunate enough to have been raised in a poverty region.

Some observers suggest that these poverty regions are not the inevitable results of an efficient economic system but are instead the effects of *systematic exploita-*

2. In Figure 1 a net poverty gap or deficit is defined as the situation in which the money necessary to bring all families up to the non-poverty threshold could not be raised by transferring money from the wealthy in those areas.

*tion* by larger urban centers, by other sectors of the economy, or by the capitalist economic system itself. The paper by Peet in this section demonstrates this view in reference to rural and regional planning problems in the U.S., and presents a nice contrast in approach to the Mera paper preceding it.

Farming regions, usually the lowest in income, respond to changes in agricultural prices, which are largely determined in the major urban areas by commodity traders, the "futures" market, and government policies. It is therefore the "terms of trade," for example, the relative price of turnips, that impoverish such areas. If oil can triple in price, why not lettuce, or clothing, or shrimp, or coal? Any of these price shifts would significantly alter the income levels of different regions. Such price shifts simply require a modification in the distribution of economic power and a change in the ability of these regions to bargain effectively and to eventually determine pricing decisions themselves.

Income differentials, then, are a simple and fundamental measure of urban-system problems, but they stem from several different sources, many increasingly rooted in the dynamics of the urban system. Almost every kind of change in the urban system—inflation, migration, urbanization, industrialization, or the introduction of any form of national economic policy, such as a tariff, a subsidy, or tax structure—redistributes income within the urban system. Sometimes the incomes of different regions converge as new income growth is more evenly distributed between the wealthier areas and the poor. This has happened in many western European countries (Thirlwall, 1974) and among the major regions of the United States over the last few decades (Perin and Semple, 1976). This result supports one thesis of traditional economic-development theory, which suggests that an urban system must first diverge in terms of income during the early stages of development and then slowly converge as economic growth accelerates (Kusnets, 1955).

More often, however, the total effect is one of divergence, through a process of "cumulative and circular causation," as Myrdal called it, or *capital accumulation* as Marx argued (Harvey, 1975). The disadvantages of backward and peripheral regions often increase over time, as capital investment and political power are centered in the core. There are no necessary conditions for the creation of regional income equality. It can only improve if the forces encouraging economic and spatial decentralization are greater than those of centralization and if, as Reiner (1975) argues, questions relating to the distributional effects of policy decisions are given as much weight in the decision-making process as economic development itself. This condition applies to Socialist as well as capitalist systems.


## GROWTH AND STABILITY

These arguments about the merits of city size, the distribution of income, and economic efficiency fuel the controversy whenever a particular decision on growth policy emerges within the urban system. It is widely believed by entrepreneurs looking for profits, governments seeking revenues, and workers fearful of unemployment that increases in income require continued high rates of growth. There is considerable empirical support for this view. Rapidly growing urban centers do have significantly higher incomes.

But each community also has an opposition group, often composed of people with secure incomes, which strongly believes that a high level of local growth is too costly, both in terms of current social stress deriving from, for example, the location of new public facilities and in terms of the long-term result, i.e., a larger city with all its problems. The inevitable consequence is an ongoing conflict within and between cities in which opposing sides in the growth debate may become very highly polarized. For some, a new airport becomes the forerunner of the moral decline of society; for others, a new factory becomes the only safeguard from another economic depression.

An increasing body of literature (e.g., Lithwick, 1970; Alonso, 1975; Gans, 1975; and Section VII) suggests that both arguments are right, but that the essential indicator to be monitored and manipulated is the rate of growth, and the basic goal is one of stability. Cities that grow too slowly force out-migration, often of individuals and families that do not wish to move, and increase the tax burden on those that remain. Clearly, decisions on the supply of new public facilities and services at any one time must not be directly linked to the highly variable rates of growth or decline typical in local areas.

At the other extreme cities should not grow too rapidly. Rapid growth requires major capital inputs and often results in hasty location decisions and the waste of much of the existing physical fabric. Social services and institutions become overwhelmed. Individual cities in an urban system should not be required to undergo stress of this sort simply in order to maintain reasonable levels of income and employment.

The problem of growth then becomes twofold: first, can a national urban system be managed in such a way as to change in a stable and orderly fashion without rapid shocks and severe adjustments in local areas? Second, can a particular city adjust to a future of low or no growth within that urban system? Can decision makers, institutions, and labor accept a metropolitan area that cannot supply more of everything and can these people live with the necessity of improving what is already there, that is, of planning for redistribution rather than for growth?

## AUTONOMY

The other cluster of issues intrinsic to urban systems focuses directly on the locus of power. Inherent in any complex organization, such as in a highly integrated urban system, is a set of central mechanisms, or decision-making processes, that impose on a particular city the requirements and rules of the overall system. National commodity markets, fiscal policies, and national transportation networks, for example, to a considerable extent ordain the growth rate, income level, and social standards of all communities. Although it appears that, for the most part, people are content to enjoy the higher levels of income and the security from localized disasters that such integration usually provides, now and again the lack of local or regional control becomes irksome. The irritant may derive from real income disparities, losses of jobs, or (as in Orange County, California) it may be rooted in a particular political ideology. The countervailing trend, which has gathered momentum in the last decade, is toward political decentralization and a shift in the balance of power toward local autonomy in decision making (Livingston, 1976). The latter is in part a conservative response to increased integration and in part it is a genuine concern for the role of local communities in a rapidly changing society.

Deutsch (1963), for example, has demonstrated the existence of a close two-way relationship between the operation of the urban system and that of the political system. The tighter integration of an urban system, bringing cities into closer and closer contact, increases their interdependence and increases the acceptance of national political power. The decisions of the national government to create unifying institutions, such as a social-security program or an interstate highway network, tend to further integrate the urban system.

Suppose, though, that one city in the urban system decides to opt out. A California city says that it has enough people already. Colorado rejects its role as a national winter sports playground. Québec resists the dominance of the English-speaking culture of North America. Scotland wants a devolution of power and to keep revenues from its oil. An integrated urban system, however, can apply a great deal of economic and political pressure in such areas. The resisting region may win on a single issue, such as holding its own referendum on the environment, but finds it difficult to resist a steady stream of entrepreneurs offering new jobs and sources of tax revenue, political plums such as irrigation schemes, media saying ''grow! grow!'', and legislation framed at the national level to address national problems like the energy crisis.

The issue of urban subsystem autonomy is simply a redefinition of an age-old controversy—from colonialism, to federalism, to states' rights—of *who makes decisions*. What is the appropriate political organization of a national territory that is highly urbanized? How should different territorial interests be reconciled? It is worthwhile considering these questions here because the pressures for integration now operate largely through the organization of the urban system. New Jersey's current difficulties are essentially due to its role within the New York metropolitan region. The urban system concept at least helps us to understand by revealing some of the forces underlying such conflicts.

## THE GEOMETRY OF POPULATION

The final and probably least critical issue in this debate is the question about which map of national population distribution is the best. Should there be one large city or several? Should large cities be close together or far apart? As we saw in the introduction to Section III many alternative distributions of cities seem to be viable, but is one pattern inherently preferable to another? There is very little firm evidence on the advantages of different distributions. At a national scale, however, particularly in European countries, a clear preference has been expressed for a relatively dispersed pattern of urban development, that is, for cities scattered in a relatively uniform fashion across the nation. Sometimes the higher incomes and economic or social opportunities provided by large cities do not seem to be at issue; observers are primarily concerned that there should not be urban-rich (i.e., having a large number of cities) and urban-poor (having few cities) regions within the same country.

Among the most plausible arguments for decentralization is the one used in Sweden to justify the government's controls on Stockholm's growth and its population-redistribution policies generally. The Swedish argument is not against large cities as such, but against the concentration of a finite national inventory of public services in a few major urban regions, which would effectively disenfranchise large segments of the population living outside those regions. Hägerstrand's paper in Section VII is a good example of this kind of thinking. Perhaps, though, efforts to disperse urbanization in most countries are also a way of avoiding more controversial issues, such as the spatial redistribution of income and power.

In areas of the world with high population densities and high mobility, particularly those where nature and historical accident have enforced a striking spatial heterogeneity in the distribution of urban places, this concern has taken a specific focus. "Megalopolis," or the spatial coalescence of sprawling metropolitan areas, has become a common term and a popular concern. The identification of "Bos-Wash," the corridor along the U.S. central Atlantic coast, and "Chi-Pitts," the area around the Great Lakes, led to images of ever larger regions, and even nations and continents, being consumed by the urbanization process (Lehman and Lehman, 1976). Megalopolitan forms have also been documented in Japan (Toyko-Osaka), northwestern Europe (Eriplan, 1974), England (Hall et al., 1973), and in other areas. The Gottmann article in Section I exemplified the concern that cities, as we now know them, would blend together, if not physically then certainly in terms of interaction, and thus become more indistinquishable; while at the same time isolating their inhabitants from contact with rural landscapes and life-styles.

Recent information largely contradicts these predictions, however. Although the increasing integration of large urban regions presents some difficulties in political administration and service provision, the way of life in such cities is still strongly organized around the original centers of economic and social activity. At the same time, at least in North America, the forces that led to the earlier assertions of continued megalopolitan formation have changed dramatically in recent years, if they have not been reversed. Absolute growth rates for both population and GNP have declined. Employment in manufacturing has declined in absolute terms in most areas, but particularly in the old industrial heartlands. Energy costs are beginning to restrict travel and urban sprawl. Land costs and thus the densities of urban development have risen. Local autonomy is again in vogue. And the rate of growth itself, as noted above, is now open to debate.

These trends were first documented, as is so often the case, in the U.S. In the sixth paper in this section, Morrison shows that the growth rates of many large metropolitan areas in the U.S., notably in the "Bos-Wash" and Great Lakes megalopolises, began to decline in the late 1960s. In the 1970s these declines have become almost precipitous. Similar trends have been observed in Britain and in many parts of Europe. Not only has the rate of natural increase dropped, but migration patterns have changed dramatically. What is noteworthy in the recent figures described by Morrison is that new growth is spreading not just to commuter towns near the metropolises, as a continuation of trends in previous decades, but to small towns and rural regions well removed from the old urban heartland.

The historical pattern of increasing population concentration in megalopolitan centers and urbanized corridors has thus been reversed within a decade. For numerous and diverse reasons, many of which seem to be largely beyond the control of the public sector, a *new urban future* appears to be emerging. Berry (1976) has described this trend as one of "counter-urbanization" and population deconcentration. One result may be to lay the basis for an entirely new set of problems. Already many of our policy statements from the 1960s are dated.

## THE DEVELOPING WORLD

Although we have not said much in this volume thus far on problems in the so-called Third World, we must at least acknowledge the staggering rates and impact of urbanization in such countries (Cornelius and Trueblood, 1975; Ward, 1976). In relative terms, the urban problems of developed countries appear to be only minor annoyances—capable of solution if the will is there—compared with those of most developing nations. Particularly important is the recognition that Third World countries' paths of urbanization and their urban problems are increasingly different from those in the developed world and require different solutions.

In the last paper Mountjoy looks at one particular dimension of urbanization and migration in the developing world: squatter settlements. These settlements, he argues, are but one indication that the correlation between urbanization and modernization (industrialization) which we might expect, given the experience of Western economies (as Pederson and Friedmann also pointed out in Section IV) does not hold in developing countries. Industrialization (and therefore jobs) lag far behind urban population growth in most of the developing world. Their major cities are overwhelmed by in-migrants, while the rural areas stagnate. Spatial inequalities increase and economic development becomes highly specialized and polarized.

The dilemma is simply this: given that these cities remain the critical economic vehicle for developing countries in an increasingly competitive international power game, can they maintain if not improve this role without at the same time strangling themselves and their hinterlands through population concentration? The larger cities are the centers of innovation and social change as well as the major points of contact with the international urban system. They are also the homes for a rapidly increasing proportion of the population in the developing world.

## SUMMARY COMMENTS

Complex social systems like urban systems are not easily manipulated. In fact their growth is not, for the most part, predictable. We do not know with any certainty the growth rate of Norfolk, or Birmingham, or Calgary over the next few decades. And the sources of growth and change are so many and so different that government intervention, in any but the most heavy-handed fashion—for example, the decision of the Brazilian government to locate its new capital in the interior of the country—may not be effective.

Nonetheless, the growth of individual cities and systems of cities affect such a large portion of people's lives—the style of living they assume, their income and opportunities, their personal security, and the future of their children—that we can expect a growing concern on the part of the public and, often reluctantly, of governments and a continuing debate in the research and policy literature on the relative merits of alternative forms of urban systems. The papers in the next and last section look at some examples of those alternative forms.

## REFERENCES

Alonso, W. 1975. "City Sizes and Quality of Life: Some Observations." *Working Paper No. 245.* Berkeley: University of California, Institute of Urban and Regional Development.

Andrews, F. M. and Withey, S. B. 1976. *Social Indicators of Well-Being: The Development and Measurement of Perceptual Indicators.* New York: Plenum.

Benhayoun, G. 1976. "Salaries et Concentration Urbaine." *Cahiers d'Economie Politique,* No. 2, pp. 254–297.

Berry, B.J.L., ed. 1976. *Patterns of Urbanization and Counter-Urbanization.* Beverly Hills: Sage Publications.

———. and Gillard, Q. 1976. *The Changing Shape of Metropolitan America: Commuting*

*Patterns, Urban Fields and Decentralization Processes*. Cambridge, Mass.: Ballinger.

Borukov, E. 1975. "On the Urban Agglomeration and Economic Efficiency: Comment." *Economic Development and Cultural Change*, vol. 23, pp. 633–652.

Cornelius, W. A. and Trueblood, F. M., eds. 1975. *Urbanization and Inequality: The Political Economy of Urban and Rural Development*. Beverly Hills: Sage Publications.

Deutsch, K. W. 1963. *Nerves of Government*. Glencoe, Ill.: The Free Press.

Eriplan (European Research Institute for Regional and Urban Planning). 1974. *North West Europe Megalopolis*. Report submitted to the Commission of European Governments. The Hague.

Firestone, O. J., ed. 1974. *Regional Economic Development*. Ottawa: University of Ottawa Press.

Friedmann, J. 1966. *Regional Development Policy: A Case Study of Venezuela*. Cambridge, Mass.: M.I.T. Press.

Fuchs, R. 1967. *Differentials in Hourly Earnings by Region and City Size*. Occasional Paper No. 101. Washington: National Bureau of Economic Research.

Gans, Herbert, 1962. *The Urban Villagers*. Glencoe, Ill.: The Free Press.

———. 1975. "Planning for Declining and Poor Cities." *Journal of the American Institute of Planners*, vol. 41, pp. 305–307.

Gilbert, A. G. 1976. "The Arguments for Very Large Cities Reconsidered." *Urban Studies*, vol. 13, pp. 27–34.

Hall, P. *et al.* 1973. *The Containment of Urban England: Or Megalopolis Denied*. Vol. 1. London: Allen and Unwin.

Hansen, N. M. 1975. *The Challenge of Urban Growth. The Basic Economics of City Size and Structure*. Lexington, Mass.: D. C. Heath.

Harvey, D. 1975. "The Geography of Capitalist Accumulation: A Reconstruction of the Marxian Theory." *Antipode*, vol. 7, pp. 9–21.

———. Forthcoming. *Urbanization Under Capitalism*.

Hicks, U. K. 1975. *The Large City: A World Problem*. London: Macmillan & Co.

Kuznets, S. 1955. "Economic Growth and Income Inequality." *American Economic Review*, vol. 45, pp. 1–28.

Lehman, A. and Lehman, I. 1976. *The Great Lakes Megalopolis*. Ottawa: Ministry of State for Urban Affairs.

Lithwick, N. H. 1970. *Urban Canada: Problems and Prospects*. Ottawa: Information Canada.

Livingston, D. 1976. "Global Equilibrium and the Decentralized Community." *Ekistics*, vol. 250, pp. 173–176.

Mera, K. 1973. "Tradeoffs between Aggregate Efficiency and Interregional Equality: The Case of Japan." *Regional and Urban Economics*, vol. 3, pp. 273–300.

Morrill, R. L. and Wohlenburg, E. H. 1971. *The Geography of Poverty in the United States*. New York: McGraw-Hill.

Perin, D. E. and Semple, R. K. 1976. "Recent Trends in Income Inequalities in the United States." *Regional Science Perspectives*, vol. 6, pp. 65–85.

Reiner, T. A. 1974. "Welfare Differences within a Nation." *Papers of the Regional Science Association*, vol. 32, pp. 65–82.

Richardson, H. W. 1976. "The Argument for Very Large Cities Reconsidered: A Comment." *Urban Studies*, vol. 13, pp. 307–310.

Robinson, E.A.G., ed. 1969. *Backward Areas in Advanced Countries*. London: Macmillan & Co.

Santos, M. 1975. "Space and Domination: A Marxist Approach." *International Social Science Journal*, vol. 27, pp. 346–363.

Thirlwall, A. P. 1974. "Regional Disparities and Regional Policy in Europe." *Urban Studies*, vol. 11, pp. 1–12.

Ward, B. 1976. *The Home of Man*. Toronto: McClelland and Stewart.

Williamson, J. G. 1965. "Regional Inequality and the Process of National Development: A Description of the Patterns." *Economic Development and Cultural Change*, vol. 13, pp. 3–45.

Yeates, M. 1975. *Main Street. The Windsor to Quebec City Axis*. Toronto: Macmillan of Canada.

# Human Settlements: Crisis and Opportunity

BARBARA WARD

## The Role of Settlements in a National Development Policy

Development policy, particularly in the Third World, faces certain facts. Settlements are rising like a flood around the globe as population explodes, urban centres double, and the biggest cities double again. They do so, moreover, at a time of constant technological innovation, which changes the form, load, impact and duration of economic activities in quite unpredictable ways. Add to this the rising demands of insistent consumption and nations confront a scale of change which usually seems, and often is, largely unmanageable.

Yet the unmanaged results are not satisfactory. In developed market economies, in most developing countries, and at least in the historical location of settlements in centrally planned societies, settlements happen to be where they are largely as the unintended by-product of policies and decision making based upon a fairly narrow economic calculus. A river crossing, a sheltered bay, the opening of a mine determines the original location. Then the economics of concentrated demand, increasing infrastructure and easily mobilizable skills and supplies set in motion a reinforcing effect which, for example, turned New York from a seaport of 50,000 to a conurbation of 20 million in about a century and a half. But economic decisions, reinforced by further economic decisions, do not, of themselves, produce a humane and urbane social order. They can leave minorities in developed lands and majorities in developing areas far below the poverty line. They inflict considerable social inconvenience even on wealthy citizens. They endanger local environments by pushing them beyond the limits of their natural capacity for regeneration. They can condemn abandoned regions to wasteful decay. In short, if a primarily economic strategy had been sufficient to create just, convenient and gracious patterns of settlements, we should have them now. The crisis we face is that we do not. The opportunity to be seized is the possibility of devising better alternative policies.

The starting point for these alternatives is precisely that settlements cease to be "residuals" and become the object of positive policy. The approach has several facets.

## Social Versus Economic Indicators

Radical change is required in the use of economic and social indicators. This change is based upon a more accurate calculus, not only of economic goods and services, but of socio-economic "bads" and "disservices." Forms of city design are sought in which basic human needs for neighbourliness, privacy, personal security and access to beauty and

Abstracted from a report prepared for the United Nations Conference/Exposition on Human Settlements, Vancouver, June 1976. Published by Information Canada for the Ministry of State for Urban Affairs, Ottawa, 1974, pp. 23–29; 39–44. Reprinted by permission of the author and the Minister of Supply and Services, Canada.

open space are given as much weight as growth statistics or taxable value. Road traffic is made to bear the cost, not simply of construction, but of congestion, pollution, length of commuting, and death and injury. Industrial planning is not judged only on the basis of job creation and urban revenue but upon nuisances, noise, effluents and the local carrying capacity of airsheds and water systems.

An example of the drastic reordering in planning priorities to which such a calculus might lead would be a government decision to abandon the concept of allowing the most rapid economic growth to accelerate wherever it begins to take hold, even if some regions are then fully exposed to the reinforcing effect of growth breeding more growth while other regions lag far behind. In its place, a more general, if slower rate of economic growth would be sought for a wider cross-section of the population. In some ways, regional policies in such developed areas as the European Economic Community reflect the need for this wider spreading of development. But it often proves difficult to coax industries back to once neglected regions. There are many experiences of firms giving up and workers leaving at the first sign of difficulty or even of a relatively slow momentum of growth. New "poles of growth" or development areas then fail to prosper, do not attract educated leadership and even tend to become ghost towns before they have managed to exist.

Such an outcome, however, suggests two things. A more widespread pattern of development in the first place might have prevented the formation of depressed regions with a certain propensity for failure and discouragement. The second is the need for more sustained and systematic planning to ensure that economic, social and cultural opportunity are all carefully calculated and increase in step.

## New Approach to Spatial Planning

This kind of calculus implies, in most countries, a new approach to the concept of spatial planning and its interrelations with economic and social development at all levels: national, regional and local. In certain cases, where settlements forming continuous "systems" cross frontiers—for instance, around inland seas or in large river estuaries—the planning has to have an international dimension. This new kind of planning clearly begins with a careful assessment of the land's topography, of its present degree of development, of its urban locations and its distribution of population, of its existing economic resources and systems of communication and those still to be developed, and of the suitability of its land for a variety of uses.

Planning based on such considerations must vary enormously from country to country. Many developed lands already have such dense settlement patterns that many options are simply foreclosed. In Czechoslovakia, no settlement is further than 2.5 kilometers from any other. This creates quite different problems from those facing largely pre-industrial societies in which density of both population and settlement are still minimal. True, in such countries, with high population growth and very large internal migrations, the urban/rural relationship, dynamic in all societies, is particularly subject to change at breakneck speed.

## Policy Foresighted

Settlements policy must take full account of the future. It must attempt to answer the uncertainties of continuous and accelerating change. What is the country's rate of population increase? What increases in income have been forecasted or promised? Are there tendencies to growth or decline in different regions? How are these related to alternative and possibly more suitable uses of space? Given the world's overall tendency to greater urbanization, are urban growth centres beginning to form or spread in the best adapted regions? If so, what forces of decline are they setting in motion elsewhere? Urban and rural regions live in a condition of inescapable interchange. The only difference is that the condition can enhance or degrade both. For instance, settlements threatening to sprawl over the most productive agricultural land will not only complicate traffic but deprive citizens of the delights of fresh food. Farm land left to weeds and abandoned barns destroy the future hope of preserving lovely landscapes for recreation and refreshment. The recent rapid emptying of many country regions in Western Europe has reminded urban man of how much of the beauty which restores his spirit is the farmer's work and vanishes with the farmer. Without forward planning, such distortions of a human and viable pattern of settlements can be set into remorseless motion before the possible loss has even been realized, let alone checked.

## Settlements: A National Priority

The new approach to settlements planning rejects the concept of their "residual" character from yet another point of view. Governments are accustomed to taking major policy decisions on the basis of what are assumed to be high national priorities. A prime example is, of course, an arms industry. A country accepts the idea that it is exposed to vulnerability and risk unless it commands the weapons of war. It then decides to mobilize—by taxation, by inflation—the resources needed to create or expand an arms industry. Thereafter, a very wide range of industries and employment come to depend upon the development and continuance of such a program. In certain circumstances— for instance, the Germany of Dr. Schacht— the decision to rearm massively in a period of deflation, unused capacity and desperate unemployment has a rapid "multiplier" effect and increases economic output in many other less warlike sectors of the economy. Even without such deflationary conditions, a large vested economic and industrial interest can be created in the expansion and continuance of an arms program.

Another instance is to be found in the decision in a number of countries, but especially in the United States, to construct a full-scale highway system, financed in the main from various forms of taxation. This again, of its own momentum, becomes first a formidable mobilizer of resources and manpower and then a vast economic vested interest in its own right.

The question today is whether the construction of a systematic pattern of settlements in developing countries or systematic modification of existing settlements in developed lands might not become a comparable program of high national priority commanding a large release of resources from the national budget. After all settlements have often been used as instruments of national policy. The planned magnificence of the capitals of princes and feudal lords once expressed pride of dynasty. Now they earn a tourist income. But economics did not determine the original decision.

In the past and on into our own day, the building of settlements has been undertaken to increase the defence of border regions or consolidate a claim to disputed territory. In the peculiar geography of Canada, strung out from ocean to ocean in a narrow temperate space between the United States and the tundra, a planned dispersion of settlements is believed by many to be a precondition of effective national unity. Otherwise the entire population might be clustered together in three major conurbations with a vast empty territory to the North.

But such settlements policies are somewhat specialized. The general question posed to the Conference/Exposition is whether a coherent strategy for settlements as a whole, instead of piecemeal sectoral decisions, might not receive a priority claim on national resources at least comparable to that of defence or of a national road system. The concept is not without political appeal since the citizens' comfort, security, opportunity and culture are much more immediately bound up with the environment of their settlements than with the content of any other national program. This is a fact even if traditional thinking gives greater weight to defence or if consumer pressure tends to be concentrated, at least for the time being, on the private car. But politicians may not have explored the advantages of citizen involvement in the planning, development and enjoyment of better financed and managed settlements because they, like everyone else, are caught in the "tunnel vision" of seeing settlements as simply the residual result of other policies.

Potential economic gains are no less promising. The stimulus given by steady defence contracts for a whole range of metal-using and engineering industries—not to speak of textile firms, camp constructors, and food suppliers—explains the concentration of interest which can be built up behind the continuance of such demand. But the multiplier effect of a systematic national program for settlements could be even greater. In any economy, upwards of two-thirds of capital investment tends to occur in one form or another of construction. Four-fifths of consumers' incomes are spent on goods related to the home. Household fixtures are a direct stimulus to the producers of consumer durables. Experiments in new "city systems" for utilities or the mass cheap construction of kitchen and bathroom units might be at least as technologically stimulating as devising new weapons and would certainly bring higher human rewards. Nor should home ownership be forgotten as a mobilizer of savings. Naturally different schemes would be needed to match different levels of wealth and sophistication, from simple "roof loans" of the type pioneered in Ghana to the mortgage arrangements of developed societies. But the sheer variety of economic stimuli that could be provided by a systematic policy of settlements suggests that, however much the prime aims of such a program were social and political, the economic benefits could be as great.

## Special Problems in Human Settlements

Certain features of the technological order produce similar problems in a wide range of settlements and require separate definition.

At the core is modern society's unique combination of rising aspirations, the pressure and mobility to achieve them, and profound technological changes taking place, partly as cause and partly as result of these pressures. The very word "settlement" is in some measure a contradiction. In many ways, modern man is dealing with continuous "unsettlement." Places of work and residence, solid as they may seem, are subjected to wave after wave of people—commuters, migrants, tourists—and to a continuous process of changing functions and of being rebuilt in response to new needs. If the processes could be speeded up and seen through a radio telescope from a remote planet, the surface of the earth would look like a disturbed ant hill and cities would be seen to be spreading—and sometimes shrinking—like some kind of tough epidermis over the green earth.

If we take, as we must, the neediest people as the highest priority, the first special result of this condition of aspiration and mobility is the spread of squatter settlements throughout the developing world. The "push" that sends country people to the cities at a rate that can be three and four times higher than the general increase in population is due in part to the relative neglect of agriculture in recent development policy, in part to the existence in some areas of rigid and unproductive forms of land tenure and in others, of an economic drive to substitute machines for men in the wake of the so-called Green Revolution. The "pull" derives from the fact that as a result of past colonial administrative and trading policies, cities exist, often as seaports, far ahead of the country's general modernization. Before the First World War, for instance, when Western Europe had nearly 30 percent of its labour force in industry, it had a lower level of urbanization than Latin America, where industry still accounted for under 10 percent of the workers. These vast cities, some of them, like Montevideo, containing over half the country's population, offer at least the appearance of modernity and wage levels which permit a worker to be better off than in the countryside even if he only works for a day a month. Meanwhile, what are euphemistically called "services"—shoeshining, selling matches, guarding automobiles against car thieves—may provide a little more income. Above all, schools of a sort may be within reach. Hope for the children's future is at the root of many migrations.

Once the migrant arrives, any easy hope of betterment is brutally dispelled—by the absence of steady employment, the lack of shelter, the generally unsanitary nature of the squatter settlements. Less than half of Brazil's municipalities, for instance, have reliable water and sewage systems. The physical misery of these *favellas* of *calampas* or *bustees* or *bidonvilles* are a spreading blight on every continent. Yet is is false to see them only as disaster areas. There is enough experience now of the energy and the capacity of the squatters or, as some would call them, "urban pioneers" to suggest that the improvement and integration of squatter communities is possible even with virtually nothing more than the efforts of the people themselves. Renewal can be greatly accelerated if the authorities devise and pursue appropriate policies of support.

The most needed strategies extend, inevitably, beyond the settlements themselves. They need to reflect the growing understanding in development planning that employment and income distribution cannot be left, any more than housing or services, to appear as by-products of purely growth-oriented economic decisions. If mechanized agriculture increases output and with it the income of farmers, the gain shows up in national statistics. But the cost of now landless tenants, moving themselves to the fringe of bloated cities and leaving rural communities to steadily decay, does not. If, as a result of installing a fully automated factory, Gross National Product rises and a small group of shareholders and organized workers enjoy increased income, the economy as a whole will still be worse off in real terms if unemployment increases significantly, and the pattern of high technology and low job-creation is critically reinforced. The whole development calculus has to begin to take direct account of the new imperatives: the creation of jobs and the spread of income.

But these are overall strategies. Within the settlements, the need is to stimulate communal self-help, to provide services such as water and power and to lend or give essential housing components which allow migrants to improve their own homes. To do this, they require some form of secure tenure. Bulldozing out the shacks does not send the squatters away. It simply destroys their faith in self-help. Admittedly, some settlements have to be moved. In many cities the squatters go into disaster areas, like flood plains, simply because there is nowhere else to go. But the forced movement should not take them too far from possibilities of work. Dumped back in the villages, they return.

Experience also suggests that in many areas, if they are piled into high-rise tenements in centre cities, they also move, leaving almost irreparable squalor behind. The need is for a careful plan for the siting of migrant communities, the provision of sites and services and attention to the transport needed to get them to work. It is a question, in fact, of treating citizens as assets. Once the policy is understood, it can be self-fulfilling. Men and women are more likely to behave like assets if they are not treated as outcasts in the first place.

Migrations are not confined to the developing world. The magnet of hope and work that draws country people to the urban areas within a country operates internationally, drawing poorer and less skilled workers across frontiers to the wealthy centres of industrial growth in developed lands.

After World War II such a migration took place between the various states in the United States. Black citizens from the South moved into northern cities, usually into the substandard centre city districts already used by three or four earlier waves of migration. In Britain, a similar movement brought West Indians and Asians to the cities. Western Europe draws in the Mediterranean people as "guest workers." All these movements have features in common. The migrants usually do the low-paid, unskilled or boring assembly line work which more affluent and educated workers no longer want to do. They usually congregate in the areas of worst housing or even in camps. Their conditions of work and living thus tend to be in every way less satisfactory than those of the people they live among. They are likely to be the first to suffer insecurity of jobs and even of residence if economies cease to expand. They also face the risk that strikes to improve their condition may lead to the closing down of industries which survive chiefly on their low wages.

Their needs in many ways resemble those of squatter communities: the means of self-help, investment in services, improvement of the housing stock, access to work, help in acquiring skills and hence promotion, education for their children. The chief difference is that many "guest workers" mean to return to their own countries. Their transience lowers their ability to get a grip on their condition. However, some governments care for their migrant citizens by negotiating terms of work and wage contracts. The whole movement also raises the issue whether, in the interests of environmental balance and some dispersal of the concentrated effects of rapid industrial growth, it might not be more sane to send some of the industry to the workers and thus speed up the modernization of less developed lands.

This direction of policy deserves consideration for another reason. Migrants moving to the big centres create problems of over-concentration. But migrants leaving the country districts create the opposite problems—of rural and regional decay. Smaller towns are drained of economic and social life and leadership. They acquire a shabby, rundown atmosphere. This further depresses the life of the people who cannot move, often the elderly, the handicapped or those who lack courage and skill. Yet, as has already been suggested, it is not clear whether, if migrants were given reasonable alternatives—reformed land tenure, successful small-scale farming, work in lively regional market centres—they would inevitably move on to the great conurbations.

Once more we are up against the consequences of what were in the first place economic decisions, taken without regard for social or environmental costs and without any effort of popular consultation. The economic advantages created by high densities of consumers, suppliers and workers can be self-sustaining and draw off an undue amount of vitality from regions in which no spiral of growth is spontaneously taking place.

This is not a new phenomenon. Over 150 years ago Goethe remarked of Paris: "How much happier this beautiful France would be, if it had 10 centres instead of one all spreading their own light and riches." Nor is it self-correcting. Every nation has such disadvantaged regions where capital and housing stock deteriorate and "men decay." And so they remain unless positive policies are adopted to reverse the trend.

Today, this is happening. Goethe would no doubt be pleased to see France planning for eight countervailing metropolises—*métropoles d'équilibre*—and using tax reductions, capital grants, training schemes and resources for housing and infrastructure to lure industry and services away from Paris. The work, known as *l'Aménagement du Territoire et l'Action Régionale,* is one of the developed world's most systematic attempts to reverse old fatalities, to bring employment and opportunity back to declining regions, to rectify stagnant settlements and take the strain off overloaded central areas. One can only repeat that in the developing world, it would seem the course of wisdom not to allow the dismal combination of over-centralization and regional decay to occur in the first place. Moreover, attention to farming, well supported regional growth, investment in intermediate towns, a more balanced distribution of national population and national income are not simply a way of saving social costs. The long-term levels of economic growth may well be higher too. There is no question but that developing countries which have stimulated small-scale farming, regional market centres and local housing and services—countries such as Korea, Taiwan and Yugoslavia—have contrived higher rates of economic growth and a better distribution of income.

# Fundamental Issues Concerning Future Settlement in America

RICHARD L. MORRILL

The American landscape, the result of the imprint of man on the natural environment, is beautiful and ugly, empty and crowded, prosperous and depressed. In recent years many authors have speculated on the forms that the American landscape may take in a postindustrial age (Berry, 1970a; Ewald, 1968). Others are more concerned with the obvious ugliness, abuse, and poverty of much of the landscape, from a national to a local scale. The many strategies that have been suggested to ameliorate these problems have been, in turn, attacked as uneconomic, unconstitutional, or unrealistic.

I have tried here to evaluate possible alternative future landscapes from a broad geographic, social, and economic perspective, with as little prior bias toward particular outcomes as possible, but with a personal emphasis on national goals of equity over, if necessary, goals of efficiency.

## The Freedom of the Future Is Limited by the Decision of the Past

Our ability to determine what the landscape of the future will be like is greatly restricted because most of tomorrow's landscape will be inherited virtually unchanged from yesterday. People and their activities are located in particular places; the material investment in improvements and modifications to the land is stupendous, at least $3 trillion. The human nonmaterial investment in current place-oriented behavior is just as overwhelming. The investment of a few years can have only a marginal effect in altering the human or natural features of the landscape or modes of behavior, especially if we realize that most material and nonmaterial investment and effort is applied to the enhancement or conservation of existing investments and patterns of behavior. Over time, the landscape does change significantly, nevertheless, and we must appreciate both the probable impacts of present decision making on the landscape and the kind and magnitude of investments that would be required to effect any desired improvements or changes.

## Goals for the Future American Landscape

Goals for American society are usually expressed in a vague rhetoric of widely accepted concepts of growth, prosperity, quality of life and of the environment, equality, and freedom (Commission on National Goals, 1960; National Goals Research Staff, 1970; Eberhard, 1971; Hauser, 1971; Friedmann, 1971; Hansen, 1971). History has shown that these goals are not all easily achieved nor are they even very compatible. In practice, the overriding goals have been economic growth, a high *per capita* product, and the preservation of national independence and economic freedom. More recently, this pattern has been

From *Geographical Perspectives and Urban Problems* (Washington, D.C.: National Academy of Sciences, 1973), pp. 81–88. Reproduced with permission of the National Academy of Sciences.

modified by concern for some aspects of equality and for conservation of the quality of the environment. Many recent critics would substitute a goal of environmental quality for economic growth. Some, including myself, would make social and economic equality and justice the primary goal (Harvey, 1970). We must be realistic and realize that we probably cannot achieve all these goals equally or simultaneously. We have not even been able to maintain the legislatively ordained stable growth and full employment, let alone conserve the environment or achieve social and economic justice (U.S. Congress, 1946). What, then, are the implications of emphasizing the various goals: growth, environmental quality, and social and economic equality.

The goal of economic growth, measured by increasing annual total and *per capita* gross national product, is generally accepted by most of the effective economic and political decision makers of our society (National Goals Research Staff, 1970, p. 24; Moroney, 1970; Morrill and Wohlenberg, 1971). Pursuit of this goal has created the most affluent society in world history, at least in *per capita* terms. One serious problem of this approach is that the efficient expansion of a private economy requires concentration of power, and therefore tends to result in severe social and economic inequality, making it partly incompatible with a goal of social justice. Poverty and social injustice are not really paradoxes in our society, although they are often claimed to be: They are expected consequences of differential control over economic resources in a competitive order. As a result, achievement of minimal standards of social and economic welfare at the bottom depends on a prodigious total national product, but even so, it instills in the less successful a feeling of severe relative deprivation (Miller, 1971). This problem obtains not only within a population in a given place or region, but between different regions. Differential control and access to economic resources and markets results in severe regional social and economic inequality. The efficient expansion of the private economy has required spatial as well as distributional concentration of eco-

nomic growth and prosperity. Again, marginal regions are better off in times of general rapid growth, but suffer especially in periods of stagnation (Hansen, 1970; Morrill and Wohlenberg, 1971).

The second serious problem, to be felt even more in the future, is that the projected increase in gross national product is so enormous that many, especially those with ecological training, fear devastating and perhaps irreversible damage to the natural environment. Projected demand for fuels, water, and land resources are so great that such growth may be possible only at the expense of future generations, at the expense of less-developed countries and peoples, and at the risk of severe ecological imbalance. The severity of these risks is objectively still unknown, although it is obvious that pressure on resources will be very great. As long as the private economy does not bear the long-term social and economic costs of resource depletion, air and water pollution, congestion and overcrowding, the risk of the overuse and damage of resources is great (Jarrett, 1966). Some of these costs are being charged to the private producer, although much is being borne by the public sector. Thus, for example, petroleum consumption, automobile use, and steel consumption are overencouraged to the extent that the current price of gasoline does not reflect the real costs of air pollution, health impairment, traffic congestion, lost time, and land withdrawn from higher-valued uses (National Goals Research Staff, 1970, p. 72). Owing to the great metropolitan and regional concentration of economic activity, environmental damage is territorially limited geographically, and for that reason, it is more severe and occurs sooner in time (e.g., New York and Los Angeles air pollution, Lake Erie water pollution).

A goal of ecological balance urged by many environmental critics of society, implies an arresting of further damage to the environment, a restoration of many damaged environments, and a shift from an emphasis on annual gross national product (growth) or "throughput" to achieving a high wealth or standard of living biomass (Jarrett, 1966). An emphasis on recycling of resources, and even more, on maximizing the time horizon of a given product or resource use or investment is basically incompatible with the traditional operation of a free market economy, which requires maximizing "throughput" (annual revenues) as the main incentive for investment. However, an ecological-balance goal is no more compatible with an aim of social and economic equality because of the competitive nature of the economy. With a normal 5 percent unemployment, greater underemployment, and a chronic labor surplus as the most important causes of poverty, and even perhaps of racial discrimination, any decrease in growth or gross national product and attendant decrease in employment will only aggravate inequality and poverty (National Goals Research Staff, 1970, p. 73). As desirable as the goal is, therefore, and despite eloquent support from intellectuals (including geographers), it is not likely to gain the support of either the rich, whose power depends on growth, or the poor, whose hope also depends on growth.

A goal of social and economic equality could be partly achieved if growth were so great that full employment resulted. The ecological effects of such extreme growth, however, could be severe. The inescapable conlusion is that greater equality, without excessive growth and with a concern for ecological balance, can be achieved only by some basic shifts in social and economic values and structures. A higher degree of public interference in the economy is inevitable, but probably not as revolutionary as some hope and others fear. The wealth (and annual product) of the United States is already sufficient to afford the elimination of poverty, slums, poor health, and many other manifestations of inequality (Morrill and Wohlenberg, 1971). A simple but radical redistribution of income toward greater income equality is required; this is most easily achieved through a far more generous guaranteed-income plan, but preferably through basic reform of the processes that determine prices, employment, wages, and salaries. With respect to regional inequality on local and national scales, a solution is again not possible without greater public involvement, especially in the decisions of where to make the investment in new opportunities. A shift in values from economic efficiency toward social equity is apparent in both income redistribution and public interference in the location of economic activities, but probably both greater class and regional equality are possible with very little effect on economic efficiency or corporate profitability. It is still difficult to believe we are ready to pay such a price (Hauser, 1971, p. 17).

## Determinants of the Landscape

In a nation so characterized by individualism and the rhetoric of freedom, it must surely be true that the composite landscape is the result of countless decisions of individual citizens and that where and how the citizen lives is his choice. At a microgeographic level the landscape does bear the imprint of the traditional freedom of at least the middle- and upper-class individuals to do just as they want with their property. At the more basic level of the setting—rural, urban, or metropolitan—and the region, however, the choice of the individual becomes circumscribed. The truth is that the significant decisions on the location of economic opportunities, and therefore on where people will live, are made in the private-business sector (Perloff, 1960). In a competitive society, the rational firm or investor will expand or locate new facilities, creating new opportunities, in those locations that seem to offer secure and sizable profitability. Businesses seem to believe in and follow demographic projections of metropolitanization, thus creating, by their investment, a self-fulfilling prophecy. Over recent decades a higher and higher proportion of these new opportunities have been located within larger and larger metropolitan areas and in particularly favored regions. In general, the views and preferences of government, prospective or actual employees, and even most stockholders are irrelevant. The majority of the American population say they would prefer not to live in a metropolis (New York Times, 1969; Hansen, 1970, p. 246); various levels of government express concern for depressed regions, parts of cities, and nonmetropolitan America generally (President's National Advisory Committee on Rural Poverty, 1968; Glazer, 1970; National Goals Research Staff, 1970); but the business world makes the real decisions.

The freedom of the individual is reduced to taking it or leaving it. The displaced worker in a declining area can choose to remain there in underemployed poverty, or he can move to the metropolis; this situation contrasts with Friedmann's strange logic that since people went to the metropolis, they must love it (Friedmann, 1971, p. 19). The propriety of the fact that the important decisions are made by capital and that people (labor) are conceived as a factor of production to shift according to the needs of businesses is, in general, unquestioned. I stress the point, since it is essential to realize that the present landscape is mainly a product of private, especially larger-scale business decisions, as the future landscape will be, unless society chooses to modify the process of decision making.

The general public as individuals and as government has affected the macrogeographic landscape to some extent. Mainly through the allocation of defense expenditures and military installations, as well as highway, agricultural, and other funds, the government has been able, since 1940, to decentralize economic growth to parts of the South and West (National Goals Research Staff, 1970, p. 47–48). The Tennessee Valley Authority represented an even more direct intervention in investment decisions. Earlier government investments in economic opportunities included various irrigation and reclamation schemes, and more indirectly, the railroad land grants and the highly permissive attitude toward resource exploitation.

The determination of many people to move to California, and later to Florida and Arizona, whether or not job opportunities existed, probably did increase economic growth over what it otherwise would have

been. Having moved, the people represented both a potential labor force and market to which investors responded. This shift of population was aided by the somewhat greater freedom of part of the retired population to choose their region and place of residence (Ullman, 1954).

Within the metropolis the middle and upper classes are afforded considerable choice in residential and job location, but the poor have very restricted choice in both. Increasing separation of work and job, again a result of private-business decisions, works an increasing hardship on the poor, just as more higher-paying jobs are moving to the suburbs (Advisory Commission on Intergovernmental Relations, 1968).

## Problems and Trends of the American Landscape

Although much of the American landscape—scenic, rural, even urban—is beautiful and represents a mutually beneficial relation of man and environment, there is also much evidence of environmental abuse and neglect, misallocation of resources, unrealized potential, and human poverty. At the macro or regional scale, the fundamental issues are the problems of metropolitan and regional concentration of activities and people and their pollution as well as the concomitant rural and regional stagnation and decline. At the local level, some major issues are the frequent ugliness of the microhuman landscape, in turn a function of poverty, freedom of property, and poor taste; the relative location of jobs, residences, businesses, and social and economic groups; and the kind of transportation systems to serve them. I concentrate here on the regional problem.

*Metropolitan concentration: settlement polarization.* For at least 100 years the process of urbanization has transferred millions from rural areas and smaller settlements to towns, cities, and metropolises. The primary basis for rapid urbanization was the efficiency of manufacturing that set off a spiral of increasing demand and productivity and encouraged the commercialization and mechanization of agriculture. Commercial and service activities located together in urban settlements, for reasons of agglomeration economies; industrial activities located together for reasons of both agglomeration and scale economies. Service centers, a hierarchy of central places from countless hamlets to New York City, spread across the landscape to serve the dispersed American population. Industry located both in the better located service centers, especially ports and transport junctions, and in clusters of settlements close to water power and coalfields (Berry and Horton, 1970, pp. 21–36).

The railroads bringing cheap long-distance overland transportation, extended settlement across the country and remain a necessary condition for concentration in larger urban centers, both within the northeastern core of the nation and within regions. The accessibility of resources and markets varied greatly from place to place. The sufficient condition for concentration has been the realization of greater and greater scale economies (permitted by the cheapness of rail transport). Thus metropolitanization, the concentration of most net economic and population growth in the highest level of the urban systems, was already well under way by 1900 and was made possible by the railroad (and industry-scale economies), not by the automobiles. The car, in fact, was expected to result in decentralization, but the forces of concentration have been stronger. The car has led to the decline, relocation, or even the disappearance of countless hamlets and villages as rural residents shift their focus to larger towns; and, of course, it has led to decentralization of residences and jobs within the metropolis (Berry and Horton, 1970, pp. 207–227, 440–482).

The nature of railroad diffusion, the discriminatory pattern of rail rates; the antebellum differentiation between North and South in labor, land, immigration, and other policies, as well as in slavery; postbellum discrimination against the South; and especially the industrial head-start and concentration of capital, talent, education, and technology were among the reasons for the overwhelming dominance of the northeastern core (Anderson, 1968). Even in 1970, after at least three decades of some regional decentralization, a core region of only 15 percent of the area of the conterminous United States still has 45 percent of the population, 55 percent of the income, 65 percent of the manufacturing, and a far higher proportion of the higher levels of economic decision making (Ullman, 1958).

This historic concentration of wealth was economically rational and efficient for investors from the dominant region, but did establish the pattern of dependence of the rest of the country on resource exploitation in agriculture, mining, and forestry. Despite economic discrimination the Far West enjoyed fair incomes because a few people shared rich resources, but the absolute level of development was below potential (Perloff, 1960). In the South the excess population, racial conflict, and dependence on agriculture resulted in endemic underemployment and poverty and underutilization of human and natural resources. This long-term exploitation of the South from outside as well as by a small aristocracy inside is taking a long time to overcome (Nichols, 1969).

Since the 1940's the West and South have experienced fairly rapid development. The spectacular growth of California resulted from massive military and defense investments and migration of millions in search of amenities, whether or not jobs were available, which in turn encouraged branches of northeastern industries (National Goals Research Staff, 1970, p. 51; Berry and Horton, 1970, p. 35). To some extent the process is occurring in Florida. In Texas, moderate growth of population and industry was based more on indigenous resources, mainly petroleum, and to a considerable degree on local determination. In the Piedmont, especially, and in much of the small-town South, industries were attracted that chose not to adapt to higher-cost labor in the Northeast (Maddox and others, 1967).

*Regional inequality.* Gross regional disparities are less than they were in the 1920's, but they remain great. Figure 1 shows those areas of the country with a net poverty gap in 1960; that is, areas in which the money necessary to bring all families just up to the non-poverty threshold could not be raised by transfer from the more wealthy in those areas (Morrill and Wohlenberg, 1971, Chap. 6). This severe condition, reflecting lack of job opportunities, unfavorable industrial and occupational structures, and labor surplus, is characteristic of most of the South, much of the Plains, and evn peripheral parts of the Northeast and West. This condition occurs in two thirds of the area of the country with two fifths of the people. Despite development, income levels in the South remain far below those in the Northeast. What improvement the periphery has experienced appears to be somewhat contrary to the natural course of private economic events and to be a result of government intervention, regional determination (Texas), and irrational patterns of migration (California, Florida). The persistence of so much regional poverty over so much territory is a consequence of the imagined unprofitability of increasing the variety and quality of economic opportunities in nonmetropolitan portions of the country. It is a national problem in that millions are condemned to poverty because of their location preferences, so many human resources are underutilized, and there is no simple or automatic solution.

*Rural-urban migration.* If economic opportunities are most efficiently located in the Northeast and in other metropolitan regions, then the economically rational solution is for the surplus population to move there from the periphery. Millions have done so, especially from the South, Appalachia, and the Great Plains, but more millions have refused to move, because they prefer their home areas and because they realize that prosperity is by no means assured, even if they move to the richest northeastern metropolises, which contain absolutely large numbers of poor people themselves (Morrill and Wohlenberg, 1971).

Within regions, the upward shift of people and activities from rural and small-town areas to the metropolis has been an economically rational response to the increasing mechaniza-

tion and productivity of agriculture, forestry, and mining that has released millions from these activities. It has also been a response to the preference and seemingly optimal location of the growing sectors of the industrial and service economy for the larger agglomerations. On balance, the process of urbanization has brought tremendous benefits (Friedmann, 1971, p. 19; Ewald, 1968, pp. 138–157). Perhaps the greatest benefit has been the creation of a giant rich and productive national economy and the world's highest living standard. Concurrently it has made possible far wider access to better education and cultural opportunities and has helped to lead to liberalization of social attitudes; many costs of the imperfect process may be seen on the landscape, however.

Tens of millions have migrated from rural areas, because few alternatives appeared to replace opportunities lost in the ever more efficient primary sectors. Many become satisfied, but available data on preferences clearly reveal that today, at least, the large majority of those not native to metropolitan areas claim that they wish to leave but have been forced into the metropolis for economic survival. Millions are unable to adapt or to find higher-paying jobs and represent only a shift from rural to urban poverty (Elgie, 1970, pp. 35–54; Hansen, 1970; President's National Advisory Committee on Rural Poverty, 1968).

The results of this out-migration on the rural, small-town areas are mixed. For some, exodus of the surplus population has been sufficient to enable most of those remaining to enjoy a decent living standard on large efficient holdings (Eberhard, 1971, p. 9). In such cases, however, the absolute level of service activities and the number of places falls. Probably in the majority of rural areas, the ideal has not occurred. Instead a stagnation or relative decline in *per capita* as well as in gross levels of income and services has taken place, because too many refuse to leave and because so often the marginal members stay. The most productive and educated migrate, leaving an unfavorable aged population with high underemployment and high dependency

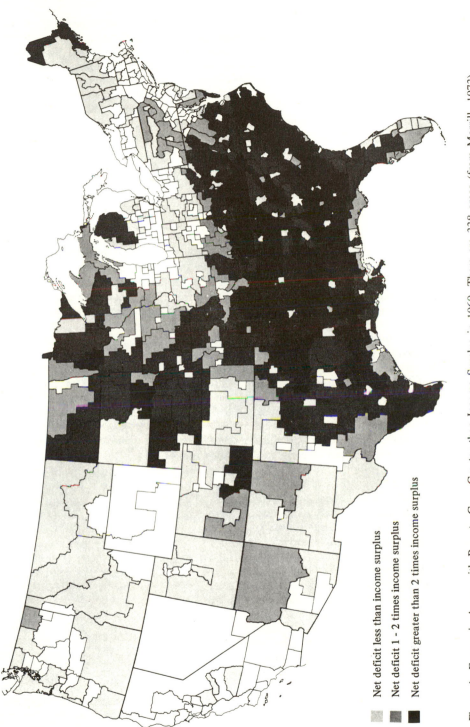

Figure 1. Economic Areas with Poverty Gaps Greater than Income Surplus in 1960. There are 338 areas (from Morrill, 1973).

Net deficit less than income surplus

Net deficit 1 - 2 times income surplus

Net deficit greater than 2 times income surplus

levels (Parr, 1966; Morrill and Wohlenberg, 1971, pp. 134–135). This condition has existed in many areas for far too long to be treated as a temporary adjustment to technological change. Partly because so many fear the metropolis and doubt their ability to compete, and because they have discovered that opportunities there are also restricted, they remain and add to the competitive weakness of labor in nonmetropolitan areas (Morrill and Wohlenberg, 1971, pp. 134–135).

In those parts of the Northeast, California, and Florida where the metropolitan areas are closely spaced (about 100 mi apart), the rural areas do not lag because people can remain in their home setting or shift to a rural setting and still commute easily to the metropolis, thus transferring income from the city. Also the farmers are conveniently situated with regard to local market and suppliers (Berry, 1970b). In much more of the country, the metropolitan areas are fewer and further apart, or lacking in opportunities themselves. About half the area and a quarter of the population are beyond commuting range to viable metropolises. This problem emphasizes the dilemma—the conflict between the desire and determination of so many people to remain in rural areas or home regions and the reality of metropolitan economic advantages. So many regions are relegated to primary activities only, and so many people are thereby denied normal participation in the nation's wealth. At present the economic consensus is that these people are irrational romantics, delaying the equilibrium process of regional income convergence.

*Conditions in metropolitan America.* At least half the problem of metropolitan concentration is the cost to the cities, not to the country. First, there are the social and economic costs of the rural migrants themselves. These are poverty jobs, underemployment and unemployment, delinquency and broken homes, the high cost to the cities of dealing with rural migrants and their problems, and the depressing effect of excess rural migration on wage levels of the unskilled (Hansen, 1970, pp. 241–244; Glazer, 1970). Next are the increasingly severe costs of pollution, waste disposal, water supply, traffic conges-

tion, and public security (because of crime and delinquency), for which the single most important variable may be the sheer population of the metropolis. The larger the city, the higher are rents and land values inflated, and the more difficult it is to ensure either the public or private space desired.

Although the largest cities are the greatest generators of wealth and culture, as well as the most profitable sites for most private economic activities, much of the great cost outlined above is not borne by the private sector, but by the public sector and by individuals (Hoover, 1968; Perloff and Wingo, 1968). The measurement of these costs is so difficult that we do not know whether metropolitan locations are actually optimum for most economic activities if all costs are considered. Sketchy evidence suggests that, on an average, unit economic costs for manufacturing, services, and transportation fall as metropolitan size increases to perhaps 1,000,000 population or more; whereas social costs of congestion, pollution, space provision, and crime begin to climb markedly after about 500,000. Although the nation would be much poorer and duller without our greatest metropolises, there is mounting reason to wish that they not become far larger yet, or that not too many more places join their ranks and assume their severe problems.

In summary, the polarization of settlement resulting in metropolitan concentration and rural stagnation is a severe problem, because of the mounting costs and disorders of the metropolis and the poverty and waste of resources of much of the countryside. Above all, in a democratic society, perhaps the wishes of many people not to live in the overcrowded giant metropolis should receive more attention.

## Prospects

Many scenarios for the American future have been suggested. Doxiadis and Gottman, extrapolating certain present trends to one extreme, project a supermetropolitan America, in which most of the population will reside in a few giant megalopolises of from 10 to 50 million people (Doxiadis, 1970). This outcome assumes a higher-than-probable total population growth, solutions to the horrendous social and transportation problems plaguing much smaller places today, the willingness or desire of the people to live in these world cities, and, I believe, a basic change in social behavior. There is no denying, however, that current trends point in this direction.

Berry, Friedmann, Meier, and Webber, extrapolating along the potential of communications and transportation innovation, project an opposite outcome; a large-scale return to country living (Friedmann, 1965). This is theoretically possible for the middle and upper classes, who will have short work weeks, who can accomplish their work by remote communication, and who will be able to commute by fast efficient means to even distant metropolises. A return to country living is also possible for the retired and for those poor who choose to live on a guaranteed income; the metropolis, then, can be abandoned to the working lower classes. This outcome rests on somewhat tenuous assumptions, especially with respect to transport technology and cost. It involves the risk of even greater social polarization.

Although it is impossible to forecast the future, the rational man has no choice but to try to anticipate it (National Goals Research Staff, 1970, pp. 23–24). Therefore, between these extremes, I shall describe the landscapes suggested by a cautious extension of trends: In the absence of radical public intervention, the future pattern of settlement may be remarkably unchanged from the present.

There are not strong reasons to expect investors to shift from the current profitable pattern: location in large metropolitan areas (over 250,000 or especially over 500,000 population), with a predominant and growing share in the fringes and a declining share in the city centers; location in towns and cities that are satellite (25–50 mi) to the largest metropolitan areas (over 2,000,000 population). These trends may produce undesirable outcomes, such as continuing job and population concentration and more rapid physical expansion of the largest metropolitan areas,

leading to aggravation of the problems associated with greater size, especially waste disposal and traffic congestion. There may be extreme pressure on land and water resources in the coalescing major metropolitan areas in the Northeast, California, and Florida. There will probably be greater class and racial polarization, with almost all the richer people moving to suburb and exurb, abandoning the central city to the elderly, jobless, poor, and black, and risking increased social and political turmoil. Population stagnation would probably result, together with continuing relative economic decline of most rural and small-town areas. Population decline may be halted as more of the elderly choose rural areas in which to retire, and if a national guaranteed income is established that is sufficient to permit those who wish to remain in or shift to rural areas to subsist in genteel poverty and not to compete for scarce jobs. These possibilities, however, will do little for the nonmetropolitan economies. Friedmann argues that greater affluence, leisure, and mobility will extend metropolitan benefits much farther (100–200 mi) in the future. I doubt that this will occur before 1985—after these rural romantics are forced from their preferred areas (Friedmann, 1965).

This effect on the landscape would be unfortunate, because of the economic costs of extreme concentration—locally and regionally—on water supply, waste disposal, transport provision and traffic amelioration, pollution control, and provision of open space. Also involved would be the corollary economic costs of underutilization of land and natural and human resources in noncongested areas; the social costs of crowding, traffic congestion, crime, and racial tension in the metropolis; and of either forced migration or of a rural life restricted by poverty. Above all, the effect on the landscape would probably be contrary to the desires of a majority of people.

The prospects and recent experience are perhaps not as extreme as painted above. In fact, in most less-successful regions of the country there are at least a few moderately growing and fairly successful cities, not prosperous enough to meet regional needs, but indicating that prospects—and potentials if the rules of the game were to change—are not really hopeless.

## REFERENCES

Advisory Commission on Intergovernmental Relations, 1968. *Urban and rural America: Policies for future growth.* Washington, D.C.: U.S. Government Printing Office. 186 pp.

Anderson, Stanford, Ed., 1968. *Planning for diversity and choice: Possible futures and their relation to the man-controlled environment.* Cambridge, Mass.: M.I.T. Press. 340 pp.

Berry, Brian, J. L., 1970a. Geography of the United States in the year 2000. *Ekistics,* 29 (1970), 339–351.

————., 1970b. Commuting patterns: Labor market participation and regional potential. *Growth and Change,* 1 (1970), 3–11.

————., and Frank E. Horton, 1970. *Geographic perspectives on urban systems: With integrated readings.* Englewood Cliffs, N.J.: Prentice-Hall. 564 pp.

Commission on National Goals, 1960. *Goals for Americans.* Englewood Cliffs, N.J. Prentice-Hall. 372 pp.

Doxiadis, C. A., 1970. Man's movement and his settlements. *Ekistics,* 29 (1970), 296–321.

Eberhard, John P., 1971. The hidden agenda. *Growth and Change,* 2 (1971), 9–13.

Elgie, Robert, 1970. Rural inmigration, urban ghettoization, and their consequence. *Antipode,* 2 (1970), 35–54.

Ewald, William R., Jr., Ed., 1968. *Environment and policy.* Bloomington: Indiana University Press. 459 pp.

Friedmann, John, 1965. The urban field. *Journal of the American Institute of Planners,* 31 (1965), 312–320.

————., 1971. The feasibility of a national settlement policy. *Growth and Change,* 2 (1971), 18–21.

Glazer, N., Ed., 1970. *Cities in trouble.* Chicago: Quadrangle Books. 276 pp.

Hansen, Niles M., 1970. *Rural poverty and the urban crisis.* Bloomington: Indiana University Press. 352 pp.

————., 1971. The problem of spatial resource allocation. *Growth and Change,* 2 (1971), 22–24.

Harvey, David, 1970. Social process, spatial form, and the redistribution of income in an urban system. *22nd Colston Symposium.* London: Butterworth and Co. 470 pp.

Hauser, Philip M., 1971. The population issues. *Growth and Change,* 2 (1971), 14–17.

Hoover, Edgar, 1968. The evolving form and organization of the metropolis. *In Issues in Urban Economics,* H. Perloff and L. Wingo, Jr., Eds., pp. 237–289. Baltimore: Johns Hopkins Press.

Jarrett, Henry, Ed., 1966. *Environmental quality in a growing economy.* Baltimore: Johns Hopkins Press, 173 pp.

Maddox, James G., E. E. Liebhafsky, V. W. Henderson, and H. M. Hamlin, 1967. *The advancing south.* New York: Twentieth Century Fund. 72 pp.

Miller, Herman P., 1971. *Rich man, poor man.* New York: Thomas Y. Crowell. 46 pp.

Moroney, J. R., 1970. Factor prices, factor proportions, and regional factor endowment. *Journal of Political Economy,* 78 (1970), 158–164.

Morrill, Richard L., and Ernest Wohlenberg, 1971. *The geography of poverty.* New York: McGraw-Hill. 148 pp.

National Goals Research Staff, 1970. *Toward balanced growth: Quantity with quality.* Washington, D.C.: U.S. Government Printing Office. 226 pp.

*New York Times,* 1969. Rural poverty. Gallup Poll, May 5, p. 41.

Nichols, V., 1969. Growth poles: An evaluation of their propulsive effects. *Environment and Planning,* 1 (1969), 193–208.

Parr, John, 1966. Outmigration and the depressed area problem. *Land Economics,* 42 (1966), 149–159.

Perloff, Harvey, 1960. *Regions, resources, and economic growth.* Baltimore: Johns Hopkins Press for Resources for the Future. 716 pp.

————., and L. Wingo, Jr., Eds., 1968. *Issues in urban economics.* Baltimore: Johns Hopkins Press.

President's National Advisory Committee on Rural Poverty, 1968. *Rural poverty in the United States.* Washington, D.C.: U.S. Government Printing Office. 641 pp.

Ullman, Edward, 1954. Amenities as a factor in regional growth. *Geographical Review,* 44 (1954), 119–132.

————., 1958. Regional development and the geography of concentration. *Papers, Regional Science Association,* 4 (1958), 179–206.

U.S. Congress, 1946. Employment Act, 79th Congress. Second Session. U.S. Code, Title 15, Chap. 21, Secs. 1021–1022.

# Economic Base and City Size: An 1811 Commentary on London*

## THE MONTHLY MAGAZINE

No question is so common as, "whence come the inhabitants of all the new houses built in the suburbs of London?" Nothing can be more rational than such an inquiry; at least one thousand houses per annum having been finished in the suburbs of London during the last forty years—yet every new house is taken and occupied before it is finished, or its walls dry! This rate of increase being ten times greater than it was between the death of Elizabeth and the accession of the Hanoverian family, the causes may be deserving of investigation not only as a matter of curiosity but with reference to their connection with the science of political economy.

As the new houses are generally of respectable size, and may be taken at the full number of eight souls to a house, the population of the metropolis is ascertained, from the occupation of the new buildings, to have increased in the present age upwards of three hundred thousand souls. So rapid an increase of inhabitants is not therefore to be accounted for on ordinary principles and it obviously involves a variety of considerations.

It is not unusual to account for the occupation of the new streets by adverting to a change of manners among the citizens and the trading classes. It is said, and with truth, that the houses of trade do not satisfy the citizens of our days, and that, to avoid the smell and bustle of the shop, the dwelling-house must be at a distance. Doubtless, from this cause, many capital houses at the west end of London are occupied by bill-manufacturers called bankers, by bank-directors, by upstart monopolists, and successful speculators in various branches of trade. These, however, are not numerous, probably they do not exceed five hundred families and, as their houses of trade are generally occupied by junior partners or head clerks, and the pupils (the fashionable city-name for shop-boys and apprentices) are domesticated there, the population of the city remains nearly the same, and is probably not affected to the number of a thousand souls by the affectation and extravagancies of this class of citizens.

The sober and more respectable city families have their country-houses at distances varying between four and ten miles from St. Paul's. These are probably ten thousand in number; but, as their houses are not an integral part of the metropolis, they form, of course, no part of the population of the metropolis because they generally dwell in their town-houses in the winter season; and in summer these are occupied by junior partners, clerks, shopmen.

I would refer to seven causes chiefly, concerned with the aggregation of the houses and population of the suburbs of the metropolis.

(1) London is not only the ancient met-

* Max R. Bloom, professor of urban land economics at Syracuse University, New York, while thumbing through *The Monthly Magazine* [February 1811, vol. 31, no. 1], an English journal published in 1811, came across the following article. It was captioned "Original Communication" and signed "Common Sense." The *Magazine* was then in its thirty-first year of publication.

From *Land Economics*, vol. 50, no. 2, May 1974, pp. 202–5. Reprinted from *The Monthly Magazine*, 1811.

ropolis of England and Wales but it is now the new metropolis of the added kingdoms of Scotland and Ireland and, moreover, of our increased colonies in all parts of the world. In the reign of Elizabeth, it was the metropolis of about seven millions of people but it is now the metropolis of an aggregation of twenty millions. It is not therefore to be wondered, without referring to other causes, that London has increased to treble its size since that time, and that the population within ten miles of St. Paul's should be four times greater. All the colonists consider London as their home; it is the focus of their correspondence and interests, their fortunes are remitted to it; and here they find pleasanter means of spending them than among their native wilds, whether in Scotland, Ireland, Yorkshire, or other districts. These persons, with their families, form, beyond a doubt, a considerable portion of the new population of the suburbs of London; probably they occupy at least five thousand of the largest new houses. I shall remark, by the bye, that they also form a considerable portion of the idle inhabitants of Bath, Cheltenham, Clifton, Brighton, and other fashionable watering-places.

(2) The increase of our government establishments: the treasury, the customs, the excise, army, navy, and tax offices; and of our great trading companies: the Bank, the India-house, and others of bill brokers, bankers, and private establishments, furnishes at least three thousand competent occupiers of our new houses. None of these establishments, or occupations, provide board and lodging for their clerks and their families; hence all houses from forty pounds to one hundred pounds per annum, in new and pleasant streets, are eagerly taken by this class and they are constantly on the increase in their departments.

(3) Persons who live upon annuities derived from the increased public funds, and from the numerous stock companies created in the metropolis within the last twenty or thirty years, are a large class of new metropolitan housekeepers. They feel a local interest and attachment; they are, besides, in general, natives, or old residents of London; and they prefer receiving their interest in person to confiding it to any agent. These occupy at least three thousand of the new built houses at rents at from fifty to two hundred pounds per annum.

(4) The general increase of the metropolis, by adding to the mass of luxury, has increased the number of artisans, and persons employed on objects of luxury, such as painters, engravers, jewelers, embroiderers, authors, designers, architects, and others of like description; and these require three thousand small habitations among the new buildings in the retired streets around the metropolis.

(5) Another distinct large class of residents, in the immediate environs of London, are French, Dutch, Spanish, German, Italian, and other emigrants who, during the late wars and revolutions, have fled to England, as a place of security, and who, by the alien laws, are attached to the metropolis. I estimate those to amount to about two thousand families; and they live in the smaller tenements, either on annuities, on the bounty of government, or by their labour in various departments of the arts.

(6) The sixth class of independent residents in the suburbs, are an increased number of persons who have made fortunes of various amounts in trade. These occupy at least two thousand of the new houses of all sizes.

(7) The enormous increase of the army and navy, and the consequent increase of officers living on half-pay, and on pensions, leads to the occupation of at least two thousand houses in the immediate vicinity of London, not only for the advantages of society, but for the convenience of receiving their annuities, and improving their interests with administration.

Hence, from these seven causes, we have no difficulty in accounting for the occupation of part of the recent forty thousand new houses, by the families of: 5000 colonists, and persons who have made their fortunes in the East or West Indies; 3000 clerks in public offices, in banking-houses, etc.; 3000 annuitants of the funds and stock companies; 3000 artists of luxury; 2000 emigrants of all nations; 2000 retired traders; and 2000 officers of the army and navy—a total of 20,000 families.

Having thus accounted for the augmented population of twenty thousand homes, it is easy to conceive that as many more are greedily taken by tradesmen and others, who propose to obtain a living out of those by trade and labour of various kinds. There will be bakers, butchers, fruiterers, grocers, public-houses, barbers, taylors, shoe-makers, hatters, carpenters, smiths, bricklayers, school-masters, lawyers, apothecaries, physicians, and all the varieties which compose the industrious and enterprising part of a community, supporting themselves out of the wants of the twenty thousand independent families, and also on the mutual wants of each other.

To what extent this increase of a metropolis can be advantageously carried, it is impossible to anticipate. Ancient Rome was said to be sixty miles round; and London is not yet more than twenty. To equal ancient Rome, it must include Stratford to the east, and Brentford on the west; Hampstead and Highgate on the north; and Clapham and Camberwell on the south; between which places and London, there now are open spaces larger than London itself.

I confess I have my doubts about the alleged size of ancient Rome; and I suspect there never existed so large and populous a city as London, or as London will be, within seven years (1818), when the new streets and squares are erected which have lately been planned on every side of the town. Twenty thousand houses are already projected in various situations; and, judging from the demand for new houses, and the uniform success which has attended building-speculations for several years past, I entertain no doubt that they will be completed and occupied within the period above-named. If we retain our foreign colonies, and the continent of Europe continues to be disturbed by revolutions and military conquest, as it has been for the last twenty years, I have no doubt but in another twenty or thirty years, the fields and roads

between London and the above-mentioned villages, will be filled with houses, and the population increased from three quarters of a million to a million and a half. This is the necessary consequence of increased empire, of insular security, of civil and religious liberty, and of public confidence.

It is idle to talk of limiting the extent or size of the town by law, unless you could prevent colonists, aliens, and annuitants, from coming to dwell among us. Whether the increased population should be provided for by improvements in the internal parts of the town, or whether by indefinite enlargement, is however a question worthy of consideration. Already the town is found to be of inconvenient size for social and trading purposes; the foreign or country trader, who has many calls to make, finds his time and labour wasted in going from one end of so large a town to the other. There has long ceased to be any common interest between the remote parts of so immense a city: the inhabitant of Mary-le-bone is a foreigner in Wapping; and so is the inhabitant of Spital Fields, in Westminster. There are thousands who have arrived at old age in one half of London, who never visited the other half; and other thousands who never saw a ship, though London is the first port in the world. Of course, these are beings of very different habits and characters; and they possess even a varied pronunciation and peculiar idioms. For convenience of trade and association, it would be desirable that the town should be more compact; but it is desirable in regard to health, that it should spread itself to the neighbouring villages.

I have often marvelled at the want of concert and general plan with which the extensive suburbs are raised, after reading the lamentations of writers in regard to the neglect of all plan, in rebuilding the city after the great fire. We see street on street raising everywhere, without any general design; every undertaker building after his own fancy, and to suit the patch of ground of which he is the master. Perhaps it is now too late for parliament to prescribe the plan of future erections; or rather, in this free country magnificence must yield to convenience, and a fancied public good, to private interest.

In conclusion, I shall observe, that great cities contain in their very greatness, the seeds of premature and rapid decay. London will increase, as long as certain causes operate which she cannot control, and after those cease to operate for a season, her population will require to be renewed by new supplies of wealth; these failing, the houses will become too numerous for the inhabitants, and certain districts will be occupied by beggary and vice, or become depopulated. This disease will spread like an atrophy in the human body, and ruin will follow ruin, till the entire city is disgusting to the remnant of the inhabitants; they flee one after another to a more thriving spot; and at length the whole becomes a heap of ruins! Such have been the causes of the decay of all overgrown cities. Nineveh, Babylon, Antioch, and Thebes, are become heaps of ruins, tolerable only to reptiles and wild beasts. Rome, Delhi, and Alexandria, are partaking the same inevitable fate; and London must some time, from similar causes, succumb under the destiny of everything human. "COMMON SENSE"

# On the Urban Agglomeration and Economic Efficiency

KOICHI MERA

## INTRODUCTION

It is often argued that today's large metropolitan areas have exceeded the "optimal" size and, therefore, development efforts should be directed toward smaller urban centers.[1] This argument is frequently based on the proposition that the economic return from investment, either private, public, or both, in large metropolitan areas is less than that in medium- and small-size urban centers. The purposes of this paper are (1) to demonstrate that this proposition cannot be supported by any available empirical analysis and that, in terms of economic efficiency, even the largest metropolitan area in the world is likely to be less than the "optimal" size; and (2) to point out that there is a legitimate objective for pursuing a decentralization policy for urbanization, that is, interregional equity, whereas in practice a decentralization policy is frequently proposed and undertaken for economic efficiency, an objective which this policy seems to affect adversely rather than favorably.

1. The argument dates back to the nineteenth century and was made popular by Utopians, social reformers, and critics such as Robert Owen, Ebenezer Howard, and Lewis Mumford. During the 1950s, the argument has been given support by academicians, typically represented by Philip M. Hauser, ed., *Urbanization in Asia and the Far East* (Calcutta: UNESCO, 1957), and has been widely accepted in practice. In recent years, supporting views were expressed with varying tones by Barbara Ward, "The Cities That Came Too Soon," *Economist* 233 (December 1969): 56–62; and E.A.J. Johnson, *The Organization of Space in Developing Countries* (Cambridge, Mass.: Harvard University Press, 1970).

Many writers have observed that the currently large metropolitan areas already have excessive population concentration. However, their assertions are rarely consistent with an economic efficiency criterion in the sense of increasing a country's total income. If they are made on the economic ground, they are not based on a systematic quantitative analysis but on either visual impressions or partial quantitative data. Only recently, sufficient quantitative data have become available to make a fairly strong judgment on the hypothesis of diseconomies of concentration. In the following discussion, empirical analyses related to this question are surveyed, and additional materials are presented.

Different areal units are used for analysis, that is, regions, states or prefectures, counties, metropolitan areas, and cities and towns. However, the intention of the paper is to measure the impact of urban agglomeration. Urban agglomeration is defined to be a contiguous area in which every part is functionally interrelated to other parts within the area, usually through commuting and trade. Such an area is usually known as a metropolitan area. The reason for using nonmetropolitan data is that metropolitan data are not so readily available as those for governmentally defined units. Therefore, in interpreting analysis with nonmetropolitan data, the relationship between the obtained result and the expected result from metropolitan data must be considered carefully.

From *Economic Development and Cultural Change*, vol. 21, no. 2, 1973, pp. 309–337. Reprinted by permission of the author and the University of Chicago Press.

## INTERREGIONAL INCOME DISPARITY AS OBSERVED

It has long been observed that the per capita income of different regions differs greatly and that the difference is related to the degree of urbanization. For example, in the United States the per capita income of predominantly urban Connecticut is slightly more than twice that of rural Mississippi,[2] and in Japan the per capita product of Tokyo Prefecture is about two and a half times that of rural Kagoshima Prefecture.[3] Similar relationships are observed in less developed countries. In Brazil, the per capita income of the South is three times that of the Northeast. If we take states as units of observation, urban São Paulo has a per capita income six times greater than that of rural Piaui.[4] In India, West Bengal and Maharashtra States which contain the two largest urban concentrations, Calcutta and Bombay, have a per capita net domestic product about 40 percent higher than the national average.[5]

Since the empirical income data overwhelmingly associate the level of per capita income with the degree of urbanization, arguments for the diseconomy hypothesis are made on one of two grounds: (1) social overhead cost is sufficiently higher in highly urbanized areas to cancel the gross-income advantage, or (2) income per capita shows only average productivity; if marginal productivity

is considered, it will be less in large metropolitan areas.[6]

## EMPIRICAL ANALYSIS: SOCIAL OVERHEAD COST

The term "social overhead cost" (SOC) is used to describe those costs of services which the public sector provides. To compare the SOC in communities of different size, differentials in the scope of the public sector, the quality of services provided, and in the prices and wages must be considered. The scope of the public sector varies from community to community and has a great deal to do with the size of the community. For example, in a small town or rural area, fresh water is supplied either entirely from a private well or largely privately by carrying from a public source of supply in the neighborhood, whereas in a large city it is usually supplied by the public sector to the individual houses. Mass transport service can be operated by the public or private sector. Schools are in the hands of the public sector to a varying degree. In measuring the social overhead cost per capita, the discrepancies due to differentials in the scope of the public sector must be eliminated.

The more difficult question is the quality differential. The quality of public services provided is determined to a large extent by the political process within the local government. The demand for public services is related to the ability of the residents to pay and to their taste. The quality of public education is known to vary among communities in a number of countries. However, for a number

2. The percentage of urban population in Connecticut and Mississippi was 78.3 and 37.7, respectively, in 1960 according to the U.S. census definition of urban population. The stated income differential holds true throughout the 1950s and 1960s. Income, here, refers to personal income (U.S. Bureau of the Census, *Statistical Abstract of the United States: 1969* [Washington, D.C.: Government Printing Office, 1969]).
3. The stated per capita product differential holds true for all recent years, although the differential has been narrowing recently. If total received income is considered, the differential is greater. Product, here, refers to income produced within the area (source: Japan Economic Planning Agency, *Chiiki Keizai Yoran: 1968* [Tokyo: Economic Planning Association, 1968]).
4. The figures are from Stefan H. Robock, *Brazil's Developing Northeast* (Washington, D.C.: Brookings Institution, 1963).
5. The figures are computed from population data in India Ministry of Information and Broadcasting, *India, A Reference Manual* (New Delhi: Government of India Press, 1967) and state net domestic product data in National Council of Applied Economic Research (NCAER), *Estimates of State Income* (New Delhi: NCAER, 1967).

6. The first point is essentially my conjecture to the reasoning of those who point out high costs of large cities as a support for the argument against large cities without sufficient reference to the difference in income. Those authors include Catherine Bauer Wurster, "Urban Living Conditions, Overhead Costs, and the Development Pattern," ed. Roy Turner, *India's Urban Future* (Berkeley and Los Angeles: University of California Press, 1962), pp. 277–98, and L. R. Gabler, "Population Size as a Determinant of City Expenditures and Employment—Some Further Evidence," *Land Economics* 47 (May 1971): 130–38. The second point is often made by economists in discussions and conversations but, to the author's knowledge, had never been rigorously presented in print.

of public services, the measurement of quality is difficult. Consequently, analysts usually use the actual cost incurred for varying levels of service without specifically considering quality differences.

The price and wage differentials are commonly thought to make a fair comparison difficult. By using the usual price index in different localities, the cost differential attributable to the price differential can be identified. However, in a country where a free market economy prevails, interregional or intercity price differentials contain meanings which should not be eliminated in a comparison. The price of an apple of specified quality may be higher in a large city because the rent and wage the retailer has to pay are higher and also because people are willing to pay a higher price for it. At the same time, such a high-cost city is not isolated from the rest of the economy. It sells goods and services in exchange for imports. Therefore, a high price index is not an accident but a sustainable property of certain cities. A higher price for a certain good at a specific location implies a relatively higher value of the good at the specific location. The same argument holds for wages. Therefore, the price differentials need not be adjusted in order to compare the SOC.

A number of studies have been done in the United States on this issue. Earlier studies tended to concentrate on specific areas.[7] Since the publication of the 1957 census of local government finance, the scope of study has expanded to the national scale. On the basis of some 3,000 counties which constitute the initial forty-eight states of the United States, Schmandt and Stephens found that total local government expenditure per capita within a county shows a U-shaped curve with respect to the population size of the county, having its bottom at $120 in the population

range 15,000–50,000.[8] The largest per capita expenditure was observed for counties of 1 million or over and was about $80 higher than the least. However, median family income is correlated to per capita expenditure to a higher degree. It was also found that the state aid is highly correlated to expenditures in selected functions such as "welfare," "highways," and "education." They concluded that the evidence supported the proposition "that wealth or resources (measured in terms of median family income and state aid) is far more important than population size or density in explaining variations in total per capita expenditures among local units." This conclusion is not unique; it confirms earlier studies which tend to show that the expenditure per capita is not very much related to the population size when the expenditure is one way or another adjusted for quality differences.[9]

Although the aggregate local government expenditure per capita rises after county size reaches a certain level, per capita income rises about four times faster than the per capita local government expenditure for the same range,[10] implying a marginal propensity to consume public services of some 25 percent. Even if the public sector services are assumed to satisfy fixed needs and, therefore, have no variation in service quality, as Alonso puts it,

7. For studies in specific areas, see Stanley Scott and E. L. Feder, *Factors Associated with Variations in Municipal Expenditure Levels* (Berkeley: University of California Bureau of Public Administration, 1957); John C. Bollens, ed., *Exploring the Metropolitan Community* (Berkeley: University of California Press, 1961); Seymour Sacks and W. F. Hellmuth, *Financing Government in a Metropolitan Area* (Glencoe, Ill.: Free Press, 1961); Robert C. Wood, *1400 Governments* (Cambridge, Mass.: Harvard University Press, 1961).

8. Henry J. Schmandt and Ross G. Stephens, "Local Government Expenditure Patterns in the United States," *Land Economics* 39 (November 1963): 397–406.

9. A number of authors found little evidence of scale economies in many of the public services by examining statistically the per capita expenditures for different functions of local governments without taking into account quality differences of services but using the family income or other resource variables as explanatory variables. The authors include Harvey E. Brazer, *City Expenditures in the United States*, National Bureau of Economic Research Occasional Paper no. 66 (New York: National Bureau of Economic Research, 1959); Scott and Feder; Werner Z. Hirsch, "Expenditure Implications of Metropolitan Growth and Consolidation," *Review of Economics and Statistics* 41 (August 1959): 232–41; and Sacks and Hellmuth. However, considering explicitly the output of public services, Henry J. Schmandt and G. Ross Stephens ("Measuring Municipal Output," *National Tax Journal* 13 [December 1960]: 369–75) found a distinct possibility that economies of scale exist for some municipal functions such as police protection, general government, education, and garbage and refuse collection and disposal.

10. William Alonso, "Urban and Regional Imbalances in Economic Development," *Economic Development and Cultural Change* 17 (October 1968): 1–14.

Table 1. Per Capita Income, Local Government Total and Investment Expenditures, and Social Overhead Capital Stock as Related to Population Density in Japan

| Population Density in 1965 (Persons per km²) | Number of Prefectures (1) | Mean per Capita Income in 1965 (1,000 Yens) (2) | Mean per Capita Local Government Expenditure in 1965 (1,000 Yens) (3) | Mean per Capita All Government Investment Expenditure in 1966 (1,000 Yens) (4) | Mean per Capita SOCS in 1963 (1,000 Yens) (5) |
|---|---|---|---|---|---|
| Less than 200 | 17 | 188.0 | 50.8 | 32.8 | 268.5 |
| 200–300 | 15 | 197.6 | 46.7 | 27.3 | 244.8 |
| 300–600 | 8 | 209.1 | 43.2 | 27.6 | 206.4 |
| 600–1,000 | 3 | 228.0 | 41.9 | 27.5 | 205.3 |
| 1,000–3,000 | 1 | 280.0 | 53.7 | 40.5 | 178.4 |
| 3,000 or greater | 2 | 340.0 | 56.1 | 39.4 | 188.0 |

Note: All computed from figures in Japan Economic Planning Agency, *Chiiki Keizai Yoran: 1968* (Tokyo: Economic Planning Association, 1968) except col. 5, which is based on (1) SOCS figures in Japan Economic Planning Agency, *Supplementary Data to the Report of the Regional Subcommittee of the Economic Council* (in Japanese) (Tokyo, 1968), and (2) the population of 1960.

the optimal size "is far likelier to depend on the productivity-per-capita function than on the cost-per-capita function."[11]

The case of Japan presents a similar situation but supports more strongly Alonso's hypothesis. In table 1, the combined per capita expenditures (including investment expenditures) of prefectural and subprefectural governments for all forty-six prefectures are grouped by the population density of the prefecture. Population density for the entire prefecture is used here as an indication of metropolitan population concentration. The per capita government expenditure shows a U-shaped curve as in the United States. The higher expenditures in less densely populated prefectures seem to reflect the national government's greater assistance to those less developed regions as well as diseconomies of dispersion. The prefectures in the least-expenditure class are much more urban in Japan than the counties in the United States. Of the three prefectures in this class, one is within commuting distance from Tokyo; one has two large cities of about 1 million; and the other has one 2-million city. In addition, the per capita expenditure differential is much

11. Alonso, p. 4.

less in Japan. The highest is only 34 percent greater than the lowest in Japan; the corresponding difference in the United States is 67 percent. This seems to reflect the characteristics of the Japanese public resource allocation system, which depends more on the discretion of the national government than on the willingness of the residents to pay. Consequently, the Japanese data is considered to reflect the quality-adjusted cost curve more closely. The two most densely populated prefectures are those of Tokyo and Osaka. If we interpret the increase in the per capita expenditure from the least to the highest level as entirely a result of the difference in the income level, the marginal propensity to consume public services turns out to be 13 percent, much less than that found for the United States.

The social overhead capital stock (SOCS) in all prefectures was recently estimated by the Economic Planning Agency of Japan. Table 1 also shows per capita SOCS and also the per capita government capital expenditure during 1966 for all levels of government, including the national government. In terms of the stock of social overhead capital, there are substantial economies of higher density. The least stock per capita is observed in the second highest density class consisting of only one prefecture which is directly south of, and has commuting zones to, Tokyo. In terms of the per capita investment expenditure, high-density prefectures show higher values, but they are principal receivers of interprefectural migration. The prefecture with the highest per capita investment expenditure had a 2.8 percent increase of population due to migration alone during 1960.[12] Therefore, it is reasonable to state that investment expenditure is related more to the rate of population growth rather than to the diseconomies of large urban agglomerations. Thus, the Japanese case reinforces the argument that the "optimal size is more likely to be determined by the productivity per capita basis rather than the cost per capita basis."

For India, Bhatia reports that the cost of public utilities per worker was Rs. 210 in Bombay state and Rs. 30 in Orissa and Rajasthan States in 1956–57.[13] Since the labor-participation ratio was higher in Bombay than in Orissa or Rajasthan, the per capita cost differential is greater than these numbers indicate. In view of the better access and availability of public utilities in urban areas, the cost difference is not surprising. For example, the number of telephones per capita in Greater Bombay is nine times greater than the national average,[14] and the number of hospital beds per 1,000 persons in 1968 was 0.787 in Maharashtra (into which the State of Bombay merged), 0.362 in Orissa, and 0.515 in Rajasthan.[15] A study by the Stanford Research Institute found through empirical research on India's urban centers that, when the quality of services is held constant, the incremental infrastructure cost per capita declines rapidly as the population size of the city

increases to 130,000 and thereafter remains relatively constant, although it declines slightly to the largest observed city which had a population of 1 million.

The per worker product in the Bombay area is greater than that in other areas by more than the difference in the per worker cost. The per worker product of Maharashtra for the same year was Rs. 850, whereas that for Orissa and Rajasthan was Rs. 570 and Rs. 580, respectively.[16] Although data for less developed countries are not abundant, it is highly likely that the cost hypothesis cannot be supported for other developing countries as well.

## EMPIRICAL ANALYSIS: MARGINAL PRODUCTIVITY

The other hypothesis is that the marginal productivity of an input declines after the urban size reaches a certain scale and that the current large metropolitan areas have already reached this critical scale. A significant contribution to this hypothesis was recently made by Fuchs.[17] Using the one-in-thousand United States census sample of 1959, he divided the labor force by sex, color, age, and education. He still found significant regional differences in the hourly wage rate which could not be attributed to the differences in the labor composition. For example, the actual hourly earnings of white and nonwhite workers in the South were, respectively, about 10 and 20 percent below the rates which would be expected from the composition of the labor force, classified by the four criteria, in the region. He proceeded to relate the hourly wage rate for each type of labor with the size of the city population. Actual hourly earnings were compared with the expected hourly earnings by city size. They are shown in table 2.

In order to interpret the results, he tested the hypothesis that the higher earnings in the

12. Japan Economic Planning Agency.
13. S. K. Bhatia, "National Cost Approach for a Balanced Regional Economic Development of India" (Ph.D. diss., Netherlands School of Economics, 1965).
14. The number in Greater Bombay refers to 1964, and the national average, to 1965–66. Source for the former is Municipal Corporation of Greater Bombay, *Report on the Development Plan for Greater Bombay—1964* (Bombay: Government Central Press, 1964); and that for the latter, India Ministry of Information and Broadcasting.
15. India Finance Commission, *Report of the Finance Commission: 1969* (New Delhi: Government of India Press, 1969).

16. Derived from India Ministry of Information and Broadcasting, and National Council of Applied Economic Research.
17. Victor R. Fuchs, *Differentials in Hourly Earnings by Region and City Size, 1959*, National Bureau of Economic Research Occasional Paper, no. 101 (New York: Columbia University Press, 1967).

Table 2. Ratio of Actual to "Expected" Hourly Earnings, by City Size, 1959

| | Rural | Urban Places | | | Standard Metropolitan Statistical Areas | | |
| | | Under 10,000 | 10,000– 99,999 | Under 250,000 | 250,000– 499,999 | 500,000– 999,000 | 1 Million and More |
| --- | --- | --- | --- | --- | --- | --- | --- |
| White males | 0.83 | 0.84 | 0.91 | 0.97 | 0.97 | 1.02 | 1.12 |
| White females | 0.83 | 0.84 | 0.88 | 0.94 | 0.96 | 1.03 | 1.13 |
| Nonwhite males | 0.78 | 0.75 | 0.76 | 0.84 | 1.04 | 1.07 | 1.10 |
| Nonwhite females | 0.76 | 0.63 | 0.78 | 0.76 | 0.90 | 1.00 | 1.19 |

Source: Victor R. Fuchs, *Differentials in Hourly Earnings by Region and City Size, 1959,* National Bureau of Economic Research Occasional Paper, no. 101 (New York: Columbia University Press, 1967).
*Note:* "Expected" hourly earnings were obtained by multiplying the national average hourly earnings of each color, age, sex, and education by the annual hours worked by members of that cell in the region, summing across all cells in the region and dividing by the total manhours of the region.

large cities might be attributed to unionization or size of employer, but the regression analysis rejected both. As to the cost of living differences, although I reject the appropriateness of the concept itself, he states that "intercity differences in cost of living appear to be small relative to differences in hourly earnings." Then, he states "one of the most promising hypotheses to explain the city-size differential is that it reflects differences in labor quality not captured by standardization for color, age, sex and education. This might take the form of better-quality schooling, more on-the-job training, selective immigration to the big cities of more ambitious and hard-working persons, or other forms." Irrespective of these reasons, since the wage rate is likely to be highly correlated positively with the marginal productivity of labor, it can be stated fairly confidently that the marginal productivity of labor increases as the size of the urban center increases throughout the observed range.

It is possible to interpret the result of the Fuchs study that the labor force in large cities is more productive, not because a large city offers a highly productive environment, but because a large city *attracts* high-quality workers and that the supply of high-quality

workers is independent of the size distribution of cities. If this hypothesis holds, a policy that discourages the growth of large cities does not reduce the supply of high-quality workers. This hypothesis may be plausible. However, it would seem more plausible to theorize that potential high-quality workers are given opportunities for greater development in large cities than in small cities because of the diverse opportunities and severe competition that are only available in large cities.

Another significant contribution was made by the Economic Research Institute of the Japan Economic Planning Agency.[18] An elaborate multiregional econometric model was constructed from regional data for 1954–62 by dividing the country into nine regions. The model, which consists of fifty-seven equations, contains such important functions as interregional migration, employment, production and income generation, flow of commodities, and private and government investment. The supply of social overhead capital, the intergovernmental transfer of government funds and interre-

18. Japan Economic Planning Agency, *Studies on Japan's Nation-wide Regional Econometric Model* (in Japanese), Institute of Economic Research Series, no. 18 (Tokyo: Economic Planning Agency Institute of Economic Research, 1967).

gional transfer of industrial capital are considered as the key government-policy variables. Several alternative policies in regard to centralization/decentralization were tried, and the 1970 economy was predicted. In general, it was found that *an increase of GNP is associated with an increase of interregional disparity of income*. Specifically, the following findings were obtained.

(1) The most effective policy for reducing interregional disparity of income has been the increased distribution of industrial capital to less developed regions. But interregional equity is achieved at a cost to GNP. Specifically, in comparison with the "neutral" projection (based on the extrapolation of current policies), the coefficient of variation (c.v.) of per capita incomes of regions is reduced from 0.212 to 0.145, but the GNP is reduced by 4.1 percent.

(2) On the other hand, further centralization of industrial capital increases the GNP almost 1 percent above the neutral level, but the coefficient of variation increases to 0.229.

(3) Intergovernmental transfer of funds is an effective tool for changing the distribution of per capita incomes without affecting much the aggregate efficiency of the economy. Without appreciably changing the GNP, it has been demonstrated that the c.v. can be reduced to 0.204 with a decentralization policy and increased to 0.225 with a centralization policy.

(4) Interregional transport investment tends to produce desirable results on both accounts. Under a policy of improving the accessibility of the less developed regions to the developed regions, GNP is predicted to increase 1 percent over the neutral level, with a c.v. of 0.202; and, with a general improvement of accessibility roughly in proportion to the current pattern, the GNP is predicted to increase 2 percent over the neutral level, with a c.v. of 0.205. However, in these cases, population migration is accelerated, and the predicted distribution of population is quite similar to that obtained with other centralization policies.

Related research for Japanese regions has also been done by me,[19] using the same regional and prefectural data collected for the above study. To examine the effect of urbanization or concentration of activities on productivity, the analysis uses spatial density variables; that is, both the output and the three kinds of inputs (labor, private capital, and social overhead capital) are measured in terms of per square kilometer for the geographical unit considered. Relevant conclusions follow.

(1) By estimating production functions for the three major sectors (primary, secondary, and tertiary) from the regional data, it was found that there are diseconomies of concentration in primary-sector production but economies of concentration in the secondary and tertiary sectors.

(2) For the forty-six prefectures, clear relationships were observed between social overhead capital and labor and private capital inputs. The density of either of the two private inputs is very much related to the density of social overhead capital.

(3) For the same prefectural data, it was also found that both the wage rate and return to private capital are higher in areas of higher social overhead capital density.

(4) Consequently, the higher per capita income in high-density areas can be explained by both savings in social overhead capital cost and increased efficiency of inputs.

(5) Therefore, policies to develop less developed regions tend to reduce the economies of concentration. If per capita income in the three sectors were to be equalized for the nine regions by a hypothetical instantaneous redistribution of social overhead capital where the distribution of labor and private capital remain the same, it is estimated that national income would drop about 30 percent.

(6) On the other hand, when labor and private capital respond to the redistribution of social overhead capital, the cost of national income for achieving equality of per capita

19. Koichi Mera, "Regional Production Functions and Redistribution Policies: The Case of Japan," Harvard University Program on Regional and Urban Economics Discussion Paper, no. 45 (Cambridge, Mass.: Harvard University, 1969).

incomes is less. Such an experiment for forty-six prefectures gave a drop of national income of about 15 percent from the current observed level.

The findings by Fuchs, the Japan Economic Planning Agency, and Mera all indicate that, on the whole, large urban centers are more productive than smaller ones.[20] Since the average productivity is found to be higher in larger urban centers, there is no reason to believe that the marginal productivity in large metropolitan areas is less than that in smaller urban centers.

## EMPIRICAL ANALYSIS: DEVELOPING COUNTRIES

The empirical analyses presented above are derived primarily from observations in the developed countries. There are good reasons to believe that situations are different in the less developed countries. Below, some research findings are presented, all of which tend to reaffirm the results derived for developed countries.

A study by Fukuchi[21] indicates that in Brazil there is a large technological gap between the developed and underdeveloped regions. The technological gap is shown by comparing output per worker in different regions, while capital per worker is held constant. For example, the technological efficiency of the South is approximately twice as large as that in the Northeast.

Williamson contributed to this question by examining regional disparities of income with respect to the degree of economic development.[22] His findings can be summarized as follows: (1) from international cross-section

data, it was found that the degree of regional inequality increases as the degree of development increases until the level of development reaches Kuznets's middle-income class which includes Italy, Spain, Brazil, and Colombia, and thereafter it declines; and (2) from time-series data of several countries it was found that "increasing regional inequality is generated during the early development stages, while mature growth has produced regional convergence or a reduction in differentials." Although the study does not explicitly deal with urban concentrations, from the association of urban concentration with higher income levels it can be interpreted that, at least at the early stage of development, urban concentration seems to be a necessary condition for economic development.[23]

Another relevant study is that of El Shaks which is cited by Alonso. "El Shaks finds that a cross-section of the world's nations results in a near-normal curve of primacy on economic development.[24] That is to say, primacy is rare in very underdeveloped countries, rises during the take-off stage, and decreases thereafter. His time-series studies of developed countries also support this view, although not as neatly as the cross-section data." This study reinforces the interpretation derived from the Williamson study; urban concentration is a necessary condition for economic development in an early stage. The relative advantage of urban concentration is greater in less developed countries than in developed countries. However, this statement should not be taken as implying that the advantage of urban concentration disappears once a country reaches a certain stage of development. The findings for the United States and Japan show that there are still observable advantages in concentration.

20. The traditional location theory is still relevant. Some industries such as resource-oriented industries are not necessarily attracted by large cities.
21. Takao Fukuchi, "Regional and Sectoral Projection of the Brazilian Economy" (Santiago: United Nations Economic Council for Latin America, Economic Projection Center, 1969).
22. J. G. Williamson, "Regional Inequality and the Process of National Development: A Description of the Patterns," *Economic Development and Cultural Change*, vol. 13, no. 4, pt. 2 (July 1965).

23. From this study, one cannot derive the conclusion that urban concentration is less in high-income countries, because the reduction of regional disparity at this stage is caused largely by a growing scarcity of labor in underdeveloped regions due to increasing employment opportunities in the modern sector and the increased mobility of labor. See below the discussion on the studies by Sovani and Kamerschen.
24. "Primacy" is used here to imply the degree of concentration of urban population.

It has been demonstrated convincingly by Sovani and Kamerschen that industrialization and urbanization are highly correlated, particularly in early stages of economic development.[25] However, the relationship which existed in the currently developed countries during the late nineteenth century differs from that which exists now in the currently developing countries. Kamerschen goes further to relate urban concentration with the level of economic development. The population of the largest city as a percentage of the total population of the four largest cities in a country was used to measure urban concentration, and per capita GNP was used to measure economic development. Using cross-section data for eighty countries during the 1955–56 period, he found that for developed countries urban concentration was negatively correlated with the level of development, but for developing countries it was positively correlated with the coefficient of correlation of .10. The correlation is not impressive, but this analysis fails to explore the dynamic relationship between the urban concentration and economic development. The issue is whether further urban concentration is conducive to economic development for each country. To determine this relationship from a simple cross-section analysis requires the rather strong assumption that every country follows a more or less similar path of urban concentration in the process of economic development. The degree of urban concentration crucially depends upon the structure of the economy and on the size of the country. In addition, it depends upon the jurisdictional boundary of the cities.

In order to examine the relationship between urban concentration and economic development without being affected much by intercountry differences in the structure of the economy and the political unit of cities, I conducted an analysis relating the growth rate

of a country to the difference in its urban concentration over time. The degree of urban concentration, primacy, was measured by the share of a certain number of largest cities in the country population. The change in the share, $\Delta p$, was computed for a recent seven-year period for all less developed countries for which reliable data were available.[26] If urban concentration of population increases efficiency, those countries which showed a large positive change in the primacy should have increased national product more than those which did not, other things being equal. Therefore, the hypothesis is that the growth rate of per capita GDP is positively related to the change in primacy. In table 3, countries are grouped by the change in the primacy measured by the population share of the *largest* city, $\Delta p_1$, for countries which had populations over 1 million in 1960.[27] The median growth rate of per capita GDP is shown for each group. The table supports the hypothesis. Specifically, those countries for which the change in primacy is less than 1.0, in general, had a substantially lower growth rate of GDP per capita than that of any other group. The group of countries for which the change in primacy is more than four percentage points has a growth rate of GDP per capita markedly higher than that for any other group. Excluding the exceptional case of Libya, which is growing at a phenomenal rate since a recent discovery of oil deposits, the GDP per

25. N. V. Sovani, "The Analysis of Overurbanization," *Economic Development and Cultural Change* 12 (January 1964): 113–22, and David R. Kamerschen, "Further Analysis of Overurbanization," *Economic Development and Cultural Change* 17 (January 1969): 235–53.

26. Population figures for cities were taken from the U.N. *Demographic Yearbook*. Those countries which did not have population figures at two different dates for the largest city or largest three cities, whichever the case may be, were excluded, as were those for which figures were not sufficiently recent, were apart from each other in time, or were not meaningful or comparable. Specifically, in order to be acceptable, (1) city-population figures for the initial year must be for 1955 or more recent; and for the terminal year, for 1960 or more recent; (2) there must be at least a four-year time span between the two dates for which city-population data were available; (3) any estimate must have at least two digits which are meaningful and sufficiently reliable; and (4) however the city population is defined, for city proper or for the urban agglomeration, the population figures for any single city at two observation dates must refer to the same geographical area. Whenever data were available for both city proper and agglomeration for an urban center at two observation dates, the figures for agglomeration were used.

27. The exclusion of small countries is to eliminate the impact of extreme volatility which primacy in these countries may exhibit.

Table 3. Per Capita GDP Growth Rate for Countries Grouped by the Change in the Primacy of the Largest City

| $\Delta p_1 \leq 0$ | | $0 < \Delta p_1 \leq 1$ | | $1 < \Delta p_1 \leq 2$ | | $2 < \Delta p_1 \leq 4$ | | $4 < \Delta p_1$ | |
|---|---|---|---|---|---|---|---|---|---|
| Algeria | -3.3 | Madagascar | -0.5 | Honduras | 1.9 | Dominican Rep. | -0.7 | Ecuador | 1.0 |
| Morocco | 0.3 | Butundi | -0.1 | Guinea | 2.5 | Ghana | -0.1 | Korea | 4.8 |
| India | 0.9 | Sudan | 0.2 | U.A.R. | 2.7 | Colombia | 1.5 | Puerto Rico | 6.2 |
| Cambodia | 1.1 | Cameroon | 0.6 | Peru | 2.9 | Cost Rica | 1.7 | | |
| Ceylon | 1.3 | Indonesia | 0.6 | Panama | 4.8 | Jamaica | 1.7 | | |
| Iraq | 1.9 | Philippines | 0.8 | Jordan | 5.8 | Guatemala | 1.9 | | |
| Mexico | 2.8 | Kenya | 1.1 | Spain | 6.9 | Chile | 2.3 | | |
| Portugal | 5.1 | Nigeria | 1.1 | | | Ireland | 3.1 | | |
| Libya | 21.4 | Venezuela | 1.1 | | | Nicaragua | 4.1 | | |
| | | Brazil | 1.2 | | | Iran | 4.8 | | |
| | | Vietnam, Rep. of | 1.8 | | | Ivory Coast | 5.4 | | |
| | | El Salvador | 2.4 | | | | | | |
| | | Pakistan | 2.9 | | | | | | |
| | | Turkey | 3.1 | | | | | | |
| | | Syria | 3.9 | | | | | | |
| | | Thailand | 3.9 | | | | | | |
| | | Taiwan | 6.7 | | | | | | |
| Median | 1.3 | | 1.1 | | 2.9 | | 1.9 | | 4.8 |

Source: U.N. *Demographic Yearbook* (New York: United Nations, annual) for population, and International Bank for Reconstruction and Development (IBRD), *World Tables* (Washington, D.C.: IBRD, 1969) for per capita GDP growth rates.
Note: The countries are grouped by the change in the primacy of the largest city, $\Delta p_1$, which is defined to be the change in population share of the largest city in percentage points during a recent seven-year period.

capita growth rate, $r$, was regressed on the change of the largest-city primacy for the remaining forty-six countries:

$$r = 1.763 + .411\Delta p_1; \quad R = .297. \quad (1)$$
$$(4.388) \quad (2.064)$$

The number in the parentheses is the $t$-value for the estimate directly above. The coefficient of $\Delta p_1$ is positive at the 2.5 percent level of significance.

In order to eliminate further the volatile impacts expected of smaller countries, the same regression equation was estimated for the countries which had a population of 10 million or over in 1960. Nineteen countries were observed, and the result was

$$r = 1.305 + .859\Delta p_1; \quad R = .503. \quad (2)$$
$$(2.328) \quad (2.401)$$

The correlation coefficient was higher and the coefficient of $\Delta p_1$ was greater than for the larger sample. Therefore, the hypothesis is supported more strongly for larger countries which are affected less by "accidental" developments. The result may also imply that primacy of larger cities is more conducive to economic development than primacy of smaller cities, as the largest city in a large country tends to be greater than the largest city in a small country.

In order to view urban concentration effects in a wider context, primacy was then measured by the share of the three largest cities in the country's population. The change of this primacy index for the same seven-year period, $\Delta p_{1-3}$, was used as the independent variable to explain the per capita GDP growth rate. Because of the increasing paucity of data, only twenty-one countries were observed. The result was

$$r = 1.422 + .600\Delta p_{1-3}; \quad R = .441. \quad (3)$$
$$(2.320) \quad (2.144)$$

The coefficient of $\Delta p_{1-3}$ was positive at the 2.5 percent level of significance. However, the result was not significantly different from

the one obtained in the preceding paragraph, using the largest city alone.

Attempts were made to separate the impact of the growth of the second and third largest cities from that of the largest city. It was found that both the change in the primacy of the second and third cities together and that of the largest city are positively related to the per capita GDP growth rate, the former having a slightly higher significance level.[28] However, this distinction should not be taken as conclusive. First, the two variables are positively correlated (with a correlation coefficient of .252); and, second, the measurement of the change in the primacy is biased more heavily with the largest city than with smaller cities because the city population is frequently measured within a political boundary rather than for the metropolitan basis; the metropolitan population is overflowing the political boundary to a greater extent with the largest city. This bias in the measurement is confirmed by the regression analysis similar to equation (1) but using only those observations in which $\Delta p_1$ is defined on the metropolitan basis: both the regression and correlation coefficients are high.[29]

The foregoing analysis confirms the results of earlier studies which tend to support positive correlation between the growth of large cities and economic development in developing countries.

## CONCLUSIONS

It has been observed that the per capita cost of government expenditure for public services is least for cities having a population under several millions. However, higher expendi-

---

28. The obtained equation for twenty-one countries was:

$$r = 1.428 + .454\Delta p_1 + 1.229\Delta p_{2,3}, \quad R = .487,$$
$$(2.320) \quad (1.281) \quad (1.600)$$

where $p_{2,3}$ is the change in the primacy of the second and third largest cities together, i.e., $\Delta p_{2,3} = \Delta p_{1-3} - \Delta p_1$.

29. Nineteen countries were qualified out of the original forty-six countries, and the estimated equation was

$$r = 1.271 + .678\Delta p_1, \quad R = .484.$$
$$(1.926) \quad (2.283)$$

tures in large cities are attributable more to the greater willingness of large city residents to pay for public services than to diseconomies of large scale. In addition, the difference in income greatly exceeds the difference in cost. Therefore, if there is any optimal size, it is likely to be determined more by productivity than by cost.

The available empirical analyses presented above show that large cities are more productive and that the largest cities are likely to be particularly more productive relative to others in a less developed country. Therefore, a decentralization policy of investment and population distribution over the country cannot be encouraged, particularly for less developed countries, if the national goal is to maximize the growth rate of national products.

However, it is known that urbanization generally increases per capita income of the areas affected. Therefore, if the national goal is to achieve a more equitable distribution of income over different regions, even at some sacrifice to the GNP growth rate, then a policy directed toward the development of underdeveloped regions can be justified.

In sum, a decentralization policy may be effective for achieving a more equitable distribution of income over different regions, but is not likely to be a desirable policy for the aggregate efficiency of the economy for most underdeveloped countries.

# Rural Inequality and Regional Planning

RICHARD PEET

Capitalist economic development has produced a certain kind of material affluence in America, but it has also resulted in growing inequalities. Well-known are income, status and power differences between classes, between blacks and whites, between the elderly and the young, and between women and men. An additional dimension to social inequality is between people living in different regions of the country, and especially inequalities between rural and urban dwellers. In general, incomes are about one-third higher in metropolitan areas than in rural areas. While eight percent of urban families are below the official, subsistence poverty level, fifteen percent of the rural families are among the subsistence poor. But such gross statistics gloss over the extremes of rural deprivation. For the depths of American poverty are found in the most peripheral, isolated regions, occupied (inevitably) by racial and cultural minority groups. Today, a decade after the ''Skirmish on Poverty'' began, there are great clusters of counties in non-coal field Appalachia, the South and Southwest, and around Great Plains Indian reservations, in which between a quarter and a half of the people somehow exist on incomes below the official subsistence level. Many, if not the majority, of these people are excluded even from the most basic, poverty-alleviating programs, such as food stamps or commodity distribution. Children still die of hunger in shacks at the edge of southern fields.

## THE COMPARATIVE POVERTY OF RURAL AMERICA

As one moves away from large American cities, a series of zones are encountered in which social environmental conditions become worse, income falls, and the incidence of poverty rises. This is shown in the most general way by Figure 1. While the majority of the people now live in and around large cities, 40 percent of the population still reside in the smaller cities and towns, and farm and non-farm rural areas (Figure 1a). The environment of jobs surrounding this forty percent is one of sparser and inferior jobs—hence, participation rates in the labor market are lower and the jobs obtained are more likely to be in the blue-collar and service categories (Figures 1b, 1c, 1d). Social services tend to be poorer, with many of those who have received the benefits of social-service investment migrating out to the large cities. Hence educational and vocational training levels are lower in small cities and rural areas (Figures 1e, 1f). Yet, fertility is higher leading to a constant pressure of people on the services and jobs available (Figure 1g). As a result, median family income in 1970 fell from almost $12,000 per family in the suburbs of large cities, to $8,000–$9,000 in the small cities and towns, and $7,000–$8,000 in rural areas (Figure 1h). This skewing down of the income distribution produces a considerably higher incidence of subsistence

From *Antipode*, vol. 7, no. 3, December 1975, pp. 10–24. Reprinted by permission.

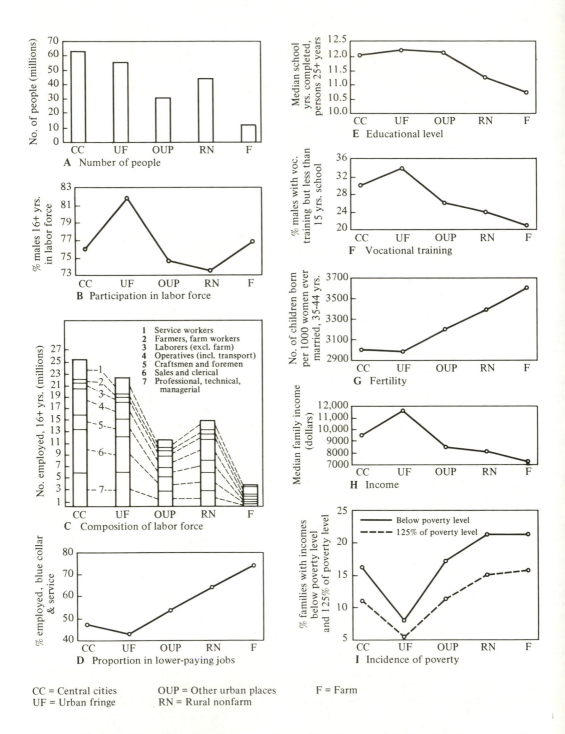

**A** Number of people

**B** Participation in labor force

**C** Composition of labor force

1 Service workers
2 Farmers, farm workers
3 Laborers (excl. farm)
4 Operatives (incl. transport)
5 Craftsmen and foremen
6 Sales and clerical
7 Professional, technical, managerial

**D** Proportion in lower-paying jobs

**E** Educational level

**F** Vocational training

**G** Fertility

**H** Income

**I** Incidence of poverty

Below poverty level
125% of poverty level

CC = Central cities          OUP = Other urban places          F = Farm
UF = Urban fringe           RN = Rural nonfarm

Figure 1. Characteristics of the Population by Place of Residence, 1970. (Statistical source: 1970 Census, U.S. Summary, General Social and Economic Characteristics.)

poverty—the chances of living in poverty are three times as high for a farm resident as they are for a suburbanite (Figure 1i).

We can examine these gross trends in more detail in Figure 2. The diagrams are derived from the 1970 census simply by arraying all counties on a line between certain major cities and entering the relevant social or economic data for each county, or city, on the graph. In Figure 2, comparisons can be made between central cities, suburbs, and rural areas in one of the poorest areas in the United States— Alabama, northern Mississippi and south-eastern Arkansas.

In Mississippi and other remote peripheral areas there are economic problems of a severe lack of jobs *and* the poor quality of the jobs available. In these areas adult male labor force participation rates approach the national average (77%) only in the infrequently-occurring cities (Figure 2a) while in the most remote, backward pockets a disastrous situation exists in which only just over one half of the adult males are able to participate in economic production.

Educational levels are higher in urban areas and drop to extremely low levels in the poorest rural areas (Figure 2b) where less than one-third of the adult population are high-school graduates. Low educational levels result in part from out-migration by the better-educated rural youth, but rural areas also have school drop-out rates about 33% higher than urban areas.[1] Rural adults are in poorer health and rural children prone to death at an earlier age than their urban counterparts. Even after illness rates have adjusted for age, it is found that 15.4% of the farm population and 14.1% of the rural non-farm population have activity-limiting chronic health conditions, compared with 9.8% of people living in large metropolitan areas.[2] Infant mortality rates rise as one moves into areas of low income and longer distances separating patients from doc-

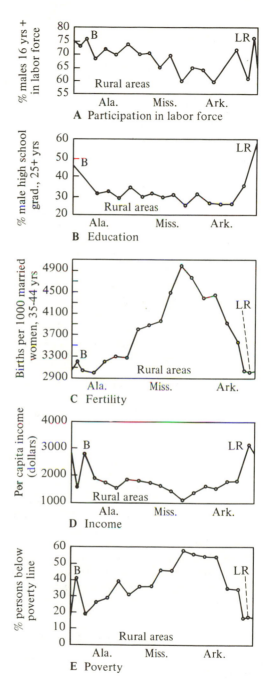

Figure 2. Social and Economic Characteristics of a Cross-section of Counties, Birmingham, Ala. (B), to Little Rock, Ark. (LR), 1970.

1. U.S.D.A., Economic Research Service, *Characteristics of School Dropouts and High School Graduates Farm and Non-farm, 1960*, Agricultural Economic Report No. 65, 1964, p. 3.
2. U.S.D.A., Economic Research Service, *Rurality, Poverty and Health: Medical Problems in Rural Areas* (Washington: 1970), p. 2.

tors. Similarly, maternal deaths (many of which can be prevented) are higher in isolated rural areas.[3]

Two-thirds of the substandard housing in America is in non-metropolitan America, despite the fact that only just over one-third of all housing units is located there. Consequently, 14% of the non-metropolitan population continue to live in such housing—and 55% of the non-white people—compared with 4% of the metropolitan population—and 11% of the non-white people.[4] An even higher proportion lives in housing which lacks bathrooms, running water, or other plumbing taken for granted in the cities.

These factors are summarized in the income and poverty diagrams (2d and 2e). Per capita income is low in the central cities, then soars in the suburbs, only to fall precipitously in areas such as rural Alabama. Small cities push annual per capita income up by $500–$750, while around large metropolitan areas per capita annual income is $1,000 a year, or more, higher than the surrounding rural areas. Correspondingly, the incidence of subsistence poverty falls from 15%–20% in the central cities, through valleys of 5%–10% in metropolitan suburbs, then rises to 30%–60% in the rural South.

In such rural areas, the President's National Advisory Commission on Rural Poverty[5] found hunger and widespread malnutrition, startlingly high rates of disease and premature death, major problems of underemployment, poor schools and housing, and the disappearance of the community as an effective institution. A survey of household food consumption, made in 1965 and 1966, showed that 30% of the rural farm population and 26% of the rural non-farm population of the South

had "poor" diets (i.e., supplied less than two-thirds of allowances for one or more nutrients), compared with 22% of the southern urban population. Among the southern rural poor, 42% of the rural non-farm and 43% of the rural farm households had poor diets.[6] It was in this population that the Board of Inquiry of the Citizens Crusade Against Poverty was surprised to find widespread malnutrition and evidence of kwashiorkor and marasmus, severe protein deficiency diseases thought previously not to exist in the United States. On the basis of low income, high postneonatal mortality rates, and low or nonexistent participation in welfare and food programs, a large number of rural countries were designated emergency hunger areas by the Board. Field investigations by six physicians in the area of the Delta country of Mississippi confirmed that children were indeed dying from hunger; because the father was declared "able-bodied," families were ineligible for welfare, while food programs were not reaching them. The physicians concluded that "welfare and food programs (including the commodity food program) are in the hands of people who use them selectively, politically, and with obvious racial considerations in mind".[7] For those people who would comfort themselves that poverty in America is not the same poverty as that of the "underdeveloped" countries, the answer is that for some groups, in some areas, people do not receive the minimal food and shelter necessary for human survival; there, the level of absolute poverty had indeed been reached.

## RURAL SUBCULTURE AS A TRANSMISSION AGENT

Poverty is transmitted intergenerationally through a number of devices, among which is the subculture of poor people. This transmis-

3. A. P. Lesser and E. P. Hunt, "Maternal and Child Health Programs and Rural Areas," in President's National Advisory Commission on Rural Poverty, *Rural Poverty in the United States* (Washington: 1968), pp. 333–355.
4. "Prepared Statement of George W. Rucker, Research Director, Rural Housing Alliance," in *Nutrition and Human Needs—1970*, Hearings before the Select Committee on Nutrition and Human Needs, U.S. Senate, Part 7, pp. 2004–2013.
5. President's National Advisory Commission on Rural Poverty, *The People Left Behind* (Washington: 1967), p. x.

6. U.S.D.A., Agricultural Research Service, *Dietary Levels of Households in the South*, Spring 1965 (Washington: 1970), p. 7.
7. Southern Regional Council, *Hungry Children* (Atlanta: 1967), p. 9. See also Citizen's Board of Inquiry into Hunger and Malnutrition in the United States, *Hunger, U.S.A.* (Boston, 1968).

sion mechanism is often mistaken for the *cause* of poverty. Thus rural poverty is blamed on the nature of rural people themselves, or on rural subcultures, just as poverty in America in general is explained in terms of the existence of an inhibiting "lower-class" subculture. This ideological argument runs more or less as follows.

Rural America is characterized by smaller communities and lower population densities than urban America. Rural society is composed of fewer and more rigid social classes, while rural regions tend to have ethnically more homogeneous populations. As a result of these factors, rural social interaction is distinguished from its urban counterpart by fewer, more personal, more lasting and less-differentiated contacts drawn from a smaller geographic area.[8] In particular a great deal of the rural individual's time is spent within the family; hence, rural people are said to be more "familistic" than urban people,[9] while outside the family much interaction takes place with kin.[10] Rural areas are relatively isolated from urban centers of social and technological change. Compared with urban people, therefore, rural "folk" are said to live in closed worlds in which traditional ideas are passed from generation to generation with minimal inputs from outside. Hence, rural people are portrayed as less materialistic, less aggressive in their pursuit of goals, more concerned with personal relationships, less spatially mobile, less convinced of the value of formal education than urban people. They are more humane humans, but they are therefore out of tune with the requirements of "modern industrial society"; their characteristics help to isolate them from the income benefits of that society.

All of this is highly generalized. More specifically, how does a rural upbringing contribute as a "cause" of poverty among rural people? One chain links the characteristics of rural social life with limited educational and occupational aspirations among rural youth, lower levels of educational achievement, less ability to compete for income compared with urban youth raised in social environments which infuse higher levels of educational and occupational aspiration into their youth, and therefore worse jobs, lower pay and a higher incidence of poverty. For example, a study of farm, village and urban high school seniors in Wisconsin found that lower proportions of rural youth planned on going to college and aspired to professional and white-collar occupations than was true for urban, and especially large-city students. The study suggested that rural students, especially those from farms, were less academically oriented, less able, and less convinced of the value of higher education than urban youth. Rural youth found themselves in school and community environments with less potential for arousing and maintaining high levels of educational and occupational aspiration. Most important of all, rural youth came from lower-status families with lower educational attainments. Their parents were less likely to have discussed and encouraged going to college with them. In short, rural students had not been taught to value high education and to strive for prestigious occupations to the extent that urban students had.[11] And it is this lack of striving that accounts for the relative poverty of rural populations.

Obviously the tendency here is to "blame" rural people for their poverty. This is a sophisticated line of thinking backed by considerable rural sociological research. But social research once started along a certain path tends to have predictable, if more quantified results, and the path of research is often set by the pre-disposition of key research workers. In this case, the predisposition was to look for the *causes* of rural social problems in the inherent nature of rural people themselves, a common enough tendency in the late 1950's

8. T. Lynn Smith and Paul E. Zopf, *Principles of Inductive Rural Sociology* (Philadelphia: 1970), pp. 23–34.
9. James H. Copp, "Family Background of Rural Youth," in Lee Burchinal, ed., *Rural Youth in Crisis: Facts, Myths, and Social Change* (Washington: 1965), p. 38.
10. Murray A. Straus, "Social Class and Farm-City Differences in Interaction with Kin in Relation to Societal Modernization," *Rural Sociology* 34, 4 (December, 1969), pp. 476–495.

11. William H. Sewell and A. O. Haller, "Educational and Occupational Perspectives of Farm and Rural Youth," in Burchinal, *Rural Youth in Crisis*, pp. 149–169.

and for much of the 1960's. Alternatively, we can seek the causes of rural poverty in certain tendencies inherent in capitalist production, and see rural subculture only as one, fairly unimportant, transmission agent. For, faced with a situation in which economic "opportunity" does not exist, or is difficult to reach, rural people may well react temporarily by adjusting their aspiration levels towards the levels of accomplishment which they can possibly attain.[12] This does *not* mean that "reduced aspiration" is in any way an inherent characteristic of rural people. It merely reflects the realities of the rural situation. Values and aspiration levels may be passed down from one generation to the next, and thus help to transmit inequality within the family, but they are subject to rapid change should circumstances change. Rural subculture is not a cause of inequality, only an expression of prior-existing inequalities.

## THE RURAL SOCIAL ENVIRONMENT

Inequality is transmitted also through the social-service environment. Generally speaking it is more expensive to provide services to a small, scattered, and often declining rural population than to a not-too-large, concentrated, urban population. A given expenditure on social services will result in lower-quality services in rural areas. For example, low densities of population affect educational costs and the variety of courses which schools can offer. Large schools offer substantial economies through bigger classes and the spreading of overhead costs over more students. But large school districts, needed to support large schools, also involve higher transportation costs for getting students to centralized schools. Trade-offs between the two factors of economies of scale and increasing transportation costs determine optimal school size. When the density of student population is low, high transportation costs prevent the accumulation of large numbers of

students sufficient to justify an extensive and varied curriculum, including vocational training.[13]

Such problems particularly affect people in the lightly populated areas west of the "institutional fault" running from Texas to the Dakotas[14] but affect most rural areas to one degree or another. Problems are also encountered in attracting urban-trained professional people to rural areas. Perhaps "rural conservatism" has restricted the amount spent by local governments for services to their populations. Financial inability, however, is the most important factor. As compared with urban people, rural people have been concentrated in low-paying occupational groups and rural populations also contain greater proportions of people outside the labor force because of age. Add the final link, that 70% of all local government revenues still originate in the local community, and it becomes clear that the lower incomes and smaller tax bases of rural areas will usually be unable to support lower social-service investments per person, and lower quality services than urbanized areas.[15]

Thus in education one study carried out during the 1950's found lower expenditures per pupil, lower teacher salaries and smaller proportions of schools with kindergartens in rural, as compared with urban, school systems.[16] Other comparisons of state expenditures per pupil find lower spending levels in states characterized by a high degree of rurality.[17] Opportunities for youth to participate in

12. Harry K. Schwartzweller, "Regional Variations in the Educational Plans of Rural Youth: Norway, Germany and the United States," *Rural Sociology*, 35, 2 (Summer, 1973), pp. 140–156.

13. Fred White and Luther Tweeten, "Optimal School District Size Emphasizing Rural Areas," *American Journal of Agricultural Economics* 55, 1 (February, 1973), pp. 45–53.
14. John Muehlbar, "Problems that Persist in the Great Plains," *American Journal of Agricultural Economics* 51 (1969), pp. 1089–1096.
15. Thomas R. Ford, "Rural Community Institutions and Poverty, with Special Reference to Health and Education," in *Rural Poverty in the United States, op.cit.,* pp. 78–80; Thomas R. Ford, "Rural Poverty in the United States," in Task Force on Economic Growth and Opportunity, *Rural Poverty and Regional Progress in an Urban Society* (Washington: 1969), especially pp. 163–170.
16. U.S. Advisory Commission on Intergovernmental Relations, *Urban and Rural America: Policies for Future Growth* (Washington: 1968), p. 22.
17. U.S.D.A., Economic Research Service, *Rural People in the American Economy,* Agricultural Economic Report No. 101, 1966, p. 22.

vocational and technical programs are severely restricted in rural as compared with urban areas. High school enrollment in vocational education courses as a proportion of total course enrollment decreases as the size of community gets smaller.[18] Altogether, rural education and job training facilities are probably inferior to urban facilities, with the gap being widest in the preparation of students for industrial occupations.

Rural-urban differences occur also in the provision of health services. There is a rapid drop-off in the number of health personnel and the number of hospital beds per capita as one moves out of greater metropolitan areas into smaller cities and rural areas. Rural areas have as many general practitioners per 100,000 population, but the number of specialists is far less.[19] Rural doctors also tend to be older, less energetic and more isolated from new scientific advances. Given the smaller number of doctors available, their lower levels of competency, greater distances separating physician and patient, it is no wonder that the general quality of health care in many rural areas is totally inadequate, and that rural people are able to visit health facilities less frequently than urban people. However, where access is further restricted by severe transportation problems, by particularly low income, or racial discrimination, the problem has become critical.[20] In such areas of America, the opportunity to lead a healthy life simply does not exist.

Rural people suffer from the fact that advancement in the techniques of providing of services tends to favor urban populations. The large school, the great hospital, the group practice all require threshold populations which are difficult to reach in rural areas. To achieve the economies of scale and advantages from specialization of the big high school, rural school committees have to

bus-in children from a wide area so that the disadvantages of two hours each way on the school bus have to be balanced against the advantages of spatial concentration. What is clearly needed is a new technology of decentralization directed at overcoming the spatial disadvantages of rural societies. More efficient media communications can be substituted for the spatial movement of children or doctors. But the problem is that the direction of technological growth is determined by the needs of the established course of economic development. And this course favors urban over rural areas, and develops urban-serving technologies before rural technology. This is merely a different way of saying that the qualities of social reproduction systems are set by the needs of the economy: that economy determines priorities, which social technology then meets. The low quality of rural social reproduction schema is thus merely a reflection of the low priority put on investment in, and improvement of, the labor resources of rural areas.

Rural inequality is transmitted from one generation to the next by rural subculture and the environment of social services. But where does inequality come from in the first place and why does it persist (thus necessitating its reproduction)? These are far more crucial questions than the matter of social reproduction. Indeed the answer to the question of original and perpetuating causes of rural inequality provides a framework in which transmission mechanisms must be placed for their role to be understood. Hence, it is to this question—the economic origins of rural inequality—that we must now turn.

ECONOMIC ORIGINS OF RURAL INEQUALITY

We must look at the spatial structure of the economy to find the origins of spatial inequalities. When we examine the capitalist space-economy we find that "industrialization typically leads to a concentration of investments upon one or two areas, while much of the remaining national territory becomes

18. Earl H. Knebel, "Vocational and Technical Education at the Post High School Level for Rural Youth," in Burchinal, *Rural Youth in Crisis*, p. 81.
19. U.S.D.A., Economic Research Service, *Rurality, Poverty and Health*, Agricultural Economic Report No. 172, 1970.
20. Milton Roener, "Health Needs and Services of the Rural Poor," in *Rural Poverty in the United States*, pp. 311–332.

locationally obsolete. A dualistic structure is thus imprinted upon the space economy, comprising a "center" of rapid, intensive development and a "periphery" where the economy, imperfectly related to this center, is either stagnant or declining."[21] But as this "contradictory metropolitan centre-peripheral satellite relationship... runs through the entire world capitalist system in chain-like fashion from its uppermost metropolitan world centre, through each of the various national, regional, local, and enterprise centers,"[22] and as it has existed for at least the last five hundred years[23] a few skeptical scholars have begun to doubt the validity of the claim that underdevelopment in peripheral regions is due to their "imperfect" relationship to central regions. Our claim instead is that dualism perfectly reflects the nature of capitalist development, that capitalism automatically creates spatial inequality, indeed that the development of urban centers is based on underdeveloping the geographic peripheries.

Let us start with Marx's proposition that the accumulation of capital is the driving, motivating force of the capitalist system. Such is the power of this driving force that barriers to rapid accumulation are barriers that the system will burst apart, spatial forms which obstruct the accumulation process are forms which will be changed, and spatial patterns which facilitate accumulation are patterns which will be seized upon, improved and made typical. For surplus value to be realized, and capital accumulated, commodities must be moved from point of production to point of consumption. This process, called circulation, obviously has costs attached to it, which capitalists try to reduce, for these costs come, in part, out of surplus value, constitute a drain on surplus value and restrict capital accumulation. Long distance

marketing of commodities increases the turn-over time of capital (turn-over time being the time capital is used in production and circulation), and the longer the turnover time of a given capital, the smaller is its annual yield of surplus value. "The need to minimize circulation costs as well as turnover times promotes agglomeration of production within a few large urban centres which become, in effect, the workshops of capitalist production."[24] In these centers are concentrated people, the eventual market for commodities, and producers, who interchange semi-finished commodities. Their agglomeration reduces the distance between production and consumption, reduces the drain of surplus value caused by transport, and maximizes the rate of surplus value formation as capital may be turned over more rapidly.

What this means to the rural periphery is that industrial and service jobs congregate in the urban centers leaving the periphery to specialize on a narrow range of agricultural and resource-extraction functions; for example, in the contemporary United States, almost three out of four manufacturing jobs are located in the 193 largest labor markets formed by the giant metropolitan areas.[25] These metropoli have traditionally been concentrated in the northeastern states and in the West Coast, leaving large stretches of rural America with only the occasional presence of a large city to relieve their rurality. Despite the growth of metropolitan areas on the fringes of the American South and at certain points on the Great Plains and in the Mountain states, and despite the slightly more rapid growth of manufacturing employment in small as compared with large labor markets in the last decade, the prevailing pattern remains one of geographical concentration of alternative employment to agriculture and resource extraction in the rural periphery. For most rural Americans employment means agriculture, agriculture-related jobs, or nothing.

21. John Friedmann, *Regional Development Policy: A Case Study of Venezuela* (Cambridge, Mass.: 1966), p. 9.
22. Andre Gunder Frank, *Capitalism and Underdevelopment in Latin America* (Harmondsworth, England: 1971), p. 34.
23. Richard Peet, "Influences of the British Market on Agriculture and Related Economic Development in Europe before 1860," *Transactions*, Institute of British Geographers, July 1972, pp. 1–20.

24. David Harvey, "The Geography of Capitalist Accumulation: A Reconstruction of the Marxian Theory," *Antipode* 7, 2 (September 1975), p. 12.
25. Claude C. Haren, "Rural Industrial Growth in the 1960's," *American Journal of Agricultural Economics*, 52 (1970), p. 432.

What kinds of wages does agriculture pay? In the early part of this century agricultural wages were about one-half those in manufacturing; since then agricultural wages have fallen even further behind.[26] How can we account for this? In conventional economics wages are set by the interaction of the supply and demand for labor, and low wages result from an over-supply of labor. However, this tells us only the superficial mechanism which sets the level of wages. It tells us nothing about the forces which determine the extent and type of labor demand and the volume of labor supply. Marxist theory, by contrast, goes deeper, into population theory and the resultant supply of labor. For Marx "relative surplus-population is . . . the pivot upon which the law of demand and supply of labor works. It confines the field of action of this law within the limits absolutely convenient to the activity of exploitation and to the domination of capital." A reserve army of labor is maintained which "during the periods of stagnation and average prosperity, weighs down the active labor-army; during the periods of overproduction and paroxysm, it holds its pretension in check."[27]

A particularly large "agricultural reserve army" has been maintained—in two ways. First, the American agricultural labor force has always received a steady input of particularly cheap immigrant labor: examples are indentured servants from Britain, black slaves from Africa, Chinese sharecroppers, Chinese and Japanese farm workers, Hindustanis, Filipinos, three waves of Mexicans in the early twentieth century before large-scale immigration ceased, *bracero* labor from Mexico up to 1964, and smaller numbers of Puerto Ricans, French Canadians, West Indians, and Mexicans who are still brought in each year. These groups have frequently been played off against each other and against the indiginous American labor in a successful effort to keep agricultural wages down.

Second, agricultural mechanization has been particularly rapid since the late nineteenth century. For example, the number of man hours needed to raise 100 bushels of corn has dropped from 135 just before the First World War to less than seven now, while machinery and developments in planting and weed control have reduced the amount of labor needed to produce a bale of cotton from 270 man hours to less than 30. With mechanization, the number of farms has fallen from 6.5 million in 1920 to less than 3 million, the farm population from 32 million to 9 million, while the demand for hired agricultural labor has also fallen precipitously (from thirteen millions of workers in 1932 to four millions today).* Mechanization and the concentration of ownership into a few hands have thus ejected millions of farm families and farm workers into the already-swollen ranks of the agricultural reserve army; with a massive, increasing supply of labor and a decreasing demand controlled by a few owners of means of production, agricultural wages and small-farm incomes have been kept at a level which just allows rural labor to survive and reproduce.**

Further than this, attempts to increase agricultural wages and small-farm incomes through the formation of unions have been met by the use of ruthless and overwhelming

*When mechanization occurs, which class obtains the income produced by the machines? Under certain circumstances, a highly organized labor force may be able to control the conditions under which capitalists introduce machinery, obtain a shorter working week and higher wages, and thus a share in the productivity of the machines. But agricultural workers and small farmers' unions have been suppressed with a ferocity experienced in few other situations. As a result, as agriculture has become mechanized, the relative share of labor in the income produced has decreased dramatically (from 72% in 1949 to 33% in 1968) while the relative share of the owners of the means of production (land and machinery) has increased correspondingly. Hired workers suffered from stagnant wages while small farmers, in an attempt to compete with agribusiness, have been compelled to exploit the labor of their families and to accept very low wages themselves.[28] As usual, this has been a mechanical "revolution" which has greatly benefited agribusiness, but has done nothing for owners of mere labor power and small landowners.

28. T. P. Lianos and Q. Paris, "American Agriculture and the Prophecy of Increasing Misery," *American Journal of Agricultural Economics,* November 1972, pp. 570–577.

**The agricultural reserve army is replenished also by high birth rates in rural areas, a consequence not of a desire for large families, but of the inadequacy of health services, lack of birth control information, and absence of agencies distributing birth control devices.

26. U.S. Department of Commerce, *Historical Statistics of the United States* (Washington: 1960), p. 95.
27. Karl Marx, *Capital* (New York: 1967), I, p. 639.

capitalist force. For example, more than one hundred rural blacks who had formed a union were killed in the Elaine Massacre. Strikes organized by the Southern Tenant Farmers Union in eastern Arkansas in the 1930's were put down with the connivance and help of local officials—with the aid of postal employees, the planters conducted mail-opening campaigns to discover which tenants were union members. A strike by the Mississippi Freedom Labor Union in 1965 was met by evictions of workers from their homes and eventual collapse of the strike. The long and violent struggle by Cesar Chavez to form the United Farm Workers will be well known to most readers.

## DEFECTS IN THE MOBILITY PROCESS

There is yet another element to be added to the explanation of rural income inequality. In contrast to urban areas, where the mechanization or decline of one industry is to some extent compensated for by increasing labor demands elsewhere in the city economy, the mechanization of agriculture has released farm labor into an economic vacuum. Many rural regions do not even have a well-developed structure of towns and cities which might provide alternative jobs. Hence the only outlet has been interregional rural-to-urban migration, a much more difficult mobility process than moving from one job to another within a city.

It has been suggested that it is the unwillingness of farmers and farm workers to move out of agriculture and out of their home regions that leads to the piling up of a low-income rural non-farm population. They thus create the conditions for their own poverty. What a strange piece of ideology this is! For the truth is that farmers and hired agriculture workers *do* respond to economic inducements to move out of farming.[29] The problem is that when farm workers leave agriculture their

incomes hardly rise at all; in fact in the period 1957–1960 more than 40% of those leaving farming in each year had *lower* incomes in their non-farm occupations the following year.[30] Out-of-farming movers are concentrated in the traditional working class (craftsmen and foremen, operatives, laborers and farm laborers), especially in the South and West.[31] When the unemployment rate in the economy is higher than 5%, the low number of job openings in bluecollar occupations is a major factor limiting migration.[32]* As Fuller[33] puts it "the 'push' forces compounded out of labor-diminishing farm technology together with willingness of farm people to adjust—have not been matched by 'pull' forces in the non-farm economy for the capabilities that ex-farm people have to offer, or have the abilities to offer effectively," for farm people have found that urban needs for their skills have been reduced by the industrial equivalent of the very same mechanization process which pushes them from the land.

Who does get out of farming successfully? Who does make the transition to city life? Hathaway and Perkins'[34] analysis of Social Security data for the period 1957 to 1963 shows that 14.2% of those employed in farming in one year had left farming by the next year, an extremely high proportion; 12.4% had moved into farming from other occupations in that year. Young people had the highest out-of-farming mobility rates; blacks had higher mobility rates than non-blacks; those who derived income from non-farm jobs as well as farm wage work had higher mobility rates than those employed only in

29. L. E. Galloway, "Geographic Flows of Hired Agricultural Labor: 1957–1960," *American Journal of Agricultural Economics*, 50 (1969), pp. 199–212.

30. Dale Hathaway and Brian Perkins, "Occupational Mobility and Migration from Agriculture," in *Rural Poverty in the United States*, p. 203.
31. Larry Sjaastad, "Occupational Structure and Migration Patterns," in Iowa State University, Center for Agricultural and Economic Adjustment, *Labor Mobility and Population in Agriculture* (Ames, Iowa: 1961), pp. 20–26.
32. C. E. Bishop, "Dimensions of the Farm Labor Problem," in C. E. Bishop, ed., *Farm Labor in the United States* (New York: 1967), pp. 12–13.
*The latent reserve of urban labor formed by rural people is called into the active labor army by changes in unemployment rates.
33. Varden Fuller, *Rural Worker Adjustment to Urban Life: An Assessment of the Research*, Policy Papers in Human Resources and Industrial Relations No. 15 (Ann Arbor: 1970), p. 40.
34. Hathaway and Perkins, *op.cit.*, pp. 186–191.

farming; and those people living within 50 miles of large cities had slightly higher rates of movement out of farming than those living more than 50 miles away from a large city. Out-of-farming mobility rates were *not* higher in low-income as compared with high-income rural areas. In addition, economic recession slowed out-of-farming mobility more in low-income rural areas, and for blacks, than in high income areas, and for whites. The data indicate that the very poorest farmers (incomes under $3,500) move out of agriculture quite slowly—mobility rates out of farming (10.3% a year) being almost matched by mobility rates into farming (9.9% a year). In conjunction with the data on mobility by age of farmer, the low income mobility rates indicate that unless poor farm people leave while young, and most employable, they become more or less trapped in agriculture by the lack of jobs elsewhere. Death and retirement, rather than occupational mobility, are the main agents of occupational removal for the aging farm poor.

The poverty problem in isolated rural regions is aggravated by low out-migration rates for those who *do* manage to leave farming. Of those occupationally mobile out of farming, Hathaway and Perkins found that only about one-third left the county in which they had been farm-employed. Migration rates were higher for blacks, who also moved further than whites; migration rates were higher for young people than for old; lower-income people moved at slightly higher rates but over shorter distances than higher-income people; and those located within 50 miles of large city moved out of county more than those living farther from a large city. The occupationally mobile are thus not particularly spatially mobile. Many of those who are ejected from farming find little to attract them away from the county in which they farmed. They therefore remain, becoming a part of the swelling rural non-farm labor reserve, among whom subsistence poverty is almost as prevalent as in the farm population. Population decline still occurs in rural poverty areas but it is the result of out-migration on the part of farmers' and ex-farmers' children rather than

the older part of the population. Hathaway and Perkins conclude that the mobility process works least well for those who need it the most. It widens gaps between blacks and whites, between high- and low-income farm people, and between high- and low-income areas. It contributes to the intensification of spatial inequalities.

## URBAN DEPENDENCY IN RURAL AMERICA

Capital is most efficiently accumulated in a centralized space economy, creating dualistic spatial structures composed of urban-industrial center and rural-agricultural periphery in the capitalist countries in general, and the United States in particular. The spatial division of labor inherent in dualism leads to conditions of a mass of jobs of different types in cities, but "monoconomy"—that is only one type of job—in the periphery. In this monoconomy, the maintenance of an enormous agricultural reserve army, through immigration, high birth rates, and mechanization, ensures that wages will be low and incomes small compared with urban areas. With the use of this labor, the rural periphery supplies cheap food and raw materials to cities in support of further surplus-value formation there. In fact, the flow of food is also a flow of surplus value extracted from rural labor, some of which value is "liberated" by the rural elite, some by urban middle men, and some eventually by the urban bourgeoisie. Accumulation in the geographic center is thus partly supported by the rural-urban flow of surplus value; or as Frank puts it:

the metropolis expropriates economic surplus from its satellites and appropriates it for its own economic development. The satellites remain underdeveloped for lack of access to their own surplus and as a consequence of the same polarization and exploitative contradictions which the metropolis introduces and maintains in the satellite's domestic economic structure. The combination of these contradictions, once firmly implanted, reinforces the process of development in the increasingly dominant metropolis and underdevelopment in the ever more dependent satellites until they are resolved through the abandonment of capitalism by one or both interdependent parts.[35]

Poverty in the periphery thus becomes functional to urban capitalist development: indeed rural underdevelopment becomes one of the very bases of urban development. Dependency is embedded into rural economic and social structures and into rural culture. Dependency and inequality are transmitted through rural culture and social institutions and come to be a way of life, one disturbed only occasionally by flashes of anti-urban consciousness.

## REGIONAL PLANNING

With this as background, we would expect that regional planning aimed at rural economic development would be approached in a half-hearted way, with an eye more on appeasement than real change. But American regional planning exceeds even our worst expectations! Let us admit that regional planning could do little to counteract the most fundamental causes of rural underdevelopment, for this would mean revolutionary change in the entire social and economic structure of the country which is beyond either the scope or purpose of intracapitalist planning. But even at the level of apparent causes, rural antipoverty planning efforts have been meager and misdirected.

It is obvious even from superficial analysis that antipoverty planning of all kinds should be directed at improving the social and economic environments surrounding low-income people. Given that unemployment rates are usually at least twice as high in the United States as in other economically-advanced countries, one would further think that particular emphasis would be placed on job creation programs—bringing the jobs to those that need them. But the basic assumptions behind American antipoverty "planning" stem from

35. Frank, *op.cit.*, p. 33.

what can only be described as blind faith in the culture of poverty hypothesis—it is the poor themselves that have to be changed so they may fit into environments of opportunity which already exist. Hence the planning emphasis on that panacea for every social problem—"education"—together with manpower training, child care, rural-urban mobility projects, employment outreach centers and similar programs designed to smooth the relationship between the poor and jobs which are presumed to already exist. Only a small proportion of total antipoverty funds has gone into increasing the supply of jobs in areas where the poor can reach them—in the central cities and in growth centers in the rural peripheries. And even these funds are not directly invested in new employment opportunities. Thus, in the rural areas a series of giant planning agencies started in the middle 1960's—Economic Development Administration, Appalachian Regional Commission, and several small regional commissions—invested in roads, industrial parks, sewers, health centers, manpower training; they also offered loans to industrialists willing to locate in depressed or otherwise poor areas; but they relied on private entrepreneurs to make the actual decisions to build the plants and operate the businesses. "Regional development planning" thus ended up as one more way of using public money to enhance the profit-making potential of private industry. To put it more bluntly, regional development planning essentially consisted of a system of bribes offered to private industrialists in an effort to get them to make location decisions "in the public interest."

What did the rural unemployed get out of this? Rural areas offer two main attractions to industry: natural resources and cheap labor. Many of the jobs which planning agencies claim they have brought in are economic activities which in fact wished to exploit raw materials or cheap labor and which treated planning inducements merely as a way of making higher profits. Keith Dix of the People's Appalachian Research Collective analyzed the new jobs "created" in West

Virginia and central Appalachia during the first five years of the Appalachian Regional Commission, and found that the number of new jobs was only a fraction of the number needed, that a large proportion of the jobs were located on the fringes rather than in the mountain heartland where the need was greatest, that much of the new investment was still in coal and the extractive industries (reinforcing a pattern of domestic imperialism that has characterized Appalachia for decades), and that many of the other jobs were in apparel, textiles and other low-wage industries.[36] In other words, the rural unemployed got a few thousand low-wage secondary labor-market jobs out of a decade or more of antipoverty regional planning. The main beneficiaries of this "planning" were the resource and land corporations, fly-by-night industries, construction companies and those academic mercenaries who will go anywhere, study anything, and come to the right conclusion for the right price.

## PRINCIPLES FOR AN ALTERNATIVE PLANNING

Rural inequality cannot and will not be planned away when that inequality is so highly functional to capitalism. Those of us, radicals and liberals, who are interested in rural problems must combine to expose the deep origins of rural inequality. We need theories of rural underdevelopment and domestic imperialism specified to the American condition. This body of theory is essential to back up our demands for fundamental change. But we should also operate at the pragamatic level, criticizing existing "programs" and suggesting alternatives which while not contradicting the aim of long-term fundamental change have some chance of being adopted and of improving the situation in rural areas. These short-term policy alternatives should contain the seeds of our pro-

36. Keith Dix, "Appalachia: Third World Phillage," *Antipode* 5, 1 (1973), pp. 25–30. For a competent but conventional analysis of rural regional development see Niles Hansen, *Rural Poverty and the Urban Crisis* (Bloomington, Ind.: 1970).

posals for long-term change. With this as introduction, I would like to propose five social and political principles on which a new type of regional antipoverty planning might be based.

*1. Ownership of the means of production.* The rural poor have suffered more than any other group from the system of private ownership of natural resources and the means of rural production. Private entrepreneurship for black sharecroppers, migrant farmworkers, and Appalachian miners has meant low wages, minimal or nonexistent labor rights, and precarious working conditions. Private ownership perpetuates the extremes of the rural class structure, for it produces great incomes for a few, and extremely low incomes for the rural masses. In addition rural America has suffered from absentee ownership of resources, from domination by, and dependence on, urban economic decision makers. Hence planning for a more socially just future must be based on *local, collective worker-ownership of the means of production.*

*2. The nature of economic development.* Federal, and especially state, development agencies planning the economic growth of rural areas frequently act on the philosophy that any economic activity is better than none. This results in active governmental encouragement for low-wage, temporary, nonunionized industries to locate in the small cities of rural areas. This belief in any kind of "growth" should be abandoned. Only those economic activities which can support labor at a comfortable standard of living should be considered as components of regional economic development planning. The capital necessary for starting and, in some cases, permanently subsidizing rural production must come from taxes on the majority urban population and especially taxes on corporations profiting from the direct use of natural resources. Hence, the second principle is that the *economic activities planned for rural areas must be nonexploitative and, at least initially, subsidized by urban and corporate taxes.*

*3. Regional culture and social networks.*

Mass migration out of rural regions and the assimilation of rural migrants in cities leads to the disappearance of regional cultures and to cultural homogenization. Interregional migration also breaks long-established and fundamentally significant rural and small town social networks. With the social objective of maintaining cultural pluralism, future economic activity should be distributed in such a way as to remove the need for long distance rural-to-urban migration. This means a system of decentralized industry in which some of the economies of scale and external and urbanization economies are sacrificed to maintain cultural heterogenity, ways of life which otherwise would be lost, and social systems which would otherwise be fragmented. The third principle is therefore *economic decentralization for the purpose of preserving rural-regional culture*.

*4. The nature of socio-economic planning.* In the past, development planning has either been based on specific development projects, has been restricted to economic planning alone, or dealt only with specific areas, or types of areas, within regions. Such planning deals only with one, or a few, components in an interrelated social and economic system. Yet change in one part of the system, even when planned, sets off changes in other parts of the system. The assumption seems to be that change elsewhere in the system will take care of itself though the normal adaptation of "free decision-making" by individuals. The problem is that to make free adaptive decisions one needs money resources, and for low-income populations these resources do not exist. Rural poor people have suffered from changes elsewhere in the socio-economic system to which they cannot adapt, not because they do not want to adapt, but because they have not had the resources necessary for successful adaptation. Piecemeal planning must therefore be abandoned in favor of *comprehensive, dynamic social and economic planning*.

*5. Decision-making in the planning process.* In traditional development planning, policy decisions are made by a trained centralized bureaucracy, backed by the academic mercenaries of the universities and research institutes. If local people are consulted, it tends to be members of the local elite who are flown to Washington and even they legitimize, rather than participate in, the decisions that are made. Effecting planning is, of course, a highly complex, technical operation for which specialized training is needed. But the great policy decisions involve the consideration of a number of alternatives, each of which has arguments for and against; there is rarely a single optimal solution. The local people who are affected should decide between policy alternatives, partly for reason of participatory democracy, but also for the pragmatic reason that with their vast storehouses of experiential knowledge they can see which alternative best fits the local situation. The fifth principle is *control of the formation and implementation of planning policy by the people affected by that policy*.

Comprehensive, regional social and economic development plans should be drawn up via people's planning groups, with the guarantee that government will accept the resulting plans without significantly altering them. These plans should, of course, deal with the essential questions of the future of rural regions—the direction of economic development, ownership of rural resources, the extent and type of urbanization, ways of providing essential social services, the survival of the regional way of life, etc. But the single, most important objective of rural development planning must be to change the relationship between low-income people and the means of producing income. This entails both changing the social organization (mode) of production, to allow a more equal distribution of the income flowing from rural economic activity, and increasing and diversifying production in poor rural areas to raise and stabilize the volume of income available.

## RURAL COOPERATIVES

One proposal which fills these objectives is a system of cooperatives started with federal financial and technical aid. The system would be composed of farm, rural-urban, and urban production cooperatives. In cooperative economic activity all members participate in policy-making and all share in the proceeds from the sale of output according to some prearranged formula (such as hours of labor performed, equal shares for all members or, ideally, family need). The advantages of cooperatives are that the workers are able to collectively control the conditions under which their labor is performed, there is no special class of people which owns the means of production, surplus value is retained and shared and income equalized. Cooperatives can be formed from existing groups of people who share a common set of experiences and can be used to maintain regional subcultures. They can be fitted into the existing pattern of social networks rather than disrupting these networks. At the same time, cooperative production generates income and reduces poverty.

Cooperatives have a long history in rural America.[37] They have usually been more successful among large and middle-sized farmers, than among small producers, but this should come as no surprise in an era of monopoly capitalism. However, one million low-income people were in cooperatives established by populist groups in the South in the late nineteenth and early twentieth centuries. During the New Deal, the Farm Security Administration was responsible for the formation of 25,000 poor people's cooperatives, with federal money being used to purchase plantations (which were turned over to small farmers), lease land, purchase machinery and develop facilities. This movement died after World War II when opposition developed from the conservative agricultural establishment, including the Department of Agriculture. A new black rural cooperative movement grew out of civil rights organizing in the South during the 1960's, and especially from the activities of a black priest, Father A. J. McKnight in rural Louisiana. These are predominantly black, low-income farmers'

37. Ray Marshall and L. Godwin, *Cooperatives and Rural Poverty in the South* (Baltimore: 1971).

cooperatives, along with some consumers', credit union, handicraft and small industry, and fishing co-ops. Financial aid has come from the Farmers Home Administration, the Office of Economic Opportunity, Economic Development Administration, and private foundations. There is a Federation of Southern Cooperatives which represents most of the co-ops formed so far. An embryonic cooperative movement already exists therefore, while the principle of federal aid to cooperatives has already been established. A program of cooperative development has some chance of being adopted by a left-liberal government.

The optimal arrangement would be a regional association of cooperatives in which, for example, food and raw materials produced on cooperative farms would be processed in small-town co-ops and passed on for further manufacture in larger regional cities, with products being returned down the chain of co-ops. Surplus products would be exchanged with other regional cooperative associations through the medium of a cooperative federation. Low-income people would thus become equal members of an alternative, cooperative economy which would provide the essentials of food, shelter and free social services to its members. Although cash incomes would probably remain somewhat lower than for other sectors, cooperative control over the conditions of one's own life would partially compensate for a lack of money. Socialization of control over the means of production removes the psychological need for large money incomes.

## CONCLUSION: THE NEED FOR ACTION

The problems of rural America come from the operation of the capitalist system as a whole. These problems cannot be solved without destroying the originating causes and conditioning factors of the rural poverty cycle. Regardless of politics, anyone who has seriously analyzed the condition of rural America is forced by knowledge and experience into a radical critique: that is a critique aimed at root causes in the American social and economic system. It is imperative that we develop a set of theories which offer a deeper and more penetrating analysis than the theories which now echo through the state agricultural schools and the regional planning offices. But in addition we should criticize programs and policies which we know are doomed to failure from the start and which we suspect may be designed to do nothing but create the illusion of improvement. We should put forward policy and planning alternatives which embody radical social and political principles. With more powerful explanatory theories, and with an attractive set of alternative planning models, we can take on the corporate-state-academic establishment which presently feeds conservative explanations and ideas to rural America. For, as resource and food prices increase, yet rural inequality remains, the contradictions inherent in American economic development will become more obvious. This will promote a condition of "conflict consciousness"[38] as rural workers come to realize their common exploitation by an increasingly corporatized, rural ownership structure. The potential exists for a new rural radicalism and it is up to us to help crystallize this potential into political action.

38. I am following the terminology developed in Anthony Giddens, *The Class Structure of the Advanced Societies* (London: 1973), pp. 114–117.

# The Current Demographic Context of National Growth and Development

PETER A. MORRISON

## POPULATION DECLINE IN METROPOLITAN AREAS

Most Americans now live in metropolitan areas but avoid their central cities. This longstanding urbanization trend—toward the metropolis but away from its core—was evident during the 1960s when the central cities' share of the steadily increasing metropolitan population fell from 50 to 46 percent. Rising incomes and extensive highway building within and to metropolitan areas permitted more and more people to move out to the suburbs and indulge their taste for detached single-family homes with yards. As a result, an unprecedented number of the nation's central cities not only ceased to grow but lost population during the 1960s.

The trend away from the urban core is behaving somewhat differently in the 1970s. Entire metropolitan areas, not merely their central cities, are registering absolute population declines. Only one of the nation's 25 largest Standard Metropolitan Statistical Areas (SMSAs) decreased in population during the 1960s. By 1974, fully 10 of the largest 25 had joined the list of metropolitan areas without growth.[1] Overall, one-seventh of the nation's 265 SMSAs are now losing population, and one of every three Americans in a metropolitan area resides in a declining one.

1. These 10 SMSAs are: New York, N.Y.-N.J.; Chicago, Ill.; Los Angeles-Long Beach, Calif.; Philadelphia, Pa.-N.J.; Detroit, Mich.; St. Louis, Mo.-Ill.; Pittsburgh, Pa.; Cleveland, Ohio; Seattle-Everett, Wash.; and Cincinnati, Ohio-Ky.-Ind.

The accompanying map shows that the declining areas tend to be those located in the Middle Atlantic and East North Central states.

These new developments must be interpreted carefully, for the declining SMSA conceals considerable diversity. Within its broad statistical aggregate, the growth of many municipalities continues and may even have accelerated. But the general areawide pattern foreshadows an increasing incidence of a common need to adapt to decline, or at least to a halt in growth. The effectiveness of that adaptation will hinge partly on how clearly the necessary political choices are recognized and made.

What the new statistics are registering is a rising incidence of zero or negative population change in metropolitan territory outside central cities. This does not mean that suburban communities are uniformly losing population, but that the longstanding trend of out-migration from central cities now applies also to the suburbs immediately surrounding the city limits.

There are two noteworthy points about this migration. First, *as birth rates have subsided, the previously obscured effect of migratory departures has become apparent in many places.* During the 1960s, nearly 4 of every 10 SMSAs recorded net out-migration, but in virtually all cases this outflow was fully offset by natural increase (the excess of births over deaths). Accordingly, these areas registered population increases even while migrants

From The Rand Corporation Publications, P-5514, September 1975, pp. 3–13. Reprinted by permission.

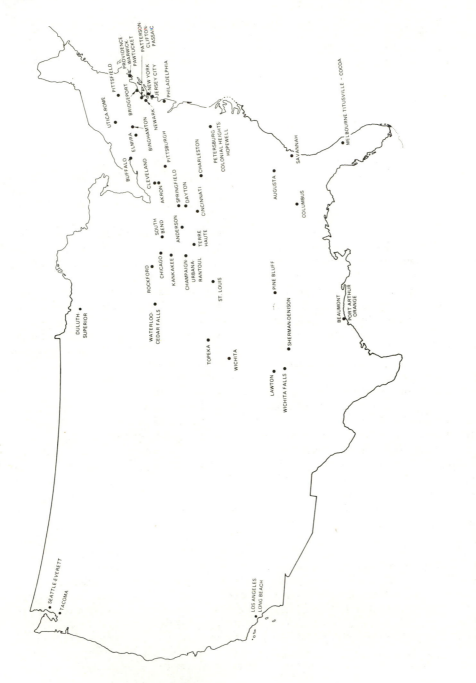

Figure 1. Standard Metropolitan Statistical Areas with Declining Population since 1970.

were leaving. That configuration of demographic forces now has changed, bringing growth to an abrupt halt in many such areas.[2]

Exacerbating this arithmetic effect is a second development: *the acceleration of migratory loss in many of the SMSAs whose magnetism for migrants was initially weak or negative.* Metropolitan areas that are losing migrants appear to be diverging from those that are gaining, even as the rate of natural increase in all areas has subsided. That divergence foreshadows sharply different futures for the two groups.

For suburban municipalities, the prospect of growthless metropolitan populations poses new kinds of problems, already beginning to be felt at the local level. Fundamentally, the *shift* from growth to decline necessitates adaptation; yet school districts, municipalities, and other legal entities are institutionally ill equipped to reduce services and expenditures in an orderly way.

In the past, planners have had no cases for study of U.S. metropolitan areas that combine local zero population growth with economic well-being, and hence have had no basis for anticipating what pathologies or opportunities might accompany them.[3] We can only speculate about possible changes in fiscal conditions or service needs and the policy responses they will engender. Several broad features can be anticipated:

(1) *They will contain proportionally fewer young children than do metropolitan areas with positive growth.* This development will result not from lower fertility (which makes for an across-the-board reduction of the young) but from age-selective out-migration, which carries away disproportionate numbers of young adults and their young children. (Nearly one-third of all migrants are in their

20s—the peak childbearing ages—and an additional 23 percent are children 4 to 14 years old.) This will bring relief to formerly overcrowded schools; it will also demand difficult administrative decisions: whether to reduce teaching staff or increase teacher-pupil ratios, whether to close some schools for economy or keep them open for convenience to the community, whether to submit to contraction or seek new ways to use school facilities and faculties.

(2) *The local economy and occupational structure will evolve more by substitution and less by new additions.* This will put a damper on the construction sector and industries closely tied to it. Flows of occupational mobility may grow sluggish for blue-collar workers and others who customarily limit their search for employment to the local labor market.

(3) *Competition for older housing stock will lessen, affording the average family more space.* This development may stabilize some neighborhoods by increasing owner-occupancy rates; it may destabilize others by threatening housing abandonment.

(4) *Local governments will face a period of necessary fiscal adjustment, marked by problems and also possibilities.* One source of pressure for adjustment is a possible disjunction between revenues acquired and services to be provided. Whether or not a disjunction develops, and the magnitude of its effect, will depend largely upon the way in which negative growth is manifested—who is leaving, what types of industries are most vulnerable to the effects of population loss, and the impact on the commercial sector. The experiences of declining central cities suggest the "budget squeeze" that results. The central city, however, can be a narrow and restrictive model when applied to declining suburbs, where the population's socioeconomic composition may not change adversely. Indeed, some of these places may be on the way to a situation of prosperous stability or decline—if they can capitalize on the potential advantages of not growing.

The halt in population growth, then, will alter local demands for public services. It *may*

2. The Buffalo, N.Y. SMSA, for example, experienced a net outflow of 84,000 migrants (about 6 percent of its entire population) during the 1960s. Still, metropolitan Buffalo increased by 42,000 residents because births exceeded deaths by 126,000. Between 1970 and 1973, net out-migration has removed 16,500 Buffalonians but natural increase has added only 20,700, leaving Buffalo with a net increase of only 4,200.
3. See William Alonso, "Urban Zero Population Growth," *Daedalus*, Vol. 102, No. 4 (Fall 1973), pp. 191–206; Edgar Rust, *No Growth. Impacts on Metropolitan Areas.* (Lexington, Mass.: Lexington Books, 1975).

affect the jurisdictions' fiscal capacity to provide them, depending on how the local population's socioeconomic composition changes. In any case, choices will have to be made among such alternatives as:

(1) Postponing or canceling previously planned increases in service levels;

(2) Reorganizing service programs through integration or centralization of services, or changing fiscal jurisdictions;

(3) Increasing service efficiencies through productivity gains, reductions in the rate of pay, or other efficiency measures whereby essentially similar service levels are maintained but at reduced budgets;

(4) Reducing services provided through personnel cutbacks or transfers of programs to other levels of government or to the private sector.

These choices will be welcomed by some and opposed by others, depending largely on where they happen to reside.

Different kinds of responses will be devised and tried out in various places. Their comparative effectiveness and ease of implementation under differing local circumstances will come to be known only gradually. Consequently, there is a risk that, in place after place, local policy response to vanishing growth will be haphazard and will be formulated in ignorance of lessons already learned the hard way elsewhere.

Beyond these immediate pressures, the demography of urban population decline imposes other more enduring changes. Persistent and severe out-migration is invariably selective, and gradually alters the composition and structure of the local population. Specifically, such out-migration produces an increasingly disadvantaged population whose needs mount as the municipality's capacity to meet them erodes. Problems of dependency and poverty—not inherent problems *of* the affected municipality—come increasingly to be located *in* it.[4]

Declining population, a phenomenon of the central cities during the 1960s, shows signs of becoming a metropolitan-wide concern in the 1970s. Some of the reasons for this concern are the same: the need to adapt the urban fiscal system to zero or negative change in property values and tax revenues; to provide several types of local public services for which the per capita demand typically rises with changing mix in population; and to manage the problem of excess housing, schools, and other capital stock. Other reasons, however, are new: the recognition that, with some planned adaptations, decline may offer opportunities.

## REVIVAL OF NONMETROPOLITAN GROWTH

A trend even more remarkable than the cessation of population growth in many SMSAs is the revival of growth in nonmetropolitan areas, even those that lie outside the influence of metropolitan centers. For the first time in this century, the nonmetropolitan population growth rate exceeds the metropolitan, and migrants are flowing from city to country. The nation's nonmetropolitan counties (current definition), which registered a net out-migration of 300,000 per year during the 1960s, are now *gaining* about 350,000 migrants per year.[5]

Some notion of how dramatic these changes are can be gained from Table 1, which compares the directions of population change in the decade of the 1960s with those between 1970 and 1974, the latest date for which data are currently available. It can be seen that annual rates of population growth have fallen disproportionately in metropolitan counties as compared with nonmetropolitan. During the 1960s the metropolitan rate led by a considerable margin (1.6 versus 0.4 percent); between 1970 and 1974, however, it lagged (0.8 versus 1.3 percent).

This reversal of a long-standing urbaniza-

4. These problems are now evident in most older cities; in some they are quite advanced. For a case study of the demography of urban population decline, see Peter A. Morrison, "Urban Growth and Decline: San Jose and St. Louis in the 1960s." *Science*, Vol. 185, August 30, 1974, pp. 757–762.

5. Calvin L. Beale, *The Revival of Population Growth in Nonmetropolitan America*, ERS-605, Economic Development Division, Economic Research Service, U.S. Department of Agriculture, June 1975.

Table 1. Components of Population Change for Groups of Metropolitan and Nonmetropolitan Counties, 1960–1970 and 1970–1974

| Population Category | 1974 Population (000's) | Annual Population Growth Rate | | Annual Natural Increase Rate | | Annual Net Migration Rate | |
|---|---|---|---|---|---|---|---|
| | | 1960–1970 | 1970–1974 | 1960–1970 | 1970–1974 | 1960–1970 | 1970–1974 |
| United States | 211,390 | 1.3 | 0.9 | 1.1 | 0.7 | 0.2 | 0.2 |
| Inside SMSAs (Metropolitan) | 154,934 | 1.6 | 0.8 | 1.2 | 0.7 | 0.5 | 0.1 |
| Outside SMSAs (Nonmetropolitan) | 56,457 | 0.4 | 1.3 | 0.9 | 0.6 | −0.6 | 0.7 |
| *In counties from which:* | | | | | | | |
| ≥ 20% commute to SMSAs | 4,372 | 0.9 | 2.0 | 0.8 | 0.5 | 0.1 | 1.5 |
| 10%–19% commute to SMSAs | 9,912 | 0.7 | 1.4 | 0.8 | 0.5 | −0.1 | 0.8 |
| 3%–9% commute to SMSAs | 14,263 | 0.5 | 1.3 | 0.9 | 0.6 | −0.4 | 0.7 |
| <3% commute to SMSAs | 27,909 | 0.2 | 1.1 | 0.9 | 0.6 | −0.8 | 0.5 |
| *Entirely rural counties* [a] | | | | | | | |
| not adjacent to an SMSA | 4,618 | −0.4 | 1.4 | 0.8 | 0.4 | −1.2 | 1.0 |

Sources: Richard L. Forstall, Population Divison, U.S. Bureau of the Census, unpublished statistics; and Calvin L. Beale. "A Further Look at Nonmetropolitan Population Growth Since 1970," review draft, August 1976.

*Note:* SMSAs as currently defined.

[a] "Entirely rural" means the counties contain no town of 2500 or more inhabitants.

tion trend is so utterly without precedent that a common first reaction to these latest figures is sheer disbelief. They must be, it is said, a statistical artifact of large metropolises spilling over into their surrounding territory—not everything labeled "nonmetropolitan" is necessarily free from metropolitan influence.

But, in fact, the growth in nonmetropolitan areas is not simply the latest manifestation of urban sprawl—it affects areas well removed from metropolitan influence. Data shown in the lower half of Table 1,* enable us to examine separately several different types of counties within the broad "nonmetropolitan" classification, including:

(1) The nation's 171 nonmetropolitan counties (containing about 4.4 million residents) from which 20 percent or more of the work force commute to jobs in metropolitan areas. These include places like Frederick County, Maryland (northwest of Wash-

*The original Table 1 has been replaced here by a more recent table, which includes rates of natural increase and net migration, prepared by the author of this essay for the Regional Science Association Meetings, Toronto, Nov. 1976.—Eds.

ington, D.C.); Sussex and Hunterdon Counties, New Jersey (adjacent to the New York-Newark metropolitan complex); and Yamhill County, Oregon (between metropolitan Portland and Salem).

(2) The 315 nonmetropolitan counties (containing another 9.9 million residents) with 10 to 19 percent of the work force commuting to metropolitan jobs—for example, Hunt County, Texas (east of metropolitan Dallas); Douglas and Leavenworth Counties, Kansas (west of metropolitan Kansas City); Cape May County at the southern tip of New Jersey; and the mid-Hudson Counties of Orange and Ulster in New York.

(3) Finally, the larger number of counties in the next two categories (in which the remaining 42.3 million nonmetropolitan Americans reside) from which only minimal commuting occurs—less than 10 percent. These counties include most of the nation's open country. They represent such diverse circumstances as are found in the Great Plains, the deep South, north-central Pennsylvania, northern New Hampshire and all of Vermont, and Cape

Cod. They permit few if any sweeping generalizations, except to say that by definition they are remote from the arena of daily metropolitan activities.

Notice the dramatic change in the growth pattern of those counties with the *least* commuting. Comparing their pre- and post-1970 population growth rates, we see that these areas have picked up considerable momentum. The post-1970 rate of increase was nearly as high as the rate for those counties with more commuting. The category "Entirely rural, nonadjacent" affords a slightly different perspective: these are counties which, in addition to being distant from any metropolitan area, have no town of even 2500 inhabitants. In sharp contrast to their absolute population loss during the 1960s, these counties show a dramatic reversal since 1970.

Analysis of this change reveals that in the first third of the 1970s, net out-migration has undergone a reverse—most dramatically in those counties with the *least* commuting to metropolitan areas and in those classified rural nonadjacent. That component of change, in those two categories of counties, carries the clearest message: the more remote kinds of places—those that as a group used to be regarded as "nowhere"—have today become "somewhere" in the minds of many migrants.

A distillation of recent studies of the economic changes under way in nonmetropolitan America suggests some of the reasons for the new growth there:[6] decentralization of employment, easier access to open space for recreation or residence, and the spread of

retirement settlements beyond the traditional areas of Florida and the Southwest. All in all, these factors probably generate growth in different ways in different parts of the nation. In some nonmetropolitan areas, growth may be due mainly to the retention of native residents who no longer feel compelled by economic pressures to migrate—to be pushed away; in other areas, growth may be due to urbanites from outside who are drawn there for a variety of reasons—being pulled to those areas.

The revival of growth in nonmetropolitan areas carries important implications for the future. It also may pose difficult problems of which we have already had some taste.

1. *Many small nonmetropolitan governmental jurisdictions will experience growth of varying intensity and rapidity which they are ill equipped to cope with and which their residents may vigorously oppose.* With increasing numbers of amenity-seekers and with newly awakened economic interest in an area's natural resource endowment, issues of access—by whom, to what place, and for what purpose—are likely to intensify. Evidence of this is already apparent in the widely publicized resistance of many communities (such as Petaluma, California) to accepting the costs and benefits that an influx of migrants confers. Traditionally, migratory growth has been beyond local control, but attempts to regulate it have raised two questions: How far does a community's right to control its own growth extend? In attempting to control its growth, does a community infringe on the freedom of individual citizens to migrate?

2. *Regionalism centered on newly valuable energy resources is likely to intensify.* In the near future, Colorado, Montana, New Mexico, North Dakota, Utah, and Wyoming will become significant sources of coal, synthetic petroleum liquids, and natural gas. Typically, these newly found energy supply areas are sparsely populated and lack the legal and institutional structures for coping with the impact of major energy-producing activities. Local recognition that these areas enjoy an especially advantageous endowment of

6. I have drawn here primarily on Beale, op. cit., as well as the following other studies: Niles M. Hansen, *The Future of Nonmetropolitan America: Studies in the Reversal of Rural and Small Town Population Decline* (Lexington, Mass.: D. C. Heath, 1973); Richard F. Lamb, "Patterns of Change in Nonmetropolitan America, 1950–1970," draft manuscript, n.d.; Fred K. Hines et al., *Social and Economic Characteristics of the Population in Metropolitan and Nonmetropolitan Counties, 1970,* Agricultural Economic Report No. 272, Economic Research Service, U.S. Department of Agriculture, March 1975; *The Economic and Social Conditions of Nonmetropolitan America in the 1970's,* Committee Print prepared by the Economic Research Service, U.S. Department of Agriculture, for the Committee on Agriculture and Forestry, U.S. Senate, May 30, 1975.

highly valued resources has already fostered regional awareness and focuses attention on issues of access. The prospect of sharp population increases, and their attendant demands for public services, is likely to intensify such issues. Currently, the most noticeable aspects of uncontrolled growth through migration are evident in the boom areas spawned by the Alaska pipeline construction.

3. *The scale of nonmetropolitan settlement will assume increasing importance.* In future years, talent will be offered increasingly in "joint supply"—an educated husband *and* an educated wife will both seek suitable employment. Areas remote from a metropolitan labor market and lacking sufficient urban scale may find it more and more difficult to recruit doctors, lawyers, and other professionals. However, some important options may promote the long-term viability of smaller settlements in remote areas. For example, promising new technologies will enable radical innovations in the delivery of services—in many cases, through telecommunication and computer-processing of information.[7]

## THE USES OF A REPORT ON NATIONAL GROWTH AND DEVELOPMENT

The forces feeding national growth and development are as potent and ineluctable as deep ocean currents and, like them, require of the navigator an abiding respect and an instinct for change of pace and direction. We have learned, at some cost, to respect the extent to which growth and hence population movement are channeled by a host of nominally unrelated policies concerned with highway building, defense expenditures, taxation, and the like. "National growth and development" really means directing these "hidden" forces to advance conscious objectives.

7. For example, audio and video satellite communications are being used experimentally for health care and education in remote areas. See Albert Feiner, "Health Care and Education: On the Threshold of Space," *Science*, Vol. 186, No. 4170, December 27, 1974, pp. 1178–1186.

# Urbanization, the Squatter, and Development in the Third World

ALAN B. MOUNTJOY

The developing countries, who form what is termed the Third World, are now passing through an "urban revolution" that is beginning to call into question the generally accepted belief, based upon Western experience, that urbanization brings modernization. In the Third World the city is still the main point of contact with the modern world and it is in the cities that socio-economic changes and innovations first appear, but the character of many of these cities may now be changing.

An analysis of this urban growth in the developing world shows first that the process is gathering speed, second that a major part of its city growth is due to migration and third, that migration to the towns is selective: it is the larger towns, often the capital cities, that show the greatest attractive forces, and this is leading to a growing imbalance in the urban structures. We find, for example, in the case of the recently decolonised African states that often only the capital city (which may also be the chief port) can offer the infrastructure and services that European-type manufacturing industry and commercial undertakings require, and can supply the amenities and activities that would be attractive to European expatriates. Thus modernisation does not spread its effects throughout the urban fields and migrants are drawn in particularly to the major centres.

The United Nations Demographic Yearbook now includes lists of towns of over 100,000 inhabitants. Between 1960 and 1970

the number of such cities in the developing world increased from 249 to 837, a 336 per cent increase. This indication of the high rate of urbanization in the developing countries is reinforced if the data on cities with over a million habitants is extracted (Mountjoy, 1968). These cities are fewer and more prominent, and there is likely to be greater accuracy in numbers than with the smaller towns. The most recent "million city" data has been graphed beside that for 1920 and 1950 (Fig. 1). It will be seen that since 1950 the number of such cities has increased from 80 to 151. Among the many features apparent from the diagram one is especially noteworthy: that the mean latitude of the world's "million cities" has moved nearer the equator with each decade. In the zone from the equator to the 35th parallels there were in the early 1950s, 31 "million cities" with a total population of 83 millions; by 1970 in this zone there were 68 "million cities" holding a total population of 167 millions. Particularly it is notable that 51 of these 68 low latitude "million cities" are in the developing countries. Berry in a recent book points out that during the last 50 years the world's urban population has increased by four times, but closer examination shows that the developed world's urban population grew by two-and-three quarter times, that of the developing world by six-and-three quarter times. (Berry, 1973).

Normally one would regard an increase in urban population as a natural concomitant of

From *Tijdschrift voor Economische en Sociale Geografie*, vol. 67, no. 3, 1976, pp. 130–37. Reprinted by permission.

Population
x  1 to 3 million
●  3 to 5 million
■  Over 5 million

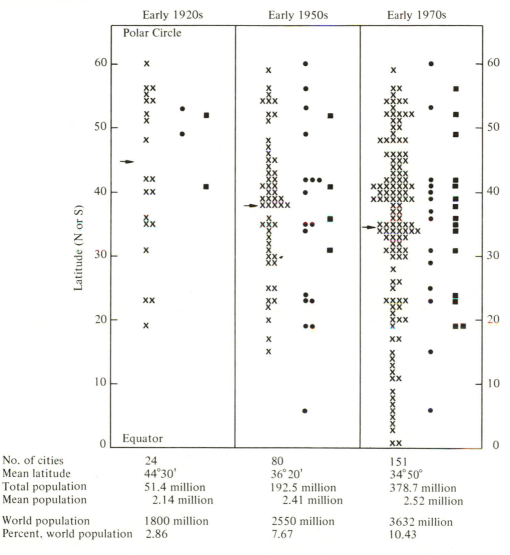

| | Early 1920s | Early 1950s | Early 1970s |
|---|---|---|---|

| | No. of cities | Mean latitude | Total population | Mean population |
|---|---|---|---|---|

| | Early 1920s | Early 1950s | Early 1970s |
|---|---|---|---|
| No. of cities | 24 | 80 | 151 |
| Mean latitude | 44°30' | 36°20' | 34°50° |
| Total population | 51.4 million | 192.5 million | 378.7 million |
| Mean population | 2.14 million | 2.41 million | 2.52 million |
| World population | 1800 million | 2550 million | 3632 million |
| Percent, world population | 2.86 | 7.67 | 10.43 |

Figure 1. Million Cities, 1920-70.

economic growth, but in the present situation this is rarely so and the astonishing and ac-celerating pace of the movement to the towns is now creating problems of crisis proportions in the developing world. The figures shown in Table 1 indicate that a very large part of the current rapid urban growth is due to in-migration, and sustain the view that since the end of the Second World War the trickle of people leaving the countryside and moving

Table 1. Migrants as a Percentage of Population Increases

| City | Period | Total pop. increase (thousands) | Migrants as a percentage of total pop. incr. |
|------|--------|---------|---------|
| Abidjan | 1955–63 | 129 | 76 |
| Bogota | 1956–66 | 930 | 33 |
| Bombay | 1951–61 | 1207 | 52 |
| Caracas | 1960–66 | 1088 | 52 |
| Djakarta | 1961–68 | 1528 | 59 |
| Istanbul | 1960–65 | 428 | 65 |
| Lagos | 1952–62 | 393 | 75 |
| Nairobi | 1961–69 | 162 | 50 |
| São Paulo | 1960–67 | 2543 | 68 |
| Seoul | 1955–65 | 1697 | 63 |
| Taipai | 1960–67 | 326 | 43 |

Source: World Bank Operations, *Background data on Urbanization Annex. 1*, (Baltimore, 1972).

into towns has become a flood. Numerous examples may be cited to demonstrate the enormous pace of city expansion. In the decade 1962–72, Kinshasa quadrupled its population (from 400,000 to 1.6 million) to become Tropical Africa's first "million" city; Lagos grew two and a half times and Rangoon doubled its population. Not every large Third World city is expanding at such speed, nevertheless the rate of urban growth, generally in the less developed countries at over 6 per cent per annum and accelerating, is far greater than the rate of natural increase of the population. Indeed, many of the rates of urban growth now being recorded in the cities of the developing world (e.g., the population of São Paulo increasing at more than 350,000 a year) would prove greater than our own advanced economies could deal with.

Almost universally development plans in the Third World have favoured industry and its infrastructure rather than agriculture, and this has favoured the largest towns. In them industrial and commercial enterprises, banking and insurance established their headquarters and foreigners with their higher standards of living have taken residence as well. These largest towns also are frequently the seats of administration and judiciary. The outward signs of development, from prestigious build-ings to modern shops, schools, health clinics, hospitals appear first in the main towns and are part of the magnetic pull they exert on the countryside. The rural areas are little affected by the modernization and opportunities for advancement are poor. Subsistence agriculture prevails over much of the developing world and agrarian overpopulation often leads to the farming of unsuitable land, to exhaustion of soil and possibly to erosion and general land degradation. The incidence of drought and pests all contribute to make farming a hazardous way of life. It is against a background of chronic rural poverty, of a stagnating countryside, that the economic and social attractions of the towns may appear so alluring.

The gap between the real income of the peasantry and of the town workers noticeably widens. In 1968 the average Zambian small farmer was less than half as well off as the urban worker with whom he had been equal in 1964. In Uganda in 1966 the cash and kind income of the average farmer was £60 per annum, whereas the average unskilled urban worker earned £125 per annum. Annual incomes per urban worker are generally two to three times those of the agricultural worker: here is the core of the "pull" the towns exert on country folk. The drift from the land of the younger and more active people has been inevitable.

A typical result of this is demonstrated in Fig. 2 where the graphs show the shortage of men—especially of the active ages—in Rhodesian Tribal Trust lands and their disproportion in the urban area. The diagram suggests that the countryside is losing its most active workers—the more ambitious and usually the better educated—and that agriculture is becoming left in the hands of less capable people. The movement to the towns also imposes a heavy burden of dependents upon the smaller numbers remaining in the countryside. The tragedy is that the floods of migrants pouring into the towns and cities of the Third World greatly exceed the amount of employment that is available, for here unlike in Western Europe, urbanization is preceding industrialization and far outpacing it. The

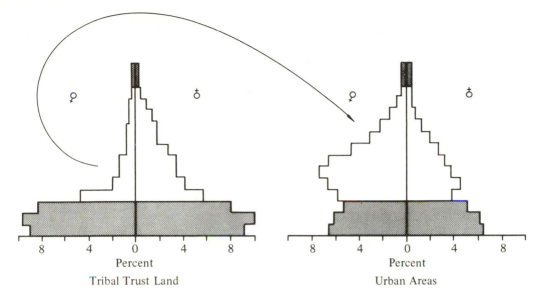

Figure 2. African Population, 1969. Age and Sex Distribution in Rhodesian Tribal Trust Areas and Urban Areas (from J. Hanks, "The population explosion in Rhodesia," *Rhodesian Sci. News*, vol. 7, 1973, p. 253).

result is the exchange of underemployment in the village for unemployment in the towns.

The impact of the vast and accelerating numbers of in-migrants is changing the character of Third World cities. These changes may be studied under a number of heads: political, social, and economic, as well as from an urban morphological point of view. Here it is proposed to examine in some detail the character and geographical implications of the growing squatter settlements (spontaneous settlements as they are coming to be called) which now have attached themselves to all the major towns of the Third World and have come to be regarded as the direct expression of the great movements in from the countryside. They have become distinctive elements with their own physical, social and economic characteristics. Local names for the urban squatter colonies have become accepted: the *favelas* of the main Brazilian cities, the *ranchos* of Venezuela, the *barriadas* of Peru, the *bustees* of India, *gourbivilles* of Tunisia and *bidonvilles* of Algeria and Morocco.

So far only a few geographers have directed their attention to the study of shanty-towns, the squatter settlements in the Third World, and one must augment their work with the more plentiful studies by anthropologists and sociologists (e.g., Abu-Lughod, 1961). There is general agreement on the definition of squatter settlements: that they are makeshift dwellings that are erected without official or planning permission and on land to which the squatters hold no title. Dwellings are constructed of any available materials, flattened petrol tins, packing cases, cardboard cartons, straw mats, sacking. There are no norms or minimum standards, the construction is largely uncontrolled, the sites lack all the expected services of an urban environment—water supplies, lighting, sewerage.

Squatters settle on any vacant plots within the cities, in places even parks have been taken, but the majority of sites necessarily are peripheral: some on hillsides, as at Lima and Rio de Janeiro; on the desert edge as at Khartoum and Omdurman; or amid marshy and malarial valleys as around Bahia; or even on or over rivers, canals and lagoons, as in Saigon and Bangkok. Numerous cases are cited, especially in Latin America, of highly organised operations whereby large numbers of squatters seize a plot of ground and hastily erect shanties in the course of one night, so that the authorities are presented with a *fait accompli* the following morning (Mangin, 1967).

Thus the cell-like accretions to the city proper increase in size and present problems to the administration that are becoming insoluble. Immigration into Rio de Janeiro of the

order of 5000 people a week is the kind of pattern that has to be grappled with by the largest of the Third World cities. Squatters now make up almost 40 per cent of the population of Caracas, 30 per cent of the population of Djakarta, now over 40 per cent of the population of Lima and 25 per cent of the population of Casablanca (Table 2). In the majority of the cities of the Third World it is probable that the squatter element already accounts for at least 30 per cent of their populations.

When we examine the origins of the squat-

Table 2. Extent of Slums and Uncontrolled Settlement in Various Cities in Developing Countries

| Country | City | Year | Uncontrolled settlement | |
| | | | Total (000s) | % city pop. |
|---|---|---|---|---|
| Senegal | Dakar | 1969 | 150 | 30 |
| Tanzania | Dar es Salaam | 1967 | 98 | 36 |
| Zambia | Lusaka | 1967 | 53 | 27 |
| Afghanistan | Kabul | 1968 | 100 | 21 |
| Ceylon | Colombo | 1963 | 30.5* | 44 |
| India | Calcutta | 1961 | 2220 | 33 |
| Indonesia | Djakarta | 1961 | 725 | 25 |
| Iraq | Baghdad | 1965 | 500 | 29 |
| Malaysia | Kuala Lumpur | 1961 | 100 | 25 |
| Pakistan | Karachi | 1964 | 752 | 33 |
| Philippines | Manila | 1968 | 1100 | 35 |
| Rep. of Korea | Seoul | 1970 | 137* | 30 |
| Turkey | Ankara | 1970 | 750 | 60 |
| | Izmur | 1970 | 416 | 65 |
| Brazil | Rio de Janeiro | 1961 | 900 | 27 |
| | Recife | 1961 | 396 | 50 |
| | Brasilia | 1962 | 60 | 41 |
| Chile | Santiago | 1964 | 546 | 25 |
| Colombia | Cali | 1964 | 243 | 30 |
| | Buenaventura | 1964 | 88 | 80 |
| Ecuador | Guayaquil | 1968 | 360 | 49 |
| Mexico | Mexico City | 1966 | 1500 | 46 |
| Peru | Arequipa | 1961 | 54 | 40 |
| | Luna | 1969 | 1000 | 36 |
| Venezuela | Barquisimento | 1963 | 12.5* | 41 |
| | Caracas | 1964 | 556 | 35 |
| | Maracaibo | 1966 | 280 | 50 |

Source: U.N. General Assembly, *Housing, Building and Planning problems and Priorities in Human Settlements*. Annex III, p. 55, 1970.
*Dwelling units.

ters some interesting and significant variations appear. Authorities who have studied squatter settlements in Latin America and the Caribbean make it clear that the shanty-towns are not settling basins for the new arrivals from the country. New arrivals go directly into the city, if only to be close to employment opportunities; therefore, it is the tenement slums that act as settling basins for new migrants and it is from these slums that they later move out as squatters to create illegal settlements. Thus such squatters may have considerable experience of urban conditions before becoming shanty dwellers, many have jobs and move out—perhaps when starting a family—to save paying rent, to escape the squalor and overcrowding of the slums, and to start building their own homes (Mangin, 1967; Clarke, 1974; Eyre, 1972). Once the settlements are firmly established and a reasonable security of tenure can be assumed, such squatters begin investing their money and labour in improving their houses and in communal services. These, indeed, are rightly termed "improving" spontaneous settlements, or settlements of hope: they are not dens of crime, vice and disease but contain enterprising, well organized, responsible citizens who by community self-help have accomplished striking improvements in their conditions, once given understanding and a minimum of aid from the municipal authorities.

Squatter settlements in Africa, broadly, are in a different category. The migrant from the country generally moves directly into a squatter settlement, often to join others of his family or tribe; sometimes this is because the poorest and slum areas of the city are already overcrowded (Harrison, 1967). Density of population in African shanty towns is often extremely high, poverty is more acute, social disorganisation in terms of crime and delinquency, vagrancy and prostitution would seem to be more marked than in the Latin America counterparts where these evidences of social disorganization are to be found more in the inner-city slum areas.

Neither are the southeast Asian examples of the "improving" type that seem more typical of Latin America (Dwyer, 1972). While some rural migrants go directly into the cities, the growing congestion is forcing increasing numbers into peripheral squatter settlements (Jackson, 1974). Here the acute poverty, as in India, and the lower proportion of families as opposed to single young males, as in Africa, contribute to a more passive hopelessness. In many of the Indian *bustees* accommodation is rented out by the earlier squatters or absentee landlords, a situation imposing additional burdens and not typical of Africa and Latin America. The large Chinese squatter colonies, offshoots of the overcrowded Chinatowns in southeast Asia, show some of the densest spontaneous settlements and they are characterised by the emergence of a multiplicity of workshop industries (Jackson, 1974). McGee in his study of the southeast Asian city holds the view that new migrants to the city move into the squatter settlements (McGee, 1967).

The largest shanty towns provide some local employment. Many families make an income by running bars and shops in their homes and many domestic industries emerge, including re-use industries such as collecting and sorting old bottles for re-use, making sandals from old motor tyres, collecting and sorting rags and garments for resale, in addition to the running of pavement workshops for repairs, metalwork and carpentry.

The squatter settlement problem arises because of the poverty of the rural in-migrants, because of their huge and growing numbers, and because of the inability of municipalities to find the money and means of expanding housing, urban services and utilities at a sufficient pace to cope with them.

Earlier, insufficient resources were devoted to housing expansion, the return on investment in housing being low. About 1960 the United Nations set targets related to a standard of 10 houses for every 1000 inhabitants for housing in the developing countries. Up to 1965 only 2 new dwellings per 1000 inhabitants had been built in many developing countries, yet residential construction was absorbing *ca* 20 per cent of their total capital investment, and to these high costs should be added those for services and utilities. Now the scale of the housing problem has grown beyond the scope of any available means so long as traditional forms of building and the enforcement of minimum standards continue.

Unhygienic and squalid conditions in squatter settlements are sometimes overstressed (many Latin American *favelas* are superior to the inner city slums) but examples such as the three water standpipes at Duala (Cameroons) to supply 50,000 squatters are numerous. At Duala the squatters also dig shallow wells for water and these become contaminated by percolation from the open latrines (Edimo, 1975). Thus with such rudimentary sanitation there is the constant danger of epidemics, such as typhoid infectious diseases and smallpox epidemics which have occurred in the *bidonvilles* of Tripoli since the war (Harrison, 1967). The prevalence of delinquency, and the harbouring of criminals are among the reasons cited by authorities in favour of anti-squatter policies. Authorities have also become increasingly conscious of the political danger of having poverty-stricken and deprived masses around their major towns, suspecting that they are fertile ground for revolutionary propaganda. The threat to orderly and controlled physical development of these cities by indiscriminate squatting is becoming reality as these squatter settlements increase in size and power and resist removal. The fact that very often squatters have voting rights brings the democratic process to their support and enables them to restrict vigorous policies against them. Rarely have policies of eviction proved successful, instead disturbance and riots have occurred and a settlement that is bulldozed rapidly springs up somewhere else.

It is not surprising that a re-thinking and a re-shaping of policies towards Third World shanty settlements is now taking place. The improvements in shanty dwellings made by individuals and community self-help works, establishing roads, installing electric lights and so on, where municipalities have eventually condoned the illegal squatting and have encouraged such improvements, indicate advantages that the award of legal ownership might bring. The planning and building codes, often based upon European and American examples and designed to improve modern housing standards, and already flouted by the squatters, need to be relaxed in furthering and supporting self-help housing projects. Squatters prefer to live in large unfinished shacks rather than in small finished houses; they can improve and complete their houses as their fortunes improve. For them, hopefully, housing is "a vehicle of social change." As Turner expresses it, referring to the *barriadas* of Lima: "They build even in the barriades for their children, and hope and expect their children will attain a higher social status. They are less worried about what they will build than where they will build it, and less concerned with initial standards than with initial lay-out. Squatter houses will improve with time, especially if given secure title to the plot" (Turner, 1970).

These more liberal views, expressed in Latin America, arise from and give emphasis to the critical situation that is fast approaching most cities in the Third World: they are on the brink of crisis. Firstly, what has to be accepted is that the fact that squatter shanty towns are no longer temporary phenomena; they are a permanent and a growing part of Third World cities and now are beginning to contain second generation squatters. Consequently, we must recognise that they are changing the character of Third World cities. Most of those cities have developed from the European model and are of colonial foundation or adaptations of precolonial settlements. It is the fabric and sinews of such cities that are now over-stretched and breaking down. The shantytowns are growing and spreading as indigenous growths and soon will contain the majority of the population of many of the larger developing-world cities. The growth rates of squatter settlements in many developing countries is now in excess of 12 per cent per annum—more than twice that of city growth as a whole. It has been calculated on present conditions that by 1990 75 per cent of

Lima's then six million inhabitants will be squatters. We must recognise that squatting provides the only method by which rapid urban growth with low income families can be accomplished. Thus it becomes clear that in a variety of ways city growth in the developing world is not repeating the pattern of growth exhibited by the European cities: growth is faster, it is unplanned and uncontrolled; it is uncharacteristic in its frugal simplicity, being devoid of services and utilities accepted as the attributes of urbanism.

The second situation that must be accepted is that in Africa and in southeast Asia (and perhaps to a lesser degree in parts of Latin America) we are no longer seeing the urbanization of rural migrants but rather the growing ruralisation of the towns. The expanding shanty-towns are becoming re-creations of the village, with narrow streets and alleys not designed for motor traffic, but rather a meeting place, a playground, an area for animals to be tethered or to scavenge. For the majority of rural migrants a change of dwelling does not urbanise them. Tribal and family ties do not become severed by the move to the city, for there they tend to coagulate into family and tribal groupings and they are becoming less and less assimilated into the fully urban way of life. Instead, they foster a replica of the customs and culture they have grown up with, in the village, and ties with the home area remain. In the Shambat shanty-town at Khartoum North the 20,000 squatters were organised into tribal and village groups, headmen being elected to act as spokesmen in dealings with the municipal authorities. As Breese expresses it, they may be *in* the city, but they are not *of* the city (Breese, 1966). Recent comparative studies of urban and rural conditions in the Indian sub-continent show that in social, demographic and economic aspects there are more similarities than differences between conditions in cities and the countryside, and that it would be wrong to view such urbanization as the catalyst for modernization (Qadeer, 1975).

The third feature now becoming apparent arises from the second, and that is the effects upon the urban way of life of this increasing ruralisation. Toennies has reminded us that in the history of all great cultural systems two periods are discernible: in the first, the basic unit is the family or kin-group where traditional authority defines roles and responses. In the second, the individual is supreme: social and economic relationships are based on contractual obligations, among individuals roles become more specialised and competitive (Toennies, 1955).

This concept explains the fundamental contrast between the countryside and the town. The town represents a concentration of population of diverse elements. It facilitates a great volume of human interactions which become impersonal and temporary. The individual's position in society reflects the skills he acquires through the wages he commands in a competitive market place. Thus characteristics of urban life are a closely settled mixed society, impersonal relationships, tolerance to change and innovation. These are the very qualities urgently needed for the acceptance and promulgation of modernisation and planned measures of economic development. It is these characteristics that are now threatened by the ruralisation of towns; and if they succumb it may well reduce the pace of economic and social betterment in the less developed countries.

The large towns are major points of contact with the outside world. They provide the centres of modernisation in the economies of less developed countries: they are the growth poles for both economic and social patterns; they are centres for change and the acceptance of the new: new occupations, new social and economic values, new patterns of organisations and responsibilities. The speedy transformation of poor traditional economies throughout the Third World relies upon the towns as instruments of change and development: but this function is already impeded and may be reduced if the nature of these towns continues to change. Thus it seems that while the urban crisis now facing the Third World has many facets, the vital question that is now posed to us all—and which is likely to be answered by the end of the decade—is whether the large Third World cities will succumb to creeping paralysis or whether they can continue to be agents of social and economic transformation.

# REFERENCES

Abu-Lughod, J. (1961), Migrant Adjustment to City Life: the Egyptian Case. *American Journal of Sociology* 67, pp. 22–32.

Berry, B.J.L. (1973), The Human Consequences of Urbanization. London.

Breese, G. (1966), Urbanization in newly developing Countries. London.

Clarke, C. G. (1974), Urbanization in the Caribbean, *Geography* 59, pp. 223–232.

Dwyer, D. J. (1972), The City as a Centre of Change in Asia. Hong Kong.

Edimo, S. N. (1975), A Shanty-Town Area and the Health of the Children. *Env. in Africa* 1, pp. 81–90.

Eyre, L. A. (1972), The Shanty-Towns of Montego Bay, Jamaica. *Geographical Review* 62, pp. 394–413.

Harrison, R. S. (1967), Migrants in the City of Tripoli. *Geographical Review* 57, pp. 397–423.

Jackson, J. C. (1974), Urban Squatters in southeast Asia, *Geography* 59, pp. 24–30.

McGee, T. J. (1967), The Southeast Asian city. London.

Mangin, W. (1967), Squatter Settlements. *Scientific American* 217, pp. 21–29.

Mountjoy, A. B. (1968), Million cities: Urbanization in the Developing Countries. *Geography* 53, pp. 365–374.

Qadeer, M. A. (1975), Do Cities 'modernize' Developing Countries? *Ekistics* 39, pp. 229–235.

Toennies, E. (1955), Community and Association. London.

Turner, J. C. (1970), *In:* W. Mengin, Peasants in Cities. Boston.

**7**

# POLICY: ALTERNATIVE SETTLEMENT STRATEGIES AND PLANNING EXPERIENCE

# Introduction

Intervention into the operation of such complex urban systems as described in previous sections of this book is not an easy task. Over the last thirty years almost every nation has tried in some fashion to alter the process and outcomes of urbanization (see Cameron and Wingo, 1973; Friedmann, 1971; Berry, 1973; Hansen, 1974; Friedly, 1975; Swain, 1975; Swain and MacKinnon, 1975). Although most have focused on the size distribution, differential rates of growth, or income levels of its cities, the range of issues is immense. Every nation sees its urban problems and potential solutions differently. Yet there is at least an underlying consensus, even if some governments are only satisfying public whims, that greater public intervention in the evolution of national settlement patterns is both necessary and appropriate.

As the papers reprinted in this section suggest, the methods and results of these interventions are by no means clear-cut. At the one extreme Khodzhaev and Khorev present a calm, almost detached discussion of how readily a formal reordering of Soviet urbanization into what they call a "unified settlement pattern" can be carried out. According to their interpretation of Marx, a unified settlement pattern eliminates the rural-urban dichotomy and the exploitation of the former by the latter. At the other extreme, Blumenfeld points out the relatively low priorities that such strategies have with most governments of any persuasion, and in his opinion, will continue to have. Berry's paper takes a middle ground. He describes the manifold complexities of planning at this level and notes the substantial progress in different countries and different social systems toward implementation of strategies for urban development at the national level. All of these papers attest to the importance of setting any discussion of national urban strategies in their appropriate political context.

The universal tendency in this literature has been, consciously or unconsciously, to narrow the area of discussion to the role of direct rather than indirect policies. By direct policies we mean those that are intentionally urban or regional in name and purpose. Consequently, the literature is dominated by debates on "decentralization policies," "new towns," "growth centers" (or "poles") and other locationally specific regional planning techniques. Only recently (see especially the

490

comprehensive review by Brookfield [1975] entitled *Interdependent Development*) has there been a concern with the full range of government activities—taxes, tariffs, transportation, for example—and their combined implications for urban and regional development. The totality of these government actions Morrison calls an "implicit" urban policy. If the full efforts of governments could be mobilized to achieve a particular settlement pattern or redistribution of income, the scope of national urban policy would be broadened enormously. Let us examine this wider perspective first, and then return to a discussion of the alternatives for direct intervention in national urban development.

## IMPLICIT NATIONAL URBAN POLICIES

Virtually every action, or calculated inaction, on the part of a national government alters the urban system in some fashion. A new defense policy, for example, changes the distribution of military bases and requires the development of new weapons systems that benefit the economies of certain localities. A new tax structure alters the relative income levels of poor areas and rich areas. So too does a shift in emphasis from one given policy area to another. The decision to shift money from urban or welfare-related problems to environmental problems, for instance, may benefit California while harming New York City.

To the extent that the space economy is specialized spatially and incomes vary from place to place, and given that social problems are as diverse as those of the poor in Harlem or the elderly in St. Petersburg, the political system is inherently spatially redistributive. Money taken from a pocket in one locality ends up in a pocket somewhere else. Politicians know this: they represent different locations, and the specialized nature of their district converts them into spokesmen for particular interest groups.

Briefly, what we mean by a hidden or "implicit" urban policy is that one result of these varied actions of government, in total, is to design unintentionally an urban system and a national pattern of settlement. Alonso (1971) has argued this point convincingly. In one area or country that design might encourage a highly centralized system, dominated by the capital city or by one or two regions. In another country the result might be a decentralized pattern of development. In any case, few governments have made these effects explicit. Few have asked themselves, What effects are our current policies and practices likely to have on the pattern of urbanization? Where are we leading the urban system? (Not all of their actions, however, are unintended or even implicit—witness the attitude of the U.S. government to the plight of its larger cities.) Our point is that the sum of the current range of policies and practices is unintended. A sufficient rationale for encouraging further efforts at national urban strategies would be simply to ask governments to make these effects explicit. Changes in policy would surely result.

## THE POSSIBILITIES FOR GOVERNMENT INTERVENTION

As the role of government increases, the impact of public policy on urban systems increases as well, as Berry suggests in his paper. In some societies the opportunity exists, as Rodwin (1970) and Strong (1971) have shown, if sufficiently high priority is given, to ordain any one of a wide variety of possible urban systems. Almost any spatial geometry, any distribution of city sizes, and any degree of urban specialization appears possible, at least in the longer term.

Two real constraints exist on the degree of policy intervention however. The efforts of policy are restricted first by the pre-existing urban system. As has been pointed out frequently in earlier sections, the effects of economic agglomeration and the importance of accessibility to markets—effects which are embedded in the present distribution of cities and intercity contacts—can be very powerful constraints. The second set of forces, also largely beyond policy influence, are those unpredictable external events constituting the "turbulent" environment we discussed in Section I. For small nations, a change in the foreign policy, in commodity markets, or in the trading strategy of a neighbor may seriously affect the urban system. For larger nations currency fluctuations, oil cartels, wars or the threat of war, social change, or a shift in political power or preferences may contradict policies aimed directly at the urban system.

We can contrast, then, three different components of change in urban systems: 1) an essentially *random urban system,* which is sensitive to these external events; 2) the more *predictable urban system* in which the growth of that system at time $t + 1$ follows inexorably from the state of that system at $t$; and 3) *the controlled urban system* in which the will of the government (however defined) largely determines the structure and behavior of cities.

The relative importance of these aspects of urban system change is not well known. We suspect that rapidly growing systems are less bound by the past and that growth dependent on foreign capital or international migration is less predictable, and perhaps less controllable, than growth deriving from sources internal to a country. The key to control, as Rodwin (1970) has noted, is the will to intervene, particularly the will of governments to pursue goals related to the urban system itself and to spatial equality, rather than to use the urban system as an intermediate step for achieving other goals such as national defense, or increased productivity, or short-term economic stability (U.S. National Goals Staff, 1970).

Perhaps the most useful analytical tool at this stage of policy development is a model or models that would permit us to simulate the response of the urban system to alternative governmental policies. What happens in Burbank or Gary if the U.S. Federal Reserve Bank increases interest rates? Our model would likely suggest that the effects of existing federal policies on the urban system, in most Western countries at least, are not cumulative and in fact are often contradictory. Effects are complicated further by the various activities of state, regional, and municipal governments. At any rate, such a model would help us to identify and understand the interconnections of the urban system, including the extent to which cities or regions are able to control their own destiny and the complexity of factors that link them to other elements in the system.

Although we do not have such a model at our disposal, we can nonetheless utilize the urban-system concept as a framework against which to compare and to evaluate national urbanization strategies (see Goddard, 1974; Bourne, 1975). Figure 1 outlines one possible framework. Five components are represented in this framework:

(1) the framework of *concepts, values,* and *ideas,* which circumscribe plausible alternative strategies for setting urban-growth policies, including the goals to which those policies are directed;

(2) the *input variables,* both internal and external to the system under study, which policies must treat, exploit, and shape to achieve such goals;

(3) the typical "black box," in the center of the illustration, denoting the *interrelationships* between the policies applied and the processes by and through which the urban system is evolving;

(4) the range of *outputs,* or *side effects,* both anticipated and unanticipated, which are attributable to the application of urban policies; and

(5) the available *mechanisms* by which such output results in feedback on subsequent decisions in the specification of goals and for defining treatments of the variables themselves.

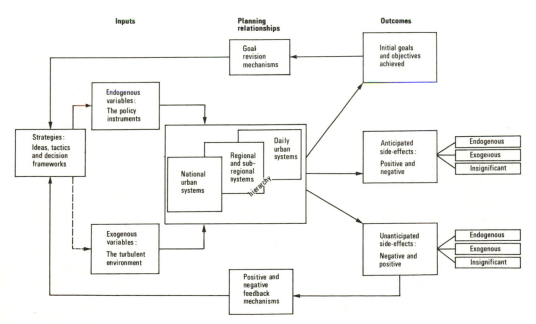

Figure 1. A Schematic Design for Urban-System Strategies.

Two aspects of this illustration necessitate elaboration. The first point is the recognition it gives to the importance of events (variables) deriving from sources (or territorial units) external to the political process under study. The second point relates to the problem that decisions on regulating urban growth will have varying impacts at different spatial and hierarchical levels of the settlement system. This is in fact the purpose of the specific design of the central box in Figure 1. The box illustrates the hierarchical levels of urban spatial organization specified initially in the Introduction to this volume. But how does the political decision-making process correspond to this or any other hierarchy? How do decisions at one level affect growth at other levels? Is it appropriate to think in terms of a hierarchy of national urban strategies with each level of policy goals and instruments tailored to the spatial expression of urban problems and social inequalities?

## THE FORMS OF DIRECT INTERVENTION

The treatment by most Western governments of regional and urban inequalities is analogous to their traditional treatment of the poverty problem in general. Direct, locally visible forms of aid are clearly preferred to more profound changes in the economic system and in the social organization—changes that might lead to a basic redistribution of income and opportunities. It is usually easier, for example, to pay welfare rather than to guarantee jobs or to alter the income differentials among occupations and social classes. It is easier to subsidize highways and industries than to alter the relative prices of cotton and automobiles or, more generally, to reallocate the national income on a spatial or on any other basis.

The range of direct policies for national urban systems are demonstrated in the articles below. Since every nation takes a different approach, given its social and political climate and its particular institutional forms, only selected examples of this range could be included here.[1] The policy options vary in terms of purpose, instruments used, focus (population or economic structure, for instance), spatial form, and level of refinement. Few nations, it seems, have an ideal construct of what their national urban systems should look like to guide the identification of goals and the implementation of policy.

Among the options we could examine here (with relevant examples) are: 1) regional systems of urban hierarchies (i.e., the Soviet Union); 2) new towns and the containment of metropolitan growth (Britain); 3) infrastructure equalization (West Germany); 4) growth poles and "alternative" metropolises (France); 5) the uniform city-size distribution (Sweden) and 6) the "laissez-faire" option of maximum social choice (Canada, U.S., and Australia). Given space limitations our review is highly selective.

---

1. Materials in this section have been largely adapted from Bourne (1975). For comparative reviews of urban-policy experience at the national level the interested reader is also referred to Hansen (1974), Goddard (1974), Friedly (1975), Swain (1975), and Swain and Logan (1975).

Among these alternatives new towns are probably the most widely advocated solution to urban problems. All new town programs have a variety of planning objectives—social (the provision of new housing) and economic (jobs), as well as health (slum clearance), environmental (conservation), and design (comprehensive planning)—but with increasing emphasis on broad social considerations (Wirz, 1975). These are all valid objectives. But in terms of a national urban-system perspective they are basically a cosmetic solution, aiming at a more orderly intra-regional landscape without altering the basic outlines of the urban system.

In this section two papers review the objectives of new town programs from contrasting perspectives. Schaffer summarizes the evolution and rationale of the British new town movement, perhaps the most widely quoted and extensive new town program undertaken anywhere. Its impact on the British landscape has been profound (see Evans, 1972 and Figure 2). In a second paper, Alonso addresses a number of basic questions to this approach: What are new towns for? Whom do they serve? Can they achieve their objectives? Are they in fact necessary? He

Figure 2. Location and Projected Size of New Towns in Britain (from Bourne, 1975).

concludes that they are not an efficient solution to urban problems, are not necessary, and cannot meet their objectives. Whether one agrees with Alonso or not, his provocative views challenge much of the conventional wisdom of urban planning at this geographic scale. These same concerns are the basis of a fascinating and long-standing debate, which is clearly not yet resolved (Merlin, 1971; Perloff and Sandberg, 1973; Clawson and Hall, 1973; Neutze, 1974; Robinson, 1975; Town and Country Planning, 1976).

Infrastructure investment, including the improvement and equalization of social-service systems and transportation networks, is important as a policy variable mainly in those urban systems that retain a high degree of regional variation in such services (such as Brazil and the U.S.), or in those in which the national inventory of such services is severely limited. A new highway in an undeveloped area of an African or South American country, where subsistence agriculture is still dominant, can have a revolutionary effect. In contrast, a third interstate highway added to the extensive highway system of Appalachia changes very little, and may even have a negative effect (Gauthier, 1973).

Growth centers (or poles) are one of the most widely discussed forms of governmental intervention to change the geography of urban and regional development (Hansen, 1972; Thomas, 1975). The literature is complex, as the Hansen paper in this section suggests, but the idea is straightforward: to shift to (or create at) a new location in an underdeveloped region some of the advantages of agglomeration and accessibility which, as noted above, tend to maintain the dominance of existing large cities. The intention is that of generating higher rates of urban growth and regional prosperity in the underdeveloped region which, in theory, will become self-sustaining in the long-term. The result should be to change the geometry and operation of the urban system, and thereby to redistribute income and wealth. To be most effective, of course, the strategy requires that the application of restraints on development in established cities and more properous regions be combined with an array of incentives to encourage development in the lagging regions. While growth centers and development incentives are usually popular, restraints are generally not popular nor are they often seriously applied. Consequently, the effects of such policies tend to be less than initially expected, and in some instances with the absence of effective controls may become counterproductive (Hansen, 1974; Stöhr, 1975).

The overriding issue in this debate, as the Hägerstrand paper ably demonstrates, remains the question of equity. Although Hägerstrand's suggestion of a uniform distribution of city sizes is but one dimension of the equity question, and a rather extreme one at that, it does emphasize the importance that must be attached to understanding how inequities are created through the operation of large-scale urban systems in particular, and of national development processes in general. As both our economy and social order become increasingly urbanized, the role of processes operating through rather than on urban systems increases.

## ZERO GROWTH

One of the planning alternatives we can readily dismiss, at least as a deliberate strategy, is that of zero growth. In part the popularity of this position reflects a widespread confusion over what is meant by the term "growth," and the differing scales in both space and time at which growth is measured. At one end of the scale is the debate on the existence of finite limits to long-term global economic growth. This debate, highlighted by the first Club of Rome report (Meadows *et al.*, 1972), has generated a substantial and often contradictory literature on the subject of growth.[2] Although the question of whether these limits exist in any practical sense or not is important for global peace, it is unlikely to directly affect urbanization in the foreseeable future. Our scale of analysis, the urban system, is in both space and time, very different from that of the global theorists. The increasing urban problem in many parts of the developed world, as Morrison's paper in the last section indicates for the U.S., is how to live with *decline* and *stagnation* rather than with growth (see Sternlieb and Hughes, 1975).

The point we have stressed throughout this volume, and Alonso (1973) emphasizes, is that even if absolute urban growth rates decline, problems associated with *structural change within urban systems will continue*, if not accelerate. Moreover, as we have previously noted, growth at one geographical scale may in fact represent decline at other scales, and vice versa. The impacts of slower growth in the overall system will also be distributed in different ways than those resulting from more rapid growth, and will often affect different people (Rust, 1975). Unless we devise better methods of dealing with social and spatial inequalities, deliberate attempts to slow growth any further may simply create new sources of inequalities and entrench the old.

## A MATCHING OF ISSUES AND RESPONSIBILITIES

Returning to the point raised earlier in this introduction, we might ask the question, How then should governments react? In his review of the problems of formulating national urban development strategies, Wilbur Thompson (1972) argued that a higher priority might be given to devising an optimal system of government than to finding an optimal city size or size distribution for cities. Part of the task of improving governmental responsiveness to issues such as those described in previous sections is to bring management practices and political responsibilities into clear correspondence with the geographical scale at which these needs are

---

2. The interested reader is referred to criticisms of the first Club of Rome report (see Cole *et al.*, 1973) and to the second report (Mesarovic and Pestel, 1974) for further details. As examples of the continuing debate readers are also referred to Beckerman (1975) for a defense of economic growth and to Kahn (1976) for an optimistic view of the world's potential. The subject is much too complex to debate here.

likely to be manifest. Since the boundaries of future urban issues are increasingly diffuse, this task will not be easy.

One possible distribution of policy responsibilities in such a management framework is described in Table 1. The purpose here is not to argue for new governmental units as such. Rather it is to inventory what instruments might be useful for influencing urban systems and how and at what level of system organization these instruments might apply and for what purposes. The concept of a hierarchical national urban system is employed as the point of departure. For each level in this hierarchy, selected examples are given of possible regulatory strategies, appropriate goals, policy instruments, and the type of procedure best suited to implementing such instruments. The international urban/economic system level (i.e., the turbulent external environment) is added to the hierarchy in terms of its importance as a focus of concern for national governments. Note that the essence of the proposed framework is not the hierarchical form of the urban system itself, but the nesting of problem sources and policy responsibilities within that system.

Three points in the table are worth stressing. First, as was argued earlier in this Introduction, many government policies that are neither explicitly urban nor spatial in name or focus have substantial impact on urban growth. The list of relevant instruments for influencing urban growth in Table 1 testifies to the diversity of "indirect" policy instruments currently available.[3] We do not need new policy instruments as much as we need better use of existing instruments. Second, to the editors at least, a national urban settlement strategy is essentially (but, of course, not exclusively) a spatial strategy. Thus, national efforts at regulating urban growth cannot be successful without coordinated efforts in certain other critical sectors of national interest, notably policies relating to population, immigration, transportation, industrial development, social-service provision, infrastructure investment, and housing. The third point which brings us back full circle to our introductory remarks, is the widely quoted assertion that a comprehensive strategy for regulating urban systems requires nothing less than a theory of the entire spatial and national development process.

## CONCLUDING COMMENTS

We do not contend in concluding this book that urban systems are the paramount source of social inequalities or of economic development problems. Nor do we contend that managing urban systems appropriately will, by definition, remove such inequalities. It is also unrealistic to argue that a single national urban strategy, based on the concept of the urban system or any other concept for that

3. An interesting and useful summary of legislative developments in the U.S. concerned with national urban policy is provided in an annual series of review papers by N. Beckman (see Beckman et al., 1975 as an example).

Table 1. Possible Hierarchical Components of National Settlement Strategies in a Spatial Context

| Focus of Settlement Policy | Types of Regulatory Strategies | Specific Goals and Objectives | Examples of Potential Policy Instruments | Implementation Principles |
|---|---|---|---|---|
| External environment: International urban/economic systems | Anticipation; monitoring consequences of change at boundaries of national system; smoothing external fluctuations | Survival; minimize environmental turbulence; coordination of foreign activities with national systems and needs; maintaining boundaries | Tariff and development policies; monetary reform; corporation taxes; immigration and emigration policy | Policies must be creative and persuasive, priming decisions; emphasis on sectoral and regional coordination |
| National urban and regional system | Redistribution of social opportunities and welfare; designing futures, national sectoral, socio-economic, and environmental planning; emphasis on long-term and goal-directed actions | Social investment; equity; economic growth targets; specific welfare balance; national unity, continuity and internal stability; social conservation and renewal | The national economy; population policy; public investment allocation; fiscal transfers and taxation; transport and communication; housing finance; employment location, information compilation and distribution; interregional locational assistance | |
| Regional (provincial/state) urban subsystems | Redesigning and articulating national frameworks, initiating strategic physical and environmental planning, both long- and short-term | Social-services provision; intraregional equity and balance; orderly urban development; regional growth and viability; environmental protection; land-use rationalization between urban and non-urban uses | Budgeting local government expenditures; regional public investment and transport policy; housing loans and construction; employment location decisions; regional land policy; educational facilities; intraregional locational assistance | Policies can be more specific; linking national and local priorities; intermunicipal coordination, emphasis on program evaluation |
| Daily urban (city) systems | Redesigning and implementing national and regional policy frameworks; initiating physical and allocative social-services provision, both short- and long-term planning | Specific social-service delivery; intraurban equity, orderly physical development; containing local externalities; viability of urban services; community stability | Local land use and location of services controls; building code enforcement, design and construction; traffic planning; local educational facilities; site location assistance | Policies specific in aggregate, allowing for some community autonomy |
| Communities and urban activity systems | Microscale planning linked to the above | | | |

Source: After Bourne (1975).

matter, is feasible in the immediate future. In fact the idea of a single overall plan, given the complexity documented in previous sections, is most unlikely. The recent shift of political interest in some countries away from such strategies, although in our opinion a temporary shift, is due in part to these strategies being oversold.

Instead we have simply argued that the urban-system perspective, as a way of thinking of urbanization, is valuable in defining and documenting the processes involved and in understanding the issues that result. We have also argued that it must be a component in any set of national strategies for reducing such problems—whatever form those strategies eventually take. The readings in the volume demonstrate some of the aspects of urban systems that must be considered in educating ourselves to the task of designing and evaluating these strategies.

## REFERENCES

Alonso, W. 1971. "Problems, Purposes and Implicit Policies for a National Strategy of Urbanization." *Working Paper No. 158.* Berkeley: University of California, Institute of Urban and Regional Development.

————. 1973. "Urban Zero Population Growth," in *Daedalus,* "The No-Growth Society," vol. 102, pp. 191–206.

Beckerman, W. 1975. *Two Cheers for the Affluent Society: A Spirited Defense of Economic Growth.* New York: St. Martin's Press.

Beckman, N. *et al.* 1975. "National Urban Growth Policy: 1974 Congressional and Executive Action." *Journal of the American Institute of Planners,* vol. 41, pp. 234–249.

Bourne, L. S. 1975. "Conceptual Issues in Designing and Evaluating Strategies for National Urban Settlement Systems," in H. Swain, ed. *National Settlement Strategies: East and West.* Laxenburg, Austria: International Institute for Applied Systems Analysis, pp. 86–118.

Brookfield, H. 1975. *Interdependent Development.* London: Methuen.

Cameron, G. and Wingo, L., eds. 1973. *Cities and Regions.* Edinburgh: Oliver and Boyd.

Clawson, M. and Hall, P. 1973. *Planning and Urban Growth: An Anglo-American Comparison.* Baltimore: Johns Hopkins University Press.

Cole, H.S.D. *et al.* 1973. *Models of Doom: A Critique of Limits to Growth.* New York: Universe Books.

Evans, H., ed. 1972. *New Towns: The British Experience.* London: C. Knight and Co.

Friedly, P. H. 1975. *National Policy Responses to Urban Growth.* Report to O.E.C.D. Environmental Directorate. London: Saxon House.

Friedmann, J. 1971. The Feasibility of a National Settlement Strategy for the U.S.," *Growth and Change,* vol. 2, pp. 18–21.

Gauthier, H. L. 1973. "The Appalachian Development Highway System: Development for Whom?" *Economic Geography,* Vol. 49 (Apr.), pp. 103–108.

Gilbert, A., ed. 1976. *Development Planning and Spatial Structure.* New York: Wiley.

Goddard, J. B. 1974. "The National System of Cities as a Framework for Urban and Regional Policy," in M. Sant, ed. *Regional Policy and Planning for Europe.* London: Saxon House, pp. 101–127.

Hansen, N. H. 1971. *Intermediate-Size Cities as Growth Centers.* New York: Praeger.

————., ed. 1972. *Growth Centers in Regional Economic Development.* New York: The Free Press.

————., 1974. *Public Policy and Regional Economic Development: The Experience of Nine Western Countries.* Cambridge, Mass.: Ballinger.

Kahn, H. *et al.* 1976. *The Next Two Hundred Years.* New York: Morrow and Co.

Lecomber, R. 1975. *Economic Growth vs. the Environment.* New York: Wiley.

Meadows, D. H. *et al.* 1972. *Limits to Growth.* New York: Universe Books.

Merlin, P. 1971. *New Towns: Regional Planning and Development.* London: Methuen.

Mesarovic, M. and Pestel, E. 1974. *Mankind at the Turning Point*. New York: E. P. Dutton.

Neutze, G. M. 1974. "The Case for New Cities in Australia." *Urban Studies*, vol. 11, pp. 259–275.

Perloff, H. S. and Sandberg, N., eds. 1973. *New Towns: Why—And for Whom?*. New York: Praeger.

Rodwin, Lloyd. 1970. *Nations and Cities*. New York: Houghton Mifflin.

Robinson, A. J. 1975. *Economics and New Towns. A Comparative Study of the U.S., U.K. and Australia*. New York: Praeger.

Rose, R., ed. 1974. *The Management of Urban Change in Britain and Germany*. Beverly Hills: Sage Publications.

Rothblatt, D. N. 1974. *National Policy for Urban and Regional Development*. Lexington, Mass.: D. C. Heath.

Rust, E. 1975. *No Growth: Impacts on Metropolitan Areas*. Lexington, Mass.: Lexington Books.

Sternlieb, G. and Hughes, J. W., eds. 1975. *Post-Industrial America: Metropolitan Decline and Interregional Job Shifts*. New Brunswick, N.J.: Rutgers University, Center for Urban Policy Research.

Stöhr, W. 1975. *Regional Development: Latin America*. The Hague: Mouton.

Strong, A. L. 1971. *Planned Urban Environments*. Baltimore: Johns Hopkins University Press.

Swain, H., ed. 1975. *National Settlement Strategies: East and West*. Laxenburg, Austria: International Institute for Applied Systems Analysis.

_____., and Logan, M. 1975. "Urban Systems: A Policy Perspective." *Environment and Planning A*, vol. 7, pp. 743–756.

_____., and MacKinnon, R. D., eds. 1975. *Issues in the Management of Urban Systems*. Laxenburg, Austria: International Institute for Applied Systems Analysis.

_____., Cordey-Hayes, M., MacKinnon, R. D., eds. 1975. "Selected Papers from IIASA Conference on National Settlement Systems and Strategies." *Environment and Planning A*, vol. 7 (special issue).

Thomas, M. D. 1975. "Growth Pole Theory, Technological Change and Regional Economic Growth." *Papers of the Regional Science Association*, vol. 34, pp. 3–25.

Thompson, W. R. 1972. "The National System of Cities as a Object of Public Policy." *Urban Studies*, vol. 9, pp. 99–116.

*Town and Country Planning*. 1976. "New Towns Special: Evidence from four continents concerning the recent wave of reappraisal, adaptation, and innovation in settlement planning." *Town and Country Planning*, vol. 44 (entire issue).

U.S. Advisory Commission on Intergovernmental Relations. 1969. *Urban and Rural America: Policies for Future Growth*. Washington: U.S. Government Printing Office.

U.S. National Goals Staff. 1970. *Toward Balanced Growth: Quantity with Quality*. Washington: U.S. Government Printing Office.

Wirz, H. M. 1975. *Social Aspects of Planning in New Towns*. Lexington, Mass.: D. C. Heath.

# 7.1
# Comparative Urbanization Strategies

BRIAN J. L. BERRY

To entitle this paper "Comparative Urbanisation Strategies" undoubtedly is presumptu-
ous, for it implies that there are in the world
today identifiably-different policies regarding
urban growth and development, that these
policies are being translated into workable
programs, and that the policies and programs
lend themselves to worthwhile systematic
comparison because they are altering urban
growth directions. For this to be so, something significant must have happened in the
past quarter-century. As Lloyd Rodwin remarked in *Nations and Cities*,[1] "before
World War II almost no one wanted the central government to determine how cities
should grow." But he did go on to say that
"radical changes in technology and in analytical and planning methods now make significant changes in the urban system not only
feasible, but to some extent manipulable,"
and, because of this, "today, national governments throughout the world are adopting
or are being implored to adopt urban growth
strategies."

Rodwin put his finger on two important
bases of comparison of urbanisation
strategies, the planning method and the political process, linked as they are ideologically in
terms of world view, which involves both the
perception of urban problems and the specification of goals to be achieved, and practically

in terms of the power to implement the means
thought likely to achieve the ends. Societies
differ in their planning capabilities, and this
introduces one important element of differentiation of urbanisation strategies. But
more importantly, cultural differences have
produced divergent goals, divergent planning
methods, divergent plans, and now divergent
paths being followed by urban development
in the world today.

I will thus begin my comparative analysis
of urbanisation strategies by examining their
socio-political bases, turning thereafter to the
question of planning styles and details of
strategies, for they are firmly derivative of the
cultural context. It will be evident that I find
no reason to change what I set down in 1973 in
my book *The Human Consequences of Urbanisation*[2] when I concluded:

The diverse forms that public intervention is taking, the variety of goals being sought, and the
differences in manipulation and manipulability
from one society to another are combining to
produce increasingly divergent paths of deliberate
urbanisation. This makes it all the more important
to understand the relations between socio-political
forms and urbanisation, because the socio-polity
determines the public planning style. Urbanisation, in this sense, can only be understood within
the broad spectrum of closely interrelated cultural
processes; among these processes, planning in-

---

1. Rodwin, Lloyd. *Nations and Cities*. Boston: Houghton
Mifflin Co., 1970.

2. Berry, Brian J. L. *The Human Consequences of Urbanisation*. London: Macmillan & Co., 1973.

From H. Swain and R. MacKinnon, eds., *Managing Urban Systems* (Laxenburg, Austria: IIASA, 1976), pp.
66–79. Reprinted by permission.

502

creases rather than decreases the range of *social* choice as modernisation takes place, while simultaneously restricting the range of *individual* choice to conform to the social path selected. . . . Images of the desirable future are becoming the major determinants of that future in societies that are able to achieve closure between means and ends. Political power is thus becoming a major element of the urbanisation process. Combined with the will to plan and an image of what might be, it can be directed to produce new social forms and outcomes, making it possible for a society to create what it believes *should be* rather than extending what *is* or what *has been* into the future.

## SOCIO-POLITICAL FORM AND URBANISATION PROCESS

### Free Enterprise Dynamics

At one end of the urbanisation spectrum are free-enterprise, decentralised, market-directed societies. Traditionally in such societies, decisions are made by individuals and small groups, and interact in the marketplace through free interplay of the forces of demand and supply. Economic and political power, vested in claims of ownership and property, are widely dispersed and competitively exercised. The instruments of collective or government action are used only to protect and support the central institutions of the market and to maintain the required dispersion of power. Thus, the public role is limited to combating crises that threaten the societal mainstream, as privately-initiated innovation produces social change. Legal systems are mainly regulatory, too, functioning to preserve established values; thus, to cite one example, the reliance of American law upon the regulatory approach to city building has meant the atrophy of city planning as a constructive element in social change.

One consequence is to be seen in North American political science, in which there has developed an explicit belief system concerning the process by which policies change, which in turn influences the way in which a problem is perceived. The dominant mode of

thought on this subject in American political science is that of *incrementalism*. As Charles E. Lindbloom said in 1963: "Democracies change their policies almost entirely through incremental adjustments. Policy does not move in leaps and bounds." The political processes of bargaining, log-rolling, and coalition-building are the major factors producing a situation in which past decisions are the best predictors of future ones. Under such conditions, no explicit policy guides urban growth. Impetus for growth derives rather from preoccupation with economic achievement, and this limits urban planning to an ameliorative problem-solving role, which is reinforced by an attitude that accepts the *inevitability* of a continuation of the processes inherent in the present.

What are some of these process? Increasing organisational scale and concentration of power is a dominant characteristic of today's post-industrial democracies. As the scale of economic and bureaucratic organisation increase, changes are taking place in the dynamics of social and economic change. Increasing numbers of the more salient developmental decisions are made by negotiation among large-scale autonomous organisations and by voluntary associations, profit-oriented but not necessarily maximisers, countervailing and countervailed against, negotiating together and existing in a context of negotiated relationships, rather than delivered by the guiding hand of an unseen and more neutral market. Power is determined as a matter of policy or agreed upon by counter-balancing powers. Under such conditions there is organisation of production by large corporations run for the benefit of stockholders, while labor negotiates wages through large-scale unions. The consumption of end products is partly determined by individual choice, and partly by governmental policy. The collective power of organisations, collective power of the government, and the free choice of individuals are all part of the system.

Hence, the "market" is no longer the single master. Rather, elaborate negotiation for "satisfactory" solutions tends to prevail; instead of maximisation, there is "satisficing'' and, increasingly, each of the large-scale organisations engages in planning in terms of corporate goals, often with systems analysis staffs at their disposal to help them select desirable courses of action. The resulting combination of scale, power and corporate planning means that developmental leadership, the innovative ''cutting edge'' of urbanisation, is now more frequently in the hands of corporate oligarchs, responding to their particular economic agendas, for in spite of the opportunity for the collective power of the government to be exercised as a significant countervailing force—Canadian and Australian experiments notwithstanding—no governmental bodies can be credited with the development and execution of an urban policy in the world's free-enterprise societies at the present time. What substitutes is a complex set of uncoordinated and often contradictory public policies and programs provided in the wake of strong economic forces which set the agenda for urban growth. Thus, if in the past urbanisation has been governed by any conscious public objectives at all, these have been on the one hand, to encourage growth, apparently for its own sake; and on the other, to provide public works and public welfare programs to support piecemeal, spontaneous development impelled primarily by private initiative. In contrast, development of a national urban policy suggests a shift in the locus of initiative, imposing on public authorities an obligation to orient, rationalise, and plan the physical, economic, and textual character of urban life. Thus, through a complementary set of policies and programs, an urban policy represents an explicit statement of the purpose of urbanisation, its pace, its character, and values that are to prevail.

## Public Counterpoints in the Redistributive Welfare State

It has been the greater radicalism of the welfare states of western Europe that has produced modification of the free enterprise system (and its large-scale twentieth-century heirs) by governmental action, to reduce social and spatial inequities and to provide every citizen with minimum guarantees for material welfare—medical care, education, employment, housing and pensions. This has been achieved most usually through differential taxation and welfare payments, but it also increasingly involves extension of more centralised decision making designed to make the market system satisfy social goals in addition to its traditional economic functions. In this way, what has emerged are mixed economies, the hallmarks of which are pluralistic societies with multiparty governments, relatively high levels of development and per capita output and built-in capacity for continued growth, but with substantial public sectors alongside elaborate private markets and ''modern'' economic institutions.

Public involvement in urbanisation in the mixed economies is to be seen as more than merely a counterpoint to private interests, however. By directing society towards goals of redistribution and equity, the competitive drive is reoriented. By constructing a large share of all housing in existing towns, and by constructing new towns, the public exercises developmental leadership. Urbanisation is deliberately led in new directions.

The particular form of policy varies from country to country. Ebenezer Howard's new towns philosophy and the apparent successes of British planning have induced other countries to attempt to control physical development, to direct new settlement away from congested metropolitan centres, and to stimulate economic and urban growth in peripheral regions. For example, the French have been concerned for a decade and a half over the steady concentration of people and economic activity in Paris. The Finns have seen the population of the northern half of their country pour into Helsinki or leave Finland entirely. The Swedes are concerned because most of their people are concentrated in Stockholm and two other metropolitan areas of southern Sweden. They are not concerned because their metropolitan centres are too big, as the French are over Paris, but because the depopulation of the Swedish north threatens to erode the social structure in that section of their nation. The Hungarians share a similar concern over the domination of their national economy by Budapest. Only the Poles are unconcerned with the outflow of rural people into their metropolitan areas. Lagging behind the rest of Europe in their rate of modernisation, the Poles see metropolitanisation as a process essential to absorb a "surplus" rural population.

Despite these differences in forms, however, the central concern of urban policy in all of Europe is the regional distribution of growth. Economic growth is viewed as the basic means to achieve social objectives such as improved income, housing, education, health, welfare, and recreational opportunity. European growth policies are intended to ameliorate disparities in income and welfare between regions of the country and, to a lesser extent, to minimise deleterious effects of economic growth on the natural environment.

As noted, the goals and objectives of urban growth policies vary from country to country, but to some degree all are aimed at: (1) *balanced welfare*—achieving a more "balanced" distribution of income and social well-being among the various regions of the country, as well as among social classes; (2) *centralisation/decentralisation*—establishing a linked set of local and national public institutions which make it possible to develop, at the national level, overall growth strategies, integrated with regional or metropolitan planning and implementation that is partly a product of a reformed local governmental system and is directly accountable to local officials and the affected constituency; (3) *environmental protection*—channelling future growth away from areas suffering from environmental overload or which possess qualities worthy of special protection, towards areas where disruption of the environment can be minimised; (4) *metropolitan development*—promoting more satisfactory patterns of metropolitan development through new area-wide governmental bodies and the use of special land use controls, new towns, housing construction, new transportation systems, and tax incentives and disincentives; (5) *non-metropolitan development*—diverting growth into hitherto by-passed regions by developing "growth centres" in presently non-metropolitan regions, con-

structing new transportation links between such regions and centres of economic activity, using various incentives and disincentives to encourage or compel location of economic activity in such areas, and forcibly relocating certain government activities into them.

Given such goals, the urban future that is unfolding in each case, represents a delicately-orchestrated balance between individual and corporate interests on the one hand, and the collective power of the state at the other. Much of this power is exercised in a negative fashion, to constrain individual or corporate drives, but the best appears when the public sets in motion new growth directions by exercising developmental leaderships, thereby initiating new and exciting trends.

## Directed Change in the Socialist State

From a public counterpoint and developmental leadership, the next step is to the command structure of the socialist states, where monolithic governmental systems are dominated by a single party, there is state operation of non-agricultural industries (in some, agriculture, too), and centralised direction of the economy. Each of the socialist nations shows strong commitment to economic growth, but on the social side there is also a desire for elimination of most of the status differences based upon economic rewards that are the hallmark of free-enterprise competition. A greater uniformity and lack of specialisation is to be seen in the urban fabric, alongside more highly regimented life styles and building patterns. It is easier to command with an explicit set of rules and procedures to be followed; in this way urban development has been both bureaucratised and standardised under socialism.

This should be no surprise. The Communist Revolution of 1917 marked the beginning in Russia, and later in eastern Europe, of yet another path in urban development. The revolutionaries had great faith in the power of the government to transform society for the betterment of man, in seizing the government not to restrict its power but rather to use it.

They aspired to remould society through a state monopoly of the production of goods, of means of communications, of education, and of science.

The great modernising revolutions that took place much earlier in the west and at a more leisurely pace of gradual transition came concurrently in the Soviet Union and took a more dramatic and radical form. The religious revolution, which in the west found expression in the Reformation, the Counter-Reformation and the gradual secularisation of most aspects of life, took the form in the Soviet Union of militant atheism. The economic revolution, which as the Industrial Revolution in the west extended over more than a century, took the form in the Soviet Union of state ownership and management of the entire economy to promote social goals and to speed industrialisation. The democratic political revolution, which found expression in the west in the American and French revolutions and the gradual diffusion of political power in Britain through a series of reforms, in the Soviet Union took the form of transfer of power from the autocracy of the Tsars to the dictatorship of the proletariat through the leadership of the Communist Party with centralised authority but democratic participation. The intellectual revolution, which in the west flowered in the Age of Reason and in which faith developed in the perfectibility of man and social institutions, in the ability of man by rational thought and scientific investigation to improve himself and society and to rule the universe, in the Communist Revolution took the form of an optimistic faith in the ability of the Party and the government, through science and industrialisation, to transform society and social relations and to create a rational communistic world order.

What has been sought in urban development was what Lenin had called "a new pattern of settlement for mankind," the city of socialist man. The classic writings of Marxism-Leninism suggested ways in which the goal might be achieved: planning was to create cities without social or economic divisions; there was to be a commitment to the socially integrative value of housing and a wide range of social services; city planning was to be responsive to economic planning, which would determine industrial location and set limits to the rate of urbanisation in developed regions and major urban complexes; and thus city planning per se was to be restricted to a basic physical-engineering-architectural profession, providing high-density new developments in approved styles.

The accomplishments of the Soviets in urban development are unquestionable. During the Soviet period the USSR has been transformed from a rural society to a predominantly urban one, through a combined process of industrialisation and urbanisation achieved as the outcome of a series of five-year plans. The authoritarian role of the central government and the priority of the economic goals of the state have been expressed at all levels of urbanisation, down to the precise physical nature of the new urban developments that have been built.

The resulting spatial patterns are held to be consistent with socialist principles of urban development (the antithesis of the European industrial urbanisation of the nineteenth century that so angered and repelled Marx and Engels). The "principle of social justice" is realised, for example, by using the official norms and standards which determine per capita living spaces, population density, and quantity of services, without class distinctions. The only basis for differentiation of available environment among urban families is the biological characteristics of the families. Similarly, the functional and the spatial structure of new residential areas and towns correspond, according to the conception of a socialist urban community.

## The Third World: Fragmented Centralisation

Increasingly affirmative and effective planning and action to eliminate problems perceived to be the products of colonialism is something to which all of the countries of the Third World aspire. But the Third World countries constitute a diverse mosaic in which traditional self-perpetuating, self-regulating, semi-autonomous, pre-industrial "little" societies welded by colonial powers into ill-fitting states, coexist with and are being changed by post-war modernisation. Traditional forms of authority and the centralised controls of colonialism have been replaced by one-party governments or military dictatorships. There is frequent instability, and limited capacity for public administration. The public sectors are small. There is fragmentation of economies along geographic, ethnic and modern-versus-traditional lines, imperfection of markets and limited development of modern economic institutions, limited industrial development and continued predominance of agriculture, low per capita product and market dependence on foreign economic relations.

The urge for more and better control of urban development results from accelerated urban growth, a compounding of the scale of the primate cities and their associated peripheral settlements, perceived increases in social pathologies, growing attachment to national urban planning as a means of securing control of social and economic change, and an increasing willingness to experiment with new and radical plans and policies. The countries of the Third World are reaching for powers, controls and planning best exemplified by the welfare states of Western Europe on the side of innovative planning, and by the command economies of Eastern Europe and the USSR in the sense of more complete and effective controls. At the same time many are seeking to preserve significant elements of their traditional cultures, so that modernisation and westernisation are not synonymous.

A variety of radical solutions to urban development are being proposed, but what characterises most of the planning efforts in the Third World is the absence of a will to plan effectively, and more often than not, political smoke-screening. Most urbanisation policy is unconscious, partial, unco-ordinated and negative. It is unconscious in the sense that those who effect it are largely unaware of its proportions and features. It is partial in that few of the points at which governments might act to manage urbanisation and affect its course and direction are in fact utilised. It is unco-ordinated in that national planning tends to be economic, and urban planning tends to be physical, and the disjunction often produces competing policies. It is negative in that the ideological perspective of the planners leads them to try to divert, retard or stop urban growth, and in particular to inhibit the expansion of metropolises and primate cities.

Elsewhere, in Maoist China for example, this anti-urban bias is also clear. In China, it has obvious historical roots in the history of the Chinese Communist Party and its struggle for power before 1949 and in the modern history of a China dominated by treaty-port colonialists who controlled and shaped nearly all of its large cities. These cities were also the homes of the Chinese bourgeoisie. They were felt to have been reactionary in the past, potentially revisionist now and in the future, and alienating at all times. Thus, their growth in China continues to be controlled by an unprecedented policy which limits their size and which channels new industrial investment into new or smaller cities in previously remote or backwards areas, or into rural communes, which are to be made industrially as self-sufficient as possible without acquiring morally corrupting and alienating qualities of big cities, nor their damaging effects on the environment. City-dwellers, especially white collar workers, must spend a month or more every year, whatever their status, in productive physical labor in the countryside, where they may regain "correct" values. The distinctions between mental and manual labor, city and countryside, "experts" or bureaucrats and peasants or workers are to be eliminated. The benefits and the experience of industrialisation and modernisation are to be diffused uniformly over the landscape and to all of the people, while the destructive, dehumanising, corrupting aspects of over-concentration in cities are to be avoided.

## PLANNING STYLE AND URBANISATION STRATEGY

The keys to the Maoist reconstruction of China have been a will to plan, clear objectives, and totalitarian powers, and indeed, wherever there has been affirmative pursuit and a modicum of success with an urbanisation strategy the necessary ingredients have been future-orientation, agreement upon goals, and the power to act.

An urbanisation strategy is, axiomatically, concerned with the future. It involves goals; it involves motivated and informed decision makers; it involves the will to act and the power to achieve. A society with an urbanisation strategy is, necessarily, a planning society.

But the nature of planning varies with socio-political structure, as does the nature and degree of future-orientation and the capability to achieve consensus on goals. In consequence it is possible to identify a sequence of planning styles—and by extension, of urbanisation strategies and of determinants of the future—roughly paralleling the sequence from free-enterprise conditions to the directed state.

The simplest, as outlined in Table 1, is simply *ameliorative problem-solving*—the natural tendency to do nothing until problems arise or undesirable dysfunctions are perceived to exist in sufficient amounts to demand corrective or ameliorative action. Such "reactive" or "curative" planning proceeds

Table 1. Four Policy-Making Styles

| | Planning for Present Concerns | Planning for the Future | | |
|---|---|---|---|---|
| | Reacting to Past Problems | Responding to Predicted Futures | | Creating Desired Future |
| | Ameliorative Problem-Solving | Allocative Trend-Modifying | Exploitive Opportunity-Seeking | Normative Goal-Oriented |
| | Planning for the Present | Planning towards the Future | Planning with the Future | Planning from the Future |
| Planning Mode | Analyse problems, design interventions, allocate resources accordingly. | Determine and make the *best* of trends and allocate resources in accordance with desires to promote or alter them. | Determine and make the *most* of trends and allocate resources so as to take advantage of what is to come. | Decide on the *future desired* and allocate resources so that trends are changed or created accordingly. Desired future may be based on present, predicted or new values. |
| "Present" or Short Range Results | *Ameliorate Present Problems* | *A Sense of Hope*<br><br>New allocations shift activities | *A Sense of Triumphing Over Fate*<br><br>New allocations shift activities | *A Sense of Creating Destiny*<br><br>New allocations shift activities |
| "Future" or Long Range Results of Actions | *Haphazardly Modify the Future* by reducing the future burden and sequelae of present problems | *Gently Balance and Modify the Future* by avoiding predicted problems and achieving a "balanced" progress to avoid creating major bottlenecks and new problems. | *Unbalance and Modify the Future* by taking advantage of predicted happenings, avoiding some problems and cashing in on others without major concern for emergence of new problems. | *Extensively Modify the Future* by aiming for what could be "Change the predictions" by changing values or goals, match outcomes to desires avoid or change problems to ones easier to handle or tolerate. |

by studying "problems," setting standards for acceptable levels of tolerance of the dysfunctions, and devising means for scaling the problems back down to acceptable proportions. The focus is upon present problems, which implies continually reacting to processes that have already worked themselves out in the past; in a processional sense, then, such planning is past oriented. And the implied goal is the preservation of the "mainstream" values of the past by smoothing out the problems that arise along the way.

A second style of planning is *allocative trend-modifying*. This is the future-oriented version of reactive problem-solving. Present trends are projected into the future and likely problems are forecast. The planning procedure involves devising regulatory mechanisms to modify the trends in ways that preserve existing values into the future, while avoiding the predicted future problems. Such is Keynesian economic planning, highway building designed to accommodate predicted future travel demands, or Master Planning using the public counterpoint of zoning ordinance and building regulations.

The third planning style is *exploitive opportunity-seeking*. Analysis is performed not to identify future problems, but to seek out new growth opportunities. The actions that follow pursue those opportunities most favorably ranked in terms of returns arrayed against feasibility and risk. Such is the entrepreneurial world of corporate planning, the real-estate developer, the industrialist, the private risk-taker—and also of the public entrepreneur acting at the behest of private interests, or the national leader concerned with exercising *developmental leadership,* as when Ataturk built Ankara, or as the Brazilians are developing Amazonia today. It is in this latter context in already-developed situations that the concept of strategy planning was developed.

Finally, the fourth mode of planning involves explicitly *normative goal-orientation*. Goals are set, based upon images of the desired future, and policies are designed and plans implemented to guide the system to-wards the goals, or to change the existing system if it cannot achieve the goals. This style of planning involves the cybernetic world of the systems analyst, and is only possible when a society can achieve closure of means and ends, i.e., acquire sufficient control and coercive power to ensure that inputs will produce desired outputs.

The four different planning styles have significantly different long-range results, ranging from haphazard modifications of the future produced by reactive problem-solving, through gentle modification of trends by regulatory procedures to enhance existing values, to significant unbalancing changes introduced by entrepreneurial profit-seeking, to creation of a desired future specified ex ante. Clearly, in any country there is bound to be some mixture of all styles present, but equally, predominant value systems so determine the preferred policy making and planning style that significantly different processes assume key roles in determining the future in different societies.

The publicly supported private developmental style that characterises the American scene, incorporating bargaining among major interest groups, serves mainly to protect developmental interests by reactive or regulatory planning, ensuring that the American urban future will be a continuation of present trends, only changing as a result of the impact of change produced by the exploitive opportunity-seeking planning of American corporations.

On the other hand, hierarchical social and political systems, where the governing class is accustomed to govern, where other classes are accustomed to acquiesce, and where private interests have relatively less power, can more readily evolve urban and regional growth policies at the national level than systems under the sway of the market, local political jurisdictions, or egalitarian political processes. This is one reason urban growth policies burgeoned earlier in Britain than in the United States. Controls are of several kinds. Most basically, use of the land is effectively regulated in conformity to a plan that codifies some public concept of the desirable future and welcomes private profit-seeking development only to the extent that it conforms to the public plan. Such is the underpinning of urban development in Britain, in Sweden, in France, in the Netherlands, in Israel's limited privately owned segments or within the designated white areas of South Africa. Such a situation also obtains, it might be added, in the planning of Australia's new capital, Canberra. To understand the developmental outcome in these circumstances, one must understand the aspirations of private developers or of public agencies involved in the development process on the one hand, and the images of the planners built into the Master Plan on the other. It is the resolution of the two forces that ultimately shapes the urban scene. In Britain, the planners' images of the desirable future have been essentially conservative, aiming to project into the future a belief that centrality is an immutable necessity for urban order, leading to the preservation of urban forms that are fast vanishing in North America. Thus, the utopian image that becomes embedded in the specific plan and the efficacy with which the public counterpoint functions to constrain private interests, are the key elements.

Nowhere has the imagery of the social reformers been more apparent than in Soviet planning for the "city of socialist man." Reflecting the reactions against the human consequences of nineteenth-century industrial urbanisation, the public counterpoint of the "mixed" economies has been the realisation that such sought-after futures can be made to come true.

Images of the desirable future are becoming determinants of that future in societies that are able to achieve closure between means and ends. Political power is becoming a major element of the urbanisation process, and can be directed to produce new social and spatial forms and outcomes, making it possible for a society to create what it believes *should be* rather than extending into the future what *is* or what *has been*.

# The Concept of a Unified Settlement System and the Planned Control of the Growth of Towns in the USSR

DAVID G. KHODZHAEV and BORIS S. KHOREV

The purpose of the present study is to present a general concept of the development of settlement[1] in the USSR, and through this to work out the basic policy assumptions for controlling the growth of towns and other settlements. Without this concept it would be difficult to carry out rational regional and urban planning. The concept of settlement development should, on the one hand, have a theoretical basis, and on the other, be based on an analysis of the empirical trends in modern settlement networks.

Theoretically, the Marxist thesis about eroding the differences between town and country during the building of communism, is very important.

The division of settlement types into urban and rural results from the social and territorial division of labour, and particularly from the separation of industry and agriculture.

This division went hand in hand with the class differentiation of society. "The division of labour in any society leads above all to the separation of labour in industry and trade from that in agriculture, and similarly to the separation of town and country."[2] In a class society this division creates an antagonism between town and country. With the liquidation of the class structure, and with the rebuilding of society along communist lines, the existing differences between town and country will gradually be eroded. However, certain features of agricultural production and its related form of settlement will remain, distinguishing this from other branches of the national economy, above all from large scale industry and its related forms of settlement.

The important points about long-term changes in the growth of towns is that the erosion of the differences between town and country will lead to a *unified system of settlement;* the planned control of this system may avert the lively and uncontrolled growth of towns. In a bourgeois society the town governs the country. According to Engels the elimination of the old division of labour in a classless society, will signify "the fusion of town and country."[3] This does not mean the absorption of the country by the town, as some urbanists hold, but the fusion of these two forms within the unified system of settlement. In the country man is usually subject to nature, but in the town he is unnaturally cut off from it; in the future unified system of

1. The term *rasseleniye naseleniya* in our literature can refer to both the process of the distribution of population over an area and to the result of this process (the settlement network). Such a wide term has no equivalent as far as we know, in English. In Polish literature, the term *rasseleniye* meaning a settlement network, is *osadnictwo* (one can correspondingly distinguish the term *geografia osadnictwa—geografiya rasseleniya* in Russian—see for example M. Kielczewska-Zaleska, *Geografia osadnictwa* (Settlement geography), Warszawa 1969.

2. K. Marks, F. Engels, *Sochineniya* (Works), 2nd ed., vol. 3, p. 20.
3. K. Marks, F. Engels, *Sochineniya* (Works), 2nd, ed., vol. 20, p. 308.

From *Geographia Polonica,* vol. 27, 1973, pp. 43–51. Reprinted by permission of PWN, Polish Scientific Publishers and the authors.

settlement man will be in harmony with nature.

Engels' thesis about the liquidation of the differences, and the subsequent merging of town and country, is sometimes taken to be a distant goal, removed from our time. One often hears that Engels' remarks on this question were accidental. Both these views are completely erroneous. In his work "The Question of Housing," and particularly in "Anti-Dühring" he not only puts forward, but also justifies his thesis about eroding the boundaries between town and country. The justification of his thesis is all the more remarkable in that it takes up economic, sociological and ecological standpoints all at the same time. At the same time it is connected with the urgent tasks of social development. From the economic standpoint "liquidating the antagonism between town and country is not only possible, but it becomes a necessity for both industrial and agricultural production."[4] "The prospect of eliminating the old division of labour stands before us" Engels emphasised, "this and the division between town and country."[5] From the sociological standpoint, the task of eliminating the antagonism between town and country is justified by Engels by the necessity "of plucking the agricultural population from its isolation and dullness in which it has vegetated for thousands of years,"[6] i.e., the life-style of the rural population can now actually be called "urban." From the ecological standpoint the elimination of the antagonism is, according to Engels, "necessary in the interests of social hygiene. Only by merging town and country can the present poisoning of air, water and soil, be eliminated."[7]

The works of Marxism-Leninism classics not only justify the necessity of eliminating the antagonism between town and country

and their subsequent fusion, but they also outline how this can be achieved: (1) the harmonious development of productive forces according to a single overall plan; (2) a greater equalization of the distribution of large-scale industry and of the population over the country; (3) achieving strong internal links between industrial and agricultural production; (4) the development of communications; (5) overcoming the excessive concentration of population in large cities (as the capitalist means of production is eliminated). Socialism will lead to "a new settlement pattern of mankind (with the elimination of both rural neglect, isolation from the world, its barbarism, and of the unnatural concentration of huge populations in the large towns)."[8] The need "to strive with every effort . . . for the rational distribution of workers" was expressed in the Party Programme, accepted at the 8th Congress of the RKP(b), and worked out on V. I. Lenin's directives.[9] An important methodological recommendation of V. I. Lenin's is "the unconstrained distribution of population throughout Russia" connected with "the rational economic use of the outlying areas of Russia."[10]

In directing these theoretical legacies, the party does a lot of the work through the rational and planned development of the economies and cultures of the peoples of the Soviet Union, through locating production and distributing settlements throughout the country. The question of rational settlement is referred to in the Programme of the CPSU, accepted by the 22nd Party Congress: "The developed building of Communism requires an even more rational distribution of industry which will ensure an economy in social endeavour, the integrated development of regions and specialization of their economy, will eliminate excessive concentration of population in large towns, will help overcome

4. F. Engels, Anti-Dühring, in: K. Marks, F. Engels, *Sochineniya* (Works), 2nd ed., vol. 20, pp. 307–308.
5. Ibid., p. 308.
6. F. Engels, K zhilishchnomu voprosu (On the housing question), in: K. Marks, F. Engels, *Sochineniya* (Works), 2nd ed., vol. 18, p. 277.
7. F. Engels, Anti-Dühring, in: op. cit., p. 308.

8. V. I. Lenin, *Poln. sobr. soch.* (Complete works), 5th ed., vol. 26, p. 74.
9. *Programma RKP(b)* (Programme of RKP(b)). V. I. Lenin, ibid., vol. 38, p. 443.
10. Ibid., vol. 16, p. 227.

the existing differences between town and country, and will make the level of economic development of regions more equal."[11]

These propositions are of prime importance for working out the scientific concept of the distribution of population.

Socialism was the first system to assume an end to the antagonism between classes, opening the era of the classless society, and predetermining the possible liquidation of the conflict between town and country. The formation of a single communist ownership, the linking of agricultural labour with industrial, and the transformation of the former into a variant of the latter, the establishment of the social equality of urban and rural workers, these are the socio-economic pre-conditions for eliminating the differences between town and country. In our country the general socio-economic process of eroding the boundaries between town and country is found in many phenomena, including: the mechanization and industrialization of agriculture (the change to a greater industrialization of the livestock branch of agriculture in recent years has been particularly important in the current plan); the spread of agro-industrial combines; the growth of "urban" occupations in the village, and as a result of this the increasing homogeneity of urban and rural workers; the growing local movement of population and increasing journey to work between village and town; making the flows of information more equal; spreading the network of developed urban centres so as to draw the large rural population into its economic and social orbit; making the small towns more active, and so on.

In this connection we must turn our attention to certain principal changes in the development and distribution of the forces of production in our country, which are important for solving the problems of settlement.

(1) It is well known that in the USSR there is an increasing number of large towns. In recent decades particularly, an important as-

11. *Programma Kommunisticheskoy Partii Sovetskogo Soyuza* (The Programme of the Communist Party of the Soviet Union), Moskva 1969, p. 72.

pect of this process has appeared. This is that the development of a network of large towns proceeds according to the principle of an "expanding geography of productional forces," helping the economic activations of formerly backward regions. The importance of large towns in the population structure of the country is gradually decreasing. Thus the proportion of the population of the seven "old" million-cities—Moscow, Leningrad, Kiev, Tashkent, Baku, Kharkov and Gorki—in the total population of large towns has changed during the Soviet period, from 60% in 1926, to 40.7% in 1939, 29.4% in 1959, and 23.4% in 1970.

(2) In recent decades there has been a significant increase in the urbanization of formerly backward developed *oblasts* and republics of the country. This is well seen in the data of the 1959 and 1970 population censuses. The higher growth rates of the total urban population in usually found in those *oblasts* with a low proportion of urban population, which testifies to an intensive "pulling-up" process of the urban network to a higher level in previously backward *oblasts*. There are now hardly any weakly-urbanized *oblasts* with a low rate of urbanization. The urban population rose by 36% from 1959 to 1970, and the proportion of urban population reached 56%. Out of 138 *krays, oblasts,* Autonomous Republics, and Union Republics which have no *oblast* divisions, the proportion of urban population exceeded 55% in 49 (we will call this the first group). It was between 50 and 55% in 13 (the second group), and less than 50% in 76 (third group). Lower than average rates of growth took up 65.3% of the administrative-territorial units in the first group, 38.5% in the second, and only 18.4% in the third.

The current growth of large towns testifies to a more equal distribution of the forces of production over the country. It does not testify, as some economists who limit themselves to a superficial look at the process of the concentration of population in large towns, believe, to a deepening of an inherited "inequality" of development.

(3) In recent years, and particularly in the 1966–1970 five year period there have been fundamental changes in the distribution of industry. These have come about through the establishment and construction of branches and separate sections of large industrial enterprises in developed industrial centres of the country in many peripheral towns (of both small and medium size). This phenomenon was a small scale one before 1966, but during the period 1966–1970 become a very large-scale one. Branches sprang up not only in towns and villages near Moscow, Kiev, Riga and other cities, but also in far-off regions of the European part of the country. For example in the Mari A.S.S.R. there are branches of head factories in Yoshkar-Ol, Kazan and even in Leningrad, Kharkov and Kuznetsk (Penzen *Oblast*). Two branches were located in such towns as Volzhsk and Kosmodemyansk, and one in the worker settlements of Krasnogorskiy and Morki. This phenomenon represents a serious step forward in solving the so-called ''problem of small towns,'' which possess free labour resources, but do not have the level of technology for modern industrial production. It is to these factories which do have the required technology that young people go with their high hopes after finishing middle school. Having come up against a labour deficit in the large towns and the difficulty of attracting supplementary labour from elsewhere, industry (especially the labour-intensive machine building industry) goes to the labour reserves in outlying areas. Thus the branches of such factories as the Moscow ZIL were located in a series of towns in many *oblasts* in the European part of the USRR.

(4) The practice of organizing separate scientific-research and project institutes in small towns, whose main branches are usually located in large towns is becoming more frequent; those in the small towns have different productional objectives. There are also those towns whose development entirely depends on the establishment of scientific-productional complexes in them. This is a very important trend in the current scientific-technological revolution.

(5) In recent years in the USSR, as in other countries of the world, there has been a great increase in the mechanization and industrialization of the livestock branch of agriculture (through the construction of large livestock complexes and poultry farms—instead of the previously small-scale dairy farming—pig farms and so on). The collectivization of agriculture in its time led to crop mechanization and helped to solve the grain quality problem. The current changes can be seen as the second very important step forward, which along with an increasing use of chemicals and other processes, testify to an important spread of the technological revolution in our agriculture. This very important qualitative change will greatly influence the distribution both of basic capital in agriculture and of the rural population.

(6) Since 1950 there have been significant qualitative changes in the local mobility of population (inter-village labour movements and cultural-everyday life links in different, regional settlement systems). These changes result particularly from the great effort put into developing sub-urban and inter-urban transport, especially bus transport. Whereas in 1950 51.9 million passengers used the inter-urban bus routes, in 1960 there were 551.3 millions, and by 1968 this figure had doubled.[12] These seemingly trivial indices of the development of inter-urban communication (the increasing number and distances of bus routes, and of passenger movement, etc.), in fact hide great progress in the general life-style of the population, particularly, that of the rural population. The wide development of bus communication and local aeroplane services in a short time changed the life-style of many rural areas, clearly increasing the mobility of the rural population and linking it with the town, and breaking with the concept of the ''deep province.'' An increase in the scale of commuting to work is connected with this. This commuting is made up of inter-settlement labour links from village to

12. Narodnoye Khozyaystvo SSSR v 1969 (Soviet national economy in 1969), *Stat. yezhegodnik*, Moskva 1970.

town. At present this process involves 3 million people throughout the USSR.[13]

(7) The wide development of channels of information and communication also help to change the style of life of people in outlying regions, and bring it closer to that of the capital cities.

These important changes are already greatly influencing (and this will increase still more in the future) all aspects of the process of the development and distribution of productional forces in our country. They are undoubtedly helping to make this distribution and development more equal, and are eroding the boundaries between town and country.

In looking at the historical aspect of the question of the development of the forces of production and social relations, one can distinguish two basic trends which strongly affect the process of settlement. An increasing territorial division of labour and differentiation of the distribution of the products of this labour result in a concentration of industrial production and urban population. This can be seen in the rapid growth of large towns. Revolutionary changes in management, in the techniques of distribution and exchange, and in inter-settlement links lead to the establishment of a unified settlement system. Its basic features are: first, a freer distribution of population over wide areas which form communities of interests and are characterized by intensive interrelations rather than intensive forms of urban development. Second, there is a more equal distribution of production and population throughout the country. It is possible to glimpse the outline of the future "unified settlement system" in the regulation and combination of the various types of settlement distribution. In the trend towards an increasing radius of large-scale settlement of workers in places which act as supplementary sources of labour and development of commuting due to the increasing speed of transport, one can see the future map of the world.

On this map settlement will not have to depend on the distance to places of supplementary labour.

It is necessary to have a general concept of the development of settlement particularly for working out the long-term control of the development of the forces of production and of the process of urbanization. Such studies are traditional in our country (one should especially mention N. Milyutin's work in the late 1920's on several important theses).[14] In recent years interest in the long term settlement problems has grown considerably. This is partly due to the preparation of a general scheme for the distribution of productional forces in the USSR up to 1980 under the direction of the all-Union Gosplan. Thus we have the task of scientifically working out a general scheme of settlement over the USSR, for the Economic Regions and Union Republics up to 1980.[15] The scientific subdepartments of the all-Union Gosstroi are working out forecasts for the development of Soviet urban growth for even longer periods (a special conference in February 1970 in Moscow was given over to this problem).[16] Because of the need to work out the long term distribution of population, Soviet geographers and urbanists have done a lot of work, especially, in the last ten years, on questions of group and agglomeration settlement distribution and on analysing territorial systems of settlement (notably the work V. G. Davidovich and his followers). At present we can already speak about a definite concept of the long-term distribution. However, it still needs a theoretical foundation (from the standpoints of urban science, sociology, economics and geography). We will call this the concept of a unified settlement system (*jedinnoi sistemy rasseleniya*), abbreviated to JSR. In general, this term is taken to mean the

13. B. S. Khorev, T. K. Smolina, A. G. Vishnevskiy, Mayatnikovaya migratsiya v SSSR i ee izuchenye (Commuting in the USSR and its study), in: *Problemy migratsii naseleniya i trudovykh resursov*, Moskva 1970.

14. N. Milyutin, *Sotsgorod*, Moskva 1930.
15. D. G. Khodzhaev, Nekotoriye problemy regulirovaniya rosta gorodov i razvitiya naselennykh mest (Some problems of controlling urban growth and development of urban settlements), *Problemy gradostroitelstva* 1, Kiev 1970.
16. Perspektivy razvitya sovetskogo gradostroitelstva (On the perpsectives of the development of Soviet town planning), *Arkhitektura SSSR*, 6, 1970.

functionally differentiated and structurally interlinked network of all the settlements in a given large area. The network is established through several subordinate stages and is being evenly developed and controlled through planning for society as a whole, and is part of a unified system of regional planning.[17] The essence of the concept is that in the long term, through the regional distribution of the forces of production of separate regions, the historically formed settlement pattern (both its concentrated and dispersed forms) will be transformed into integrated regional systems of settlement units which are socially and economically interlinked; their size will depend on local conditions. These units will together form the unified (economic) system of settlement.[18]

The political aim in establishing the JSR is to secure the necessary comparable conditions of work and style of life for all the components of the system.[19] This does not mean, however, that the conditions of settlement in an existing small town will become like those in a large town. Within the system the very structure of settlement distribution must change significantly.

There are several types of permanent inter-settlement links which have a great influence on the structure of settlement distribution: (1) productional, (2) cultural and everyday-life, (3) labour, (4) recreational and (5) informational. The development of these various types of link proceeds unevenly in

time and space. This is the reason for the difference in the level of development and structure of settlement systems. The intensive development of the different types of inter-settlement links leads to the transformation of existing towns into agglomerations and "settlement region." These can be taken as new units of territorial and urban planning with their own peculiar internal structure. Z. N. Yargina has demonstrated one of the possible lines this transformation may take.[20] As a practical example of solving the internal structure of the JSR we can take the work of Lithuanian scientists and planners on a scheme for regional planning in their republic (the main ideas in this work can be found in the doctoral dissertation of K. Sheshelgis, "A uniform system of settlement in Lithuanian SSR," 1967).

Under the concept of the JSR the importance of separate urbanizing factors on the development of a given settlement is altered. Industry is no longer the basic and mandatory factor in each settlement. Learning, internal transport, a zone of recreation, and even a complex of institutions maintaining the important inter-urban services, can all act as an urbanizing base for the various types of settlement within the system. A change in the role of the separate factors in the whole system naturally changes the normative importance of their combined influence in calculations on the total population of particular towns. Such calculations must be carried out above all for the system (region) as a whole. Even in the near future the basic "urbanizing" or "town-forming" factors must be examined in the wider regional aspect as "region-forming" factors. We entirely agree with the well-known Polish urbanist K. Dziewoński, when he writes that with an increasing mobility of the population, of goods and information, and with the growing area of the towns, potential fields of urbaniza-

17. B. S. Khorev, Rasseleniye naseleniya: kriterii i kontseptsii (Population distribution: criteria and concepts), in: *Materialy Vsesoyuznoi nauchnoi konferentsii po problemam narodnonaseleniya Zakavkazya,* Erevan 1968; Rasseleniye i territorialnosistemnaya organizatsiya proizvoditelnykh sil (The distribution and the territorial-system organization of productive forces), *AN SSSR, ser. geogr.,* 2, 1971.
18. N. Baranov, Problemy perspektivnogo razvitiya sovetskogo gradostroitelstva (Problems of the perspective development of Soviet town planning), *Arkhitektura SSSR,* 4, 1970; Articles by N. A. Solofnenko, S. I. Soldatov, V. S. Ryazan, G. A. Kaplan and others, in: *Nauchniye prognozy razvitiya i formirovaniya sovetskikh gorodov na baze sotsialnogo i nauchno-tekhnicheskogo progressa* (Scientific predictions concerning the development and the forming of Soviet towns on the basis of social and scientific-technical progress), 3, Moskva 1969.
19. The reason why the necessary living and working conditions are described as comparable is due to differences in the natural environment, so that it is impossible to achieve complete equality.

20. Z. N. Yargina, *Sotsialniy progress i nekotoriye voprosy perspektivnogo rasseleniya* (doklad na VII Mezhdunarodnom sotsiologicheskom kongresse, Varna 1970) (Social progress and some questions on the perspective settlement network. Paper presented to the VIIth International Sociological Congress, Varna 1970), Moskva 1970.

tion arise. As a result the "opening-up" of a town increases, and the urbanizing base increasingly assumes functions which are not limited to a defined area.[21] This important theoretical observation can be found in Gorynski's concept of a "regional-urban model."[22]

The formation of the JSR represents a new stage in the development of settlement, and also a step forward compared with the universally observed expansion of uncoordinated settlement forms of local combinations of settlements including large-town agglomerations. The nature of the emergence of agglomerations and the JSR is the same—the intensification of inter-settlement links. But there is an essential difference between them. A well organized and regulated agglomeration can be one of the components of the JSR, but the system as a whole represents a higher stage in the development of inter-settlement links. The JSR presupposes a certain intensity of these links (given a suitable technical standard to these links) and a certain level in the network of services, which will ensure comparable opportunities for using all the services and places of recreation by all the inhabitants of the regional system. In the Soviet Union, especially in the older developed regions this means that as well as improving the transport one should also create appropriate networks of focal centres of population in which various service institutions would be concentrated. Their distribution should ensure that they will be equally accessible to the whole population. The large urban agglomeration with its centripetal tendencies can be distinguished from the JSR by the way it divides the adjoining areas into those privileged nuclei with services and the remaining outlying areas without services. Under the JSR this

division is overcome and the conditions for a "more equal distribution" of productional forces are created, as advised by Engels. However, it is often mistaken for the process of deconcentration of these forces, and thereby contrasted with the "law of concentration."

Two basic types of settlement network formation can be distinguished, occurring in the process of concentration of population itself (and in the concentration of the forces of production in general):

(1) Concentration in the chief, often excessively developed, centre, or in the chief town and its satellites. Example: the concentration in a country's capital or in the administrative centre of a region (or in a corresponding agglomeration) under the slackening development of "residual" settlement networks.

(2) Concentration in both the chief centre and several additional centres. Example: concentration proceeds in a country not only in its capital or in its 2 or 3 chief towns if it is a large country, but in all its large towns—the regional centres; or concentration proceeds in a region not only in its central towns but in several additional centres of average size.[23]

We think that type 2 can be the policy basis of the formation of the JSR in most older-developed regions of the USSR. In the European part of the country the development of settlement, according to this line, can lead, as Z. N. Yargina correctly pointed out, to the formation in the next 50–100 years of equal living conditions over the whole territory from the point of view of accessibility to centres of social activity. Only under these conditions can the excessive and disproportionate growth of individual large centres be overcome, which today seems to be an unavoidable evil.

Under the concept of the JSR one cannot speak about a contrast between the life styles of large towns and agglomerations and small towns, as erroneously held by some writers

21. K. Dziewoński, The concept of the urban economic base: overlooked aspects, Reg. Sci. Ass. Papers, 18, 1967; Present needs and new developments in urban theory, 21st Intern. Geogr. Congress, India 1968, Abstracts of Papers, Calcutta 1968.

22. J. Goryński, Problemy gradostroitelstwa v svete sovremennoi urbanizatsii (The nature and character of the urbanization process), Trudy Kom. po delam Territ.-Ekonom. Razvitiya Strany PAN, 16, Warszawa 1967 (in English: Studies, Committee for Space Economy and Regional Planning of the Polish Academy of Sciences, 19, Warszawa 1968).

23. In the USSR towns of "average size" in a system are those with between 50 and 250,000 inhabitants (formerly up to 500,000). These towns are more economic from the point of view of expenditure in the urban economy.

(for example V. I. Perevedentsev, A. S. Akhezer and A. V. Kochetkov). One must emphasise the background of this exclusive approach, which appeared in the Soviet Union in recent years in the problem of limiting the growth of very large towns, and also in the fate of small towns, and more precisely towns requiring development. It resulted directly from the social "demand" made of our scientific and planning departments. This "demand" appeared in several party and government resolutions. There has been a lot of practical work in the last decade, and particularly in the 1966 to 1970 period, in activating those towns requiring development. This was indispensable at this stage in the formation of the JSR for increasing the role of individual areas in the national economy.

The direction of the national economic planning of the forces of production and distribution of settlement over the country undergoes important changes in the various stages of the development of society. Thus in the political background to the formation of the JSR in the post-war years one can distinguish: a stage of the extension of the network of large towns—the local centres of *oblast* rank—through strengthening the industrial development of several "provincial" centres in the *oblasts* and Autonomous Republics (e.g., Ryazan, Kaluga, Cheboksary, Kurgan); the stage of increasing economic activation of small and middle-size towns; the stage of the formation of a network of important focal centres within an *oblast*. These are the so-called regional centres where new industrial investment is now being concentrated as well as services to meet the needs of the entire population of the region within the *oblast*.

A very important practical political task in establishing the JSR is the control of the distribution of production and population in all the developed parts of the USSR. This task is difficult when dealing with local combinations of settlements. Under the JSR, recreational areas such as national parks, reserves and areas set aside for tourism and leisure, are as important in planning as industry, agriculture science and education. This will be very effective in improving the ecological situation. The JSR is a form of spatial organization which must be an organic combination of the natural and artificial environments.

The basic geographical problem of the JSR is the economic regionalization of the country. Only through this is it possible to distinguish regional systems of settlements of various rank, and to carry out a regional-network analysis which above all tries to define the location of the focal centres of population in the whole system. In economic planning the formation of the JSR is one of the tasks behind the politics of the distribution of productional forces. We should point out here that the formation of the JSR requires special criteria.

One is correct in assuming that the general criterion of the rational distribution of the forces of production is an increase in the effectiveness of the whole of production. This in its turn helps raise the standard of living of the population. This criterion is normally used in assessing the rational distribution of population and of the development of a settlement network. However we think this criterion is insufficient for the latter problem. One should take as a second criterion an improvement in the standard of living and the creation of opportunities for comparable living conditions for the population in the various regions and settlements of different size and type, from the village to the large town, throughout the settlement system.

One must see that the universal creation of comparable working and living conditions for the population is the most radical solution of the problems of rationalizing the distribution of production and regulating the growth of towns and so decreasing the demographic pressure on large towns. At present, the rational and even distribution of production is unquestionably one of the important conditions for levelling the standard of living and for developing towns. This means that these economic and social problems must be treated together.

# Toward a Policy Planner's View of the Urban Settlement System

PETER A. MORRISON

## INTRODUCTION

Since its earliest stages, national urban policy in the United States has been marked by grandiose schemes and ill-defined objectives. A proposal in 1969, for example, envisioned a national program to build from scratch 10 new cities with populations of at least one million, and 100 new cities with populations of at least 100,000.[1] The logic of this proposal appeared to be: if cities are overcrowded, siphon off the excess people by building new cities. Bankers, government officials, and other people in powerful positions took the new-cities idea seriously because it was an appealing solution to a new "problem."

Other problem-solvers catered to the national nostalgia for an earlier and simpler era. Alarmed by the exodus of population from rural America—as though "rural America" were all one kind of place—they called for a policy of "balanced growth." No one yet has precisely defined "balanced growth" or the social purposes it would serve.[2] In his first annual report to the Congress last January, the Secretary of Agriculture seemed to say that it means creating a job for everyone, regardless of where he lives, and reversing the longstanding trend of rural out-migration.[3]

These problem-solving ideas show a remarkable absence of appreciation of the constraints that demographic processes—migration in particular—impose on the attainment of stated or implied objectives. In the realm of urban growth policy, at least, policymakers have too often pretended to knowledge and power they simply do not possess. They have made a caricature of the real, enormously complex system of urban settlement by reducing it to a set of repetitive orderly relationships.

In retrospect, it is apparent that the objectives of these schemes were murky, that the views of how the urban settlement system works were oversimplified, that the sense of what policy has in its power to do was exaggerated. But out of these exercises in urban policymaking has come a recognition that if we are to have an explicit national urban policy, it must be development-oriented rather than problem-oriented; it must build on processes of change under way instead of ignoring or attempting to thwart them, and it must evolve as understanding evolves instead of succumbing to the penchant for master plans.

In the United States, we are beginning to

1. National Committee on Urban Growth Policy, "Key National Leaders Recommend Large Program of New Cities for U.S.," Washington, D.C., Urban America, Inc., news release dated May 25, 1969.
2. These issues are explored systematically in William Alonso, "Balanced Growth: Definitions and Alternatives," unpublished paper dated September 1973 (mimeo).
3. *Rural Development Goals*, First Annual Report of the Secretary of Agriculture to the Congress (Washington: U.S. Department of Agriculture, 1974), pp. 1–5.

From The Rand Corporation Publications, P-5357, 1975, pp. 1–15, 18–19. Reprinted by permission.

appreciate the interplay of three types of influence that affect the national system of urban settlement:

(1) *Cultural predispositions,* the basic values and axioms that define a society's aspirations and direction, even though they may seldom describe its actual performance;

(2) *Migratory predispositions,* the highly focused but as yet inactivated streams of potential migration that are defined by the history of past population movements;

(3) *Governmental activities and programs,* whose inadvertent secondary effects exert a powerful but undirected influence on the redistribution of population.

This paper reviews what we know, and still need to know, about these factors in order to discern the *implicit* urban policy that now exists and to evolve broader strategies that are process-perfecting rather than problem-oriented.

## CULTURAL AND MIGRATORY PREDISPOSITIONS

Policy planners need to understand something of their culture to get a "feel" for the dynamics of its urban settlement system. I use the word "feel" because gleaning the salient aspects of a culture that bear on urban policy requires a mixture of interpretive insight and scientific skill. This mixture does exist in, for example, the work of Alonso, Beale, Berry, Boorstin, Lee, Pierson, Zelinsky, and others.[4] I have taken the liberty of embellishing

several cultural motifs suggested by Zelinsky to show how directly germane they are to the dynamics of an urban settlement system as policy planners must view it—that is, in terms of leverage points and constraints.

One motif is the intense *individualism and privatism* that are part of the American national character. Both characteristics are expressed through migration rooted in the earliest history of U.S. settlement and nurtured by an expanding national frontier, and still recur in many facets of personal and political life. The spatial fragmentation of political authority is a case in point. The U.S. metropolis, however unified a socioeconomic entity, is balkanized into dozens and sometimes hundreds of politically sovereign entities. The atomistic strain in the American national character evidenced in this patchwork of governing bodies does not necessarily prevent government agencies from charting long-range social and economic plans, but it generally blocks the effective execution of such plans, as many programs of the last decade show.

Another facet is the relentless American pursuit of a neo- or perhaps pseudo-rural residential setting. To opinion surveyors, Americans state a strong desire to live in rural and small-town settings. But further probing and careful analysis reveal that their anti-urbanism is qualified: the settings favored by most such respondents lie within 30 miles of a big city.[5] Americans, then, do not want to live *in* big cities, but neither do they want to be very far from one.

The rapid territorial expansion of the U.S.

4. William Alonso, "Balanced Growth: Definitions and Alternatives"; Calvin L. Beale, "Rural Development: Population and Settlement Prospects," *Journal of Soil and Water Conservation,* Vol. 29, No. 1 (January–February, 1974), pp. 23–27; idem, "Rural and Nonmetropolitan Population Trends of Significance to National Population Policy," in U.S. Commission on Population Growth and the American Future, *Population Distribution Policy,* Sara Mills Mazie, editor, Vol. V of Commission Research Reports (Washington: Government Printing Office, 1972), pp. 665–677; Brian J. L. Berry, "The Geography of the United States in the Year 2000," *Transactions of the Institute of British Geographers,* Publication No. 51, November 1970; Daniel J. Boorstin, *The Americans: The Democratic Experience* (New York: Random House, 1973); Everett S. Lee, "The Turner Thesis Reexamined," *American Quarterly,* Spring 1961; idem, "Migration in Relation to Education, Intellect, and Social Structure," *Population Index,* Vol. 36 (October–December 1970), pp.

437–444; George W. Pierson, *The Moving American* (New York: Alfred A. Knopf, 1973); Wilbur Zelinsky, "Selfward Bound? Personal Preference Patterns and the Changing Map of American Society," *Economic Geography,* Vol. 50, No. 2 (April 1974), pp. 144–179; idem, *The Cultural Geography of the United States* (Englewood Cliffs, N.J.: Prentice-Hall, 1973).

5. Glenn V. Fuguitt and James J. Zuiches, "Residential Preferences and Population Distribution," *Demography* (forthcoming). Other revealing studies are: Donald A. Dillman, "Population Distribution Policy and People's Attitudes: Current Knowledge and Needed Research," paper prepared for the Urban Land Institute, dated October 15, 1973 (mimeo); Donald A. Dillman and Russell P. Dobash, "Preferences for Community Living and Their Implications for Population Redistribution," Bulletin 764, Washington State College Agricultural Experiment Station, Pullman, November 1972.

metropolis since World War II shows how people have managed to have their cake and eat it, too. But the outward extension also has given rise to functional reorganization of metropolitan activities into daily urban systems that reach far beyond the defined boundaries of metropolitan areas. In the non-metropolitan hinterland of the daily urban system, a particular locality's growth has come to depend chiefly on its distance from the metropolis and its endowment of natural amenities.[6]

Cultural predisposition, coupled with hidden policies (to be discussed further on), has decisively shaped patterns in and around metropolitan centers that will linger on for years. Further generations will have to contend with a low-density, spread-out, energy-inefficient system of settlement whether they subscribe to present priorities for urban organization or not.

Individualism and privatism are likely to persist as salient motifs of the American national character, but how they will be expressed in the future is a matter for speculation. Cultural predispositions seem to have gained prominence as transportation technologies have reduced the relative importance of transportation costs as a locational constraint. Likewise, communication innovations may allow previously repressed locational desires to dictate new settlement patterns. Telecommunication policy could well have as profound an impact on settlement over the next two decades as transportation and housing programs have had during the past two.[7]

Over most of history, efficient interaction among people has depended on spatial proximity. Advanced communication technologies have weakened this dependence.

In the United States, this communication function no longer occurs within the narrow or sharply delineated frame of the past core-oriented city. Time-saving and space-spanning communication technologies, along with easy access to once-distant places, have dissolved the core-oriented city in space.[8] Telecommunication may enable the U.S. population finally to reconcile what seem to be two fundamental but conflicting needs in American society: access to others and separation from them. It may hasten the advent of what one observer described as its destiny: an urban civilization without cities.[9]

Interesting new manifestations of atomism are detectable now at a collective level, where communities' growing recognition that they can lose control of their individual destinies through demographic excess has fostered attempts to restrict further growth.[10] Reacting to such symptoms of overpopulation as congestion in urban spaces and environmental decay—or to the threat of them—some communities have tried to slow or block in-migration by restricting the number of new dwelling units that can be built; others have adopted ordinances that would force newly-arrived migrants to leave. The courts deny communities the right to enact such measures on the grounds that citizens have a right to settle where they please. But tenacious champions of local self-rule reject the idea that a community has to make room for newcomers without limit.

Americans' predilection for *mobility and change* is, in fact, a second cultural predisposition suggested by Zelinsky. The typical American's life resembles a prolonged odys-

6. Richard F. Lamb, "Patterns of Change in Nonmetropolitan America, 1950–1970," University of Chicago, pp. 237–253.
7. This remains largely a speculative topic. See Peter C. Goldmark, "Communication and the Community," *Scientific American*, September 1972, pp. 143–150. For an exhaustive review and synthesis of the literature, see Richard C. Harkness, "Telecommunications Substitutes for Travel: A Preliminary Assessment of Their Potential for Reducing Urban Transportation Costs by Altering Office Location Patterns," unpublished Ph.D. dissertation, Department of Civil Engineering, University of Washington, 1973.

8. A major factor in this dissolution has been the proliferation of controlled-access highways. Within the daily urban system, proximity to a highway is an important determinant of small-town growth or decline. Detailed evidence on this point is given in Craig R. Humphrey and Ralph R. Sell, "The Demographic Impact of Controlled Access Highways on Nonmetropolitan Communities, 1940–1970," n.d. (mimeo).
9. Irving Kristol, "An Urban Civilization Without Cities," *The Washington Post*, December 3, 1972.
10. Earl Finkler and David L. Peterson, *Nongrowth Planning Strategies* (New York: Praeger, 1974). For the demographic perspective on this issue, see Peter A. Morrison and Judith P. Wheeler, *Local Growth Control Versus the Freedom to Migrate*, P-5330, The Rand Corporation, December 1974.

sey. Marriage, childbearing, military service, higher education, changes of employment (or shifts from one plant or office location to another with the same employer), divorce, retirement—all are likely to entail changes of residence and locale.

Migration itself is deeply rooted in the American experience. Now as in the past, people continue to migrate for reasons that are connected with the workings of national economic and social systems. A characteristic of modern economies is the quick exploitation of newly-developed resources or knowledge, a process that requires the abandonment of old enterprises along with the development of the new. Such economies depend on migration to alter the labor forces of localities more quickly than could be accomplished by natural increase. Without a tradition of migration, which moves people from areas where jobs are dwindling to places where workers are needed, U.S. economic growth would be sluggish and less efficient than it actually has been.

Migration is also an important vehicle of social mobility. Many people are prevented from bettering their circumstances, less because of inherent personal limitations than because of rigidly drawn social barriers in their communities. The generally positive experience of blacks who have left the rural South and of ethnic groups that have left city ghettos confirms the value of geographic mobility as a means of access to conditions fostering improvements in personal status.[11]

The policy planner's view needs to recognize that the migratory dynamics of the national settlement system in the United States are to a considerable degree attuned to this cultural predisposition for upward social mobility, in distinct contrast to some other societies. But migration may be equally noteworthy as a sorting mechanism, filtering and sifting the population as its members undergo social mobility.[12] This possibility

recalls a central ambiguity: whether the act of migration, by freeing an individual's energies, leads to subsequent observed improvements in his life; or whether, as a prism separates light, the act is merely selective of certain persons who would have improved their status irrespective of the decision to migrate.

A look at two competing models that describe the placement of migrants in the urban class system will flesh out this point.[13] According to the "urban escalator" model, newcomers start at the bottom of the economic ladder and edge up as they learn city ways, leaving their low-level jobs to succeeding groups of newcomers. By contrast, what might be called the "filtering" model sees migrants as distinctive types of persons selected from the population at large. Such persons circulate among the cities, tending toward certain ones.

Although these two models are not incomptatible, each has a distinctive emphasis and implication. According to the "urban escalator" model, migration is noteworthy as a means of upward social mobility. With the "filtering" model, what is noteworthy is the possibility that distinctive types of persons may become concentrated in the places to which migrants flow the fastest.[14] Together, these two models imply that migration sorts

11. Evidence on this point is discussed in Peter A. Morrison, "Population Mobility: How the Public Interest and Private Interests Conflict," in U.S. Commission on Population Growth and the American Future, op. cit.

12. There is, at best, only fragmentary evidence on this point.

See, for example, Charles W. Mueller, "City Effects on Socioeconomic Achievements: The Case of Large Cities," *American Sociological Review*, Vol. 39 (October 1974), pp. 652–657.

13. Stephan Thernstrom, *The Other Bostonians: Poverty and Progress in the American Metropolis, 1880–1970* (Cambridge, Mass.: Harvard University Press, 1973), pp. 30–33.

14. Today's migrants to urban centers tend to rank higher in education and work experience than do their residents. See Peter M. Blau and Otis Dudley Duncan, *The American Occupational Structure* (New York: John Wiley and Sons, 1967); Charles Tilly, "Race and Migration to the American City," in James Q. Wilson, ed., *The Metropolitan Enigma* (Cambridge, Mass.: Harvard University Press, 1968), pp. 135–157.

The case of black migration from the South to the North appears to be more complicated. See Larry H. Long, "Poverty Status and Receipt of Welfare Among Migrants and Nonmigrants in Large Cities," *American Sociological Review*, Vol. 39 (1974), pp. 46–56; Larry H. Long and Lynne R. Heltman, "Income Differences Between Blacks and Whites Controlling for Education and Region of Birth," paper prepared for the annual meeting of the Population Association of America, April 18–20, 1974, New York City.

people out spatially as the more mobile individuals seek to elevate their status.

## UNDIRECTED MIGRATION CURRENTS

If important self-selections come into play as the population circulates among cities, migration may present significant opportunities for guiding redistribution. Zelinsky gives the name "voluntary regions" to areas where most people are there by migratory choice rather than reproductive chance.[15] When combined with the view of migration as a sorting process, his concept contains certain policy implications that I would like to explore.

One possibility is that through self-selection, the labor markets of some areas may acquire greater resiliency to change than do others. It is known that a large part of the moving that occurs in the United States is done by a small part of the population, who migrate repeatedly and frequently. Consequently, the population in places that have grown through waves of past in-migration acquires a characteristic structure differing from that in places which have grown principally through the simple lottery of birth.[16] Specifically, areas of intense migratory growth become heavily weighted with the most footloose members of society, many of whom subsequently move on. The places through which they pass resemble, demographically, a pool that a stream flows into at one end and drains at the other. Accordingly, it would be expected that adjustment to changes in the overall demand for labor, or to shifts in the mix of required skills, could occur promptly because of the brisk inflow and outflow of workers. By providing settings for voluntary job turnover, such contexts also may be conducive to occupational mobility.[17]

Another possibility is that by recognizing impending tendencies for people to sort themselves out among places, it may be feasible to strengthen or guide these tendencies according to a deliberate plan. The phenomenon of return migration is one such tendency which, until recently, has gone largely unnoticed.

"Return migration" means migration back to an area in which a person formerly resided. (In conventional usage, the area has been defined as a county, metropolitan area, state, or region.) In the United States, return migration is a phenomenon of growing demographic significance. During the 1955–1960 interval, return movers constituted 17 percent of all white movers and 14 percent of all black movers in interstate migration. By the 1965–1970 period, these percentages had risen disproportionately to 20 percent for whites and 21 percent for blacks.[18] Although only about one-fifth of all migrants are returning to a place they once lived, a fuller understanding of their actions would illuminate the prospective actions of the considerably larger segments of the population who are *potential* return migrants to somewhere. Many past migrants, especially those who have left rural areas, maintain connections with their hometowns through family and friends, and some look forward to returning there one day. What mechanisms or policies—inadvertent or deliberate—might translate such latent impulses for migration into action? By examining individual motives for return migration, we may gain some insights into these questions.

Predispositions to return somewhere appear to depend upon a complex interplay of economic, sociological, and cultural factors. Return migrants, like others, mix economic and non-economic reasons for moving, but seem to be directed somewhat more by family considerations or life-cycle-related factors, such as retirement. There is evidence that the decisionmaking of return migrants differs from that of non-return movers: there is a general lack of consideration of alternative

15. Zelinsky, *The Cultural Geography of the United States*.
16. Peter A. Morrison, "A Method for Estimating and Projecting Metropolitan Area Migration Flows," unpublished paper.
17. M. Cordey-Hayes, "Migration and the Dynamics of Multiregional Population Systems," reprinted in Section V of this book.

18. Anne S. Lee, "Return Migration in the United States," *International Migration Review*, Vol. 8 (Summer 1974), pp. 283–300.

locations and virtually no reliance on alternative information sources among returnees.[19]

Evidence of the potential for return migration is also revealing, although generalizations in this instance are restricted to certain classes of rural-urban migrants who were asked on surveys to contemplate the possibility of returning. Studies by both Price and Collignon indicate that a sizeable minority of rural-urban migrants desire to move back to their area of origin and can describe circumstances that would cause them to do so.[20]

From the standpoint of places, several additional points are germane. The "population at risk" for return migration (i.e., the pool of ex-residents) varies widely by place. Not only are numbers different, but the intent to return also differs by type of stream: for example, 26 percent of Appalachian outmigrants, but only 7 percent of black outmigrants, indicate a desire to move back to their former place of residence.[21]

Owing to its extensive history of migration, a considerable fraction of the U.S. population qualifies at any given time as potential return migrants to somewhere. The presence of these masses of like-minded but "as-yet-unmigrated" persons with common affinities for place has potentially dramatic implications. This can be grasped if, for a moment, we imagine that the complex odysseys that have marked 20th century U.S. history were to reverse themselves. The migration of young blacks from the South would become a return of retirees; the California-bound exodus from the rural Ozark-Ouachita region in Missouri, Arkansas, and Oklahoma in the 1930s would become a return to common rural affinities.[22]

Contemporary migration patterns offer striking evidence that long-standing directions of movement are in fact reversing. The historically dominant northward stream of black migrants is now exceeded by its counterstream: between 1970 and 1973, five blacks migrated from the North to the South for every three who followed the traditional path in the opposite direction.[23] Both diminished out-migration and increased return migration account for this reversal.[24]

Other recent net reverses have been documented, but the extent of return migration involved cannot yet be established.[25] The Ozark-Ouachita region now withdraws many more migrants from California than it sends there: between 1965 and 1970, two persons migrated from California to this region for every one who followed the traditional path leading west. During that period, over one-third of the region's net migratory gain originated in California alone.

Such examples of areas in which decades of out-migration have reversed suggest that the paths beaten by migrants can run both ways. It is worth considering whether and how the sentiments for other kinds of return migration might be translated into action. Policies might deliberately foster selected return flows by building on rural proclivities embedded in the American national character and strengthen-

19. John B. Lansing and Eva Mueller, *The Geographic Mobility of Labor* (Ann Arbor, Mich.: Survey Research Center, Institute for Social Research, 1967).
20. Daniel O. Price, *A Study of Economic Consequences of Rural to Urban Migration,* Office of Economic Opportunity, Washington, 1969, Vol. III, Chapter 13; Frederick C. Collignon, *The Causes of Rural-to-Urban Migration Among the Poor,* Institute of Urban and Regional Development, Berkeley, 1973; also see Gene B. Petersen and Laure Sharp, *Southern In-Migrants to Cleveland* (Washington: Bureau of Social Science Research, 1969).
21. Collignon, op. cit.
22. This epic and highly focused movement is treated in Walter

J. Stein, *California and the Dust Bowl Migration* (Westport, Conn.: Greenwood Press, 1973).
23. Daniel M. Johnson et al., "Black Migration to the South: Primary and Return Migrants," *Phylon* (in press). It should be noted that for the periods 1955–60 and 1965–70, about two-thirds of the blacks who migrated from the North to the South were returning to their region of birth. This return migration appears to select persons quite unlike those who are migrating, but not returning, to the South. The return migrants tend to be less youthful and frequently more elderly than the primary migrants (although the majority of both groups are 20 to 34 years old).

Other studies of this phenomenon are: Rex R. Campbell et al., "Return Migration of Black People to the South: Data from the 1970 Public Use Sample," *Review of Public Data Use* (in press); Daniel M. Johnson, "Black Return Migration to a Southern Metropolitan Community," unpublished Ph.D. dissertation, University of Missouri—Columbia, 1971; Gary J. Stangler et al., "Black Return Migration to Two Rural Areas of the South," n.d., mimeo, University of Missouri—Columbia; Larry H. Long and Kristin A. Hansen, "Trends in Return Migration to the South," 1974, mimeo.
24. Long and Hansen, op. cit.
25. Beale, "Rural Development: Population and Settlement Prospects."

ing the process whereby sentiments for return migration come to be translated into action. The above examples of spontaneous reverse movements, which echo earlier epic migrations, demonstrate that it may at least be possible to stimulate reversal.

One group—those who are in or near retirement—merits close attention as potential return migrants. With a steady income assured regardless of location, people are economically footloose. Those who migrated as young adults during the 1920s and 1940s, when the flow of rural-urban migrants was numerically large, have been approaching the retirement age since the 1960s. Where they choose to live and how many of them return to their regions of origin are matters of considerable import.

New sources of income such as the federal Supplemental Security Income program[26] and other income maintenance programs likely to be enacted in coming years, will expand the options of this group and may be viewed in the present context as a potential new hidden policy of population redistribution. They could create a population of floating consumers predisposed to migrate in highly directed ways to locales offering a favorable cost of living. These locales often may be the same places such people departed from in their youth.

All of these points suggest that analysis of a settlement system's past evolution may reveal subtle and possibly effective ways to guide its future growth by a selective strengthening of cultural and migratory predispositions. Such predispositions might even afford opportunities to plan and program the evolution of "voluntary regions." By drawing like-minded individuals together from widely scattered origins, certain policy objectives might be furthered simply by activating latent sentiments for migration.

These interesting possibilities pose a more general question: What does a nation need in the way of new places and regions? Are there "gaps" in the national system of settlement? It would be unsafe to presume that existing population centers (a legacy from the industrial age) have necessarily filled all the best sites of the impending post-industrial age, with its anticipated higher incomes, earlier retirement, and orientation toward recreation and retreat.[27]

## "HIDDEN" POLICIES AFFECTING URBAN SETTLEMENT

In addition to considering a society's cultural and migratory predispositions, policy planners must allow for the arbitrary and (in the U.S., at least) overwhelming influence of "hidden" policies. Agencies that build highways, award defense contracts, and choose locations for federal installations are simultaneously redistributing employment and altering incentives for private investment. These and other programs and activities, although uncoordinated, tend to accumulate and exert a powerful but undirected influence on migration. (The influence of U.S. aerospace and defense expenditures were, without doubt, major factors drawing population to the nation's Gulf Coast and Southern California.)

Efforts to intervene in any nation's system of urban settlement must begin with an assessment of such hidden policies—a difficult task, given the range and diversity of what governments do and the complex linkages through which settlement patterns come to be influenced. To cite three of the best-known examples of major federal programs that were undertaken for "non-urban" purposes, but that have decisively affected U.S. metropolitan settlement.[28]

(1) Federal welfare programs, enacted to

---

26. The Supplemental Security Income (SSI) program replaces federal and state programs of aid to the aged, blind, and permanently and totally disabled. In general, SSI yields an increase in cash income for the aged poor, and eligibility conditions for the program are uniform across the nation.

27. Wilbur Thompson, "New-on-Old Towns in the System of Cities," Chap. 15 in Harvey S. Perloff and Neil Sandberg, eds., New Towns: Why—And for Whom? (New York: Praeger, 1973).
28. These examples and the following discussion of impact assessment are drawn from an unpublished paper by my Rand colleague, Stephen M. Barro.

support minimal living standards for poor families, have encouraged the concentration of low-income and minority populations in the cities and thereby created the demographic basis for some of the nation's most intractable urban problems.

(2) The federally aided interstate highway program, created to improve the U.S. transportation system, has been instrumental in determining the growth patterns of metropolitan areas and the roles of cities relative to their suburbs. "The city determines the road," it is said, "and the road recreates the city."

(3) Federal income tax deductions for homeowners and federal support for mortgage credit, both intended to improve the nation's housing, have provided overwhelming economic incentives for middle-class families to move to surburban, owner-occupied housing, thereby weakening the central cities economically and strengthening tendencies toward racial and economic segregation.

The officials who designed and implemented these policies did not intend and were not aware that their actions would have profound consequences for settlement patterns. Nevertheless, each of the programs or policies mentioned above has probably had a greater impact on American cities than all the explicitly urban programs combined.

If there is to be such a thing as coherent urban policymaking at the federal level, a major concern of the policymakers will have to be assuring that major programs not specifically designated "urban" have desirable rather than counterproductive effects on the settlement system. But that presupposes a capability for identifying and assessing the urban impacts of a wide variety of existing and proposed policies. No such capability is now available to policymakers. It is likely, however, that many of the analytical models and other components that would be needed to create an impact assessment capability do exist in some form, although probably not in forms suitable for policy analysis and, of course, not in any overall integrative framework.

## CONCLUSIONS

In the United States, fertility decline has enlarged the relative importance of migratory growth. More so in the future than in the past, an area's population may be shaped by a process of deliberate and self-selected migration as well as by the simple lottery of birth. Whereas in the past the traditional flows of rural-urban migration and high fertility bestowed some measure of growth everywhere, many localities will now experience rates of growth hovering around zero.

Through decades of migration, particular regions have become differentiated according to their migratory histories. As forcefully as its current circumstances, an area's past settlement (or resettlement) may limit or enlarge possibilities for change. Each of the individual centers comprising a national settlement system must be considered with the following questions in mind:

1. *What fraction of the population consists of recent settlers from elsewhere rather than native or long-term residents?* Centers with a large fraction of recent settlers are high flow-through areas, which pass more people through the filter of place.

2. *Why did the settlers come?* Although economic impulse is dominant, the exceptions to the rule are what matters. The motives for moving shed light on the assortative forces operating—hence the kinds of like-minded people around whom "voluntary regions" are taking shpae.

3. *What fraction of the population has left, and for where?* The special significance of this question, of course, is the potential for return migration: an earlier odyssey lays the foundation for potential new directions of redistribution.

Finally, the recognition that a nation may have a significant cultural geography suggests that one worthy policy objective may be to nurture rather than eradicate the distinctive complexions that become attached to places (for whatever reasons). Such complexions signal purposes, as evidenced by the long list of places which serve the diverse needs of retirees (Arizona), the environmentally concerned (Oregon), and the religiously united (Utah's Mormon region). Explicit recognition of a nation's *emergent* (as well as apparent) cultural geography, coupled with sensitivity to its underlying values, may clarify the purposes that territorial policy might serve. Once it is recognized that places change people, as well as vice versa, then it may be that in strengthening the separate identities of the former, we serve the diverse ambitions, tastes, and needs of the latter.

# The New Town Movement in Britain

FRANK SCHAFFER

In a sense, new towns are as old as the history of man. The Romans, the Greeks—and no doubt the Chinese and others before them—wrote philosophical treatises. British and other writers through the years had utopian visions. The sixteenth and seventeenth-century explorers founded the cities of the New World and left them to grow. Enlightened industrialists in Britain built good houses for their workers at places such as Bournville and Port Sunlight. But the new town movement as we know it today was something different—it was the planning and building of a whole new environment.

The starting point came in 1898 with the publication by Ebenezer Howard—then a shorthand writer in the Law Courts—of his now famous book *Tomorrow: a Peaceful Path to Real Reform*.[1] I like to think of him as a young man in revolt though in fact he was by then nearly 50 and had seen the world; yet he had the enthusiasm of youth in his eloquent condemnation of the smoke and squalor of our industrial towns—"ulcers on the face of our beautiful island" he called them. And he had the vision of the prophet in his plans for a better way of life.

To Howard new towns were the way of escape from the congestion and social evils of urban life in Britain at the turn of the century. He saw a town as a complete social and functional structure, with sufficient jobs to make it self-supporting, spaciously laid out to give light, air and gracious living and surrounded by a green belt that would provide both farm produce for the population and opportunity for recreation and relaxation. Half a dozen such towns, separate but linked by a rapid transport system, should, he suggested, form a "social city" catering for the complete needs of around a quarter of a million people (Figure 1).

## "DO IT YOURSELF"

To gain support and to help propagate his ideas Howard founded the Garden City Association; but writing and talking were not enough. He believed in showing the way by example. "If you wait for the authorities to build new towns," he told Frederic Osborn, "you will be older than Methuselah before they start. The only way to get anything done is to do it yourself." So in 1902 he got sufficient backing to start building his first garden city at Letchworth, some 30 miles from London, and in 1920 he started the second garden city at Welwyn. They were brave ventures and, despite many financial and other troubles, the towns slowly but

1. Reissued with slight revisions in 1902 under the title *Garden Cities of Tomorrow*. Now available in paperback with a preface by Sir Frederic Osborn and an introductory essay by Lewis Mumford, Faber and Faber, 1965. The book has been translated into five languages including Japanese.

From "The New Town Movement," *New Towns: The British Experience*, H. Evans, ed. (London: C. Knight and Co., 1972), pp. 11–15, 17–21. Reprinted by permission.

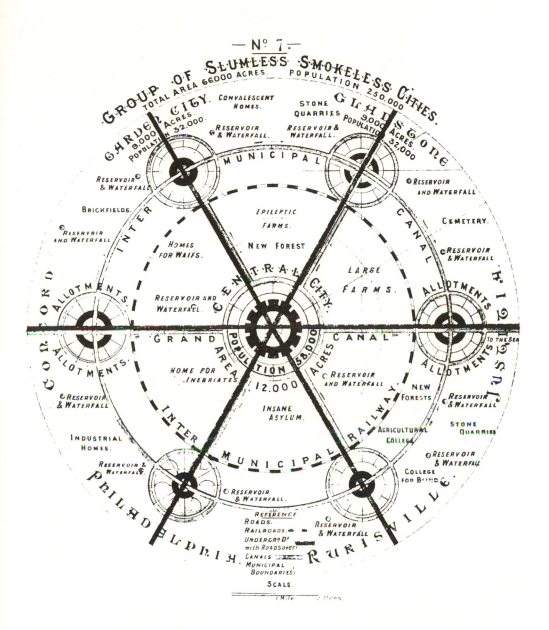

Figure 1. Diagram No. 7 from the first edition (1898) of *Tomorrow: A Peaceful Path to Real Reform*. Ebenezer Howard omitted the diagram from the revised edition (re-named *Garden Cities of Tomorrow*) in 1902 as too visionary even for sympathetic readers.

It is clear from the text of the 1898 edition that Howard saw the cluster city as the next stage after the first garden city demonstration. "Let me here present a diagram, No. 7, representing a series or cluster of towns . . . the idea of a carefully planned town lends itself readily to the idea of a carefully planned cluster of towns . . . so that the advantages which a large city presents in the higher forms of corporate life may be within the reach of all. . . ."

529

surely established themselves. They proved, in a very practical way, that his ideas were fundamentally sound.

In starting the second garden city, Howard wanted to show the Government how to solve the massive housing problem that faced Britain after the first world war. We needed a hundred of these new towns, he said, and he urged the Government to build them. Like so many prophets before him he was in advance of his time, but his pleas did not fall on entirely deaf ears. In 1921 the Government set up a committee under the chairmanship of Neville Chamberlain which reported in favour of the idea and in the next Housing Act local authorities were given powers to buy land for the purpose. But the powers were never used.

Ten years later, with London rapidly expanding, the Greater London Regional Planning Committee, in a special report by Raymond Unwin, again recommended the building of new towns as a matter of urgency. The Government responded by setting up yet another committee under Lord Marley. This committee discussed the matter for four years and its report in 1934 again recommended in favour of new towns; but again nothing was done.

## THE TCPA's CAMPAIGN

Throughout these years the association founded by Howard in 1898, under its new name of the Town and Country Planning Association, waged a constant campaign and when Howard died in 1928 it found equally powerful and determined advocates in Mr.—now Sir—Frederic Osborn, the first secretary and estate manager of the Welwyn Garden City Company, Captain R. L. Reiss, Dr. Norman Macfadyen and Gilbert and Elizabeth McAllister—to mention only a few of the stalwart supporters. The need for new ways of tackling the national problem of overcrowding and urban sprawl was in any case being clearly demonstrated by events, and by the late 1930s the problems of planning—or lack of planning—had become

acute. More and more people were drifting away from the northern counties in search of jobs. London was still expanding; and with war on the horizon the concentration of people and industry in the South became a cause for such concern that in 1938 the Government set up the Royal Commission on the Distribution of the Industrial Population under the chairmanship of Sir Montague Barlow. The report of this commission, published and pigeonholed just as war broke out, recommended the establishment of a central planning authority and a further examination of the land problem; but in a minority report some members again pressed for a more forthright programme, including the building of garden cities and satellite towns.

## 1930s: "AN ALL-TIME LOW"

Thus for nearly 40 years new towns were just talked about, with Letchworth and Welwyn Garden City struggling ahead but little known outside a few professional circles. Meanwhile the suburban rash of jerry-built houses spread across our countryside, with ribbon development along the main roads and bungaloid settlements of converted buses and railway coaches only 20 miles from London. And the big local authorities sought to solve the housing crisis by building massive one-class housing estates without jobs and without the score of other things a society needs. In the 1930s we really reached an all-time low. Everyone said it was wrong; but it took another war and another housing crisis to get anything done.

When the bombs started falling on London, and the amount of destruction that would take place was quite unpredictable, Winston Churchill, who was by then Prime Minister, appointed Lord Reith to advise on the problems of post-war reconstruction. He collected together a small band of experts, put in hand a study of the controversial subject of compensation and betterment[2] and an examination of

2. *Final Report of the Expert Committee on Compensation and Betterment* (Chairman, Mr. Justice Uthwatt) 1942, Cmd. 6386.

the problems of the rural areas,[3] commissioned Professor Abercrombie and J. H. Foreshaw to prepare a new plan for London[4] and later asked Professor Abercrombie to prepare a plan for the whole of the Greater London area.[5] The examples of the garden cities, the studies of the 1930s, the limited planning experience of the pre-war years, all came under intensive examination in this far-reaching review of the problems that would have to be faced in Britain when the war was over. They all pointed inescapably to the need for a national planning policy and a more effective and positive machine for controlling and directing post-war development.

Lord Reith very quickly secured government acceptance of the need for national planning and in 1943, at the height of the war, a new Ministry—the Ministry of Town and Country Planning—was set up to prepare for the post-war situation. Within a year legislation was passed through Parliament enabling the war-damaged areas to be bought, replanned as a whole and rebuilt; but the rest had to wait until peace was restored.

## 1945: NEW TOWNS A PRIORITY

With the end of the war in Europe and the Labour Party's victory at the polls in 1945, Clement Attlee, the new Prime Minister, appointed Lewis Silkin as Minister of Town and Country Planning. Swift action followed. With the thousands of servicemen returning home and a desperate housing shortage, new towns became a priority. Much preliminary work had already been done by the newly-formed Ministry. A committee of officials under George Pepler had worked out the basic principles for planning new towns and the various possible ways of getting them built. But Silkin quickly saw that to convince his colleagues in the Government that it could be done and to get the necessary legislation through a crowded session of Parliament, a

departmental report was not enough. He needed the backing of influential and experienced people in the outside world of administration and finance.

Lord Reith, creator of the BBC, famed for his organising genius and first Minister in charge of post-war reconstruction (though inexplicably removed from the job by Churchill after only a brief period) was an obvious choice. Under his chairmanship and with a galaxy of talent to support him, an advisory committee was quickly set up, not this time to advise on *whether* to build new towns but *how*. This time the Government really meant business.

In framing his main recommendations Lord Reith clearly drew heavily on his BBC experience where a semi-independent government-appointed broadcasting corporation had proved its worth in both peace and war. Under his guidance the committee drew up a blueprint for somewhat similar government-appointed agencies for building new towns. These development corporations, too, have proved their worth over a quarter of a century as the most effective instrument yet devised for undertaking development projects on a massive and comprehensive scale.

Speed was essential. Lord Reith knew that recommendations were urgently needed and his first report[6] on the question of agency was produced in three months—a tremendous *tour de force*. The second report,[7] dealing in detail with the legislation needed, followed a few weeks later and the final report,[8] containing a remarkable exposition of the planning principles and of the organisation needed, was completed in another three months. Legislation was drafted even while the committee was still sitting and the New Towns Act, 1946,[9] was one of the earliest social measures to be passed by the new Parliament.

---

6. *Interim Report of the New Towns Committee,* Cmd. 6759, HMSO, 1946.
7. *Second Interim Report,* Cmd. 6794, HMSO, 1946.
8. *Final Report,* Cmd. 6876, HMSO, 1946.
9. The 1946 Act, together with the 1959 Act which set up the Commission for the New Towns—see p. 36 in original text—are now consolidated in the New Towns Act, 1965. Separate Acts apply in Scotland and Northern Ireland.

---

3. *Report of the Committee on Land Utilisation in Rural Areas* (Chairman, Lord Justice Scott) 1942, Cmd. 6378.
4. *The County of London Plan,* Macmillan & Co., 1943.
5. *Greater London Plan,* 1944. HMSO, 1945.

# GREATER LONDON PLAN

### THE FOUR RINGS

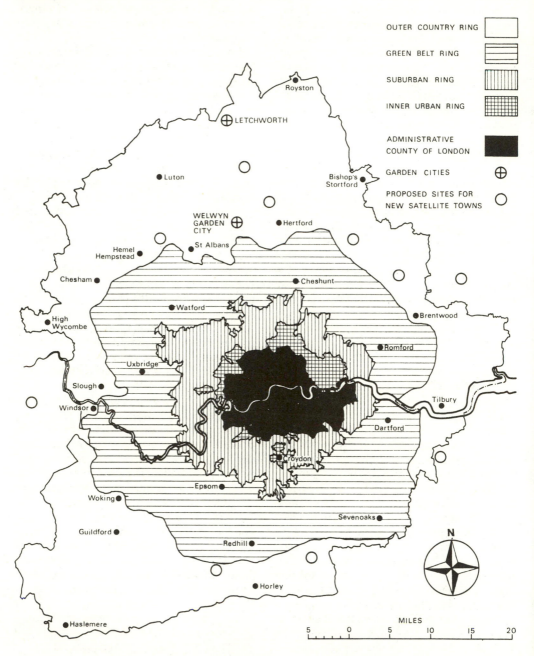

OUTER COUNTRY RING

GREEN BELT RING

SUBURBAN RING

INNER URBAN RING

ADMINISTRATIVE
COUNTY OF LONDON

GARDEN CITIES

PROPOSED SITES FOR
NEW SATELLITE TOWNS

Royston

LETCHWORTH

Luton

Bishop's
Stortford

WELWYN
GARDEN
CITY

Hertford

Hemel
Hempstead

St Albans

Chesham

Cheshunt

Watford

Brentwood

High
Wycombe

Uxbridge

Romford

Slough

Windsor

Tilbury

Dartford

Croydon

Epsom

Woking

Sevenoaks

Guildford

Redhill

Horley

Haslemere

MILES

5   0   5   10   15   20

N

Figure 2. Proposed siting of eight to ten new satellite towns and reservation of country belt in Professor Sir Patrick Abercrombie's *Greater London Plan (1944)*.

## THE FUTURE ASSURED

There were a few opponents and some scep-tics; and there were many who were con-vinced that the new towns would never in fact be built. Others predicted they would be the "greatest white elephants of all time." Yet, despite the cries of the Jonahs, they went ahead. It was not all plain sailing. In some areas local opposition was intense. Lewis Silkin had to face stormy meetings and the first three designation orders were challenged in the Courts, one of them right up to the House of Lords, before any progress could be made. Thereafter the opposition died away. Between 1946 and 1950, 14 towns were started,[10] eight of them to take "overspill" from London, one for Glasgow and five to meet other specific needs, such as housing the steel workers at Corby, the coalminers at Peterlee and Glenrothes, the workers in the factories in the East Monmouth valley and the war-time factory estate at Aycliffe that was being rapidly converted to peace-time produc-tion.

For the "overspill" towns, attraction of industry was the key to success. People would not move without jobs. At first, industrialists were hesitant: to build a new factory in green fields 30 miles from the capital took more faith than courage. But the publication of the master plans, the building of roads and the opening up of attractive factory areas began to reassure them. A few industries in the crowded areas of London, short of space and manpower, seized the chance of expanding in more spacious surroundings. The new and rapidly growing post-war industries wel-comed the opportunity of cheap land and government capital for factory building. The first small trickle soon became a steady stream and in a few years the future of the towns was no longer in doubt.

There were growing pains, of course. It

10. One of these was Welwyn Garden City. Because of shortage of capital in the early post-war years, the Government thought the Garden City Company would not be able to complete the town quickly enough and it was accordingly taken over by a develop-ment corporation for completion as part of the London "over-spill" programme.

took time for the development corporations to create their organisations and reach an under-standing with the Ministry on the financial and other controls. There were false starts in one or two towns, when grandiose and im-practicable plans were drawn up and had to be abandoned. It was a bad time, too, to start. Bricks, cement, timber and steel were all rationed; building labour was scarce; money was certainly short; the financial implications were a matter of sheer guesswork; and the first of the economic freezes and squeezes all but brought the programme to a complete halt. But these were short-term problems. It was the long-term vision that mattered. If the first post-war Government had lacked the courage to start when they did, if they hadn't been ready to take a risk and learn by experience, the chance would have been lost and the old apathy would have taken over again.

## AN ALL-PARTY PROGRAMME

In the ups and downs of the post-war econ-omy, there were fears that the Conservative Government that succeeded the Attlee Gov-ernment would reverse the policy and aban-don these projects completely. Harold Mac-millan, who became Minister in 1951, quickly recognised the contribution they could make to the housing shortage and gave them every encouragement, yet with the single exception of Cumbernauld, started in 1955 to relieve the extreme housing pressure in Glasgow, it was 10 years before any more new towns were designated. In 1961–64, under the mounting pressure of housing short-age, the Government ventured on a second series of new towns at Skelmersdale, Dawley (now renamed Telford), Runcorn and Red-ditch, to help solve the overcrowding prob-lems in Birmingham and Merseyside, and started another town at Livingston in Scot-land. Labour came back to power in 1964 and adopted proposals already in hand for a town at Washington, close to Tyneside; and Irvine, the fifth new town in Scotland, followed two years later.

By this time extensive regional investigations had demonstrated the need for an even more radical approach to the problems that lay ahead. The new towns were acknowledged to be successful in economic, financial and social terms, and the machinery had stood the test of time. Wider use was clearly indicated. In 1967 the first ''new city'' was started at Milton Keynes for a quarter of a million people and the new town procedure was used to double the size of the ancient city of Peterborough, to add 100,000 people to the nearby town of Northampton and another 100,000 to Warrington to relieve pressure on Manchester. In 1971—and although the investigation started under Labour the decision was taken after the Conservatives came back to power—35,000 acres of Central Lancashire were designated under the New Towns Act to provide a growth point for the economic revival of the area where a population growth of over two million is expected by the end of the century. Two more towns of the traditional type were also announced—Llantrisant in Wales and Stonehouse in Scotland.

In Northern Ireland, too, the new-town machinery was accepted as a way of meeting the urgent need for new housing, new industry and urban rebuilding. Under legislation passed by the Northern Irish Parliament in 1965 development commissions have been set up in Lurgan and Portadown (to become the new city of Craigavon), in Antrim and Ballymena, and in Londonderry.

Thus new towns are no longer a political issue. They are now a well-tried instrument of physical and economic progress, accepted and supported by all the political parties. Regional plans for other areas are demonstrating the need for more new centres of development in which new towns must surely play a part; and when we begin in Britain, as we soon must, to tackle seriously the problem of tearing down the obsolete and decaying areas of our older towns and cities and rebuilding them in a way that will match the economic and social needs of the twenty-first century, the new town experience of comprehensive development over the past 25 years will be invaluable.

## BIRTH OF A NEW SCIENCE

It seems a long time ago now since those exciting early days when the blueprints for the post-war world were being hammered out and the vision of a new and rebuilt Britain emerged. The vision has sometimes become a little blurred as new economic restraints have crowded in and practical difficulties have imposed a seemingly never-ending brake on progress. Yet 25 years is so brief a period. Measured against progress in any earlier generation the achievement is tremendous and the increasing momentum is opening up wider horizons. In the sphere of professional thought and activity new and far-reaching planning ideas have been developed, with a better understanding of people's needs and sophisticated methods of analysis, prediction and financial appraisal. A whole new science has been born.

And the impact has been world-wide. Every year thousands of foreign visitors come to see the British new towns. Almost every country in the world has sent official delegations to find out more about them and to see how it is done. Scores of countries are now following our lead—a lead born of the vision and despair of a humble London shorthand-writer 70 years ago.

Ebenezer Howard did not live to see any spectacular results in his lifetime. Even though he received a knighthood in 1927 in recognition of his services to planning, he must have died a disappointed man. Thirty years of propaganda and only two half-built towns to show for it. But ideas—good ideas—live on. He made a greater contribution to mankind than he ever knew.

# What Are New Towns For?

WILLIAM ALONSO

Calling for new towns has long been a favourite activity of architects and architectural critics, but in recent years just about everyone in the United States seems to be advocating the development of new towns. The list of proponents is staggering and includes giant corporations, real estate developers, the American Institute of Planners, the *New York Times,* the current and former Vice Presidents of the United States, the former President, the Urban Affairs Council of the current President, the legislatures and planning or development agencies of several states, several Cabinet members, and the National Committee on Urban Growth Policy which includes in its membership and represents on this issue prominent congressmen, senators, governors, mayors, county commissioners, the National Association of Counties, the National League of Cities, the United States Conference of Mayors, and Urban America. Television shows and feature stories in newspapers and magazines have brought the general idea into pop culture. Hippies are forming communes reminiscent of the utopian communities of the last century.

The causes behind the interest in new towns in this country are intriguing but elusive. Some of the advocacy may be self-serving, as in the case of congressmen or federal agencies seeking to maintain constituencies diminishing by out migration, or of professional groups interested in extending their role and influence, or of industries after new markets. In other cases, the images of glimmering and simpler future Camelots are a marriage of American nostalgia for the small town and escapism from the biting complexity of our real urban problems. But mostly, it seems that the very idea of new towns holds some magic that quickens the pulse and fires the imagination, a Promethean impulse to father a better place and way of life, a calm and healthy utopia of crystalline completeness.

But it is not my purpose here to analyse such causes for new town proposals; rather, I will try to examine the stated purposes of a new towns strategy in America as a rational policy in the public interest: What are new towns for? The romantic parentage of new towns concepts makes this difficult because it has established a style of advocacy which is hortatory, metaphorical, and often without specific meaning. When a cabinet member speaks of "avoiding chaos," "organic balance," "creative possibilities," "building poems," "communities of tomorrow," and the like, he is reading burnished but rather empty rhetoric taken by his speech writer from current exponents of a long tradition of architectural and utopian writers. Further, certain code words are commonly used. For instance, one of the most frequent reasons for wanting new towns is that they will be "planned" (a word used in urban matters as a term of praise acceptable to both the political right and left). But the fact *per se* that something is to be planned is of interest only to the professionals who get the work and also to later chroniclers. To others, such planning is

From *Urban Studies,* vol. 7, February 1970, pp. 37–45. Reprinted by permission of the University of Glasgow.

an input and the question is one of output: what does such planning do to what the new town will do? In this particular case, "planning" stands for certain land use and circulation features, lower costs through reduction of uncertainty in infrastructure investment, and so forth. Some other code words are "balanced," "exciting," "variety," "living environment," "choice," "human scale." I have tried to interpret fairly these meanings into language that is clearer. I have also had to use my judgement in distinguishing between purely instrumental objectives and their intended purposes. For instance, it is frequently said that new towns will distribute the population more equally across the national territory. In such cases I have tried to get at why such a population distribution should be wanted and have referred these instrumental objectives to more general ones such as mental health or economic development. In all, I have discovered some two dozen principal objectives, some with several variants. I shall present these with some commentary in the coming pages.

In fairness to the reader, I must state my principal conclusions: There is little force in the arguments for a major commitment of effort and resources to direct a substantial portion of our urbanisation into new towns. On the other hand, there may be some sense in the limited use of new towns for the testing and development of technological, physical, and institutional innovations which might be applicable to the expansion and rebuilding of existing cities. These conclusions are presented more fully at the end of the paper.*

A definitional interlude is necessary. Some have tried to draw a distinction, but "new town" and "new community" are currently used almost interchangeably, although the term "community" is gaining in accordance with the present fashion of using it to indicate approval of two or more people or of a place. "New community" also has a slightly wider meaning, and is often used for the promotion of subdivisions which would not be called new towns by anyone. This confusing usage

*Not reprinted here—Eds.

may be illustrated by a passage from President Johnson's Message on Housing and Cities to the 90th Congress (February 1968):

But there is another way as well, which we should encourage and support. It is the new community, freshly planned and built. These can truly be the communities of tomorrow—constructed either at the edge of the city or farther out. We have already seen their birth. Here in the nation's capital, on surplus land once owned by the government, a new community is springing up. In other areas, other communities are being built on farm and meadow land. The concept of new community is that of a balanced and beautiful community—not only a place to live, but a place to work as well. It will be largely self-contained, with light industry, shops, schools, hospitals, homes, apartments, and open spaces.

This paper reserves the terms new towns and new communities to those that are to be built at some distance from existing urban areas, and will not discuss except in passing new communities which are extensions of the territorial margin of existing settlements or reconstruction of the internal structure of cities. Although terms such as "new towns in town" are gaining currency, they seem to be attempts to make use of a fashionable label to promote large projects which, regardless of their merits, are not new towns.

New towns may be "independent" if they contain the employment of their own residents, or be "satellite" if there is to be a substantial amount of commuting to existing centres.[1] Thus, Reston and Columbia, the best known current new towns, are satellites, as have been most of the other well-known ones over the decades: Radburn, Forest Hills, the Green Belt towns. Historically, independent new towns have been quite numerous. In a sense, of course, almost every American city has been an independent new town founded within the last three and a half centuries. But, in addition, the nineteenth cen-

1. Some authors use the term "satellite" for towns which are self-contained labour markets but whose residents make some use of the facilities of a nearby metropolis. It seems clearer to use the term "independent" for towns with substantial closure of their labour market, and "satellite" for those with a more open labour market.

tury saw a great many company-run towns, such as Lawrence, Lowell, and Pullman, and a substantial number of utopian and religious new settlements; also, the railroads planned and developed a very great number as they spanned the continent. Present-day independent new towns are most frequently resort or retirement towns, or such special cases as towns that originated as housing for workers in large projects (Boulder City and Norris) or atomic-energy towns (Oak Ridge and Los Alamos).

Although there has been some slight association between the new town ideas and the concept of growth centres or poles, especially by some federal agencies, there are enough differences that I shall concentrate on the new town idea as such. The principal differences are: (1) new town proposals are for newly built settlements, while growth centres usually deal with the expansion of an existing centre to bring it to sufficient size to afford the economies of scale and externalities needed for self-sustaining growth; (2) new town proposals often stress self-containment as a labour market, while growth centre proposals often stress the role of providing jobs for those living in the surrounding region; and, perhaps most important, (3) new town proposals are based on steering growth *away* from urban areas which are regarded as too big, while growth centres are viewed as steering growth *toward* underemployed populations (or, in the case of frontier regions, toward some unexploited resource). There is an obvious complementarity between new town policies that aim at deconcentration of urbanisation and growth centre policies that aim at an increase of urbanisation in underdeveloped regions. This complementarity has received increased recognition in recent years in some European and developing countries, but in this paper I shall concentrate on new towns proposals—that is to say, on the *elsewhere* or deconcentration argument.

Although much of the following analysis would apply to a policy of directing all further urban growth to new towns, the discussion will focus on proposed policies of directing to new towns only a substantial portion of that

growth. There are two reasons for this. First, that with journalistic exceptions there are no proponents of a commitment to channel all further growth to new towns. Second, that it is inconceivable that such a policy be feasible. The British experience is instructive. As of December 1967, after twenty years of sustained effort, the population of the new towns had grown by only 554,373, which is only one percent of the national population. During 1967, the population of the new towns grew by 34,577, which is less than 10% of the yearly British population growth (Town and Country Planning, 1968).

I shall group into three categories the principal objectives for new towns which I have found in the literature and in discussion with their proponents: (1) macro geo-economic purposes, (2) social policy purposes, and (3) production and physical purposes.* These categories are not entirely satisfactory, but they serve to cluster the arguments.

## MACRO GEO-ECONOMIC OBJECTIVES

It is common to argue that present urban areas cannot cope with the expected growth of urban population. A recent and significant statement of this type was made by the National Committee on Urban Growth Policy (1969). They predicted that by the year 2000, U.S. urban population would grow by 100 million, and recommended that to help accommodate this growth, we build one hundred new towns, each of at least 100,000 population, and ten new cities, each of at least one million population.[2] The very roundness of these figures suggests their tentativeness and leads one to wonder how the proposals might have differed if men had six fingers on each hand. Nonetheless, accepting these targets, the year 2000 would see only 7% of

---

*Only the first set of purposes is discussed in this reprint—Eds.
2. National Committee on Urban Growth Policy, "Key National Leaders Recommend Large Program of New Cities for U.S." (Washington, D.C.: Urban America, Inc., news release dated 25th May 1969). The story was carried by all major papers on that date; it was based on D. Canty (ed.), *The New City* (New York: Praeger, 1969).

the 300 million population residing in these new settlements and 80% of the foreseen growth in existing ones. If replacement of one-third of the existing dwellings is taken into account, almost 90% of new housing would be produced in existing urban areas. Thus, the National Committee's proposal, as radical as it first seems, would affect only a small part of our population and an even smaller part of our housing production. A programme so marginal in its effect cannot stand very high in the list of our priorities. Further, it would seem that, within the uncertain state of our knowledge, we cannot say that existing urban centres can absorb 80 but not 100 million persons. If each of our smallest two hundred metropolitan areas took in a half million persons, we could hold the 100 million without any of these areas exceeding two and a half million. The argument is further weakened when we examine the growth assumption: our national rate of population growth has declined steadily for the past fifteen years and currently stands at one per cent. At this rate, by the year 2000 the increase will be only 75 million—5 million less than the growth allocated to existing areas.

Less crude than the "lack-of-room" arguments are those holding that further growth of large urban areas is inefficient. In brief, such arguments state that urban costs per capita rise with increasing urban size or, equivalently, that marginal costs increase with population.[3] A considerable literature addresses itself to the shape of this cost curve and the location of its bottom, but has not settled the question of whether costs rise beyond a certain population for a given level of service. Whether they do or not, when the city is compared to a firm or unit of production (as this argument does), an analysis based only on costs is incomplete in its own terms: the objective of a unit of production is to make money, not to save it. The point of minimum costs is relevant only if we assume constant product per inhabitant. It appears that "product" per inhabitant rises

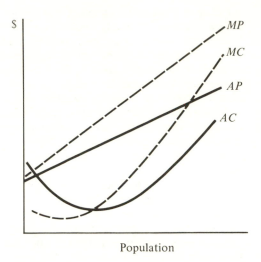

Figure 1.

faster than "cost."[4] The situation may be seen in Fig. 1, where $AP$ and $MP$ are average and marginal product and $AC$ and $MC$ average and marginal costs. Let us define net national product so as to exclude such goods and services as travel to work, fire protection, pollution control, etc., which are here viewed as costs instrumental to the production of ultimate consumption or investment. A national objective of maximising net national product would optimise at the city's population size where marginal product equals marginal costs, if we assume a national labour surplus. If there is full employment, the optimum would occur at the population where the difference between marginal product and marginal cost is equal to opportunity costs similarly defined at another location. If product per capita rises with urban scale, this

3. According to this line of reasoning, urban areas grow beyond their least cost point because arriving people or firms pay average costs as private costs in taxes, congestion, etc. These are lower than the marginal or social costs that their arrival imposes.

4. Costs are traditionally measured by local government expenditures, and these do rise. However, the level of services is not controlled in such crude tests. The cost of living, which is available for the larger U.S. metropolitan areas and which includes transportation, housing, etc., is associated only weakly with population size and shows an extremely low elasticity. For the "product" side, we would like to have gross regional product or value added for the urban areas. This information is not available for U.S. cities, but family income rises steeply with population size, with a far greater elasticity than municipal costs or the cost of living. Fragmentary data for other countries repeat this pattern.

population level is obviously far higher than that at which average costs are minimised.[5] The point is that efficiency arguments for diverting growth away from existing urban areas depend upon new towns having a greater difference between marginal product and marginal cost, while in fact the opposite seems to be the case if we judge by existing cities of a size comparable to that of the proposed new towns.

There are frequent suggestions that the new towns would intercept migrants from the rural areas to the large cities and provide a "domestic detente" (American Institute of Planners, 1968) to give our metropolitan areas time to absorb, culturally and economically, their earlier migrants. However, the image of a flood of rural migrants is by now out of date. Migration of farm population to metropolitan areas has dropped to an insignificant trickle, largely because there are so few farmers left. Migration plays a decreasing role in metropolitan growth. Of the 10.9% growth of metropolitan areas during the 1960–1966 period, only 22.6% came from immigration as compared to 35% for the 1950–1960 period. Most of the domestic migration came from smaller urban places, rather than from farms, and migration proceeds upward through the hierarchy of urban places. But beyond this, the picture is very confused. For example, compare the yearly rate of 492,000 migration into metropolitan areas with the rate of 138,000 migration out of non-metropolitan areas and the rate of 377,000 civilian immigration into this country during the 1960–1966 period. I cannot discover an analysis of the interaction of these flows, but these figures strongly suggest that nearly three-fourths of the migratory increase into

metropolitan areas is international in origin, and that only 6% of their population growth comes from domestic flows.[6]

Many metropolitan areas are, in fact, losing population through out-migration. The cross currents among metropolitan areas may make it difficult to form a clear image. The fastest growing metropolitan areas, and strongest magnets to migrants in proportion to their size, are those between 200,000 and 2,000,000, while those over 2,000,000 were attracting only 0.2 migrants per hundred population per year, and those under 200,000 had net out-migration.[7] Nine areas[8] accounted for 81% of all net migration, leaving an average of less than 500 migrants per year entering each of the others. Or, put another way, twenty-eight metropolitan areas in the South, South-west, Mountain States, and Pacific Coast accounted for 99% of the net migration (A.C.I.R., 1968).

Because the concern with intercepting migrants has a great deal to do with the racial question, some examination of black flow is of interest. Black migration to metropolitan areas during the 1960–1966 period averaged 145,000 yearly—about 30% of all net migration—down from a 172,000 yearly rate during the 1950–1960 decade.[9] From 1960 to 1966, migration accounted for some 34% of

---

5. If instead of maximising net national product (which would be a national objective) we sought to maximise the net product per capita in the city (which would be an objective of the city's residents), we would be seeking to maximise the difference between average product minus average cost. This would occur at a lower population level than the national product maximisation, but at a higher population level than the point of minimum costs per capita. This can be proved formally, but it is enough to refer to the diagram. The curious point is that, despite the locals' optimum occurring at a lower population level than the nation's, most cities want to grow while many national governments are trying to stop or slow this growth.

6. The figures on domestic migration are calculated from data in U.S. Bureau of the Census, *Current Population Reports*, Series P-25, No. 427, "Estimates of Population of Counties and Metropolitan Areas, July 1, 1966: A Summary Report," U.S. Government Printing Office, Washington, D.C., 1969. The figures on international migration are calculated from data in the *U.S. Statistical Abstract*. Some uncertainty exists in the analysis. If suburban growth has spilled strongly over the boundaries of the metropolitan areas, as defined by the Census, the real domestic migration into metropolitan areas, which is a net figure, would be an understatement.

7. Computed from *Current Population Reports*, op. cit., p. 5.

8. Los Angeles-Orange County; New York-North Eastern New Jersey; San Francisco-Oakland-San Jose; Washington, D.C.; Philadelphia; Houston; Miami-Fort Lauderdale; San Bernardino-Riverside; and Dallas.

9. These figures are derived from census population data by applying the rate of growth of all black population to its components and attributing the differences at a later period to migration. This crude technique may understate rural-to-urban migration slightly if rural birth rates are higher. However the most recent estimate places the total flow of blacks into metropolitan areas for 1960–1969 at 800,000 or 100,000 per year. (Statement by Conrad Taeuber, Associate Director, Bureau of the Census, before the House Committee on Banking and Currency, 14th October 1969.)

the growth of black metropolitan population, but only 31% of the black migrants (44,000 per year) were from farms. The black population is already far more urbanised than the white, and the shifting proportions of blacks among urban areas of diverse sizes indicates that, on the whole, they are moving upward along the urban-size hierarchy faster than whites. This is understandable because the percentage of blacks below the poverty level declines as size of urban place increases (A.C.I.R., 1968).

On the basis of this brief review, three questions may be posed: (1) Is the flow of migrants so large that we should undertake a reorganisation of our system of urban places to gain a "domestic detente"? It would appear not. If we exclude the twenty-eight metropolitan areas in the developing and urbanising crescent from the South to the Pacific States, the other metropolitan areas are either trading already urban migrants with each other or they are trading ex-migrants for new migrants. Black migration from the farms is relatively small and declining, and the other black migration is primarily from small urban places to urbanised areas. (2) If new towns were developed, would they attract these migrants? Again, it would appear not. New towns or even new cities would of necessity be smaller, at least in the beginning, and the pattern of migration, especially for blacks, is away from smaller urban places toward bigger ones. Of course it might be that new towns of extraordinary amenity, offering strong inducements and having a credible guarantee of future size, might succeed in attracting people, but there is no assurance that these arrivals would be the same migrants that are to be intercepted.[10] Further, it may be that the cost of inducements to effect a geographic shift might be better used directly for the welfare and acculturation of the intended populations. (3) If the new towns can attract population, would they do so in time? From the present stage of vague discissions and the experience of such programmes as urban re-

newal, one may estimate that ten years from now there may be some small beginnings on the ground, and that it would be another decade before the new towns would involve enough people to affect significantly the migration flows to metropolitan areas. Of course, a determined federal government could act much faster, breaking ground within a year and promoting fast growth by hot-house techniques. But this would make extremely unlikely those elements of amenity, detailed programming, technical and institutional innovation, private-public cooperation, and so forth, that are integral to most new town proposals. The dilemma is that quickly-developed towns would be new but not innovative, and a poor magnet for migrants if we are to judge by existing cities of comparable size. On the other hand, innovative new towns would have a long gestation in research, development, and organisation. Two decades from now, of course, we shall be far more urbanised; migration to metropolitan areas then will be smaller in absolute figures and quite small indeed as a relative number. Further, it is to be hoped that our national conscience and political necessity will have led us to improve the cultural and economic capacity of those future migrants to a level well above that of today.

A variant of the objective of intercepting migrants for the relief of urbanised areas is the positive statement that industrial new towns be developed in rural areas or other areas of declining employment in primary production in order to provide jobs that offer people a permanent alternative to out-migration from their district. This variant was advanced by the U.S. Department of Agriculture during the Johnson administration under the label "urban-rural balance" (U.S. Dept. of Agriculture, 1968). The proposals included new towns, growth centres based on existing communities, and "new communities" that would encompass several counties in ways which were not clear. Although these proposals were not very specific, they apparently called for new towns that would be quite small, just large enough to absorb the district's surplus population. Standardised pro-

10. The British experienced a similar missed population target in their new towns (Heraud 1968).

cess manufacturing has been leaving the larger metropolitan areas, moving to smaller ones and cities, but it is doubtful that enough plants could locate in rural surroundings or small towns as would be necessary for such a policy to be effective. Also, because the size of a plant typically increases with decreasing urban size, this suggested pattern would lead to a very large number of one-company new towns under absentee ownership. But, more important, it appears that the rate of out-migration does not vary with local hardship; rather, migrants leave at a steady rate regardless of local conditions, while local conditions affect the rate of in-migration (A.C.I.R., Lowry, 1966; Lansing, 1963). These findings have strong policy implications. They suggest that population maintenance and jobs-to-people programmes, if successful, may in effect bring new people to depressed areas (which are usually labour surplus) rather than retain the original residents who are leaving. It is well known that those who leave these areas are younger and better educated than those who stay behind, so that their departure weakens the local economy out of proportion to their number. Unfortunately, it appears the migrants entering depressed areas are more like the stayers than the movers (older, less educated, and less skilled) (Social Security Bulletin, 1967), so that the newcomers do not replace the qualities lost through out-migration.

It is sometimes suggested that new towns are needed to preserve agricultural land, an argument which derives from the British. But in this country, where historically we have been abandoning agricultural land, the argument lacks force. To accommodate 100 million people at suburban densities (with homes, factories, and so forth) would take about 14 million acres. This is a fraction of 1% of U.S. land territory (excluding Alaska and Hawaii), less than 2% of the present area in forests, and less than 5% of the area in crops. It is also only about one-half the decrease in planted crop acreage that occurred during the 1959–1964 period. The territory to be occupied by urban growth is relatively small, but beyond this one must question whether new towns would take up less space. It is hard to believe that they would. Densities are likely to be low as the American preference for large lots meets low land prices, and most descriptions of new towns stress the land-consuming amenities that will be found there (such as parks, playing fields, artificial lakes). Some designers advocate very high density towns, but it is doubtful that these would prove attractive. Some point out that growth at the margin of existing urban areas overruns some of the most valuable and productive agricultural land; but the value and productivity of this land derives not from its intrinsic fertility but from the more intensive use of capital, labour, and other inputs on land valued for its adjacency to urban markets. Growth of existing areas would merely slide the von Thunen rings outward.

Another conservation-of-land argument is based on the sprawl of marginal urban growth. Sprawl is an ill-defined word, referring to a condition characterised by very large lots, or by a ribbon development along major highways, or by the leap-frogging of clustered development which results from speculation. Thus, by thin development or by leaving gaps, sprawl covers more land than continuous compact development. I am unaware of studies showing the extent to which by-passed land is withdrawn from agricultural production; the one study I know of that attempts an economic analysis of how sprawl functions concludes that it may be an effective way of withholding land from premature development at low densities (Harvey and Clark, 1965; Lessinger, 1962). This depends, of course, on whether growth eventually backtracks to fill in the gaps at higher densities when demand has ripened. My impression is that this does occur, but I do not know of systematic studies of the process. Even if sprawl is dysfunctional, however, it would seem that the effects of redirecting a fraction of urban growth to new towns would be correspondingly small. It would be more effective to use direct strategies based on taxation of land and capital gains, on land banks, on the pricing of public services, and on direct regulation.

A frequent argument for new towns is that sprawl is expensive because of additional utility and street costs. Although the proposition is plausible, studies show these costs to be quite insensitive to alternative forms of development (Kain, 1967). Even if these costs did vary, they are so small that their marginal changes with urban form would not justify much of anything. For instance, the 1966 per capita expenditures of local governments were $31 for utilities (including debt maintenance and transit) and $22 for streets. This point will be further discussed below under control over development.

It is often suggested that new towns will stimulate the economy, presumably by their contribution to demand. Such an argument is often advanced by the very ones who promise that new towns will be cheaper to develop and to run than the corresponding extension of existing urban areas. Such inconsistency aside, if new towns are to be used to stimulate the economy during recessions, their rate of development must conversely be slowed when the economy is working at full capacity. But new towns could not very well be used as a balance wheel for the cyclical control of the economy. Their lead times for decision and for action are far too long, and the success of various aspects of their development depends upon keeping to a time schedule. The heavy front-end investment which characterises them presents critical cash-flow problems for the private developer, and a slowdown would be disastrous for him. From the public point of view, a slowdown would be extremely costly in terms of the opportunity costs of idle capital.

Most new town proposals stress that they will be as self-contained as possible, providing housing, jobs, schools, and shops for their residents, even when the proposals are for new towns on the edge of existing cities or in central city redevelopment projects (see the passage previously quoted from President Johnson's message to the 90th Congress). The purpose of this closure, often called "balance," is not altogether clear. It seems to stem in part from a desire to produce a sense of community that combats alienation—this will be discussed later—and in part from the

intention of reducing commuting costs and congestion by reducing distances involved. Two questions may be raised in this respect: (1) Does this make economic sense? and (2) Would it work? As mentioned earlier, the cost-minimising strategy makes sense only if productivity is fixed; in fact, income and most other measures of material welfare rise strongly with urban size. This is not the place to present a lengthy discussion of the reasons for this rise. They have to do with adaptability and innovative power and, in general, with the advantages of high connectivity for actual and potential interaction within a large system. In these terms, seeking closure at a small scale may economise on certain inputs (such as those of commuting) but results in lower per capita production (and lower disposable income after accounting for commuting costs) as well as the risks of instability and low adaptability which affect small cities. In small cities a declining firm can be a local disaster, new firms are less likely to develop because of the sparseness of linkages, a dismissed worker has fewer chances for reemployment, a boy has fewer career opportunities, a woman fewer choices for shopping, and so on. In short, trying to save on transport costs may be penny-wise and pound-foolish.

But could such self-contained new towns be achived? It seems to be quite hard. Several of the much admired European new towns, such as Tapiola, have about as many jobs as they have workers, but in fact, residents work outside and outsiders commute to work inside. The British experience demonstrates how difficult it is to keep labour market closure. British authorities have had extraordinary power since, in the face of a crushing housing shortage, they made the award of housing in new towns conditional on local employment and vice versa. The British new towns still show about the same number of jobs as workers but, after some years, 7.3 workers enter and leave the town in their daily trip to work for every 10 who live and work in the same new town.[11] People seem unwilling

11. Computed from A. A Ogilvy, "The Self-Contained New Town: Employment and Population," *Town Planning Review* (April 1968).

to constrain themselves to a localised and therefore small range of choices; they avail themselves of outside opportunities.[12] It is extremely doubtful that new towns fairly near metropolitan or other urban areas could maintain self-contained labour markets, with their residents making only occasional trips to the larger cities for special services and facilities. Yet, if the new towns are not independent or self-contained, the space that intervenes between them and other opportunities can only lengthen travel and make it more costly. Thus a new town pattern of development might have an effect opposite from that intended, lengthening travel except for those new towns in remote areas which are free from temptation. Yet virtually all our national territory, with the exception of some of our great deserts, is within commuting range of some existing urban centre (Friedmann and Miller, 1965).

The last two geo-economic arguments can be dealt with briefly:

In the early years after World War II there was considerable interest in dispersing populations in order to reduce potential damage from nuclear attack; some saw a silver lining in such dispersal in that it clearly pointed to the breakup of large cities and the development of new towns across the nation. This line of argument has virtually ceased, perhaps because bigger bombs and ubiquitous fallout would destroy us, whether we were clustered in cities or sprawled out in towns.

Some take up the Henry George argument that, with public ownership of the land retained, fresh starts in new towns would permit society to recapture the increase in land values. The difficulties with the Henry George argument are well known: On the one hand, if land is publicly owned and its price determined by bureaucratic procedures, we forgo

the cybernetic mechanism of the market for setting prices and, quite possibly, the entrepreneurial search for new uses—a matter of great importance since land rent is primarily a reflection of opportunity costs as determined by alternative uses. On the other hand, ad valorem taxation in effect socialises as much of this value as desired if the land is properly assessed.[13] It should be noted that this argument is currently a minority one. Most advocates speak of a mixture of private and public participation in which the increases in land value are one of the primary incentives for private participation.

## REFERENCES

Advisory Commission on Intergovernmental Relations (A.C.I.R., 1968). *Urban and Rural America: Policies for Future Growth.* Washington, D.C. G.P.O.

American Institute of Planners (1968). *New Communities.* Background Paper No. 2. Washington, D.C.

Bogard, G. T. (1969). Construction Market Development. Remarks at Utility Conference. Appliance Park. February.

Eichler, E. (1968). *The Community Builders.* Berkeley, University of California Press.

Friedmann, J.R.P. and Miller, J. (1965). The Urban Field. *Journal of the American Institute of Planners.* November.

Harvey, R. O. and Clark, W.A.V. (1965). The Nature and Economics of Urban Sprawl. *Land Economics.* February.

Heraud, B. J. (1968). Social Class and the New Town. *Urban Studies* 5.1. February.

Kain, J. F. (1967). *Urban Form and the Costs of Urban Services.* Discussion Paper No. 6. Harvard University Programme of Regional and Urban Economics.

Lansing, J. B. et al. (1963). *The Geographic Mobility of Labor.* A First Report. Survey Research Center. Ann Arbor, Michigan.

Lessinger, J. (1962). The Case for Scatteration.

12. The probabilistic nature of social behaviour where there is choice is well illustrated in such findings as these: at low rural densities, shoppers for a particular type of store break into discrete market areas as deterministic location theory would have it; but at dense urban areas, when more choices are easily accessible, market areas diffuse through each other in accordance with the probabilistic Huff model (B.L.J. Berry, *Geography of Market Centres and Retail Distribution* [Englewood Cliffs, N.J.: Prentice-Hall, 1967]). Ogilvy, *The Self-Contained New Town,* finds a similar pattern in the commuting new towners.

13. For instance, if the rate of return on a piece of land is $20, and the discounted value of this stream $200, the value of the land in the absence of taxes is $200. A 10% tax will, in effect, half-socialise the land, driving the money price down to $100 (the other $100 of the economic value belonging now to the public sector) and dividing the yearly $20 equally between owner and government.

*Journal of the American Institute of Planners*. August.

Lewis, O. (1965). Further Observations on the Folk-Urban Continum and Urbanisation with special reference to Mexico City. In P. Hauser and L. Schore, *The Study of Urbanisation*. New York, Wiley.

Lowry, I. (1966). *Two Models of Migration*. San Francisco, Chandler.

Mills, E. (1970). Urban Density Functions. *Urban Studies*, Vol. 7:1 pp. 5–20.

Moynihan, D. P. (1969). Press Conference. Office of White House Secretary. 22nd May.

Rosenberg, G. (1968). High Population Densities in Relation to Social Behaviour. *Ekistics*. June.

Schmitt, R. C. (1966). Density, Health, Social Disorganisation. *Journal of American Institute of Planners*. January.

Schorr, A. L. (1968). Housing the Poor, in *Power, Poverty and Urban Problems*. Ed. Bloomberg, W. and Schmandt, H. J. Sage Publications.

Social Security Bulletin (1967). Vol. 30 No. 3. March.

U.S. Department of Agriculture (1968). Secretary Orvil's statement. National Growth and its Distribution. Washington, D.C. G.P.O.

Werthman, C. S. (1968). The Social Meaning of the Physical Environment. Ph.D. Dissertation. University of California.

# An Evaluation of Growth-Center Theory and Practice

NILES M. HANSEN

## INTRODUCTION

Allowing for the fact that any significant body of knowledge or theory has numerous relevant historical antecedents, it may be stated with some confidence that the growth-center literature originated two decades ago in the seminal work of Perroux (1955), Hirschman (1958), and Myrdal (1957). In the mid-1960s I argued that while the growth-center approach represented a substantial advance over both static location theory and the balanced growth and steady growth approaches, it nevertheless could not "be emphasized too much that the theory of development poles is badly in need of a thorough semantic reworking; the concepts and language which characterize it need more precise definition and more consistent usage. Even the notion of a development pole itself suffers in this regard" (Hansen, 1968). In more recent years numerous critiques have sought to remedy this fault (Lasuén, 1969; Moseley, 1973a; Todd, 1974; Moore, 1972).[1] Most of these contributions have been valuable in their own right, but viewed as a whole they indicate that the growth-center approach is still in a disordered state. Nevertheless, despite genuine difficulties that have arisen from particular empirical and theoretical contexts, major themes of the

growth-center literature still have relevance to regional policy.

## SPONTANEOUS AND INDUCED GROWTH

It has been alleged that some of the difficulty has come about because the growth-center label has been attached to different concepts, but that "Introduction of William Alonso's and Elliott Medrich's useful categorization of growth centers as *spontaneous* or *induced* appears to resolve the conflict" (Collier, 1973). In their scheme, induced growth centers are those in which public policy is trying to promote growth; there is a normative element in the designation of a locality as a growth center. Spontaneous growth centers, in contrast, are growing without the benefit of special assistance, or at least without the benefit of conscious or explicit policy (see Alonso and Medrich, 1972, in Section V).

At this point it must be emphasized that the growth-center literature originated largely as a response, or better a reaction, to the deductive models of classical location theory, as well as to highly simplified and abstract models of economic growth. The growth-center approach was supposed to be more oriented toward immediate policy issues, in particular the overconcentration of people and economic activity in one or a few large urban areas and the problems of stagnation or de-

---

1. It may be noted that growth-center theory has now entered the field of vision of the "radical geographers." For several prime examples of rediscovering the wheel, see *Antipode* (1974).

From *Environment and Planning A: Special Issue,* Selected papers from IIASA conference on national settlement systems and strategies. © IIASA, Laxenburg, 1975, vol. 7, pp. 821–32. Reprinted by permission.

cline in some nonmetropolitan areas. More-over, it has obvious relevance to efforts to bring about "concentrated decentralization," a strategy which, it has been widely felt, "will surely prove more effective in promoting various development goals than would either entirely dispersing growth or entirely concentrating it in very large cities" (Rodwin, 1970).

In view of these considerations there can be no doubt that the growth-center approach was concerned primarily with induced growth centers, as means both for slowing the growth of one or more spontaneous growth centers and for promoting growth in other areas. More recently, however, this normative concern has tended to give way to positive approaches related primarily to spontaneous growth centers. Thus one of the most recent major contributions to the literature limits its emphasis explicitly to "natural growth poles" (Parr, 1973; see also Casetti *et al.*, 1971; Robinson and Salih, 1971). While there is of course nothing wrong *per se* with positive analyses of spontaneous growth centers, they do shift the ground from the major issues that originally were the main *raison d'être* for the growth-center notion.[2] The point is not that spontaneous growth centers should be neglected, but rather that a great deal of sterility can be avoided by viewing them in a policy context.

It is somewhat ironic that I have been accused of neglecting induced growth centers in favor of studying spontaneous growth centers (Collier, 1973), because I proposed a growth-center strategy for the United States based on spontaneously growing inter-mediate-size cities. My major point, however, was that it appears economically

rational to accelerate (induce) growth in such places because they have more opportunities in terms of existing external economies than do smaller towns and rural areas, and fewer diseconomies than do the largest cities. The accelerated growth of intermediate centers would be made conditional on the granting of newly created employment opportunities to a significant number of workers from lagging regions, who could either commute or migrate (Hansen, 1971).

Similarly, the distinction between spontaneous and induced growth centers made by Alonso and Medrich (1972) was not intended to shift emphasis from normative to positive considerations. Rather, they argued that spontaneous growth centers should be studied "both for the lessons they may hold for inducing growth where it does not occur spontaneously and for their own sake as a valid subject of national developmental policy, since growth also has its problems."

## GROWTH CENTERS, CENTRAL PLACES, AND THE URBAN HIERARCHY

Although growth-center theory began in large part as an attempt to grasp the complex technical origins and dynamic interrelations of the growth process, expositions of the theory were generally presented in an input-output framework, usually in terms of a regionalization of the basic Leontief-type model, or by applying modifying vectors or matrices to the basic model. Unfortunately it was frequently not possible to quantify the modifying variables. Thus, while some contributions were made to operationally meaningful theory, an approach that was supposed to deal with the polarization process in fact dealt largely with static effects.[3] Other elements in early works

2. While it is true that Perroux's initial paper on growth poles (1955) neglected the spatial dimension and was not directly concerned with policy matters, the output of the French School almost immediately became oriented to policy issues in a spatial context. The original work of Hirschman and Myrdal was clearly concerned from the start with regional policy. Thus I do not hesitate to use the terms "growth pole" (which to some writers implies intersectoral relations abstracted from space) and "growth center" as equivalent expressions implying regional policy concerns.

3. Another difficulty is that "If homogeneous regions are good candidates for input-output models, strongly nodal regions may be poor candidates unless the boundaries of the region conform closely to the outer limits of the gravitational field of influence of the dominant node, and even then an important condition must be that this 'force field' should not overlap with that of a node outside the region" (Richardson, 1972).

included such well-known analytic devices as location coefficients, simple graph theory, and shift-share breakdowns of employment change.

Eclecticism continues to characterize the growth-center literature, but with a relative shift in emphasis. The early seminal works were written by economists and emphasized economic variables, economic relations, and economic growth. In the past decade geographers (and economists more interested in location theory than in growth) have entered the lists in increasing numbers, and it may properly be said that their studies have, for a time at least, dominated the field. In consequence, less weight has been given to economic analysis and more to relationships of growth centers to central place theory and city size distributions. The positive side of this phenomenon is that greater attention has been focused on the "where" of economic activity, which is of course what regional economic policy is about. On the other hand, it also represents something of a return to the static approaches against which the original growth-center writers were reacting. I say "something of a return" because this literature is not limited to static-descriptive studies of central places and urban hierarchies. It significantly adds dynamic notions of filtering and spread within urban systems. Before examining this point further it would be instructive to note the generally ambiguous empirical role of central place hierarchies.

Berry (1961), for example, has found that "There are no relationships between type of city size distribution and either relative economic development or the degree of urbanization of countries, although urbanization and economic development are highly associated." Böventer (1973) has convincingly argued on theoretical grounds that satisfactory economic growth and the personal well-being of a country's citizens are compatible with wide differences in the degree of spatial concentration of population and economic activity; particular rank-size distribution parameters are no help in national planning decision processes. In a somewhat narrower

vein, it has been shown that the central place schemes of Christaller and Lösch, with their concentration on market-oriented functions, contain restrictive assumptions which render them "inadequate as a general theoretical framework for analyzing the diffusion of growth, especially in the case of highly developed economies" (Parr, 1973, page 202).

Nevertheless, by relaxing the assumptions of the classical approaches, a central place model can be used as a kind of landscape in which development-related diffusion processes operate (Parr, 1973). This appears to be what Berry (1973) has in mind when he maintains that there are two major elements in the way in which economic activities in space are organized around the urban system. The first is a hierarchical system of cities, arranged according to the functions performed by each city; the second is a corresponding set of urban areas of influence (urban fields) surrounding each of the cities in the system. What Berry terms "impulses of economic change" have, he finds, been transmitted simultaneously in the system along three planes: first, outward from heartland metropolises to those in large regional hinterlands; second, from higher to lower urban centers in the hierarchy, in a pattern of hierarchical diffusion; and third, outward from urban centers into their surrounding urban fields in the form of radiating spread effects, of which more will be said in the following section. In this context modern growth theory, as described by Berry, would suggest that:

continued urban-industrial expansion in major metropolitan regions should lead to catalytic impacts on surrounding areas. Growth impulses and economic advancement should filter and spread to smaller places and ultimately infuse dynamism into even the most tradition-bound peripheries. Growth center concepts enter the scene if filtering mechanisms are perceived not to be operating quickly enough, if "cumulative causation" leads to growing regional differentials rather than their reduction . . . or if institutional or historical barriers block diffusion processes. The purpose of spatially-selective public investments in growth centers, it is held, is to hasten the focused extension of growth to lower echelons of the hierarchy in outlying regions, and to link the growth centers more closely into the national system via higher-echelon centers in the urban hierarchy (Berry, 1973).

This position is consistent with the contention that "the role played by growth centers in regional development is a particular case of the general process of innovation diffusion," and that therefore "the sadly deficient 'theory' of growth centers can be enriched by turning to the better developed general case" (Berry, 1972). Yet this approach is not without its own ambiguities. For example, modern growth theory asserts that within urban-regional hierarchical systems "impulses of economic change are transmitted in order from higher to lower centers in the urban hierarchy," so that "continued innovation in large cities remains critical for extension of growth over the complete economic system" (Berry, 1973; 1972). There is considerable evidence that the advantages which larger cities have as centers of innovation are closely bound up with the production of information and communications (Hansen, 1975). In addition, it has been argued that no matter where a growth-inducing innovation takes place in the nation's system of cities, it is likely to appear soon in some or all of the largest cities because of the high contact probabilities which the latter have with many other places (Pred, no date). However, it is one thing to say that large cities are prime candidates to adopt innovations made in smaller centers, and quite another to say that innovation *in* large cities is critical, and that the transmission process works only in order from higher to lower centers.

Moreover, it is not always clear what is being transmitted through the urban hierarchy. For example, in certain of his earlier general discussions, Berry seems to break away from the confines of that concentration on market-oriented functions which, as Parr correctly points out, make the central place approach inadequate as a general theoretical framework for analyzing the diffusion of growth. In this broader context Berry talks about the transmission of rather general entities such as "innovations" or "impulses of economic change." But in attempting empirical verification of his argument, he has given prominent attention to the diffusion of television stations and sets—an extremely market-oriented phenomenon (Berry, 1972). Similarly, in developing a growth-center strategy for the Upper Great Lakes he leaned heavily on the hierarchy of market-oriented central places in the region (metropolis, wholesale-retail center, complete shopping center, partial shopping center, convenience center) (Berry, 1973). Again, apart from television diffusion, one searches in vain here for concrete examples of the transmission of specific "innovations" and "impulses of economic change."

To summarize, it would appear that reliance on a traditional, market-oriented hierarchy of central place schemes does not provide an adequate growth model. On the other hand, if one is concerned with innovations and impulses of economic change, and is using the central place model as a locational matrix or landscape, it should be recognized that "information can be exchanged between centers of the same size; innovations can be diffused laterally within the hierarchy (that is, between centers of the same level); the diffusion process can even operate in an upward direction, as opposed to the more likely downward direction" (Parr, 1973).

As pointed out later in this paper, recent studies by Pred, Törnqvist, and Goddard indicate that these issues may be clarified by shifting the focus of attention to organizational information flows within urban systems. In any case, it is clear that urban and regional growth issues need to be viewed in the context of the national urban system, even though it is premature to be overly doctrinaire about the precise functioning of dynamic processes within the system.[4]

4. Rogers and Shoemaker (1971). Although this study does not give much emphasis to the spatial transmission of innovations, it clearly illustrates the complexity and ambiguity of innovation diffusion processes.

## THE QUESTION OF SPREAD EFFECTS

Regional policies aimed at promoting growth in lagging regions have been largely responsible for the considerable international interest shown in induced growth centers as generators of spread effects. In the United States the Economic Development Administration, US Department of Commerce, attempted to apply this strategy on a national scale. It was not successful because development funds were too widely and thinly dispersed. The Department of Commerce, in a report prepared jointly with the Office of Management and Budget, pointed out that:

The policy of dispersing assistance rather than focusing on those [areas] with the greatest potential for self-sustaining growth has resulted in much of EDA's funds going to very small communities. Over a third of its public works funds have gone to towns with less than 2500 people, and over half to towns with less than 5000 population. There are relatively few kinds of economic activities which can operate efficiently in such small communities, so the potential for economic development in the communities is relatively small.[5]

The question remains: what would have happened if EDA outlays had been concentrated in larger centers? Would the basic rationale for the strategy have produced positive results, in terms of center growth and spread effects, if larger centers had been used? Before examining relevant evidence, the rationale itself can be briefly presented by reference to figure 1, which shows a "typical" EDA multicounty district containing a mix of distressed and relatively healthy counties. Ideally, the growth-center's hinterland benefits from the spread of services, secondary jobs, and development expertise from the center, as well as from opportunities made available to hinterland residents who commute or migrate to the core. It may be noted that what one chooses to call a spread effect often depends on the particular perspective of

5. See *Report to the Congress on the Proposal for an Economic Adjustment Program*, 1974. For further details concerning the failure of EDA's growth-center policy see Milkman *et al.* (1972).

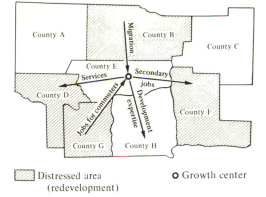

Distressed area (redevelopment)   o Growth center

Figure 1. Economic Development Administration: Development District and Growth-Center Concepts (from Milkman *et al.*, 1972).

the viewer. For example, from the perspective of county B in figure 1, it is not clear that migration will be beneficial, whether the migrants go to the growth center in county E or leave the district altogether. If the migrants were unemployed, or if unemployed workers with similar skills could replace the employed workers who migrate, the total output of county B would not or should not fall. Because the unchanged output is now divided among fewer people in county B, the average real *per capita* income will be higher than before. This may be regarded as a spread effect. On the other hand, the out-migration of skilled workers who were employed in county B (or for whom employment would soon be found), and who were earning an income higher than the county average, would result in a decline (or prevent as high a rise as otherwise possible) in the average real *per capita* income of the people remaining in county B; it would also adversely affect the overall skill composition of its economy. This would be a backwash effect, in Myrdal's terminology (cf. Salvatore, 1972). Of course, if migrants from county B go to the district growth center they may spend more of their earnings in county B than if they had migrated to more distant places. The leakage from county E would benefit county B but would obviously not affect the district. Finally, apart from these economic considerations there are those of a political and social nature. Out-migration is often regarded as undesirable by people living in an area, whether or not the economic consequences are desirable for the people left behind. Here too the results would vary depending on whether one adopted the perspective of a single county, a single district, or a geographically wider frame of reference.

The notion of spread effects is most commonly associated with the induced generation of "secondary jobs" in hinterland counties such as county F in figure 1. This is largely because of a pronounced tendency to identify the induced effects of an economic activity with *locally* induced effects. However, the great weight of the empirical evidence indicates this view to be mistaken. For example, Beyers' analysis of interindustry purchases and sales relationships in the Puget Sound region showed that regional interindustry connections were weak compared to interregional interindustry relations. Value added and personal consumption were the most important regional linkages for many sectors. His data "suggest that Perroux's conceptualization of a growth pole, with its heavy emphasis on growth stimuli being transmitted via forward and backward interindustry linkages, is probably more applicable at a broad national level than at the small regional scale (Beyers, no date; see also Erickson, 1974). Gaile's (1973a) growth-center test of the Milwaukee area led to the finding that "the concept of concentric 'spread' of growth from the 'growth center' has not been proven." In another paper, Gaile (1973b) reviewed seventeen studies using the growth-center concept, and concluded that if a trend was discernible it was that spread effects were smaller than expected, limited in geographic extent, or less than backwash effects. A study by Gray (1969) of the employment effect of a major new aluminum reduction and rolling mill at Ravenswood, West Virginia, fifty miles north of Charleston, found that the induced employment attributable to the plant's operations could be traced mainly to Ohio (power) and

Louisiana (bauxite), but very little was discernible around Ravenswood.[6]

There is even a case to be made for investing directly in hinterland areas on the ground that such outlays might benefit "growth centers" as much as the hinterlands. Nichols's (1969) analysis of the propulsive effect of growth poles suggests that investments be concentrated in towns with the strongest linkages to hinterlands but, if these linkages are weak as the foregoing evidence would indicate, "there are also advantages to be gained from injecting capital in lower order centres, or even the agricultural base, because increases in incomes in these places will generate strong income multipliers in higher-order centres but not the other way round." Moseley's studies of the spatial impact of Rennes, France, and of spatial flows in East Anglia also cast doubt on the notion that spatial concentration of investment will inevitably benefit much wider geographic areas. He concludes that "given an objective to foster the economic development of a number of small towns in a region, then direct investment in those towns would appear to be required. 'Trickle down' cannot be relied on. If 'some growth' is required throughout an urban hierarchy, then there is a case of neglecting the larger settlements to which some 'trickle up' might normally be expected" (Moseley, 1973b).

In the light of this evidence it would be difficult to justify growth-center policies for lagging areas on the basis of spread effects. This is not to say that cities in general do not generate spread effects. Clearly larger cities do so in urban systems where one or two cities are not in a position of unmistakable dominance (Berry, 1973; Hansen, 1973a); the problem is that larger cities are rarely found in lagging regions.[7] However, the case for growth-center strategies aimed at helping people in lagging areas does not necessarily depend on the spread effect justification. If it can be shown that large numbers of poten-

6. For a comparable Flemish example, see Vanneste, 1971.
7. The case for smaller growth centers in lagging areas is relatively well stated in Morrill (1973). However, a more persuasive contrary argument is given in Lamb and Gillard, 1973.

tially mobile persons in lagging areas would *prefer* to move to intermediate-size growth centers rather than stay at home or move to large metropolitan areas, the case for settlement pattern strategies oriented towards the development of intermediate-size cities would be reinforced. There has been very little research in this regard, but findings based on surveys in the United States indicate that such preferences do in fact exist (Hansen, 1973b).

Of course, not everyone can or should leave lagging regions, because of the profound historical, social, and political realities which must necessarily temper policies based on economic criteria. Fortunately, some of these regions have benefited and will benefit from the extension of urban fields and the decentralization of manufacturing (Hansen, 1973a; Lamb, 1975). But these phenomena will not automatically solve the problems of all lagging areas. While some consideration might be given to the promotion of smaller growth centers, provided they have genuine growth potential, policies for lagging areas should be focused mainly on the development of service centers oriented toward upgrading human resources and the quality of life. Improved health, education, and other service delivery systems are likely to result in increased migration to places with greater economic opportunity. This should be viewed as a social gain rather than a cause for alarm, at least in so far as regional policy aims at increasing individual welfare rather than maintaining or expanding the number of persons resident in a given area. In the long run, however, out-migration may be expected to decline. Many persons who benefit from social investments will choose to remain in lagging regions because of attachment to family, friends, surroundings, etc. These persons eventually will constitute a body of qualified labor sufficient to justify increased public-infrastructure development and expanded directly-productive activities. This general approach probably would not produce dramatic short-run changes (a political liability), but it would permit a gradual adaptation of regional population to regional resources.

In summary, then, while it is difficult to justify economically a growth-center strategy on the basis of spread effects, this is not the case for a strategy based on the expansion of economic infrastructure and directly productive activities in intermediate-size cities, coupled with emphasis on improved human-resource development systems in lagging regions. Admittedly, though, attempts at implementing such a strategy would meet with political resistance, for example from politicians losing constituents in lagging regions, and from "no-growth" advocates in intermediate growth centers.

## DIRECTIONS FOR GROWTH-CENTER RESEARCH

The foregoing analysis would suggest that in growth-center research less emphasis be placed on the delineation of urban hierarchies and central place schemes, and more on the costs and benefits associated with various types of public and private investments in various city sizes (taking account also of cities' access to opportunities in other areas, which can be estimated with gravity models), and on the nature and significance of people's location preferences.

More generally, I would argue that the lack of a unifying theory in growth-center research is attributable primarily to its ambitious scope; it is no simple task to bind together such concepts and issues as the roles of external economies and diseconomies, economies of scale, regional and urban growth thresholds, propulsive sectors and their multiplier effects, interindustry linkages, growth transmission in spatial terms, migration and commuting patterns, and the induced and inducing nature of public investment. Some writers even urge that "psychological polarization" is a key element in the growth of both industry and tourism (Vanneste, 1971). The fact that no one has succeeded in combining all these factors within the framework of an operationally feasible model should not rule out efforts to build from more modest bases.

It was pointed out earlier that growth-center analysis was supposed to provide a dynamic alternative to static location models. Yet the French school of regional economists tended to fall back on static models. More recently, geographers have shed valuable light on spatial diffusion of innovation processes, though sometimes within the framework of rather rigid, market-oriented hierarchical central place schemes. Thomas (1972; 1975) represents a notable exception in this regard. Building from the work of Perroux and Hirschman, he has emphasized the economics of why, how, and where a growth center grows; and he has convincingly urged that specific industry growth patterns need to be examined for clues to improve our conceptual framework for dealing with the disequilibria of propulsive industries, internal and external economies, technological change and productivity growth, innovation, and the diffusion of new techniques. Fortunately, this work has been extended in range and depth by numerous researchers involved in the University of Washington's Growth Pole and Regional Development Project.[8]

Lasuén (1973) has also made important contributions to the elaboration of a dynamic growth-center theory based on the complex interaction between economic growth and spatial organization. Like Thomas, he begins with the work of Perroux and attempts to reorient growth-center theory by developing a neglected but essential hypothesis due to Perroux:

Following Schumpeter's lead, Perroux stated that economic development results from the adoption of innovations; then extending Schumpeter's view, Perroux implicitly advanced the main hypothesis that innovations in several subsidiary lines will follow in the wake of an innovation in a dominant industry, and that these innovations would be located in geographical clusters around the same industry.

Lasuén recognizes the value of central place theory in helping to understand service activity location,

8. At the time of this writing the project has resulted in twenty-seven published papers and seven dissertations. Hopefully an effort will be made to synthesize the project's findings.

But for the explanation of the evolution of the system of cities we need the growth pole approach, for no other framework is as well fitted to explain why and how the newer activities will come about and locate. Thus, it can easily be hypothesized that the present system of poles is the result of the impact of a past system of innovations and that newer systems of poles will be brought about by newer systems of innovations (Lasuén, 1973).

In Lasuén's analytic framework, economic development results from the adoption of successive packages of innovations in dominant industries. Moreover, these sectorially clustered sets are also geographically clustered. Functional and spatial impacts produce disturbances in the sectorial and geographic distribution of activities. The diffusion and adoption of successive sets of innovations follow similar patterns, resulting in a fairly stable system of poles. Over time, successive innovations demand greater scales of operation and larger markets; they also come at shorter intervals. Larger cities are the earliest adopters of innovations, which then diffuse gradually to the rest of the urban system. As a consequence of this process, the system of growth poles becomes increasingly hierarchic in nature (Lasuén, 1971).

Lasuén also places great emphasis on the international, rather than national, generation of innovations, and on the importance of business organization in the polarization process. If innovation diffusion is delayed because of inadequate organizational arrangements, then appropriate changes need to be made in order to minimize the costs and risks inherent in the learning process.

At present, the emphasis of development policies (national, regional, and local) is placed on production. Policies are geared to promote producers. According to our analysis the emphasis should be placed on marketing and technical know-how. The provision of facilities warranting complete commercialisation of the products: commercial credit, publicity, marketing, sales-servicing, etc., and of the know-how required to start a smooth and standardised production—via licensing contracts, custom manufacturing agreements or technical assistance and research and development programmes, is a round about but most effective way of guaranteeing the promotion of specific productions (La-suén, 1973).

Lasuén (1973) reaches an extreme of audacity among urban economists when he proposes that the adoption of innovations in industry and services could be furthered by learning from the experience of agricultural extension programmes, and particularly from the way in which they have reduced the risks of adopting agricultural innovations.

Emphasis on business organization also characterizes important recent efforts by geographers to analyze the nature and significance of information flows for the urban system. Pred, for example, argues that if policymakers wish to reduce regional employment inequalities, and if they wish to provide new jobs that do not require out-migration from rural areas, they should take two coordinated measures. These would be:

(1) To promote urban production and *administrative* activities which not only will give rise to regional exports, but *intra*regional urban interdependencies as well; and
(2) To improve air or other communications between the existing cities selected for the location of new activities, and between those locations and major metropolitan centers elsewhere in the country. That is, insofar as possible large non-local multipliers ought to be internalized within the target region and concentrated at a limited number of spatially dispersed cities that are made more accessible to one another in terms of the ease of making face-to-face organizational contacts. This should not only mean more new jobs in the short run. To the extent that new functional linkages and communications possibilities generate spatial biases in the availability of specialized information, the two steps should improve long-run development prospects by increasing subsequent probabilities both for the intraregional diffusion of growth-inducing innovations and for the organizational selection of intraregional operational decision-making alternatives. On the other hand, if intraregional urban interdependencies are not created, and if interurban communications are not improved, the short-run multipliers and long-run employment benefits will leak out of the region to an unnecessary degree, mostly to major metropolitan areas located in other regions (Pred, no date).

Pred further suggests that policies aiming at concentrated decentralization should

create new interdependencies between selected small metropolitan areas, regardless of whether or not they are located in the same broadly defined region. In particular, if the policy is to increase its probability of long-run success through circular and cumulative feedbacks, some high-level organizational administrative activities—with their characteristically high local multipliers—should be among the activities located at the decentralization foci. The artificially created interdependencies associated with such a policy would, in turn, require improved air connections between the selected "intermediately-sized" cities so as to facilitate the non-local face-to-face exchange of non-routine specialized information. Thus, to take a totally hypothetical example, if Fresno, California, and Chattanooga, Tennessee—two cities in Hansen's suggested 200,000–750,000 population range—were among a small set of cities designated as "intermediately-sized" growth centers, it would be necessary to subsidize or create frequent non-stop air service between them and thereby eliminate time-costly plane transfers at San Francisco, Atlanta, or some other intervening large metropolitan area.

Goddard (1974), in a synthetic study based on evidence concerning information flows in Great Britain, the United States, and Sweden, derives similar policy conclusions.[9]

Increasing research on information flows obviously is serving to correct an unjustly neglected area in the growth-center literature. Yet the emphasis given to the functioning of the "postindustrial society" should not detract from the opportunities that manufacturing decentralization represents for many rural areas. In fact, better access within national communications networks can be of considerable help to rural areas, not only in attracting more manufacturing activity, but in upgrading its quality. This in turn depends on the ability of rural people to take advantage of opportunities, that is, on the quality of rural human resources. The failure of most growth-center theory and practise to include explicitly human resource and manpower di-

9. See also Törnqvist (1973, 1974).

mensions is at least equal to the neglect of information circulation.

## REFERENCES

Alonso, W., Medrich, E., 1972, "Spontaneous growth centers in twentieth-century American urbanization," in *Growth Centers in Regional Economic Development,* Ed. N. M. Hansen (Free Press, New York).

*Antipode,* 1974, *A Radical Journal of Geography,* 6 (2).

Berry, B.J.L., 1961, "City size distributions and economic development," *Economic Development and Cultural Change,* 9 (4), 587.

———., 1972, "Hierarchical diffusion: the basis of developmental filtering and spread in a system of growth centers," in *Growth Centers in Regional Economic Development,* Ed. N. M. Hansen (Free Press, New York).

———., 1973, *Growth Centers in the American Urban System,* Volumes 1 and 2 (Ballinger, Cambridge, Mass.).

Beyers, W. B., no date, "Growth centers and interindustry linkages," unpublished paper, Department of Geography, University of Washington, Seattle.

Böventer, E. von, 1973, "City size systems: theoretical issues, empirical regularities, and planning guides," *Urban Studies,* 10 (2), 145–162.

Casetti, E., King, L., Odlund, J., 1971, "The formalization and testing of concepts of growth poles in a spatial context," *Environment and Planning,* 3 (4), 377–382.

Collier, G. A., Jr, 1973, "On the size and spacing of growth centers: comment," *Growth and Change,* 4 (4).

Erickson, R. A., 1974, "The regional impact of growth firms: the case of Boeing, 1963–1968," *Land Economics,* 50 (2), 127–136.

Gaile, G. L., 1973a, "Growth center theory: an analysis of its formal spatial-temporal aspects," unpublished paper presented at the Southern California Academy of Sciences Annual Meeting, Long Beach, Calif., May, 1973.

———., 1973b, "Notes on the concept of 'spread,'" unpublished paper, Department of Geography, University of California, Los Angeles.

Goddard, J. B., 1974, "Organizational information flows and the urban system," paper presented at the Conference on National Settlement Systems and Strategies, International Institute for Applied Systems Analysis, Laxenburg, Austria, December 16–19, 1974.

Gray, I., 1969, "Employment effect of a new industry in a rural area," *Monthly Labor Review,* 92 (6), 29.

Hansen, N. M., 1968, *French Regional Planning* (Indiana University Press, Bloomington, Ind.).

———. 1971, *Intermediate-Size Cities as Growth Centers* (Praeger, New York).

———., 1973a, *The Future of Nonmetropolitan America* (D. C. Heath, Lexington, Mass.).

———. 1973b, *Location Preferences, Migration, and Regional Growth* (Praeger, New York).

———. 1975, *The Challenge of Urban Growth: The Basic Economics of City Size and Structure* (D. C. Heath, Lexington, Mass.), chapter 5.

Hirschman, A. O., 1958, *The Strategy of Economic Development* (Yale University Press, New Haven, Conn.).

Lamb, R., 1975, "Metropolitan impacts on rural America," research series monograph No. 162, Department of Geography, University of Chicago.

———. Gillard, Q., 1973, "Growth center schemes evaluated," in B.J.L. Berry, *Growth Centers in the American Urban System,* Volume 1 (Ballinger, Cambridge, Mass.), pp. 165–187.

Lasuén, J. R., 1969, "On growth poles," *Urban Studies,* 6 (2), reprinted 1972 in N. M. Hansen, *Growth Centers in Regional Economic Development* (Free Press, New York).

———. 1971, "An open-system model of multiregional economic development," unpublished paper, Autonomous University of Madrid.

———. 1973, "Urbanisation and development—the temporal interaction between geographical and sectoral clusters," *Urban Studies,* 10 (2), 163.

Milkman, R. H., Bladen, C., Lyford, Beverly, Walton, H. L., 1972, *Alleviating Economic Distress* (D. C. Heath, Lexington, Mass.).

Moore, C. W., 1972, "Industrial linkage development paths in growth poles: a research methodology," *Environment and Planning,* 4 (3), 253–271.

Morrill, R. L., 1973, "On the size and spacing of growth centers," *Growth and Change,* 4 (2), 21–24.

Moseley, M. J., 1973a, "Growth centres—a shibboleth?", *Area,* 5 (2), 143–150.

———. 1973b, "The impact of growth centres in rural regions," *Regional Studies,* 7 (1), 93.

Myrdal, G., 1957, *Rich Lands and Poor* (Harper, New York).

Nichols, Vida, 1969, "Growth poles: an evaluation of their propulsive effect," *Environment and Planning,* 1 (2), 193–208.

Parr, J. B., 1973, "Growth poles, regional development, and central place theory," *Papers of the Regional Science Association,* 31, 175.

Perroux, F., 1955, "Note sur la notion de pôle de croissance," *Économie Appliquée,* 307–320.

Pred, A. R., 1973, "The growth and development of systems of cities in advanced economies," in A. R. Pred and G. Törnqvist, "Systems of cities and information flows: two essays," in *Lund Studies in Geography Series B,* number 38 (Gleerup, Stockholm).

*Report to the Congress on the Proposal for an Economic Adjustment Program,* 1974 (Department of Commerce and the Office of Management and Budget, Washington, DC).

Richardson, H. W., 1972, *Input-Output and Regional Economics* (John Wiley, New York).

Robinson, G., Salih, K., 1971, "The spread of development around Kuala Lumpur: a methodology for an exploratory test of some assumptions of the growth pole model," *Regional Studies,* 5, 303–314.

Rodwin, L., 1970, *Nations and Cities* (Houghton Mifflin, Boston, Mass.).

Rogers, E. M., with Shoemaker, F. F., 1971, *Communication of Innovations,* second edition (Free Press, New York).

Salvatore, D., 1972, "The operation of the market mechanism and regional inequality," *Kyklos,* 25 (3), 518–536.

Thomas, M. D., 1972, "Growth pole theory: an examination of some of its basic concepts," in *Growth Centers in Regional Economic Development,* Ed. N. M. Hansen (Free Press, New York), pp. 50–81.

———. 1975, "Growth pole theory, technological change and regional economic growth," *Papers of the Regional Science Association,* 34, 3–26.

Todd, D., 1974, "An appraisal of the development pole concept in regional analysis," *Environment and Planning A,* 6 (3), 291–306.

Törnqvist, G., 1973, "Contact requirements and travel facilities," in A. R. Pred and G. Törnqvist, "Systems of cities and information flows: two essays," in *Lund Studies in Geography Series B,* number 38 (Gleerup, Stockholm).

———. 1974, "Swedish industry as a spatial system," paper presented at the Conference on National Settlement Systems and Strategies, International Institute for Applied Systems Analysis, Laxenburg, Austria, December 16–19, 1974.

Vanneste, O., 1971, *The Growth Pole Concept and the Regional Economic Policy* (De Tempel, Bruges).

# An Equitable Urban Structure

TORSTEN HÄGERSTRAND

The authorities responsible for the formulation of regional policy are faced with a whole range of distribution problems arising from the primary task of locating employment; these problems include the distribution of public sector services, transport amenities, and information and participation in the framework constituted by our inherited settlement pattern. Both the present principles of distribution and the settlement pattern must then be adjusted so as ultimately to provide a regional structure that meets the demand for equality of status for people in different parts of the country as regards access to the fundamental utilities.

An individual or a household, wherever they or it resides, is surrounded by a pattern of supplies, distributed in space and time, that he or she must rely on in order to satisfy his or her needs and desires. The term "supplies" in this context is used in a most general sense, and covers, for instance, employment opportunities, services, information, social contact, and recreation. These are, however, not freely accessible at any particular moment; they are located at a distance and are almost invariably behind other more or less easily penetrable barriers. The pattern of supply points and barriers, as seen from the standpoint of the individual or household, will be referred to below as the "environmental structure."

To start with, mention will be made of factors that tend to give rise to differences in accessibility to supplies of various kinds,

supplies which, with the existing population distribution, must be made available in a system of central places of different ranks, and which will differ in their accessibility according to the transport cost—in time and money—entailed in reaching the supply points' outlets. Since nearly all supplies consist of indivisible, elementary units—many of which, moreover, are constantly increasing in size—the number of possible supply points is limited. It follows that some inhabitants will be favorably and others unfavorably located as regards accessibility to the supplies. Any tolerably close equality of status for people in this respect is a physical impossibility unless the whole population is collected in a few urban units, each with a large enough population to support a complete range of supplies.

The location dilemma is complicated further by the appearance and gradual development of new activities, whether commercial or community services. There are at first usually only a few service units to locate, and then the first ones will be sited so as to obtain as large a population as possible in the units' immediate area of influence. This can be achieved only if the first unit is placed where the population density is greatest, that is to say, in the area of the capital, the second unit where the population density is next greatest, and so on. This way of calculating the population basis means that metropolitan areas, especially Stockholm, will be accorded priority. From the standpoint of each field of activity this approach is, of course, justifi-

From Report to E.F.T.A., Working Party on New Patterns of Settlement, Geneva, 1972. Reprinted by permission.

able, if not the only conceivable one, but when the various fields are considered together great differences in environmental structure between urban units build up with time.

The places obtaining everything first will come to own everything and will always be ahead of the others in their range of choice. Other regions (containing just as large populations) will always come last and always be the least well equipped.

Any attempt at modifying the settlement structure should not be based on the problematic aspects of the individual city; rather, the task should be considered as one of distribution. A large agglomeration has too many advantages that benefit only a small section of the population. Against an optimal settlement pattern in the narrow economic sense, which leads to wide differences, can be set another which is designed so as to result in a uniform distribution of welfare both within and between regions. One might speak of an equitable settlement pattern from the labor market point of view, and from both social and cultural aspects.

The discussion on optimal town size, especially as far as essentially metropolitan questions are concerned, has been concerned primarily with frictions and their economic consequences. A less well-explored approach is that concerning distribution. Equality between people is not achieved simply by leveling out income, by treating all according to the same legal code, or by reforming titles; when all this has been done there remains the task of reorganizing the environmental structures in order to offer everyone the same or equivalent combinations, both in daily life and in the longer time perspective. To attempt to bring about this situation is certainly not simply a matter of formal justice but one of economic, social, and cultural development with time.

## AN EQUITABLE SETTLEMENT PATTERN

Just what essential meaning one ascribes to the term "equitable" is, of course, ultimately a matter of personal appraisal; but these relative aspects do not preclude a theoretical consideration of the consequences for location and transport policy of placing, as optimal goals, the distribution of social supplies on which no price is set before the production of business supplies on which a price is set. Any solution that will work in practice will inevitably be a compromise. A one-sided household-oriented approach would thus be unsatisfactory as a model of a possible reality—we cannot conceive, for example, so perfect a society that each household has its own doctor. But the one-sided business-oriented approach to location problems has hitherto been so predominant that it would do no harm to take a few steps towards the opposite extreme for once.

## A DRAFT MODEL

Though not claiming to represent a formally satisfactory analysis, a draft model is presented here, which shows the distinguishing features of an equitable settlement pattern.

Equality of status implies that, so far as the daily routine is concerned, the environmental structure shall offer the same range of supply alternatives to everybody. The first condition for households to be able to enjoy such equal opportunities in order to benefit from the environment is that they should all possess the same potential local mobility, for otherwise the range of supply alternatives available to the individual households will vary according to the location of the dwelling.

The supplies in demand at any given time may be assumed to compose a series of classes that are not mutually exchangeable, but the variety for each is great enough to satisfy the different needs and preferences of individuals. It will be generally agreed that the more important supply classes are housing, employment, consumer goods, information, welfare, social contact, and recreation. It is impossible to compensate for, say, a shortage of work by providing a superfluity of recreation. In an equitable urban structure the intraclass variation must, however, completely reflect the national variation (if we accept, for the sake of argument, that equitability stops at the national frontier). Thus, the environmental structures must not be such that some urban units have only an elementary school while others have a complete educational spectrum up to university level. One should also expect that higher education for adults can be pursued simultaneously with gainful employment.

Experience shows that even with an extremely high level of physical mobility there is a tendency to increase the possible combinations of activities by packing them in different urban units. The term "urban unit" will be used below to denote a dominating employment center with its commuting hinterland. A completely diffuse spread probably cannot be obtained until an extremely high degree of mobility is reached and aids are acquired that greatly reduce the need for personal contact. The equitable settlement pattern thus cannot be conceived as a continuum but must be composed of a number of equivalent urban areas, each with its well-defined center.

## Divisibility of Supplies

Let us suppose that in order to accommodate a certain population a country is to be built up from the beginning without inherited encumbrances. The first thing to be decided is how many urban areas must be provided. The smallest conceivable number is obviously one, as long as no boundary may be crossed with resulting internal differences between population groups. The greatest possible number of urban areas is determined by the limit of divisibility for the smallest divisible unit of supply to which all shall have equal access.

From the standpoint of the household, the labor market is, of course, the most important of the supply classes. In fact, the degree of divisibility of the labor market possibly determines the greatest number of urban areas in the equitable settlement pattern. Households have the right to expect that the region shall afford security of employment not only for the conventional breadwinner but for other members of the household, too, so that temporary unemployment shall not necessitate a change of dwelling. This is not to say that such a move should be impossible, but in the equitable settlement pattern it is reasonable that it shall be undertaken on the household's own initiative and that it not be dictated by shortcomings of the environment.

Other critical supply items are the large, specialized educational and medical service institutions. If there is only sufficient economic accommodation for, say, ten first-rate hospitals, the equitable settlement pattern cannot contain more than ten urban areas. For instance, everyone shall have an intensive-treatment unit within easy access.

For other types of supplies divisibility is a less critical factor, either because the limit to divisibility is very high or because there are acceptable substitution possibilities. This is particularly the case for consumer goods and recreational facilities. There may also be unconventional technical solutions to the problem of divisibility and access—for instance, mobile suppliers. It would not be reasonable to allow exclusive supplies with low divisibility to govern the number of urban areas. But the manner in which they are made available might be reexamined. In the equitable settlement pattern cultural supplies, such as the opera should, of course, move around.

## Interregional Passenger Transport

With the above conception of the population in an urbanized country divided into a number of urban units that are equivalent from the aspect of the supply structure, it is pertinent to examine the effects of such a physical dispersal on the economic, political, scientific, and cultural coordination of activities in the various regions. How shall the centralized decisions be made and how would other organizational collaboration be effected in a decentralized physical shell?

It will, of course, be technology and the costs of transport that will decide what is possible. Information in the form of words, figures, and images hardly provides any problem today. In any case within a single country access can be obtained without "distance friction," especially if the principle of standard postage rates is extended to other types of transport and communication. A major problem is presented by the kind of information that depends on direct personal contact. The ideal is, of course, for one to be able to travel between the regions from any origin to any destination without needing to rely on a schedule-operated land- or air-transport system. Just as at the intraregional level free access is assumed to all the supplies from all dwellings, wherever situated, so at the interurban level there should be complete freedom of movement between centers. These journeys would not need to take much longer than the internal trips across a particular urban area. The functionaries that need to be in close contact with each other would then not have anything particular to gain from concentration at a chosen administrative center.

In an equitable settlement pattern it would not be necessary to have a special capital, since its very existence would inevitably introduce interregional differences as regards the working population's opportunities for maintaining personal contact with the decision makers, whether they belong to administration, the business world, or the supply organizations. The transport apparatus and the secretariat organization must be such as to allow the population group that needs to maintain interurban contact to be able to operate in a "town without geographical position." This is, moreover, a condition—and perhaps the most important one—for urban areas remaining equal in size. One consequence of this approach is that it must not be taken for granted that institutions of "national interest" must be located at the same place as the central government.

## Upper and Lower Limits of City Size in a Modification of Existing Urban Systems

The Utopian conception of an equitable settlement pattern can indicate certain criteria for estimating the upper and lower population thresholds in an existing urban system to be reconstructed on the basis of a welfare-oriented approach rather than on one governed purely by considerations of business economics. It is accepted as an inevitable feature of the economic system that less efficient units are eliminated, whether in a small community or in a larger urban unit. But it is the broad, fundamental idea of the welfare state that despite this one individual shall not be restricted through circumstances beyond their control, so far as access to the fundamental requirements of life are concerned. It follows that an attempt should be made to provide environmental structures that, in the first place, have a large and varied enough labor market to provide stability even in the case of rapid reorganization of the economy, and also that afford opportunities for members of the same household to take jobs in quite different occupational fields. In the second place, access to community services and cultural sources should be such *that one person is not worse off then another because of where he or she lives*. We cannot obtain these conditions in the short run if we are bound by the restrictions of the past, but the question may be discussed as a possible long-range goal.

To consider first the upper limit for the size of the urban unit, growth is mainly due to an increase in the number of employment opportunities. At the same time the labor market usually becomes increasingly differentiated; for a person seeking a career, or simply wishing to change jobs, eligible vacancies occur at an increasing rate, and members of a particular household will also gradually find it easier to get work locally even if they seek quite different occupations. The available range of consumer goods will likewise broaden and the community services and available cultural resources and activities will become increasingly varied, often increasing in volume in relation to the population basis. The flow of information in all these sectors will increase. In brief, there will be an excess of worthwhile combinations of jobs and cultural activities, perhaps more than anyone can reasonably need—even more than is good for some households. (Combinations in the environmental structures of the large metropolis are themselves neutral as regards what may be considered good or evil; even the criminal enterprise is better off there than anywhere else.)

If it is stipulated that there shall be internal equitability, the whole range of supplies should be available on an equal basis to all households in the urban area, irrespective of the position of the dwelling. The ideal is random accessibility.

In reality it is impossible to disregard transit time, but we shall stipulate that for a particular daily program the daily travel expenditure for the various households shall not have too great a spread above or below the mean. For this to be possible it is necessary in turn that all the households shall have access to the same transportation combinations.

As is evident from observations, uniformly distributed random access is easiest to approach in the smaller urban units. A village and a town of 50,000 inhabitants do not differ greatly. There the bicycle and the motor car are roughly equivalent; everyone has the same chances of competing for the supplies and no supply point is actually uncomfortably located in relation to any dwelling. There is nothing in the actual size of the urban unit that promotes economic and social segregation of the inhabitants through accessibility; where this happens it has other causes. On the other hand, the supply alternatives are limited.

A further increase in the population and the number of supply alternatives will be accompanied by an increasing conflict between space and time. To secure space it is necessary to accept greater distances. The inhabitants are divided up into well- and less well-situated groups and into more or less mobile classes, depending on the kind of transportation at their disposal. Somewhere a limit is ultimately reached at which, for given transportation conditions, some households are so peripherally located that they are in practice able to benefit from only a small part of the region's supply. This situation is of course most painfully felt when the labor market ceases to be randomly accessible as a whole. Size itself now constitutes a segregation factor. The peripherally located household will feel the effect of the breakdown in the random

access long before the centrally located enterprises and organizations.

People try to offset the disadvantages associated with growth by obtaining their own individual means of transportation. This, however, is in itself a process that gradually reduces the mobility of everybody. The community can attempt to restore the homogeneity of the region by investing in transport apparatus, but because of their need for geometric structure, new networks tend to place the profits in one place and the costs (in environmental nuisance) in quite a different one. This situation as a rule is not covered by the usual economic compensations.

The benefits of the new apparatus will, moreover, be only temporary. Whatever advanced transport amenities are provided in a growing metropolis, the relief will not be permanent unless the establishment of new activities is controlled at the same time.

We can speculate that the size limit for a town might be reached when the newly formed household finds an environmental structure that offers as large a range of alternatives as the suburb and a more random access of desired supplies and when it settles in a locality that is still small enough to permit unhampered use of the private vehicle. This conclusion is, of course, a speculative one and it would be interesting to investigate on an empirical basis the size limit at which an urban unit begins to lose its homogeneity in terms of the characteristics of its residents, and hence be a community only in name.

In the growing town the labor market is the first supply factor whose accessibility is critically affected by expansion. Commuting time is an important item in the community's total transport budget and its prolongation will eventually curtail all other freedom of movement in the working day. On the other hand, as a metropolitan area grows, the range and volume of supplies in the commodity, service, and culture sectors increase to the point where the smaller urban units cannot do better. It is not likely that any household in the region is worse off because of the growth in this respect, however far it may go. On the other hand, the opportunities of reaching the countryside for recreation are generally diminished, and likewise the psychological distance to the centers of the regional power structure increases, though not because of greater internal transport distances, but because of the anonymity in social relations that inevitably results from an increase in population.

The interest of the community in the distribution of growth between regions within the existing settlement pattern is not, however, in the first place concerned with the intraregional differences that may exist in a metropolitan area. Rather it is with eliminating, as far as possible, the interregional differences that tend to widen the spread between the present pattern and an equitable settlement pattern. It is important, then, to ensure that the range of supplies at as many places as possible approaches that for the best-off metropolitan area.

As regards the lower threshold value for what can be achieved in the way of uniformity, the labor market affords no absolutely precise criteria, given the present state of our knowledge. The range of alternatives, will, of course, diminish as the population basis falls, but it is impossible to say, on a theoretical basis, what the minimum population must be in order to ensure security of employment. Nor does the commodity supply approach afford a clear indication of the alternatives. The assortment of supply alternatives falls off steadily in breadth and depth. The critical lower threshold is probably reached only in the small urban places.

The more critical supplies in the public sector, on the other hand, decrease in a more stepwise fashion as the population basis is diminished. It follows that when a list has been made of the supplies to be included in the comparison it is possible to indicate directly how far down the series of existing urban areas the equitable settlement pattern can extend. The more technology advances in different fields—especially in education and in health services—leads to an increase or a decrease in the number of supply units and to a smaller number of regions in which the equality criteria can be fulfilled.

## Conclusion

The above argument, stressing as it does the fact that the regional policy must, for reasons of distribution, aim at the construction of a number of well distributed centers with supplies of the type found in the present metropolitan area, should not be misconstrued as meaning that in practice the goal is necessarily to collect all the inhabitants in such agglomerations. There are many reasons why a household or an enterprise may be willing to sacrifice accessibility to the metropolitan supply, for example, in order to secure space and other advantages offered by a smaller town, or even a rural area. The point is, however, that it is far easier to maintain an acceptable standard of services and favorable conditions for economic growth in a smaller town if there is a large center nearby than if there is not. The large town offers two indispensible things, namely, a good range of supply of goods and services and links with the national and international transportation system. These are essential if the small town is also to be incorporated in a wider economic, social, and cultural context.

# The Effects of Public Policy on the Future Urban System

HANS BLUMENFELD

## INTERNATIONAL EXPERIENCE

### Distribution of Growth on a National Scale

In surveying the policies related to the national distribution of urban growth, it is striking to note that all governments concerned with these questions—in "developing" and in "developed" nations, in countries with "free enterprise" and those with "centrally planned" economies—without exception proclaim the two closely related goals of regional equalization and of restraining the growth of their largest cities, in particular of their primate city.

The United Kingdom, following the recommendations of the "Barlow Report" of the 1930s, has attempted to counteract the growing concentration in the Southeast and in the Midlands, centred on London and Birmingham respectively. However, despite some successes in stimulating the growth of other areas, these two regions continue to grow at a faster rate than the balance of the country.

France has long been concerned about the historical overcentralization of national life in Paris, popularized by the slogan "Paris et le desert Français." The government has attempted to build up eight of the largest provincial centres into "countermagnets" to Paris. Again, while some of these centres are developing rapidly, the Paris region continues to grow at a considerably faster rate than the rest of the country.

The Netherlands government has been concerned with the growing together of its largest cities into a contiguous urban area called the "Randstad," as well as with underdevelopment in the northeastern provinces. A multifaceted policy, consistently pursued over a quarter of a century, has succeeded in stimulating the northeast and in reducing the growth of the Randstad to a rate just a shade below the national average. However the northeast as well as the Randstad show a modest net migration loss, while a migration gain is noted in the southeast, which lies in the periphery of Europe's strongest urban field, the Rhine-Ruhr area.

In the developing countries the primate cities are everywhere growing at an alarming rate, often concentrating the majority of the nation's urban population. Sometimes they account for over a quarter of the entire national population.

In countries with a centrally planned economy the situation differs. Despite the fact that their primate cities are also the seats of government and the leading industrial centres, they account for less than 10 per cent of the national population, except in Hungary, and grow at a somewhat lower rate than the total urban population. However the planned limits of city size have been exceeded in practically all cases.

Because of similarities in size of area,

From L. S. Bourne et al., *Urban Futures for Central Canada* (University of Toronto Press, 1974), pp. 194–98, 205–8. Reprinted by permission.

location, and climate, the experience of the Soviet Union is of particular interest to Canada. Its goal of industrializing the entire country has been largely achieved. However, contrary to notions widespread in Canada, the Soviet Union has not set an example of "northern development." In fact during the last intercensal period (1959–70) population growth in Siberia was even nominally lower than in the European part of the Russian Republic (10.3 per cent versus 10.8 per cent); and practically all of this growth was concentrated in the large cities on the southern edge of Siberia. By contrast, population increased by 42.8 per cent in the Central Asian Republics and by 28.2 per cent in the Caucasus. In the European part of the Soviet Union the three southernmost regions, North Caucasus, Southern Ukraine, and Moldavia, increased at twice the average of the other regions. This substantial southward shift, only partly due to differences in the birth rate, had been neither planned nor foreseen by the Soviet government. It seems that even in a centrally planned economy the locational preferences of individuals have a substantial impact on the pattern of urban growth.

As to population distribution by city size, the Soviet Union has since its inception pursued the goal of limiting the growth of its largest cities, and for several decades Soviet theory has proclaimed a size of about a quarter of a million as optimal. In fact the population of the 31 cities which in 1927 had populations between 100,000 and 500,000 had almost quadrupled by 1970, while Moscow had grown by 246 per cent and Leningrad by 134 per cent. Total population of towns under 100,000—many of them, of course, new— had grown even faster; their share of total urban population increased from 62.1 to 73.9 per cent during these 43 years, while that of Moscow has dropped from 7.7 to 5.2 per cent.

However this relative success should not obscure the fact that the repeated attempts to fix an upper limit on the size of Moscow, as on a number of other cities, have universally failed. In recent years many voices have been raised to advocate abandoning this policy as unrealistic and harmful. A respected Soviet economist claims that productivity in Moscow is 40 per cent higher than in cities of "optimal" size. While this estimate, like similar ones made in other countries (e.g., 15–20 per cent for Stockholm), is controversial, there is little doubt that the agglomeration economies of big cities are substantial, and continue to promote the universal "trend to the metropolis."

The reasons for the failure of all governments to bring into effect their proclaimed policies are highlighted by the experience of West Germany, where governments and public opinion have been particularly vocal in condemning the large "Ballungen" (concentrations). As a result of the phasing out of coal mining the Ruhr area, by far the biggest of these concentrations, a few years ago showed sluggish growth. Far from welcoming this, both the provincial and the federal governments rushed in to promote other industries in order to take up the slack in employment.

It may sound cynical, but it is safe to predict that governments and political parties everywhere will continue in the foreseeable future to proclaim their devotion to decentralization at the national level but will do little about it. The goal will always be highly popular with everyone in the regions and smaller towns which desperately want growth and with many in the big cities who suffer from congestion. It is not difficult to think of any number of incentives and disincentives to implement such a policy. But substantial migration will come about only if and when living conditions, in particular employment opportunities and earnings, are continuously and substantially less favourable in big metropolitan areas than they are in the rest of the country. So far such a situation has not been acceptable to any government.

The contrast between the success of decentralization within metropolitan regions discussed below and the failures of decentralization on a national scale also reflect the fact that the latter runs counter to economically determined "natural" trends, while the former is in conformity with them. There is no indication that Canada's future will be an exception and that government policies will have more than a marginal effect on future population distributions on a national or provincial scale.

## Distribution of Growth within Metropolitan Regions

In contrast to the universally proclaimed goals concerning the distribution of urban population on a national scale, there is no consensus on its distribution within metropolitan regions. This has generally been determined by market forces, more or less modified by local planning, without national directives. The one major exception is the United Kingdom which since the end of the war has consistently pursued a policy of "decanting" the population growth of large urban centres into "satellite towns." The main instruments of this policy are Crown corporations which assemble and hold large tracts of land, at distances averaging about 30 miles from the city centre, erect industrial and commercial as well as residential and public buildings, and promote their sale or lease. More than two dozen "new towns" have been successfully launched by this method, with a total population of about one million. However this accounts for less than one-sixth of total postwar urban growth.

This experience has led to some significant modifications. Originally these towns were conceived to be "self-contained" and commuting was frowned upon; now they are seen as constituent parts of their metropolitan regions, and commuting, not so much to the central city as to and from other places in the region, is accepted as normal.

Originally great stress was laid on a rigidly fixed upper limit of population; now growth beyond the planned limit is accommodated. The "planned" size itself has continuously been revised upward, from the 32,000 proposed by Ebenezer Howard to 50,000 to 60,000 in the first government-built new towns, to 100,000 to 250,000 in those such as Milton Keynes, presently in process of development.

Several other governments have also experimented with various types of "new towns," without, however, developing any clear and consistent policies. The frequent assertion that the Scandinavian countries follow such policies is an error; it is based on a misinterpretation of developments such as Vallingby at Stockholm. Thanks to a policy of large-scale assembly of surrounding land areas, initiated by a conservative city government at the beginning of this century, Stockholm has been able to create well-planned settlements for about 50,000 to 100,000 people at distances of about 10 miles from the city centre. These settlements are not "new towns" they might be called "new boroughs." They are not intended to be self-contained, but on the contrary, are connected as closely as possible to the central city by both rapid-transit lines and freeways. They were expected to provide employment locally for about one-half of their residents; in fact, the percentage is lower, as a result of a great deal of "in-" as well as of "out-" commuting. The easy access to a wide range of employment opportunities as well as of services has enabled these "new boroughs" to avoid some of the difficulties experienced in "new towns," in particular during their early years.

## CONCLUSIONS

It is probable that public land ownership for urban development, by whatever level or combination of levels, will play an increasing role in the future form of urban development in North America, as it already does in Europe. It may be significant that it is now being strongly advocated by the Dean of American Land Economists, Homer Hoyt. If and when—and only if and when—it become public policy in Canada, the Vallingby-Stockholm model, advocated by some observers (Lithwick, 1970), may become—in many and widely modified forms—the model for the future development of our urban areas.

A substantial modification of future population distribution within urban fields might thus come about. In place of the present scatteration, the indiscriminate mixture of urban and rural land uses, there would be fairly large contiguous urban areas in planned satellite boroughs and satellite towns, surrounded by even larger contiguous rural areas.

Presumably life in the developments would be more attractive for both households and enterprises than the alternatives now available in urban-metropolitan fields. If the claims of their advocates that they combine the advantages of small-town and of big-city life should be confirmed, this would imply that the relative attractiveness of isolated small towns would be further reduced—contrary to declared government policy. The success of redistribution within metropolitan regions in the future would contribute to the failure of redistribution on a national (or provincial) scale, as may have been the case in the United Kingdom.

## REFERENCES

Friedmann, J., and Miller, J. 1965. "The Urban Field," *Journal of the American Institute of Planners,* 31: 312–90.

Lithwick, N. H. 1970. *Urban Canada: Problems and Prospects.* Ottawa: Queen's Printer.